W9-CUG-417

To Gladys

A History of the
GREEK CITY-STATES
ca. 700 — 338 B.C.

ΗΡΟΔΟΤΟΣ

A History of the
GREEK CITY STATES
ca. 700 – 338 B.C.

Raphael Sealey

University of California Press

Berkeley · Los Angeles · London

ARCHBISHOP ALEMANY LIBRARY
DOMINICAN COLLEGE
SAN RAFAEL, CALIFORNIA

938
Se15h

Frontispiece:

Portrait bust of Herodotus. Roman copy (second century A.D.*) of a Greek sculpture (late fifth century* B.C.*).*

[Courtesy The Metropolitan Museum of Art, New York, Gift of George F. Baker, 1891.]

University of California Press
Berkeley and Los Angeles, California

Unversity of California Press, Ltd.
London, England

Copyright © 1976, by
The Regents of the University of California

Library of Congress Catalog Card Number: 75-27934
Printed in the United States of America

97815

Contents

Maps

Some of the information given in Maps 1–7 was drawn from maps published in G. W. Botsford and C. A. Robinson' *Hellenic History* (fifth edition, revised by D. Kagan; Copyright, The Macmillan Company, New York, 1969) and in J. B. Bury's *History of Greece* (fourth edition, revised by R. Meiggs; Copyright, Macmillan and Company of London and St. Martin's Press of New York).

Map 8 reproduces by permission with minor modifications the map published by W. K. Pritchett in Studies in Ancient Greek Topography Part II = University of California Publications in Classical Studies, volume 4 (1969), figure 1 on page 10.

Illustrations

Abbreviations

Harpocration:	Valerius Harpocration (first, second or third century A.D.), wrote a *Lexicon of the Ten Orators*
Hdt.:	Herodotus
Hell. Oxy.:	*Hellenica Oxyrhynchia*, ed. V. Bartoletti (Leipzig 1959)
Hyp.:	Hypereides
Eux.:	*For Euxenippus*
Isoc.:	Isocrates
Just.:	Justinus, Justin
Lyc.:	Lycurgus
Leocr.:	*Against Leocrates*
Lys.:	Lysias
Nepos:	Cornelius Nepos (first century B.C.) a Roman friend of Cicero and Catullus; he wrote biographies, including those of several famous military men of the past.
Tim.:	*Life of Timotheus*
Paus.:	Pausanias
Philoch.:	Philochorus
Phot.:	Photius
Pind.:	Pindar
Nem.:	*Nemean Odes*
P.:	*Pythian Odes*
Plat.:	Plato
Plut.:	Plutarch
Alc.:	*Life of Alcibiades*
Alex.:	*Life of Alexander*
Arist.:	*Life of Aristeides*
Cim.:	*Life of Cimon*
Dem.:	*Life of Demosthenes*
Lyc.:	*Life of Lycurgus*
Lys.:	*Life of Lysander*
Pelop.:	*Life of Pelopidas*
Per.:	*Life of Pericles*
Phoc.:	*Life of Phocion*
Sol.:	*Life of Solon*
Them.:	*Life of Themistocles*
Thes.:	*Life of Theseus*
Mor.:	*Moralia, Moral Treatises*
Pollux:	Julius Pollux (second century A.D.), wrote an atticizing lexicon called *Onomasticon*

Polyaen.: Polyaenus
Polyb.: Polybius
Str.: Strabo
Syncellus: Georgius Syncellus, Byzantine monk (late eighth–early ninth century A.D.), wrote a chronographic summary of world history
Theophr.: Theophrastus
Char.: *Characters*
Thuc.: Thucydides
Vitruvius: Vitruvius Pollio, architect and military engineer under Augustus, wrote a treatise *de architectura*
Xen.: Xenophon
Anab.: *Anabasis*
Hell.: *Hellenica*

MODERN WORKS OFTEN CITED

ATL: B.D. Meritt, H.T. Wade-Gery and M.F. McGregor, *The Athenian Tribute Lists,* 4 vols. (Cambridge, Mass. 1939–53)

CAH: J.B. Bury and others (edd.), *The Cambridge Ancient History* (Cambridge, Engl. 1923–39)

Davies, *APF*: J.K. Davies, *Athenian Propertied Families 600–300 B.C.* (Oxford 1971)

Ehrenberg Studies: E. Badian (ed.) *Ancient Society and Institutions: Studies presented to Victor Ehrenberg* (Oxford, Blackwell 1966)

F.Gr.Hist.: F. Jacoby, *Die Fragmente der griechischen Historiker*, I–II (Berlin 1923–26), III (Leiden 1940–58)

French, *Growth*: A. French, *The Growth of the Athenian Economy* (London 1964)

Gomme, *Comm.*: A.W. Gomme, *A Historical Commentary on Thucydides,* I–III (Oxford 1945–56)

Gomme/Andrewes/ Dover, *Comm. 4*: A.W. Gomme, A. Andrewes, and K.J. Dover, *A Historical Commentary on Thucydides IV* (Oxford 1970)

Hammond, *Studies*: N.G.L. Hammond, *Studies in Greek History* (Oxford 1973)

Hignett, *HAC*: C. Hignett, *A History of the Athenian Constitution* (Oxford 1952)

Hignett, *XIG*: C. Hignett, *Xerxes' Invasion of Greece* (Oxford 1963)

Hill: G.F. Hill, *Sources for Greek History between the Persian and the Peloponnesian Wars*, new edition, revised by R. Meiggs and A. Andrewes (Oxford 1951)

I.G.:   *Inscriptiones Graecae* ed. A. Kirchoff and others, I– (Berlin 1873–   )

I.G. I², II²: *Inscriptiones Graecae I and II*, editio minor, F. Hiller von Gaertringen and J. Kirchner (edd.) (Berlin 1924–40)

Larsen, *GFS*:   J.A.O. Larsen, *Greek Federal States* (Oxford 1968)

Meiggs, *AE*:   R. Meiggs, *The Athenian Empire* (Oxford 1972)

Meiggs/Lewis: R. Meiggs and D. Lewis, *A Selection of Greek Historical Inscriptions to the end of the fifth century B. C.* (Oxford 1969)

RE: A. Pauly, G. Wissowa and W. Kroll, *Realencyclopädie der classischen Altertumswissenschaft* (Stuttgart 1894–   )

Ruschenbusch, *SN*:   E. Ruschenbusch, *Solonos Nomoi: Die Fragmente des solonischen Gesetzeswerkes mit einer Text–und Überlieferungsgeschichte* = *Historia Einzelschriften* Heft 9 (Weisbaden 1966)

Ryder, *Koine Eirene*:   T.T.B. Ryder, *Koine Eirene: General Peace and Local Independence in Ancient Greece* (Oxford 1965)

Sealey, *Essays*:   R. Sealey, *Essays in Greek Politics* (New York 1967)

Tod.:   M.N. Tod, *A Selection of Greek Historical Inscriptions*; vol. I², *To the End of the Fifth Century B.C.* (Oxford 1946); vol. II, *From 403 to 323 B.C.* (Oxford 1948)

Wade-Gery, *Essays*:   H.T. Wade-Gery, *Essays in Greek History* (Oxford, Blackwell 1958)

JOURNALS REFERRED TO BY ABBREVIATIONS OR TITLES

ABSA: *Annual of the British School at Athens*

AHR: *American Historical Review*

AJA: *American Journal of Archaeology*

AJP: *American Journal of Philology*

Autochthon

BCH: *Bulletin de Correspondence Hellenique*

BICS: *Bulletin of the Institute of Classical Studies* (University of London)

Classica et Mediaevalia

CP: *Classical Philology*

CQ: *Classical Quarterly*

CQ NS: *Classical Quarterly,* New Series
CR: *Classical Review*
CSCA: *California Studies in Classical Antiquity*

Hermes
Hesperia
Historia

HSCP: *Harvard Studies in Classical Philology*
JHS: *Journal of Hellenic Studies*
JRS: *Journal of Roman Studies*
Num. Chron.: *Numismatic Chronicle*
PACA: *Proceedings of the African Classical Associations*

Philologus
Phoenix

REG: *Revue des Etudes Grecques*

Rheinisches Museum
Talanta

TAPA: *Transactions of the American Philological Association*

MISCELLANEOUS

anon.: anonymous
ed.: editor, edited by
fr.: fragment
hyp.: hypothesis, used of the argument or summary sometimes prefaced to ancient works in Byzantine manuscripts
ibid.: ibidem, at the same place
loc. cit.: locus citatus, the place cited
op. cit.: opus citatum, the work cited
sc.: scilicet
schol.: scholion, scholiast
s.v.: *sub verbo*, under the word (cited in lexica)

Preface

This book is intended to introduce readers to the study of Greek history. It tries to acquaint them with important problems and with significant hypotheses; or, to speak honestly, it discusses the problems which I consider important and the hypotheses which I find illuminating. It is in the main a product of the teaching I have done in California since 1967; for patient hearing and comments I thank many undergraduate and graduate students and not least those few who seemed to hold me personally responsible for everything that went wrong in antiquity.

I am happy to express gratitude to many who have helped me: to the University of California Press and its readers for constant courtesy and valuable suggestions; to Mr. George L. Cawkwell, who first introduced me to the study of ancient history; to Professors Darrell A. Amyx and W. Kendrick Pritchett for helping with the illustrations; to Mrs. Adrienne Morgan, who designed seven of the maps; to my wife, whose critical questioning clarified some obscurities; to Professor Erich S. Gruen, whose encouragement was the more effective for being unobtrusive; and above all to Miss Helle B. Jacobsen, whose assistance kept me on the job just when I was inclined to give up.

RAPHAEL SEALEY
Berkeley, September 1975

I

The Development of the City-State and the Persian Wars

Note

For convenience the literary sources for the history of archaic Greece will here be classified under several headings: poets, historians, orators, writers of Roman date, and Byzantine scholars.

POETS

The poems attributed to HOMER are primarily the two long epics, the *Iliad* and the *Odyssey*. Modern research has shown that these were originally composed without the aid of writing. The poet composing verse orally relied on an elaborate equipment of stock-phrases or "formulas;" this technique took many generations to develop. It is widely believed that the *Iliad* and the *Odyssey* were composed in something like their present form within the period 750–650*, and that is not unlikely. But the poems remained highly fluid until they were reduced to writing, a process probably carried out in Athens in the sixth century, when the Panathenaic festival was reformed to include competitions in reciting Homeric verse. Some items in the poems come from earlier dates; indeed, the poems contain a few recollections of artifacts used in the late bronze age (see also chapter 1, p. 15).

In antiquity several other poems were current under the name of Homer. Among these were a number of shorter epics, telling the remaining episodes from the Trojan cycle of myth and the legends of Thebes and Argos. These epics have been lost except for quotations and summaries. But a number of Homeric hymns, each praising a god, have been preserved. Like the shorter epics, these were probably composed later than the Iliad and the Odyssey, but their date is uncertain.

The practice of composing verse with the aid of writing began not later than the seventh century. The earliest known poet of this kind was ARCHILOCHUS of Paros, on whom see chapter 1, p. 28. His works, and those of the other lyric and elegiac poets of the seventh and sixth centuries, have mostly been lost except for fragments quoted by later writers, but some of the quotations are extensive.

* Dates in this book are B.C. unless otherwise indicated.

Mention may here be made of Tyrtaeus, Solon and Theognis. TYRTAEUS was active in Sparta in the seventh century and took part in the fighting against the Messenians. His poems included exhortations for warfare and passages about Spartan institutions. The Athenian statesman SOLON (see chapter 5) wrote elegiac and iambic verse on various themes; the fragments dealing with contemporary politics are moderately extensive but disappointingly vague. THEOGNIS of Megara, who was active in the middle of the sixth century, wrote elegiac verse on moral and political themes. The collection preserved under his name includes work by other poets, and the question of authorship of specific lines is often insoluble.

The Boeotian poet PINDAR (518–438) composed lyric verse for specific occasions. Hellenistic scholars collected his works and arranged them in seventeen books; four of these, consisting of choral odes in honor of victors in the Panhellenic games, have been preserved. For the most part these odes say little about contemporary events, but they provide insight into the aristocratic values which developed in the archaic period. BACCHYLIDES of Ceos, a contemporary of Pindar, likewise wrote lyric poetry of various kinds; a papyrus discovered in 1896 contains fourteen of his odes for victors in the games along with other of his poems. In Athens choral performances were held at the spring festival called the Dionysia, and the final step in developing tragedy from these was taken by AESCHYLUS (525/4–456). He drew the material for most of his plays from legends and myths, but of the seven plays extant one, *The Persians*, dealt with recent history, namely with the Persian invasion and especially with the battle of Salamis.

HISTORIANS

By far the most valuable source of information on the archaic period and the Persian Wars is the History written by HERODOTUS (ca. 490–ca. 430). The author was born at Halicarnassus, a Dorian city in southwestern Asia Minor. His extensive travels took him to Egypt, Syria, probably Babylon, parts of Thrace and the coasts of the Black Sea. He spent some time in Samos and he undertook journeys in European Greece, where he probably made Athens his base. When in 443 the Athenians sent a new settlement to Thurii in southern Italy, Herodotus joined the venture probably at its start, and he stayed in Thurii as a citizen of that city.

The work which he wrote was a lengthy history of Persian expansion and of the wars between Persia and the Greek cities. Modern study has thrown a good deal of light on his intellectual development. (A good introduction is C. W. Fornara, *Herodotus* [Oxford 1971].) He seems to have begun his literary activity

by compiling accounts of the nations he visited outside Greece. In this he followed the tradition begun late in the sixth century by writers who are commonly
called "the Ionian logographers;" they collected and wrote down geographical
and historical information about places which they knew or visited. But later, perhaps during his stay in Athens, Herodotus conceived the novel idea of writing a
connected account of a single historical event, namely the warfare between
Greeks and Persians. He retained his accounts of non-Greek nations by linking
them together on the theme of Persian history; that is, he gave an account of each
nation at the point in his narrative where the Persian Empire first came into
contact with it; the first contact was usually a Persian attempt at conquest. So the
first half of his final work was a history of Persian expansion and included
accounts of the geography, customs, history and wonders of Lydia, Egypt,
Scythia, Thrace and other places. The second half was a history of the Persian
Wars, beginning with the antecedents of the Ionian Revolt.

Herodotus drew his historical information almost entirely from oral tradition.
There were few, if any, documentary sources available to him. Obviously oral
traditions could err, and they could relate events from partial viewpoints. A few
of Herodotus's statements, notably the figures he gives for the expeditionary
force which Xerxes brought to Greece, are incredible. But his evidence is of
outstanding value for two reasons: First, he wrote down faithfully the information that was told to him; he did not try to modify it to suit a scheme or a theory.
Second, he lived and wrote before the art of writing history, as pursued by many
later practitioners, had fostered habits of speculation and controversy. Herodotus's information is raw in the sense that it has not been influenced by the theories
and arguments of his predecessors; in the strict sense he had no predecessors.
Accordingly when his statements conflict with those of later authors, the
evidential value of his account is usually better.

On THUCYDIDES, who provides some information on the archaic period, see
"Note on the Literary and Epigraphic Sources for Part II."

The philosopher ARISTOTLE (384–322) included politics among the many
subjects he studied. He compiled a general treatise, *Politics*, in which he dealt with
such subjects as the different kinds of constitutions and the best ways to preserve
each, the nature of strife within cities, and the ideal state. This treatise cited
numerous historical events as examples, but often the references are allusive and
difficult to interpret. He and his pupils compiled accounts of the constitutions of
158 Greek states. A papyrus preserved in the British Museum in London and first
published in 1890 contains much of Aristotle's account of the *Constitution of the
Athenians*; a few fragments from another papyrus copy of the same work are
preserved in Berlin and are of some help towards recovering the text. Assessment
of Aristotle's quality as a historian depends on this work. The first part of the

treatise is a history of the Athenian constitution up to 401/0; the second is a description of it as it was in his own time. The value of the historical part as evidence for the archaic period depends on the quality of its sources; except where Aristotle or the Atthidographers whom he followed could draw on documents or institutional survivals, his statements must be viewed with scepticism. (See further chapter 4, pp. 89–91.)

ORATORS

By the later part of the fifth century public speaking had become a refined and complex art. One hundred and thirty-nine speeches by Athenian orators have been preserved and they span the period ca. 420–322. Many of them were composed to be spoken in lawsuits, several were pronounced in debates in the Athenian public assembly, and a few were written as part of the celebrations at festivals. They are an important source for the history of their own period, but they sometimes mention earlier events and institutions surviving from archaic conditions. So it will be convenient to review them here.

ANTIPHON (ca. 480–411) composed speeches professionally for other men to deliver. He took part in the revolution of 411; indeed Thucydides says that he was the brain behind the seizure of power by the Four Hundred. When the Four Hundred were overthrown, he was tried and executed. The extant speeches concern cases of homicide.

ANDOCIDES (ca. 440–ca. 390) was accused of taking part in the mutilation of the Hermae and the parody of the Eleusinian mysteries in 415, and so he was driven into exile. The second of his three extant speeches was delivered some years later, when he applied unsuccessfully for permission to return. Eventually he came back to Athens under the general amnesty of 403. In 400 his political enemies seized an opportunity to bring up the scandal of 415 against him afresh; he was prosecuted but he defended himself successfully with the speech preserved as the first in the collection. In 392/1 he served as one of four envoys sent to Sparta to negotiate for peace; on his return he delivered Speech 3 to advocate acceptance of the proposed terms, but the Athenian assembly rejected them and drove the four envoys into exile.

LYSIAS (ca. 459–380) was the son of Cephalus, who migrated from Syracuse to Athens. In 404 the oligarchy of the Thirty attacked Lysias and his elder brother Polemarchus in order to seize their property; Polemarchus was executed, and Lysias was arrested but escaped to Megara. He returned in 403. He composed speeches for clients to deliver, but two of the extant speeches were delivered by Lysias himself against members and agents of the Thirty after their overthrow.

Except for these two, very few of the extant speeches attributed to Lysias can be pronounced with confidence to be his work; the collection current under his name is a selection of speeches by various Athenian orators of the late fifth and early fourth centuries. (For a good introduction both to Lysias and to Athenian oratory in general see K.J. Dover, *Lysias and the Corpus Lysiacum* [Berkeley and Los Angeles 1968].)

Very little is know about ISAEUS (ca. 420–ca. 350). Eleven speeches and a fragment of a twelfth have been preserved; all these are court speeches on cases of inheritance. They throw some light on Athenian social institutions.

ISOCRATES (436–338) composed speeches for clients early in the fourth century, but ca. 392 he opened a school of rhetoric in Athens and he continued to teach there until after 351. Several of his extant speeches were composed on a current or recent event and were probably intended for circulation in writing. These speeches can be useful sources for the state of opinion at the time of composition, but some of them are difficult to interpret.

DEMOSTHENES (384–322) was active in Athenian politics from the middle of the fourth century until his death. The sixty speeches preserved under his name are a valuable source for the history of his time. Sixteen of these were designed for delivery in the public assembly; four of the sixteen are of doubtful authenticity, but at least one of the four is a genuine speech by a contemporary of Demosthenes. Most of the remaining forty-four speeches were composed for delivery in lawsuits; several of them are by Demosthenes and most of the others are by contemporaries of his. Speeches composed for lawsuits where political interests were at stake and the speeches composed for the public assembly are especially useful to the historian.

AESCHINES (ca. 390–after 330), an opponent of Demosthenes, pursued a political career with intermissions. His three extant speeches were spoken in trials arising from his disputes with Demosthenes. In 346 the latter and Timarchus brought a charge against Aeschines because of things he had allegedly done on his embassy to Macedon. Aeschines countered by bringing a charge of immoral living against Timarchus. The case against Timarchus was heard in the winter of 346/5; Aeschines spoke the first of the three extant speeches and secured a conviction. The case against Aeschines because of the embassy of 346 eventually came to trial in 343/2; Aeschines spoke the second of the three speeches in his own defense and won an acquittal. In 337 Ctesiphon proposed a decree granting Demosthenes a crown in recognition of his long and devoted services to the Atheian state; Aeschines prosecuted him on the grounds that the proposal was contrary to the laws. This case was tried in 330; Aeschines failed to secure a fifth of the votes of the jury and had to go into exile. He liked to boast of his education and he included some digressions on early history in the speeches; among the more useful are a digression on the Delphic Amphictyony in speech 2 and one on the First Sacred War in speech 3.

LYCURGUS (?-324) associated with Demosthenes in politics in the late 340s. From 338 until 326 he was in effect in control of the finances of Athens, although the nature of the office or commission he held is not wholly clear. Only one of his speeches has been preserved; Lycurgus delivered it in 330, when he prosecuted a certain Leocrates on a charge of treason for fleeing from Attica after the battle of Chaeronea.

HYPEREIDES (389-322) associated to some extent with Demosthenes and Lycurgus. Several of his speeches, mostly for lawsuits, have been discovered on papyri since 1847. They supply information about the politics of his own time.

DEINARCHUS (ca. 360-after 292) was a Corinthian who settled in Athens and composed speeches for clients. The three extant speeches concern a scandal which occurred in 324. In that year Harpalus, the treasurer of Alexander the Great, fled from Babylon to Greece and sought refuge in Athens. Eventually the Athenians excluded him, but it was alleged that some Athenian politicians had accepted bribes from him. An investigation was held and several suspects were brought to trial. The extant speeches of Deinarchus were delivered in the prosecutions of Demosthenes and two other suspects.

From the middle of the first century B.C. onwards teachers of rhetoric increasingly favored the simpler or "Attic" style of oratory and turned away from the more florid or "Asianic" style previously fashionable. Consequently they studied the Athenian orators of the classical period as models. Caecilius of Caleacte, who taught rhetoric at Rome in the time of Augustus, drew up the above list of ten orators and their speeches came to be accepted as canonical. Later in the Roman period selections of their speeches were made for literary and rhetorical study, and the practice of schools in the Roman Empire is the ultimate reason why speeches have been preserved only of these ten among the Athenian orators.

WRITERS OF ROMAN DATE

The Hellentistic period, a term given approximately to the third, second and first centuries B.C., saw the rise of scholarly research into Greek authors whose works were already considered classical. The most important center of such research was the Library founded at Alexandria by Ptolemy II, who ruled Egypt from 285 until 246. The works of the Hellenistic scholars have been almost entirely lost, but they were accessible to educated men in the ensuing Roman period.

On the whole, whereas Hellenistic scholars engaged in original research into literature and history, their successors of Roman date were content to compile compendiums of the information already ascertained. One such compendium is the work begun by DIOGENES LAERTIUS perhaps in the third century A.D. It attempted a history of philosophy in the form of brief accounts of successive philosophers; each account summarized the life and opinions of its subject and often gave remarks attributed to him. The author tried to be comprehensive and included not only philosophers but also men famous for ancient wisdom, such as the Spartan statesman Chilon.

An earlier author of a different kind was DIODORUS SICULUS. He composed a history of the world from the earliest times until 54 B.C.; he was at work on it ca. 60–ca. 30 B.C. For each major part of his subject Diodorus tried to rely on a single standard work. For events in Greece proper (apart from Sicily and south Italy) in the classical period he drew heavily on EPHORUS. The latter was a native of Cyme in northern Asia Minor and flourished in the early and middle part of the fourth century; his most ambitious work was a general history, beginning with the return of the Heracleidae and ending with the year 341. Ephorus's work was widely consulted in antiquity, and so considerable fragments have been preserved in quotations or recovered on papyri. Ephorus arranged his material according to subject matter; Diodorus tried to rearrange it chronologically in order to give a narrative of events year by year; in the process his dating of some events became confused. Moreover Diodorus was uncritical and some blunders are easy to recognize. But sometimes Ephorus drew on good sources, and so his statements and those of Diodorus are occasionally valuable.

In the Roman Empire there was a revival of Greek letters. It produced writers of many kinds, historians, rhetoricians, and men of general learning. Three of them call for note here. PLUTARCH (ca. A.D. 45–after 120) was a native of Chaeronea in Boeotia. He traveled widely and studied in libraries during his travels. His most ambitious work was the *Parallel Lives,* a series of biographies of famous Greek and Roman statesmen, mostly arranged in pairs. He also composed a large number of shorter treatises, many in the form of dialogues; collectively these are called the *Moralia.* Not infrequently a piece of information given as a moral example in the shorter treatises occurs also in the *Lives.* For study of the archaic period the *Lives* of Lycurgus and of Solon are the most useful. Plutarch's main concern was ethical; he tried to assess the character of his subjects as possible models for conduct. Living under Roman rule, he had little understanding of the political conditions of the free Greek cities of the past. But he drew on a great wealth of erudition, and he preserves plentiful items of information which would otherwise be lost.

PAUSANIAS, who was active in the middle of the second century A.D., traveled widely in Greece and beyond. He wrote a *Periegesis* or "Description of Greece," dealing in turn with the different parts of the mainland. He included historical information, which seems to have been drawn from local sources and from standard works, such as Ephorus's history.

ATHENAEUS of Naucratis in Egypt flourished about A.D. 200 and his surviving work is called *Deipnosophistae* or "The Learned Banquet." In form it is an account of a dinner party lasting several days with numerous guests present. In fact the table talk is a vehicle of erudite information on a great variety of subjects. Athenaeus often names his sources. For the student of classical Greek politics he can be particularly useful when he preserves information from Hellenistic historians.

BYZANTINE SCHOLARS

In the Byzantine Empire there was a revival of scholarship in the ninth century. It was led by PHOTIUS, the patriarch of Constantinople, and its effects continued until the capture of that city by the Turks in 1453. Photius read and wrote widely. His most important undertaking was the *Bibliotheca*, which comprised summaries of 280 works which he had read. In many cases Photius's summary is the sole source of information about a lost work.

Byzantine scholars produced works of two related kinds, which are useful for the historian of classical Greece. First, they compiled lexica, which often included historical information and sometimes named their sources. Photius himself compiled a lexicon, based on earlier ventures of the same kind. A more ambitious lexicon was compiled about the end of the tenth century and called the *Suda* or "Fortress." Second, Byzantine scholars continued the practice of copying classical texts and including explanatory notes in the margins or sometimes between the lines. These notes are called "scholia" and their authors are called "scholiasts." Occasionally the same note occurs both in a lexicon and in a scholion to a classical author. Much of the information was drawn from earlier compendia, and some of it rested ultimately on Hellenistic scholarship. The scholia to the works of Homer and Pindar are the richest; those to Aeschines also offer a good deal of historical information.

1

Greece ca. 700

European Greece is the southern part of the Balkan range of mountains, and at its extremities some of the mountains have been submerged by the sea, so that they appear as islands. Inlets of the sea divide mainland Greece into three parts. The most southerly of these is the Peloponnese or "island of Pelops." It is linked to the rest of the mainland by a land bridge or isthmus; properly speaking the term "isthmus (of Corinth)" applies to the narrowest part of the land bridge. The inlets of the sea abutting on the land bridge are the Gulf of Corinth in the west and the Saronic Gulf in the east. The district extending northwards from these inlets as far as the Gulf of Malis may be called central Greece; at its eastern end is Attica, the territory dependent on Athens. The large island of Euboea lies stretched out near the northeast coast of central Greece; the channel dividing it from the mainland, the Euripus, could be crossed easily in places, and the fortunes of Euboea usually went with those of its mainland neighbors. The Greek district north of the Gulf of Malis is Thessaly, a large plain surrounded by ranges of mountains.

Most of the Greek mainland is divided by irregular highlands into small cantons. Hence settlers in antiquity tended to concentrate in inland valleys and coastal plains. Communications by land were difficult. Thus the terrain favored the development of a large number of independent communities or city-states. But it should be noted that there was a natural route leading through the length of European Greece. More than one pass led southwards from Macedon into

Thessaly. After crossing the Thessalian plain the traveler could proceed round the head of the Malian Gulf. Soon afterwards he came to the pass of Thermopylae, a narrow defile with mountains on the one side and the sea on the other. From the pass he could proceed through central Greece in any of several directions. If he made for the isthmus of Corinth, he would there find himself again in a narrow defile between mountains and the sea. After reaching Corinth, he could continue southwestwards, cross the Arcadian highlands in the center of the Peloponnese, arrive at Sparta and proceed southwards to the sea. Most invaders of Greece have taken this route. Moreover, by commanding strategic positions on the route an ambitious city could gain access to considerable areas. Hence the route was the scene of many battles, both against invaders and between Greek cities.

Most of the Greek islands may be classified in three groups. (1) Well to the south of the Peloponnese is the large island of Crete; in the historic period its cities played little part in the general political development of Greece. (2) A large number of islands are scattered through the heart of the Aegean; collectively they are called the Cyclades. Many of them are very small and none is very large, although some developed flourishing cities. (3) Off the west coast of Asia Minor there are a series of larger islands; proceeding from north to south, the chief of these are Lesbos, Chios, Samos and Rhodes. At an early period Greeks settled in these islands and on the neighboring west coast of the mainland; henceforth the fortunes of the islands and of the coast were closely linked.

The climate of the Greek area is characterized by mild winters and hot summers. The rainfall in most of Greece is adequate for agriculture but nearly all of it comes in winter. This combination of temperature and rainfall constitutes a climate of the type often called "Mediterranean" or "Californian." In antiquity a climate of this kind encouraged farmers to grow fruit trees, especially the vine and the olive; these could send down deep roots and in summer draw on reserves of moisture stored up since winter in the lower reaches of the soil. The climatic conditions are most severe in Attica, where the annual rainfall is only sixteen inches. Accordingly Attica came to produce wine and olive oil for export, and by the fourth century, perhaps a good deal earlier, nearly all of its grain was imported. But the vine and the olive tree take several years to grow to maturity and begin bearing fruit. Hence communities relying in part on these were peculiarly vulnerable to attack; by cutting down the fruit trees a hostile army could inflict damage, from which the victim would suffer for a long time.

GREEK ORIGINS[2]

Human habitation is attested in Greece as early as ca. 70,000 B.C., but palaeolithic man was a food gatherer, who used up the supplies of animals, fish or wild fruits in one district and then moved on to another. Neolithic villages first appeared in

Greece in the sixth millennium; they mark the beginnings of sedentary life and of rudimentary political organization. Such conditions made possible further material improvements, such as the introduction of pottery and the use of bronze. But the beginning of the bronze age in Greece, which may be placed very approximately near the year 3000, did not mark any major cultural change.

The earliest inhabitants of Greece did not speak Greek. A relic of their language was preserved into the historic period by those place-names which used the non–Indo-European suffixes –nth– and –ss– (–tt– in Attica), for example, Corinth, Erymanthus, Ilissus, Parnassus, Sphettus, Hymettus, Lycabettus. It is suggestive that the same suffixes appear in Asia Minor (Caryanda, Telmessus), Crete (Cnossus, Tylissus), Sicily (Agrigentum), south Italy (Tarentum, Beneventum) and even on the middle Danube (Carnuntum). But about 2000 there was a major change in mainland Greece. Invaders coming from the north destroyed most of the previous settlements; they brought in a new type of pottery and a distinctive plan for building dwellings. It is probable that the invaders were the first speakers of Greek to settle in Greece. Their arrival marks the beginning of the Middle Helladic period, or middle bronze age of Greece.

In the Middle Helladic period and above all in the early part of the Late Helladic (ca. 1600–ca. 1100) period Greece was influenced much by the Minoan civilization, which flourished in Crete. In the late bronze age Greece had an advanced civilization with a luxurious and martial culture; most of the settlements were towns clustering round elaborate palaces, which directed the economy; the population was as large and as widely spread through the different parts of Greece as in the classical period. But a protracted series of migrations and invasions, beginning rather before 1200, afflicted the whole of the Near East, including Greece, Asia Minor and the Levant. Little is known about the origin or national composition of the invaders, and as destruction advanced, they probably drew recruits from among the settled populations which they subverted; accordingly it is convenient to call them "land- and sea-raiders," a term based on Egyptian documents. The raids began to affect Greece a little before 1200 and in a couple of generations Late Helladic civilization was destroyed; the activities of the several settlements had been highly centralized and they collapsed, once the upper layers of the palace bureaucracies were removed. Henceforth for a long time Greece was a land of villages and hamlets; it had a much smaller population than before, the art of writing was lost, and there was no further building in stone in Greece until the late seventh or early sixth century.

The migrations lasted a long time and carried different groups of people in different directions. Perhaps ca. 900 settled conditions began to emerge. Later Greek tradition called the invaders Dorian Greeks and said that their home just before the migrations was in the border district between Epirus and Thessaly. A less useful legend said that those Dorians who came to the Peloponnese were led by the descendants of Heracles, a mythical hero associated primarily with places in the Peloponnese, and thus in this southern theater the migration was called "the return of the Heracleidae." Information drawn from the distribution of dialects in the historical period can be combined with the tradition of a Dorian invasion to give a plausible reconstruction of the migrations, although it must be admitted that the result is a hypothesis and not the only possible one.

The Greek language in the historical period was divided into a multiplicity of dialects. These varied from canton to canton, but they fell into two major divisions, East Greek and West Greek. The East Greek dialects may well have been descended from the type of Greek which was first brought into Greece ca. 2000; their chief subdivisions were Aeolian, Ionian and Arcado-Cyprian. West Greek was the type of speech brought to Greece by the invasions at the end of the bronze age; its chief subdivisions were Dorian and North West Greek. The distribution of dialects in the historical period suggests that the invaders, speaking West Greek dialects, had come from the north and proceeded towards the south and the east. They occupied most of central Greece and the Peloponnese. Going further by sea, they occupied Crete; in the Cyclades they seized the small islands of Melos and Thera; and proceeding southeastwards, they settled in Rhodes, Cos and some sites nearby on the Asiatic mainland.

Speakers of East Greek survived in a few parts of the European mainland and retreated to the islands and the coast of Asia Minor. In the Peloponnese they were confined to Arcadia, the mountainous center, which had a dialect akin to that spoken in Cyprus; this fact suggests that speakers of Arcado-Cyprian or its ancestor had held part at least of the east coast of the Peloponnese in the late bronze age, when Greek settlement in Cyprus began. In Central Greece Ionian dialects were spoken in Attica and in the island of Euboea. Indeed a tradition, which may be correct in outline, said that Ionians fled to Athens from the Peloponnese because of the Dorian invasions and that they sailed eastwards from Athens to the Cyclades and Asia Minor. In Boeotia, the district northwest of Attica, a mixed dialect emerged, containing both Aeolian and North West Greek elements. In Thessaly too there was a mixed dialect, combining these elements. Mixed dialects doubtless reflect intermingling of the invaders with the previous inhabitants, and probably such intermingling took place in other districts as well as Boeotia and Thessaly; thus Laconian, the Dorian dialect spoken in the southeastern part of the Peloponnese, had a few East Greek features.

Ionians occupied most of the Cyclades. On the west coast of Asia Minor and in the offshore islands three dialectal groups appear distinctly. In the north speakers of Aeolian held Lesbos and part of the mainland shore, where the chief city was Cyme. In the center Ionians held Chios, Samos and a long strip of the coast. This part of the coast included rich alluvial plains at the mouths of major rivers, such as the Hermus, the Cayster and the Maeander, which drain much of Asia Minor. Some of the Greek settlements in mainland Ionia probably originated in the late bronze age, although they may have been reinforced during the migrations. Further south Dorians settled in Rhodes and some smaller islands, such as Cos, and on the neighboring coast.

Greeks in the historical period were conscious of belonging to groups such as Dorians and Ionians. Each group was based on a fiction of common origin and a fact of common customs; for example, each Ionian city celebrated the festival of Apatouria. Sometimes, as will be seen in chapter 2, these divisions among Greeks had political consequences. To the modern student dialect is the chief indication of these affiliations, but to the contemporary Greek his affiliation also brought a rich heritage of custom and legend. The heritage was complex as well as rich. For example, the inhabitants of a northern part of the Peloponnese along the coast of the Gulf of Corinth believed that they were descended from the pre-Dorian population and they called themselves Achaeans, a word used in the Homeric poems for those who dwelled in Greece before the Dorian invasions; but the dialect of Achaea was a form of North West Greek.

The student of historic Greece must ask the question of continuity: Was anything inherited from the Bronze Age civilization? It is clear that in mythology and religion a great deal survived. The sites most celebrated in Greek legend were powerful centers in the bronze age, whereas some of them, such as Mycenae, were insignificant in the historical period. Some cult practices of the later period had a bronze-age origin. But political continuity is another question. In most of Greece there was destruction ca. 1200 and this led to complex and protracted migrations; such conditions did not favor the survival of political institutions. The question is most acute in relation to Athens, for there the acropolis was a civilized center in the late bronze age and this site did not suffer destruction. Indeed in the ensuing period, often called the Greek dark ages (ca. 1150–ca. 750), Athens was comparatively prosperous. But Athens could not remain unaffected by the turbulence in the rest of Greece. When the political affairs of Athens begin to become clear in the seventh and sixth centuries, they do not reveal any feature compelling a hypothesis of political continuity from the bronze age. Accordingly, it is a good working hypothesis to suppose that the political institutions of Athens and of the rest of Greece were new creations of the iron age. In other words, nothing excludes the view that, as the invasions proceeded, all former features of political organization were destroyed and, when conditions eventually became more settled, the Greeks began creating political institutions anew with nothing more to start from than the monogamous family and the fluid institutions of migrating tribes.

In connection with the question of continuity some attention must be given to the Homeric poems. In the present century it has been shown by Milman Parry that the *Iliad* and the *Odyssey* were composed orally by means of a traditional technique. Each poet learned the technique from his predecessors and could hope to elaborate it only a little; the development of the art of oral composition must have taken many generations. Hence it is understandable that the poems mention artifacts belonging to very different periods; a few of these can be dated by archaeological parallels to the late bronze age. This should be borne in mind before attempting to use the sporadic indications which the poems provide about social and political conditions. Some scholars have tried to reconstruct "Homeric society" by collecting these indications and assigning them all to one period. How mistaken this method is can be seen by considering the treatment of metals in the poems. The poets were familiar with the use of iron and in the poems tools are usually made of that metal; but the poets claimed to sing of a heroic age long past and so they speak of the weapons of their heroes as made of the more romantic metal, bronze. Yet there never was a society which used iron for tools but bronze for weapons; on the contrary, since iron is more difficult to work but tougher, it was first used for weapons, once the skill to work it was acquired. Accordingly, when the indications in the poems of social and political conditions are studied, an eclectic method may be recommended; if a feature in the poems shows resemblance or affinity to an institution attested later in historic Greece, the Homeric item may be used with caution to illuminate the origin of the institution. But this procedure, which will be followed below, does not imply that a date can be assigned to the Homeric feature or that all Homeric features of social organization belonged to one period or one society.

POLITICAL GEOGRAPHY OF THE EUROPEAN MAINLAND[3]

The earliest inscriptions in the Greek alphabet come from the eighth century, and the ensuing period may be called historic, in contrast to the "dark ages" which precede. It is convenient to give the name "archaic" to the early part of the historic period, until approximately the end of the sixth century; the period from then until the time of Alexander the Great (336–323) is often called "classical." The political geography of the Greek homelands in the Balkans and Asia Minor underwent comparatively little change in the archaic and classical periods. A brief survey will be made here of the chief cities, as they emerge in the archaic period.

In the Peloponnese the Dorian city of Argos was one of the more powerful states in the seventh century. It sought to reduce to dependence the lesser cities of the Argolid peninsula, which extends towards the southeast, and sometimes it tried to win leadership of the Peloponnese. Argive ambitions were achieved in part under king Pheidon, who may belong to the second quarter of the seventh century (see chapter 2, pp. 40–45). Some time later the power of Argos declined as that of Sparta rose, and thereafter Argos was a constant, but usually ineffectual, rival of Sparta.

In the southern part of the Peloponnese Mount Taygetus runs southwards from the Arcadian highlands and divides Laconia on the east from Messenia on the west. Dorians settled these two districts during the age of migrations and a good many small towns arose. Sparta gained ascendancy over the other towns of Laconia at an early stage and the state which she thus built up was called Lacedaemon. Later Sparta set about conquering Messenia; the consequent struggle was long, beginning in the second half of the eighth or perhaps in the seventh century, but by 600 Messenia had been conquered and absorbed into Lacedaemon. During the sixth century Lacedaemon extended its influence in the Peloponnese by creating and developing a league; it inflicted a defeat on Argos about the middle of the century, and by 500 it was the strongest power in Greece.

Arcadia, the mountainous center of the Peloponnese, evidently had little attraction for the Dorian invaders. Although it had forests and upland pastures, it was relatively poor by nature, and it became the only Peloponnesian district where an East Greek dialect survived. The strongest among its several towns were Tegea, which lay due north of Sparta, and Mantinea further north. Attempts were made from the fifth century onwards to set up an Arcadian federation, but such attempts were impeded by rivalry between the two chief towns.

Elis held considerable territory west of Arcadia; is land consisted of the foothills of the highlands and of a coastal plain. Two rivers flowed westwards across the territory. The city of Elis stood on the bank of the more northerly river, the Peneus, but the sanctuary of Zeus at Olympia was beside the other river, the Alpheus. Elis, as far as is known, did not advance much in political organization and its chief importance for the rest of Greece lay in the Olympian sanctuary.

The narrow coastal plain extending along the northern shore of the Peloponnese was called Achaea. Local tradition said that originally there were twelve units in Achaea but two of these became submerged by the sea. The towns of Achaea formed an organized federation as early as the fifth century and perhaps earlier; indeed the federation probably developed from a tribal settlement which was older than the several towns.

East of Achaea and divided from it by a spur of the Arcadian highlands lay the harbor city of Sicyon. In the archaic period this Dorain city developed considerable trade, but it was usually overshadowed by its more prosperous easterly neighbor, Corinth. The latter, also Dorian, held extensive territory, including harbors both on the Saronic and on the Corinthian Gulfs. It commanded the narrowest part of the isthmus. Thus it was well placed for control of communications, and during much of the archaic period pottery made in Corinth was exported more widely than that of any other Greek city. The acropolis, called Acrocorinth, and the residential city were in the southwestern part of the territory.

North and east of the Corinthiad, the remaining part of the land bridge linking the Peloponnese to central Greece constituted the territory of Megara. This district was technically outside the Peloponnese, since it lay beyond the isthmus proper, which was the narrowest part of the land bridge, but its political fortunes often went with those of the Peloponnese. In the eighth and seventh centuries Megara was sufficiently powerful to send out colonies, but later it was often dominated by its wealthier neighbor, Corinth. In the fifth century, after Athens had become a leading power, rivalry between Athens and Corinth for influence in Megara can be traced in some detail; control of the Megarid was strategically valuable because it stood on routes leading to Attica, Boeotia and the Peloponnese.

Attica, the territory of Athens, was one of the largest expanses of land controlled by a single Greek city. The district was divided by uplands into a number of plains. In chapters 4, 5 and 6, attention will be given to the questions of how this whole territory came to be united and what were the political effects of the subjugation of the outlying townships to the city of Athens. Here it need only be noted that for a long time in the archaic period Athens was of little consequence in the interstate affairs of Greece. During the sixth century her prosperity grew and under the control of the tyrant Peisistratus (546–528) she may first be said to have developed a foreign policy. At last in the first quarter of the fifth century she became a leading power, when she seized opportunities to enlarge her fleet.

To the west and north of Attica lay Boeotia, which comprised about a dozen cities. Much of the land consisted of two river basins, those of the Asopus in the south and the Cephisus further north. Correspondingly, the strongest cities of Boetia were Orchomenus, which lay near the Cephisus, and Thebes not far north of the Asopus. There was frequent rivalry between the two. Whatever the condition may have been in the bronze age, in the historical period Thebes was usually the more powerful of the two cities. Eventually and probably in the sixth century the Thebans began to build up a federation of Boeotia. This federal union, though repeatedly disbanded, was restored in varying forms; at times, particularly in the second half of the fifth century, it was perhaps the most promising attempt to draw together a regional group of Greek cities, while allowing them reasonable control of local affairs.

West and north of Boeotia a large strip of territory, running from the

Corinthian Gulf to the Euboean channel, was divided between Phocians and Locrians. Both these peoples spoke North West Greek dialects, but probably the Locrians came at a relatively early stage in the migrations and at first held the whole territory; the Phocians came later and seized the central part, thus dividing the Locrians into two non-contiguous sections. East Locris held part of the coast by the Euboean channel; its chief city was Opus, which became the seat of a well-developed federation. West Locris was a looser federation of several cities, such as Amphissa, Naupactus and Chaleum. East and West Locrians remained conscious of their kinship and kept up close relations at least into the fifth century. The heart of Phocis lay in the upper valley of the Cephisus river, but a small extension ran southwards to the Corinthian Gulf and included Delphi. Phocis developed into a federation of about twenty townships. Delphi with its sanctuary of Apollo was at first a Phocian city, but it was made independent at a time not later than the First Sacred War (ca. 595-586; see chapter 2, p. 47). The land at the source of the Cephisus river was held by Doris, a union of four villages, insignificant except that other Dorian states claimed it as their mother city and used the claim as a pretext to intervene in Central Greece. Likewise Aeniania and Malis, the two states occupying the valley of the Spercheus river, were too small to leave much imprint on interstate relations.

Thessaly was potentially the dominant power in northern Greece. It consisted of a large plain, drained by the Peneus river and its tributaries and surrounded by mountains. Conditions here differed from those in the rest of Greece; the extensive plain allowed grain growing and horse breeding on a large scale; the climate was continental. Thessaly emerged from the dark ages as a land of large estates, where each of several princely families held much land and controlled many *penestai* or serfs. Cities developed later than in much of Greece and each Thessalian city may have begun as a creation of the local dynasty, which continued to influence its affairs. A Thessalian union of some kind was formed by the beginning of the sixth century and perhaps a good deal earlier. It was marked by an elective monarch, who bore the title of *tagos*. Tradition said that the first *tagos* was Aleuas the Red of Larisa; it credited him with introducing the division of Thessaly into four territorial parts, called *tetrarchiai*, and it said that he assessed the whole plain for supplying cavalry and infantry. At an early stage Thessaly conquered the inhabitants of the surrounding mountains, which were called its *perioikis*. Then it extended its ascendancy southwards into Central Greece; it gained control of Phocis and played a decisive part in the First Sacred War. Eventually the Phocians rebelled; little is known of the struggle, which may have been protracted; the Phocians finally secured their freedom by defeating the Thessalians in two battles in Phocis not many years before 480. During the fifth century the continued growth of cities in Thessaly weakened the federation and the *tageia* fell into abeyance.

INSTITUTIONS[4]

The characteristic forms of Greek settlement emerging after the dark ages were the *polis* or city-state and the *ethnos* or tribal community. Like a modern city, the *polis* (plural *poleis*) included a cluster of dwellings but it had several distinctive features. First, it had a dependent territory; in antiquity people commonly went out to work in the fields in the daytime and returned to the town for safety at night. In large *poleis* the territory sometimes included subordinate villages, but political institutions and authority were concentrated in the city. Second, with rare exceptions the *polis* had a defensible citadel as its heart. Indeed the word *polis* originally meant "citadel," and in Athens as late as the fifth century it was used for the acropolis. Corinth, one of the larger *poleis,* illustrates the typical features well. The hill of Acrocorinth with precipitous slopes provided a natural citadel. The residential and commercial town clustered at its foot; and the dependent territory was extensive, including both ends of the isthmus and several villages. Apart from such general characteristics the nature of the *polis* varied a great deal from place to place. Many *poleis* were small, consisting of a single valley or coastal plain, but some, like Athens and Sparta, were large. Many were near the sea and came to rely much on maritime communications, but some, like those of Arcadia, lay inland.

The other type of settlement was the *ethnos* (plural *ethne*). A good example is Aetolia. Thucydides, recording Aetolian resistance to an Athenian attack in 426, says: "The Aetolian nation (*ethnos*), although numerous and warlike, yet dwelt in unwalled villages scattered far apart, and had nothing but light armor." From Thucydides's account it appears that the Aetolians constituted three tribes and each of these held a different part of the territory. They resisted the Athenian invasion successfully and afterwards they sent three envoys, one from each tribe, to Corinth and Sparta for help. It is to be noted that the Aetolians lacked any fortified city and their common institutions were probably sufficient only for making war and alliances. Probably many other tribal states, such as Phocis, Locris, Achaea in the northern Peloponnese and Acarnania west of Aetolia, at first had equally rudimentary institutions, but cities developed in many of them. For example, Polybius in the second century said that Achaea had consisted of twelve cities; three centuries earlier Herodotus said that Achaea consisted of twelve parts, and although some of the parts may already have been cities, his choice of the word "part" may indicate that some of them were mere districts. Even when cities developed within tribal states, some common organs were often retained and formed the starting point for a remarkable development of federal institutions in the third and second centuries. But in the archaic and classical periods the political development of *ethne* was usually less advanced than that of *poleis*.

Athens. The Acropolis seen from the Pnyx. [Photo by Hirmer Fotoarchiv, München.]

Athens. The southwest side of the Acropolis seen from the monument of Philopappus. On the left the Propylaea and temple of Athena Nike. In the center the Erechtheum. On the right the Parthenon. [Photo by Hirmer Fotoarchiv, München.]

The Acropolis of Athens. The west front of the Parthenon. [Photo by Hirmer Fotoarchiv, München.]

Within the *polis* early in the archaic period public authority was weak and political institutions were rudimentary. An illustration is provided by Ithaca in the Homeric *Odyssey*. While the paramount chief, Odysseus, was away, the public assembly failed to meet for twenty years, and this fact is mentioned by the poet in passing; the audience required no explanation. Society was agrarian and each community had people of very different status, wealthy landowners, small farmers, landless laborers, artisans, and in some places serfs bound to the soil under locally varying conditions. The strong unit was the family; that is, a powerful family attracted to itself numerous and varied dependents, who sought protection or economic help from it and contributed in turn to its strength. A man of modest standing directed his political loyalty not towards other men of the same class but towards his protector. Hence the divisions in political society were vertical, not horizontal; conflicts were usually not between disparate classes but between groups, each of which was led by a prominent family or a few prominent families and held many humbler followers.

The resulting institutions are best attested in Athens, where they retained some significance for religion and for social prestige as late as the fourth century; so they are mentioned by the orators and in inscriptions. Two related items, the *genos* and the *phratria*, stand out and, although much about them remains obscure, an approximate account of their nature can be given. The *genos* or clan was a family or, perhaps more often, a group of families, which claimed descent from a common ancestor and was held together by common cults. In a few cases the cult practiced by a clan won recognition and support from the Athenian state; thus the clans called Eumolpidae and Ceryces supplied priestly officials for the Eleusinian mysteries. The *phratria* or phratry seems to have grown up early in the archaic period as the group of men attaching themselves to a clan. The name comes from the Indo-European word for "brother" and it may have been used for associations of some kind from very early times, but in the Homeric poems phratries are mentioned only rarely; the poets did not keep returning to phratries as a crucial item in social structure. Therefore it is likely that the phratries, as attested in classical Athens, were being fashioned and built up at a period late in comparison with many conditions described in the poems. In the fourth century, in the case of some phratries at least it could be said that one clan held a privileged position within its phratry; for example an inscription of 396/5 gives, on the most defensible interpretation, rules adopted by a phratry called Deceleieis, but it reveals that the list of members of the phratry was kept by the clan of the Demotionidae; moreover, claimants to membership in the phratry were examined according to criteria called "The Law of the Demotionidae" and claimants rejected by the Deceleieis could appeal to the Demotionidae. Probably these prerogatives of the clan were relics from a time when its position within the phratry was not merely privileged but leading and dominant.

Membership of a phratry, like membership of a clan, was hereditary; so was membership of a larger unit, the tribe (*phyle*). In each Greek city the citizens were divided into several tribes, and some of these were common to several cities. Thus three tribes with the same names, Hylleis, Pamphyli and Dymanatae, are attested in several Dorian cities, including Sparta, Argos and Sicyon; evidently these tribes were constituent units of the Dorians before they settled in their historic cities. For Ionian cities the situation was more complex. Athens had four tribes, called Geleontes, Hopletes, Argadeis and Aegicoreis, and these are sometimes called the four Ionian tribes, but the term is inaccurate. Cyzicus, a colony of Ionian Miletus, had four tribes with these names and two others called Boreis and Oenopes; Miletus certainly had Oenopes, Boreis and Hopletes, and probably the other three as well. The explanation for the complexities should be sought in the period of migrations, as the tribes appear to have been older than the cities. One may call to mind the three tribes attested by Thucydides among the Aetolians, although he does not use the word *phyle* of them.

Thus society in the archaic city was built up from several hereditary groups; as late as the fourth century membership in a phratry could be cited as proof of Athenian citizenship. The central institutions usually found in the city were a king, a council and an assembly. These developed understandably from conditions in the age of migrations. At that earlier period each migrating group had a military commander; before taking decisions he usually consulted the leaders of powerful subdivisions of the group; and he summoned a parade of the whole army to announce decisions and orders. When the group ceased migrating and became sedentary, the military commander became a hereditary king; he continued to consult an advisory council, consisting doubtless of the heads of powerful households; and an assembly of adult male citizens was summoned to hear decisions. Several passages of the Homeric poems illustrate these institutions. The Homeric king consults advisers, who are called "elders" (*gerontes*) or "kings" (*basileis*); sometimes they are called "a council of elders" (*boule geronton*); he announces his decision to an assembly of troops or subjects and often it applauds but sometimes opposition is expressed. Even allowing for the imaginative character of the poems, the institutions portrayed must bear some relation to reality.

Perhaps the most noteworthy feature of the institutions shown in the poems is their fluidity. Sometimes the Homeric king consults the council before summoning the assembly, but sometimes the order is reversed. Neither the council nor the assembly takes a vote, although there is sometimes a shout of approval in the assembly. Decisions are taken by the king, but the poems avoid the question whether the king could override determined opposition from his advisers. The nearest approach to such a conflict occurs among the gods, when Zeus considers saving a beloved mortal, Sarpedon, from the death which awaits him in battle. Hera expostulates; she says that Zeus may do as he wishes, but the other gods will not approve; if he saves Sarpedon from his appointed death, other gods will likewise wish to save mortals whom they cherish; finally she suggests that Zeus should let Sarpedon die but have his body conveyed to his home for funeral rites. Zeus yields to Hera (*Iliad* 16.431–461). Possibly this scene reflects conditions obtaining for a time in human societies: there was no institutional check on the king, but the force of custom and convention was strong enough to restrain him from outrages.

In sedentary conditions the relations between king, council and assembly changed. Although the council began merely as the king's advisers, it was more resilient than the monarchy. The king might be a minor or a man of weak character, or there might be a disputed succession. Although in some cities an office with the title of king (*basileus*) was kept, its authority decreased; sometimes the office became elective and its term was limited to one year. Moreover, as the state slowly extended its authority by acquiring additional functions, new officers were created to discharge these. Thus at Athens by ca. 632 and perhaps much earlier the monarchy had been replaced by an annual board of nine elective officials; one of them bore the title of king.

An important passage of the *Iliad* (18.497–508) is suggestive for the way the assembly developed. It comes from the account of the designs wrought by the divine smith Hephaestus on the shield which he made for Achilles. The scene showed a dispute between two men about the wergild or payment due for a man who had been killed. One of the parties offered to pay in full, but the other refused to accept anything. The elders sat on polished stones in a circle; each of them offered his verdict in turn. A prize of two talents of gold was to be given to the elder who offered the most just verdict; doubtless the most just verdict would be defined in practice as the one which both the parties were willing to accept. Furthermore, the people stood around and shouted, some for the one party and others for the other.

Plastic art is regrettably static. One can only imagine how the dispute portrayed on the shield of Achilles might proceed further. It is at least conceivable that none of the elders could devise a verdict satisfactory to both parties; then each of the two might appeal to those of the people who shouted for him and try to assert his right by force. Thus the scene on the shield is not far removed from a general fight. But the imagination can go one step further. If one side in a fight is much more numerous than the other, the former usually wins; in such a situation, all the interested persons might agree to count the strong right arms instead of wielding them. Thus the general fight is not far removed from the practice of taking a vote in a public assembly. As Santayana pointed out, the habit of taking decisions by majority vote is not self-explanatory.

The development suggested in the preceding paragraph is not wholly imaginary. The crucial element, the threat of appeal to a violent mob, is attested as a constitutional device in Tegea. As Xenophon relates (*Hellenica* 6.5.6–9), at Tegea in 370 a party led by Callibius and Proxenus tried to launch a proposal for setting up a federation of Arcadia, but they could not gain a majority among the body called the *thearoi*, which may have been a council of officials. So, expecting to have a clear majority in the assembly, they carried out their weapons. Thereupon their opponents, led by Stasippus, armed themselves and proved to be no less numerous. Fighting ensued. Thus the appeal to force, in connection with taking an issue to the assembly, is known to have occurred in Tegea.

Taken together, the scene on the shield of Achilles and the events at Tegea in 370 suggest how a major change came about in the function of the public assembly. In the Homeric poems the assembly was essentially a meeting to receive the king's orders, even though some approval or opposition might be expressed. In Greek cities of the classical period, on the other hand, final decisions were normally taken by vote of the public assembly; that is, the assembly had become sovereign. The process of change cannot be traced in detail; but if it was in outline as suggested above, an important consequence follows. At Tegea in 370 the initiative in transferring the issue from the *thearoi* to the assembly was taken, not by the mass of the common people, but by Callibius and Proxenus. Likewise in the scene on the shield of Achilles a similar initiative might be taken, not by the people who shouted for the parties to the lawsuit, but by the parties themselves. Thus the sovereignty of the assembly was not the result of a class struggle of commoners, who attended the assembly, against an aristocracy, which worked through a council; it came about because of conflicts between political leaders, who appealed severally to their followings among the common people. In other words, the sovereignty of the assembly does not necessarily imply that the common people had achieved class consciousness.

ORIENTAL INFLUENCE[5]

As settled communities developed in Greece in the dark ages, it should be presumed that their outlook was highly conservative; people did things one way because they believed that this was the way things had always been done. A recurrent phrase in the *Odyssey* illustrates this attitude. When Odysseus calls up the shades of the dead and tries in vain to embrace that of his mother, she explains: "This is the way (*dike*) of mortals, whenever someone dies. The muscles no longer have flesh and bones; those parts are overcome by the powerful might of blazing fire, once the breath of life leaves the white bones, but the ghost like a dream departs in flight" (*Odyssey* 11.218–222). Elsewhere in the poem various

Early Corinthian kotyle. [Courtesy Staatliche Kunstsammlungen Kassel and D.A. Amyx.]

modes of behavior are commended as "the way (*dike*)" of old men (24.255), of kings (4.691), of slaves (14.59), and so on. The word *dike* already had powerful overtones, implying good order and justice. To say that such and such conduct was "the way (*dike*)" of a specific group was an unanswerable exhortation, in the eyes of those audiences for whom the *Odyssey* was composed.

In a period of about a hundred years beginning ca. 750 Greek conservatism was disturbed by a number of changes, most of which were prompted by oriental influence. For example, there was a change in the type of designs painted on pottery. In the dark ages decoration of pottery was geometric; it made use of highly formalized representations of men and animals, alongside of geometric figures, such as triangles, circles and spirals. Peasant cultures in many parts of the world have used similar ornamentation. But in the second half of the eighth century more naturalistic styles began to appear in some Greek cities; collectively these are called "orientalizing." The new styles differed from place to place; Rhodian, Chiote, Sicyonian and other types of pottery can be distinguished. The most important of the new styles were those produced in Corinth ca. 725–ca. 550; Protocorinthian and Corinthian wares came to be exported more widely than those of any other Greek city.

Another import from the east was the alphabet. The earliest Greek inscriptions are to be dated rather before 700; apparently the alphabet was adopted in the eighth century, perhaps in the second half of the century, and different cities may have adopted it independently of one another. Some features show that the source of the Greek alphabet was Semitic. The Greek names of the letters have no meaning in Greek, but they are drawn from names which have a meaning in the Semitic languages; alpha and beta, for example, are mere letter-names in Greek, but in Semitic besides designating letters they mean "ox" and "house" respectively. Again the order of the letters is the same in the Semitic alphabets and in Greek. It is not so clear which of the Semitic peoples was the immediate source of the Greek alphabet; the Phoenicians perhaps, since they traded extensively by sea.

The Greeks may have borrowed the Semitic alphabet originally for commercial purposes, but it made possible a new development in literature. Previously the highest form of literary entertainment was orally composed epics; the chief surviving specimen is the Homeric poems. The oral poet used a traditional technique; he relied on an elaborate series of formulaic phrases, which his predecessors had built up to meet the combined demands of narration and meter. The subjects too, both the legends and the characters, were traditional; each successive poet might make at most minor modifications in the formulaic technique and the content of the lays. But with the introduction of the alphabet writing became available as an aid to composition. This does not mean that a new art of written composition was grafted on to the traditional technique of oral epic. On the contrary, written verse differed as much from oral verse as did verse from prose. The poet who used writing could select each word with care. The first such poets in Greece abandoned the hexameter, the meter of oral epic, and developed new meters, namely, elegiacs, iambics and lyric meters. Moreover, where oral epic had kept to customary ideas, the new poets could express their individuality; they could challenge convention and voice their own loves and hates.

The earliest known poet to use writing as an aid to composition was Archilochus of Paros. The approximate date of his activity is known, since he mentioned a solar eclipse of 648. The extant fragments of his work sometimes challenge established views. Thus Archilochus joined the expedition sent from Paros in the Cyclades to colonize the island of Thasos in the northern Aegean; thence a force crossed to the mainland and fought against a local Thracian tribe, the Saeans. In the fighting Archilochus fled and threw away his shield. In flight a shield was a heavy encumbrance; to throw it away was a disgraceful deed, the mark of a coward. Archilochus boasted of his deed, saying (fr. 6):

One of the Saeans prides himself on my shield, which I left beside a bush. . . but I'll get another just as good.

This, like other challenges to convention, became a new convention. In the first half of the sixth century the poet Alcaeus of Mytilene fought in a war against the Athenians and threw away his shield. More than five centuries later the Roman poet Horace, an admirer of Alcaeus, fought at the battle of Philippi and threw away his shield, or at least he said so; what else could a self-respecting poet do?

Another literary feature belongs to oral epic but shows oriental features. Aside from the Homeric poems parts of another corpus of oral verse have been preserved; they are the compositions attributed to the Boeotian poet, Hesiod. The most popular of these, the *Works and Days*, collects together moral and practical precepts for the good farmer on the occasion of a dispute between the poet and his brother. More significant here is the Hesiodic poem called the *Theogony*. This tries to state the origin of all the many gods. The central narrative tells of three successive generations of gods, who ruled in heaven. It is a barbarous story, in which Cronus, the chief of the second generation, castrates his father and swallows his own children, until he is overcome by the youngest of them, Zeus. A Hittite poem, first published in A.D. 1945 and often called *The Epic of Kumarbi*, tells of four successive generations of gods. Kumarbi, the chief of the third generation, castrates his father and swallows the children of Earth, until he is overthrown by the youngest of them. There are more similarities of detail; for example, in the *Theogony* the male god of the first generation is Uranus, a word meaning "sky"; in the Hittite epic the chief god of the second generation is Anu, a word of Sumerian origin meaning "sky." But the oriental elements in the *Theogony* are composite. The instrument used by Cronus to attack his father is a knife called *harpe*, which is not a native Greek word; it may be derived from the Semitic word *ḥ r b*, meaning "sword." The lines of transmission linking the *Theogony* to the *Epic of Kumarbi* must have been complex. Some further elements in early Greek mythology seem to depend on oriental sources. Thus the *Theogony* (line 123) mentions something called Erebus, saying that it and black Night came into being from the primeval Void. The Hebrew word *'ereb* means "evening," "sunset" or "the west." Again in the *Odyssey* (4.561–569) the Elysian plain is mentioned as a place of happiness, where privileged persons go at the end of their lives. *El* is a Semitic word for "god" and the Ugaritic texts from Ras-Shamra mention an obscure "field of El."

The time of composition of the *Theogony* is not clear; a date in the eighth or seventh century can be defended. But the date when it reached its present form may not be important, since it was composed orally in a traditional technique. It presents ideas of the kind which could reach Greece at the time when the alphabet was borrowed and orientalizing styles of pottery began. It is indeed conceivable that the story of the successive generations of gods was borrowed as early as the late bronze age, to which the Hittite text of the *Epic of Kumarbi* belongs, but this is less likely; the complexity of the story would not be easy to preserve in Greece of the dark ages, when contact with eastern lands was slight. The proper conclusion is that in the early archaic period, as in the late bronze age, Greece belonged to the single cultural and intellectual circle of the Near East.

A change in the mode of fighting battles began in the seventh century and owed something to oriental models. In the sixth and fifth centuries the typical mode of Greek warfare employed hoplite tactics. The troops were heavily armed infantry or hoplites, with a thrusting spear and a sword for attack, but their characteristic equipment was defensive armor, including a plate corslet, greaves, a closed helmet and a large round shield (*hoplon*) with an armband and a handgrip. Moreover, the men fought in close formation as a *phalanx* or series of rows in depth; the front row advanced and tried to push the enemy off the field, and the other rows kept close order behind it and added their weight to the impact. In the eighth century fighting was conducted by an earlier method, which is known from the Homeric poems, from Archilochus and from representations on vases. Fighting was on foot but was carried out by a relatively few leading warriors; they had a shield, a sword and a throwing spear, but except for the shield they had little defensive armor for the head and body. These warriors were not organized in a phalanx; each fought largely on his own, and a Homeric battle tended to become a series of duels.

Until a few years ago it was believed that all the items of hoplite equipment and with them the hoplite phalanx were adopted within a few decades a little before or after 700; and once one city adopted them, the others had to do likewise in order to survive. But recent study of vases has led to different conclusions. It now appears that the several items of hoplite equipment were adopted piecemeal; none of them is attested before 750, but all of them appeared by 700. However, at first they were used separately, not combined into a complete set of equipment; the full hoplite panoply is first shown on a vase ca. 675. Further, the adoption of hoplite equipment did not at once bring a change in tactics; men using some or all the items of hoplite equipment continued to fight in the less organized fashion of the eighth century. The hoplite phalanx does not appear on vases before ca. 650.

This change in conclusions about the date of adoption of hoplite tactics affects the question of their possible social effects. While the view was current that the hoplite phalanx was introduced ca. 700, it was possible to see in this a cause of subsequent revolutionary chages, the establishment of some regimes called tyrannies; it was argued that hoplite tactics spread the burden of fighting to a wider class, the substantial peasant farmers, than before, that this class accordingly demanded a share in political power and that some tyrants rose as its champions. It was further maintained that a constitutional reform was carried out in Sparta during the seventh century and achieved a satisfactory compromise between the conflicting interests. Now that the adoption of hoplite equipment and hoplite tactics proves to have been a more gradual process, completed at a later date, the difficult problem of the dates of the early tyrannies acquires new importance and the evidence for constitutional reform in Sparta has to be reexamined. Besides, it has been urged that the substantial peasants, who supplied the hoplite phalanx, were likely to be a conservative force; they would dislike military disturbances as threatening their land and taking them away from tillage. So they might well be a force making for stability, not revolution. These questions will require further attention in chapters 2 and 3.

Some items of hoplite equipment indicate Greek knowledge of foreign artifacts. The development of the corslet was influenced by the metal-working cultures of Central Europe and Italy. But the closed helmet and the large round shield with armband and handgrip were derived from oriental models. During the reign of Tiglath-Pileser III (745–727) Assyrian forces approached the Syrian coast of the Mediterranean; hence it was possible for Greek travelers and traders to see Assyrian equipment.

COLONIZATION[6]

From ca. 750 onwards the founding of colonies by Greek cities indicates that economic changes were occurring. A Greek colony (*apoikia*) differed from a modern colony. A Greek colony was an organized group of settlers, sent out from a city to found a new city at a distance and usually overseas. The old city dispatching the settlement was called the *metropolis* or mother city; sometimes two or more cities cooperated to provide settlers, but one of them supplied leadership and organization. The new city or colony was fully equipped with the institutions and political life of its period; accordingly it could behave as an independent state, although some colonies retained ties with their mother cities. It is permissible to speak of an age of colonization ca. 750–ca. 550. Greek cities continued to found colonies right through the classical period, but by ca. 550 Greeks had reached all the main areas where they settled before the reign of Alexander the Great (336–323). The age of colonization constitutes a recognizable stage in Greek expansion; it brought Greeks far away from their homelands, so that they settled on the coasts of the Black Sea and most of the shores of the Mediterranean.

Usually the immediate reason for sending out a colony was land hunger, when population in the mother city had grown beyond the local means of subsistence. An example is the foundation of Cyrene (ca. 630) in North Africa, as described by Herodotus (4.150–158). The original settlement was sent from the island of Thera after a prolonged famine and it sailed in two penteconters; the men were chosen by lot and dispatched under compulsion; they probably numbered two hundred. But if land hunger was the general cause of colonization, a further question arises. It is at least conceivable that, as settled conditions developed, in much of Greece population outran local means of subsistence long before ca. 750 and for a long time there was a high rate of early mortality; one can only conjecture why from ca. 750 a constructive effort was made to dispose of surplus manpower by colonization.

The question of a causal connection between colonization and trade is not simple. Often the foundation of colonies had the effect of promoting trade, especially that of the mother city; and probably trade, as well as piracy, was a source of information about sites suitable for prospective colonists. But it does not follow that a desire to expand trade was a predominant cause of colonization. It is noticeable that the sites chosen for many colonies were plains well suited for agriculture, and this fact supports the view that land hunger provided the driving motive. Even so, a few colonies were founded for purposes of trade. A clear example is the settlement at Naucratis in Egypt. Herodotus (2.178) mentions it and says that a sanctuary, the Hellenium, had been founded there by people from several Greek cities, namely Chios, Teos, Phocaea, Clazomenae, Rhodes, Cnidus, Halicarnassus, Phaselis and Mytilene. He adds that three separate sanctuaries also had been founded there, by people from Aegina, Samos and Miletus. Doubtless Herodotus is right in saying that the settlement at Naucratis was founded with the permission of the pharaoh, but he errs in saying that it was Amasis (569–525); the earliest Greek pottery found at Naucratis is dated ca. 615/610. Evidently the settlement was essentially commercial. The same is true of the settlement at Al Mina (Sueidia), in northern Syria. It is known solely from excavation and its history can be traced from the second half of the eighth century. It was a small trading post, well placed for access to routes into the Fertile Crescent.

The most acute problem about colonization is chronology. Thucydides (6.3–5) gives dates of foundation for most of the Greek colonies in Sicily. But for colonies founded elsewhere literary evidence of date comes from much later sources; indeed the most plentiful dates are given by Eusebius, a bishop active early in the fourth century, A.D. and some of his dates are surprisingly early. It is, for example, incredible that Cumae in south Italy was founded in 1051. Archaeological evidence gained by excavating the sites of colonies could be decisive, but a complication arises in using it. The successive styles of orientalizing, and especially of Protocorinthian and Corinthian, pottery can be arranged in a relative sequence on internal grounds, but this sequence does not of itself provide dates. To gain absolute dates for the sequence one must assume that Thucydides's dates for foundation of colonies in Sicily are correct and that the type of pottery found in the lowest layer of the excavated sites among these was the type current at the time of foundation. The sequence of pottery styles can then be used to date the foundation of colonies elsewhere, by noticing what type of pottery is found in the lowest layers at these sites. This method and the assumptions on which it rests may be accepted as a working hypothesis; it has not led to contradictions.

Surveying the chief colonies by area, one may start in the west. In Sicily Greek settlers acquired most of the eastern part of the island, including good agricultural plains, and penetrated westwards along the coasts. Many Greek cities founded settlements in Sicily. Naxus, the oldest Greek colony there, was founded in 734 from Chalcis in Euboea. Syracuse was founded from Corinth in the next year. In the ensuing century and a half other Sicilian sites attracted settlers from many parts of Greece, including Megara, Euboea, Rhodes and Crete. The island of Corcyra near the approach to the Adriatic was colonized from Corinth and according to a tradition preserved by Strabo (6.2.4, p. 269) the settlement was founded in the same year as Syracuse; that may be approximately correct, since Corcyra lay on one of the sea routes to Sicily. Tradition provided less information about the colonies in south Italy. Cumae, the most northerly of these, was reputed to be the oldest Greek colony in the west; it may have been founded ca. 750, and the settlers came from Euboea. Other colonies followed, until Greeks held the southern coasts as far as the heel of Italy. Several of the colonies were founded by people from Achaea in the northern Peloponnese; they included Sybaris and Croton, which became the leading cities of south Italy during the second half of the sixth century. Tarentum was the only colony founded from

Sparta; its earliest pottery is dated ca. 700/650. Beyond Sicily the western basin of the Mediterranean was opened up to Greek enterprise by men from Phocaea in mainland Ionia: they founded Massilia, the modern Marseille, ca. 600. The Massiliotes in turn founded dependent settlements for trade as far as the northeast coast of Spain.

Among districts to the north and east of the Greek mainland, numerous colonies were founded in the three-pronged peninsula which came to be called Chalcidice, because many of the settlements were from Chalcis. But some were from the island of Andros near Euboea. Possibly Chalcis in many cases provided leadership but drew additional colonists from other cities. Poteidaea, holding an important position at the isthmus of Pallene, the westernmost prong, was exceptional; it was founded from Corinth in the late seventh or early sixth century (see chapter 2, pp. 51–52). Otherwise the colonies in Chalcidice were probably founded in the seventh century, but no more precise date can be given with any confidence. Further east at the Bosporus Calchedon was founded by the Megarians on the Asiatic shore and had good agricultural land. Byzantium on the European shore was founded seventeen years later, also by the Megarians; it was less well placed for agriculture but in time it grew more prosperous, because it held a crucial position on the route from the Black Sea. The interval of seventeen years is given by Herodotus(4.144.2); the absolute dates offered by Eusebius, 685 and 659, may not be far wrong but they lack confirmation. A great many colonies were founded on the coasts of the Propontis and the Black Sea, and most of them traced their foundation to Miletus. Perhaps the latter city gave leadership but drew some colonists from other cities of Ionia. For many of these settlements Eusebius gives dates, sometimes two for the same colony, in the eighth and seventh centuries. At three of the Black Sea colonies, Istrus, Olbia and Apollonia Pontica, the archaeological record is adequate to provide some indication; the earliest pottery found at these three colonies is dated ca. 610/600.

PARTICULARISM AND PANHELLENISM[7]

In the introduction to his history of the Peloponnesian War Thucydides argued that in early times warfare in Greece was conducted only on a small scale. On land there were border disputes between neighboring states, but no city attracted a large number of allies so as to form a major center of power. Thucydides indicated economic and political causes of weakness, and another can be specified; in the archaic period the institutions of the *polis* were rudimentary and weak, and therefore there were few relations of war or of alliance between cities. Powerful families in different cities developed relationships of friendship, marriage and rivalry; many of the odes of Pindar were composed for such families and they indicate, in a loose sense, a leading class which was international. Ties between families powerful in different cities could affect the fortunes of the cities but they did not necessarily lead the cities to develop policies of their own.

In the same context Thucydides said that the nearest approach to a general Greek conflict occurred in connection with the war between Chalcis and Eretria, as many other cities joined the one side or the other. Chalcis and Eretria were the leading cities of Euboea and the war has come to be called the war of the Lelantine plain, because at least one issue between the two cities was control of the plain of the Lelantum River. Geographically the plain belongs to Chalcis; it lies just east of that city and ends when half the journey to Eretria is done. Herodotus says that Samos was an ally of Chalcis and Miletus an ally of Eretria. The conflict between Samos and Miletus may suggest that the Lelantine war was more a series of local conflicts than a general war. Although Samos and Miletus were divided by the sea, they were not far apart and as late as 441 they went to war for control of Priene, which lay between them.

The date and nature of the Lelantine War are obscure. Nowadays it is commonly believed that the war was fought late in the eighth or early in the seventh century and that it had to do with disputes arising from colonization. There is a good case for this view, but a date as late as the sixth century can be defended. Even the outcome of the war is uncertain. In the fifth and fourth centuries Chalcis was usually stronger than Eretria, and during the war Chalcis with help from Pharsalus in Thessaly defeated the Eretrians in battle, but it does not necessarily follow that Chalcis won the war. It may be more to the point to note the pottery series at Chalcis. Although the city has not been excavated, considerable finds have been made in a quarry, which probably lay within the ancient city. The geometric pottery belongs mostly to the eighth century; few, if any, of the fragments extend the series into the seventh century. Of the later pottery none need be earlier than the middle of the sixth century. Thus there is a gap which suggests that Chalcis was somehow eclipsed in the seventh and early sixth centuries, whether because of the Lelantine War or other causes.

Although local particularism was acute in early Greece, some customs drew men of different cities together. Usually the occasions for coming together were religious, but religious associations sometimes acquired political functions. An example is provided by the Ionian cities of Asia Minor, which built a temple, the Panionium, to Poseidon on the northern slope of Mount Mycale. The twelve cities whose people gathered there for periodic festivals were Samos, Chios and ten cities of the mainland. When the Ionians felt themselves threatened by the expansion of the Persian Empire ca. 544, they gathered at the Panionium for political deliberation. A religious association of a different kind was the League of Amphictyones, comprising mostly states in central and northern Greece from Boeotia to Thessaly. The members were not cities but tribal groups, such as the Thessalians, the Boeotians, the Locrians and the Phocians. This League arose originally to protect and administer the sanctuary of Demeter at Anthela near Thermopylae, but it later acquired control over the sanctuary of Apollo at Delphi. The oath of the members included a promise not to destroy any city of the Amphictyones or cut off its water supply. From time to time Amphictyonic meetings were a scene of political rivalry between the Thessalians, the Boeotians and the Phocians.

With or without a league of protectors, some oracular sanctuaries acquired more than local reputation and hence provided links between Greeks of different cities. At Delphi there was already an oracle in the late bronze age but the deity consulted was Earth and the sanctuary may have been frequented only by people from its immediate neighborhood. The cult of Apollo was introduced not later than the middle of the eighth century. Somehow the colonization movement brought about regard for the Delphic oracle in all parts of Greece; a city founding a colony regularly sought divine approval beforehand and often the god consulted was Apollo of Delphi.

The sanctuary of Zeus at Olympia in the territory of Elis provided an oracle and a festival with competitions of several kinds. The list of Olympic victors, drawn up about 400, said that the festival was begun in 776; until 736 the victors came from the western Peloponnese and chiefly from Messenia, but afterwards competitors came from further and further afield. The reliability of the early dates in the Olympic list is a difficult question (see chapter 2, p. 42); perhaps the dates should be somewhat later. But it is doubtless true that at first the festival attracted people mainly from the western Peloponnese and only later acquired wider popularity. The festival was finally reorganized in 580, although it is not clear whether this was a cause or a consequence of its panhellenic popularity. A few years later Cleisthenes the tyrant of Sicyon, seeking the best man in Greece as bridegroom for his daughter, chose the Olympic festival as the occasion to announce the competition for her hand (see chapter 2, p. 46). Evidently this festival had become an occasion recognized by all Greeks. Persons not Greek were excluded from the competitions. The other major panhellenic festivals were founded in the first half of the sixth century, the Pythian games at Delphi in 582, the Nemean games at Cleonae between Sicyon and Argos in 573, and the Isthmian games at the isthmus of Corinth in 582. These foundations attest some growth in panhellenic consciousness; they also mark a growth in wealth associated with the period of the early tyrants.

NOTES

1. See M. Cary, *The Geographic Background of Greek and Roman History* (Oxford 1949) 1–56.

2. Perhaps the best short introduction to the study of bronze-age Greece is provided by S. Dow, "The Greeks in the Bronze Age," *Rapports (II) du XIe Congrès International des Sciences Historiques* (1960) 1–34. See also A. E. Samuel, *The Mycenaeans in History* (Englewood Cliffs, N.J. 1966); E. Vermeule, *Greece in the Bronze Age* (Chicago 1964). Traditions about the Dorian Invasions are given by Herodotus (1.56) and Thucydides (1.12.3); those about Ionians and Aeolians are given by Herodotus (1.145–151). On dialects the standard English handbook is C.D. Buck, *The Greek Dialects* (Chicago 1955). The survival of bronze-age mythology in Greece was established by M.P. Nilsson, *The Mycenaean Origin of Greek Mythology* (Berkeley and Los Angeles 1932). Milman Parry expounded his discovery in *L' épithète traditionnelle dans Homère* (Paris 1928) and in numerous articles, which were published in *HSCP* 41 (1930) 73–147; 43 (1932) 1–50; *TAPA* 59 (1928) 233–247; 64 (1933) 179–197; *CP* 28 (1933) 30–43. A good introduction to Homeric problems is provided in the chapters by E.R. Dodds in M. Platnauer (ed.), *Fifty Years of Classical Scholarship* (Oxford 1954). A.J.B. Wace and F.H. Stubbings, *A Companion to Homer* (London 1962), is disappointing. For conspicuous examples of bronze-age artifacts mentioned in the Homeric poems see H.L. Lorimer, *Homer and the Monuments* (London 1950) 211–219 and 328–335 (on the boars' tusk helmet and the "cup of Nestor"). On bronze and iron in the poems see D.H.F. Gray, "Metal-Working in Homer," *JHS* 74 (1954) 1–15.

3. See M. Cary (supra n. 1) 57–102. On Thessaly, Phocis and Locris see Larsen, *GFS*, 12–26 and 40–58. The defeats of the Thessalians by the Phocians not many years before 480 are known from Hdt. 8.27–28.

4. A general account of the *polis* is offered by V. Ehrenberg, *The Greek State* (London, 2nd ed. 1969). Much information about *ethne* is provided by Larsen, *GFS*, 3–103. Attic use of the word *polis* for the acropolis is attested by Thuc. 2.15.6. His account of the Athenian attack on Aetolia in 426 is at 3.94–100. On the twelve cities or parts of Aetolia see Polyb. 2.41.7; Hdt. 1.145. The failure of the public assembly in Homeric Ithaca to meet for twenty years is given in *Odyssey* 2.26–27. For a good, brief account of archaic social structure see Forrest, *Emergence* 45–58. The view taken here about clans and phratries is based on A. Andrewes, "Philochoros on Phratries," *JHS* 81 (1961) 1–15 and "Phratries in Homer," *Hermes* 89 (1961) 129–140; for an earlier and different view see Hignett, *HAC* 55–57, 313–315 and 390–391. The interpretation of the decree concerning Deceleieis and Demotionidae is based on Wade-Gery, *Essays* 116–134 = "Studies in the Structure of Attic Society: I. Demotionidae," *CQ* 25 (1931) 129–143. For the three Dorian tribes see Hdt. 5.68; Tyrtaeus fr. 1, line 51. On Attic and Ionian tribes see Hignett, *HAC* 50–51. The chief Homeric passages illustrating the council and the assembly are: (1) assembly alone: *Iliad* 1.54–305; 19.40–237; 20.4–40; Odyssey 2.1–257; 8.1–45; (2) council and assembly: *Iliad* 2.48–399; 9.9–174; meetings resembling a council occur also at *Odyssey* 8.389–399 and 13.13–16.

5. On the alphabet see L.H. Jeffery, *The Local Scripts of Archaic Greece* (Oxford 1961). The fragments of Archilochus are to be found in E. Diehl, *Anthologia Lyrica Graeca*, vol. I (Leipzig, 2nd ed. 1936); on his date see F. Jacoby, "The Date of Archilochos," *CQ* 35 (1941) 97–109. The flight of Alcaeus is mentioned by Hdt. 5.95. The Epic of Kumarbi is to be found in J.B. Pritchard, *Ancient Near Eastern Texts relating to the Old Testament* (Princeton, 2nd ed., 1955) 120–125; see also H.G. Güterbock, "The Hittite Version of the Hurrian Kumarbi Myths," *AJA* 52 (1948) 123–134. The current view on the introduction of hoplite equipment and hoplite tactics is owed to A.M. Snodgrass, "The Hoplite Reform and History," *JHS* 85 (1965) 110–122. The earlier view was that of H.L. Lorimer, "The Hoplite Phalanx," *ABSA* 42 (1947) 76–138. Following Lorimer's view, A.

Andrewes, *Probouleusis* (Oxford 1954), developed an important thesis about the social effects of hoplite tactics; for criticisms see Sealey, "Probouleusis and the Sovereign Assembly," *CSCA* 2 (1969) 247–269.

6. The article by R.M. Cook, "Ionia and Greece in the Eighth and Seventh Centuries B.C.," *JHS* 66 (1946) 67–98, has fundamental importance for colonization and especially for its chronology. Cook's arguments have been criticized by A.J. Graham, "The Date of the Greek Penetration of the Black Sea," *BICS* 5 (1958) 25–42. See also A.J. Graham, *Colony and Mother City in Ancient Greece* (Manchester 1964). On Cyrene see L.H. Jeffery, "The Pact of the First Settlers at Cyrene," Historia 10 (1961) 139–147. A. Blakeway, "Prolegomena to the Study of Greek Commerce with Italy, Sicily and France in the Eighth and Seventh Centuries B.C.," *ABSA* 33 (1932–33) 170–208, argued that a major reason for founding colonies in the West was a desire to promote trade, but some of his dates for pottery were insecure. On Al Mina see C.L. Woolley, "Excavations at Al Mina, Sueidia, I–II," *JHS* 58 (1938) 1–30 and 133–170, and J.D. Beazley, "The Excavations at Al Mina, Sueidia, III. The Red-Figured Vases," *JHS* 59 (1939) 1–44.

7. The chief sources on the Lelantine War are Hdt. 5.99.1; Thuc. 1.15.3; Str. 10.1.11–12.448; Plut. *Mor.* 760e–761b. For discussion see J. Boardman, "Early Euboean Pottery and History," *ABSA* 52 (1957) 1–29, also D.W. Bradeen, "The Lelantine War and Pheidon of Argos," *TAPA* 78 (1947) 223–241. Warfare between Samos and Miletus in 441 is recorded by Thuc. 1.115.2. The case for a later date for the Lelantine War rests mainly on Theognis 891–894, which seems to associate the destruction of the Lelantine plain with the Cypselidae; see E. Will, *Korinthiaka: Recherches sur l'histoire et la civilisation de Corinthe des origines aux guerres médiques* (Paris 1955) 391–404. On Ionia and the Panionium see Hdt. 1.141–148. On the Amphictyonic League see Aeschin. 2.115–116. On the oracle at Delphi see Aesch. Eum.1–11; Homeric Hymn to Apollo; W.G. Forrest, "Colonisation and the Rise of Delphi," *Historia* 6 (1957) 160–175.

2

Tyranny in the Early Peloponnese

In the course of his introductory survey of early Greek history (1.1–19), Thucydides remarked on the rise of tyrannies: "As Greece grew more powerful and the standard of wealth rose, tyrannies were established in the cities for the most part, the revenues being large (previously there were ancestral kingships with specific privileges)" (1.13.1). The modern meaning of the word "tyranny" must be avoided here; in the seventh and sixth centuries rulers of a new type arose in many cities, and subsequent Greek tradition, preserving information about them, called them "tyrants" (*tyrannoi*). Thucydides noticed that tyrants arose in many different cities within a single period and he associated their appearance with a growth in wealth.

The origin of the word can be traced. It is not Indo-European. In Greek it first occurs in a poem by Archilochus. The nature of the poem is not wholly clear, but apparently Archilochus made a character called Charon, a carpenter, speak the four lines which are preserved (Archilochus fr. 22 = Ar. *Rhet.* 3.1418b28):

I care not for the things of Gyges of much gold; I am not seized by jealousy; I do not gaze in envy at godlike works, nor do I long for a great tyranny; for it is far from my eyes.

Gyges was king of Lydia and a contemporary of Archilochus. He overthrew his predecessor and founded a new dynasty. He and his successors developed relations with Greek cities and oracles, and Greeks were much impressed by their wealth. The passage of Archilochus suggests that *tyrannos* was the Lydian word for king; moreover, it shows that Greeks associated the word with oriental wealth and with display of wealth. Charon's remark can be paraphrased: "I don't want to be a pasha."

In Greek the word "tyrant" acquired subtle and complex implications. Generally the term was used of rulers who had no hereditary or legal claim to rule in their cities, although Pheidon, who will be discussed below, constituted an exception to this. Again, the tyrant usually did not take any official position as his mode of rule. The tyrants of the fourth and third centuries in the Greek cities of Sicily did take such a position, but generally the rule of a tyrant was not exercised through any office but was an informal and extralegal preeminence in the affairs of his city; the modern parallel that springs to mind is the boss of a town. The rule of a tyrant was not necessarily oppressive or unpopular; some of the early tyrants were remembered for the benefits they had brought, and it has been held that some may have risen as champions of popular movements. Indeed, the word "tyrant" continued to be used in verse as a neutral term for "monarch." Yet side by side with this neutral usage the word acquired pejorative implications. These can first be recognized in an Athenian drinking song, composed about the end of the sixth century in honor of Harmodius and Aristogeiton; in 514 they had killed Hipparchus, the younger brother of the tyrant then ruling Athens, and the song praised them as liberators:

Your fame will last forever, beloved Harmodius and Aristogeiton, because you killed the tyrant and made Athens equal in law.

(See also chapter 6, p. 145.) By the time of Herodotus the Spartans boasted of their constant hostility to tyranny. Public life in the classical Greek city was highly competitive, and when one competitor far outdistanced his rivals, they felt that they no longer had a fair chance; they used the term "tyrant" to express their disapproval of his excessive preeminence.

Since a good many tyrannies were set up in Peloponnesian cities in the seventh and sixth centuries, the question arises whether they were due to common causes. Among theories which have sought to answer this question two merit special attention. One, the "pre-Dorian" theory, recognizes that in most Peloponnesian cities a privileged or ruling element traced its origin to the Dorian invasions, but a pre-Dorian element in the population survived; the theory maintains that some at least of the tyrants rose to power as champions of the pre-Dorian element against Dorian aristocracies. The second theory, the "hoplite" theory, claims that the introduction of hoplite tactics had large social effects. The military power of the state, it is urged, came to depend on a wider class than before, namely, on a class of substantial peasant farmers; these accordingly claimed a voice in running the affairs of their cities, and the tyrants rose to power by championing their political aspirations. In order to test these theories and consider the question of common causes, the present chapter will survey the early Peloponnesian tyrannies, so far as known; it will deal in turn with Pheidon of Argos, Cleisthenes of Sicyon and the Cypselidae of Corinth.

The sources on these rulers are distressingly scanty. The most valuable is the work of Herodotus, who provides digressions on Cleisthenes and the Cypselidae and an allusion to Pheidon. Although Herodotus lived long after the events, he was free from the fourth-century desire to systematize early history. Aristotle in the *Politics* says a little about the early tyrants and his statements on chronology are especially important. The question of his reliability is difficult; it is not clear whether his information was drawn from historians of his own age or rested on research conducted independently in his school. In the fourth century Ephorus wrote the first general history of Greece from the dark ages until his own time. To some extent it reduced early history to a pattern and, unlike Thucydides, it offered no challenge to conventional opinions; it achieved lasting popularity and was used in full or in summaries to instruct the young for many centuries. Probably much of the information provided by late authors, such as Pausanias, rests directly or ultimately on Ephorus. The student of the early tyrannies must repeatedly face the question, how far he may use authors of the fourth century and later to supplement Herodotus.

PHEIDON[2]

Pheidon was hereditary king of Argos at an early date. Aristotle (*Pol.* 5.1310b 26–28) makes the curious remark that Pheidon became a tyrant from being king. He does not substantiate the statement; on the contrary, he makes it to justify his claim that tyrants sometimes arise from kings. It follows that Aristotle could expect his readers to accept as already known the view that Pheidon became a tyrant; in other words, this view was not Aristotle's own conclusion but was drawn from his sources. Speculation about the identity and date of those sources would perhaps not be profitable, but by reviewing the recorded activities of Pheidon it may be possible to discover what was meant by calling him a tyrant.

In a brief digression Herodotus (6.127.3) says that Pheidon "performed a greater outrage than any other Greek; he expelled the Elean presiding officers and presided himself at the competition in Olympia." Late sources reveal a pattern of events to which this occurrence belongs. The population of the territory of Elis formed two groups. One, the Eleans, was a privileged body; they alone provided the presiding officers for the Olympic festival in the classical period, and they were doubtless descended from those who had conquered the land in the age of migrations. The town of Elis on the Peneus river in the northern part of the territory was their city. The other group, the Pisatans, was underprivileged and belonged to rural districts; they were akin to the Arcadians across the border and were descended from those who held the territory before the Elean conquest. The sanctuary of Zeus at Olympia, together with the town of Pisa nearby, lay close to the Alpheus river in the southern part of the territory. The late sources (Strabo, Pausanias, Eusebius) say that the Eleans controlled the festival from its inception, supposedly in 776; but they give varying accounts of a period of Pistan control in the seventh century. It is clear that the Eleans finally recovered control in time for the festival of 580; but previously, whether for a protracted period or intermittently, the Pisatans provided the presiding officers for the festival. Statements of Eusebius and Pausanias can be combined to yield the result that the Pisatans first secured control of the festival in 668 with help from Pheidon. Tradition spoke further of a series of Pisatan tyrants, although it preserved little reliable information about them beyond their names (Pantaleon, Damophon, Pyrrhus). The sources concerned themselves mainly with the presidency of the festival, but probably the intervention of Pheidon had also a secular effect, enabling the Pisatans to achieve some degree of autonomy under a dynasty of tyrants.

If Pheidon's intervention at Olympia is correctly dated to 668, another statement of Pausanias becomes important, since it seems to belong to the same chronological scheme. Without naming Pheidon, Pausanias (2.24.7) says that in 669 the Argives defeated the Lacedaemonians at Hysiae. Hysiae lay in the plain of Thyrea, the border district between Lacedaemon and the territory of Argos; the issue at stake in the battle was control of this plain. That is, Argos and Lacedaemon had each expanded until they came into conflict for the plain of Thyrea. Indeed Herodotus says (1.82.2) that at one time Argos controlled the east coast of the Peloponnese southward as far as Cape Malea and even the island of Cythera opposite that Cape. If this is correct, it is difficult to discover any period other than the reign of Pheidon for this expansion of Argive power. But it is also difficult to believe that Lacedaemon was driven back from so much land; perhaps the tradition followed by Herodotus was grossly inflated, and towards the south the Argos of Pheidon actually may have won little beyond the plain of Thyrea.

If Pheidon won the plain of Thyrea, one may accept in substance the statement of Ephorus (*F.Gr.Hist.* IIA 70F115) that he regained the lot of Temenus, although its language was drawn from legend. The story of the return of the Heracleidae said that they came to the Peloponnese in three companies and these shared out their conquests; one company took Messenia, one took Lacedaemon, and the company led by Temenus took the Argolid. Ephorus believed that after the time of Temenus the Argive kingdom fell apart and was eventually reunited by Pheidon. If the mythical element is removed from this account, there remains a tradition that Pheidon unified the Argolid; that is doubtless correct, if he proceeded to advance beyond the Argolid into the plain of Thyrea. But it is not clear how extensive was the Argolid as unified by Pheidon; that is, it is not clear how far he extended his rule eastwards in the Argolid peninsula. Traditions associating him with Aegina may have some basis (see below).

So far Pheidon emerges as a man who brought much territory around Argos under his rule, defeated the Lacedaemonians at Hysiae in 669 and intervened at Olympia in 668. There is no good reason to doubt that he did these things, but the dates are less than secure. They appear to rest on the Olympic victor list, which recorded a period of Pisatan control starting in or about 668. The list of Olympic victors was published by the sophist Hippias about 400 or soon after, and the latter part of the list from the reorganization of 580 was reliable. But doubt may be entertained about the earlier part of the list. It is not clear that Hippias had sound information for victors before 580; these entries may rest on speculative reconstruction. The list gave 776 as the year of the first celebration of the festival, but the accuracy of this was a subject of discussion in antiquity. The tradition on the interlude of Pisatan control was not uniform. Possibly during the first period after its inception the Olympic festival was celebrated at intervals more frequent than once in four years.

The question of the reliability of the Olympic victor list is important for several problems of seventh century chronology and it remains unsolved. The problem of the date of Pheidon is especially embarrassing, because Herodotus (6.127.3) says that Pheidon's son Leocedes was a suitor for Agariste, the daughter of Cleisthenes of Sicyon; the wooing of Agariste took place towards 570 (see below, p. 60). This would imply that Pheidon was active late in the seventh century or early in the sixth. But it is surprising to find an Argive among the suitors for Agariste, since Cleisthenes developed bitter hostility towards Argos; possibly Leocedes was the son of another Pheidon, whom Herodotus confused with the famous one.

In his short but informative digression on Pheidon of Argos (6.127.3), Herodotus implies an approximate date for the ruler's activities; he mentions the intervention at Olympia, and he adds one further item: Pheidon struck measures for the Peloponnesians. In the classical period a common system of weights and measures was used in most cities of the Peloponnese, though not in Corinth; it was called Pheidonian. Herodotus's word may comprise measures of weight as well as measures of length. Later sources say more. According to Ephorus (*F.Gr.Hist.* IIA 70F115 and 176) Pheidon made measures and also struck coins in Aegina; according to Aristotle (fr. 481), he invented coins, striking them in Aegina, and dedicated short spits (*obeliskoi*) at the Argive temple of Hera.

Coinage in precious metals was invented in the kingdom of Lydia and the earliest coins used to be dated ca. 700; but more recent studies, appearing since 1951, have shown that the earliest Lydian coins were struck ca. 630. Greek states adopted the invention gradually; the first coins to be struck in European Greece were made in Aegina in the last quarter of the seventh century. If Pheidon intervened at Olympia in 668, his reign was too early to have anything to do with coinage. But before the introduction of coinage, unstamped pieces of iron were used as a medium of exchange in Greece; they were of various shapes, short spits or *obeliskoi* being popular, and these gave their name to a small and common denomination of silver coin, after the introduction of coinage. Short iron spits have been found by excavation at the Argive temple of Hera; conceivably Pheidon dedicated some to establish a standard of size.

When Pausanias mentions the Argive victory at Hysiae, he fails to name Pheidon. In some other incidents Pheidon is not named by the source, but his presence has sometimes been suspected. One of these concerns relations between Corinth and Megara. Border disputes between these two cities were frequent at an early period and by the classical period Corinth was the stronger power. Pausanias (6.19.12–14) describes the treasury built by the Megarians at Olympia and says that above the pediment a shield was dedicated, recording that the treasury was built from spoils taken from the Corinthians. He indicates a very early date for the treasury, before the Athenian eponymous archons became annual (see chapter 4, p. 95), and he adds: "It is said that the Argives joined with the Megarians in the action against the Corinthians." Evidently Argive participation was not recorded in the dedication but was attested only by an oral tradition. Study of colonization may suggest a date for the Megarian victory. In the last third of the eighth century Megara was one of the cities which sent colonists to the eastern part of Sicily, but the best sites were secured by other cities, such as Chalcis and Corinth, and the Megarians had to be content with an inferior position at Megara Hyblaea. But in the seventh century colonists from Megara occupied good sites in the northeast at Calchedon and Byzantium. The apparent rise in the fortunes of Megara may reflect the victory over Corinth. Thus that victory may belong to the period of Pheidon. But any attempt to associate him with the victory is clearly a flimsy reconstruction; and the belief that he concerned himself with the affairs of Corinth and Megara is strengthened only slightly by the assertion of a late author (Nicolaus of Damascus *F.Gr.Hist.* IIA 90F35), that Pheidon was killed in Corinth when he came to the aid of one side in civil strife there.

The other sphere where Pheidon's activity may be suspected concerns Epidaurus, Aegina and Athens. Herodotus (5.82–88) tells a strange story about early relations between these cities. The Epidaurians, he says, built two cult images of olive wood to escape a famine; they obtained the wood from Athens and agreed to pay an annual rent. Later the Aeginetans, previously dependent on Epidaurus, rebelled and took away the two images, and so the Epidaurians stopped paying rent. The Athenians complained to Epidaurus and were referred to Aegina, but they were rebuffed by the Aeginetans and prepared to raid the island. The Aeginetans, however gained help from Argos; Argive troops traveled through Epidaurus to Aegina and inflicted a severe defeat on the Athenians there.

The story is on the whole credible and Athenian fortunes may suggest a date in the first half of the seventh century. In the dark ages Athens had been more prosperous than most Greek states, but in the seventh century she failed to send out any colonies and export of Attic black figure vases only begins ca. 610; these facts may indicate that the Athenians suffered a major setback in the early part of the century. If the affairs of Epidaurus, Aegina and Athens, as related by Herodotus, belong to the time of Pheidon, his participation may be suspected at more than one point and may have to do with recovering "the lot of Temenus." But he is not named.

There is nothing improbable in supposing that Pheidon made his weight felt extensively in the northeastern part of the Peloponnese, but the positive case for associating him with the affairs of Corinth, Megara, Aegina and Epidaurus is not strong. Interpretation of his reign and of his "tyranny" must rest on those activities of his which are attested with certainty; in practice this means the activities mentioned by Herodotus, namely the making of standard measures and the intervention at Olympia. The introduction of standard measures for Argos and its territory marks a significant growth in the self-assertiveness of public authority; the fact that many other Peloponnesian states adopted the same standards provides some testimony to the respect felt for Pheidonian Argos. The intervention at Olympia was more spectacular and so it may provide a clue to explain why Pheidon came to be called tyrant.

The several theories of tyranny must be compared with his known actions. Advocates of the "hoplite" theory can see in Pheidon primarily a military figure; before intervening at Olympia he must have extended in influence widely by military means. But the hoplite phalanx is not attested before ca. 650; unless the late date implied for Pheidon by Herodotus is correct, he cannot have gained his successes by using the hoplite phalanx or by taking advantage of its social effects. Those who follow the "pre-Dorian" theory can draw attention to the period of Pisatan ascendancy, which followed Pheidon's intervention at Olympia; Pheidon himself was Dorian, but by supporting Pisatan claims he acted in favor of the pre-Dorian element in the population of the Peloponnese. Possibly this view of his career lies behind the assertion that he was a king who became a tyrant.

But there is a more likely possibility. The incident at Olympia not only shows the power of Pheidon; it also reveals him making an ostentatious display of power. The note of magnificence, as it may be called, can be traced in the activities of all the early tyrants. If Pheidon's reign spanned the year 668, he was an approximate contemporary of Gyges, who founded a new and prosperous dynasty in Lydia. The description of Pheidon as tyrant may or may not come from his own time; even if it does not, it may mean simply that Pheidon's display reminded people of the Lydian potentate.

CLEISTHENES OF SICYON[3]

Herodotus provides two digressions on Cleisthenes, the tyrant who ruled Sicyon early in the sixth century. In one of these (5.67–68) he expounds a change carried out by Cleisthenes in the tribal organization of his city. Cleisthenes, he says, was at war with Argos and carried out various acts of internal policy to voice his hostility. Thus he put an end to rhapsodic competitions in Sicyon, because the "Homeric epics" sung by the rhapsodes almost continually praised Argives and Argos. (This suggests that the "Homeric epics" known in Sicyon belonged to the Theban cycle of legend, not the Trojan cycle.) Again, Herodotus continues, Cleisthenes sought to expel the Argive hero Adrastus, who had a sanctuary at Sicyon in the market place. After inquiring of the Delphic oracle and receiving an unfavorable response, Cleisthenes brought in the hero Melanippus from Thebes and gave him a sanctuary within the office building of the Sicyonian magistrates. According to the legend Melanippus had been an inveterate enemy of Adrastus. Cleisthenes transferred most of the cult of Adrastus to Melanippus, but the tragic choruses, with which the Sicyonians had previously honored Adrastus, were henceforth to be performed in honor of the god Dionysus. Finally Cleisthenes altered the names of the tribes at Sicyon, so that they would not be the same as at Argos. He renamed his own tribe *Archelaoi* ("Rulers of the People"), and he called the other three *Hyatai* ("Pig-ites"), *Oneatai* ("Ass-ites") and *Choireatai* ("Swine-ites"). Herodotus adds that the Sicyonians continued using these tribal names during the lifetime of Cleisthenes and for sixty years after his death; then they changed the names to Hylleis, Pamphyli, Dymanatae and Aegialeis, the last being named after Aegialeus, who in legend was the son of Adrastus.

The three names Hylleis, Pamphyli and Dymanatae, were the names of the Dorian tribes. Before the work of Cleisthenes the population of Sicyon evidently had a Dorian element, which was divided into these three tribes, and a pre-Dorian element, which constituted the tribe of Aegialeis. The pre-Dorian element was at a disadvantage, possibly solely through being relegated to a single tribe. Cleisthenes carried out a change in the tribal system and thereby elevated his own tribe, the Aegialeis. Obviously the change must have been something more substantial than a change of names. But the tradition as it reached Herodotus was halfway to becoming anecdote or myth, and it does not seem possible to guess the content of the reform. At least it must have been a major internal change. Herodotus explains it as caused by the war with Argos, but more probably it was due to internal causes; in specifying causes Herodotus generally deals more in justifications than in motives of a kind which would be recognized today. In short, Cleisthenes appears as a social reformer of the type envisaged by the "pre-Dorian" theory of tyranny. The reform was doubtless the source of his continued power.

In the other digression (6.126–130) Herodotus tells how Cleisthenes set about giving his daughter Agariste in marriage. At Olympia, after winning a victory in the chariot race, he issued a proclamation, inviting any Greek who would be a suitor to come to Sicyon within sixty days. Herodotus gives a list of the suitors. Some came from as far away as Sybaris and Siris in Italy, Crannon in Thessaly, and the land of the Molossians in Epirus. When they had arrived, Cleisthenes inquired into their descent and kept them with him for a year; he tested them in all manner of gentlemanly exercises and observed their social behavior. As the time for making his choice approached, he was most pleased by the two Athenian suitors, Hippocleides the son of Teisander and Megacles the son of Alcmaeon, and of them he was inclined to prefer Hippocleides. But at the feast at the end of the year, Hippocleides began to dance; then he called for a table, leaped upon it and danced Laconian and Attic dances; finally he stood on his head on the table and danced with his legs in the air. Cleisthenes restrained his indignation at first, but when he saw Hippocleides dancing on his head, he could contain himself no longer. "O son of Teisander," he exclaimed, "Thou hast danced away thy marriage." But Hippocleides retorted: "Hippocleides doesn't care." So Cleisthenes gave his daughter in marriage to Megacles.

The story does more than illustrate Herodotus's sense of humor. Hippocleides came of an ancient family, tracing its descent from the legendary hero Philaeus; the ancestry of Cleisthenes, as traced by Herodotus, went back only three generations. Hippocleides had no need for a marriage alliance with an upstart. By the same reckoning Cleisthenes had reason to make a great display. An Olympic victory was not enough; an ostentatious proclamation and lavish hospitality to the suitors might get a good match for his daughter.

There may have been a political calculation in Cleisthenes's final choice. In Herodotus's list of suitors Athens is the only city to supply two. They came from different parts of Attica: Megacles of the Alcmaeonidae came from the neighborhood of the city of Athens; Hippocleides of the Philaidae came from Brauron in eastern Attica, a district divided from the city by hills. Since the institutions valid for the whole of Attica were located in the city of Athens, the leading families of the city had an advantage; if Cleisthenes made a political calculation, the choice of Megacles was shrewd. By the irony of history the choice did not turn out well; within a generation the men of eastern Attica, led by Peisistratus, gained ascendancy in Athens (see chapter 5, pp. 123–128).

Late sources attest the participation of Cleisthenes in another incident, the First Sacred War. The war, beginning ca. 595, concerned the Delphic sanctuary. The previous condition of the town and sanctuary is not certain; originally they were controlled by Phocis and they may have remained so until the beginning of the war. After the war, if not before, Delphi became an independent city and the sanctuary was put under the control of the League of Amphictyones (see chapter 1, pp. 17–18). Thessalian forces played a major part in the war. But in its late stages the war became a protracted siege of Cirrha; this was a city on the northern shore of the Gulf of Corinth and it controlled one of the main routes to Delphi. The victors represented the war as retaliation for Cirrhan exploitation of pilgrims. Cirrha was able to hold out for a long time because it received supplies by sea. But Cleisthenes equipped a fleet for operations in the Gulf and used it to stop the transport of supplies to Cirrha. That city fell in 591/0; pockets of resistance held out until 586, and the Pythian festival was definitively organized in 582. At the festival of that year Cleisthenes's team won the chariot race.

Sicyonian pottery was exported on a considerable scale, and it is sometimes conjectured that Sicyon joined in the war against Cirrha in order to remove a commercial rival. That is possible, but there is nothing to support it, and the thirst for power and prestige accounts adequately for the participation of Cleisthenes. His share in the First Sacred War indicates the power he achieved for his city more clearly than does his war against Argos, which may not have been entirely successful for Sicyon; an occurrence at Cleonae may be significant. That city lay approximately midway between Sicyon and Argos, and the Nemean Games were founded there in 573; the site was associated with the seven heroes who in legend attacked Thebes, their leader being Adrastus, the Argive hero whose cult Cleisthenes drove out of Sicyon.

Judgment on Cleisthenes in relation to theories of tyranny is not difficult. Although the record is incomplete, there is at least no indication that the Sicyon of Cleisthenes achieved major successes as a land power; there is no reason to associate the tyranny with hoplite tactics. The "pre-Dorian" theory, on the other hand, finds its firmest support in the tribal reform of Cleisthenes. The execution of the reform must have brought a social upheaval on a considerable scale, and so it illustrates an important feature of the early tyrannies; not infrequently the tyrants, while pursuing more specific aims, in effect brought about a growth in the authority of the state within its territory. The note of magnificence is patently present in the chariot victories of Cleisthenes and in the steps he took to find a husband for his daughter.

THE CYPSELIDAE OF CORINTH[4]

Herodotus gives two digressions on the tyranny which arose at Corinth, but he is less illuminating than on Cleisthenes. One of the digressions (5.92) is in form a speech professedly delivered by the Corinthian delegate at a congress at Sparta near the end of the sixth century (see chapter 6, p. 148); the Spartans had proposed to restore the former tyrant Hippias to Athens, and to dissuade them the Corinthian expatiated on the evils of tyranny by describing the example of the Cypselidae. Thus the digression has the character of an exhortation or even of a sermon; nonetheless it provides some useful information, especially on the origins of the Corinthian tyranny.

According to the digression, Corinth before the tyranny was controlled by a group called the Bacchiadae, and the group was so exclusive that its members married only members of the group. But an exception was made in the case of Labda, who was born into the Bacchiadae; she was lame, and so she was given in marriage to Aetion, who was not one of the Bacchiadae. Indeed Aetion traced his descent to the Lapiths, a mythical people who in legend fought against the Centaurs. Before Labda gave birth to her son, Cypselus, the Delphic oracle made utterances portending his future power. Warned by these utterances the Bacchiadae sent men to Petra, the village where Aetion lived, to kill the infant, but Labda hid him in a grain bin (*kypsele*). So Cypselus grew up and made himself tyrant of Corinth; he exiled some Corinthians, deprived others of their property and killed others.

Some comments may be made on this account. The story of concealment in the bin was patently invented to explain the name of Cypselus, but the rest is credible. The Bacchiadae were an especially exclusive example of a Dorian aristocracy; the name shows that they claimed descent from a common ancestor. Aetion belonged to the pre-Dorian element in the population, since he claimed descent from the Lapiths. Possibly Cypselus rose as a leader of the pre-Dorian element. The story implies a further possibility too. One of the oracles foretelling the birth and greatness of Cypselus addresses its warning to "You Corinthians, who dwell around fair Peirene and beetling Corinth." "Beetling Corinth" must mean Acrocorinth, the acropolis on a very steep hill; the town of Corinth arose at its foot, and the dependent territory, the Corinthiad, was extensive. Peirene was the name of a spring on Acrocorinth. The village of Petra, to which Aetion belonged, lay within the Corinthiad at some distance from the town of Corinth;

for according to the story the Bacchiadae sent men on a journey to Petra to destroy the infant Cypselus. It is conceivable that there was tension between the town of Corinth and the dependent villages; possibly Cypselus rose as a leader of the men of the villages. A political factor of this regional kind in a large state will become familiar, when attention is given to archaic Athens.

Herodotus continues his digression (5.92) by saying that Cypselus died, after ruling for thirty years, and left his tyranny to his son Periander. The latter was at first milder than his father, but he became much more cruel after he received advice from Thrasybulus, the tyrant of Miletus. For he sent a herald to Thrasybulus to ask how best to preserve his rule. Thrasybulus led the herald to a field of grain and cut off the highest ears. When the herald returned to Corinth and reported this, Periander understood; he killed or exiled all outstanding citizens. Further, Herodotus adds, to honor the spirit of his wife Melissa, whom he had killed, Periander invited all the women of Corinth to the temple of Hera one day, as if to a festival, and sent his bodyguard to take away their clothes, which he burned as an offering to Melissa.

The digression is told skillfully to point the moral, that power seized unlawfully shows its true nature in the end. Periander became the most famous of the early tyrants and the tradition grew more unfavorable as time passed; a century after Herodotus Aristotle (*Pol.* 3.1284a26–33) told the story of cutting off the highest ears of grain, but in his version the roles are reversed and Periander sends the advice to Thrasybulus. Such material reveals little about the nature of the Corinthian tyranny or the source of its power.

The other digression introduces an important theme, the relations of the tyrants with Corinthian colonies. Herodotus (3.48–53) gives the digression when he narrates a Spartan expedition of ca. 525 against Samos and seeks to explain why the Corinthians joined in the expedition; the explanation takes him to a complex series of events occurring a generation earlier. Periander married Melissa, the daughter of Procles tyrant of Epidaurus, but later he killed her. Then Procles sent for the two sons of Periander and tried to turn them against their father; he had some success with the younger, Lycophron. So Periander quarrelled with Lycophron and sent him away to Corcyra, which Periander controlled. Then he marched against Procles, overcame Epidaurus and captured Procles alive. But as time passed and Periander grew old, he decided to recall Lycophron and make him his successor in Corinth. Lycophron was at first reluctant but finally they reached an agreement that Periander should move to Corcyra, while Lycophron should return to Corinth and succeed to the tyranny. But the people of Corcyra did not want to receive Periander, and so they killed Lycophron. In retaliation Periander seized 300 of the children of leading Corcyreans and sent them as a present to Alyattes, king of Lydia. But when the party put in at Samos on the

Corinthian Gold Bowl. The inscription says: "The sons of Cypselus dedicated [this bowl] from Heraclea." Heraclea is probably the town of that name on the Gulf of Ambracia. [Courtesy Museum of Fine Arts, Boston. Francis Bartlett Donation.]

journey, the Samians enabled them to escape. After the death of Periander tension persisted between Corinth and Corcyra, and so the Corinthians continued to bear a grudge against Samos a generation after the original offence.

Much of the motivation in this story may be fictitious; the intimacies of Periander's family life were not a matter of record. But the public facts in the story are credible. They indicate Periander's varying relations with Procles and his desire to foster good relations with Lydia. Further they show his dealings with the Corinthian colony of Corcyra: he controlled it and sent his son Lycophron to rule it, and when the Corcyreans rebelled and killed Lycophron, Periander attacked Corcyra and exacted 300 hostages. Relations with the colony were a matter of major concern to Periander.

Corinthian colonization was extensive and began long before the foundation of the tyranny. Thucydides (6.3.2) says that Syracuse was founded from Corinth in 733 and the leader of the expedition was Archias, who claimed descent from the Heracleidae; that is, he belonged to the Bacchiadae. The geographer Strabo, writing at about the beginning of the first century A.D., says (6.2.4, p. 269) that Archias on his journey left a party under Chersicrates to settle Corcyra, Chersicrates being also descended from the Heracleidae; Strabo may draw his information from Ephorus. A fragment of the historian Timaeus (*F.Gr.Hist.* IIIB 566F80), who wrote in the third century B.C., confirms that Chersicrates belonged to the Bacchiadae and says that he led the colony to Corcyra 600 years after the Trojan War. Since Hellenistic scholars believed that Troy fell in 1184, Timaeus's statement indicates an impossibly late date for the foundation of Corcyra; the figure "600" may be corrupt. Because of Strabo's statement modern historians generally believe that Corcyra was founded at about the same time as Syracuse. It must still be admitted that no easy emendation will bring the fragment of Timaeus into agreement with the date implied by Strabo; there may be real divergence on the date. But in any case Corcyra was founded before the time of the tyrants; for tradition usually associated the names of the tyrants with colonies founded by them, and it would be especially likely to do so in the case of so important a colony.

Under the tyrants a number of colonies were founded in the northwestern part of European Greece. Strabo (10.2.8. p. 452; 7.7.6, p. 325) says that Cypselus and his son Gorgus founded colonies at Leucas, Ambracia and Anactorium. Thucydides (1.24.2) says that Epidamnus, much further north on the Adriatic coast, was founded by the Corcyreans, but in accordance with custom they invited their own mother city, Corinth, to supply the leader, and the man sent was a descendant of Heracles. Thucydides does not give the date of foundation or associate the tyrants with it. Eusebius and St. Jerome give the date of foundation as 626 or 625, and these years fall within their dates for the rule of Periander. The implication, that Epidamnus was founded in the time of Periander, derives some slight support from an argument from geographical probability; settlers looking towards the mainland in the northwest would be likely to occupy sites nearer the heart of Greece, such as Ambracia, before they went so far afield as Epidamnus. If Periander sent a descendant of Heracles, that is, one of the Bacchiadae, to lead the settlement to Epidamnus, this might be his way of removing a man whom he found embarrassing; it was a method showing more clemency and more confidence than the grim story of exiles and executions, told by Herodotus in the digression discussed first above. Only geographical probability can provide a date for the foundation of Apollonia, which stood on the Adriatic coast rather south of Epidamnus; Strabo (7.5.8, p. 316) says that it was founded by Corinthians and Corcyreans.

Apart from foundations in the northwest, Corinthians founded a colony in the northeast, namely, Poteidaea. Thucydides (1.56.2) calls Poteidaea a Corinthian foundation. Nicolaus of Damascus (*F.Gr.Hist.* IIA 90F59), in a somewhat confused passage about the sons of Periander, says that one of them, Euagoras, led the colony to Poteidaea and died there. The choice of the site can perhaps be explained by reference to Apollonia and Epidamnus. These cities held the western ends of the sole natural route leading eastwards across the Balkans into Macedon, the route taken in Roman times by the Via Egnatia. Poteidaea held a strong position on the isthmus of Pallene; it was not too far from the mouths of the rivers Axius and Strymon, and their valleys provided routes into Macedon. The location of the three colonies suggests that in the time of Periander Corinthians were interested in opening up the interior of Macedon to trade, although doubtless that was not the only reason for the foundations.

The record of Corinthian colonization may be incomplete; in particular, unsuccessful ventures may have been forgotten. But the record is full enough to allow drawing a conclusion important for understanding the tyranny. Corinthian colonial enterprise began long before the tyranny was founded and continued under the tyranny. That is, the tyranny did not mark a change in the direction of Corinthian development; it marked a continuation and an intensification of previous policies. The archaeological record tells a similar story. The styles called Protocorinthian began in the last quarter of the eighth century and gave way during the seventh to those called Corinthian, which continued to flourish into the sixth; ware of these kinds was exported more widely than the contemporary ware of any other Greek city, although it did not by any means enjoy a monopoly.

Some of the policies adopted by the Corinthian tyrants probably had the effect of encouraging trade. Good relations were maintained with non-Greek powers of the Near East. This is shown in the case of Lydia by the story of the 300 Corcyrean captives sent as a present to Alyattes. Good relations with Egypt are implied by the Egyptian name of Periander's nephew and successor, Psammetichus; it occurs repeatedly in the Saite dynasty (663–525). Commercial considerations may have played a part in the building of the *diolkos*, a stone causeway for hauling ships across the isthmus of Corinth. The date of this used to be uncertain, but excavation in 1956 discovered letters incised by the builders on some of the stones as a guide to their correct placing; the letters are decidedly archaic in character and support the view that the diolkos was built by the tyrants.

Commercial motives may have contributed to the work of the Corinthian tyrants in colonization and diplomacy, but it is difficult to say how much the commerical factor counted for. Considerations of power and display may also have played a part. Some actions of the tyrants did not promote trade but they illustrate the note of magnificence. This is true of some buildings which they erected. As Herodotus (1.14.2) pointed out, the building known in his time as the Corinthian treasury at Delphi was in fact the work of Cypselus. Tyrants of some Greek cities served as patrons to poets; Herodotus (1.23–24) says that the poet Arion spent much of his life at the court of Periander and made significant developments in the dithyramb.

CHRONOLOGY AND CHARACTER OF THE TYRANNY AT CORINTH[5]

Herodotus (5.92) says that Cypselus ruled for thirty years. Fuller data on the duration of the tyranny are offered by Aristotle (*Pol.* 5.1315b22–26), who cites them to show that the rule of the Cypselidae was the longest lasting tyranny except for that of the Sicyonian dynasty. The whole tyranny, he says, lasted seventy-three years and six months. He adds that Cypselus ruled for thirty years; Periander ruled for forty-four years; and Psammetichus the son of Gorgus ruled for three years. Since the figures do not add up correctly, Aristotle's figure for the duration of Periander's rule is often emended to "forty and a half years."

Most modern historians draw dates for the tyranny from Eusebius, who makes three statements about it. First, under the year 658 he says that Cypselus ruled the Corinthians for twenty-eight years; St. Jerome gives the same observation under the year 659. Second, under 630 Eusebius says that Periander ruled the Corinthians; St. Jerome puts the same note under the year 628. Third, under 587 Eusebius says that the tyranny at Corinth came to an end. Putting together the statements of Aristotle and Eusebius, most historians believe that Cypselus ruled ca. 658–ca. 628, Periander ruled ca. 628–ca. 588, and Psammetichus ruled ca. 588–ca. 585. It should be added that Eusebius's dates form part of a system. Periander mediated in a war between Athens and Mytilene, a war in which the Mytilenaean poet Alcaeus took part (Hdt. 5.95.2; see below, p. 142); Alcaeus was a contemporary of Pittacus, the tyrant of Mytilene, and of Sappho. Eusebius gives dates for the activities of Pittacus, Alcaeus and Sappho, and these fall within his dates for the rule of Periander. Dates for the activities of Pittacus, Alcaeus and Sappho are also given by Diogenes Laertius and by the Byzantine lexicon called the *Suda*; these agree, within a year or two, with the dates given by Eusebius. Thus the system is self-consistent.

Accepting the Eusebian dates, some historians have tried to draw a further consequence. Thucydides (1.13.4) says that the earliest naval battle known to him was between the Corinthians and the Corcyreans and that it was fought ca. 260 years before the end of the war whose history he was writing. His work in its final plan was intended as a history of the Peloponnesian War, which ended in 404. So some have suggested that Corinth suffered a severe setback in a battle with the Corcyreans ca. 664; this weakened the ascendancy of the Bacchiadae, and so Cypselus was able to overthrow them a few years later ca. 658. Against this reconstruction it has been pointed out (by W.G. Forrest) that Thucydides does not say which side won the battle, and his date may rest on a count of generations and hence be unreliable.

Two passages of Herodotus conflict with the Eusebian system. First (3.48.1) he says that the Corinthians joined the Spartans in an expedition against Samos ca. 525, because of an injury which the Samians had inflicted on the Corinthians "a generation before." The injury was the release by the Samians of the 300 Corcyreans, whom Periander intended as a present to Alyattes of Lydia. Herodotus adds that the Samians inflicted this injury on Corinth about the same time as they stole an ornamental bowl, which the Spartans were sending as a present to Croesus. Croesus succeeded Alyattes as king of Lydia ca. 560 or a few years later. Thus Herodotus implies that Periander sent the 300 Corcyreans late in the reign of Alyattes and towards 560.

In the second passage (5.94–95) Herodotus tells of a war between Athens and Mytilene. Peisistratus the Athenian captured Sigeum from the Mytilenaeans, and this led to a long war between them and the Athenians; eventually peace was mediated by Periander. Peisistratus tried three times to make himself tyrant of Athens, his first attempt being in 560. But his first two periods of rule were brief; he gained secure and lasting control of Athens at his third attempt in 546 (see chapter 5, pp. 123–128). Conceivably his war for Sigeum was fought when he was not tyrant, possibly even in his years of exile from 556 to 546; but since Herodotus calls one party in the war "the Athenians" simply, it is easier to believe that the war was fought when Peisistratus controlled the Athenian state after 546. In short, Herodotus's account of the war for Sigeum implies that Periander was still alive at a date which was scarcely earlier than 560 and probably towards 540.

Thus there is conflict between the "low" dates implied by Herodotus and the "high" dates of Eusebius. Something can be said against the reliability of Herodotus on sixth century chronology. He has at least one blunder: he says (6.125) that Alcmaeon the Athenian visited Croesus of Lydia, but in fact Alcmaeon belonged to an earlier generation. Graver doubts may be entertained about the Eusebian system. On the one hand it is difficult to imagine what good evidence for chronology could survive, apart from the oral traditions collected by Herodotus; on the other hand it is very easy to imagine that in or after the fourth century B.C. the traditions were reduced to an artificial system by speculation and theorizing. Herodotus's indications about the dates of Periander's activity do not arise from a theoretical system; they are embedded in the stories which the historian collected. That is the reason for preferring them.

The problem of chronology has a bearing on the question of the nature of the Cypselid tyranny. If the "high" dates are correct, then in the present state of archaeological discovery the rise of Cypselus cannot have been a consequence of the introduction of hoplite tactics, for the hoplite phalanx is not attested before ca. 650. If the "low" dates are correct, there is no chronological objection to seeking in the "hoplite" theory an explanation for the rise of Cypselus. But there is little to commend such an explanation. Obviously Cypselus succeeded in mobilizing people who supported him in preference to those whom he killed or exiled; but the record of his activities and those of his son does not furnish any ground for seeing in these supporters a class of substantial peasant farmers, newly burdened with an obligation of hoplite service.

The record of the Corinthian tyrants scarcely furnishes more comfort to advocates of the "pre-Dorian" theory. Cypselus stood outside the Bacchiad aristocracy and on his father's side he traced descent from pre-Dorian inhabitants of Greece. But he may have seen his exclusion from the ruling group just as easily in regional as in hereditary terms: he belonged to Petra and opposed the men of "beetling Corinth." Moreover, as far as is known, neither he nor Periander carried out a social upheaval after the manner of Cleisthenes of Sicyon; none of their actions was an attempt to elevate the group from which they had risen, whether they identified that group as a pre-Dorian section or as the men of the villages.

Positively, the record suggests a different explanation for the tyranny. Under the Bacchiadae Corinth sent out colonies; under the Cypselidae she sent out more colonies. Corinthian trade had flourished since the last quarter of the eighth century; and although the motives of Cypselid policy may have been mixed, surely commercial considerations were among them. It is a story, not of revolution, but of continuity; the Cypselidae pursued the same policies as the Bacchiadae, but they pursued them rather more effectively. Perhaps more stress should be laid on the maternal descent of Cypselus. He should not be regarded as an outsider who rejected the whole outlook of the ruling group; rather he arose on its fringe and forced his way to the center of power. He and his son achieved greater success and influence for Corinth than she had known before. This should be explained, in the first place, by the cumulative effect of the economic expansion, which had begun in the eighth century; furthermore, if the "low" dates for the tyranny are correct, the adoption of hoplite tactics may have had social effects which had nothing to do with any class struggle. In the hoplite phalanx the citizen learned to fight in a much more disciplined and organized way than before; he learned to obey orders and cooperate with his fellows. If he carried these habits over, even in part, into civil life, the consequence would be an increase in the effectiveness of state authority.

THE NATURE OF TYRANNY[6]

A little, but only a little, is known about other tyrannies in the Peloponnese in the archaic period. Procles of Epidaurus has been noticed in connection with Periander and nothing more is recorded about him; his varying relations with

Periander show at least that there was no constant alliance of Peloponnesian tyrants against a common enemy. Megara stood technically outside the Peloponnese, but its fortunes were much influenced by Corinth. Theagenes as tyrant of Megara supported an Athenian revolutionary, Cylon, who had married his daughter; when Cylon tried to seize the acropolis in 632 or a little later, Theagenes sent him troops (Thuc. 1.126; see chapter 4, pp. 98–99). From the Megarian point of view this unsuccessful venture was an attempt to gain influence in Athens by supporting a promising candidate for tyranny there. There is also one item of information about the domestic policy of Theagenes; according to Aristotle (*Pol.* 5.1305a24–26), he caught the herds of animals belonging to the wealthy beside the river and killed them. By the fifth century Megara exported wool on a considerable scale. Aristotle's story may be a somewhat colored version of an attack on men who were developing the wool trade; but it is not clear whether these men were a traditional aristocracy or a group newly come to wealth.

The names of Theagenes and Procles, considered in conjunction with the better known tyrants, suggest that tyranny was widespread in the Peloponnese in the late seventh and sixth centuries, and this encourages the quest for common causes arising from the social situation. But tyrannies were established in the same period outside the Peloponnese in states where social conditions were somewhat different. The tyranny at Athens will be considered in chapters 5 and 6. Thrasybulus of Miletus, who allegedly sent advice to Periander, has already been mentioned; under his leadership the Milesians concluded a defensive war of twelve years against the kings of Lydia by making an alliance with them (Hdt. 1.17–22). Perhaps the war gave Thrasybulus the opportunity to begin or confirm his ascendancy. Scarcely anything substantial is known about Pittacus, the tyrant of Mytilene. He was attacked in the poems of his contemporary, Alcaeus; later tradition said that he made laws for Mytilene and laid down his tyranny after ruling for ten years.

Tension between Dorian and pre-Dorian elements in the population may be suspected in Peloponnesian states, but there had been no Dorian conquest in Athens, Miletus or Mytilene. The "pre-Dorian" theory has only been proposed as an explanation for tyrannies within the Peloponnese. But since tyrannies arose outside the Peloponnese in the same period, one may seek common causes of greater generality. To say this is not to deny the value of the "pre-Dorian" theory. Tension between Dorian and pre-Dorian elements is illustrated by the struggle between Eleans and Pisatans; it appears with clarity in the work of Cleisthenes at Sicyon; and it may explain some features of Spartan foreign policy (see chapter 3, pp. 83–84).

Advocates of the "hoplite" theory, on the other hand, will find little to help them in the preceding survey of archaic tyrannies. If Pheidon is rightly dated in the second quarter of the seventh century, his successes were earlier than the earliest known vases attesting the hoplite phalanx. If a later date for Pheidon is correct, he may have achieved his military successes by recognizing the merits of hoplite tactics at an early date; but that does not mean that he exploited the discontent of a hoplite class. Cleisthenes championed the pre-Dorian element in the population of Sicyon, but there is neither evidence nor probability in favor of identifying this element with any supposed hoplite class of substantial peasants. Nor does the record for Cypselus and Periander associate them with any such class of men. Information about the Peloponnesian tyrants is admittedly scanty, but the silence of the record is so impressive that one should doubt the presuppositions of the "hoplite" theory; that is, one should doubt the hypothesis that the introduction of hoplite tactics, spreading the burden of military service among a relatively wide class of substantial peasants, led that class to demand a share in political power.

The adoption of hoplite tactics may have had social effects of quite a different kind. Substantial peasant farmers, the class from which most hoplites were drawn, probably desired stability, not revolution, as their first care was to cultivate and harvest their crops. In the eighth and seventh centuries, while public authority was weak, the military force of a city can have been little more than a collection of private armies, each controlled by a family powerful in a section of the state. Indeed in some cities hoplite tactics may have been first introduced, not by public decision of the city, but on the initiative of sectional leaders who dominated parts of the city's forces. But tyranny increased the power of the state; that was indeed its most lasting effect. When one ambitious leader displaces his rivals and asserts his sole control, his influence may be in theory private and extralegal, but his subjects identify the greater obedience he demands with obedience to public authority. Besides, most of the tyrants pursued an ambitious foreign policy, and this enhanced the subject's sense of belonging to his own city rather than to its neighbors. Meanwhile the adoption of hoplite tactics also contributed to the growth in the power of the state, since it schooled the troops in habits of obedience and cooperation. The historian should imagine complex causal interaction, of which the details are lost, between the domestic measures taken by the tyrants to establish themselves, the foreign policies they pursued, the spread of hoplite tactics and the growth in the power of the state.

One feature common to the early tyrants is ostentatious display, whether evidenced in public buildings, in participation in panhellenic festivals, or in maintaining a court and keeping poets there. This note of magnificence is doubtless the reason why Greeks, impressed by the wealthy kings of Lydia, borrowed the word for them and applied it to men ascendant in their own cities.

To explain why Greek tyranny first arose in the seventh century is to explain why ostentatious splendor on a new scale became possible then, and the answer must clearly be sought in the growth of prosperity under oriental influence since late in the eighth century. Within this general picture there was room for plentiful differences between tyrannies because of local conditions and local causes; according to a remark quoted by Herodotus (3.53.4), "Tyranny is a fickle mistress, and many are her lovers."

Yet the origin of Cypselus may suggest something more. His father, Aetion of Petra, was surely a man of some wealth and local power, or the Bacchiadae would not have chosen him as husband for Labda. In short, Cypselus belonged to the not quite privileged fringe of a privileged group. He can hardly have been the only member of such a fringe; in the villages of the Corinthiad there must have been other wealthy men, who were locally powerful and resented the superiority of the leading men of "beetling Corinth." Furthermore, the record of colonization and trade shows that Corinthian power and prosperity were already growing under the Bacchiadae; consequently it is conceivable that the Bacchiadae had achieved their ascendancy by being the first to exploit the political possibilities that came with economic growth.

To put the matter another way, it should be supposed that in the dark ages there was little cohesion within the Corinthiad; different families had predominant influence in different parts of the territory. With economic growth in the late eighth and seventh centuries the Bacchiadae gained some superiority over other leading families. In consequence of their ascendancy public authority grew a little more articulate and effective. That ascendancy was resented by other ambitious families, who had wealth and local influence; Cypselus seized power as the champion of this resentment. In other words, the conflict between the Bacchiadae and Cypselus may have been, not a struggle between an upper class and a relatively humble class, but a struggle between rival groups within an upper class; each group had a following in the humbler levels of society. To say this is not to deny that within the supposed upper class one group, the Bacchiadae, had outdistanced its rivals, until Cypselus discovered how to make their discontent effective.

It must be admitted that this hypothesis about the Corinthian tyranny, like any other, includes a good deal of speculation; at least it does justice to the remarkable continuity of Corinthian policy between the Bacchiad and Cypselid eras. Can the hypothesis be generalized? That is, should the early tyrants in general be regarded not as leaders of the masses, however conceived, but as leaders of disadvantaged aristocrats? Obviously the hypothesis overlooks local factors, such as the pre-Dorian element at Sicyon, although it does not exclude them. One consideration tells in favor of generalizing the hypothesis. The archaic tyranny for which information is most plentiful is the one exercised by Peisistratus and his sons at Athens. It will be examined in chapters 5 and 6, and the view will be defended that the Athenian tyranny arose in consequence of struggles between locally powerful families which were dominant in different parts of Attica.

NOTES

1. The article by H.W. Pleket, "The Archaic Tyrannis," *Talanta* 1 (1969) 19–61, illustrates well the present state of discussion about tyranny. R. Drews, "The First Tyrants in Greece," *Historia* 21 (1972) 129–144, argues that the early tyrants were simply ambitious men who used small forces of hoplites. For the Greek view of the Lydian dynasty founded by Gyges see Hdt. 1.6–58; 1.69–81; 1.84–91; Bacchylides 3. The song about Harmodius and Aristogeiton is to be found in Oxford Book of Greek Verse, No 230. The alleged Spartan hostility towards tyrants is stated by Thuc. 1.18.1 and implied allusively by Hdt. 5.92a.1; a list of tyrants supposedly overthrown by the Spartans is given by Plut. *Mor.* 859d (= *Concerning the Malignity of Herodotus* 21). The "pre-Dorian" theory of tyranny was offered by H.T. Wade-Gery, *CAH* 3.539–569. The "hoplite" theory was first offered by A. Andrewes in his inaugural lecture, *Probouleusis* (Oxford, 1954), and in parts of his book, *The Greek Tyrants* (London, 1956); it has found many followers, for example, Forrest, *Emergence* 88–122. P.N. Ure, *The Origin of Tyranny* (Cambridge 1922) argued that the tyrants arose as captains of industry, who turned large labor forces to political use; this theory must be rejected, since Greek industry was not organized in large factories, but the book is a useful collection of material and indicates the connection of tyranny with wealth. For an illustration of the way Ephorus systematized early history see A. Andrewes, "Ephorus Book I and the Kings of Argos," *CQ*, N.S. 1 (1951) 39–45.

2. To accept 668 as the date of Pheidon's intervention at Olympia and make this the basis for dating his reign is perhaps the commonest view among modern historians; it is defended by A. Andrewes, "The Corinthian Actaeon and Pheidon of Argos," *CQ* 43 (1949) 70–78. G.L. Huxley, *Early Sparta* (London 1962) 28–30, argues for an eighth-century date for Pheidon. A useful and sceptical discussion of the Olympic victor list is given by F. Jacoby, *F.Gr.Hist.* IIIb (*Kommentar*) 221–228. Pisatan claims in the fourth century are known from Xen. *Hell.* 3.2.31; 7.4.28. The traditions on the Pistan interlude at Olympia are given by Str. 8.3.30.355; Paus. 5.9.4–5; 6.22.2–4; Euseb. *Chron.* 1.196. Leocedes, who according to Herodotus was a suitor for Agariste and a son of Pheidon of Argos, may possibly have been a son of Pheidon of Cleonae, for whom see Meiggs/Lewis 9. On the beginnings of coinage see E.S.G. Robinson, "The Coins from the Ephesian Artemision Reconsidered," *JHS* 71 (1951) 156–167; *idem*, "The Date of the Earliest Coins," *Num. Chron.*, 6th Series 16 (1956) 1–8; C.M. Kraay, "The Archaic Owls of Athens, Classification and Chronology," *Num. Chron.*, 6th Series 16 (1956) 43–68; R.M. Cook, "Speculations on the Origin of Coinage," *Historia* 7 (1958) 257–262; W.P. Wallace, "The Early Coinages of Athens and Euboea," *Num. Chron.*, 7th Series 2 (1962) 23–42; C.M. Kraay, "The Early Coinage of Athens: A Reply," *Num. Chron.*, 7th Series 2 (1962) 417–423. On the border disputes of the Megarians see also Paus. 1.44.1; *I.G.* VII, 52.

3. For the descent of Hippocleides see Pherecydes, *F.Gr.Hist.* I 3F2 = Marcellinus, *Life of Thucydides* 3. The most informative source on the First Sacred War is schol. Pind. *Nem.* 9 inscr.; the

earliest account is Aeschin. 3.107–112; see also Paus. 10.7.4–6. For discussion see T.J. Cadoux, *JHS* 68 (1948) 99–101; G. Forrest, "The First Sacred War," *BCH* 80 (1956) 33–52. The date of foundation of the Nemean Games is from St. Jerome; their connection with Adrastus is known from schol. Pind. *hyp. Nem.* On the question of Cleisthenes's predecessors and successors in the tyranny see Appendix to this chapter.

4. On the *diolkos* see M.S.F. Hood, "Archaeological Reports 1956," Supplement to *JHS* 77 (1957) 7.

5. Most modern historians accept the "high" dates for the Corinthian tyranny. The "low" dates are defended by K.J. Beloch, *Griechische Geschichte* II². 2 (Strassburg 1913) 274–282; E. Will, *Korinthiaka: Recherches sur l' historie et la civilisation de Corinthe des origines aux guerres médiques* (Paris 1955) 363–440; Sealey, *REG* 70 (1957) 318–325. For Forest's observation on the battle of "664" see *Emergence* 109. Those who accept the "high" dates face a difficulty concerning Athenian foreign policy; they have to explain Herodotus's statement that Periander mediated in the war between Athens and Mytilene. One solution consists in supposing that, besides the war fought in the time of Peisistratus, there was an earlier war between Athens and Mytilene for Sigeum, the earlier war being fought late in the seventh century and brought to an end by the mediation of Periander; see, for example, G. Glotz, *Histoire Grecque* I (Paris 1948) 427.

6. For traditions on Pittacus see Ar. *Pol.* 2.1274b18–23; 3.1285a33–1285b1; Diog. Laert. 1.75; 1.79; cf. D. Page, *Sappho and Alcaeus* (Oxford, 1955) 149–158.

APPENDIX

THE ORTHAGORID DYNASTY AT SICYON

The known activities of Cleisthenes imply approximate dates for his ascendancy. He gained control of Sicyon not later than the nineties of the sixth century, since he intervened in the First Sacred War at a decisive stage. His daughter Agariste and her husband Megacles had a son, called Cleisthenes after his grandfather; the younger Cleisthenes was head of the Alcmaeonid clan and very active at Athens in the last decade of the century. So the marriage probably took place not much before 570. Evidently Cleisthenes controlled Sicyon for more than twenty years, perhaps a good deal more. (For discussion of the chronology of his reign see M.F. McGregor, "Cleisthenes of Sicyon and the Panhellenic Festivals," *TAPA* 72 (1941) 266–287.)

Herodotus (1.126.1) gives the descent of Cleisthenes according to the following stemma:

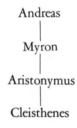

Andreas

|

Myron

|

Aristonymus

|

Cleisthenes

Cleisthenes is the only member of the family whom Herodotus calls tyrant. Later authors have much more to say about the predecessors of Cleisthenes. Aristotle is the earliest of them. He says (*Pol.* 5.1315b12–14) that the tyranny at Sicyon lasted longer than any other; it was held by the children of Orthagoras and by Orthagoras himself; and it lasted a hundred years. He adds (*ibid.* 1316a29–31) that sometimes one tyranny changes into another, as at Sicyon the tyranny of Myron changed into that of Cleisthenes. Plutarch (*Mor.* 553b) repeats part of this information; he says that at Sicyon Orthagoras became tyrant and after him Myron and Cleisthenes. A papyrus from Oxyrhynchus (*P. Oxy.* 1365 = *F.Gr.Hist.* IIA 105F2) gives an account of the rise of Orthagoras and says that he was the son of Andreas. Nicolaus of Damascus, who wrote a universal history at about the end of the first century B.C., says (*F.Gr.Hist.* IIA 90F61) that Cleisthenes had two brothers, Myron and Isodemus; Myron ruled as tyrant for seven years and was succeeded by Isodemus; after a rule of one year Isodemus was overthrown by Cleisthenes, who ruled for thirty-one years. Finally Pausanias (6.19.1–2) says that Myron was tyrant and won the chariot race at Olympia in 648; he adds that Myron built at Olympia the treasury known later as the treasury of the Sicyonians.

These data can be put together to give a stemma, if two assumptions are made. (1) It must be assumed that Orthagoras had a daughter, from whom subsequent tyrants were descended; this step is necessary to reconcile the stemma given by Herodotus with the assertions that the tyrants were descendants of Orthagoras (Ar. *Pol.*, loc. cit.) and that Orthagoras was a son of Andreas (*P.Oxy.* 1365). A stemma has been reconstructed by H.T. Wade-Gery (*CAH* 3.570); his crucial conjecture is that the daughter of Orthagoras married Aristonymus. (2) It must be assumed that the family included two men called Myron; one was the son of Andreas (Hdt., loc. cit.) and the other was the brother of Cleisthenes (Nicolaus, loc. cit.). The two men would be grandfather and grandson; in Greek practice a boy was often named after his grandfather. But it should be noted that Pausanias is the only author to call Myron I tyrant and the date of Myron's chariot victory depends on the problematic part of the Olympic list (chapter 2, p. 42).

Late sources say something about the end of the tyranny. Pseudo-Plutarch (*Moralia* 859d = *Concerning the Malignity of Herodotus* 21) gives a list of nine tyrants overthrown by the Spartans; one of them is Aeschines of Sicyon. One may suppose that Aeschines was a descendant of Cleisthenes, especially as a scholiast (to *Aeschin.* 2.77) says that the Spartans deposed the descendants of Cleisthenes.

Present-day historians usually put these data together in order to reconstruct the dynasty to which Cleisthenes belonged. To ascertain the dates of the dynasty use is made of a papyrus of the second century B.C. (*P.Rylands* 18 = *F.Gr.Hist.* IIA 105F1). The extant fragment probably comes from a work composed about 300;

the work discussed the Seven Wise Men and tried to show that the contemplative life is superior to the active life. The papyrus has been reexamined by D.M. Leahy ("Chilon and Aeschines," *Bulletin of the John Rylands Library* 38.2 [1956] 306–335). The text is uncertain at some points, but the most probable readings give the following sense:

.... crossed to the mainland (?) and settled much land in the coastal foothills—Chilon the Laconian as ephor and military commander and Anaxandrides overthrew the tyrannies among the Greeks—in Sicyon Aeschines, Hippias (the son of) Peisistratus (at Athens?) ...

Anaxandrides was king at Sparta in the middle of the sixth century. Chilon is recorded as ephor at Sparta by Diogenes Laertius (1.68) within the fifty-sixth Olympiad (556–553). So it is argued that Aeschines, the last of the Orthagorids, was overthrown by the Spartans ca. 556/5; then, since Aristotle gives the tyranny a duration of a hundred years, it was founded by Orthagoras ca. 656/5.

This view has been defended by D.M. Leahy ("The Dating of the Orthagorid Dynasty," *Historia* 17 [1968] 1–23). He adds an argument based on a study of Spartan foreign policy in the sixth century. In the middle of the century Sparta used heroic mythology for diplomacy, trying in particular to appropriate pre-Dorian heroes; the incident of the bones of Orestes, which enabled Sparta to win the alliance of Tegea (Hdt. 1.66–68; see chapter 3, pp. 83–84), is the best known but not the sole example. Leahy finds another example in the transferral of the bones of Teisamenus from Helice in Achaea to Sparta (Paus. 7.1.8; Leahy, "The Bones of Tisamenus," *Historia* 4 [1955] 26–38); Teisamenus was a pre-Dorian hero, and by this gesture the Spartans sought to win an alliance with Helice, but the latter town refused the offer. Leahy finds this use of mythology so distinctive that he attributes it to a single period and probably a single statesman. Thus the Spartan overture to Helice, not dated by Pausanias, would occur towards the middle of the sixth century within the same period as the making of the Tegean alliance. Sicyon stood next to Achaea and was more powerful; when the Spartans concerned themselves with Achaea, they would be likely to give at least as much attention to Sicyon. Hence the Spartan intervention at Sicyon should belong to a period towards the middle of the sixth century.

Leahy's supporting argument is not strong. Use of heroic mythology in diplomacy was peculiar neither to Sparta nor to the middle of the sixth century. Late in the century, when the Thebans had been defeated by the Athenians, they appealed to Aegina for help. The Aeginetans sent them the Aeacidae, that is, relics or images of heroes. When the Thebans had suffered a further defeat, they returned the Aeacidae and asked the Aeginetans to send men (Hdt. 5.80–81). Moreover, Spartan statesmen continued to exploit their pre-Dorian associations a generation after the time of Anaxandridas. Towards the end of the sixth century Cleomenes, the son of Anaxandrides, went to Athens to support Isagoras (see chapter 6, p. 147); among other actions he tried to enter the sanctuary of Athena on the acropolis. The priestess obstructed him and said that Dorians were not allowed to enter. Cleomenes replied: "Madam, I am not a Dorian but an Achaean" (Hdt. 5.72.3). Thus the development of Spartan policy would allow a much later date than that suggested by Leahy for the intervention at Sicyon and for the abortive relations with Helice.

Indeed, a further consideration about Spartan policy suggests a later date for intervention at Sicyon. In order to reach Sicyon Spartans had to march a long way north and expose their flank to possible attack from Argos. It would be foolish to do this before the Spartans gained the upper hand in rivalry with Argos; they achieved this at the so-called "battle of the champions," which Herodotus synchronizes with the fall of Croesus (Hdt. 1.82-83; see chapter 3, p. 84). Croesus was overthrown ca. 544. Admittedly strategists sometimes do foolish things and suffer no consequences. Even so, this strategic consideration suggests a date not earlier than the late 540s for Spartan intervention at Sicyon.

Any attempt to date the fall of Aeschines from the Rylands papyrus must confront a major difficulty. The papyrus seems to attribute the overthrow of Hippias, as well as that of Aeschines, to Chilon and Anaxandrides. But Hippias, the son of Peisistratus and tyrant of Athens, was overthrown by Cleomenes, the son of Anaxandrides, in 510. It still can be imagined that the Hellenistic author of the text, citing examples of overthrown tyrants to illustrate his point about Chilon, gave the first correctly but erred in his subsequent examples; but to admit this is to weaken the evidential value of the text drastically.

A different interpretation of the papyrus was proposed by Mary White ("The Dates of the Orthagorids," *Phoenix* 12 [1958] 2-14). Punctuation being uncertain, she suggested that a sentence ended with the statement that Chilon and Anaxandrides overthrew the tyrannies among the Greeks. The new sentence, referring to Aeschines and Hippias, had a new subject, namely Cleomenes; it said that Cleomenes overthrew them. The author's train of thought would be that the Spartan policy of overthrowing tyrants was initiated by Chilon and Anaxandrides, although the best known illustrations of that policy belonged to the activity of Cleomenes. So Miss White dated the overthrow of Aeschines from that of Hippias and held that the Orthagorid tyranny belonged to the period ca. 615-515/510. Since Cleisthenes ruled in the first few decades of the sixth century, Miss White could accommodate Herodotus's statement (5.68.2) that the Cleisthenic tribal names were kept for sixty years after his death; they would be abandoned at the point when the Spartans overthrew Aeschines.

Miss White's interpretation makes the papyrus somewhat circumlocutory.

Moreover it is difficult to accommodate the names of the known tyrants within her scheme. She holds that the tyranny continued for sixty years after Cleisthenes's death and that Cleisthenes ruled ca. 600–570; Nicolaus of Damascus gives him a reign of thiry-one years. This leaves very little time for the predecessors of Cleisthenes. The difficulty can be put another way, allowing for possible inaccuracy in the late sources: the tradition remembered at least the names of several predecessors of Cleisthenes but only one successor, yet on Miss White's view the tyranny had a much longer duration after Cleisthenes than before him.

If Miss White's solution is accordingly rejected, it becomes impossible to accept and reconcile all the evidence. At the very least the author of the Rylands papyrus erred in citing the overthrow of Hippias to illustrate the policy of Chilon and Anaxandrides. Since he erred on that point, it is less than circumspect to accept him on the overthrow of Aeschines. But if an author at work ca. 300 could blunder on sixth century chronology, Aristotle's statements on Orthagorid chronology deserve to be reexamined; he was at work only a generation before the author of the papyrus, and why should his statements about early Sicyon be less subject to criticism than his statements about early Athens?

Some items in the late sources fail to inspire confidence. Nicolaus of Damascus gives a total of thirty-nine years to the reigns of the three brothers, Myron, Isodemus and Cleisthenes; that is suspiciously close to the standard figure of forty years for a generation. The Oxyrhynchus papyrus gives an account of the rise of Orthagoras: Sicyon had border disputes with Pellene in Achaea and so it maintained a force of border police (*peripoloi*); Orthagoras distinguished himself in this force, so he was made its commander (*peripolarchos*); he continued to distinguish himself, so he was made commander of all the armed forces (*polemarchos*), and he used his control of the armed forces to make himself master of the state. This is a familiar story; it is the stock motif of the military tyrant, a motif which owes something to the fourth-century tyrants of the Greek cities in Sicily. In short, if an author of the fourth century or later did not know how Orthagoras rose to power but tried to make up an account, he would tell the sort of story that is given in the Oxyrhynchus papyrus. By contrast, Herodotus's picture of Cleisthenes is highly individualized; a war with Argos, an animus against the hero Adrastus, a curious set of tribal names, a daughter to be given to the most accomplished suitor, these are not stock motifs.

Possibly modern historians have erred in assuming that Herodotus and the post-Herodotean sources preserve parts of a single tradition and that they should be combined. At Athens there were divergent traditions about the fall of the tyranny there; since tyranny and its overthrow were matters arousing political passions, surely the presumption should be that at Sicyon too the traditions about the tyranny were not uniform.

There is a special reason for treating with caution the data about the predecessors of Cleisthenes. Herodotus's account of the latter is not merely individualized but illuminating; it enables the reader to ascertain the significance of the tyrant's rule and the source of his power. In particular, it appears that the tribal reform constituted something in the nature of a social revolution and the successful execution of this measure ensured the continued ascendancy of Cleisthenes. It follows that his predecessors had not carried out the tribal reform; in other words, they had not taken a drastic step to elevate the pre-Dorian section of the population. Since tyranny was not an office, there was not necessarily any clear cut answer in any specific case to the question of what constitutes the establishment or the fall of a tyranny. That is, since Aristotle reckoned that the tyranny was established by Orthagoras and lasted a hundred years, Aristotle must have attached significance to an act of Orthagoras and to another act which occurred a hundred years later, but one cannot be sure what either act was. By modern standards the activities of Orthagoras may not have been important; they were certainly less important than the tribal reform of Cleisthenes.

There remains the question of the fall of the tyranny. There is no suggestion in the sources that Cleisthenes himself was overthrown, and the argument from silence has some force, since a disaster overtaking so powerful and popular figure would be memorable. Hence it is likely that Cleisthenes had at least one successor in the tyranny. Consequently there does not seem to be strong reason to reject the statements that a successor of his, called Aeschines, was overthrown by Spartan intervention. Little can be said about the date when the tyranny collapsed; but because of the strategic argument given above it is likely, though not by any means certain, that the tyranny lasted until some time after the battle of the champions.

3

Early Sparta

South of the central highlands of the Peloponnese, Dorian invaders reached the two plains of Laconia and Messenia during the age of migrations, and a great many townships arose. The earliest Laconian pottery of Protogeometric type belongs to the period ca. 1000–950; it may mark the beginning of settled conditions. Among the townships of Laconia, Sparta became the strongest and reduced the others to a dependent condition, a process completed perhaps in the eighth century. The resulting political unit, consisting of Sparta and its dependencies, was called Lacedaemon; at first Lacedaemon embraced only Laconia, together with the Malean promontory and the island of Cythera.

Thus constituted, Lacedaemon was a large state with a growing population. It founded only one colony, namely Taras (Tarentum) in South Italy; the earliest pottery discovered there belongs to the period 700–650. For the most part Lacedaemon tried to meet the problem of overpopulation by conquest of neighboring land. An advance towards the northwest brought the Lacedaemonians into conflict with the Argives, who defeated them in the battle of Hysiae (669? see chapter 2, pp. 41–42). The alternative was to cross the Taygetus range and invade Messenia; this led to a long struggle, and the outcome was that Lacedaemon conquered and absorbed Messenia.

Data on the course of the struggle for Messenia must be treated with caution. Long afterwards, in the winter of 370–369, Epaminondas led the forces of Thebes and her allies into the Peloponnese; he invaded Laconia and he restored the independence of Messenia. Thereafter the Messenians were successful in preserving their independence, and so their early history had to be written. The fourth century historian Callisthenes included in his *Hellenic History* a digression on an early Messenian War and its hero, Aristomenes. Ephorus, a contemporary of Callisthenes, distinguished two early Messenian Wars; the first lasted twenty years and culminated in the conquest of Messenia by the Lacedaemonians; some time later a Messenian revolt precipitated a second war, in which the Messenian hero was Aristomenes. In the first half of the third century that poet Rhianus wrote a historical epic, *Messeniaca*, which dealt mainly with the Second Messenian War.

In an attempt to prune away inventions and discover reliable data, it is best to start from a statement of Epaminondas. He said that he had founded Messene after 230 years. Evidently Epaminondas thought that the early struggle had come to an end ca. 600. Considerable fragments are preserved of the poems of Tyrtaeus, who lived during warfare between Lacedaemon and the Messenians and exhorted the Spartans to fight well. In one poem (fr. 4) he speaks of "our king, Theopompus, through whom we captured Messene;" he continues by saying that "the fathers of our fathers" fought for Messene for nineteen years; at last in the twentieth year the defenders fled from the Ithomaean mountains. The interval between fighting grandfather and fighting grandson is about half a century. Tyrtaeus's statement is compatible with the belief, held by most modern historians, that there were two early Messenian Wars, though it does not imply that; Tyrtaeus might mean that a twenty-year struggle for the stronghold on Mt. Ithome was a distinguishable incident in a long period of warfare.

Many modern historians believe that a First Messenian War lasted ca. 736–ca. 716; the argument for this rests in large part on the Olympic victor list (on which see chapter 2, p. 42). Hence they date a Second War, with Tyrtaeus alive, ca. 660–650, and they need a further hypothesis to account for Epaminondas's statement. An important observation, made by F. Jacoby, suggests a different approach: writers of the fifth century, and later writers drawing on them, do not distinguish a specific number of Messenian Wars; instead they recognize a reduction of Messene, which should be identified with the twenty-year struggle, and this was followed by a lasting but delicate situation, in which the descendants of the vanquished rose intermittently in local revolts.

The only certainty is that the conquest of Messenia was complete by ca. 600; henceforth Lacedaemon held all the southern part of the Peloponnese, beyond the territories of Elis, Arcadia and Argos. The basic structure of the state recognized people of three different status, namely, Spartiates, perioeci and helots. The Spartiates were the citizens of Sparta itself. The city of Sparta arose from the union of four neighboring villages, Pitana, Mesoa, Limnae and Conooura, and from an early stage it included the town of Amyclae, which was a few miles further south in the valley of the Eurotas river. In Hellenistic times a wall was built round the four villages. The institutions of Sparta managed the affairs of Sparta and had overriding authority over the other towns of Lacedaemon; they also had sole direction of foreign policy. The free inhabitants of the other towns were perioeci or "dwellers round about;" there were many perioecid towns in Laconia and some in Messenia. Each such town had its own institutions to manage local affairs. The helots were serfs bound to the soil. Each adult male Spartiate had a *kleros* or allotment of land, some allotments being in Laconia and some in Messenia. The allotment was tilled for the master by helots, so that he would be free to devote himself to public and military affairs. Helots were not privately owned slaves; the Spartan master, on whose estate a party of helots worked, controlled them in most respects, but could not alienate them from the land.

The question arises, How severe was the condition of the helots and how acute was their discontent? In some lines that are often quoted, Tyrtaeus (fr. 5) compares them to donkeys, worn down by heavy burdens, and says that they surrendered a half of the produce of the soil. Other evidence suggests that this is exaggerated, at least as a description of a lasting condition. Plutarch (*Lyc.* 8.4) says that each allotment was required to provide its master with a fixed and uniform amount of produce; apparently the helots could keep any surplus. For the battle of Plataea in 479 (see chapter 8, pp. 223–225) Sparta supplied five thousand Spartiate hoplites and seven helots for each Spartiate (Hdt. 9.10.1.). These helots did not have hoplite equipment; they were service troops, not fighting troops. Even so, before the invention of the machine gun it would have been folly to send on campaign seven unarmed men with every armed man, if the unarmed men hated him. Probably relations between Spartiates and helots grew much worse in consequence of the unsuccessful Messenian Revolt, which broke out in the 460s and lasted a good many years (see chapter 9, pp. 255–256). Later in the fifth century Thucydides (4.80.3) observed: "The Lacedaemonians constantly take most of their decisions with a view to precautions against the helots"; this remark may not be valid for the period before the revolt.

A related question concerns artistic and commercial life in Lacedaemon. Some modern writers have supposed that after the reduction of Messenia Sparta devoted her whole effort to maintaining a strong military force against the disaffected helots, and there could be no creative achievements in such an atmosphere of fear and distrust. But Pindar, writing in the first half of the fifth century, described Sparta as the place "where the counsels of the old men and the spears of the young excel, as do dances and the Muse and splendor" (fr. 199 Snell

= Plut. *Lyc.* 21.6). Artistic work and trade were presumably conducted by perioeci, and the reduction of Messenia did not bring a decline; export of Laconian vases and bronzes continued right through the sixth century. Laconian vase painting, though not among the best in Greece, reached its highest level ca. 560–550; its subsequent decline was not as acute as in the case of Corinthian pottery and can best be explained by the competition of Attic ware. Laconian craftsmen continued producing bronze figures of good quality into the first half of the fifth century. On the whole sixth century Lacedaemon was not an unhappy place to live.

THE SOURCES

Enough is known about early Sparta to arouse curiosity, but a special difficulty arises in evaluating the sources. In the third century B.C. there was a movement for reform of Spartan society; it culminated in the work of the kings Agis IV (244–241) and Cleomenes III (235–222). The reformers recommended their measures by alleging that these would restore the original and pure condition of Spartan society. So it is not unlikely that the reformers invented some features and attributed them to the pristine constitution. Accordingly, statements made by writers later than the third century B.C. about the early condition of Sparta deserve special scrutiny; if they can be supported by allusions in earlier writers, they should be accepted, but otherwise they are highly suspect.

It happens that the sole full account of the Spartan constitution to survive is provided by a late author, namely, Plutarch in his *Life of Lycurgus.* Lycurgus was the legendary lawgiver to whom the Spartans attributed their institutions. An example may be cited here of the uncertainties that arise in using Plutarch's work. Since much of the best land in Laconia and Messenia was distributed to Spartiates, and since these allotments were considered equal, it would be useful to know how many adult male Spartiates there were. Plutarch (Lyc. 8.3) gives the figure of 9,000, and many modern historians have accepted this. But it should be noted that in 243 Agis sought to redistribute the Spartan land in Laconia in 4,500 lots. By then Messenia was independent; it may have been assumed that, while Lacedaemon controlled Messenia, there were as many allotments in Messenia as in Laconia. Possibly Agis had good evidence for an original figure of 9,000 and hence proposed 4,500 lots; alternatively the figure of 9,000 may have been invented in connection with Agis's proposal. In short, the original number of allotments remains unknown.

Among writers at work before the third century four deserve to be specified. Herodotus provides a good deal of information about Spartan foreign policy in the sixth century; he says less about internal conditions, but he gives a digression

on the powers of the Spartan kings (6.56-60). On Spartan domestic affairs
Thucydides provides information incidental to his narrative; one of the more
notable passages describes a meeting of the Spartan public assembly (1.67-87).
Aristotle (*Pol*.2.1269a29-1271b19) gives a critical survey of the Spartan constitution. Unfortunately he is more concerned to say what was wrong with the
Spartan constitution than what it was, but he provides some valuable information; for example, he remarks that Spartan citizens were forbidden by law to buy
or sell land but they were allowed to give it away or bequeath it, and so
inequalities of wealth arose. Finally Xenophon wrote a treatise, *The Constitution of
the Lacedaemonians*. It is largely concerned with private habits and military
discipline, but it offers some important information about political conditions;
for example, Xenophon (10.2) notes that the council of elders served as a court to
hear capital cases.

The present chapter will consider the political and social institutions of early
Sparta and the main problems about them. Then it will look into Spartan foreign
policy of the sixth century; thanks to Herodotus, this is the aspect of archaic
Spartan life that is best attested.

POLITICAL INSTITUTIONS[2]

As in many ancient states, so in Sparta it is convenient to look for a king, a council
and an assembly. Sparta had not merely a king; she had two hereditary kings
drawn from two royal families. Moreover she differed from other Greek states in
that she preserved this institution for a long time. In Athens at an early stage the
king ceased to be hereditary and became one among several elective magistrates,
holding office only for a year; in Sparta the hereditary kingship persisted till the
second half of the third century B.C.

The Spartans had a legend tracing the descent of the two royal families to two
brothers (Hdt. 6.52). Nowadays it is often supposed that the dual kingship arose
from the early amalgamation of two communities. The royal powers are listed by
Herodotus (6.56-60). The most important of these was command in war. Indeed,
Herodotus says that the kings have the right "to make war on any country they
choose, and no Spartiate may obstruct this." Elsewhere (5.74.1) Herodotus
mentions an occurrence late in the sixth century: King Cleomenes "gathered an
army from the whole Peloponnese, without revealing the purpose for which he
was gathering it," and led it against Attica. But it should be observed that the
other king went with Cleomenes on this expedition and, when the second king
withdrew, the federal force dispersed. The authority of the king over the forces of
the Peloponnesian League will require attention below (p. 85); here it suffices
to say that after the reign of Cleomenes (ca. 520-ca. 490) no case is known where

the king made war of his sole authority. In the time of Thucydides and Xenophon the decision leading to war was taken by the public assembly and as the next step the ephors, a board to be considered shortly, called up troops for the specific campaign. This does not mean that the royal prerogative of declaring war was specifically abrogated; rather as public authority grew more articulated, it became customary for other organs to have a share, eventually a predominant share, in deciding questions of war and peace. The king continued to serve as a military officer exercising command in the field, though for some campaigns the Spartans chose other commanders.

The domestic powers of the king, as listed by Herodotus, are less impressive. They enjoyed some priesthoods and perquisites, such as the first portions at public banquets. They were members of the council of elders, but there is nothing to indicate that this was a source of special influence. Further, they exercised judicial authority in cases of three kinds: if a man died leaving an unbetrothed heiress, the kings decided who she should marry; they judged cases concerning public roads; and adoption of sons could only be performed in the presence of the kings. In the archaic state judicial powers concerning heiresses and adoption were especially important. Public authority was still weak and the effective social unit was the family; childlessness and the lack of male heirs threatened the survival of the family and its estate, and in Sparta it was the kings who intervened to meet crises of these kinds. Later, as the state acquired more functions, it tended to exercise them through other officers.

The council consisted of thirty members, including the two kings. It was called the *gerousia*, or council of elders (*gerontes*). Its twenty-eight nonroyal members had to be at least sixty years old; they were chosen by acclamation in the public assembly and they retained office for the rest of their lives. Membership of the council was highly honorific, but only a little can be said about its specific powers. As already noted, the council served as a court to hear capital cases. Herodotus (5.40; see below, p. 73) mentions a case in which the council advised a king to take a second wife and backed up their advice with a threat. It is often supposed that the council had the task of preparing business for the public assembly, and that is likely enough, although the main evidence, the so-called Great Rhetra, will require discussion.

The public assembly could be attended by all adult male Spartiates. It elected gerontes and ephors and it had the ultimate decision on matters of legislation and policy. The usual mode of voting was by acclamation, but this was not invariable. Thucydides (1.87.2), describing a debate of 432 on relations with Athens, says: "They decide by acclamation, not by casting pebbles," but he adds that on that occasion the presiding officer, an ephor, wanted to make the outcome patently clear, so he designated two places and told those present to go to the one or the other, according to the view they took on the issue. It is impossible to guess how often a division was taken in this way.

It used to be believed that in Spartan practice the real decisions were taken in the council and the assembly merely ratified them. This was Aristotle's view (*Pol.* 2.1272a10–12; 1273a9–13); likewise Plato (*Laws* 691d–692a) and Plutarch (*Lyc.* 5.6–6.1) talk in strong, though vague, terms about the ascendancy of the council. Recently this view has been challenged (by A. Andrewes). Aristotle expresses his view while drawing comparisons between Sparta, Crete and Carthage, and these passages have grave difficulties of interpretation. The best sources, Thucydides and Xenophon (in the *Hellenica*), record frequently that real issues were brought to the Spartan assembly for decision, but they say very little about the council. As described by Thucydides (1.67–87), the debate in the assembly in 432 on relations with Athens was lively and it is difficult to discern any point where the council could exert decisive influence.

Apart from the kings Sparta had another group of executive officers, the ephors. There were five of these each year; they were annual, and they were elected by acclamation in the public assembly. In the fifth and fourth centuries they transacted a good deal of day-to-day business. They presided at meetings of the assembly and perhaps at those of the council. They received foreign envoys. They transmitted orders to commanders in the field, although it is not clear whether such orders originated with the ephors or with some other body, such as the public assembly.

Questions about the origin and specific powers of the ephors are difficult. They can best be approached by asking what was the relationship of power between the kings and the ephors. As Xenophon records (*Constitution of the Lacedaemonians* 15.7), every month the kings and the ephors exchanged oaths; the king swore on his own behalf to rule according to the established laws; the ephors swore on behalf of the city to preserve the kingship undiminished, provided that the king observed his oath. Since these oaths were exchanged every month, they may go back to a very early period, when the moon but not the sun was used for calendric purposes. They appear to reflect an early struggle between the kings and the community, but their origin is too early to throw light on the position of the ephors in the historic period.

Tradition said that the significance of the office was enhanced by an ephor called Chilon. The latter was regarded as one of the Seven Wise Men, and so Diogenes Laertius (1.68) provides an account of him. This account gives a date, since it says that Chilon was ephor in the fifty-sixth Olympiad (556–553), but it is disappointing, as it is little more than a collection of witty sayings attributed to Chilon. Its sole statement on constitutional matters is: "And he was the first to introduce the practice of associating the ephors with the kings." Diogenes does not say whether the ephors were associated as equals or as subordinates. The sentence suggests a remark of Herodotus (6.63.2): in the middle of the sixth century news was brought to king Ariston of the birth of a son when he was "sitting on a seat with the ephors." Perhaps it was a seat of judgement, but it is still not clear whether the ephors were present as the king's equals or his subordinates.

Thucydides (1.131.2) says that the ephors have power to imprison the king. In the context this is a power to arrest, not a power to judge and condemn. An occurrence narrated by Herodotus (5.39–40) shows how far the ephors could go in trying to persuade the king. In the middle of the sixth century King Anaxandrides had a wife but no children. So the ephors urged him to divorce his wife and marry another, but he refused indignantly. Then the ephors and the elders together took counsel and urged Anaxandrides to keep his present wife and marry a second one in addition; they warned him that, if he refused, the Spartiates might consider some unusual action against him. Anaxandrides did as they advised.

This incident shows that the ephors could not coerce the king. It suggests that the king would bow to the combined will of the ephors and the council of elders; possibly when complaints arose against the king, the ephors served as mere complainants and the elders as judges. But the incident is ambiguous in its implications. Anaxandrides yielded to the wish of the ephors and the elders, but he yielded when they suggested that the Spartiates might take action. Did a power to coerce the king reside in the council of elders or in the assembly of adult male Spartiates?

It should perhaps be added that a somewhat similar incident occured three centuries later. The reform proposals of Agis IV led to tension and violence in 241; one of the ephors, Amphares, arrested him, in order to take him before the board of ephors, and with the help of other Spartiates put him in prison. The other king, Leonides, surrounded the prison with troops. The ephors went into the prison and summoned some of the elders thither to hold a trial: Agis was condemned to death. Agis's relatives outside the prison demanded that he be tried before his fellow citizens. Instead, Amphares executed Agis; then he admitted the relatives to the prison and killed them. The incident is reported by Plutarch, *Agis* 18–20. So turbulent a situation cannot reveal much about legal rules; although Agis was effectively condemned by ephors and elders together, his claim to trial before the Spartiates may have been valid. At least in his case, as in that of Anaxandrides, the ephors could not take final action until they had the cooperation of some of the elders.

It used to be fashionable to suppose that the ephors constantly pursued a corporate policy over a long period and that this policy involved them in a protracted struggle with the kings. Such a view is implausible; since new ephors were elected each year, and since there were five of them, it is more likely that there was diversity of policy among the ephors. Any politically ambitious group would strive to get some of its spokesmen elected to the ephorate. Those who offered theories of corporate hostility between ephors and kings tended to regard the reign of Cleomenes I as crucial, but on one of the few occasions when Herodotus mentions ephors, he reports collaboration between Cleomenes and them (3.148.2). He refers to an occurrence of ca. 518, when Maeandrius of Samos, driven from his native island by Persian forces (see chapter 7, p. 174), came to Sparta and appealed to Cleomenes for help. The king would not give help and he feared that Maeandrius might win sympathy in Sparta; so he went to the ephors and told them that it would be better if the stranger were to leave. The ephors expelled Maeandrius.

Expulsions of foreigners (*xenelasiai*) were one of the many executive tasks of the ephors. Enemies of Sparta made the most of such expulsions, although in fact a good many foreigners are known to have visited the city. In general, the strong position of the ephors in classical Sparta should not be explained as the result of a long struggle with the kings. A better explanation consists in saying that, as public authority asserted itself in more spheres of activity, the ephors acquired a miscellaneous bundle of powers and administrative functions. Hence any man who happened to be in office as ephor was well placed for influencing the process of reaching political decisions; in other words, the ephorate was an invitation to political intrigue.

THE GREAT RHETRA[3]

Plutarch (*Lyc.* 6) quotes in full a document which purports to throw light on the relationship between the council and the assembly and, more generally, on the political institutions of Sparta. He introduces it to show the importance which Lycurgus attached to the council. Plutarch says that the document was an oracular response brought by Lycurgus from Delphi and that it was called *rhetra* by the Spartans. In fact, *rhetra* was a word used in Sparta for "law" or "enactment." Opinions have differed on the question whether the text was a Spartan enactment, made perhaps in response to the advice of the Delphic oracle, or an oracular utterance, which led the Spartans to make an enactment or some enactments.

The text is uncertain at some points, but probable readings allow the following translation:

After the people has set up a sanctuary of Zeus Syllanios and Athena Syllania, after the people has arranged itself by tribes and obes, after the people has set up a council (*gerousia*) of thirty including the kings (*archagetai*), let them gather from season to season for the festival of Apellai between Babyka and Knakion; let the elders introduce proposals and decline to introduce proposals; but let the people have the final decision.

Commenting on the text, Plutarch says that later two kings, Polydorus and Theopompus, added a further clause. This addition, now often called the rider, runs as follows:

But if the people make a crooked utterance, let the elders and the kings (*archagetai*) decline it.

Plutarch draws on Aristotle explicitly for his explanations of some items in the text; this suggests that he found the document in Aristotle's treatise on the Lacedaemonian constitution.

The Rhetra, considered without the rider, appears in its crucial clauses to regulate the procedure for making laws and deciding policy. The procedure is to have two stages. First the council of elders is to make proposals or decline to make proposals; then the public assembly, meeting from season to season (monthly?) in a festival called Apellai (a festival of Apollo?), is to have final decision on those proposals. How far the power of the assembly extends is not wholly clear; in particular, the question whether the Rhetra allowed a possibility of amendment in the assembly depends on uncertain readings in the text and on interpretation of the rider. But at least the Rhetra empowered the assembly to accept or reject proposals of the council; the assembly was to have a yea-or-nay competence.

On this minimal interpretation, the Rhetra plays an important part in a theory about Greek constitutional development and the social effects of the introduction of hoplite tactics (see chapter 1, pp. 29–30). The theory claims that the introduction of hoplite tactics had large social effects; as the military strength of the state came to rest on a relatively large class of substantial peasant farmers, this class claimed a share in political power and came into conflict with the relatively narrow aristocracy, which had previously been in control. In some cities the conflict issued in tyranny, but Sparta found a solution, which was embodied in the Rhetra. The procedure, whereby the council introduced proposals but the assembly had at least a yea-or-nay competence of final decision, proved to be a satisfactory compromise. The theory concludes by saying that other states adopted this solution from the Spartan model; for example in Athens early in the sixth century Solon, it is said, introduced a council of four hundred to prepare business for the public assembly.

The theory is impressive because it subsumes a whole range of phenomena under a single explanation. Each item in the theory deserves separate consideration; something has been said in chapters 1 and 2 about hoplite tactics and tyranny, and the question of a Solonian council will be discussed in chapter 5. Here attention will be given to the Spartan part of the theory. It should be noted that there is good evidence for social strife in seventh-century Sparta; Aristotle (*Pol.* 5.1306b37–1307a2) says that "during the Messenian War" some people in Lacedaemon demanded a redistribution of land. He refers to Tyrtaeus as his source. Economic discontent of this kind could not be satisfied by the merely political provisions of the Rhetra, but those provisions might reapportion power so that measures could be passed to solve the economic problem. No doubt the demand for redistribution of land was ultimately met by allocation of allotments in Messenia.

The Rhetra has several troublesome features. Apart from the central clauses about meetings of the assembly and its authority, the document has a series of opening clauses, which deal with three items: foundation of a sanctuary of Zeus Syllanios and Athena Syllania, arrangement of the people by tribes and obes, and establishment of a council of thirty. Either the Rhetra first introduced these three provisions, or it referred to them as things already established by earlier legislation. In the former case the wording of the document is inadequate; more needs to be said, for example, to specify the composition of tribes and obes and the way of choosing the elders. If, on the other hand, the opening clauses refer to institutions already established, the item about the council is relevant to the procedure of legislation, but the other two opening clauses do not have anything to do with the central provisions about the manner of taking decisions; when Thucydides (1.67–87) reports a debate and vote in the Spartan assembly, he leaves no room for use of tribes and obes in the procedure. In short, some difficulty of interpretation arises because the Rhetra includes several disparate subjects in a single document. Possibly this difficulty can be escaped by supposing that the Rhetra is not an enactment but an oracle, recommending general lines for legislation; but in that case the Rhetra is one step removed from Spartan enactments and is so much the less reliable as a key to Spartan institutions.

Greater difficulties appear when the diction of the Rhetra is studied. It uses the word *archagetai* for the Spartan kings, but this word does not mean "king;" it means "founder" and was used of the founder of a cult or of a colony. Some have tried to defend the use of *archagetai* in the Rhetra by saying that the two kings reigning at the time were founders of a new constitutional dispensation, embodied in the document, and of a sanctuary of Zeus Syllanios and Athena Syllania. But the Rhetra does not refer specifically to the kings reigning at the time; it lays down a procedure to be followed permanently. Moreover other features of diction in the Rhetra are proper, not to a legal document, but to a literary composition. For example, the opening clauses ("after. . .after. . .after. . ." in the translation above) do not use connecting particles; the phrase mentioning tribes and obes uses two nouns and two verbs which rhyme; and the phrase used for "from season to season" is poetic.

The difficulties of content and especially those of language strongly suggest that the Rhetra is not authentic. Many scholars have accepted the Rhetra as genuine because they have thought to find an allusion to it in six lines composed by Tyrtaeus and quoted by Plutarch (Tyrt. fr. 3 = Plut. *Lyc.* 6.7). The text has at least one serious uncertainty, but on a probable reading it allows this translation:

After listening to Phoebus they brought home from Pytho the oracular responses and perfect words of the god: "Let the initiative in deliberation be taken by the god-honored kings, who have care of the lovely city of Sparta, and by the elderly gerontes, and then let men of the people answering with straight enactments . . . "

Plutarch understood that "they" in the opening sentence were two Spartan kings. In Plutarch's version the text breaks off at the end of the six lines, when a verb is needed; another version of the fragment, preserved by Diodorus (7.12.6), supplies a verb but is much inferior as verse. The general sense is clear. This passage of Tyrtaeus is much more monarchical in spirit than the Rhetra; and if Tyrtaeus had in mind the provision of the rider as well as those of the Rhetra proper, his allusion to the rider is compressed into the single work "straight." Even so Tyrtaeus describes a procedure in which the first step in deliberation is taken by the kings and the elders and it is followed by a response of the common people. A procedure of this kind is laid down by the crucial clauses of the Rhetra. Hence many people have supposed that the passage of Tyrtaeus guarantees an early date for the Rhetra. One hypothesis, which follows these lines but recognizes the difficulties in the Rhetra, supposes that the Rhetra was forged by reformers at an early date, before the time of Tyrtaeus; the reformers persuaded the Spartans to accept their proposals by alleging that these had been laid down in an oracle or enactment which had been issued long before and subsequently neglected.

But a radically different approach to the problem is possible. A two-stage procedure of legislation, with a council making proposals and forwarding them to a sovereign assembly, is attested in other societies. Tacitus mentions it as customary among the Germanic tribes of his own time; he says (*Germania* 11.1): "The magnates deliberate on lesser affairs and all members of the community deliberate on greater affairs, but with the proviso that even the subjects on which the common people have the decision are first discussed by the magnates." In Rome of the middle and late Republic new legislation customarily began with a decree of the senate, which was technically a recommendation; then at the second stage a bill embodying the content of the decree was proposed to the public assembly. In Rome certainly and probably among the Germanic tribes the two-stage procedure arose by custom; it did not originate from a specific enactment laying it down. That the two-stage procedure in Greek cities arose likewise from custom, not from specific enactment, is suggested by a passage of the *Iliad* (2.48–399). There Agamemnon, the supreme commander of the Greek forces at Troy, wishes to propose a course of action. First he summons a "council of elders" (*boule geronton*) and tells them of his plan; they listen and one of them comments on it. Then Agamemnon addresses the whole host of fighting men; they hear his proposal and begin to act on it. This occurrence in the *Iliad* differs from the fully developed procedure known later in Greek states, since no vote is taken on Agamemnon's proposal in the council or in the assembly of the host. But how voting came to be adopted is another question; the passage in the Iliad shows that, in Greek states including Sparta, the two-stage procedure might have a customary origin.

If that is so, Tyrtaeus's six lines may describe a customary procedure, though they describe it with a monarchical bias; they no longer guarantee the prior existence of the Rhetra or of an enactment based on it. The difficulties in the text of the Rhetra lead to the hypothesis that it was a forgery. Suspicion is strengthened by the fact noted above (p. 72), that in the best accounts of Spartan procedure, from Thucydides and Xenophon, the council does not predominate over the assembly; yet Plutarch cites the Rhetra to illustrate the importance attached by Lycurgus to the council, and the rider gives the council a power of veto over actions taken in the assembly. If the Rhetra was a forgery, it was composed early enough to impose on Aristotle, but that may allow a date as late as the early fourth century. The question of the motive for forgery must be asked, and more than one answer can be offered, since the Rhetra deals with more than one subject. Possibly a clue to the correct answer can be found in what the Rhetra omits; it says nothing about ephors. Perhaps it was composed during a conflict when one side happened to control the board of ephors; then the other side produced a document purporting to show that the ephors had no place in ancestral procedure.

SOCIAL INSTITUTIONS[4]

Sparta developed an elaborate system of public education and discipline for citizens. The only full account of it to survive is given by Plutarch (*Lyc.* 10–12, 14–25). At birth a child was examined by "the oldest among its fellow tribesmen" (*ibid.* 16.1), who decided whether to rear or expose it. Until the age of seven the child was under the care of its mother and nurses. On reaching seven years, boys were formed into units called "herds" (*agelai*); the members of each herd lived and exercised together. At the age of twelve a more severe stage began with new groupings; each boy was allowed only one tunic each year and no cloak. The content of education included music and poetry as well as physical exercises and games. The whole system of education was under the direction of a public official called the *paidonomos*.

Serious military training came in the last two years of education. After that, at the age of twenty, a boy was held to have reached maturity, but he still was not free. He now sought admission to one of the living and eating units called *phiditia*; each of these had about fifteen members, who each month contributed fixed amounts of food to the common stock. Each *phidition* served as a unit on military campaigns; the members' habit of consorting together at home was expected to foster mutual loyalty in the field. When a new applicant sought admission to a phidition, the members voted and a single adverse vote sufficed to exclude him and led to diminution of his civic rights. If the applicant was accepted, he lived mostly in the phidition until he reached the age of thirty and in this period he was available constantly for military service. After the age of thirty he had more freedom, but he usually devoted much of his time to public affairs and he could be called out for military service, if the emergency justified it. For girls there was public education, including gymnastic exercises, but they became free from public discipline when they reached maturity.

The above account rests largely on statements by Plutarch, but some items can be confirmed from sources earlier than the reformers of the third century. Thus Xenophon (*Constitution of the Lacedaemonians* 2–4) describes a system of public education in Sparta; his account is less systematic, but he mentions some significant details, for example, the paidonomos. He describes (*ibid.* 5) the practice of taking common meals in the phiditia, although again he is less informative than Plutarch and does not mention the procedure of admission. Aristotle (*Pol.* 2.1269b19–22) remarks of Sparta: "The lawgiver wanted the whole city to be hardy, and in the case of the men he was obvious in his aim, but he neglected it as concerns the women." Aristophanes (*Lys.* 82) makes a joke about the gymnastic exercises practised by Laconian women. For military service Spartans were grouped in year-classes, so that men of one age constituted one class. Xenophon (*ibid.* 11.2) says that as the first step towards a campaign the ephors declared which year-classes were required. He gives details of mobilization at several points in the *Hellenica*; hence it appears that, when a battle was begun, the force first sent into action consisted of the youngest ten year-classes, that is, Lacedaemonians aged twenty to thirty, although the force sent out on a campaign often included some additional year-classes; and men who had reached the age of sixty were no longer compelled to serve outside Lacedaemon.

Thus the essentials of the system of public education and discipline are attested for the fifth and fourth centuries, even though by the time of Plutarch some details of practice may have been added and literary tradition about it may have become embellished. The origin of the system must be sought in the archaic period. Some features indeed suggest initiation ceremonies stemming from a very early period, but the ultimate origins of individual features matter less than the question, When was a comprehensive system of public discipline devised? The system trained Spartiates as hoplites; it emphasized mutual cooperation and loyalty, attitudes which were not so necessary in the less organized type of fighting which preceded the introduction of hoplite tactics. So the system probably was not introduced before the middle of the seventh century. On the other hand, the date probably was not later than the middle of the sixth century, when Sparta defeated Argos and began to emerge as the dominant power in the Peloponnese (see below, pp. 84–85). The introduction of the system may have to do with a change in the divisions of the citizen body, which requires attention next.

TRIBES AND OBES[5]

In a fragment preserved on papyrus Tyrtaeus (fr. 1) talks about men going into battle; he refers to them as "separately the Pamphyli and the Hylleis and [the Dymanes]." The context of the line is not certain, but the passage seems to be an exhortation, and so in it Tyrtaeus probably addresses the Spartans of his own time. The three names are those of the three Dorian tribes, which have already been met in Sicyon and Argos (chapter 2, p. 45). The line of Tyrtaeus is the sole but sufficient evidence to show that the Spartans were at some time divided into the three Dorian tribes.

Inscriptions of Roman date reveal a different classification of citizens. Some of the inscriptions record victories in competitive games and a few honor local magistrates. Each unit winning victories or granting honors is called an "obe" (*oba*). This term is used of Limnae and Amyclae. Further, on different inscriptions the teams of Conooura, Pitana and Neapolis are said to have "won (the competition of) the obes." Finally an inscription from Amyclae honors someone described as a man of Mesoa. As already observed (above, p. 68), historic Sparta comprised the four villages of Pitana, Mesoa, Limnae and Conooura, and the town of Amyclae. The name Neapolis means "new town," so it may mark a new foundation of Hellenistic or Roman date. Thus historic Sparta would appear to consist of five obes and membership of these would depend originally on residence in the appropriate village or town. Aristotle in a fragment of his treatise on the *Constitution of the Lacedaemonians* (fr. 541) says that Sparta had five "ancestral regiments" (*lochoi*) and he names them; only one of them, Mesoa, has a regional name, coinciding with one of the obes, but it should follow that all five regiments were originally regional in composition, even though four of them had nonregional names. Possibly it should be noted that at the battle of Plataea in 479 the Spartiate force, brigaded separately from perioeci, numbered 5,000 (Hdt. 9.10.1). There were five ephors each year and their number may reflect the division of the Spartan citizens into obes.

On this basis Wade-Gery (in 1944) proposed a hypothesis on the following lines. Spartiates were originally divided into the three Dorian tribes; membership was hereditary and the tribes were preserved from the age of migrations. But under settled conditions a purely hereditary division of citizens has disadvantages. Absorption of new immigrants is difficult; moreover, because the units are hereditary, they are likely to become unequal in numbers, and so if public burdens, such as military service, are distributed equally among the units, they will be distributed unequally among the citizens. In Rome at an early period and in Athens towards the end of the sixth century (see chapter 6, pp. 151-155) considerations of this kind led to the introduction of a new division of the citizen body; membership in the new tribes depended on residence in the several areas into which the territory of the state was divided for the purpose of the reform. Wade-Gery's hypothesis said that the Spartiates underwent a change similar in principle; the new units were obes, and membership of these depended on residence in the five districts which constituted historic Sparta. The Rhetra, discussed above (pp. 74-78), requires the people of Sparta to arrange themselves by tribes and obes; Wade-Gery, accepting the Rhetra as authentic, saw here references to the traditional Dorian tribes and to the new system of obes.

This hypothesis was seriously impaired in 1951, when Beattie published a new study of an early Laconian law. The law was inscribed on stone but the inscription has been lost; it was copied and published in the nineteenth century, and the report on the lettering suggests that the original belonged to an early date, probably to the fifth or sixth century B.C. The law dealt with matters of cult and much of the text is uncertain; one of the certain passages is a reference to "the obe of the Arkaloi." Thus even if Neapolis was a new creation of Hellenistic or later date, the five other obes attested in the Roman period together with the obe of Arkalia amount to six obes. Hence since 1951 Wade-Gery's hypothesis of five obes has seemed to be no longer tenable.

Recently an ingenious theory has been proposed by Huxley. He suggests that the three Dorian tribes were kept but, as the territory inhabited by Spartiate citizens grew, it was divided into an increasing number of obes. At one stage the obes numbered five and now the number of ephors became fixed. Later, by 676, the number of obes was increased to nine. In 676 the festival called the Karneia was reformed and it is described by Demetrius of Scepsis, an antiquarian of the second century B.C. He says that for the festival the Spartans used nine tentlike structures and the representatives of three phratries met in each. Thus there were twenty-seven phratries in all, and Huxley sees here a combination of the hereditary division by three tribes with the territorial division by nine obes; the ultimate unit was the phratry, and to define the membership of any one phratry it was necessary to specify both a tribe and an obe.

Demetrius does not mention tribes or obes and his use of the word "phratry" may not be technical. No parallel from any other ancient republic has been cited for combining the hereditary and the territorial principles of division in the way Huxley suggests. Moreover, it is difficult to see any reason for adopting so complex a scheme. By introducing a division of citizens on a purely territorial basis, the state could equalize the burden of military service and hence draw more fully on the military potential of the citizens; but if the hereditary principle of division was integrated into the new system, the phratries preserved the inequalities of the three hereditary tribes.

For this reason Huxley's hypothesis should be rejected. A return to Wade-Gery's theory, in a modified form, may be recommended. The figure five was significant in Spartan institutions. Five ephors took office each year. Heredotus (1.67.5) mentions an annual group of five *agathoergoi* ("*good-service men*"); they were chosen from among those retiring from a career of service in the royal bodyguard, which was called "horsemen" although it fought on foot, and the men selected served for a year as messengers of state. Considered in conjunction with these offices, the five "ancestral regiments" mentioned by Aristotle suggest that at some period Spartiates were divided into five units for military service. Possibly those units were called "tribes" (*phylai*) and were based on territorial divisions, with obes as subdivisions of the tribes. Such a hypothesis may derive some slight support from the Rhetra; even if it is a forgery, the author was evidently familiar with Spartan institutions, and as he mentioned tribes and obes in the same breath, they were presumably elements coordinated in a single system. The inscriptions of Roman date show that obes were based on territorial divisions, even if the system had been revised drastically by then.

If this hypothesis is on the right lines, it remains to ask, When was the five-fold division into territorial tribes introduced? Two indications suggest limits. First Tyrtaeus (fr. 1) seems to refer to his own time when he speaks of troops organized according to the three Dorian tribes. After the new system was introduced, the Dorian tribes still may have been recognized for some religious purposes, but the five new tribes were used for military organization. Secondly, Herodotus mentions the five agathoergoi in connection with the conclusion of the Spartan war against Tegea; that war was brought to an end ca. 560–550.

FOREIGN POLICY IN THE SIXTH CENTURY[6]

So far, this chapter has had to deal with matters which, however necessary for understanding Lacedaemon, are obscure and speculative. But Herodotus provides information which permits reconstruction of a relatively clear and intelligible picture of sixth-century policy. The subjugation of Messenia was completed by ca. 600 (see above, pp. 66–67). Thus Sparta had extended her rule successfully to the west. As a next step she looked northwards; by following the route which led up the valley of the Eurotas and beyond into Arcadia, she came into conflict with Tegea.

Herodotus's account of the Tegean War (1.65–68) indicates that it was long and difficult for Sparta. It began under one pair of kings, Leon and Agesicles, but was concluded in the reigns of the next pair, Anaxandrides and Ariston. In view of the databable activities of their descendants, the war must have lasted ca. 590/580–ca. 560/550. Herodotus at the beginning of his account says that in consequence of the war the Lacedaemonians gained superiority over the Tegeates, but as his account develops, it reveals something more subtle. At a late stage in the war the Spartans, advised by the Delphic oracle, set about finding the bones of the legendary hero Orestes to bring them to Sparta. A further utterance of the Delphic oracle promised that Sparta would become "protector" of Tegea. At last an ingenious Spartan discovered the bones of Orestes and brought them to Sparta; Herodotus adds that thereafter the Lacedaemonians were successful in battles against the Tegeates. It should further be noted that, during the campaign of 479 at Plataea (see chapter 8, pp. 223–225) the Tegeates said that among the allies of Lacedaemon they traditionally had the privilege of taking the place of honor on the wing in the battle line (Hdt. 9.26.2).

In short, the war led, not to the subjugation of Tegea, but to an alliance between that city and Lacedaemon. When the war began, the Spartans may have hoped to treat Tegea as they had treated Messenia; they may have expected to absorb its territory and reduce its inhabitants to dependent status. But Tegea proved too tough to conquer, perhaps because of the difficulty of campaigning in the highlands of Arcadia; and on the other hand the Lacedaemonians were too formidable for the Tegeates to refuse all relations with them. The solution found was an alliance. Moreover, in the diplomacy leading to the alliance the Spartans enunciated a new claim. Orestes, who was worshipped in Arcadia, was a hero revered by the pre-Dorian element in the population of the Peloponnese. It was observed in chapter 2 that tension between Dorian and pre-Dorian elements was a lively issue in some parts of the Peloponnese as late as the sixth century. By adopting ostentatiously the cult of Orestes Sparta, although a Dorian state, posed as the protector of the pre-Dorian element. It was at least partly through this claim that the Spartans succeeded in winning many permanent allies in the ensuing half-century.

But before Sparta could win many allies, she had to deal with Argos, her chief rival in the Peloponnese. Herodotus (1.82) tells how tension between the two powers came to a head ca. 544 and was decided for a long time by a battle fought for control of the plain of Thyrea. The battle can be called "the battle of the champions;" each side chose three hundred protagonists to fight and thus spare the others, but when the survivors could not agree who had won, the armies fought a further battle to decide the issue. After the Spartan victory it is not clear whether a formal treaty of peace was made, but the question scarcely matters; nothing further is heard of fighting between Argos and Lacedaemon until ca. 494. A more important question concerns the extent of Argive power immediately before the battle of the champions. Sometime in the seventh century Pheidon had made Argos the strongest power in the Peloponnese; early in the sixth century Argos fought a war against Sicyon with an outcome perhaps not wholly unfavorable for Argos (see chapter 2, pp. 42 and 45), but that is all that can be affirmed about the power of Argos between the death of Pheidon and the battle of the champions. So it is not clear whether at that battle Sparta confronted a power of almost Pheidonian scale or one which had already lost much of its former possessions and influence.

In the ensuing generation Sparta brought many of the states of the Peloponnese into her alliance. Herodotus (1.68.6) appends to his account of the war with Tegea a statement that by ca. 546 Sparta had gained leadership over most of the Peloponnese, but he anticipates. A clear date in the growth of the Spartan alliance is provided by the campaign waged by king Cleomenes in 510; he led an army across the isthmus of Corinth to overthrow Hippias, the tyrant of Athens. This implies that Sparta had the good will of Corinth and Megara. Quite possibly by 510 she had won alliances with Elis and Sicyon, with some Arcadian towns in addition to Tegea, with small towns near Argos like Mycenae and Tiryns, and with cities further east like Epidaurus and Troezen and perhaps the island of Aegina. At some time, perhaps in the sixth century, Sparta tried to win alliances in Achaea by bringing from Helice to Sparta the bones of the pre-Dorian hero Teisamenus; in legend Teisamenus was the son of Orestes, and the Spartan approach followed the pattern set in her dealings with Tegea, but Helice refused the offer of an agreement. In seeking allies Sparta doubtless made the most of her position as a Dorian state which championed pre-Dorian Peloponnesians.

The resulting sum of alliances is often called the Peloponnesian League. The name is modern; the ancient name was "the Lacedaemonians and their allies." It arose from a series of bilateral treaties between Sparta and other cities; the alliance with Tegea was probably the first of these and launched Sparta on the course of winning allies instead of absorbing territory, as she had done in the seventh century. But at some time the bilateral treaties were replaced by a multilateral agreement; this bound all members of the League to accept any decision reached by a majority at a federal congress, to which the several member states would send deputies.

Possibly the change from bilateral to multilateral obligations was carried out at a congress held at Sparta very late in the sixth century. In any case that meeting was important in the development of the League, although Herodotus's account of it (5.90–93) raises some questions. Shortly before, Cleomenes had led a Pelo-ponnesian force against Athens, but at Eleusis the Corinthian contingent mu-tinied and went home. Then the other Spartan king, Demaratus, deserted the expedition; thereupon Cleomenes retreated and disbanded the force. Herodotus (5.74–75) says that because of this divergence between Cleomenes and Demara-tus the Spartans made a law that henceforth only one of the kings should serve on any one expedition; and he reports a congress at Sparta, where the Spartans proposed a new policy towards Athens which the allies rejected. A difficulty arises because of a further incident recorded by Herodotus (6.50; 6.61–73) as occurring about ten years later. In 491 Cleomenes went to Aegina and tried to exact hostages, but a leading Aeginetan defied him and alleged that the Aeginetans were not bound to obey, as the order had been issued by only one of the Spartan kings. So Cleomenes went home and, after intrigues, came back to Aegina with a second Spartan king; then the Aeginetans gave the hostages required.

The incident of 491 throws some light on the behavior of Demaratus at Eleusis. Perhaps there was a rule that the allies must obey an order issued by both the kings. When the Corinthians refused to proceed further against Athens, Demaratus withdrew, so that only one king was left in command and the allies were no longer bound to obey; one way of dealing with a mutiny is to invalidate the disobeyed order. But if both kings eventually proceeded to Aegina in 491, it is unlikely that a rule had been adopted ten years before to the effect that only one king should serve on each expedition. It should further be noted that the incident at Aegina in 491 is the last occasion on which both kings are known to have served abroad together.

It would be bold to insist on any one interpretation of the organizational changes carried out in the Peloponnesian League late in the sixth and early in the fifth century. All that can be asserted is that in that period the Spartans and their allies gave a great deal of thought to federal organization and at least one congress was held. And that much is important. The Peloponnesian League was a lasting organization; it did not disintegrate until 366/5. But it did not arise from mere local ties reinforced by a belief in common descent; it was an artificial creation, brought into being by political power. A league of this kind was a new experiment among the Greek city-states; there would be further attempts to found such leagues and they would draw on the experience of the Peloponnesian League.

One further aspect of Spartan foreign policy in the sixth century deserves attention here. Relations were opened with some of the non-Greek powers of the east. Herodotus (1.56.1; 1.69–70) tells of dealings with Lydia. Croesus, he says, prepared to go to war against Cyrus of Persia (ca. 544) and sent to Sparta for an alliance. The Spartans remembered a benefit he had previously conferred on them; when they required gold to build a statue of Apollo and sought to buy it in Sardis, Croesus gave it to them free. So the Spartans agreed to ally with him and sent him an ornamental bronze bowl as a present. When the war with Cyrus went against Croesus and the latter was besieged in Sardis, Herodotus (1. 81–83) says that he sent to his allies for help. The Spartans were preoccupied with the war with Argos, but allegedly prepared a force of ships; however, before it could sail, news came that Sardis had been captured and Croesus was a prisoner. In this story one must be aware of the account of unrealized intentions. Indeed the supposition of military or naval considerations in the relations between Sparta and Lydia is improbable. But the exchange of presents is credible.

The bronze bowl intended for Croesus traveled no farther than Samos. An act of Samian piracy is the occasion for Herodotus (3.47) to mention Spartan relations with Egypt. Amasis, king of Egypt, sent the Spartans a present consisting of a linen corslet, elaborately embroidered and trimmed with gold. It was stolen by the Samians in the year before the disappearance of the bronze bowl.

Thus Herodotus indicates that the Spartans opened relations with Egypt and with Lydia. These relations are merely incidental to his main narrative, so there may have been more exchanges of presents than he mentions. The ceremonial nature of the relations should not blind the reader to their political significance. Rather he should call to mind the relations which Periander of Corinth had cultivated with Lydia and Egypt (see chapter 2, p. 52); such dealings contributed to the magnificence of the Corinthian tyrant. From some tyrants, such as Cleisthenes of Sicyon, the Spartans learned to pose as the champions of pre-Dorian Peloponnesians; they also learned the lesson of magnificence, whether they copied it from the tyrants or simply conformed to a Greek taste which they shared. By the end of the sixth century Sparta was the strongest power in Greece, and her ascendancy rested primarily on her army and her diplomacy. But ostentation, evidenced in Spartan dealings with oriental powers, was impressive and politically advantageous. Pageantry is a not unimportant part of history.

NOTES

1. Recent years have seen numerous works on Sparta. Mention may be made of G. L. Huxley, *Early Sparta* (London 1962); A.H.M. Jones, *Sparta* (Oxford 1967); and W.G. Forest, *A History of Sparta 950–192 B.C.* (London 1968). Many of these try to extract more historical information about the period before 600 than is attempted in the present chapter. For example, Huxley (op. cit. 19–25) accepts Pausanias's account (3.2) of the early expansion of Sparta in the Eurotas valley; there is indeed no geographical objection to the account, but that may only show that it is a plausible fiction, and it is difficult to see that the ultimate source could be anything better than oral tradition. A good introduction to the problems of chronology of the Messenian Wars is provided by H.T. Wade-Gery, "The 'Rhianos-Hypothesis'" *Ehrenberg Studies*, 289–302. The argument for dating the First War ca. 736–ca. 716 is given by Wade-Gery, *CAH* 3.537–538. On the chronological problems fundamental importance belongs to the observations of F. Jacoby, *F.Gr.Hist.* IIIa (*Kommentar*) 112–119 (on Rhianos, *F.Gr.Hist.* IIIA 265F38–46); cf. IID (*Kommentar*) 425 (on Callisthenes, IIB 124F23–24). Epaminondas's remark is known from Plut. *Mor.* 194b and Aelian, *V.H.* 13.42. The fragments of Tyrtaeus are available in E. Diehl, *Anthologia Lyrica Graeca* I³ (Leipzig 1949) 4–18. On artistic work in Laconia see R.M. Cook, "Spartan History and Archaeology," *CQ.*, N.S. 12 (1962) 156–158.

2. This section owes much to A. Andrewes, The Government of Classical Sparta, *Ehrenberg Studies*, 1–20. For theories attributing a corporate policy to the ephors see G. Dickins, "The Growth of Spartan Policy," *JHS* 32 (1912) 1–42. The way hostile propaganda used and perhaps exaggerated Spartan expulsions of foreigners is illustrated by Thuc. 1.144.2. For an intrigue illustrating the value of the ephorate in political maneuvering see Thuc. 5.36.

3. The literature on the Great Rhetra is enormous. Ed. Meyer (*Die lykurgischen Rhetren, Forschungen zur alten Geschichte* I² [Halle 1892] 261–269) attacked the nineteenth-century view that the Rhetra was the foundation-document of the Spartan constitution; his arguments show that, if the Rhetra is so understood, it must be a forgery. The nineteenth-century view has been revived by Hammond, *Studies* 47–103 = "The Lycurgean Reform at Sparta," *JHS* 70 (1950) 42–64. Wade-Gery (*Essays* 37–85 = "The Spartan Rhetra in Plutarch *Lycurgus* IV," *CQ* 37 [1943] 62–72; 38 [1944] 1–9 and 115–126), answering Meyer, argued that the Rhetra is not a foundation-document but carried out a reform in an existing constitution; his study of the text was thorough and superseded many previous discussions. L.H. Jeffery ("The Pact of the First Settlers at Cyrene," *Historia* 10 [1961] 139–147, especially 145–147) raised linguistic objections to authenticity; W.G. Forrest ("The Date of the Lykourgan Reforms in Sparta," *Phoenix* 17 [1963] 157–179) tried to answer them and dated the Rhetra to 676. D. Butler ("Competence of the Demos in the Spartan Rhetra," *Historia* 11 [1962] 385–396) made an important suggestion about procedure in the Spartan assembly. Other studies which may be mentioned are G.L. Huxley, *Early Sparta*, 37–52; A.H.M. Jones, "The Lycurgan Rhetra," *Ehrenberg Studies* 165–175; Sealey, "Probouleusis and the Sovereign Assembly," *CSCA* 2 (1969) 247–269.

4. Texts illustrating the use of year-classes in mobilization include Xen. *Hell.* 2.4.32; 3.4.23; 5.4.40; 6.4.17. The exemption of men over sixty years old from foreign service is attested by Xen. *Hell.* 5.4.13. For further references on Spartan education see G. Busolt and H. Swoboda, *Griechische Staatskunde* II³ (Munich 1926) 694–703.

5. For the four villages constituting Sparta see Paus. 3.16.9. The inscriptions of Roman date attesting obes are *I.G.* V (1), 26; 32; 34; 472; 480; 515; 564; 566; 675; 676; 681; 682; 683; 684; 685; 686; 688; 834; 917. Wade-Gery developed his theory of tribes and obes in *Essays* 66–85 = "The Spartan Rhetra in Plutarch *Lycurgus* VI: What is the Rhetra?, *CQ* 38 (1944) 115–126. For the obe of

the Arkaloi see A.J. Beattie, "An Early Laconian 'Lex Sacra'," *CQ*, N.S. 1 (1951) 46–58. For Huxley's view see his *Early Sparta*, 47–49; a similar theory is offered by Forrest, *A History of Sparta 950–192 B.C.*, 42–46. The statement of Demetrius of Scepsis about the Karneia is preserved by Athen. 4.141e–f.

6. On the Tegean War, the bones of Orestes and the beginnings of the Peloponnesian League see Wade-Gery, *CAH* 3.565–569. On the Spartan approach to Helice see Paus. 7.1.8; D.M. Leahy, "The Bones of Tisamenus," *Historia* 4 (1955) 26–38. The ultimate extent of the Peloponnesian League can be learned from Thuc. 2.9. Its organization has been discussed by J.A.O. Larsen, "The Constitution of the Peloponnesian League," *CP* 28 (1933) 257–276; 29 (1934) 1–19. That the members were explicitly bound to accept a majority decision is known from Thuc. 5.30.1. For examples of congresses of the League see Thuc. 1.119–125; Xen. *Hell*. 5.2.11–24.

4

The Beginnings of the Athenian State

THE LITERARY SOURCES[1]

For the history of Athens extant information is more plentiful than for that of any other Greek city. A comparatively clear picture can be reconstructed of Athenian behavior in the late fifth and fourth centuries; this is due to the survival of histories, like those of Thucydides and Xenophon, and speeches, such as those of Lysias, Demosthenes and Aeschines, and to the recovery of numerous, though often fragmentary, inscriptions. Unfortunately the institutions of the Athenian state had for the most part reached lasting form before the period for which evidence is relatively plentiful; and so the inquiry into the political forces which shaped those institutions is tantalizing.

The term "Atthidographers" is used of those who wrote histories of Athens. The first to do so was Hellanicus of Lesbos, who compiled chronological accounts of several cities in the fifth century. One fragment of his work on Athens deals with an event of 407/6; evidently he brought his account down to a date late in the fifth century, but hardly anything more can be said about its character. The other Atthidographers were Athenian citizens. The earliest of them was Cleidemus or Cleitodemus. Even the form of his name is uncertain; his *Atthis* appeared at about the middle of the fourth century. The next in the series of Atthidographers was Androtion, a man who had a political career. His last recorded political activity was in 344/3; thereafter he withdrew from Athens to Megara and wrote his *Atthis* in exile. Little is known of the next three Atthidographers, Phanodemus, Demon and Melanthius, but a good many fragments survive from the last *Atthis*, that of Philochorus. This author lived in the third century and brought his account down to the year 263/2, the end of the Chremonidean War. The *Atthis* of Philochorus became one of the standard reference works of antiquity and so it is often quoted by later writers. For events of the fourth century the extant fragments are a valuable source; those dealing with earlier periods are rather less informative.

A writer close to the Atthidographic tradition was Aristotle. In the course of his political studies he compiled, perhaps with the aid of pupils, accounts of the constitutions of 158 Greek states. Extensive parts of his account of Athens were found on papyrus and first published in 1891. This work, the *Athenaion Politeia* ("The Constitution of the Athenians,") is divided into two parts; the first is a narrative and the second is an account of the constitution as its was in Aristotle's time. The narrative varies in value and betrays the influence of Aristotle's theories about political development.

The excitement caused by the discovery of Aristotle's treatise was partly responsible for the popularity of a theory which would have given it enormous evidential value. The theory said that from early times an official chronicle was kept by religious officials in Athens; this chronicle then would be the source for much of Aristotle's work, whether he drew on it directly or through the accounts of Hellanicus, Cleidemus or Androtion. Positive evidence for the existence of an official chronicle is lacking. The hypothesis of an official chronicle has been attacked, particularly by F. Jacoby; he pointed out that acutely divergent accounts of the overthrow of the Peisistratidae could not have arisen and persisted, if an official chronicle had been available to settle the question.

Although little is known of the works of the early Atthidographers, it is clear that they and Aristotle sometimes disagreed with one another. For example, Aristotle's account of the economic work of Solon differed from that given by Androtion, whose *Atthis* was the most recent when Aristotle composed his treatise. Again Aristotle said that in 480, when the Athenians were preparing to evacuate Athens in face of Persian attack, the Areopagite Council provided and distributed money, thus making embarkation possible; Cleidemus said that Themistocles provided the money by a trick. Jacoby tried to show that divergences between Cleidemus and Androtion in their *Atthides* reflected a divergence of opinion on contemporary politics. The evidence may be too slight to establish such a thesis; the divergences among the Atthidographers and Aristotle may reflect controversies that were strictly literary and scholastic. At least their work was influenced by speculation and by outlooks proper to the fourth century.

Although there was no official chronicle available to the Atthidographers, there was an official list of the annual eponymous archons. Plato (*Hippias maior* 285e) remarked that it was possible to trace the annual archons back to Solon (594/3); his language does not indicate whether one could take the count further back. Excavation has recovered four small fragments of an archon list inscribed about 425, and study of these has led to an important conclusion: if the proportions of the stone were similar to those of other fifth-century inscriptions, the list it bore went back beyond Solon to Creon (682/1), whom tradition regarded as the earliest of the annual archons. Yet a caution must be uttered. In the narrative part of *The Constitution of the Athenians* Aristotle tries to state the intervals of years between the successive events mentioned from 594/3 to 401/0, when the narrative ends. Enough is extant of the opening sections of the treatise to show that Aristotle did not give intervals of years for events before 594/3, or at least did not give such intervals regularly. If the archon list available gave entries going right back to Creon, one wonders why Aristotle did not use the entries for the years before 594/3; perhaps he considered them unreliable.

The Atthidographers and Aristotle were influenced by speculation and controversy. Accordingly, special importance attaches to literary sources composed before their period. One of these, the poems of Solon, proves to be disappointing. Considerable fragments of his poems survive, many being preserved in Aristotle's *Constitution of the Athenians*; but little can be learned about political forces from such a passage as fr. 5 (*AP* 12.1):

> I gave the *demos* as much honor as suffices, neither depriving it of prestige nor inciting it to seek more. As for those who had power and were admired for their wealth, I ensured that they should not undergo anything iniquitous. I stood and put a strong shield round both and I did not let either win victory unjustly.

Even since the notion of extremism was introduced into political discourse, all statesmen have professed moderation. Moreover, because of the scarcity of contemporary literature, the meaning of some of Solon's crucial terms is uncertain. This is particularly true of the word *demos*, which occurs in the passage cited above. It is usually taken to mean "the common people," a sense which it often has in later political literature and which appears as early as the Homeric poems. But in the Homeric poems it is also well attested in the sense of the rural territory of a city as distinct from the residential town; this may be the ancestor of the special sense which the word acquired in Attica in consequence of the reforms of Cleisthenes, for there it was used of the several villages or parishes into which the whole territory was divided. Accordingly, it is possible that in Solon's poems the word *demos* indicates people of the countryside, or some part of it, as distinct from people of the town.

The other literary sources written before the age of speculative Atthidography are some passages of Herodotus and Thucydides. The latter provides valuable digressions on the unification of Attica, on Cylon and on the Peisistratidae. Herodotus narrates the rise of Peisistratus and elsewhere gives an account of the fall of his sons. It is difficult to conjecture the sources used by these writers beyond saying that they drew on oral traditions and perhaps especially on the traditions of families whose ancestors had been powerful in the sixth century. Doubtless the hazards of oral transmission harmed the traditions which reached them. Very occasionally the reader may think he has discerned a dubious item; for example, when Herodotus describes the rise of Peisistratus and attributes to him three successive attempts at tyranny, one may feel that this is suspiciously schematic. Even so, the relevant passages of Herodotus and Thucydides are the best evidence surviving on early Athens.

Among late sources Plutarch (ca. A.D. 46–after 120) deserves mention. He read very widely and on early Athens his *Lives* of Theseus and Solon are useful; he drew on Aristotle and on other writers now lost. He is especially valuable when he records institutional survivals. This chapter and the next will try to show that a credible account of the political forces in Athens of the seventh and sixth centuries can be given, mainly on the basis of Herodotean evidence; negatively these chapters will try to reject other accounts, which depend more on Aristotle.

For possible documentary sources see Appendix to chapter 5.

THE UNIFICATION OF ATTICA[2]

Among the city-states of European Greece classical Athens with its territory, Attica, was large. It could compare with Boeotia, which was a federal state, and with Lacedaemon, where the supremacy of Sparta was somewhat tempered by the local authority of the perioecid towns. But Athens in and after the fifth century was a unitary state, where local organs, the village or parish units called demes, had only rudimentary powers. So it is a proper question, How did so large a territory come to be so closely controlled from a single center? This result was brought about by a complex series of developments, concluding with the work of Cleisthenes. The first step was formal unification, whereby the organs of the city of Athens asserted sovereignty over the whole territory. But this first step was little more than formal, since the organs of the city could still be challenged successfully, as is shown by the rebellion of Peisistratus.

Geographically Attica may be divided into three or four plains separated by hills. The central plain held the city of Athens and a strip of coast, including the bay of Phalerum. Further west was the plain of Thria; here the largest settlement was Eleusis. The eastern section of Attica consisted partly of low-lying territory and partly of hills and it included several settlements, the most noteworthy being at Brauron and at Marathon. Athens was an important site in the late bronze age, but the territorial extent of its authority is not clear. Some passages in the Homeric poems imply that Athens already controlled a wide expanse of land; in the Catalogue of Ships (*Iliad* 2.546–556) Menestheus is said to have brought fifty ships from Athens to Troy, and in the Odyssey (3.278) Sunium is described as "the promontory of Athens." But whatever view is adopted about the origin of the poems, these passages may have been composed as late as the sixth century and may have exaggerated the former greatness of Athens to please audiences at the Panathenaic festival.

Athens was one of the few sites where habitation was not interrupted at the end of the bronze age. Indeed, it was comparatively prosperous in the Protogeometric and Geometric periods. But in all probability any hegemony which Athens had built up was lost and for a time in the dark ages Attica was a land of many independent towns and villages. So much may be inferred from the persistence into the historic period of recollections of such a former condition. Thucydides (2.15.1–2) says that until the time of the legendary king Theseus Attica was divided between several independent states and there were wars between some of them, for example, between Athens and Eleusis. The "Homeric" *Hymn to Demeter*, a poem of very uncertain date, tells at length of Demeter's sojourn in Eleusis but has no hint of any Eleusinian subjection to Athens. A few institutional survivals reflect former independence. Plutarch (*Thes.* 13.4) observes that there was no intermarriage between the demes of Pallene and Hagnous. Both were in the central plain and the custom of avoiding intermarriage indicates a time when even that plain had not yet been united under Athens. Again at irregular intervals Athens sent to Delphi sacred envoys as a deputation called the *Pythais*, and on these occasions the four villages constituting the Tetrapolis of Marathon sent separate envoys of their own.

It should be conjectured that Athens first united the villages of the central plain, while Eleusis gained similar control in the west and one or two predominant centers arose in the east; then at a second stage of unification Athens brought the outlying plains under her own control. Something can perhaps be ascertained about the date of this second stage. For the western plain the archaeological record is suggestive. Geometric graves at Eleusis were marked probably by a mound of earth and some small stones, occasionally by a plain slab of stone or a vase; there is nothing at Eleusis resembling the large Dipylon vases used as grave markers in Late Geometric Athens. This has been regarded as indicating a lack of connection between Eleusis and Athens in the eighth century. Again a Late Geometric building at Eleusis has been identified as a Sacred House for worship of ancestors. It was destroyed early in the seventh century; at the beginning of the sixth century a small chamber with an altar was built in front of the wall of the court of the former Sacred House. Could the destruction reflect the overthrow of a locally powerful family during the final stage of the unification? For the unification of the eastern district with the central plain some entries in the list of archons of the seventh century are suggestive. They are:

669/8 Peisistratus
664/3 Miltiades
659/8 Miltiades.

The reliability of entries in the archon list for years before 594/3 is not wholly clear (see above, p. 91); but at least these entries may show that the names Peisistratus and Miltiades occurred among the archons well before 594/3. In the middle of the sixth century men called Peisistratus and Miltiades became prominent; the former certainly and the latter probably came from Brauron (see chapters 5 and 6, pp. 123 and 141).

It is reasonable to conclude that the unification of the plain of Eleusis and of the eastern districts with the central plain took place not later than the first half of the seventh century and perhaps not much earlier. Even in the sixth century the borders of Athenian authority were not permanently fixed. There was a struggle, probably protracted, with Megara for control of Salamis; perhaps this should be regarded as continuing that movement of Athenian expansion which had absorbed Eleusis. There were conflicts with Boeotian cities on the northern border, especially over Oropus, a township which remained in dispute for centuries.

It is important not merely that unification was comparatively late but that local and separatist memories and traditions survived. Some of these have already been noticed and others may be mentioned. Legend said that the village of Deceleia in northern Attica had resisted king Theseus of Athens; accordingly when the Tyndaridae brought an army to Attica in search of Helen, the people of Deceleia welcomed them and led them to the village of Aphidna, which was betrayed to them. This legend was remembered early in the Peloponnesian War and was alleged by the Spartans as their reason for sparing Deceleia, when they ravaged other parts of Attica. On inquiring into their real reason one may remember that much later in the war, in 413, they fortified and garrisoned Deceleia. Thus separatist legends could be used to political purpose. Some legends bearing on localities enhanced the status of powerful families. For example, the clan called the Gephyraei lived in northern Attica; one branch, or perhaps all its branches, belonged to Aphidna, which lay a little to the east of Deceleia. The clan claimed to have come from Euboean Eretria and their cults suggest ties with Tanagra in Boeotia. In 514 two members of the clan, Harmodius and Aristogeiton, were sufficiently powerful and ambitious to quarrel with Hipparchus, the brother of the ruling tyrant Hippias, and assassinate him.

If in the process of unification northern districts like Deceleia, Aphidnae, Rhamnous and Marathon became attached to Athens, not to Eretria or Tanagra, this was a result not of geographical predetermination but of historical accident. The modern student of archaic Athens suffers from knowing what happened next; he tends to assume that the primary loyalty of all the free inhabitants of Attica was towards Athens. This temptation must be resisted; in many parts of Attica there were local traditions, local cults and locally powerful families, and factors of this kind commanded the primary loyalty of the locality. In terms of political power, local ties had the effect that different families predominated in different parts of Attica and had the first claim on the devotion of humbler families and persons in their several regions. The thesis of this and the next two chapters is that "regionalism," rivalry between strong families powerful in different regions of Attica, is the clue to Athenian political history until the time of Cleisthenes.

INSTITUTIONS OF THE UNITED STATE[3]

Thucydides (2.15.1-2) discerned the political character of the unification. Previously the several cities of Attica each had their own council chambers and boards of magistrates; the unification abolished all except the council chamber and board of magistrates of the city of Athens, and thus these became institutions valid for all the communities of Attica. But the unification did not mean a concentration of population in Athens; most of the inhabitants continued to live scattered over the extensive territory of Attica. It may be inferred that the unification brought political advantage to powerful families of the central plain, as opposed to powerful families of more distant regions; the former could more easily participate in the institutions of the city of Athens.

In studying those institutions one may look for the three items, king, council and assembly. In Athens by the time of Cylon in the second half of the seventh century the king had been replaced by a board of annual magistrates, the nine archons. Tradition recorded by Aristotle (*AP* 3.1-5) said that once there had been kings ruling for life. Then the office of polemarch, or war-commander, was created to take over military functions from the king; rather later that of archon was created for other functions. Likewise the term of office was decreased from life to ten years and then to one year. The six officers called *thesmothetai* ("setters of verdicts") were created after the others had become annual. Their name may indicate that from the first they were conceived as primarily judicial officials. Modern writers have doubted some items in the Aristotelian account; they ask if the office of polemarch was created before that of archon, and if there were ever archons holding office for life or for ten years. The account may rest more on reconstruction than on knowledge, but speculation here is fruitless. The result of the development, the existence of nine annual archons, is clear.

The Athenian council came to be called the Council of the Areopagus, since it held some of its meetings on that hill. It consisted in later times of all who had held any of the nine archonships; probably this had been its composition ever since the nine archons came into being, as Aristotle indicated (*AP* 3.6). Likewise, a public assembly of some kind doubtless existed from time immemorial; indeed when a massed gathering of Athenians opposed the rebel Cylon and entrusted dealings with his forces to the nine archons, this should probably be regarded as the action of a rather disorderly public assembly (see below, pp. 98–99). Further, it is likely that the public assembly elected the nine archons. Aristotle says in the *Politics* (2.1274a1–2 and 15–17) that the nine archons were elected by the assembly and that Solon made no change in this. This seems credible. In the *Constitution of the Athenians* (8.1–2) he says that at first the Council of the Areopagus chose the archons and Solon replaced this procedure with selection by lot from among candidates approved by the tribes. But it is difficult to see how Aristotle could have reliable grounds for these statements in the *Constitution of the Athenians*; the statements may spring ultimately from a fourth-century desire to find Solonian precedent for sortition.

Among the institutions of the archaic state the Council of the Areopagus was the strongest in personnel. There was a minimum age limit for election to the archonships. At least in the fifth century thirty years was the minimum age for jurors in the courts and for members of the new Council of Five Hundred; probably this limit was valid for all major offices and went back to the archaic period. Once elected to one of the nine archonships a man could expect thirty years or more of active life in the Areopagite Council; Solon in a poem on the ten ages of man (fr. 19) reckoned that, when a man reaches the age of seventy, it is time for him to die. A member of the board of nine archons had only one year in office, too short a time to launch extensive plans, and he was in contact with the Council of his seniors, to whose revered company he was about to be admitted. It is difficult to specify functions of the early Areopagus. Later Athenian tradition remembered that the Council had once been the dominant organ of state, but attempts to list its early powers were mere rationalization (see, for example, *AP* 3.6; 8.4). If it had begun as a body from which the king sought advice, it may have remained in principle advisory to the nine archons, but few archons would dare to go against its recommendations. Thus the preeminence of the Areopagite Council in the archaic state rested on the personal quality of its members and their relationship to the archons.

SOCIAL STRUCTURE[4]

Yet the formal institutions of the state were not sources of power but a framework, in which real forces worked. Diverse interests came into conflict in the Council of the Areopagus; sometimes, perhaps in more extreme cases, the scene of conflict was the public assembly. The real centers of power in the dark ages were strong households. If a household or group of households retained economic and social power through several generations, it came to constitute a *genos* or clan, and its humbler dependents came to be grouped around it in a hereditary organization called a *phratria* or phratry (see chapter 1, pp. 22–23). The names of several clans are known, for example Eumolpidae, Ceryces, Eteoboutadae, Bouzyges, and Lycomidae. Information about clans and phratries comes mainly from inscriptions and speeches of the fourth century, when they no longer had political significance, although association with a clan could bring social prestige. By the fourth century these units had become formalized; for example, a distinction had arisen between a clan and a family, although it is not clear what the distinction was or when it developed. Late in the dark ages, when the structure of clans and phratries was emerging, it may have been less formalized, more diverse, and more significant for political power. What matters most is that in the fourth century the clan had, at least in some cases, a special and privileged position in its phratry. This suggests that in the seventh and sixth centuries the clan had a much more predominant position within its phratry, for after the sixth century the general tendency in Athenian institutional development was towards leveling of social distinctions.

The importance of the phratry can be approached by considering the notion of Athenian citizenship. All Athenian citizens belonged to phratries, and in the classical period a man whose citizenship was challenged could prove it by showing that he was a member of a deme or of a phratry. The demes were first recognized by the reforms of Cleisthenes late in the sixth century. Membership of a phratry was the older ground of citizenship. This statement can be translated into the terms of the seventh century, when public power was still weak and no clear concept of citizenship had emerged: a man's status depended on his connection with a powerful family, and this connection was realized in the institution of the phratry. Early Attic society should be pictured as a collection of strong households, each having numerous and multifarious dependents. A man

Attic Geometric neck-amphora, often called the "Baring" amphora. Warriors riding in chariots. Now in Hearst State Monument, California. [Courtesy California Department of Parks and Recreation and D.A. Amyx.]

who had no links to any such household was weak and vulnerable. Accordingly, it should be expected that political struggles in the archaic state were struggles between the clans.

CYLON[5]

The rising of Cylon was an extreme example of struggle of this kind. Cylon had won an Olympic victory, a source of honor, and had married the daughter of Theagenes the tyrant of Megara, a source of power. Gathering together his friends and a force from his father-in-law, he seized the acropolis during a subsequent Olympic festival. But the Athenians came in mass from the fields and besieged the Cylonians on the acropolis. After a time they entrusted the siege to the nine archons. Cylon and his brother escaped, but his followers ran short of food and water; so they made terms with the nine archons, who agreed to spare their lives. Then, as the Cylonians came down from the acropolis, the nine archons killed them. Those responsible for the breach of faith later were exiled as being accursed, but later still they were allowed to return.

It is often supposed that Cylon's rebellion took place in or near the year 632, since his Olympic victory was recorded under the year 640. This raises the question of the reliability of the Olympic victor list in its seventh-century entries (see chapter 2, p. 42). A date a little later for Cylon's attempt cannot be excluded. Unfortunately the question is not indifferent; if Cylon's rising was as early as 632, the consequent bitterness and feuding may have provoked the legislation attributed to Dracon in 621 (see below, pp. 99–105), but if Cylon's rising was later than 621, no such causal link can be discerned.

Perhaps the rising of Cylon is not a particularly edifying subject of study. Attempts to recognize in him a champion of popular discontent are not convincing. Doubtless he was motivated by personal ambition; the record does not prove anything more. A little can be said about his enemies, the men who killed his followers and hence fell under a curse. More than once the scandal was revived against the descendants of the original slayers and, when revived, it was directed strictly against "the Alcmaeonidae and their partisans" (Hdt. 5.70.2). This suggests that the Alcmaeonidae and their partisans predominated among the nine archons of the year of Cylon's rising. The Alcmaeonidae were a family belonging probably to the central plain (see chapter 5, p. 124). Accordingly, a conjecture may be made about the type of discontent voiced by Cylon. He received a military force from Theagenes of Megara and led it to the acropolis, before he suffered any effective check. This would be easy to do, if Cylon's home was in the western part of Attica. Thus it is possible, though only possible, that the rising was "regionalist" in character; Cylon may have expressed the resentment of leading families of the Eleusinian plain towards the political effects of the unification.

DRACON[6]

In the classical period many Greek states claimed that their laws had been drawn up by an early lawgiver. Such lawgivers included Lycurgus at Sparta, Zaleucus at Locri Epizephyrii in Italy and Charondas at Catane in Sicily. How far these men were real and how far legendary is a difficult question. The Athenians were exceptional in claiming that their laws were the work of two successive lawgivers, Dracon and Solon. The tradition was that Dracon wrote down the laws, but later Solon rewrote all except the laws on homicide; hence the classical Athenians attributed their homicide laws to Dracon and their other laws to Solon. It is a strange story, and the few references to laws of Dracon on subjects other than homicide do not help. A partial explanation will be offered below (p. 104).

Aristotle (*AP* 4.1) says that Dracon made his laws in the archonship of Aristaechmus. Authors of Roman and Byzantine date give the year as 621/0; it has been shown recently (by R.S. Stroud) that apparent divergencies on the year

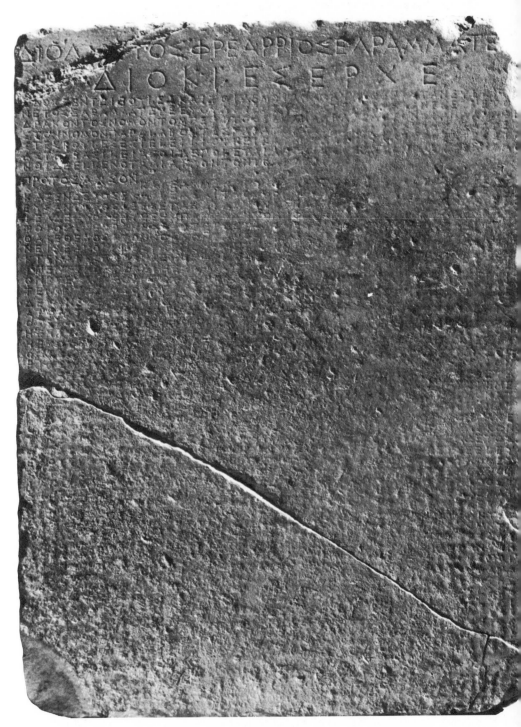

Extant part of the inscription of 409/8, republishing Dracon's law on homicide. [Courtesy R.S. Stroud.]

are due to errors in copying manuscripts and the tradition is in fact uniform. Although some general doubt may be felt about dates from the archon list before 594/3 (see above, p. 91), a date so shortly before 594/3 is not likely to err by any large amount. Nothing is known about Dracon except this date and his legislation; to accept the date 621/0 is to assign a substantial part of the Athenian laws on homicide to that year.

The sources for the early Athenian law of homicide are remarkably good. First there is an inscription of 409/8; it is the work of a commission which had been ordered to republish "the law of Dracon concerning homicide;" the opening and an important part of the law are preserved. In places the text can be supported from quotations in fourth-century speeches (especially *Dem.* 23 and Pseudo-*Dem.* 43). Other passages in the orators, and in lexicographers such as Pollux who had access to a much larger corpus of speeches than is now extant, add more information, and it is possible to trace a uniform pattern of ideas on homicide. Finally there is the evidence of institutional survivals; Aristotle (*AP* 57.3–4) gives a list of the homicide courts as they were in his own time and a similar list is given by Demosthenes (23.65–79), although it is not clear how many of these items come from Dracon, that is, from 621/0.

The inscription of 409/8 has a preamble, recording the order to reinscribe the law. Then the text begins as follows with provisions about any person who commits involuntary homicide.

The First Axon. And if anyone kills anyone without intention, let him go into exile. Let the kings adjudge responsible for killing either. . .or the man who planned the killing, and let the *ephetai* reach a decision. Let pardon be granted, if a father survives or a brother or sons, by them all, or the one who opposes pardon shall prevail. If these do not survive, let pardon be granted by relatives as far as cousin's son and cousin, if they all are willing to grant it; the one who opposes pardon shall prevail. If none of these survives but he kills involuntarily and the fifty-one *ephetai* decide that he killed involuntarily, let ten of the *phrateres* admit him, if they are willing; let the fifty-one choose these according to their worth. And let also those who killed previously be bound by this law.

Some readers have been struck by the fact that the text begins with a provision about involuntary homicide, where provisions about voluntary homicide might be expected to come first; but perhaps that is to import modern expectations of order into an ancient text. It is more striking that the section begins with the word "and": "And if anyone kills anyone without intention. . . . " Surely the word "and" implies a preceding clause, not included when the text was reinscribed in 409/8. To escape this implication Stroud has observed that the words often translated as "and if" can equally well mean "even if." This linguistic point is sound, but the implication still stands; a concessive clause, beginning with such words as "even if," implies that the hearer has recognized previously the alternative possibility. *Timeo Danaos et dona ferentes* presupposes the reader's knowledge that I fear the Greeks also when they do not bring gifts. Admittedly, the logic of concessive sentences does not necessarily require that the "previous possibility" be made explicit. Yet the original Draconian law is likely to have made the "previous possibility" explicit, for otherwise the text would have been very obscure indeed; it would have taken for granted the provisions about voluntary homicide.

Thus the opening words, "and if" or "even if," in the inscribed text suggest that the original text had a preceding clause about voluntary homicide. Now Plutarch (*Sol.* 19.3), who may have had access to a fuller version of Dracon's laws, remarks that Dracon in his laws never mentions the Areopagite Council but speaks only of the *ephetai*. In classical Athens cases of voluntary homicide were tried by the Council of the Areopagus. Accordingly, the conjecture has been made that in the laws of Dracon the *ephetai* dealt with voluntary homicide as well as with involuntary homicide; some time later cases of voluntary homicide were transferred to the Council of the Areopagus, and since Dracon's provision on voluntary homicide was thus repealed, it was not reinscribed with the rest of his law in 409/8.

At this point two further lines of reasoning should be introduced. The law reinscribed in 409/8 provides that the man who has committed involuntary homicide must go into exile. Demosthenes (23.72; cf. 23.73; 23.28) quotes an early law about involuntary homicide, without attributing it to Dracon; it provides that a man convicted of involuntary homicide must leave Attica by a fixed route and within a stated period, and must stay in exile until the relatives of the deceased grant him pardon. In the fourth century this provision may have been understood as a sentence of exile, but the details suggest that it was originally conceived as something else. The fixed route and the stated period sound like a safe-conduct to leave the territory.

The second line of reasoning concerns wergild, the practice whereby the killer compensates his victim's relatives with a payment of valuables and brings the incipient blood feud to an end. This practice is recognized in the Homeric poems, where wergild is the normal meaning of *poine*. For early Attic law wergild is attested by the Byzantine lexicographers (Photius 437.20 = Ruschenbusch, *SN* F11; Bekker, *Anec.* 1.428.9 = *Suda* 1.334, ed. Adler = *SN*. F12); they cite the words *poinan, apoinan* and *apoina* from the laws of Solon. Pollux (9.61 = SN. F10) mentions "a twenty-oxen penalty" in the laws of Dracon. This may have been compensation for homicide or for a severe injury.

On the basis of these considerations E. Ruschenbusch offered the following hypothesis. Until the work of Dracon any act of homicide entitled the victim's relatives to retaliate, unless the killer paid them wergild and was thus admitted by them to pardon. But Dracon introduced a distinction according to the intention of the killer. He set up a court, the *ephetai*, to discover that intention, and if the *ephetai* found that the act of homicide was involuntary, then by Dracon's law the Athenian state guaranteed the killer a safe-conduct to leave the country. By implication Dracon issued a whole law of delict, since he left the former procedures of retaliation and wergild in force except where the killer's act was found to have been involuntary. The material change he made in the law was small, but its implications for the future were large. He introduced consideration of intention, as distinct from act, into Athenian procedure. He instituted a jury, the *ephetai*. Above all he asserted the claim of the state to intervene in the blood feud. The claim was at first a modest one; the state was not strong enough to do anything more than offer the involuntary killer a safe-conduct to the borders; but its strength would grow.

This hypothesis is attractive: it subsumes a variety of evidence under a single explanatory theory. One may be tempted to attach the date 621/0 to the small but pregnant change wrought by Dracon and dismiss it. But evidence provided by institutional survivals suggests a further step. The survivals are the homicide courts, which were known in Athens in the fourth century and are described by Aristotle (*AP* 57.3–4). He does not attribute them expressly to Dracon, but it is clear that they are in large part archaic. He lists five courts; each of them met under the presidency of that one of the nine archons who was called the king. (1) The Council of the Areopagus sat as a court to try cases of killing with intention, wounding with intention, poisoning when it caused death, and arson. (2) A court met at the Palladium to try cases of involuntary homicide, charges against the man who planned homicide when another agent carried it out, and charges of killing a slave or a resident alien or a foreigner. (3) A court meeting at the Delphinium heard cases where a man admitted that he had killed but alleged that the act was lawful; he might, for example, say that he had caught his victim in adultery or had killed him in war, without recognizing him, or had slain him in a athletic contest. (4) A court met at Phreatto on the coast if a man already in exile for an offence which allowed pardon was accused of committing a further act of killing or wounding; in such a case the accused attended trial in a boat just offshore. (5) Animals and inanimate objects causing death were tried by a court consisting of the king-archon and the four "tribal kings," who were the heads of the four hereditary tribes into which the Athenians were divided (see chapter 1, p. 23). From the lexicographers (notably Pollux 8.125; Harpocration s. v. *ephetai*) it is known that the jurors in the second, third and fourth courts were the *ephetai*. The identity of this board is not clear; that they were a commission of the Areopagite Council is a common conjecture. Their number is given as fifty-one in the reinscribed Draconian law of 409/8 and in Pseudo-*Dem*. 43.57.

From the list it appears that the competence of the several courts was determined by a great variety of criteria. Indeed, some of the criteria spring from opposed principles. The case of a man accused of planning an act of homicide when another agent carried it out rested on a principle almost directly opposite to that arising in cases of involuntary homicide, yet cases of both types were heard at the Palladium. No single principle informs the five courts as a system. It is likely, then, that Athenian law learned to recognize the different criteria at different times and for different reasons. Among the criteria the one resting on the intention of the agent, that is, on the question whether his act was voluntary or involuntary, was especially important for the further development of jurisprudence, but it probably was not the first to be recognized. The distinction resting on the status of the victim, whether he was a free man or a slave, may well have been older. To judge from Germanic parallels the wergild of a free man doubtless differed from that of a slave already at a very early period.

Accordingly, it is likely that the series of five courts with the divergent principles determining their competence grew up over a long period and in a series of stages. Tradition associated the date 621/0 with the development of the law of homicide, and it may be true that one step in that development occurred in that year, but it is not possible to tell which step. If the law of homicide developed over a long period, longer than any man's lifetime, attention should be given to the theory of K. J. Beloch, who suggested that Dracon was not a man; *drakon* was a Greek word for serpent and the Athenians worshipped a sacred serpent on the acropolis. Perhaps "the laws of Dracon" were originally laws issued on the authority of the sacred serpent by the priests who tended it. Against this theory it has been urged that the literary tradition is unanimous in regarding Dracon the lawgiver as a man, but this objection is not conclusive; the earliest reference to Dracon seems to be a remark made by Prodicus in the fifth century (and preserved by Aristotle, *Rhet.* 2.1400b20–23), and by then the original identity of Dracon may have been forgotten. Beloch's theory provides the law of homicide with a religious source, which is not unwelcome; it explains how a long and complex development could be attributed to a single source of law; and it removes the Athenians from the exceptional position of having two early lawgivers, where other states had only one.

This discussion of Draconian law is disappointing to the student of political history. Some inferences, hitherto much favored, prove to be groundless. One can no longer say with any confidence that the troubles consequent on Cylon's escapade led to codification of the law of delict in 621/0; one can no longer say with any confidence that later Solon had to rewrite the laws because, as written in 621/0, they were too severe. What happened in 621/0 is lost beyond recovery and it may not be important. But the political historian may take comfort; he is entitled to draw an inference on something more fundamental from his study of the law of homicide. Public authority in early Attica was weak in comparison with strong households; but even so, at an early period the Athenian state tried to set up procedures for dealing with homicide; it asserted its right to restrict family feuds when these issued in killing. This claim is especially apparent in the offer of a safe-conduct to the borders for the man who committed involuntary homicide. It does not necessarily follow that the state always succeeded in enforcing its claim. But in pre-Peisistratean conditions the law of homicide may have been the field of activity in which the ordinary free man was made most aware of public power and of the unity of Attica.

NOTES

1. The fragments of the Atthidographers are to be found in *F.Gr.Hist.* IIIB 323a-329; F. Jacoby discusses them in ibid. IIIb (Supplement) 1.1-598; he offers, especially in his account of Androtion, the thesis that the works of some of the Atthidographers differed because their authors diverged on political principles. Against the hypothesis of an official chronicle, kept from early times, see F. Jacoby, *Atthis* (Oxford 1949). J. Day and M. Chambers, in *Aristotle's History of Athenian Democracy* (University of California Publications in History, vol. 73, 1962), have shown that in his reconstruction of Athenian constitutional history Aristotle was grossly influenced by his own theories of politics. On the fragments of the inscribed archon list see Donald W. Bradeen, "The Fifth Century Archon List," *Hesperia* 32 (1963) 187-208. For reconstruction of the entries in the archon list see T.J. Cadoux, "The Athenian Archons from Kreon to Hypsichides, *JHS* 68 (1948) 70-123. The fragments of Solon's poems are cited according to the numbering in E. Diehl, *Anthologia Lyrica Graeca* I³ (Leipzig 1949). Attention may be drawn here to two useful works of reference: (1) G. Busolt and H. Swoboda, *Griechische Staatskunde* II (Munich 1926) 758-1239 (these pages deal with Athens); (2) J.K. Davies, *Athenian Propertied Families 600-300 B.C.* (Oxford 1971). (Davies collects information on all wealthy Athenian families and takes the performance of "liturgies" or expensive public services as the criterion of wealth.)

2. On the unification in general see Hignett, *HAC* 34-38. On the deputation called the *Pythais* see A. Boethius, *Die Pythais* (Uppsala 1918); the inscriptions attesting the separate envoys from Marathon belong to the second and first centuries B.C. On the archaeological evidence concerning Eleusis see G.E. Mylonas, *Eleusis and the Eleusinian Mysteries* (Princeton 1962), 59-62. On Deceleia see Hdt. 9.73. On the Gephyraei see Hdt. 5.57; Plut. *Mor.* 628e; J. Toepffer, *Attische Genealogie* (Berlin 1889) 296-297; cf. Sealey, *Essays* 193 (= *BICS* 7 [1960] 38).

3. On the mode of selecting the archons see Hignett, *HAC* 321-326; for a different view see R.J. Buck, "The Reforms of 487 B.C. in the Selection of Archons," *CP* 60 (1965) 96-101. Thirty years as the minimum age for office in inferred from Aristotle, *AP* 63.3; Dem. 24.150; Xen. *Mem.* 1.2.35; cf. *I.G.* I², 10 line 10 = Meiggs/Lewis 40 line 11.

4. See the references to Forrest, Andrewes, Hignett and Wade-Gery given in note 4 to chapter 1 on p. 36. J. Toepffer, *Attische Genealogie* (Berlin 1889) tried to list all the known clans.

5. The most useful account of Cylon's rising is Thuc. 1.126.3-13. A briefer account is given by Hdt. 5.71. Plutarch (*Sol.* 12) adds a few items of uncertain reliability; for example, he says that the name of the eponymous archon was Megacles. On the date of Cylon's rising see Gomme, *Comm.*

1.428–430. M. Lang, *"Kylonian Conspiracy," CP* 62 (1967) 243–249, argues that the greater length of Thucydides's account in comparison with that of Herodotus marks merely the growth of a legend, and so the additional information supplied by Thucydides is not reliable. But the interval of time separating composition of the two accounts need not be long; indeed it cannot be proved that Thucydides's account is the later of the two. The items he gives beyond Herodotus are highly specific and this inspires confidence. The part played by Theagenes in the story, first attested by Thucydides, is treated by Miss Lang as possibly fictitious; but a legend-creating imagination would be more likely to introduce a more famous tyrant, such as Periander. The real difficulty in Herodotus's account is his designation, "the presidents of the *naukraroi*," for those who made the Cylonians leave the acropolis; this is bound to remain a difficulty, as hardly anything is known about the naukraroi. B. Jordan "Herodotus 5.71.2 and the Naukraroi of Athens," *CSCA* 3 (1970) 153–175, argues persuasively that the naukraroi were financial officials and their presidents acted on the orders of the nine archons.

6. See the valuable discussion by E. Ruschenbusch," ΦΟΝΟΣ: Zum Recht Drakons und seiner Bedeutung für das Werden des athenischen Staates," *Historia* 9 (1960), 129–154; also the studies mentioned in Appendix to chapter 5. Passages which allege laws of Dracon on subjects other than homicide are Xen. *Oecon.* 14.4–5; Ar. *Pol.* 2.1274b15–18; Plut. *Sol.* 17; these amount to little more than a tradition that Dracon's laws were severe. On the date of Dracon's work see pages 66–70 of Stroud's study (mentioned in Appendix to chapter 5). For K.J. Beloch's view on the identity of Dracon see his Griechische Geschichte 1².2 (Strassburg 1913), 258–262; it is rejected by Stroud 65–66.

5

Solon and the
Rise of Peisistratus

Herodotus (1.29) knew of Solon as a wise man who made laws for the Athenians
and then went traveling for ten years; he had much more to say about Peisistratus
(1.59–64; 5.55–65; 5.94–95; 6.34–41; 6.103–104). About a century later, when
Aristotle composed his *Constitution of the Athenians*, the tradition on Solon had
grown. Aristotle's discussion of Solon's work is comparatively extensive (*AP* 2
and 5–12) and valuable, partly because it preserves passages from Solon's poems.
Solon had become a subject of controversy among the Atthidographers; Androtion offered a novel view about the economic change he made, and one reason
why Aristotle wrote at length about Solon may be that he wished to defend his
own view against the most recent *Atthis*. If the chances of recovering papyri had
produced Androtion's *Atthis* instead of Aristotle's treatise, modern accounts of
Solon's work might be different. This chapter will try to show that the activities
of Solon are largely obscure; that he may not have made such crucial changes in
the constitution as is often believed; and that Herodotus's account of the rise of
Peisistratus allows reconstruction of a reliable and tolerably clear picture of
political struggles in archaic Attica.

THE SEISACHTHEIA[1]

One of Solon's poems (fr. 24 = *AP* 12.4) gives an account of his public work; it
has twenty-seven lines and it appears to be complete. The first seventeen lines

describe the measures he took to meet the economic crisis confronting Attica. Solon claims that he has achieved all the purposes which he cherished when he "gathered together the demos." He says that the earth itself might bear witness to this, for he has removed the "marking-stones" (*horoi*) which had been stuck in the ground in many places, and thus the earth was previously enslaved but is now free. He says that he has restored to their native land of Athens many who had been sold; some had been sold legally and others illegally, and yet others had fled into exile to escape severe need and had wandered so far that they no longer spoke the Attic dialect. Finally he mentions people who at home suffered "unjust slavery" and feared the whims of their masters; he says that he has made them "free." He adds that he has achieved all this by the power of law, fitting together force and justice, and he has accomplished his promises.

Aristotle's exposition of the economic crisis and of Solon's work (*AP* 2.2; 6.1) contains elements that appear genuine and others that may be due to speculation. He says that the poor, together with their children and wives, "were slaves to" the rich. They were called "serfs" and "sixth-parters" (*hektemoroi*), since they worked the land of the rich "at that rent." All the land was owned by a few; and if the poor did not pay their rents, they and their children were subject to personal seizure. Until the time of Solon loans could only be contracted on the security of the borrower's person. Solon, according to Aristotle, freed the demos for the present and the future, by forbidding the practice of pledging the person as security for debt. Besides issuing laws, he cancelled debts, both private and public, and this cancellation was called *seisachtheia* or "the throwing off of burdens."

Some of Aristotle's items of information cannot be impugned. The term "seisachtheia" is genuine, but it does not reveal much about Solon's actions. The term "hektemoroi" is more useful. It should be accepted as authentic, since in the subsequent history of Athens no conditions are known which could have led to inventing such a term; indeed it is not a common word in Greek at all. In virtue of its meaning, "sixth-parters," it shows either that the hektemoroi paid a sixth of their produce to their masters or that they paid five-sixths and kept only one-sixth. To Aristotle the meaning was clear and he commented: "For they tilled the lands of the rich at that rent" (*AP* 2.2). To modern readers the choice between the two meanings is not wholly clear, and parallels drawn from peasants paying dues in other cultures are not conclusive, but at least Plutarch (*Sol.* 13.4) thought that the hektemoroi paid only one-sixth of their produce.

Two items in Solon's poem summarized above deserve to be associated with the hektemoroi. When Solon speaks of people who suffered "unjust slavery" in Attica, fearing the whims of their masters, and says that he has freed them, the word "slavery" need not be technical; he probably means people who were not slaves but stood in some condition of serfdom, since he distinguishes them from people who had been sold. Likewise his reference to "marking-stones" can be associated with serfs or hektemoroi. He says that he removed the marking-stones and thus the land, previously enslaved, became free; his choice of words about "slavery" and "freedom" suggests that his liberation of the land belongs with his liberation of the hektemoroi. If these several indications are drawn together, it appears that numerous Athenian peasants lived in a dependent status, signified by the term "hektemoroi;" they were subject to masters, and the bond affected their land, which was marked with marking-stones to record the claims of the masters. Moreover Solon's choice of words shows that this dependent status was felt to be burdensome.

How had this status arisen? In the fourth century people regarded it as a consequence of indebtedness. Aristotle (*AP* 6.1) said that Solon canceled debts, both private and public, and that this was called "the seisachtheia;" Androtion (*F.Gr.Hist.* IIIB324F34 = Plut. *Sol.* 15.3–4) said that the seisachtheia consisted not in canceling debts but in limiting the rate of interest and in changing measures and coinage. Many modern writers have made debt central in theories which seek to explain the origin and nature of the crisis confronting Solon. Such a theory notes that in the late eighth and seventh centuries many Greek states had relieved the pressure of growing population on local resources by sending out colonies, but Athens had not done so. Population was doubtless growing in Attica as elsewhere, and so the land was cultivated with increasing intensity. Such cultivation diminished the fertility of the soil. A peasant, who found that his store from the last harvest would not last till the next, might borrow from a wealthy landowner by pledging part of his harvest in advance; but with intense cultivation each year brought the peasant a poorer harvest and a larger debt, until at last he entered into a permanent bond with the landowner, and this was indicated by setting marking-stones on the peasant's land.

Theories of this kind are attractive. Those who hold them tend to assume that land could not be alienated outside the family in early Attica; for if the peasant could have sold his land directly to the wealthy landowner, surely this would have been more advantageous for both. Aristotle insists that until the work of Solon debts were contracted on the security of the person; this suggests that land could not be pledged as security, that is, it was inalienable. There is no direct evidence for or against the alienability of land in early Attica, but the indirect evidence suggests that land was alienable. In particular, Hesiod (*Works and Days* 341) exhorts his brother to win the favor of the gods by sacrifices, "so that you may buy the land-allotment of others, and not see your allotment bought by another." Admittedly Boeotia was not Attica and the date of the *Works and Days* is not so securely established as is often supposed; but the line indicates that within the archaic period alienability of land was known in a district bordering on Attica.

But even if land could be sold, there may have been a strong prejudice against alienating it outside the family.

However, the economic development is not simple. During much of the seventh century Attica may well have been backward and poor, as its failure to found colonies suggests. But growth in the export of Attic black-figure vases marks a subsequent recovery. The export can be traced from ca. 610, and thereafter in each period of two decades till ca. 520 the ware reaches further and further afield, until it is found in most parts of the coasts of the Mediterranean and Black Seas. In the last decades of the sixth century Attic pottery retained its predominance but fashion changed from black-figure to red-figure ware. The development of this trade in the sixth century was at first slow but grew with increasing rapidity. The date of Solon's work is disputable (see below, pp. 121–123), but it fell within the first few decades of the century. So one may favor a view which says that the status of the hektemoroi was not a burdensome condition which had arisen recently but an old condition which people had recently learnt to consider burdensome, as prosperity began to grow.

Solon's extant poems have no certain reference to debt. Perhaps attempts to explain the origin of the hektemoroi and the nature of the seisachtheia in terms of debt are anachronistic; they may rest on nothing firmer than assumptions current in the age of the Atthidographers. As an alternative, it has been urged recently that the status of the hektemoroi was a traditional form of tenancy, arising in the period of migrations or the dark ages. Other Greek cities recognized traditional types of depressed tenancy or serfdom. The best known and perhaps most severe example is in Lacedaemon, where the status of helot persisted beyond the archaic period. Pollux (3.83) gives a list of classes intermediate between freedom and slavery. Those of his examples that belong to the European Greek mainland are the helots of Lacedaemon, the *penestai* of Thessaly, the *gymnetes* of Argos and the *korynephoroi* of Sicyon. Scarcely anything beyond the names is known about the Argive and Sicyonian examples, but those names suffice to show that a depressed or dependent status was recognized in some city-states of the archaic period; it may have been widespread.

Aristotle (*AP* 2.2) says that all the land of Attica was owned by a few; he assumes that all except the few were hektemoroi and he says that they worked the land belonging to the rich. Doubtless he exaggerates the extreme character of the situation confronting Solon; uniformity is not to be expected in so large a territory as Attica. But he may be right in implying that a great deal of land was owned by relatively few people and that the land tilled by the hektemoroi belonged, not to them, but to their landlords. This must be borne in mind in asking what Solon did for the hektemoroi. Certainly he abolished the status, but did the land which they had tilled become their property or remain that of the landlords? If Solon assigned such land to the hektemoroi, his work was in the nature of a social revolution. In favor of such a view it can be urged that Attica later had estates of very varying size; in the time of the orators there was no predominance of large estates owned by a few, even though some men owned a good deal of land, usually in scattered parcels. In his poems Solon complains of the rapacity of the rich and insists that he himself took up a firm position in the middle between conflicting interests; in Greece such language befits a man whose acts are those of a social revolutionary.

If a view of this kind about Solon's economic work is correct, further speculations may be entertained. Aristotle assumed that conditions were the same for the whole of Attica, but this is difficult to believe, since the territory was extensive and its communities had had a long period of independent development before the unification. There may well have already been free peasants owning the land they tilled. Moreover, in view of the extent and diversity of the communities, dependent peasants who paid dues may not have been subject to the same conditions in all parts of Attica or on the estates of every landlord. In other words, if some tenants paid a sixth (or conceivably five-sixths) of their produce, others may have paid some other proportion.

Perhaps it is bold to think on these lines, but the argument should be followed wherever it leads. Does sixth-century Attica show any trace of peasants paying dues in a proportion other than a sixth? A generation later Peisistratus levied a tax of a twentieth of all produce; this is the earliest known direct taxation by the Athenian state, with no apparent precedents and no direct descendents. Yet very few institutions are wholly new; one may conjecture that the levy of a twentieth began as the amount exacted by Peisistratus from the peasants on his own estates and he extended it to the whole of Attica. It would not be out of character for a tyrant to extend to the whole state a private institution orginating on his own domain. This conjecture leads to the following hypothesis: that in the early sixth century peasants traditionally paid dues to landlords, but the rate varied from place to place and estate to estate; that in some cases the rate was as high as a sixth, whether from old custom or through novel rapacity among landlords; and that Solon's measure consisted in abolishing dues levied at an excessive rate, including those levied at the rate of a sixth. This hypothesis has the slight merit of making sense of Androtion's eccentric account of the seisachtheia. Atthidographers regarded the dependent status anachronisitically as a consequence of debt, and so they regarded the dues as interest; accordingly, if Solon abolished dues levied at an excessive rate, in Androtion's eyes he limited the rate of interest.

MISCELLANEOUS MEASURES[2]

Although the precise character of the seisachtheia is disputable, there can be no doubt that the measure had a large effect; because of Solon's work the Athenian state thereafter did not have any class of citizens in dependent or semiservile status. Solon reduced the laws to writing; it is not clear whether the seisachtheia was part of this work or a separate act. Possibly Solon carried out the seisachtheia in the course of writing down the laws; he may have thought that he was restoring a pristine and just condition. Modern historians have scrutinized his activities for significant innovations, and some of their supposed findings will require attention shortly. But one may also study the tradition on his laws in the hope of discovering, not how he changed the condition of Attic society, but what that condition was. Two conclusions drawn in inquiries of the latter kind deserve notice here.

The first concerns a subsequent codification of the laws. Late in the fifth century the Athenians found that their laws needed revision. Commissioners were appointed to examine the laws in 410. The work was interrupted but was resumed in 403 and completed in 399. The result of this work was a new publication inscribed on stones of those laws which were accepted as valid. Some of the laws were inscribed on stelae; the only known example is the Draconian law on homicide (see chapter 4, pp. 101–102). But the bulk of the texts was inscribed on a series of at least three freestanding walls, which provided broad surfaces. Eleven fragments of these walls have been found; they amount only to a very small part of the original surfaces, but as they are a random sample, they may be approximately representative. They bear twenty-six passages of continuous writing; one of these is part of a secular law (about the trierarchy), and the other twenty-five are devoted to matters of sacred law, such as sacrifices. Moreover the best of the surfaces provided by the walls was reserved for a systematic calendar of sacrifices, and this was inscribed with the most handsome and conspicuous lettering. In short, as late as 399 the Athenians, on revising their laws, gave pride of place to religious matters. So it is to be presumed that when Solon first reduced the laws to writing, much of his attention was given to sacred law.

The second conclusion concerns criminal law. From a study of the extant fragments of the Solonian laws it has been argued convincingly (by E. Ruschenbusch) that the penalties were negative. The state might declare the offender an outlaw (*atimos*), that is, it might withdraw legal protection from him and leave him at the mercy of his enemies; or it might pronounce a curse against him. From these two basic penalties others could develop. For example, a man convicted of unintentional homicide was in effect required to go into exile (see chapter 4, pp. 101–103), that is, the state withdrew protection from him if he stayed in Attica; and a convicted criminal might buy himself free of one of the basic penalties by paying valuables to the state, so that in an indirect way fines could be imposed. But in Solonian law the state does not yet inflict positive penalties, such as death, imprisonment or confiscation. The negative character of the penalties illustrates the weakness of public authority in the first half of the sixth century.

Several measures attributed to Solon seem calculated to promote prosperity, but it is difficult to estimate their effect. The attribution of some of these to Solon may rest on nothing more than the later Athenian habit of attributing to him all laws, whether real or merely recommended. This should be borne in mind on reading Plutarch's statement (*Sol.* 22.1) that by a law of Solon a father had no claim on support from his son, unless he had taught the son a trade. The same considerations apply to another alleged law (*ibid.* 24.4), which offered citizenship to those aliens who settled with their families in Athens in order to pursue a trade. It is further asserted (*ibid.* 22.3) that Solon instructed the Council of the Areopagus to inquire into every man's source of livelihood and punish the idle; the tradition about this may rest on an imperfect understanding of a survey of property conducted in connection with classification of citizens (see below, pp. 115–120). The most substantial of the miscellaneous provisions attributed to Solon is a law allowing export of olive oil but forbidding export of any other agricultural produce. Plutarch (*Sol.* 24.1–2) says that this law stood on the first *axon*. Perhaps it sought to ensure a supply of grain within Attica and to encourage production of olive oil for export. But one cannot tell whether the law marked a new departure in commercial policy, since there is no way of discovering whether it was an innovation or merely renewed an existing law.

There is the further question of the coinage. Androtion said that the seisachtheia consisted in a limitation of the rate of interest together with an increase of measures and a provision about coinage. What provision he meant about coinage is not clear, as the text seems corrupt. Aristotle (*AP* 10) says that Solon carried out an increase in measures, weights and coinage; he proceeds to state the relation of the consequent Athenian measures to the Pheidonian standards, which were used in Aegina and much of the Peloponnese. Classical Athens used the standards of weight current in Corinth and Euboea. The first Athenian coins were struck ca. 570 or later. Possibly they were introduced by Solon, whose chief activity may have been in the period 580–570 (see below, pp. 121–123). Even so, it is not clear what would be the aim of provisions about measures and coinage. Besides, the association of Solon's name with weights, measures and coinage may derive merely from the later Athenian habit of attributing all customary institutions to him.

In short, the tradition credits Solon with several economic measures, apart from the seisachtheia, and although their force is difficult to estimate, they may have been intended to promote prosperity. During the sixth century Athenian prosperity rose steadily, as is shown by the growth in the export of black-figure ware. Yet it would be rash to regard the rise in prosperity as an effect, and an intended effect, of the policy of Solon. In modern states, where the executive apparatus is far more powerful and enormous sums are spent on the study of economics, the development of the economy rarely conforms to the intentions and expectations of governmental policy. Only a bold statesman launches a five-year plan; only a bold historian credits Solon with an economic policy successful for several decades.

THE CRISIS: CONSTITUTIONAL MEASURES[3]

Solon attempted a comprehensive publication of the law. Modern writers have selected those measures which seem most substantial and intelligible in the tradition about him, and they have tried to interpret the character and purpose of these. At least two of the measures associated with him, namely the seisachtheia and the division of Athenians into property classes, are promising as starting points for analysis of his work and of the situation confronting him; by choosing each of the possible starting points people have offered plausible interpretations of Solon's activities. Unfortunately, because these interpretations are indeed plausible, the reader now runs a risk of forming a "split-personality" picture of Solon; that is, there is a risk of attributing to Solon's constitutional work purposes which bear no relation to those recognized in his economic work. Clearly this danger must be avoided; a unified account must be given of the crisis confronting Solon and of the task which he set himself.

Until recently the crisis confronting Solon was commonly conceived as a class struggle; from the seisachtheia historians tried to conjecture the classes whose interests were in conflict. Lately a more sophisticated view has been offered (by Ellis and Stanton). Its champions have pointed out that, if the struggle was simply one between rich and poor, the rich landowners would have had no reason to yield and risk their future on the probity of Solon as mediator, since they were stronger in weapons, military training and wealth. Moreover, before the time of Solon Athenian political conflicts, such as the rebellion of Cylon and the ensuing events leading to the explusion of the Alcmaeonidae, were essentially rivalries between powerful clans; the political divisions of society were not horizontal lines between classes but vertical lines, separating each powerful family or group of powerful families, together with their dependents, from other powerful families with their dependents. The same is true of political conflicts after the time of Solon and especially of the conflicts attending the rise of Peisistratus. It would be very strange if a pure class conflict in the time of Solon intervened between earlier and later conflicts of a quite different type. Accordingly, the political crisis facing Solon has been reconstructed in the following way. It is supposed that the political scene was still essentially one of rivalry between powerful clans, but this rivalry grew more dangerous because some clans might exploit the grievances of the poor. The collapse of Cylon's movement and the subsequent expulsion of the Alcmaeonidae had removed two strong groups and left the balance of forces uncertain. In this situation of a scramble for power the unscrupulous leader of a clan might make large promises to the aggrieved classes and hence seize control. To escape this risk leaders of other clans might join together to entrust settlement of the predicament to such a man as Solon; perhaps they realized that they would lose something in the settlement, but they were willing to accept some losses in order to avert a tyranny.

Concerning Solon's conception of his task, it is at least a reasonable hypothesis that he envisaged it as essentially one of reducing customary law to writing. This is suggested by the comprehensive character of his law code and by the age when he worked; the state was not yet strong enough to enforce extensive changes in the law, and so the lawgiver could best hope to get his laws accepted if he presented them as a mere codification of longstanding practice. This is not to say that Solon could not conceive of statutory change in the law; the law of Dracon on homicide contained a retroactive provision, so at least one of its items must have been an innovation (see appendix to chapter 5, p. 132). But a written statement of the existing law was an improvement on the uncertainties of custom and memory.

Possibly a passage in Solon's writings can be used in support of this hypothesis about his concept of his task. The poem mentioned above (pp. 107–108), which seems to be complete and gives an account of his public work, devotes seventeen lines to the seisachtheia. Next Solon records his other legislative work in one sentence: "I wrote laws alike for the bad man and the good, fitting straight justice into each law." The sentence embraces two lines and a word. The remainder of the poem, nearly eight lines, says that another man in Solon's place would not have restrained the demos, and if Solon had favored first one side and then another, many lives would have been lost, but instead he stood firm like a wolf among dogs. If, apart from the seisachtheia, Solon had set out to introduce major innovations, surely he would have had more to say about them than two lines and a word.

Two major innovations in the constitution have often been attributed to Solon; they are the division of Athenian citizens into classes on the basis of property, and the Council of Four Hundred. Aristotle (*AP* 7.3–4) provides the crucial information on the property classes. He says that Solon divided the citizens into four classes, called *pentakosiomedimnoi, hippeis, zeugitai* and *thetes*. Those whose estates produced each year at least 500 measures of grain, wine and olive oil constituted the pentakosiomedimnoi. Estates with annual produce of 300 measures were the qualification for membership of the hippeis; estates with annual produce of 200 measures were that for the zeugitai; and the remaining citizens formed the class of thetes. The significance of the classification was that it made property the qualification for political privilege. Candidatures for the office of treasurer of Athena could be accepted only from members of the first class, the pentakosiomedimnoi; candidatures for the nine archonships were accepted probably from the first two classes, and thus the scale of privilege continued, so that the only political activity open to the thetes was participation in sessions of the public assembly, including its judicial sessions.

A theory widely held says that this classification was an innovation. Previously, it is alleged, only the members of a hereditary aristocracy, the *eupatridai*, were admitted to the nine archonships, the avenue of political privilege; but with new economic opportunities men from families outside the hereditary aristocracy attained wealth and conceived political ambitions. Solon supposedly met their desires: he replaced birth with wealth as the qualification for political office. According to this view Solon transformed Athens from a closed to an open society. To test this view it is necessary to review the evidence for the supposed class of eupatridai and reexamine the property classes. To anticipate, much of the evidence on the eupatridai is poor, although some of it is not easy to deny; but there are grounds for thinking that the property classes, as recorded in writing by Solon, were not wholly an innovation.

EUPATRIDAI[4]

Study of the eupatridai can begin with a few fragments preserved from the opening sections of Aristotle's treatise *The Constitution of the Athenians*. One of these, commonly numbered fragment 3, says that the Athenians were once divided into two classes, *georgoi* ("farmers") and *demiourgoi* ("artisans?"). A passage of Plutarch's *Life of Theseus* (25) is often printed as fragment 2 of the treatise; it may well belong to the treatise, although it does not name Aristotle. It says that the legendary king Theseus, on unifying Attica, divided the citizens into three classes, *eupatridai* ("nobles"), *geomoroi* ("landowners?") and *demiourgoi*, and the eupatridai were to provide the archons and have sole knowledge of sacred and profane law. Since fragment 3 gives only two classes, it should refer to an earlier period, probably that of the mythical hero Ion. Thus Aristotle thought that Theseus instituted the eupatridai as a hereditary order of nobility. This can be brought into relation to Thucydides's account of the unification of Attica (2.15.1–2); he says that Theseus abolished the councils and magistracies of the several towns and allowed only the council and magistracies of Athens to survive. If these indications are put together and the mythical king Theseus is omitted, it would appear that after the unification Attica had a hereditary class, the eupatridai, who were alone admissible to the nine archonships and hence to the Council of the Areopagus.

But fragment 3 of Aristotle's treatise does not inspire confidence. It proceeds to say that the Athenians were divided into four tribes: each tribe was divided into three units, called phratries and trittyes; each of these held thirty *gene* ("clans"); and each clan comprised thirty men. The four hereditary tribes are historical, and phratries and clans existed. But it is unlikely that phratries were called trittyes, a term introduced in the reforms of Cleisthenes; and the systematic numbers are obviously a fanciful reconstruction, based on division of the year into seasons, months and days. Does the alleged division of citizens into eupatridai and two other classes rest on anything better than fanciful speculation?

The word *eupatrides* could be used in verse to mean "noble" with no precise implications. Occasionally it seems to have a technical sense in prose. It is used in this way of some men active in the late fifth and early fourth centuries. Xenophon (*Symposium* 8.40) makes Socrates say that Callias is eupatrides. Callias, who served as envoy to Sparta in 371, belonged to the clan called Ceryces. Again Isocrates (16.25) says that Alcibiades was descended on his father's side from the eupatridai but on his mother's side from the Alcmaeonidae; by setting these side by side Isocrates implies that Eupatridai was the name of a clan, as distinct from a class, and this may be correct. It is recorded of Andocides, who was active in the same period, that he belonged to the eupatridai (Pseudo-Plut. *Mor.* 834b); it is not clear from the context whether a class or a clan is meant. Thus the term eupatridai is associated with Callias, Alcibiades and Andocides; all three were active in politics and all three belonged to the same social circle; the story of their relations and quarrels can be traced in part. Perhaps their claim to be eupatridai arose from speculative snobbery; several fourth-century Athenians tried to arrogate to themselves distinguished ancestors. But the claim must have meant something.

A hint of its meaning is provided by Pollux. He says (8.111) that the tribal kings were drawn from among the eupatridai. He proceeds to give the same systematic and numbered division of citizens as is stated in fragment 3 of Aristotle's treatise, and this does not inspire confidence. But the rule he states about tribal kings may be correct; and since his *Lexicon* was a guide to the Attic orators, the rule was presumably upheld in the fifth and fourth centuries. The tribal kings were the heads of the four hereditary tribes; by the fourth century their functions amounted to little more than receiving perquisites at some sacrifices. The rule about selection of tribal kings, considered together with the claims of Callias and his associates, suggests that the eupatridai of the fourth century were a half-understood relic of a hereditary governing class which had once ruled Athens.

When had that governing class held real control of the state? It is conceivable, and it is often asserted, that the eupatridai were in control after the unification was complete. But it is much more likely that their supremacy belonged to a much earlier period, when the unification had scarcely begun and the city of Athens controlled only its immediate neighborhood. At that early stage the many independent communities of Attica had different institutions; some may have had hereditary aristocracies. The long process of unification must have brought a good deal of mutual adjustment of institutions. Athens may have absorbed some communities by sheer conquest. But it is not likely that this happened in every case; probably some communities were brought into the union by persuasion and compromise; that is, influential interests in some communities probably succeeded in bargaining for some continuation of power. A hereditary ruling class, being rigid, had little chance of surviving such a process of adjustment. Surely the obvious hypothesis is that wealth replaced birth as the qualification for office, not through a deliberate reform by Solon, but because of the protracted effect of the slow process of unification.

One remaining reference to eupatridai is troublesome. Aristotle (*AP* 13.1–2) traces disturbances after the archonship of Solon (594/3): for four years there was peace, but in the fifth there was *anarchia*, that is, no archon was elected because of conflict (590/89). Another year of anarchia came in 586/5. In 582/1 Damasias was archon; he retained office in 581/0 and the first two months of 580/79. Then he was driven from office by force and ten archons were elected, five from the eupatridai, three from the *agroikoi* ("boors?") and two from the demiourgoi. How much can be learned from this record?

Aristotle probably drew, directly or indirectly, on the archon list for record of the two years of anarchia and for some of his information about Damasias, but the archon list could scarcely tell him that Damasias was expelled by force. It is not certain whether the archon list was his source for the ten archons of the last ten months of 580/79. If that information did not come from the archon list, it is difficult to imagine any source that would be reliable; on the other hand, it is difficult to imagine any occasion or reasons for inventing the record. It is not clear what the election of ten archons meant: were they to replace the eponymous archon alone or all of the regular nine archons? Was each to rule for one of the remaining ten months, or were they to rule together as a board? Was the institution of ten archons set up for only one year or was it intended as a permanent solution?

If the record of ten archons is sound, the three terms deserve attention. They show some resemblance to the terms used by Aristotle *AP* frr. 2 and 3, but *agroikoi* is not the same as georgoi or geomoroi. Agroikoi is not a neutral word for farmers or country people; it is a term of abuse for boors. Hence it should not be understood as the legal term for a recognized class; and so the words eupatridai and demiourgoi, when they occur in the record of archons for 580/79, are not legal names for recognized classes. The only way to save the credibility of the record for 580/79 seems to be to interpret the three names as the names of political groups or parties; and so the conflict of 580/79 should be interpreted in the light of the better known political struggles of the age, that is, especially of the struggle attending the rise of Peisistratus.

No discussion of eupatridai can be wholly satisfactory; the evidence is too contaminated. But the following theory cannot be proved wrong. At a very early stage, when the unification of Attica had scarcely begun, Athens had a hereditary ruling class, called eupatridai, but in the ensuing centuries of unification the institutions of the several communities were adjusted to one another. The result of these compromises was that, by the time the unification was complete, wealth was recognized as the qualification for public office. The surviving families of eupatridai retained a few religious and ceremonial privileges; these were recognized as late as the fourth century, when men like Callias put forward claims, genuine or false, to be eupatridai.

THE PROPERTY CLASSES AND THE COUNCIL OF FOUR HUNDRED[5]

The theory just stated implies that the property classes in some form were already traditional in the time of Solon. The same conclusion emerges with greater force from study of the names of the classes. The first of these, pentakosiomedimnoi or "five-hundred-measure-men," refers directly to the qualification by amount of produce. But etymologically hippeis means horsemen or knights, and zeugitai means men who could plough with a yoke of oxen; and although the etymology of thetes is obscure, in the Homeric poems the word is used of hired laborers. Commenting on the classes, Aristotle (*AP* 7.4) says that according to some people the qualification for hippeis was ability to maintain a horse; and he cites a dedication which showed a horse and bore the inscription: "Anthemion son of Diphilus dedicated this to the gods, when he exchanged the thetic class for the class of hippeis."

Even without this encouragement from Aristotle one could surely guess that there was a time when Athens had only three classes. Admission to the highest of the three, the hippeis, was achieved by maintaining a horse. The qualification for the second class, the zeugitai, was the wherewithal to plough with a yoke of oxen; and the remaining citizens were thetes. After that early stage two things happened. The qualifications for the three classes were restated in terms of annual produce, the dividing lines being set at 300 and 200 measures; and the richest men from among the hippeis were made into a separate class of pentakosiomedimnoi. These two changes may both have been carried out at the same time. Possibly they were both carried out by Solon. At least it would be otiose to seek a later time for them than his work, since no later occasion is known to which they can be plausibly assigned. Possibly they had both been introduced before Solon's time. In either case it follows that a system of property classes, whether of four classes or of three, already existed when Solon set to work. It should be added that Aristotle himself may have believed something like this; his statement (*AP* 7.3) about introduction of the property classes is: "(Solon) divided (the citizen body) into four classes, as it was divided before." But not much weight can be attached to this statement as supporting evidence, since it is difficult to see how Aristotle's view could rest on sources better than the names of the property classes.

The other major innovation with which Solon is commonly credited nowadays is the Council of Four Hundred. Aristotle (*AP* 8.4) says that Solon founded such a Council, drawing a hundred members from each tribe. Plutarch (*Sol.* 19.1) adds that its task was to prepare business for the public assembly. Neither author gives his grounds for believing that Solon created a Council of Four Hundred; Plutarch gives his statement in a passage where he also says that Solon founded the Council of the Areopagus, but this is not correct. Neither author says how long the members of the Council of Four Hundred were to stay in office or how they were to be chosen; it looks as if neither had any clear idea of the nature of the Council. If Solon founded such a Council, it was a major innovation, and so it is strange that he does not mention it in the extant fragments of his peoms, in particular the poem paraphrased above, where he summarizes and justifies his work. There is no certain reference to activity of the Council, before it was superseded by the Cleisthenic Council of Five Hundred; indeed the only possible reference to its activity is Herodotus's statement (5.72.2) that a Council resisted Cleomenes, when he came to Athens with a small force to support Isagoras (see chapter 6, pp. 147 and 149); but it is at least equally likely that that Council was the Council of the Areopagus. Although sources for the sixth century are scanty, the argument from silence has some force, since a major innovation ought to have left some trace; indeed this consideration might suggest that, if Solon founded a Council of Four Hundred, it soon petered out without fulfilling his hopes.

Support for Aristotle's statement has been sought in a Chiote inscription of ca. 575–550; it mentions *boule he demosie* which drew fifty members from each tribe. The argument is that, if Chios had so democratic an institution in the first half of the sixth century, Athens might have had one too; having taken this step, historians diverge on the question which city copied which. This argument assumes that *boule he demosie* must mean "the popular council." But the word *demos* is highly ambiguous. In the Homeric poems it often means the countryside dependent on a city, and so in the Chiote inscription *boule he demosie* might be a village council; but this is perhaps unlikely, in view of the large number of members which this Council drew from each tribe. At least Chios had a large territory and so it probably had villages with their own organs; so it is possible that *boule he demosie* meant, not "the popular council," but "the state council as distinct from village organs."

It must be admitted that considerations on the alleged Council of Four Hundred at Athens are inconclusive. The easiest hypothesis is that that Council was invented in the age of the Atthidographers. After 356 Solon came to be regarded as the founder of the democracy (see appendix to chapter 5); the Council of Four Hundred may have been invented to provide a precedent for the Cleisthenic Council of Five Hundred.

THE DATE OF SOLON'S WORK[6]

Solon was eponymous archon in 594/3 and Aristotle assumed that he carried out his political work in that year. Plutarch seems to distinguish two successive commissions entrusted to Solon. First he says (*Sol.* 14.3) that Solon was chosen "archon after Philombrotus and at the same time reconciler and lawgiver." Then he describes the seisachtheia and the comments it evoked, and after that he says (16.5) that the Athenians made Solon "reformer of the constitution and law-giver;" he proceeds to describe the legislation. Plutarch's language in reporting Solon's commissions in imprecise; the word "lawgiver" occurs in both passages and Plutarch moreover fails to give dates. In apparently distinguishing two commissions he may follow a mere surmise or mistake of his predecessors. If Solon held only one commission then perhaps the seisachtheia was carried out as part of the writing down of the law; that is, when Solon removed marking-stones and abolished the status of the hektemoroi, he may have thought that he was merely stating the ancient and true law. But it is difficult to believe that the task of writing down the law comprehensively could be completed within a single year; it is almost as difficult to believe that the regular powers of the archon sufficed for such an extraordinary task. It is far more likely that Solon received a special commission, which lasted more than a year. When Aristotle assumed that Solon's work belonged to his archonship, the assumption was a guess and an improbable guess.

There are two reasons for supposing that Solon carried out his work appreciably after 594/3. First, he went traveling afterwards, allegedly for ten years, and during his travels he visited Philocyprus, the tyrant of Solii in Cyprus. Now Aristocyprus, the son of Philocyprus, was killed in battle in or near the year 497 during the Ionian Revolt. A man killed in battle was not likely to be much older than sixty and a father was not likely to be much older than thirty at the birth of his eldest son; Philocyprus probably was at least twenty years old when he became tyrant of Solii. These figures suggest that Solon met Philocyprus not much before 567 and set off from Athens not much before 577. Second, there are the troubles recorded by Aristotle (*AP* 13.1–2) from the archon list after 594/3. There was anarchia in 590/89 and again in 586/5; in 582–580 Damasias attempted something extraordinary, perhaps a tyranny. Admittedly it is conceivable that these troubles followed the work of Solon, but surely it is more likely that his efforts at reconciliation and harmony were not a complete failure. The troubles of 590–580 may reflect the struggles which led to the appointment of Solon to write the laws down. After 580/79 no further troubles are known for nearly two decades, and even then the first attempt of Peisistratus did not shake seriously the stability of the state.

For these two reasons the probable date for Solon's work is ca. 580–570. This suggestion was made (by Hignett) as long ago as 1952. It has found little favor among subsequent historians; many have chosen to ignore it, and those who dispute it have found no more positive argument than that ancient writers assumed that Solon's reforms were carried during his archonship. The earliest writer to say this is Aristotle (*AP* 5.2), and it cannot be shown that the assumption rested on any good grounds.

One item in Solon's work refers to the year of his archonship. A law of amnesty is quoted by Plutarch (*Sol.* 19.4) from the thirteenth axon; it says:

Concerning outlaws who were outlawed before Solon was archon, let their rights be restored, except for those who, when this law was promulgated, were in exile because they had been condemned in the Areopagus or among the *ephetai* or in the Prytaneion by the kings on charges of homicide or massacre or tyranny.

The style is archaic and the law has every chance of being authentic. It may have had the effect of recalling the Alcmaeonidae and any others who had suffered in the rising of Cylon and its aftermath. If Solon carried out his work ca. 580–570, it is not clear why he chose 594/3, the year of his archonship, as epochal for the amnesty. Those who prefer the late date can admit so much with a light heart. Possibly the year 594/3 was significant for time-reckoning (see chapter 4, p. 91).

If his work should be dated ca. 580–570, its chronological context can be recognized. By that time the controversies over Cylon's rising were dead; the Alcmaeonidae could be recalled without fear. A new growth of Athenian prosperity was well under way: ambitious peasants were growing restive, and covetous landlords were growing more exacting. The years of anarchia and the rule of Damasias were symptoms of political unrest. Solon met the situation by reducing the law to writing and reforming the practices of land tenure. Such work was perhaps more modest than creating a Council of Four Hundred or inventing a series of property classes out of nothing. But his achievement was realistic and beneficial; there was comparative peace for the next two decades, and thereafter, when Peisistratus tried to disturb the situation, it took him a series of attempts and more than a dozen years to secure control. Moreover, Solon's work contributed enormously to the long-term development of Attica. It was due in part to the seisachtheia that wealth in classical Athens was well spread; Solon's codification of the law stated rules that were easy to understand and taught men from all parts of Attica to respect the law of Athens. Solon deserved his traditional place among the Seven Wise Men of Greece; the art of the possible is the art of the beneficial.

THE RISE OF PEISISTRATUS[7]

On Athenian events in the middle decades of the sixth century Herodotus provides information, and this at last is a firm basis for understanding political struggles. He begins his account of the rise of Peisistratus (1.59–64) by saying that there were two rival parties, "the men of the plain" (*hoi ek tou pediou*), led by Lycurgus, and "the men of the shore" (*hoi paraloi*), led by Megacles son of Alcmaeon, but Peisistratus created a third party, "the men from beyond the hills" (*hoi hyperakrioi*). Peisistratus had distinguished himself by leading an Athenian campaign against the Megarians and capturing Nisaea, the eastern port of Megara. Some time later he wounded himself, drove into the city of Athens on a cart and said that he had been attacked by his enemies; in this way he persuaded the assembly to give him a bodyguard of club-bearers, and with them he seized the acropolis. But soon afterwards Lycurgus and Megacles joined forces against Peisistratus and drove him out.

This first attempt of Peisistratus at tyranny was in 561/0 or 560/59 and probably it lasted only a few months. The names of the three parties deserve attention. Aristotle (*AP* 13.4–15.3) gives an account of the rise of Peisistratus which is largely based on Herodotus. His names for the parties of the plain and the shore are virtually the same as those given by Herodotus (he writes *hoi paralioi* for *hoi paraloi* and *hoi pediakoi* for *hoi ek tou pediou*). But Aristotle calls the party of Peisistratus "the men of the hills" (*hoi diakrioi*), whereas Herodotus calls them "the men from beyond the hills." On this point the witness of Herodotus is better; the oral tradition, when it reached him, was still uncontaminated by the speculations of Atthidographers. How Aristotle came to err is a difficult question. A classical Attic deme called Diakrieis is attested only by Stephanus Byzantius; if that is correct, possibly confusion with the deme misled Aristotle or his source.

As it happens, Herodotus's name for the party of Peisistratus, "the men from beyond the hills," makes very good sense. Peisistratus himself was a native of Brauron, which is in eastern Attica and is separated from the city of Athens by

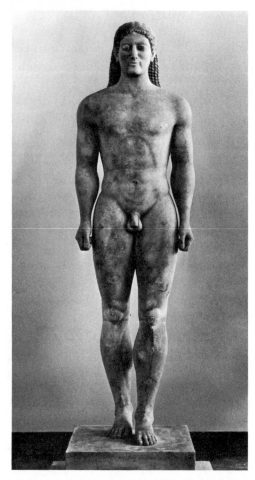

*Sepulchral monument of
Croesus the Athenian ca. 530.
From Anavyssos in Attica.
See page 130.*
[Photo by Hirmer Fotoarchiv, München.]

hills; from the point of view of the city Peisistratus was a man from beyond the hills. The other two party-names lend themselves to interpretation by locality. In Attic usage the term "the plain" without qualification meant the plain of the city of Athens; examples may be found in Thucydides's accounts of Lacedaemonian operations in Attica during the Peloponnesian War (2.20.1; 2.20.4; 2.55.1; 7.19.1). Again, in recording the Peloponnesian invasion of 430, Thucydides (2.55.1) says that the invaders came to "the so-called shoreland." From the context it appears that the district called "the shore" began on the coast near the plain of the city or perhaps within it and extended southeast towards Laureum. It should be added that the men of the shore were led by Megacles the Alcmaeonid and in the fifth century Alcmaeonidae are attested belonging to demes in the city district–Alopeke, Agryle, Xypete and perhaps Leukonoe. Lycurgus, the leader of the plain, may possibly be an ancestor of his fourth-century namesake, who belonged to the clan of the Eteoboutadae; this clan was linked to the deme Boutadae, which was probably in the city district.

On the three parties Aristotle (*AP* 13.5) makes the unexceptionable comment: "Each drew its name from the district where they tilled the soil." It should be supposed that each of the three parties was essentially local in composition; each consisted of one or a few powerful families at the head and a multitude of dependents of very varied status. The party of the plain certainly belonged to the plain of the city. The territory from which the party of the shore sprang may have extended some distance southeast towards Laureum, as Thucydides's use of the term indicates; but the fifth-century demes of the Alcmaeonidae suggest that the political center of the party was in the neighborhood of the city. If that is correct, before Peisistratus created his third party politics was moderate rivalry between two groups, both based in the plain of the city; this illustrates the effect of the unification, which gave advantage to powerful men of the city over powerful men of the outlying plains. The ambitions of Peisistratus illustrate the ultimate reaction of men of the outlying plains; he brought his followers and dependents to Athens from beyond the hills and seized the acropolis by force.

The course of his second attempt at tyranny, as given by Herodotus, supports this analysis at some points. Some time after the expulsion of Peisistratus Megacles founded himself worsted in rivalry with Lycurgus, so he made an alliance with Peisistratus; the latter was to marry Megacles's daughter. Together the confederates dressed up as the goddess Athena a woman of Paeania, a township north of the city, and she conducted Peisistratus back to Athens, where he was welcomed and recovered the tyranny; then he married the daughter of Megacles. But Peisistratus already had children and did not desire any more by his new wife. This led to a quarrel with Megacles, who withdrew his support, and so Peisistratus left Attica altogether and went to Eretria in Euboea.

Two features are to be noted in this narrative. First, the struggles were primarily personal rivalries between the several leaders. The semiscandalous story about the marital affairs of Peisistratus may have gained something in the transmission; but even allowing for that, the narrative shows that the leaders could make and break alliances at their own discretion. The loyalty of the followers may have been intense, but it was loyalty to actual leaders or their families, not to impersonal causes such as class interests. Second, when Peisistratus lost the acropolis the second time, Herodotus says that he "withdrew from the territory entirely;" he adds that Peisistratus went to Eretria and held a council with his sons. It is a much stronger phrase than Herodotus uses to record the first expulsion of Peisistratus; on that occasion Herodotus says that "the partisans of

Megacles and those of Lycurgus drove him out." It may be that at his first expulsion Peisistratus did not leave the territory of Attica entirely; he may have retired from Athens to his private estates near Brauron.

In short, the narrative of Herodotus so far suggests that the political scene was one of personal rivalries for power; Peisistratus exacerbated the struggles by injecting a "regionalist" element. But it is time to consider other views which have been held about the nature of the conflicts. Aristotle (*AP* 13.4–5) attributed distinctive constitutional programs to the three parties. According to him the men of the shore desired a "middle" constitution; the men of the plain desired oligarchy; and Peisistratus appeared most democratic. He specified further that two groups joined the party of Peisistratus; they were first those who had lost property through Solon's settlement of debt, and second, men of impure descent, who feared lest their title to citizenship be questioned. He stated his reason for believing in the existence of the latter group; after the fall of the tyranny a revision of the citizen list was held, as if many people had usurped citizen rights.

Modern writers have often used these statements to support a hypothesis of class struggle. Such a hypothesis has usually been based on interpretation of Solon's work. It has been supposed that Solon by constitutional and economic changes weakened severely a landed aristocracy and gave advantage to men who had recently achieved wealth, including those who achieved wealth by trade. Then, it is suggested, the men of the shore were the class content with the outcome of Solon's work; the men of the plain stood for the landed aristocracy and wished to reverse Solon's work; and the party of Peisistratus was largely drawn from the poorer classes and desired more radical changes than Solon had carried out.

Hypotheses of this kind have derived much of their appeal from a gratuitous assumption that political struggles are commonly the expression of divergent class interests. Methodically they are at fault in two ways. First, they try to explain the situation confronting Peisistratus, which is better known, from a reconstruction of Solon's work, which is less well known. Second, they prefer Aristotle's description of the three parties, including the term "men of the hills" (*diakrioi*), to Herodotus's account, which includes the term "men from beyond the hills" (*hyperakrioi*), although Aristotle wrote at a time when the tradition was more subject to corruption by speculation. Aristotle's description of the three parties has little to commend it. In attributing to them distinctive constitutional programs he may well have been led by an assumption that political struggles are commonly disagreements about forms of government. When he says that the party of Peisistratus attracted men who had lost property through Solon's settlement of debt, he draws an inference from the assumption that Solon's economic problem arose from indebtedness; that view has been criticized above.

His statement about men of impure descent rests patently on inference from an event occurring a generation later.

The main reason for rejecting attempts to explain the rise of Peisistratus by struggles about forms of government or by class struggles is that such theories do not do justice to the names of the three parties. Those names are drawn from localities, and it is clearly unlikely that the advocates of one form of government or the members of one economic class coincided with the men of one locality. Recently a more sophisticated attempt has been made (by R.J. Hopper) to show that the struggles arose from a difference of policy with economic implications. Negatively, it is argued that the regional associations of the parties are largely invented by later tradition; Peisistratus admittedly came from Brauron, and it is suggested that because of this, tradition later attributed distinct localities to the other leaders. Positively, Athenian policy towards Megara and Salamis is offered as the clue to the struggle within Athens. There was a long conflict between Athens and Megara for control of Salamis. The theory claims that some Athenians wished to control Salamis as a step towards commercial expansion; on the other hand a powerful landed interest opposed commercial expansion and the designs on Salamis, since it wished to produce a surplus of grain for export by oppressing the small cultivator. This landed interest, it is supposed, was championed by Cylon, and the changing fortunes of the two rival Athenian policies can be traced until the time of Peisistratus.

This theory is excessively sceptical towards Herodotus's regional names for the three parties. It assumes that the struggle for Salamis was a struggle for trade routes, but that assumption may not be correct. The theory may be excessively credulous towards Plutarch's account (*Sol.* 8–10; 12.5) of the warfare between Athens and Megara for Salamis. It takes from Plutarch the belief that, in the struggles following Cylon's rising and about the time when the Alcmaeonidae were expelled, Athens lost Salamis to Megara. But although the struggle over Salamis may have been protracted, no faith can be put in Plutarch's chronology; he makes Solon and Peisistratus capture Salamis before the rebellion of Cylon.

It must still be admitted that, in the present state of research, theories which explain Athenian politics of ca. 650–550 by differences of foreign policy offer the most serious challenge to the "regionalist" theory. Theories of both types include a large element of speculation; both succeed in explaining a considerable range of phenomena. The preference for the "regionalist" theory, adopted here, rests on the claim that it does better justice to the party-names reported by Herodotus.

On this view the first two attempts of Peisistratus at tyranny were essentially "regionalist:" because of the unification the balance of political power was weighted in favor of leading families of the city plain, and so Peisistratus tried to capture the seat of political power by seizing the acropolis. It should even so be admitted that he won some following in the plain of the city; the vote of a bodyguard by the public assembly suggests this, and his previous capture of Nisaea brought him some general popularity. But the failure of his first two attempts at tyranny can best be explained if he did not yet have much appeal to men of the city. It was probably in 556 that he withdrew from Attica entirely, and during the next ten years he gathered foreign support of various kinds. He settled at first at Rhaecelus on the Themaic Gulf and then moved to the neighborhood of Mount Pangaeum in Thrace. There he raised money, perhaps by mining operations, and hired troops. Thebes excelled among several cities which provided him with money; probably Thebes was already building a federation of Boeotian cities and therefore was interested in the affairs of Attica. For his planned return Eretria let him use its territory as a base. He was joined by a force from Argos, by an ambitious citizen of Naxos named Lygdamis, and doubtless by other adventurers. At last in 546 he brought his forces to Marathon. His landing was not opposed; indeed a good many Athenians, even some from the city, came and joined his camp. When he began marching towards Athens, his enemies from the city brought their forces against him; he defeated them at Pallenis and this ended resistance. After the battle he bade his sons ride ahead and reassure the fugitives; they were urged to return to their homes. Some Athenians withdrew into exile, but these may not have been numerous. Critics of the "regionalist" theory sometimes claim that by 546, when Peisistratus established lasting rule in Athens, he was no longer merely a champion of east Attic interests but had a broader base of support. This is in part true; evidently after the battle of Pallenis the bulk of Athenian citizens was no longer keen to resist Peisistratus. But the narrative shows that in 546 his positive sources of power were a private army and foreign support.

NOTES

1. The view here advocated, that tension arose not from debt but from a traditional system of tenancy, is based on A. Andrewes, *The Greeks* (London 1967) 104–108; cf. Forrest, *Emergence* 147–156. For a recent theory tracing the trouble to debt see French, *Growth* 10–17; cf. idem, "The Economic Background to Solon's Reforms," *CQ* N.S. 6 (1956) 11–25. An earlier such theory was offered by W.J. Woodhouse, *Solon the Liberator* (Oxford 1938). Against the view that land was inalienable see Andrewes, op. cit. 97–98; for further discussion of that view see French, *Growth* 10 with footnote 1; French entertains the possibility that there was a strong prejudice ("a taboo") against alienation, although alienation did occur. On the export of Attic black-figure ware see B.L. Bailey, "The Export of Attic Black-Figure Ware," *JHS* 60 (1940) 60–70. A different view of the seisachtheia and other things is offered by Hammond, *Studies* 104–144 = "Land Tenure in Attica and Solon's Seisachtheia," *JHS* 81 (1961) 76–98.

2. On the revision of the laws 410–399 see S. Dow, "The Law Codes of Athens," *Proceedings of the Massachusetts Historical Society* 71 (Oct. 1953–May 1957 [published 1959]) 3–36; idem, "The Athenian Calendar of Sacrifices: the Chronology of Nikomakhos's Second Term," *Historia* 9 (1960) 270–293 (with bibliography); idem, "The Walls inscribed with Nikomakhos' Law Code," *Hesperia* 30 (1961) 58–73. On penalties in Solonian law see E. Ruschenbusch, *Untersuchungen zur Geschichte des athenischen Strafrechts* (Graezistische Abhandlungen. Schriftenreihe der Arbeitsstelle für Griechisches Recht im Institut für Rechtsgeschichte und Geschichtliche Rechtsvergleichung an der Universität Freiburg/Br., Band 4, Köln 1968), 11–15. The economic measures discussed in this section are given by Ruschenbusch *SN* as F56, F75, F78c and F65. On coinage see the discussions cited in note 2 to chapter 2 on p. 59.

3. On the nature of the political crisis which brought Solon to power see J.R. Ellis and G.R. Stanton, "Factional Conflict and Solon's Reforms," *Phoenix* 22 (1968) 95–110. The classic statement of the view that Solon introduced the property classes and thereby replaced birth with wealth as the ground of political privilege is given by Wade-Gery, *Essays* 86–115 = "Eupatridai, Archons and Areopagos," *CQ* 25 (1931) 1–11 and 77–89; cf. Hignett, *HAC* 99–107.

4. On *eupatridai* see Wade-Gery, loc. cit. That the tribal kings received perquisites at some sacrifices in the fourth century is known from *I.G.* II², 1357; for their judicial function see Ar. *AP* 57.4 and above, p. 103. The *exegetai ex Eupatridon* were probably drawn from a clan, not a class, since they are attested in a way similar to the *exegetai ex Eumolpidon*; the evidence, mainly inscriptions of Hellenistic and Roman date, is collected by J.H. Oliver, *The Athenian Expounders of the Sacred and Ancestral Law* (Baltimore 1950), especially 34–45, but Oliver holds that the *eupatridai* were a caste. The record of archons for 580/79 is treated as a forgery by L. Gernet, "Les dix archontes de 581," *Revue de Philologie*, 3rd Series 12 (1938) 216–227. C. Mossé, "Classes sociales et regionalisme à Athènes au debut de VIe siècle," *L' antiquité classique* 33 (1964) 401–413, uses that record as her most substantial evidence in defending a theory of class struggle. It should be noted that in other Greek states the term *demiourgoi* occurs as a title of magistrates (L.H. Jeffery, *ABSA* 51 [1956] 164–165); so does the term *geomoroi* (Hdt. 7.155.2; Aesch. *Suppl.* 613).

5. For estimates of the real economic value of the property qualifications see French, *Growth* 18–22. The best discussion of the Council of Four Hundred is given by J. Day and M. Chambers, *Aristotle's History of Athenian Democracy* (Berkeley and Los Angeles 1962), 200–201. On the Chiote inscription see L.H. Jeffery, "The Courts of Justice in Archaic Chios," *ABSA* 51, (1956) 157–167. Later texts of the inscription are offered by J.H. Oliver, *AJP* 80 (1959) 296–301, and Meiggs/Lewis 8.

6. For the date of Solon's archonship see T.J. Cadoux, *JHS* 68 (1948) 93–99. His travels of ten years are given by Hdt. 1.29–33; Ar. *AP* 11.1; Plut. *Sol.* 25.6 His meeting with Philocyprus and the death of Aristocyprus are given by Hdt. 5.113.2; cf. Solon fr. 7. Of fundamental importance on the date of Solon's work is Hignett, *HAC* 316–321. For criticism see French, *Growth* 181. On the amnesty law see E. Ruschenbusch, *Historia* 9 (1960) 132–135; *SN* 5–8. M. Miller, "Solon's Timetable," *Arethusa* 1 (1968) 62–81, tries to spread Solon's work over the years 595/4–591/0, but does not meet Hignett's arguments. For recent defense of a late date see S.S. Markianos, "The Chronology of the Herodotean Solon," *Historia* 23 (1974) 1–20. M. Ostwald, *Nomos and the Beginnings of the Athenian Democracy* (Oxford 1969) 2 and 12–19, holds that Solon's laws were not voted by the assembly but issued on Solon's own authority, but this view rests heavily on semantic analysis; the authority sanctioning Solon's laws is not recorded.

7. That Peisistratus came from Brauron is known from Pseudo-Plat. *Hipparch.* 228b and Plut. *Sol.* 10.3. The evidence for the demes of the Alcmaeonidae in the fifth century is as follows: Alopeke: *I.G.* I², 237 line 56; 238 lines 66 and 262; 908; Ar. *AP* 22.5; Agryle: Craterus, *F.Gr.Hist.*

IIIB 342F11; Plut. *Them.* 23.1; Xypete: *Hesperia* 19 (1950) 376–390; a Megacleides of Leukonoe is known from *I.G.* I², 368 lines 3–4, but only his name suggests that he may have been an Alcmaeonid. C. W. J. Eliot, "Where did the Alcmaionidai live?," *Historia* 16 (1967) 279–286, tries to place the sixth-century home of the Alcmaeonidae in modern Anavyssos, because a sepulchral monument honoring an Athenian called Croesus has been found there and the Alcmaeonidae had dealings with the Lydian kingdom (Hdt. 6.125). His inference rests on an argument from silence; if the Alcmaeonidae and Miltiades I (Hdt. 6.37) had friendly relations with the Lydian kingdom, the presumption should be that other Athenian families too could have dealings with Croesus. The home of the Alcmaeonidae is further discussed by P. J. Bicknell, *Studies in Athenian Politics and Genealogy* (= Historia Einzelschriften Heft 19 [1972]) 56–57 and 74. On the Eteoboutadae see *I.G.* II², 3474 and Pseudo-Plut. *Mor.* 841b. Accounts explaining the rise of Peisistratus by a class struggle include F. E. Adcock, *CAH* 4.60–62; G. Glotz, *Histoire Grecque* I (Paris 1948) 443–444; Hignett, *HAC* 109–112. The view taken here owes a great deal to A. Andrewes, The Greek Tyrants (London 1956) 102–104. R. J. Hopper gives his theory in " 'Plain', 'Shore', and 'Hill' in Early Athens," *ABSA* 56 (1961) 189–219. For an earlier attempt, using the question of Salamis as a clue, see A. French, "Solon and the Megarian Question," *JHS* 77 (1957) 238–246; idem, "The Party of Peisistratos," *Greece and Rome,* 2nd Series 6 (1959) 46–57. For a recent study of economic factors see French, *Growth* 25–43. On the chronology of Peisistratus's attempts a plausible view is that offered by F. E. Adcock, "The Exiles of Peisistratos," *CQ* 18 (1924) 174–181; cf. T. J. Cadoux, *JHS* 68 (1948) 104–109.

APPENDIX

THE LAWS OF DRACON AND SOLON

Ancient writers attribute many provisions to Solon and some to Dracon. A collection of reliable citations would provide a documentary source on early Athens, but questions about authenticity arise. Several recent studies, to be noticed here, have clarified the evidence and the problems.

Statements of the Athenian orators about Solon must be treated with great circumspection. Pleading in 400/399, Andocides (1.95–96) quotes a clause from a law, calls it a law of Solon and then has the law read out in full; but into the full text he inserts a statement that the law was passed in 410/09. Moreover in an important article "(ΠΑΤΡΙΟΣ ΠΟΛΙΤΕΙΑ: Theseus, Drakon, Solon und Kleisthenes im Publizistik und Geschichtsschreibung des 5. and 4. Jh. v. Chr.," *Historia* 7 (1958) 398–424) E. Ruschenbusch collected the references of the orators to Solon. He found that Solon is mentioned only four times in the seventy-five extant speeches made before 356 but as many as thirty-two times in the sixty-four extant speeches after 356. Furthermore, speeches before 356 give Solon as the author, genuine or alleged, of specific laws; speeches after 356 cite him as a democratic model for the Athenians to follow. Evidently something happened about 356 to enlarge and corrupt the tradition about Solon.

Rather less doubt need be felt when a law attributed to Dracon or Solon is cited from the *axones* or the *kyrbeis*. These were objects preserving the texts of the laws. Axones were doubtless mounted on axles in pivots, so that they could be turned to expose their several rectangular faces; the cross-section may have been triangular or square. Kyrbeis may have been structures in which the axones were kept (in the view of Ruschenbusch) or they may have been a free-standing wall bearing the texts of other laws (in the view of S. Dow, *The Law Codes of Athens*, mentioned in note 2 to chapter 5, p. 129); another hypothesis (offered by G. Busolt, *Griechische Geschichte II* [Gotha 1895] 290–293) is that, whereas the axones held the original texts, the kyrbeis were of stone, bore copies of the texts, and stood in the royal stoa for the benefit of the king-archon, who supposedly saw to their observance. Although much is uncertain about the axones and the kyrbeis, it is likely that they were made of wood. The question arises, How well were they preserved?

Plutarch (*Sol.* 25.1) says that only small fragments of the axones were preserved in the Prytaneum in his time. In a monograph, (*Solonos Nomoi*), Ruschenbusch has collected the passages citing laws of Dracon and Solon and has discussed the transmission of the texts. He draws attention to the lost commentary of Aristotle, consisting of five books, on the axones of Solon, and he argues convincingly that later study of the texts in antiquity depended on Aristotle's work. Further, he claims that either the axones themselves or a reliable copy was accessible to Aristotle. Although he defends the authenticity of some of the laws successfully, his general claim must confront some difficulties. First, in the third century Eratosthenes and Polemo visited Athens and examined the axones but disagreed about their shape; Eratosthenes said that they were triangular but Polemo said that they were square. Ruschenbusch suggests that the cross-section of the axones was square but it looked triangular when they were turned on edge. Surely it is more likely that the disagreement arose from the already fragmentary condition of the objects. Second, even if the texts were legible in full, the language of the first half of the sixth century may have been obscure to readers in the late fifth and fourth centuries. Indeed, Ruschenbusch supposes that Aristotle misunderstood some terms in the laws (*atimos* and perhaps *stasis*: SN pp. 81 and 83, on F37a and F38a–g). Thirdly, as early as the fifth century the comic poet Cratinus (fr. 274 K = Plut. *Sol.* 25.1) makes the puzzling remark that people fry barley on the kyrbeis of Solon and Dracon. Admittedly the business of a comic poet is to make jokes and this may entail exaggeration; even so the remark suggests that the kyrbeis were not preserved with much care.

The inscription which republished the law of Dracon on homicide in 409/8 has been studied by R.S. Stroud in a monograph (*Drakon's Law on Homicide* [University of California Publications in Classical Studies, Volume 3, 1968]). By cleaning and reexamining the stone Stroud has been able to read 218 more letters than had been discerned before. Perhaps his most important single discovery concerns headings. After the prescript, which provides for reinscribing the text, there is the heading, "The First Axon," and this is followed by provisions on involuntary homicide. Lower down on the stele Stroud discerned traces which must belong to a new heading, "The Second Axon." It follows, contrary to the assumption previously made by Ruschenbusch, that the axones of Solon and the axones of Dracon were two different sets of objects. For Plutarch (*Sol.* 24.1) reports a provision of Solon about export of agricultural produce and says that it stood on the first axon; it cannot have stood on the first axon of Dracon, which dealt with homicide.

Was the text inscribed in 409/8 a true copy of the original? In favor of an affirmative answer Stroud (p. 62) appeals to Ruschenbusch's claim that the axones of Solon survived into the second century B.C. Perhaps the question does not yet allow a satisfactory answer. On most problems arising from the text reference may be made to Stroud's discussion, but it will not be amiss to raise three points here.

(1) The provisions on involuntary homicide (quoted in chapter 4, p. 101) conclude with a clause of retroaction: "Let those who killed previously be bound by this law." Stroud (p. 51) infers that the author of the original text sought not merely to write existing law down but to innovate. This inference has much force, even though the innovation may have consisted more in clarifying the law and insisting on its enforcement than in making entirely new provisions. But the question arises, What is meant by "this law" in the provision for retroaction? Did the lawgiver mean the immediately preceding clause about selection of phrateres, or the whole preceding passage about involuntary homicide, or the whole Draconian law extending over at least two axones? It is possible that the author of the original text conceived his task as mostly one of writing existing law down. Where the law was obscure, as unwritten law may often have been, he clarified it. Where opinions among judges differed as to which previous custom to follow, he made his choice and he insisted that the rule he chose from among the several already known must be applied even to men who had committed homicide previously.

(2) The same provisions on involuntary homicide begin with the phrase: "And if (even if) someone kills someone *me 'k pronoias*," and after provisions about relatives of the victim, a new sentence opens with: "But if none of these survives, and he kills *akon*." Stroud translates *me 'k pronoias* by "without premeditation" and *akon* by "unintentionally." Then (p. 41) he accepts from a modern lawyer the point that killing without premeditation is not coextensive with unintentional killing; a man may kill intentionally, in the heat of the moment,

even though he kills without premeditation, and Stroud has to ask which procedure would apply to such an act. In fact the distinction is not valid. Words like "voluntary" and "involuntary," "intentional" and "unintentional," "with/ without premeditation," derive their meaning from the contexts in which they are used and especially from the way each is contrasted with others. The logic of the provisions in the Draconian law seems to use interchangeably the terms *me 'k pronoias* ("without premeditation," "without intent") and *akon* ("unintentionally," "involuntarily").

(3) It is embarrassing that some provisions about homicide are attributed to Solon. Photius cites from him the word *andraphonon* ("of murderers:" Phot. 126.17 = *Ruschenbusch SN* F3) and the verbs *poinan* and *apoinan* (Phot. 437.20 = *SN* F11), which must have to do with wergild. Bekker's *Anecdota* cites *poina* from the laws of Solon (1.428.9 = *SN* F12); and a scholiast on the *Iliad* (2.665 = *SN* F7) says that Solon set five years' exile as the penalty for killing. This last passage may rest on a misunderstanding, for it does not accord with anything else in the Athenian law of homicide. But the remarks in the Byzantine lexica are sufficient evidence that provisions on homicide featured in the legislative work of Solon. This is striking, since Stroud's findings have shown that the axones of Solon were distinct from the axones of Dracon. It follows that the literary tradition is wrong when it asserts (for example, Ar. *AP* 7.1) that with the legislative work of Solon the Athenians ceased using the laws of Dracon except for those on homicide. It is permissible to suggest that legislation on homicide continued after the work of Dracon.

For the student of political and constitutional history the extant fragments of Solon's laws are disappointing. Very few of them deal with public institutions and even fewer with those institutions in which Solon has often been supposed to have made significant changes. The fragments show that he dealt with assessment of property (*SN* F77–78) and this probably concerned the property classes, but that is all that they reveal about the constitutional innovations now often attributed to Solon.

6

The Peisistratidae and the Reforms of Cleisthenes

The development of the Athenian constitution in the seventh and sixth centuries is sometimes described under the heading of the growth of democracy. That designation is unfortunate; the Athenians were engaged in the far more important business of building a united body politic. In the middle of the seventh century the unity of Attica could mean little to the bulk of the Athenians. Central organs, such as the magistracies and the council, mattered to those who engaged in the pursuit of power and honor, and the juridical procedure for dealing with cases of homicide and other violence was uniform for all Athenians; but for most affairs the ordinary Athenian probably found his protector and master in a family powerful in his own locality. The work of Solon marked a significant step in increasing the authority of the state. His codification of the law tried to be comprehensive; and although the problem of the hektemoroi is obscure and may have been more acute in some parts of Attica than in others, Solon's solution applied to the whole territory; thus to some extent all Athenians had the experience of a common political crisis.

Even so the Athenians were still far from achieving a common political outlook. If the "regionalist" explanation of the rise of Peisistratus is correct even in part, it follows that in rebellion he could count on the loyalty of the men of Brauron. When he finally defeated his enemies in 546, he was able to establish a lasting tyranny; he was still in control when he died in 528/7, and he passed on his rule to his sons. Thus after 546 he had time to develop a policy of his own. Human history is not fully determined in advance; it is conceivable that after 546 Peisistratus might have chosen to undo the unification and in particular to create an independent state with its center at Brauron. He did not do so; greater opportunities awaited the tyrant of all Attica than the ruler of an independent Brauron. But Peisistratus's choice was decisive for the future of Athens; by instituting uniform taxation, by building temples and fostering national festivals, and by pursuing an expansive foreign policy Peisistratus brought the people of Attica towards a more perfect union.

PEISISTRATUS: HOME POLICY[1]

Later Athenian tradition spoke favorably of the rule of Peisistratus. Herodotus, referring to the first tyranny (1.59.6), said that he "did not alter the existing positions of honor and did not change the laws, but he governed the city in accordance with established principles, ruling well and with distinction." Thucydides (6.54.5–6) gives a favorable judgement on the sons of Peisistratus as well as on their father: "In relation to power (Hipparchus) was not burdensome to the majority, and their power did not provoke opposition. Indeed these tyrants paid great attention to virtue and wisdom; they exacted only a twentieth of Athenian produce as taxation, but they decorated the city with elegance, prosecuted the wars and performed the sacrifices. For the most part the city continued to follow the established laws, except that the tyrants always ensured that there would be one of their own men among the magistrates." Aristotle (*AP* 16) gives an equally favorable account of the rule of Peisistratus and enlivens it with anecdotes and with philosophic speculation about the tyrant's motives.

Ensuring that there should be at least one of their own men among the magistrates each year was perhaps the key to continued ascendancy. The magistracies that counted were the nine archonships. If Peisistratus and his sons contrived each year that at least one of their supporters was elected, this meant that each year there was at least one archon available to propose and conduct the business they desired. But it meant more. Every man who had held any of the nine archonships became a member of the Areopagite Council, and so as the years passed there arose within that body a group of men on whom the tyrants could rely.

A fragment of the archon list, inscribed ca. 425, has been discovered and throws some light on the policy of the tyrants towards the archonship. It bears parts of six names of eponymous archons for successive years. The fourth name is Miltiades, who is attested independently (by Dionysius of Halicarnassus, *Rom. Antiq.* 7.3.1) as archon for 524/3. He is probably the man whom the Peisistratidae trusted sufficiently to send him to rule the Chersonese ca. 516 (see below, p. 140). Of the last name on the fragment only one syllable "–strat–" is preserved. The name can be restored as that of Peisistratus, the grandson of the founder of the tyranny, and although other restorations are possible, this one is reasonable, since Thucydides (6.54.6) mentions the tenure of the archonship by the younger Peisistratus.

The two most revealing names on the fragment are the second and third, Hippias and Cleisthenes. Hippias was the eldest son of Peisistratus and head of the family after his father died in 528/7. It is remarkable that Hippias was archon as late as 526/5. The minimum age for the archonship in classical Athens was thirty years; one would expect the son of a ruling tyrant to hold office very soon after he attained the legal age. But Hippias is likely to have been born a good deal before 556. Herodotus (1.61.3) indeed says that Peisistratus, when expelled from his second attempt at tyranny, withdrew to Eretria and deliberated with his sons, and Hippias persuaded him to try to recover power; but this story can be dismissed as merely illustrating the folklore motif of the "tempter." A more reliable indication of the age of Hippias is that his father was old enough to lead a campaign against the Megarians sometime before 560; accordingly the probability is that Hippias, the eldest legitimate son, was born at a date nearer 565 than 556. Furthermore, if the younger Peisistratus, the son of Hippias, was archon in 522/1 and the age limit for the archonship was observed, the birth of Hippias can scarcely have been later than 570. The early date of birth is compatible with the latest recorded activity of Hippias; in 490 he guided the Persian fleet which landed at Marathon. If Hippias was born ca. 570 and held one of the nine archonships during his father's lifetime, his eponymous archonship of 526/5 is likely to be a second tenure; he may have chosen to hold office then in order to proclaim the continuance of the regime in spite of his father's death; when Peisistratus died in 528/7, the nine archons for the coming year may already have been chosen, and so the earliest available year for Hippias was 526/5. That there was some need to display solidarity of the regime appears from an item which will be noticed below: Cimon, a wealthy man who had achieved reconciliation with Peisistratus, was murdered in mysterious circumstances shortly after the latter's death.

By far the most exciting name in the fragment of the archon list is that of Cleisthenes, archon in 525/4. There can be no doubt that the archon is identical with Cleisthenes who was head of the Alcmaeonidae in the later part of the sixth century; the name was not common in Athens and Cleisthenes the Alcmaeonid derived it from his maternal grandfather, the tyrant of Sicyon. But Herodotus says (1.64.3; 6.123.1) that the Alcmaeonidae left Athens after the battle of Pallenis and stayed in exile through the whole duration of the tyranny. Evidently

Herodotus was misinformed. It is conceivable that the Alcmaeonidae had not left Attica after the battle of Pallenis; but the alternative supposition is that they went into exile after that battle and later achieved a reconciliation with Peisistratus. This alternative is preferable in view of the parallel fortunes of Cimon. The latter went into exile because of Peisistratus, and while he was in exile, his horses won a victory in the chariot race at Olympia. At the next Olympic festival he won a second victory with the same team and announced it in the name of Peisistratus instead of his own; hence he was able to make a treaty with Peisistratus, return to Athens and recover his property. After he had won a third Olympic victory with the same horses, he was killed at night near the Prytaneum, the official building of the eponymous archon; Peisistratus was no longer alive and the tradition followed by Herodotus said that the sons of Peisistratus instigated the murder. Probable, though not certain, dates for Cimon's Olympic victories are 536, 532 and 528. During the tyranny at Athens the sons of Cimon, Stesagoras and Miltiades, held positions of power; they were successive rulers of the Athenian settlement in the Chersonese (see below, pp. 140–142).

The list of eponymous archons for 526/5–524/3 shows Hippias the Peisistratid, Cleisthenes the Alcmaeonid and Miltiades the Cimonid. Would that lists had been kept for the others of the nine archonships! But at least the meager record suggests that the rule of the Peisistratidae depended on a coalition of powerful families; the favorable judgement passed by later tradition on Peisistratus and his sons reflected the skill with which they conciliated ambitious men.

The note of magnificence, traced in the work of other early tyrants, can be found in that of Peisistratus and his sons. Poets were patronized; Anacreon of Teos, for example, was invited to the court by Hipparchus, and Lasus of Hermione and Simonides of Ceos spent some time there. A stone temple of Athena was built on the north side of the acropolis. The cult of Athena fostered a sense of national identity among the inhabitants of Attica, and their unity was celebrated in the festival called the Panathenaea. Although the details are obscure, this festival was enlarged during the sixth century. Most of the evidence concerns recitation of the Homeric poems at the festival. In 566 new arrangements were adopted whereby in that year and in every fourth year thereafter the festival was celebrated on a larger scale than before; such celebrations were called the Greater Panathenaea, whereas in the intervening years the festival, called the Lesser Panathenaea, was celebrated on the scale obtaining before 566. In 566 Peisistratus had not yet made his first attempt at tyranny, but it may be no accident that the eponymous archon of the year was Hippocleides the Philaid; like the Peisistratidae, the Philaidae came from Brauron (see below, p. 141). Later in the sixth century more rules were adopted. According to a tradition attested in the fourth century, Hipparchus introduced the rule whereby rhap-

*Attic black-figured neck-amphora.
One side shows Dionysus seated between
maenads. On the other side a figure of
disputed identity, perhaps Hephaestus or
Dionysus, rides a mule between satyrs.*
[Courtesy Lowie Museum of Anthropology,
University of California, Berkeley.]

sodes at the Greater Panathenaea were kept to a fixed order in reciting the several episodes of the Homeric poems. A further tradition, mentioned by Cicero, says that Peisistratus first arranged the episodes in a fixed order. Opinions have differed on the value of these traditions; at least they show that Peisistratus or his sons did something about rhapsodic competitions at the festival. Bearing in mind the local origin of the family, one may call to mind the remark of the lexicographer Hesychius of Alexandria (s.v. Brauroniois): "Rhapsodes used to sing the *Iliad* at Brauron in Attica." Conceivably the rhapsodic competitions were a Brauronian custom, which the Philaidae and the Peisistratidae brought to Athens.

Work on public buildings and the enlargement of the Panathenaic festival illustrate the lasting significance of the tyranny. The purposes of Peisistratus and his sons may have concerned merely the splendor and prestige of the family, but their methods were bound to reinforce a sense of unity among the inhabitants of Attica. If Aristotle can be believed, they took a major institutional step in this direction; he says (*AP* 16.5) that Peisistratus introduced the deme dicasts (*dikastai kata demous*), that is, judges who toured all parts of Attica in order to settle disputes. These judges existed in the fourth century, when they numbered forty and had authority to settle cases worth not more than ten drachmas (*AP* 53.1–2). But a difficulty arises because Aristotle also says (*AP* 26.3) that deme dicasts were reintroduced in 453/2, when they numbered thirty. If they had previously been established by Peisistratus, it is difficult to conjecture when or why the institution lapsed before 453/2; it is also difficult to see how Aristotle could have had good evidence for the earlier institution. Perhaps the attribution of deme dicasts to Peisistratus is a projection of a fifth-century institution into the past, a projection resting on comparisons drawn between fifth-century statesmen, such as Pericles, and the Peisistratidae (that such comparisons were made is known from Plutarch, *Per.* 16.1).

Only a little is known about the financial and economic base of the tyranny. Thucydides (6.54.5, cited above, p. 135) says that the tyrants exacted a twentieth of produce as tax; Aristotle (*AP* 16.4) gives the proportion as a tenth, but Thucydides, the more scrupulous historian, is likely to be correct. That Peisistratus carried out a redistribution of land, seizing some from his enemies and allocating it to peasants, is a modern conjecture without direct support in the sources, but it may be correct; there are several indications that the idea of redistributing land was discussed in sixth-century Athens; indeed, redistribution had been demanded during the crisis which Solon faced. Export of Athenian vases continued to grow during the tyranny and implies trade in other goods too. The foreign policy of Peisistratus suggests a conscious desire to safeguard commercial routes; not only did he expand Athenian influence into the heart of the Aegean; the capture of Sigeum and the settlement of Athenians in the Chersonese imply concern for the route to the Black Sea.

PHILAIDAE, CIMONIDAE AND THE CHERSONESE[2]

The account of the Athenian settlement in the Thracian Chersonese, as told by Herodotus (6.34–40; cf. 6.103–104), illustrates both the foreign interests of Peisistratus and his relations with other families. The Thracian tribe of the Dolonci held the Chersonese but, being attacked by another tribe, the Apsinthii, they consulted the Delphic oracle, came to Athens and invited Miltiades the Philaid to protect them. He took a party of Athenian volunteers, settled in the Chersonese and built a wall across the isthmus of the peninsula for protection against the Apsinthii. Then he engaged in a war against Lampsacus, a city on the opposite side of the Hellespont, and was captured by the Lampsacenes, but his friend Croesus, king of Lydia, intervened with diplomatic threats and made them release him.

Herodotus's account continues by saying that Miltiades died childless and rule of the Chersonese passed to Stesagoras, the son of Miltiades's maternal half-brother Cimon (see table B for the relationship). Indeed Stesagoras was already in the Chersonese with Miltiades before the latter's death. He continued the war against Lampsacus; eventually a man of that city, pretending to be a deserter, received asylum in the Chersonese and assassinated Stesagoras. The latter left no children, and so the sons of Peisistratus sent out Militiades II, the brother of Stesagoras, to take control of the Chersonese. He arrived there ca. 516 and established his rule by strong measures, arresting several of the leading men and maintaining a force of five hundred mercenaries. He married the daughter of the Thracian king Olorus, thus securing an ally in the neighborhood. Eventually in 493, when Persian fleet sailed northwards through the Aegean and reached Tenedos, Miltiades fled to Athens (see p. 185).

The departure of Miltiades I for the Chersonese probably occurred soon after Peisistratus began his third and final tyranny. Herodotus's account of the rulers of the Chersonese tries to suggest tension between them and the tyrants of Athens. He says that Miltiades I was willing to leave for the Chersonese because he was aggrieved at the rule of Peisistratus; he alleges that the Peisistratidae instigated the murder of Cimon. But as the Peisistratidae sent Miltiades II to so crucial a place as the Chersonese, they must have had confidence in him. Probably the suggestions of tension were exaggerated at the first trial of Miltiades II; for when he returned to Athens in 493, his enemies prosecuted him on a charge of exercising tyranny in the Chersonese. By 493 the tyranny of the Peisistratidae had been overthrown and those who had worked for its overthrow were regarded as liberators. The enemies of Miltiades, recollecting that he had been sent to the Chersonese by the Peisistratidae, may have tried to portray him as a relic of the old order; it was in his interest to dissociate himself and his predecessors in the Chersonese from the tyranny.

Miltiades I belonged to the clan called Philaidae; they traced descent to the mythical hero Philaeus, the son of Aias. Plutarch (*Sol.* 10.2) remarks that there was a deme called Philaidae at Brauron; this is the reason for supposing that the clan of the Philaidae belonged to Brauron. Cimon and his descendants were related through a woman to Miltiades I; so they should not be called Philaidae but Cimonidae. In the fifth century Cimon II, the son of Miltiades II, distinguished himself repeatedly in command of Athenian forces, and his deme is recorded; it was Laciadae, just to the west of the city of Athens, on the Sacred Way followed by travelers to and from Delphi. Deme membership was finally determined in the reforms of Cleisthenes towards the end of the sixth century (see below, p. 151) and it was hereditary. But Miltiades II was not in Attica at the time when those reforms were passed. So there are two possibilities for the local origin of the Cimonidae. The first is that Cimon I in the sixth century already belonged to Laciadae and Miltiades II in 493 returned to his ancestral home. The second is that in the sixth century the Cimonidae belonged to some other part of Attica; then Miltiades II, returning in 493, was allowed to choose his deme and chose Laciadae. A fact about Miltiades I the Philaid tells in favor of the first possibility: according to Herodotus, when the Dolonci had consulted the Delphic oracle, they traveled along the Sacred Way towards the city of Athens and they found Miltiades I sitting in the doorway of his house. Apparently he owned a house in or near Laciadae. It may be conjectured that the alliance between the Cimonidae and the Philaidae brought advantages to both parties; the Philaidae of Brauron gained a base of operations near the city of Athens, and when Peisistratus led the men of Brauron to ascendancy in Athens, the Cimonidae had a link with a leading Brauronian family.

The Chersonese was a valuable position because of its relation to the sea route through the Hellespont. By the fourth century the Athenians imported most of their grain and about half of the import came from the north coast of the Black Sea. Import of Pontic grain into some parts of Greece is attested for an earlier period by Herodotus (7.147.2); he says that in 480, when Xerxes was at Abydos on his way to European Greece, he saw ships sailing from the Black Sea and bearing grain for Aegina and the Peloponnese. It is not clear how far Athens had become dependent on Pontic grain by the middle of the sixth century. The Solonian restrictions on export of agricultural produce (see chapter 5, p. 113) suggest that there was plentiful demand for grain in Attica; and Athenian black-figure ware is known to have reached the coast of the Black Sea as early as the period 600–580. So it is credible that by 546 the grain route through the Hellespont was of concern to the makers of Athenian policy. The strategic character of the Athenian settlement in the Chersonese should not be overemphasized; since the men whom Miltiades took with him were volunteers, the settlement evidently served as an outlet for surplus population. Neither should the degree of control achieved over the grain route be exaggerated; Lampsacus, the enemy of the Athenian settlement in the Chersonese, was just as well placed for guarding or obstructing the passage of ships through the Hellespont. But the settlement founded by Miltiades established Athenians in a place whence they could easily come to the aid of grain ships against pirates and privateers.

PEISISTRATUS: FOREIGN POLICY[3]

Before the time of Peisistratus Athens can scarcely be said to have had a foreign policy. She fought a long and probably intermittent war with Megara for control of Salamis; indeed, Solon composed a poem exhorting the Athenians to seize Salamis. But that war was perhaps an extension of the process of formal unification, exacerbated by the rebellion of Cylon, rather than an act of deliberate choice. Again the Athenians took part in the First Sacred War. Later tradition said that war was declared on the proposal of Solon and the Athenian contingent was commanded by Alcmaeon; these details may merely reflect the tendency of great names to attract events, but Athenian participation is proved by an institutional survival: henceforth Athens had a place in the Amphictyonic Council, which managed the affairs of the Delphic sanctuary. It is, however, possible that the Athenians joined in the war not from a considered resolve to extend Athenian influence but in reaction against Delphic utterances that bore on the internal politics of Athens; the oracular response given to Cylon, promising that he would "take the acropolis during the greatest festival of Zeus" (Thuc. 1.126.4), comes to mind. The actions of Peisistratus, on the other hand, indicate a considered resolve to extend the influence of the Athenians and of their tyrant.

The conduct of foreign affairs by Peisistratus reveals a desire to secure positions near the Hellespont, an attempt to assert Athenian claims in the central Aegean, and a singular skill for maintaining good relations with numerous powers of the mainland. Apart from the Chersonese, a position was secured at Sigeum on the Asiatic coast near the mouth of the Hellespont. Previously Sigeum had been among the extensive possessions of the Mytilenaeans on the Asiatic mainland. As Herodotus relates (5.94–95), Peisistratus captured Sigeum and entrusted it to his son Hegesistratus, but a long war followed with the Mytilenaeans. At last the parties submitted the dispute to the arbitration of Periander and he ruled that each party should keep what it held; thus the Athenians retained Sigeum. Consequently Peisistratus and his sons could reckon with Athenian settlements at two positions near the Hellespont, namely the Cheronese and Sigeum; their interest in the grain route was overinsured. Much later, in 514 or 513, Hippias allied with the tyrant of Lampsacus, an act which was likely to offend Miltiades II in the Chersonese; he retained good relations with the Athenian settlement at Sigeum and presumably considered this a sufficient safeguard for the grain route (see below, p. 145).

In the heart of the Aegean Peisistratus could take a first step to assert Athenian influence by paying a political debt. Lygdamis, an ambitious adventurer from Naxos, had joined Peisistratus's forces in time to help in his final restoration. So it was probably soon afterwards that Peisistratus captured Naxos by warfare and entrusted the island to Lygdamis (Hdt. 1.64.2). A late source (Polyaen. 1.23.2) says that Lygdamis in turn helped Polycrates to make himself tyrant of Samos; this is credible. Polycrates, who developed the strongest fleet in the Aegean (Hdt. 3.39.3–4; 3.122.2; see chapter 7, p. 173–174), was a valuable friend.

The question arises, Did the tyrants of Athens, Naxos and Samos try to preserve the ties between them? About 525, when the Spartans and the Corinthians made an expedition against Polycrates, there is no indication that Hippias sent him help. Polycrates withstood the attack successfully, but it was probably on the same expedition that the Spartans overthrew Lygdamis. Doubtless respect for Peloponnesian power deterred Hippias from any thought of intervening. Thus relations between the three tyrants did not amount to a wholly binding and effective alliance. But one item shows that, after Peisistratus installed Lygdamis in Naxos, their friendship continued to have political value: Peisistratus took hostages from those Athenians whom he distrusted and he sent the hostages to Naxos for safekeeping (Hdt. 1.64.1).

Athens, Naxos and Samos were Ionian settlements. In the fifth century Athens claimed to be the mother city of all other Ionian cities, and the claim was already implied by Solon, who called Attica "the oldest land of Ionia" (fr. 4 = *AP* 5.2). This explains why Peisistratus carried out a ceremonial purification of Delos, removing buried corpses from within sight of the temple (Hdt. 1.64.2); Delos was the sacred island of the Ionians, where they held festivals. In conducting the purification Peisistratus behaved as one who, being newly come to power, sought wider recognition by a display of magnificence. Further, there may have been some rivalry with Polycrates; the latter dedicated the neighboring island of Rheneia to Apollo by binding it to Delos with a chain (Thuc. 3.104.1–2).

On the European mainland of Greece Peisistratus won the good will of many states. With some he had gained connections during his exile. For his final return Thebes provided money and Eretria provided a base; doubtless both of them, being near to Attica, desired a friendly regime there and judged that Peisistratus was the most promising man to support. From Argos he hired a force of troops; Aristotle (*AP* 17.4), who gives their number as 1,000, says that they came in virtue of the connection he had established by marrying an Argive woman, Timonassa. Ties were established with Thessaly. These proved fruitful in 512, when Sparta sent an expedition by sea to overthrow the Peisistratidae, but these gained cavalry from Thessaly in consequence of their alliance (Hdt. 5.63.3). But relations had been opened a generation earlier, since Peisistratus gave the name Thessalus to one of his sons.

There is evidence that the Athenian tyrants achieved good relations with Sparta. Late in the sixth century, several years after the Spartans had overthrown the sons of Peisistratus, they regretted this and they called to mind that the Peisistratidae had been their friends (Hdt. 5.90.1; cf. 5.91.2; the word *xeinos* indicates friendship of a formal kind); so they launched a plan to restore Hippias. Nothing came of that plan, but the incident indicates that there had once been friendship between the Spartans and the Peisistratidae. It is not clear whether that friendship went back to the time of Peisistratus, or whether after his death his sons maintained links with Argos. Perhaps it is better to believe that, after the battle of the champions (see chapter 3, p. 84), the Athenians lost interest in maintaining good relations with Argos and opened ties of friendship with Sparta.

THE DECLINE AND FALL OF THE PEISISTRATIDAE[4]

In 546 Peisistratus owed his restoration largely to foreign support; a generation later changes occurring outside Attica brought about the expulsion of his sons. Developments during the 520s were unfavorable to their friends in the islands of the Aegean. A Spartan attack on Polycrates of Samos ca. 525 was repulsed (see chapter 8, p. 197); but probably during the return journey of the same expeditionary force the Spartans overthrew Lygdamis of Naxos. In about 522 Oroetes, the Persian satrap of Sardeis, enticed Polycrates into a conference on the mainland and killed him (Hdt. 3.120–125).

The position of the Peisistratidae was weakened more seriously in 519. In that year the Plataeans were attacked by the Thebans, so they sought help from a Lacedaemonian force under Cleomenes, who happened to be near. But the Lacedaemonians refused to make any alliance, pointing out that their home was too far away for them to bring speedy aid to the Plataeans in future, and advised them to appeal to Athens. The Plataeans did so; the Athenians made an alliance and sent a force, which asserted Plataean independence successfully. Herodotus (6.108) reports the incident and states the Lacedaemonian motive for their curious advice to the Plataeans: they wanted the Athenians to be preoccupied with trouble with the Boeotians. This statement is suspect, since it may reflect conditions obtaining when Herodotus was writing. He finished his history by about 430; early in 431 the Thebans made a surprise attack on Plataea and began a seige, which lasted until 427; the Athenians helped the Plataeans in this conflict because of their longstanding alliance. Yet the motive which Herodotus attributes to the Lacedaemonians is not impossible for 519. Sparta was expanding her power by enlarging the Peloponnesian League; the task which brought her forces so far north in 519 may have been an attempt to bring Megara into alliance. Beyond Megara lay Athens and Boeotia, where Thebes was building a federation. By referring the Plataeans to Athens and thus making Plataea an issue of conflict, the Spartans may have hoped to weaken both Athens and Thebes. The actions of the Spartans in the last decade of the sixth century show that they wanted to gain ascendancy over Athens; so they needed an Athens less self-assertive than that of Peisistratus.

If the motive attributed by Herodotus to the Lacedaemonians in 519 is thus substantially correct, the incident was ominous for Hippias. Of the mainland powers which had befriended Peisistratus and his sons, Thebes was henceforth hostile. Argos was no longer of paramount importance since the battle of the champions; and Sparta, though technically tied by friendship to the Peisistratidae, was not well disposed. There remained Eretria and Thessaly. The Thessalians were true to Hippias until the end, but a conspiracy launced in Athens in 514 may throw indirect light on the policy of Eretria.

Hipparchus quarreled with two Athenians, Harmodius and Aristogeiton. So they made a plot to overthrow the tyranny and chose the Panathenaic festival of 514 for their attempt. Then at the last moment a misunderstanding arose; believing themselves betrayed, the plotters assassinated Hipparchus, but the bodyguards of Hippias took control of the situation. Harmodius was killed in the scuffle, but Aristogeiton was arrested and examined under torture. The subsequent investigations led Hippias to believe that the plot had many accomplices. He made his rule more severe, killing a good many citizens. Moreover, as Thucydides observed (6.59.2–3), because of the plot Hippias made a new departure in foreign policy to insure his safety; he gave his daughter in marriage to the son of Hippoclus, the tyrant of Lampsacus. This seems an excessive reaction by Hippias to an abortive plot, which his troops had easily suppressed. Indeed he had little to fear at home; a year or so later an attempt by exiles to seize Leipsydrium in Attica was defeated (see below, p. 146), and when at last Hippias was overcome in 510, this was achieved by foreign intervention. Hippias's alarm at the discovery of the plot may become comprehensible when the family origin of Harmodius and Aristogeiton is taken into account. They were members of the clan called the Gephyraei. This clan lived in the northern part of Attica; Harmodius came from Aphidna. The clan claimed to have migrated to Attica from Eretria (Hdt. 5.57.1) and they kept up their ties with that city; nearly two centuries later a member of the clan, Cydimachus, fled to Eretria when he was condemned to death in Athens. The abortive conspiracy of Harmodius and Aristogeiton may have warned Hippias that Eretria was not as favorable to his family as it had been in 546; he could no longer seek a refuge there in an emergency.

Hippias responded to the plot by allying with Hippoclus of Lampsacus. That city was on the mainland of Asia Minor and was under Persian control; Hippoclus served Darius loyally on the Scythian expedition (Hdt. 4.138.1; see chapter 7, pp. 173–174). The Peloponnesian League was growing to such an extent that a man like Hippias had to choose between Spartan and Persian protection. By allying with Hippoclus Hippias risked offending Miltiades in the Chersonese but Miltiades did not do him any harm. How much Hippias expected to gain from the Persian connection escapes conjecture; possibly Darius had already conceived a design of invading European Greece, but whether Hippias knew about that is another question. In the event what he gained was a refuge in the Persian Empire after his expulsion from Athens.

The Alcmaeonidae withdrew into exile, probably because of the deaths of Harmodius and Aristogeiton and the ensuing investigations. Doubtless they, like Hippias, could recognize the changes in Athenian relations with foreign powers. But first they tried to overthrow the tyranny without foreign help. They led a party of exiles into Attica, perhaps in 513, and they fortified a position at Leipsydrium above Paeonia; some people from the city of Athens joined them, but the forces of Hippias besieged Leipsydrium successfully. Evidently the rule of the tyrants was popular, even in its last and most severe years.

Athenian tradition, as reported by Herodotus (5.62–65), tried to attribute to the Alcmaeonidae the initiative in the final overthrow of Hippias. It said that they secured the contract for rebuilding the temple at Delphi, which had been burned down, and rebuilt it in a more expensive manner than was required; thus they gained the good will of the oracle and so, whenever Spartans came to consult it, the response included an exhortation to free Athens. Hence the Spartans sent an expedition by sea under Anchimolius and he landed in the bay of Phalerum, but the Peisistratidae with cavalry from Thessaly overcame him. The Spartans sent a second expedition under King Cleomenes by land. Cleomenes put the Thessalian cavalry to flight and besieged the Peisistratidae on the acropolis. When some of their children were captured, they agreed to leave Attica within five days. They retired to Sigeum.

Although this tradition tried to give first place to the Alcmaeonidae, it did not conceal the fact that the real initiative came from Sparta. Not that the behavior of the Delphic oracle was insignificant; the Spartans needed a religious excuse to break their ties of formal friendship with the Peisistratidae. The Spartan objective in overthrowing Hippias was surely to bring Athens within the Spartan sphere of influence; it is often conjectured that, at the expulsion of Hippias in 510, Athens became a member of the Peloponnesian League. The complexity of the situation for the Spartans and the success of Spartan policy are suggested by three hints concerning Megara. First, late in the sixth century, whether before or after 510, the Athenians passed a decree for measures to defend Salamis; evidently they thought that their possession of the island was threatened again. Second, the first Spartan expedition against Hippias traveled by sea; this suggests that the Spartans could not use the land route through the Megarid. If Sparta brought Megara into her League in 519, as supposed above, it is fully conceivable that Hippias brought about a change of outlook in Megara a few years later; in the fifth century Athens and Sparta competed frequently for influence in Megara. It should be supposed that Anchimolius sailed in 512 and the Spartans devoted the next year to restoring their influence in Megara. Third, Plutarch (*Sol.* 10.6) says that a Spartan board of five arbitrators adjudicated in the dispute over Salamis, awarding the island to Athens, and although he assigns the arbitration to the time of Solon, the last name among the five is Cleomenes. Perhaps Spartan recognition of the Athenian claim to Salamis was part of the settlement of 510. During the next ten years Sparta proved able to retain Megara in her sphere of influence, but the Athenians asserted their independence successfully.

CLEISTHENES AND ISAGORAS[5]

Herodotus (5.66–81; 5.89–94) narrates the complex events which ensued in Athens some time after the expulsion of Hippias. Rivalry developed between Cleisthenes and Isagoras and at first the latter won the upper hand. So Cleisthenes carried a tribal reform and thereby won ascendancy. Isagoras responded by appealing to Cleomenes, with whom he had contracted ties of friendship when the Spartans were besieging the Peisistratidae. So Cleomenes sent a herald to Athens with a message; it demanded the exile of Cleisthenes and of 700 families descended from those who long before had incurred a curse by slaying the followers of Cylon (see chapter 4, pp. 98–99). Cleisthenes withdrew into exile; then Cleomenes came to Athens with a small force and set about expelling the 700 families. But he went further: he tried to dissolve the council and entrust rule to 300 partisans of Isagoras. But the council offered resistance and so Cleomenes and Isagoras seized the acropolis. Thereupon the Athenians rallied in defence of the council; they besieged Cleomenes and Isagoras for two days and let them depart under treaty on the third. Now Cleisthenes and the 700 families were recalled.

Cleomenes continued his efforts to put Isagoras in control of Athens. He brought about a triple attack on Attica: the Boeotians invaded the territory from the north, the Chalcidians raided it in the northeast, and Cleomenes led the forces of the Peloponnesian League towards western Attica. But when the Peloponne-

*Attic amphora, ca. 510. The lettering
beside the horse's leg says "Hippocrates
is handsome." Hippocrates is probably
the brother of Cleisthenes and father of
Megacles. The epithet "handsome," attached
to proper names on vases, expresses
admiration which is often erotic but
sometimes, as probably here, political.*
[Courtesy Staatliche Antikensammlungen
und Glyptothek, München.]

sian force was confronted by an Athenian force at Eleusis, the Corinthian
contingent refused to fight and went home; then Demaretus, the second Spartan
king, also withdrew from the force, and the several contingents retired. The
Athenians proceeded to attack and defeat the Boeotians and the Chalcidians in
succession. The Spartans made a further plan for intervention. They summoned a
congress of the Peloponnesian League and proposed to restore Hippias, who was
present for the meeting; apparently the Spartans had realized that Isagoras was no
longer a promising candidate. But the Corinthians and then other members of
the Peloponnesian League rejected the proposal, and so the Spartans gave up their
designs on Athens.

A clue to the nature of the rivalry between Cleisthenes and Isagoras may be sought in their local origin. Cleisthenes was the head of the Alcmaeonidae, who belonged to the city (see above, note 7 to chapter 5 on p. 129). Isagoras has sometimes been claimed as a Philaid, because his father's name was Teisander and this name is attested among the Philaidae; earlier in the sixth century a Philaid Hippocleides, the son of Teisander, was archon in 566/5 and suitor for the hand of Agariste (see above, pp. 46 and 137). But the name Teisander is not sufficiently uncommon to justify the inference. Herodotus (5.66.1) reports that he could not discover the ancestry of Isagoras and adds that his relatives worshipped Zeus Carius. It has been pointed out (by D.M. Lewis) that Herodotus could surely have discovered descent from the Philaidae and that the cult of Zeus Carius is attested only at one place in Attica, namely at Icaria in the Pentelicum area. Icaria was well to the north of Athens; it lay southwest of Marathon and southeast of Deceleia. It stood on the northern slope of Mount Pentelicum and was thus cut off from the plain of the city.

If Isagoras came from Icaria outside the city plain, he may well have become the leader of men from those eastern districts which had given Peisistratus his earliest and most reliable supporters. Thus a "regionalist" explanation is available for his rivalry with Cleisthenes the Alcmaeonid. Isagoras was eponymous archon in 508/7; hence he became a member of the Council of the Areopagus. That Council probably held a group of men loyal to the Peisistratidae and to the interests of eastern Attica. From 546 until 510 the tyrants ensured that some of their supporters should be amoung the nine archons chosen each year. When Hippias was overthrown, some of his former supporters may have deserted him; but surely there remained within the Areopagite Council a substantial core of men devoted to the eastern Attic cause. That group may be the source of strength which enabled Isagoras to gain the upper hand at an early stage in his rivalry with Cleisthenes.

These considerations throw significant light on the actions taken by Cleomenes, when he came to Athens with a small force. Everything went well for him until he tried to dissolve the council; then the Athenians rallied against him. Herodotus does not say what council Cleomenes tried to dissolve. The existence of a Council of Four Hundred, created by Solon, is doubtful (see chapter 5, pp. 120–121); and although Cleisthenes introduced a Council of Five Hundred, there was hardly enough time for that Council to be established before Cleomenes arrived. By elimination the Council of the Areopagus would appear to be the one attacked by Cleomenes, and a further argument leads to the same conclusion. When Cleomenes set about dissolving the council, he also tried to entrust rule to three hundred supporters of Isagoras. That figure approximates to the probable size of the Areopagite Council, since it admitted nine new members annually and each of them could expect thirty further years or more of active life (see chapter 4, pp. 95–96). If Cleomenes tried to dissolve the Council of the Areopagus, he miscalculated the situation in Athens; he failed to see that that council was the body within which Isagoras could expect valuable support. This was a strange mistake for Cleomenes to make, since he had Isagoras to advise him. Possibly the tradition exaggerated the enormity of his attack on the Council; perhaps he attempted, not to dissolve it, but merely to modify its composition. It should further be borne in mind that supporters of Isagoras may have constituted only a minority, albeit a significant minority, in the Council of the Areopagus. Yet it must be recognized that Cleomenes committed a major blunder when he attacked the Council; until that point his intervention in Athens had been remarkably successful, but thereafter Isagoras had no further political prospects. The Areopagite Council enjoyed enormous prestige among the Athenians, and Cleomenes first had to meet serious opposition when he attacked it.

THE REFORMS OF CLEISTHENES: SOURCES AND DATE[6]

Herodotus gives an extensive narrative of the fortunes of Cleisthenes but has little to say about the content of his reforms. He says (5.66.2; 5.69.2) that previously the Athenians constituted four tribes but Cleisthenes divided them into ten; he adds that there were henceforth ten tribal commanders and that Cleisthenes distributed the demes among the tribes "in ten parts," if the emended text is right. Aristotle bases his narrative of the fortunes of Cleisthenes (*AP* 20) on Herodotus but he adds an account of the content of the reforms (*AP* 21). In this he describes the structure of the ten tribes and he says that Cleisthenes replaced the Solonian Council of Four Hundred with a Council of Five Hundred.

It cannot be proved that Herodotus or Aristotle had written documents as evidence for the reforms. Even so their statements are mostly acceptable. Herodotus attests a tradition, independent of Atthidographic speculation, that Cleisthenes introduced the system of ten tribes. That system remained in force permanently; so in describing it Aristotle was dealing with things which he could himself observe. The attribution to Cleisthenes of the Council of Five Hundred gains in credibility from a further statement of Aristotle; he says (*AP* 22.2) that in 501/0 the Council first swore the oath which it still swore in his time. Only parts of the oath have been preserved; Aristotle's ultimate source for the date 501/0 may have been a clause in the oath naming the archon of that year. A parallel is provided by the oath of the nine archons, since this mentioned the archonship of Acastus (*AP* 3.3).

If the Council of Five Hundred first swore its oath in 501/0, it follows that the Council of that year was the first to hold office and hence that the reforms of

Cleisthenes had been carried recently. It is commonly believed that the reforms were carried in 508/7; Aristotle (*AP* 21.1) assigns them to the year when Isagoras was eponymous archon, and that was 508/7. Doubtless the reforms took some time to execute; the tribal reform required a survey of the land and population of Attica, and the Council of Five Hundred presupposed the tribal reform, since it drew fifty members from each of the ten new tribes. But the interval from 508/7 to 501/0 is too long; the reforms are more likely to have been carried in 503 or 502. Aristotle's dating of the reforms to 508/7 may have rested on an assumption that the archonship of Isagoras marked the stage when he won ascendancy in rivalry with Cleisthenes. In fact it is more likely that Isagoras first became a leading figure some years after his archonship; this happened to Solon (see chapter 5, pp. 121–123) and to Themistocles (see chapter 7, pp. 184–185). If the reforms were passed in 503 or 502, the ensuing events, including Cleomenes's visit to Athens, his attempt at a triple attack on Attica and the Peloponnesian congress at Sparta, occupied a period of three or four years, ending in 499. When Hippias left the Spartan congress and retired to Sigeum, he used his influence with the satrap of Sardis to suggest a Persian attack on Athens with a view to his own restoration. The Athenians complained to the satrap but received in reply a curt demand that they should welcome Hippias back. Hence they were displeased with the Persian authorities, when Aristagoras of Miletus arrived in Athens to seek help for the Ionian Revolt (Hdt. 5.96–97). That Revolt began in 499 (see chapter 7, pp. 175–177).

THE REFORMS OF CLEISTHENES: THE TRIBAL SYSTEM[7]

Thanks to Aristotle, the structure of the new tribal system introduced by Cleisthenes is clear. Hitherto the Athenians were divided into four tribes and membership of these was hereditary. These four tribes continued to exist for some religious purposes, but Cleisthenes introduced a division of all citizens into ten tribes and this bore no relation to the four traditional tribes. The basis of membership in the new tribes was territorial; that is, a citizen belonged to such-and-such a tribe because he resided in such-and-such a part of Attica when the reform was carried out. But a complex method was adopted for assigning the different parts of Attica to the ten artificial tribes. The basic unit chosen was the deme (*demos*) and Attica was divided into these units, which numbered ca. 140. Each deme should be regarded as a village or parish with rudimentary organization for conduct of local affairs. Probably villages with some local organization had arisen in many parts of Attica before the reforms, but Cleisthenes extended the division into demes through the whole territory; the process included dividing the city of Athens into demes and perhaps modifying local organization in some other places. As a first step towards forming ten new tribes from the demes Cleisthenes divided Attica into three large regions, called "the city" (*asty*), "the coast" (*paralia*) and "the interior" (*mesogeios*). Then he divided each of these regions into ten parts, called "trittyes." Each trittys consisted of a number of demes. To form each tribe Cleisthenes put together one trittys from the city, one from the coast and one from the interior.

Thus the units in the new structure were the demes, the trittyes and the tribes. Of these, the demes had important functions. Each deme had an assembly of demesmen, that is, of adult male citizens belonging to it; and each deme had an annual headman or *demarchos*, elected by its assembly of demesmen. Moreover, each deme kept a list of its demesmen, and whenever the son of one of them reached the age of majority in his eighteenth year, his father presented him to the demesmen; if they were satisfied with his age and descent, they added him to their list of demesmen, and enrollment on the list of any deme constituted proof of citizenship. The demes varied much in size; Acharnae, the largest, constituted a whole trittys, whereas in some cases a trittys consisted of about ten demes. Membership of the several demes, and therefore of the tribes, depended on one's place of residence when the reform was carried out, but for the future it was hereditary; wherever a man might move to in Attica, he continued to be a member of the deme where his ancestor in the male line had resided in the time of Cleisthenes.

Like the demes, the tribes had serious functions. Each tribe had its own shrine and priest. Each tribe had an assembly of its adult male members and chose its own officers; in the fourth century the civil officers in charge of the tribes were called "overseers of the tribes" (*epimeletae ton phylon*). The tribes were used for military organization. Henceforth the Athenian army of hoplites was conscripted by posting ten lists of names, one for each tribe, and it was brigaded in ten regiments, each under a tribal commander (*taxiarchos*). Furthermore, the tribes were used in regulating candidatures for offices of state; in 501/0 the rule was adopted that each year the public assembly should elect ten generals (*strategoi*), choosing one from each tribe, and a similar rule was adopted for other offices (see below, pp. 154–155).

By comparison with the demes and the tribes, the trittyes had only slight functions. Admittedly, some of them owned property and developed their own cults; this indicates that some trittyes developed a sense of identity. It can be argued that Cleisthenes intended the trittyes to be more active than they in fact became. But it is difficult to see what significant tasks he envisaged for them. Consequently, it is better to follow the usual view, that the trittyes were intended essentially as a mere device for distributing demes into tribes.

The new tribal system substituted territorial divisions of citizens for hereditary divisions. Other ancient republics experienced a change similar in principle; this is probably true of Sparta (see chapter 3, pp. 80–82) and certainly of Rome, where tradition attributed the change to the early king Servius Tullius. Comparison with Rome and Sparta may suggest part of the purpose of Cleisthenes. During the sixth century Attica probably attracted immigrants; this is likely in view of the growth in prosperity, which the export of Attic vases attests. Aristotle says in the *Politics* (3.1275b36–37) that Cleisthenes enfranchised many foreigners and slaves. In another context he says (*AP* 13.5) that after the fall of the tyranny the Athenians took a vote to exclude from citizenship many people who had encroached on its privileges surreptitiously; the authenticity of this record has been doubted, but if it is correct, one may suppose that Cleisthenes championed the men whose citizenship had been brought into doubt. In any case, if population was growing by immigration, the new settlers could be absorbed more easily into a system based on territorial divisions than into one based on hereditary divisions. Moreover, since the four traditional tribes were hereditary in membership, they must have come to vary considerably in size. By introducing a new tribal system, Cleisthenes made possible a more even distribution of the burdens of citizenship, such as military service; this meant that the state could draw more fully on the military potential of the population. That may be the reason why, shortly after the reforms had been carried, the Athenians were able to win striking victories over the Boeotians and Chalcidians (see above, pp. 147–148). At Rome the tribal reform facilitated admission of recent settlers and a more even distribution of public burdens.

Considerations of this kind doubtless played a part, but they do not explain the real peculiarity of the Cleisthenic tribes. At Rome each of the Servian tribes held a compact block of territory; at Athens each tribe held three blocks of territory drawn from three different regions. Absorption of immigrants and even distribution of civic burdens could have been achieved at Athens by assigning to each new tribe a compact block of territory; why did Cleisthenes adopt a much more complex scheme?

An important observation (made by D. W. Bradeen) constitutes a first step towards an answer. In two or three cases the coastal trittys of a tribe was adjacent to the interior trittys of the same tribe. Thus in the tribe Aegeis the coastal trittys extended north from Brauron and was contiguous with the interior trittys, most of whose territory lay on Mount Pentelicum. In the tribe Aeantis the coastal trittys included Marathon and neighboring settlements; the interior trittys was adjacent to this and had its main center of population at Aphidna. The case of the tribe Pandionis is less striking. The coastal trittys was south of Brauron and extended some distance inland into the plain; the interior trittys lay further west in the plain and probably met the coastal trittys at an angle. The significance of these cases should not be misunderstood. Where two trittyes of the same tribe were adjacent, they did not constitute a compact block of political power. For example, in the case of Aeantis, the uphill journey from Marathon to Aphidnae was long and arduous and, whereas Marathon had Peisistratid connections, being used as a landing place by Peisistratus in 546 and by Hippias in 490, Aphidnae was the home of the men who assassinated Hipparchus. Even so the contiguity of the coastal and interior trittyes in a few tribes indicates something about the aims of Cleisthenes. He was not concerned to separate coastal districts from interior districts; his concern, in constructing the tribes, was with the district of the city.

Aristotle says (*AP* 21.2; cf. *Pol.* 6.1319b19–27) that the aim of Cleisthenes in introducing the new tribes was "to mingle (the Athenians) together." Some modern writers have fallen back on a view of this kind and have held that Cleisthenes tried to promote a sense of unity by bringing together men of different districts; perhaps they have despaired of diagnosing a more specific purpose in so opaque a scheme. Yet there must have been a specific purpose; the reforms were carried during a struggle with Isagoras and they enabled Cleisthenes to win ascendancy over his rival. So any hypothesis which fails to allow for a partisan element in the reforms should be highly suspect. If, as argued in the preceding paragraph, the thrust of the tribal reform concerned the city district, it should not be forgotten that the Alcmaeonidae belonged to that district, whereas the home of Isagoras was well outside the city. Can the reform be understood as giving an advantage to leading men of the city as distinct from leading men of outlying districts? A fully satisfactory answer to this question has not yet been given, but at least two hints can be offered.

One of these concerns the official centers of the ten tribes for conduct of business. With one exception each tribe had a center in the city of Athens; the exception was Hippothontis, which seems to have had its center at Eleusis. Thus the tribal assemblies of nine of the tribes met in the city of Athens; so men of the city could attend more easily and in larger numbers than men of the other trittyes. Such an arrangement would not have been possible, if each tribe had been constructed from a compact block of territory so that some of them would not have held men of the city. It must be admitted that little is heard of political activity in the several tribes, but most of the evidence on transaction of business in Athens refers to the late fifth and fourth centuries; in the few decades immediately following Cleisthenes's work the assemblies of the tribes may have counted for more, before the fifth-century growth of Athenian prosperity and power brought increased activity by the central organs of the state.

The second hint concerns candidatures for office. From 501/0 onwards the Athenians chose each year ten generals (*strategoi*), selecting one from each tribe (*Ar. AP* 22.2; cf. 61.1); the electoral body was the assembly of all Athenian citizens, but the rule of candidature was that there must be one general from each tribe. It is cometimes assumed that the generals originated as commanders of the several tribal regiments, but there is no evidence for this; in Herodotus's account of the battle of Marathon (especially 6.109–110) they appear as staff officers, not regimental officers, and this may have been their function from the beginning of the institution. They were elected as military specialists, but Athenian thought did not distinguish between such work and political activity. It is not clear how far the system adopted in 501/0 was an innovation; whether generals had been elected before, whether they had been elected every year or only occasionally, whether there had been a rule of candidature referring to the four traditional tribes, these are unanswerable questions. But for the present purpose those questions do not matter. The rule of candidature adopted in 501/0 was in appearance eminently fair; if one general was to be drawn from each tribe, every qualified man in Attica, whatever his tribe, had a chance of being elected. But since each tribe had a trittys in the city, men of the city had a chance of being elected to all ten vacancies; and since the electoral body, the public assembly, met in the city, leading men of the city had much more chance of bringing their dependents in adequate numbers to ensure election than leading men from outlying demes. Unfortunately no lists of generals have been preserved for the period immediately following the work of Cleisthenes. The earliest decade for which substantial, though far from complete, lists can be reconstructed is 441/0–432/1; those lists show a preponderance of men belonging to demes in and near the city.

Probably similar considerations apply to the nine archons. Although the name "the nine archons" was kept, the board was increased in number to ten, the additional officer being called "the Secretary of the Thesmothetae." The rule was adopted that one member of the board should be chosen from each of the ten tribes, and this was still observed in the fourth century (Ar. *AP* 55.1). The date of the change is not known, but the easiest conjecture is that it was a consequence, perhaps a part, of the reforms of Cleisthenes. Because of the apparently fair rule of candidature, men of the city had a chance to predominate among the nine archons.

THE REFORMS OF CLEISTHENES: THE COUNCIL OF FIVE HUNDRED[8]

The other new institution introduced by Cleisthenes was the Council of Five Hundred. Its membership was annual and it drew fifty members from each tribe; within the tribes each deme supplied a number of councilors proportionate to its size. Members for the Council were chosen by lot. Eligibility for repeated membership in the Council was restricted; in the fourth century each adult male citizen was allowed only two terms as councilor (Ar. *AP* 62.3), and it may be that at an earlier period only one term was allowed; the rule may have been relaxed if enough volunteers were not forthcoming in a period of financial difficulties, such as the early fourth century. The function of the Council was probouleutic: it prepared business for the public assembly, and no item could come before the assembly unless it had first been considered by the Council. In the middle of the fifth century the Athenian state took to handling much more business than before and created many additional boards of officers; the Council was the sole organ, apart from the assembly itself, which took cognizance of all departments of public business. This does not mean that the Council acquired additional functions of supervising administration and finance; those tasks were a consequence of its basic function of preparing business for the assembly.

Athenian tradition on Cleisthenes said more about the tribal reform than about the Council of Five Hundred. Herodotus (5.66.2; 5.69.2; 6.131.1) mentioned the one but not the other; Aristotle (*AP* 21) summarized in full the structure of the tribes with explanatory comments, but he devoted only one sentence to the Council. It is understandable that memory dwelt more on the tribal system. Henceforth each Athenian's affiliation to a deme was part of his official nomenclature; his membership of a deme, implying membership of a tribe, was recognized in all acts which brought him into contact with the law or with organs of state. But he concerned himself with the Council only if he took an interest in politics. Modern writers have tended to pay more attention to the tribal system than to the Council, because the intricate structure of the former makes it more problematic. Those who accept a Solonian Council of Four Hundred can, though they need not, regard the change made by Cleisthenes in the Council as merely adjusting an old institution to the new tribal system; but if there was no Solonian Council of Four Hundred, as argued above (chapter 5, pp. 120–121) the introduction of the Council of Five Hundred demands explanation.

Aristotle (*Pol.* 4.1299b30–38) thought it obvious that there must be an organ to prepare business for a public assembly, but he considered that the varying composition of such an organ made a difference to the constitution; if, for example, the probouleutic body was small in numbers, the effect would be oligarchic. Indeed, it is easy to imagine that a probouleutic Council was in a position to assert itself and encroach on the assembly's power of making real decisions, provided that it had the talent and the will to do so. But the members of the Council of Five Hundred were not men of any particular talent, since they were chosen by lot. They did not acquire expertise in conciliar business, since each of them held office for only one or at most two annual terms. Further, since the Council had five hundred members, it was too large to be dominated by any one political group. In short the Council was not likely to arrogate to itself influence over real decisions; it served to prepare business for the assembly and because of its composition it would leave real power of decision to the assembly.

The further question may be asked, Who prepared business for the public assembly before the Council of Five Hundred was created? There is no evidence and at least two answers can be suggested. Firstly, it is conceivable that business was prepared by informal groups of powerful and ambitious men; secondly, it may have been prepared by the Council of the Areopagus. In either case the preparatory body probably tried to influence the final decision; members of the Areopagite Council were ambitious, for they had atained the archonship by election, and they gained experience of public business, since they remained members of the Council for life. The introduction of the Council of Five Hundred was important, not only because it provided a probouleutic organ, but also because it excluded any other, more self-assertive body from performing the probouleutic function. If indeed the Council of the Areopagus had customarily prepared business for the assembly, and if, as argued above, in the last years of the sixth century that Council held a weighty group who owed their places to the tyrants and were willing to support Isagoras, then by establishing the Council of Five Hundred Cleisthenes diminished indirectly the functions of the older Council.

It was advantageous to city families, like the Alcmaeonidae, that real decisions should be taken in the assembly without being prejudiced by a strong preparatory body. The assembly met in the city, and therefore leading families residing in or near the city could bring their friends and dependents more easily and in larger numbers than leading families of the more distant parts of Attica. In the second half of the fifth century Cleisthenes was said to have founded the *demokratia* at Athens; Herodotus described him as "the man who established the tribes and the *demokratia* for the Athenians" (6.131.1); and in 411 an amendment to a decree instructed a board "to seek out the ancestral laws which Cleisthenes carried when he established the *demokratia*" (Ar. *AP* 29.3). Such a description of Cleisthenes's work was not wholly unreasonable, in view of the nature and function of the Council of Five Hundred, but the description concealed the irony of history. The introduction of the new Council may have been more decisive than the tribal reform; it may have counted for more in the political struggles of Cleisthenes and in the subsequent development of the Athenian constitution. But it was not the purpose of Cleisthenes to establish *demokratia*; indeed it is unlikely that the word or the notion had been invented in his time. By his reforms Cleisthenes achieved victory in a "regionalist" struggle.

THE TYRANTS AND CLEISTHENES: RETROSPECT[9]

The political slogan current in the time of Cleisthenes was not *demokratia* but probably some compound of *iso-* (= "equal"). Herodotus calls the new order *isegoria*, a word whose etymology refers to equality in speaking. More can be learned from a drinking song composed in honor of Harmodius and Aristogeiton (see note 4); it said that they "killed the tyrant and made Athens *isonomoi*" (= "equal-law"). The meaning of *isonomia* approximates to "equality before the law;" it is a condition in which all citizens have equal political opportunities, and this is contrasted with the arbitrary rule of Peisistratus and his sons.

Not that the Athenian tyrants had been particularly arbitrary. They had kept the former laws in force. As is often conjectured, Peisistratus may have redistributed some land, especially that of opponenets who had gone into exile; if so, that was perhaps his most arbitrary action. But redistribution of land for similar reasons seems to have followed the overthrow of Hippias. At least Herodotus says (6.121) that Callias bought up the property of Peisistratus at public auction when Peisistratus was expelled from Athens. Study of Callias's descendants shows that he was active not in the age of Peisistratus but in that of Cleisthenes; doubtless he bought up the property of the tyrant's family when Hippias was expelled from Athens. If the Peisistratidae had been restored after the time of Cleisthenes and had established a permanent regime, later Athenians would have called the Alcmaeonidae tyrants and the Peisistratidae liberators.

Athenian tradition on Peisistratus and his sons was ambiguous. Herodotus, Thucydides and Aristotle spoke favorably of their rule. On the other hand, the account reaching them tried to say that the Alcmaeonidae freed Athens from oppression by Hippias. Yet another tradition stressed the part played by Harmodius and Aristogeiton: statues of them were set up on the acropolis and their descendants received public honors. There were many interests to be reconciled in post-Cleisthenic Athens.

Seen from a distance, the issues between the Peisistratidae and the Alcmaeonidae take on a different significance. The choice for Athens was not between tyranny and liberation; indeed there was very little choice. Peisistratus and Cleisthenes, each pursuing his own purposes, in fact fostered a greater sense of unity among the Athenians. Peisistratus gave more meaning to membership of the Athenian state by internal measures, such as taxation, festivals and buildings, and by launching a self-assertive foreign policy; Cleisthenes achieved decisive victory for the city district in the "regionalist" struggle and weakened drastically the local associations, whence his rivals had drawn loyalty. Ever since the completion of formal unification in the seventh century the city district had had an advantage, because there the organs of the state were located. Not that the outcome of the "regionalist" struggle was predetermined. It would have been different, for example, if Peisistratus had led a separatist movement in eastern Attica, instead of making himself master of Athens. But there was little chance that an ambitious man would be content to rule in an independent Brauron. The outcome of the "regionalist" struggle was not predetermined but nearly so.

NOTES

1. The main sources on Peisistratus and his sons are: Hdt. 1.59–64; 5.55–65; 5.94–95; Thuc. 1.20.2; 6.54–59; Ar. *AP* 13–19. For the fragments of the inscribed archon list see Meiggs/ Lewis 6. Valuable discussion of politics and chronology is provided by Wade-Gery, *Essays* 155–170 = "Miltiades," *JHS* 71 (1951) 212–221. The fortunes of Cimon are given by Hdt. 6.103; cf. 6.39.1. For Anacreon and Simonides see Pseudo-Plat. *Hipparch.* 228c; for Lasus see Hdt. 7.6.3. On the Greater Panathenaea and rhapsodic competitions there the main evidence is: Pherecydes *F.Gr.Hist.* I 3F2 = Marcellinus, *Life of Thucydides* 3; Pseudo-Plat. *Hipparch.* 228b; Cic. *de orat.* 3.137; for discussion see Sealey, *REG* 70 (1957) 342–351; J.A. Davison, "Notes on the Panathenaea," *JHS* 78 (1958) 23–42. On the possibility of some redistribution of land during the tyranny see D.M. Lewis, *Historia* 12 (1963) 37 note 136. For the family of Peisistratus see Table A, p. 166.

2. On the date when Miltiades I founded the settlement in the Cheronese see D.W. Bradeen, *Hesperia* 32 (1963) 194 note 33. D.M. Lewis, *Historia* 12 (1963) 25 and 27, argues that Miltiades I did not belong to Brauron; he notes that Miltiades was sitting at the door of his house in or near Laciadae, when the Dolonci arrived, and he suggests that Cleisthenes tried to annoy the clan of Philaidae by giving their name to a distant deme in Brauron and thus fostering the cult of Philaeus far away from Laciadae. But it is not easy to see why a clan should be annoyed when a man made its name and its eponymous ancestor more widely known. On fourth-century import of grain see Dem. 20.31–32; A.H.M. Jones, *Athenian Democracy* (Oxford 1957) 77–78.

3. On the war with Megara for Salamis see Solon fr. 2; Hdt. 1.59.4; Plut. *Sol.* 8–12; there is chronological confusion in Plutarch's account. On Athenian participation in the First Sacred War see Aeschin. 3.107–112; Plut. *Sol.* 11; ways in which the Delphic oracle may have offended the Athenians were suggested by W.G. Forrest, "The First Sacred War," *BCH* 80 (1956) 33–52, especially 34–44. The view that the Athenians fought two wars for Sigeum, one late in the seventh century and one in the time of Peisistratus, rests on the "high" dating of the Cypselidae; see chapter 2, pp. 53–54. On Lygdamis see D.M. Leahy, The Spartan Embassy to Lygdamis, *JHS* 77 (1957) 272–275.

4. The date of the Athenian alliance with Plataea is given by Thuc. 3.68.5; it has been doubted; for discussion and defense see Joseph Wells, *Studies in Herodotus* (Osford 1923), 81–86; the objections are not decisive and there is no strong consideration in favor of the alternative date suggested, namely 509. The conspiracy of Harmodius and Aristogeiton is given by Hdt. 5.55–56; Thuc. 1.20.2; 6.54–59; Ar. *AP* 18. Thucydides gives his account as a correction and refutation of a version popular in Athens; the popular version is known only in part from a *skolion* or drinking song current in the fifth century (easily accessible in Oxford Book of Greek Verse, No. 230), and it does not coincide with the account of Herodotus or with that of Aristotle. Hence there is a tantalizing problem of source criticism; see C.W. Fornara, "The 'Tradition' about the Murder of Hipparchus," *Historia* 17 (1968) 400–424, where references are given to earlier discussions; see also Fornara, "Hellanicus and an Alcmaeonid Tradition," *Historia* 17 (1968) 381–383. On the Gephyraei see Sealey, *Essays* 193 = *BICS* 7 (1960) 38. The affair of Leipsydrium is given by Hdt. 5.62.2;

Ar. *AP* 19.3. For the Athenian decree about Salamis see Meiggs/Lewis 14. On Megara and the date of Anchimolius's expedition see Wade-Gery, *Essays* 161 note 2 = *JHS* 71 (1951) 216 note 19.

5. On the local origin of Isagoras see D.M. Lewis, *Historia* 12 (1963) 25–26. The cult of Zeus Carius in Icaria is known from I.G. I², 186.

6. Wade-Gery, in *Essays* 135–154 = "The Laws of Kleisthenes," *CQ* 27(1933) 17–29 showed that Aristotle drew his narrative on Cleisthenes from Herodotus. He also claimed that documentary evidence on the reforms was available to the Atthidographers; for in 411, when a decree was passed setting up a board of thirty to draft legislation, Cleitophon added a rider requiring the board to seek out the laws of Cleisthenes (Ar. *AP* 29.2–3). But people can seek for things without finding them. That Isagoras was archon in 508/7 is known from Dion. Hal., *Rom. Antiq.* 1.74.6; 5.1.1. On the date of the archonship of Hermocreon, when the Council first swore its oath, see T.J. Cadoux, *JHS* 68 (1948) 115–116; Hignett, *HAC* 337.

7. Hignett, *HAC* 124–142, in discussing the reforms of Cleisthenes seems to fall back in despair on a hypothesis of promoting unity by bringing men of different districts together. D.W. Bradeen, "The Trittyes in Cleisthenes' Reforms," *TAPA* 86 (1955) 22–30, recognized that the real peculiarity of the new tribes was the inclusion of some men of the city in each, and he saw that this affected candidatures for the generalship. The view offered here is based on Sealey, *Essays* 9–38 = "Regionalism in Archaic Athens," *Historia* 9 (1960) 155–180. An alternative view, based on a valuable study of the trittyes, is offered by D.M. Lewis, "Cleisthenes and Attica," *Historia* 12 (1963) 22–40; see Appendix A to this chapter. C.W.J. Eliot, in *Coastal Demes of Attika: A Study of the Policy of Kleisthenes* (Toronto 1962) and "Kleisthenes and the Creation of the Ten Phylai," *Phoenix* 22 (1958) 3–17, has drawn useful conclusions from a detailed study of demes but makes too little allowance for the partisan character of the reforms. The same criticism may be brought against the thesis of A.G. Woodhead, "*Isegoria* and the Council of 500," *Historia* 16 (1967) 129–140; he claims that "Cleisthenes' geographical basis for his reform had thus nothing to do with local landlords and local pressures" (page 138); he attributes to the Council an authority for which there is no evidence. On the tribes in early Rome see H. Last, "The Servian Reforms," *JRS* 35 (1945) 30–48. On demes in Attica before the reforms of Cleisthenes see A.E. Raubitschek, *Dedications from the Athenian Akropolis* (Cambridge, Mass. 1949) 467–478. On Cleisthenes's possible concern for recent settlers see D. Kagan, "The Enfranchisement of Aliens by Cleisthenes," *Historia* 12 (1963) 41–46. Authenticity of the vote allegedly taken after the fall of the tyranny about illegitimate encroachment on citizenship has been doubted by Jacoby, *F.Gr.Hist.* IIIb (Supplement) I, 158–160. For the lists of generals 441/0–432/1 see Hill, *Sources* 401–402; cf. Sealey, *Essays* 86–88 = *PACA* 1 (1958) 72–73. R.S. Stroud, "Tribal Boundary Markers from Corinth," *CSCA* 1 (1968) 233–242, suggests that Corinth may have had trittyes, but the evidence is not yet decisive. Two decrees of the tribe Hippothontis (*I.G.* II², 1149 and 1153) have been found at Eleusis; this suggests that the assembly of that tribe met there. A different approach to the work of Cleisthenes is attempted by P. Leveque and P. Vidal-Naquet, Clisthène l'Athénien (Paris 1964).

8. The probouleutic rule, that no item should be brought before the assembly unless it had first been discussed by the Council, is given by Plut. *Sol.*19.1; Plutarch speaks there of the Solonian Council of Four Hundred.

9. On the meaning of *isonomia* see M. Ostwald, *Nomos and the Beginnings of the Athenian Democracy* (Oxford 1969) 96–136; he argues convincingly that *isonomia* "is not a name for a form of government but for the principle of political equality" (p. 97; cf. p. 113 on equality of political opportunity). For the family of Callias see Table C on p. 168. On the statues of Harmodius and Aristogeiton and honors for their descendants see F. Jacoby, *Atthis* (Oxford 1949) 339 note 52; the original statues were removed by the Persians and new ones were set up in 477/6.

APPENDIX A

CLEISTHENES, THE TRITTYES AND THE COUNCIL

Two important studies suggest further lines of approach towards understanding the work of Cleisthenes; they are D.M. Lewis, "Cleisthenes and Attica," *Historia* 12 (1963) 22–40, and P.J. Bicknell, "Kleisthenes as Politician: An Exploration," in *Studies in Athenian Politics and Genealogy* (= *Historia Einzelschriften* Heft 19 [1972] 1–53, cf. Historia 23 (1974) 161 and 163. Lewis has examined the layout of trittyes in some detail. Usually each trittys held a connected parcel of territory, but Lewis draws attention to some anomalies. Two of these are especially revealing. The first concerns the coastal trittys of the tribe Pandionis. Most of this trittys lay in a block south of Brauron; but the deme Probalinthos, just south of Marathon, belonged to the same trittys, although separated from it by the coastal trittys of the tribe Aegeis. This anomaly can be explained. There was a much older unit, the Tetrapolis, consisting of the adjacent villages of Marathon, Oenoe, Trikorythos and Probalinthos; this continued to perform religious functions; indeed as late as the first century B.C., on occasions when the Athenian state sent the sacred deputation called the Pythais to Delphi, the Marathonian Tetrapolis sent its own separate envoys. Cleisthenes created a trittys consisting of Rhamnous, a township further north, and of Marathon, Oenoe and Trikorythos; this was the coastal trittys of the tribe Aeantis and took the old name Tetrapolis. But in assigning demes to trittyes Cleisthenes detached Probalinthos from the old Tetrapolis and allocated it to the more distant trittys of the tribe Pandionis. The district of Marathon had Peisistratid connections; the anomaly surely reveals a desire to prevent the old Tetrapolis from retaining political significance. It is to be noted that Probalinthos was not assigned to the adjacent trittys of the tribe Aegeis; that trittys held Brauron.

The second anomaly concerns the deme Hecale. This lay on the road from Athens to Marathon, probably in the north-northwest part of Mount Pentelicum. The neighboring trittyes were the interior trittyes of the tribes Aegeis, Cecropis and Antiochis. Hecale was not assigned to any of these but to the interior trittys of the tribe Leontis; the bulk of that trittys lay on the eastern slopes of Mount Parnes and within the northwestern extension of the central plain. Hecale had a festival, Hecalesia, celebrated by the villages around it, and there are hints of other archaic cult associations in the neighborhood. Evidently Cleisthenes wished to prevent the villages from remaining associated in the new political structure. It should not be forgotten that his rival Isagoras probably came from Icaria, which lay on Mount Pentelicum and was assigned to the interior trittys of Aegeis.

Lewis discerns two purposes in the tribal reform of Cleisthenes: "The two things which emerge most clearly are an attack on organisations which held a locality by religious ties, some of them in areas attached to political opponents of Cleisthenes, and an attempt to unify Attica by making men from different areas work and fight together" (p. 37). The first purpose is illustrated by the recognizable anomalies. As for the second purpose suggested, it can well be imagined that the new tribes had the effect of bringing together men from different parts of Attica for public service and thus achieving a greater degree of unification; it does not necessarily follow that that was the aim of the tripartite composition of the tribes. Indeed, consideration of the place of the Alcmaeonidae in the new scheme may suggest something.

In the fifth century Alcmaeonidae are attested as members of three demes in the city trittyes of three tribes, Alopece (tribe Antiochis), Agryle (Erechtheis), Xypete (Cecropis). It cannot be supposed that Cleisthenes tried to break down the power of his own clan by dividing it between different tribes; on the contrary, one may suspect that the influence of the Alcmaeonidae was somehow strengthened through being thus distributed. Lewis offers an explanation: "The Alcmeonids possessed no important local cult of their own that we know of. Their power rested solely on land and wealth, which they buttressed by looking outside Athens to Delphi, Sicyon and Lydia" (p. 37). "The trittys-lines were drawn to leave Alcmeonids in at least three different tribes, a result which might well prove fatal to a family which depended for influence on the control of a local cult, but which could be positively welcomed by a family of land and wealth which acquired the opportunity to have a hand in the affairs of three of the new tribes" (p. 39). As Lewis admits, there is only the argument from silence for saying that the Alcmaeonidae did not control an important local cult; the argument from silence has some force, since more is recorded about the Alcmaeonidae than about any other Athenian clan, but in any case a different explanation springs to mind. A group with a strong sense of cohesion might find its influence enhanced by being spread through several trittyes in or near the city, provided that the tripartite structure of the tribes was designed to increase the power of the men of the city.

The work of Bicknell concerns the position of the Council of Five Hundred and of its subdivisions, which depended on the Cleisthenic system of tribes, trittyes and demes. Lists inscribed in the fourth century show in the case of most demes how many councilors were drawn from each deme, and it appears that the number of councilors drawn from any one deme was almost constant; it did not vary from year to year by more than one. Historians have often assumed that Cleisthenes assigned places in the Council to the different demes in approximate proportion to their size. Bicknell has devised a way of testing this assumption. He worked from lists of all Athenians whose deme affiliation is known from the time of Cleisthenes until 1 B.C. Since the period covered is long, and since the Athenians of known deme affiliation are a random selection, one may suppose that, within each tribe, the proportions between the numbers of known Athenians of the different demes offer a rough guide to the proportions actually obtaining between the sizes of the demes. Since each tribe supplied fifty councilors, from the proportions between the totals of known Athenians of the different demes within any one tribe Bicknell could estimate the number of councilors to be expected from each of those demes.

Because of the imprecision inherent in working from a random selection of Athenians, Bicknell supposed that, in the case of any one deme, a difference of only one between the number of councilors to be expected on the basis of his calculation and the actual number attested in inscribed lists of the fourth century was not significant. He was able to make the comparison for 115 demes. He found that in 75.5% of these the difference between the expected number of councilors and the actual number was nothing or insignificant, but in the remaining 24.5% of the demes the difference was two, three or four.

Bicknell paid further attention to those 24.5% of the demes which showed the anomalies. The figures for the demes of the tribe Aeantis proved to be suggestive. Three of its coastal demes, Marathon, Rhamnous and Trikorythos, each had two fewer councilors than were to be expected; Peisistratid connections may be suspected in these demes. On the other hand, the interior trittys of the tribe Aeantis had only one deme, Aphidna, and this deme had four more councilors than were to be expected. Aphidna was the place of origin of Harmodius and Aristogeiton, the assassins of Hipparchus, and so its demesmen may well have had anti-Peisistratid sentiments. In general, where the number of councilors drawn from a deme differed from the number to be expected, Cleisthenes probably pursued a partisan purpose, and Bicknell concluded by asking (p. 45): "Are we on the point of running Kleisthenes the faction politician to earth, or does he remain as elusive as ever?"

Bicknell's findings are undoubtedly illuminating. They become more so on the basis of a further assumption which he made. By the middle of the fifth century the Council of Five Hundred was divided into ten parts, called prytanies; each prytany consisted of the fifty councilors drawn from one tribe and was on duty for a tenth of the year (see below, chapter 11, p. 299). The date of the introduction of this practice is uncertain; some historians hold that it was begun shortly before the middle of the fifth century, perhaps in connection with the reforms of Ephialtes; others, including Bicknell, think that it was instituted by

Cleisthenes in the course of his reforms. If the latter view is correct, then it was patently important to Cleisthenes that his potential opponents should not constitute a majority among the fifty councilors drawn from one tribe.

A further point deserves to be made in relation to Bicknell's findings. The 24.5% of demes, in which anomalies were apparent, merited attention and revealed something about the purposes of Cleisthenes. It is to be presumed that in the other 75.5% of demes Cleisthenes achieved his purposes without having recourse to anomalous distribution of places in the Council among the demes. This comes close to saying that the peculiar feature of Cleisthenes's tribal system, its tripartite structure, was well designed to achieve his partisan aims.

APPENDIX B TO CHAPTER 6

OSTRACISM

By the procedure of ostracism in the fifth century an Athenian could be made to leave Attica for ten years without any cause being stated. Each year in the sixth prytany the assembly was asked whether it wished to hold an *ostrakophoria* that year. If it replied affirmatively, a special meeting was held later in which each voter cast a potsherd on which he had written the name of the man whom he would most wish to leave Attica. For the ostracism to be valid at least 6,000 votes had to be cast at the meeting. The person receiving the largest number of adverse votes had to leave Attica for ten years, but his property was not confiscated and after ten years he could return and enjoy full rights.

Aristotle (*AP* 22.1) says that the law of ostracism was authored by Cleisthenes. He also says (*AP* 22.3–4) that the first ostracism was held in 488/7. Until recently it was believed that a quotation from Androtion (*F.Gr.Hist.* IIIB324F6), given by Harpocration, said that the law of ostracism was first passed towards 488/7. But further study of the manuscripts of Harpocration has cast doubt on the text of the quotation; it is indeed likely that on the origin of ostracism Androtion said the same as Aristotle, who may well have drawn the information from him (see J.J. Keaney, "The Text of Androtion F6 and the Origin of Ostracism," *Historia* 19 [1970] 1–11).

Yet the attribution of the origin of ostracism to Cleisthenes is puzzling. Since Cleisthenes is not known to have been active after 500, it is strange that the first recorded ostrakophoria was held as late as 488/7. Modern attempts to find a purpose for ostracism in harmony with Cleisthenes's known reforms have not been successful. Moreover, the fourth-century tradition on the origin of ostracism was not uniform. Theophrastus, a pupil of Aristotle, attributed the institu-

Ostraka from the Ceramicus. More than 4300 ostraka were discovered by the German Archaeo-logical Institute in the Ceramicus in 1966–67. UPPER LEFT: *two ostraka, inscribed "Megacles son of Hippocrates" and "Themistocles Phrearrios." Megacles was ostracized in 486. Since both sherds were broken from the same vase, they were probably both cast on the same occasion, perhaps in 486 (see page 185).* UPPER RIGHT; *two ostraka, broken from a single vase and cast against Themistocles and Cimon.* LOWER LEFT; *ostrakon cast against Callias son of Cratius, who was probably an Alcmaeonid ostracized in 485 (see Bicknell, Studies in Athenian Politics and Genealogy 64–76).* LOWER RIGHT: *fragment of an ostrakon inscribed "Menon, son of Mene-cleides, of the deme Gargettos"; although only a small part of this ostrakon is preserved, the full nomenclature of Menon can be restored, since more than 200 ostraka cast against him have been found.* [Courtesy Deutsches Archaeologisches Institut, Athens.]

tion to the legendary king Theseus. His divergence from Aristotle suggests that there was no decisive evidence available. The origin of the institution remains uncertain.

Aristotle (*AP* 22.3–7) specifies several ostracisms held in the 480s, and some others held later in the fifth century are known. The last was that of Hyperbolus, held probably in 416/5 (chapter 13, p. 353). Thereafter the procedure remained technically available but was not in fact used.

(For an introduction to the problem see Hignett, *HAC* 159–166. The quorum of 6,000 is known from Plut. *Arist.* 7.6. Philochorus, *F.Gr.Hist.* IIIB328F30, as quoted by Byzantine writers, says that 6,000 votes against a single victim were required for a valid ostracism, but Plutarch may have preserved Philochorus's information more accurately. Theophrastus's view is known from Theophr. *Char.* 26.6; Euseb. *Chron.* p. 50; schol. Aristeid. XLVI, 241, 9–11; *Suda*, s.v. Theseioisin = schol. Aristoph. *Plut.* 627; *Suda*, s.v. Arche Skyria; Eustath. I, p. 782, 52ff. Numerous ostraka have been recovered by excavation; see Meiggs/Lewis 21, and E. Vanderpool, *Ostracism at Athens* [Semple Lectures, University of Cincinnati 1970]. A full survey of the problem is provided by R. Thomsen, *The Origin of Ostracism. A Synthesis* [Copenhagen, 1972]. A brief note in a Byzantine manuscript of the fifteenth century A.D. says that ostracism originally was conducted before the Council and later transferred to the assembly [J.J. Keaney and A.E. Raubitschek, "A Late Byzantine Account of Ostracism," *AJP* 93 (1972) 87–91]; but the other historical entries in the manuscript do not inspire any confidence in its value.)

Table A: The Peisistratidae

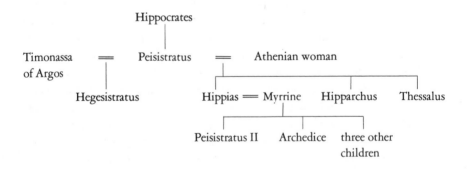

The main sources for the stemma are: Hdt. 1.59.1–3; 1.61.3; 5.55; 5.94.1; Thuc. 6.54.6; 6.55.1; 6.59.3; Ar. *AP* 17.3–4. On the sons of Peisistratus note that (1) the text of Aristotle says that Thessalus was another name of Hegesistratus, but the clause is probably interpolated (C.W. Fornara, The "Tradition" about the Murder of Hipparchus, Historia 17 [1968] 400–424); (2) Aristotle says that Timonassa bore Peisistratus two sons, Iophon and Hegesistratus; (3) among the three sons of Peisistratus and an Athenian woman, Hippias was the oldest, but it is not known whether Hipparchus was older than Thessalus.

The real problem about the family of Peisistratus is to discover the order of his marriages. The marriage to the daughter of Megacles was childless and of brief duration (Hdt. 1.60.2–1.61.2); it is tied to the second tyranny towards 556. As Herodotus remarks, at the time of that marriage Peisistratus already had legitimate children; they were probably the sons of the Athenian wife, not of the Argive, since the context implies that they would be Peisistratus's heirs, whereas Herodotus (5.94.1) calls Hegesistratus illegitimate because his mother was not Athenian. Likewise there are reasons to suppose that Hippias was born about 570 (see above, p. 136). But Hegesistratus was old enough to be put in charge of Sigeum when Peisistratus captured it; the capture led to a "long" war with the Mytilenaeans, and this was brought to an end by Periander (Hdt. 5.94–95). Periander can scarcely have been alive after 540, since the Corinthian expedition against Samos, undertaken about 525, occurred a generation later than his dealings with Corcyra (Hdt. 3.48.1). If accordingly Hegesistratus was established in Sigeum ca. 550 or a few years later, it is likely that Peisistratus's marriage to Timonassa preceded his marriage to the mother of Hippias. The alternative hypothesis, that Timonassa was the second wife of Peisistratus, would imply that Hippias was very old indeed at the battle of Marathon. (See also Davies, *APF* 444–455).

Table B: The Philaidae and the Cimonidae

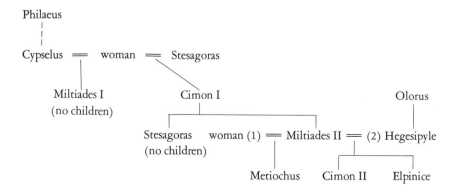

The main part of the stemma depends on Hdt. 6.35.1; 6.38.1; 6.39.1; 6.41.2; 6.103.1. For Cimon II and Elpinice see Plut. *Cim.* 4.1–3. Pherecydes, *F.Gr.Hist.* I 3F2 = Marcellinus, *Life of Thucydides* 3, traces the descent of the Philaidae as far as Miltiades I; the text is corrupt but shows that Hippocleides the archon of 566/5 was a relative, perhaps a cousin, of Miltiades. See also Wade-Gery, *Essays* 164 note 3 = *JHS* 71 (1951) 218 note 29; Davies, *APF* 293–312.

Table C: The Callias-Hipponicus family

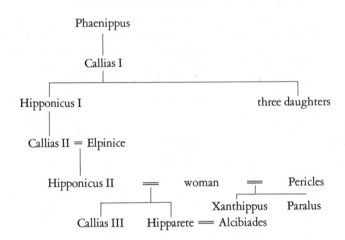

The stemma depends mainly on Hdt. 6.121–122; Plut. Cim. 4.8; Plut. *Per.* 24.8 (on which see K. J. Beloch, *Griechische Geschichte* II², 2 [1913], 35 and 44–45); Plat. *Protag.* 314e; Plut. *Alc.* 8.3–6. Approximate dates of activity may be inferred from the marriages of Callias II and of Hipparete and from the following data: (1) Callias III should be identified with the Callias son of Hipponicus who served as envoy to Sparta in 371 (Xen. *Hell.* 6.3.2–9); (2) Callias II went on an embassy to Artaxerxes at Susa (Hdt. 7.151) and should perhaps be identified with the Callias who helped to negotiate peace with Sparta in 446 (Diod. 12.7). The notorious wealth of the family is mentioned by Andoc. 1.130; Lys. 19.48; Isoc. 16.31. See also Davies, *APF* 254–270.

7

Persia and Greece I:
The Designs of the Persians

In 612 the Assyrian capital of Nineveh was sacked by the forces of the Medes and the Babylonians. This was one of the decisive military actions of antiquity. Previously the Assyrians had built up the first systematically organized empire to dominate the Near East, but their power collapsed with the fall of Nineveh, and for about half a century afterwards control of the Near East was divided between four powers. One of these, Lydia, came to hold most of Asia Minor west of the Halys river; it had frequent dealings with Greek cities and will therefore require attention below. Another, Egypt, experienced a revival under the Saite dynasty (663–525) after centuries of obscurity. Lower Mesopotamia was held by the Neo-Babylonian or Chaldaean Empire. The fourth power, the Medes, had brought together many of the tribes of Iran into a warlike kingdom; after the fall of the Assyrians the Medes ruled Upper Mesopotamia and Syria, as well as Iran; their fortunes were to be decisive for the future.

One of the tribes of Iran was the Persians, who inhabited the district of Anshan. They were closely akin in language to the Medes. They began their advance to imperial rule under Cyrus, who belonged to the Achaemenid dynasty and became their king in 559. In 550 Cyrus defeated Astyages, the king of the Medes, and thus he secured the Median Empire for the Persians. He made further conquests; in particular he overcame Lydia by warfare ca. 544, and in 539 he gained Babylon, where the populace rose against its own dynasty and welcomed

him. The power thus emerging is called the Persian Empire. But although the
dynasty was Persian, the senior administrators, provincial governors and chief
military commanders were drawn both from Persians and from Medes. The
Persian Empire was the rule of Medes and Persians over a great variety of subject
peoples.

Through the conquest of Lydia the Persians came into contact with Greek
cities. These relations grew until the Persians tried to conquer European Greece.
This and the next chapter will attempt to trace the development of Persian
purposes towards Greeks, to observe the way Greeks responded, and to note the
organization which some of them consequently formed to embrace many cities.

IONIA AND LYDIA[1]

It is often asserted that Ionia was more prosperous and more highly developed
than much of Greece in the seventh and sixth centuries. The reasons for believing
this are good, though somewhat indirect. There was good and extensive land for
agriculture in mainland Ionia and in some of the offshore islands. The dialect of
the Homeric poems is predominantly Ionian, although it includes forms from
other dialects which probably come from an earlier stage in the development of
the epic technique. Moreover, some of the similes in the poems strongly suggest
that they were composed in Ionia. The first of the Greek scientists, Thales, who
predicted a solar eclipse of 585, came from Miletus; so did his successors,
Anaximander and Anaximenes. All but one of the Greek cities using the
settlement of Naucratis in Egypt belonged to the Asiatic mainland and offshore
islands. Some sophistication of political development is suggested by an inscription of ca. 575–ca. 550 from Chios; it mentions *bole he demosie*, and although the
phrase allows more than one interpretation (see chapter 5, p. 120), the presence
of the distinguishing epithet suggests that Chios had other comparable organs
besides this council. Otherwise not much is known of constitutional innovations. Miletus, the leading city of the mainland, had a tyrant, Thrasybulus, but
little is recorded of him beyond his friendship with Periander and his war with
Lydia. Afterwards Miletus suffered civil strife for a long time, but at last a
settlement was mediated by men from Paros, and then Miletus achieved a higher
level of prosperity than ever before.

The thesis that Ionia was more advanced than European Greece has been
challenged on the basis of a study of colonization. It has been argued that the
Milesian settlements on the coast of the Black Sea were not founded until long
after the first major colonies in Sicily; it might be inferred that the economy of
Ionia did not advance sufficiently to cause colonization until much later than that
of cities like Chalcis and Corinth. It must be admitted that from archaeological
evidence the Black Sea colonies cannot be proved to be earlier than the late

seventh century. But many cities of Asiatic Ionia held the alluvial plains of major rivers; in such extensive land population could expand much further than in European Greece before pressure on local resources precipitated colonization. A political fact seems conclusive about the power of Miletus; under Thrasybulus that city emerged successfully from a war of twelve years against Lydia.

The resources of the Lydian kingdom included gold, silver and electrum, a natural alloy of both metals. By overthrowing the previous ruler and making himself monarch instead, Gyges (ca. 685–652) made the kingdom much more effective than before; the Mermnad dynasty, which he founded, apparently filled a power vacuum. Its relations with the Greek cities of the Asiatic mainland were in part hostile; Gyges himself raided Miletus and Smyrna and captured the citadel of Colophon, and his successors continued this policy. Eventually the practice of raiding was replaced by a more permanent relationship, whereby the Greek cities paid annual tribute to the Lydian kings; such an agreement was achieved, at the latest, under Croesus, the fifth and last member of the dynasty, and was evidently more convenient for both parties. But Miletus won better status; it resisted Sadyattes and Alyattes, the third and fourth members of the dynasty, in a war of twelve years and finally concluded an alliance with the Lydians.

Yet in some ways the Lydian kingdom was beneficial to the Greeks. Several of the kings made dedications at Greek shrines; tradition said that Gyges himself made such dedications at Delphi, and those of Croesus at Delphi were outstandingly valuable. This practice suggests a generally philhellenic attitude. Stories were later told of visits by famous Greeks, such as the Athenians Solon and Alcmeon, to Croesus, and although some of the stories may be exaggerated or even wholly fictitious, they presuppose that Greeks could travel freely in Lydia. Accordingly, the wealth of the kingdom, which most impressed the Greek imagination, was important as providing an opportunity for Greek commercial enterprise. The extent of the kingdom was important to Greeks for the same reason. In 585 Alyattes concluded a war of six years with the Medes; now and perhaps previously the Halys river was recognized as the boundary between the Median and the Lydian kingdoms. Possibly not all districts on the mainland west of the Halys had been reduced to subject status yet, but that process was completed by Croesus. Ionian prosperity in the first half of the sixth century was due in part to maritime trade and in part to intercourse with the Lydian monarchy.

THE PERSIANS AND THE GREEKS OF ASIA[2]

War broke out between Croesus and Cyrus ca. 544. After an indecisive battle east of the Halys river Croesus withdrew to Sardis, expecting to postpone further engagements until the next year. But Cyrus followed him to Sardis and defeated his forces there; then he captured the city after a siege of fourteen days. Thus the Persians gained formal control of Lydia; the operations of the next few years brought them into contact with Greek cities.

When Cyrus first marched against Croesus, he sent messages to the latter's Ionian subjects and urged them to rebel. So at least Herodotus says, and the report is credible. After the overthrow of Croesus the Ionians and Aeolians sent envoys to Cyrus, while he was still at Sardis, and asked him to accept them as subjects on the same conditions as Croesus had observed towards them. Cyrus renewed the special status which the later Lydian kings had granted to Miletus, but he refused to make any undertaking to the other cities. He stayed in Sardis only a short time and then marched for Ecbatana in Media; he appointed a Persian, Tabalus, to govern in Sardis, but he entrusted the treasury of the former Lydian kingdom to a Lydian called Pactyes. The latter promptly raised a revolt of the Lydians; he also visited the Greek cities of the coast and gained help from them. The combined forces besieged Tabalus in Sardis. Cyrus received the news while he was still marching upcountry and he sent additional troops against the revolt. Pactyes withdrew at their approach and the Persians recovered Lydia. Then they attacked the Ionian cities of the mainland severally. At Priene they killed the men and enslaved the women and children. They plundered the plain of the Maeander river and Magnesia. They reduced most of the cities by besieging them and building earthworks. Half the inhabitants of Phocaea fled by sea and tried to settle in Corsica; the people of Teos fled to Thrace and founded Abdera there. After overcoming Ionia the Persian forces proceeded to the southwestern part of Asia Minor, where they reduced the Carians and others; the Dorian city of Cnidus yielded without resisting.

These operations must have taken a few years; the Persians reduced the Greek cities of the Asiatic mainland by ca. 540, but Miletus continued to enjoy its privileged status. During the conquest atrocities were committed at some cities, as noted above, but not necessarily at all. The main burden imposed by Persian rule was payment of annual tribute. In addition the Persians commonly supported a tyrant in each Greek city; thus they had someone to call to account for the city's behavior. The severity of Persian rule should not be exaggerated. Even so, the behavior of the Greek cities of Asia during the conquest indicates that they preferred the Lydians; and Greek writers never remembered any Persian king with the warmth and favor they showed for Croesus.

Cyrus died in 530. His son and successor, Cambyses, devoted himself to conquering Egypt, which he invaded successfully in 525. After securing Egypt he began to consider plans for further expansion against Carthage and other places, and for these purposes he counted on the Phoenician fleet, although in the event the Phoenicians proved unwilling to sail against Carthage, as it was their own foundation. The Phoenicians had submitted voluntarily to Persian rule and probably they offered their submission to Cambyses, not to Cyrus. Theirs was the best naval contingent at the disposal of the Persian Empire. The Persians had carried out the conquest of Asia Minor without using a fleet. Their acquisition of Phoenicia might eventually be significant for people dwelling on the European shores of the Aegean.

Cambyses died in 522 after a revolt had begun in Iran. A complex series of rebellions followed; the ruler who emerged successfully from the struggles was the usurper Darius, who came of a collateral branch of the Achaemenid dynasty. Darius consolidated the Empire by further campaigns and administrative measures; under him it reached its widest extent, stretching as far as northwest India. One of these campaigns calls for note, since it has a bearing on Darius's intentions towards Europe. Perhaps in 514 Darius led an expedition against the Scythians. For this purpose a bridge was built across the Bosporus; in addition, the naval contingents drawn from the Greek cities of Asia Minor sailed under their tyrants through the Black Sea to the Danube and built a bridge across that river. Darius led his expeditionary force through Thrace and across the Danube bridge; then he advanced through Scythian territory. But the Scythians retreated ahead of his advance and, as they proceeded, they destroyed the fodder and fouled the wells in the country; they harassed the Persian troops and foraging parties by guerrilla methods. Darius had to retire to the Danube bridge and then complete his retreat. But the Scythian campaign brought at least one material advance for the Persian Empire; in consequence of it Darius established a satrapy or province in Thrace.

Herodotus (1.169.2) says that, when the Persians conquered mainland Ionia after the revolt of Pactyes, the Ionians of the islands took fright and offered their submission to Cyrus. This statement is misleading. Possibly some of the islanders opened friendly relations with Cyrus or his officers, but they had no need to subject themselves to the Persian Empire, until it acquired a fleet sufficient for operations in the Aegean. Details are recorded for one of the islands, Samos, and they show a complex development.

Samos came under the rule of the tyrant Polycrates ca. 540. He pursued a forward policy, practicing piracy and attacking many islands and cities of the mainland; he fought a successful war wagainst the Milesians and inflicted a heavy defeat at sea on their allies, the Lesbians. For a time he maintained friendly relations with Amasis of Egypt. Under Polycrates Samos became the strongest naval power in the Aegean. He may have taken advantage of a development in naval engineering. Probably in his time the trireme was invented; it was swifter and more powerful than the penteconter. At least Herodotus says at one point that Polycrates maintained a fleet of a hundred penteconters but elsewhere that he sent forty triremes to help Cambyses in the expedition against Egypt. Samian refugees, fleeing from Polycrates, persuaded Sparta and Corinth to send an expedition against him ca. 525, but although the force landed in Samos, it had to withdraw after besieging the city for forty days.

The growth of Persian power might become a more formidable threat. Perhaps Polycrates saw this; that would explain why he sent ships to help Cambyses. Towards 522 Oroetes, the satrap who resided at Sardis and governed Lydia, conceived a desire to conquer Samos; by thus enlarging the Empire he might find favor with Cambyses. So he enticed Polycrates to the mainland to confer with him; then he slew Polycrates and crucified his corpse. But before Oroetes could pursue his design further, Cambyses was overthrown, Darius established himself, and the new king had Oroetes assassinated.

On the death of Polycrates control of Samos passed to his secretary, Maeandrius. A little while later Darius took up the plan to conquer Samos and sent a special force for this task. Meanwhile internal disputes had broken out in the island, and so the Persian force landed unopposed. Presently some Samians attacked the Persians, and these responded by attacking the island. Finally the Persian force entrusted Samos to Syloson, the brother of Polycrates. Previously Syloson had been driven into exile by his brother and had made the acquaintance of Darius when the latter was serving under Cambyses in Egypt.

It should be noted that the conquest of Samos was not an easy operation. A special force was sent; a change of regime in the island and consequent disputes gave the Persians an opportunity; and a Samian exile was available as a guide. Perhaps others of the offshore islands were reduced one at a time in a similar way, although some may have yielded voluntarily. During the operations in Egypt Cambyses had at his disposal at least one ship from Mytilene; possibly the Mytilenaeans sent it for reasons like those inducing Polycrates to support Cambyses. The extent of Persian rule over Greeks at the time of the Scythian expedition can be estimated, since Herodotus gives a list of tyrants employed to build and guard the bridge across the Danube. They included men from the leading cities of the Asiatic mainland, Miletus, Phocaea and Cyme. There were tyrants from several cities on the Asiatic side of the Propontis and the Hellespont, namely Cyzicus, Proconnesus, Parium, Lampsacus and Abydus. From the European shore of the straits the only tyrants recorded at the Danube bridge were Ariston of Byzantium and Miltiades of the Chersonese. The offshore islands attested in the list were Chios and Samos. Elsewhere Herodotus says somewhat enigmatically that Coes was present in command of a Mytilenaean force at the bridge and Darius made him tyrant of Mytilene as a reward for his services on the expedition; this may indicate an increase in Persian influence in Lesbos in the aftermath of the expedition. At least the islands of Samos, Chios and Lesbos mark the westward limit of Persian ascendancy ca. 514.

NAXOS AND THE IONIAN REVOLT[3]

For perhaps a dozen years after the Scythian expedition the Persians continued to advance their power westward by relatively small steps, without launching any major new undertaking. After the expedition Darius created a satrapy of Thrace. Megabazus, the first commander of the satrapy, made a successful attack on Perinthus not far from Byzantium; then he reduced parts of Thrace and overcame the tribe of the Paeones in the valley of the Strymon River. Presently he was replaced by Otanes, who operated on both shores of the straits. Otanes captured Byzantium, whether because it had rebelled or because the Persians had become dissatisfied with the tyrant Ariston; he also captured Calchedon, Antandrus in the Troad, and Lamponium. Furthermore he gained ships from Lesbos and with them he seized the islands of Lemnos and Imbros.

Operations of this kind, though not spectacular, helped to consolidate the Persian position in the northern Aegean. They may have been part of a comprehensive plan, in which the Scythian expedition was the first step. Meanwhile other gains were achieved by diplomacy. While Megabazus was in command, the dynasty of Macedon made an alliance with Persia. Subsequently Persia gained connections with cities in the heart of Greece. Late in the sixth century Cleomenes of Sparta brought a small force to Athens and tried to expel 700 families, but the Athenians, after some hesitation, rallied against him and drove him out (see chapter 6, p. 147). Then, believing that they had antagonized the Lacedaemonians, they sent envoys to Artaphernes, the satrap at Sardis, with a request for alliance. Artaphernes required the envoys to render submission by giving earth and water, and they did so. Herodotus (5.73), relating this, adds that on their return to Athens the envoys were greatly blamed. He does not say that they were disavowed; moreover, his statement about being greatly blamed may be a later attempt to gloss over the fact that the Athenians became subordinate allies of the Persians. It is not unlikely that the Athenians, on dispatching the envoys to Artaphernes, foresaw the Persian demand for the regular tokens of submission. If Athens in the course of intercity disputes entered into such relations with Persian satraps, one may guess that some other cities of European Greece did so too.

A new stage in the development of Persian policy may be discerned in 499, when a force was sent by sea to attack Naxos in the heart of the Aegean. This was the first attempt to extend Persian rule into the Cyclades. Herodotus (5.28–35) tells the story from a Greek point of view. Histaeus, the sometime tyrant of Miletus, had received Myrcinus in the Strymon valley as a reward for loyalty on the Scythian expedition, but later Darius invited him as adviser to Susa and kept him there, and Histiaeus entrusted Miletus to his son-in-law, Aristagoras. The latter received an appeal from some Naxian exiles and made a plan for an attack on Naxos. He won the support of Artaphernes, who in turn referred the plan to

Susa for royal approval. Darius concurred; a fleet of 200 ships was assembled, largely from the Greek cities of the Asiatic mainland, although the troops to be carried included Persians; and the command was given to Megabates, a cousin of Darius. But troubles ensued; even before the fleet reached Naxos, Aristagoras quarreled with Megabates. Moreover, after the troops landed in the island of Naxos, the city withstood a siege of four months successfully. So the force withdrew and Aristagoras, fearing to be called to account, sought to bring about a revolt of the Ionian cities.

The story is told to explain the outbreak of the Ionian Revolt. It is possible to alter the perspective and see the events in part from a Persian point of view. Two hundred ships were a large force and this suggests that the first initiative was taken, not by Aristagoras, but by someone in Sardis or perhaps in Susa. In other words, it was Persian authorities who first conceived a design of attacking Naxos; in view of the rivalries prevalent within and between cities they could expect to find a party of Naxian exiles and an ambitious Greek, like Aristagoras, to guide them; the attack on Samos should be called to mind. A remark alledgedly made by Aristagoras to Artaphernes may provide a clue to Persian motives; he said that, if the Persians secured Naxos, they would be in a good position to attack Paros, Andros, the other Cyclades and then Euboea.

According to Herodotus (5.36–38), the immediate effect of the failure at Naxos was a revolt of Ionia. Aristagoras, coming back to Miletus, deliberated with his partisans and they decided on revolt. They sent an envoy to Myus, where the fleet had anchored on its return from Naxos, and the envoy arrested the Greek tyrants who were in command of the naval contingents from their cities. Aristagoras formally laid down his tyranny at Miletus, but this made little difference, as he continued in control. He handed over the other tyrants to the people of their cities. At Mytilene the tyrant Coes was stoned to death, but in most places the citizens let their erstwhile tyrants go free. Then Aristagoras traveled to European Greece to seek help.

In Herodotus's account, just summarized, the Revolt is caused by the frustrations and fears of Aristagoras and the change which the deposition of tyrants wrought in the balance of factions within the cities. This is credible. Political life in the cities was largely a series of rivalries between small groups within the governing class; the relative position of the groups could easily be altered, and such an alteration could affect the fortunes of the whole city. Modern writers have looked for deeper causes. It is sometimes suggested that there was a general hatred of tyranny, but this is unlikely, since most of the cities let their deposed tyrants go free. The possibility of economic grievances is more tantalizing. Persian rule was usually not severe. An extant inscription preserves a copy of a letter of Darius to the satrap Gadates, who governed Ionia; the king praises the satrap for promoting agricultural improvements in his satrapy. Again, as will be seen, the settlement imposed at the end of the Revolt had decidedly mild features. On the other hand Greeks had been welcome in Lydia, while it was ruled by its own kings, but nothing suggests that the Persian satraps continued this policy. The excavations at Al Mina (Sueidia), in northern Syria are suggestive. They show that Greek trade continued without interruption right through the period of warfare between Persians and Greeks; but they also show that from the later part of the sixth century Athenian pottery virtually monopolized the market. Possibly there was some economic decline among the Asiatic Greeks because of Athenian competition, and the consequent discontent was channeled into the political revolt of the Ionian cities.

In 499 Aristagoras, traveling in European Greece, received assurances of support from Athens and Eretria. The Athenians were aggrieved at Persian favor to Hippias, who had returned to Sigeum when he was rebuffed by the congress of the Peloponnesian League (see chapter 6, p. 148). Sigeum lay within the satrapy of Artaphernes and Hippias found the satrap willing to listen to him; he might hope to be restored to Athens by Persian forces. The Athenians sent an embassy to Sardis to protest against the attention given to Hippias, but Artaphernes replied with a demand that the Athenians restore their former tyrant. The Athenians were not willing to comply and so their alliance with Persia ceased to operate, although it may not have been formally revoked. When relations had thus deteriorated, Aristagoras reached Athens; he tempted his hearers with prospects of easy fighting and plentiful booty. The Athenians voted to send twenty ships. When Aristagoras appealed to the Eretrians, they voted to send five ships. Herodotus explains this as gratitude for Milesian help to Eretria in the War of the Lelantine Plain (see chapter 1, p. 34); the immediate motives of the Eretrians are not known.

Probably in 498 the Athenian and Eretrian ships sailed to Ephesus and joined the Ionians there. The combined forces marched upcountry to Sardis and captured the city, which caught fire in the confusion, but they could not take the citadel. When they withdrew to Ephesus, Persian forces caught up with them and defeated them. Then the Athenians withdrew their contingent. Even so the Ionians were able to extend their operations; there was fighting in the Hellespontine district and in Caria. Most of the cities of Cyprus joined the revolt and an Ionian fleet was sent to support them. But next year the Persians sent additional forces against the Cypriotes and reduced the island. Then they divided their land forces in Asia Minor and attacked the Greek cities severally. Finally they concentrated their land and sea forces against Miletus. The Ionians brought together all available triremes, to the number of 353, but they were defeated at sea at Lade near Miletus. Hence the Persians were able to besiege and capture Miletus; they deported the captives. The siege of Miletus, carried out in 494, brought the Revolt to an end.

Those who had fought the Persians during the Revolt included not only the Ionian cities of the mainland but also Cyme and the islands of Samos, Chios and Lesbos. The Persian authorities took military and administrative steps towards a settlement. Shortly after the fall of Miletus the Phoenician contingent from the Persian fleet restored Aeaces, son of Syloson, as tyrant to Samos and spared the island; Aeaces had persuaded the Samians to desert the Ionian cause during the battle of Lade. The Persian fleet wintered at Miletus and in 493 it sailed northwards, recovering the islands of Chios, Lesbos and Tenedos; it sailed into the straits and captured the cities of the Chersonese and other places on the European shore, such as Perinthus, Selymbria and Byzantium. Meanwhile Artaphernes summoned envoys from the Ionian cities and made them accept terms to regulate their mutual relations; the intention was that henceforth their disputes should be settled by arbitration without recourse to warfare. Artaphernes also reassessed their territory for payment of tribute; he followed more or less the previous scale and his assessment remained in force into the time of Herodotus, a fact which may suggest that it did not arouse any bitter resentment.

In 492 Mardonius, the son-in-law of Darius, brought new land and sea forces to Asia Minor. This may suggest that a new stage had been reached in Persian plans. Mardonius completed the administrative settlement of Ionia; Herodotus says that he overthrew the tyrants and set up *demokratiai* in the cities. Some readers have found this statement puzzling, since tyrants are found in Ionia some time later. But the real question is, What does Herodotus mean by *demokratiai* in this context? Possibly he means the rule of law as distinct from the arbitrary regime of a tyrant. If so, it is not incredible that the Persian authorities drew up comprehensive rules for the internal affairs of the cities; in the previous year Artaphernes had imposed terms to regulate their mutual relations.

Mardonius proceeded with his forces across the Hellespont. He reduced Thasos, which made no resistance. With his land force he operated in Macedon, where the Thracian tribe of the Brygi defeated him by a surprise attack but was soon overcome. Meanwhile, his fleet proceeded from Thasos to Acanthus and thence tried to round Mt. Athos, the easternmost of the three promontories of Chalcidice. But a storm sprang up and damaged the fleet severely; allegedly 300 ships were destroyed on the cliffs. Even so, Mardonius's expedition had done something to consolidate the Persian position on the north coast of the Aegean. Herodotus, however, says that the objectives of the expedition were Athens and Eretria; this raises the question of Persian plans.

DARIUS AND EUROPEAN GREECE[4]

When Cyrus first conquered Lydia and received an appeal of the Ionians and Aeolians, his refusal to make any undertaking to them suggests that he set little store on relations with them (see above p. 172). But by the time of Darius the Persian court was learning to value Greeks as engineers, builders, and specialists in other scientific skills. For his expedition into Scythia a bridge was built across the Bosporus, and the engineer in charge of the work was Mandrocles, a Greek from Samos. Darius built a palace at Susa and his inscription recording the work mentioned Ionian stonemasons, alongside of other artisans. Democedes of Croton served as doctor to Darius and his family for a time and was highly esteemed by the king. Contacts of this kind do not explain why Darius set about conquering European Greece, but they help to explain how Persian attention was drawn towards Greeks.

Herodotus tried to explain the eventual Persian invasion of Greece as the result of a series of hostile actions and reactions, which gave rise to a chain of grievances and counter-grievances. At an early point in his text he singled out Croesus as "the man who first began unjust deeds against the Greeks" (1.5.3); his narrative proceeded to trace how the Persians superseded Croesus and how they conquered other nations. Somehow he was unable to follow this chain through to the invasion of Greece, and so he marked a new beginning at the attack of Aristagoras and Megabates on Naxos (5.28). This, in Herodotus's view, provoked the Ionian Revolt; forces from Athens and Eretria supported the Ionians and took part in the attack on Sardis. Thus Darius had a grievance against the Athenians and the Eretrians; Herodotus says that, when Darius received news of the burning of Sardis, he told one of his servants to say to him three times at dinner each day: "Master, remember the Athenians" (5.105). Accordingly, Herodotus supposes that the expedition of Mardonius in 492 was directed against Athens and Eretria but was frustrated by the storm off Mt. Athos. A subsequent expedition by sea in 490 was indeed directed against Athens and Eretria, but it was defeated by the Athenians at Marathon. This defeat increased the Persian grievance; according to Herodotus (7.1.1), when Darius received news of the battle of Marathon, he became much more keen to march against Greece. His plan was eventually launched after his death by his son Xerxes in 480 and 479.

Such is Herodotus's picture of the causal chain. Even within his terms of thought the explanation is imperfect; the operations of 480 and 479 were directed not merely against Athens and Eretria, the states against which Darius had a grievance because of the burning of Sardis, but generally against the cities of European Greece, except for those which offered submission. But it is important to recognize Herodotus's terms of thought. Habitually, he explains an act of violence by citing another act of violence committed previously in the opposite direction. For example, when the Aeginetans went to war against the Athenians late in the sixth century, Herodotus explains that they called to mind a war fought between the two states more than a century before (5.81.2; 5.82–89). He extends this mode of explanation even to natural history; among the winged serpents of Arabia the female kills the male immediately after intercourse but is subsequently killed by her offspring, and Herodotus regards her death as "compensation" to the father (3.109.2). An explanation of this kind gives, not what would now be called a cause, but a justificatory grievance. The habit of thinking in terms of justificatory grievances appears frequently in the literature and diplomatic practice of the Greeks, although it is more evident in the work of Herodotus than in that of many authors. But even though Greek cities often cited prior grievances to justify them in going to war, it does not follow that such grievances determined their actions, much less those of the Persian king.

Herodotus's explanation for the Persian attack on European Greece can perhaps be put into modern dress. That is, it can be suggested that minor incidents on the Greek fringe of the Persian Empire grew, until the king lost patience and decided to terminate them with a large expedition. But such an explanation is not satisfactory. The scale of the expedition which Xerxes led to Greece in 480 shows that it was not a punitive operation, intended merely to inflict damage; the aim was conquest. The ultimate reason for the Persian invasions can only be discerned in general and somewhat uninformative terms; one may speak of the tendency of empires to expand or note that the Persian ruling class set a value on conquest. It is more pertinent to ask why the invasions came about when and as they did. Here the Scythian expedition of Darius offers a clue.

Herodotus assumed that the aim of the expedition was the conquest of Scythia; if so, it failed completely. But the course of events allows and perhaps suggests a different interpretation. The lasting result of the expedition was the establishment of a satrapy in Thrace, and the commanders sent there consolidated their territory by seizing adjacent places. Perhaps the Scythian expedition was part of a plan for expansion into Europe, that is, towards European Greece. The satrapy of Thrace secured the first stage on the land route, which led thence past Chalcidice and southwards into Thessaly and beyond. If this is correct, the expedition into Scythia was a preventive raid, intended to impress the Scythians and intervening tribes so that they would not threaten the land route along the north coast of the Aegean. The expedition was successful in this aim; when Persian forces used the land route, they are not known to have suffered any flank attack from the north.

On this interpretation, the Scythian expedition presupposes a Persian design to advance towards European Greece. In 514 the design may have still been embryonic; the immediate prospect was merely to expand beyond the neighborhood of the straits. Once that stage had been achieved through the consolidation of the Thracian satrapy and the alliance made with Macedon, the makers of Persian policy could look further afield. They could also consider alternative routes. The land route along the north coast of the Aegean was the route eventually taken by Xerxes in 480, but it posed a major problem of commissariat, since travel by land was slow. It would have been much quicker and cheaper to transport the expeditionary force by sea from Ionia directly across the Aegean. The Persian high command apparently considered using the sea route. That explains why an expedition was sent against Naxos in 499; if a force was to be transported to the European mainland, it would be advantageous to hold some of the islands on the route. As Aristagoras allegedly pointed out to Artaphernes, if the Persians once held Naxos, they could easily take others of the Cyclades and eventually Euboea. The latter island could provide a base for disembarkation close to the mainland.

The expedition against Naxos failed and the Ionian Revolt impeded the development of Persian plans. After its suppression the high command seems to have wavered between choosing the land route or the sea route. By 492 the Persians could resume the initiative in armed operations; Mardonius brought additional forces to Asia Minor and advanced along the north coast of the Aegean. Evidently this route was now favored. Mardonius's achievements were considerable, but the damage suffered by his fleet off Mt. Athos was serious. So in the next years attention shifted to the possibility of using the sea route. In 490 an expedition was sent by sea across the Aegean. It secured Naxos and other places among the islands, but its goals were Eretria and Athens. It can best be understood as preliminary to a planned conquest of European Greece. If a power holding Asia Minor wishes to advance into European Greece, it must first secure bases on the western shore of the Aegean in order to land its expeditionary force. Antiochus III faced the same problem in 192, when he sought to weaken Roman influence in Greece; he could only bring his troops across the Aegean after the Aetolian League had seized Demetrias in Thessaly and offered it to him as a base. In 490 the Persians tried to seize Athens and Eretria because they would need these bases for disembarking an eventual expeditionary force.

ATHENIAN POLICY BEFORE MARATHON[5]

In 491 Darius, developing his designs on Greece, sent heralds to the Greek cities to demand earth and water. Some cities gave these symbols of submission but others did not; when a party of Persian heralds reached Athens, the Athenians threw them into the pit where they normally executed criminals. It is appropriate to ask how Athenian policy had developed to such a vehemently anti-Persian position. The problem is difficult, because only a few Athenian events are known from the period between the work of Cleisthenes and the battle of Marathon. Historians have given a good deal of attention to these events, and it used to be supposed that the divisions among Athenians were divisions on broad issues, rather like those professed by modern political parties. It was suggested, for example, that the Athenians divided into pro-Persians and anti-Persians or pro-Spartans and anti-Spartans; or it was held that they divided on the constitutional question, some preferring aristocracy and others democracy, while yet others hoped for a restoration of tyranny, and attempts were made to discover how these supposed groupings took stands on the broad issues of foreign policy. But no theory of this modernist kind was sufficiently persuasive to win wide acceptance. Moreover, the supposed broad groupings of Athenian opinion have failed conspicuously to leave traces in the evidence; in particular, when Herodotus mentions the internal politics of any city, he usually conceives the scene in highly personal terms. Accordingly more recent studies of post-Cleisthenic Athens have looked for personal conflicts and for divergences on immediate and specific issues.

If the view expounded above (chapter 6, pp. 151–157) about the reforms of Cleisthenes is correct, henceforth Athenian affairs were dominated by the city families and the Alcmaeonidae were likely to be prominent. But Hippias had received asylum at Sigeum and the protection of Artaphernes, the satrap of Lydia (see above p. 177); he could hope to be restored to Athens with Persian support. In 490, when he at last accompanied a Persian naval expedition to Attica, he guided it to land at Marathon, the place where his father Peisistratus had landed in 546; apparently Hippias could still expect some sympathy in eastern Attica. Thus, once Artaphernes committed his support to Hippias, an Athenian accommodation with Persia would mean a revival of the eastern Attic cause and an end to the ascendancy of the city families; Athens could not accept such a condition, because the city families had been dominant since the reforms of Cleisthenes. Thus in a sense the anti-Persian stand of the Athenians was already determined, once Artaphernes bade them restore Hippias. So much may be apparent to the historian, who knows what happened afterwards, but it can only be apparent to him; to contemporary Athenians the situation may have been less clear, since they were preoccupied with events occurring nearer Athens.

One such event was a war with Aegina, beginning towards the end of the sixth century. The opportunity for the Aeginetans was provided by a Boeotian appeal for help; when Cleomenes organized unsuccessfully a triple attack on Athens in support of Isagoras, the Boeotian force taking part in this operation was defeated (chapter 6, pp. 147–148), and so the Thebans sought aid from Aegina. The Aeginetans hesitated at first, but after the Thebans suffered a further defeat by the Athenians and renewed their appeal, the islanders raided Phalerum and many parts of the Attic coast. The causes of the ensuing war may have been more complex than the opportunity; on many occasions in the fifth century hostility between Athens and Aegina is attested in varying forms. Commerical jealousies may have been a cause of the war. The early growth of Aeginetan trade is proved by the Aeginetan establishment maintained at Naucratis (see chapter 1, p. 31); but Greek trade with Egypt had decreased since its conquest by the Persians in 525. Meanwhile, in the late sixth century the Athenians were achieving something like a monopoly in the export of vases.

The Aeginetan War lasted intermittently until 481. It was a matter of raids and counter-raids. Most of the information Herodotus provides about it concerns setbacks for the Athenians; so the war was frequently a major claim on Athenian attention. Yet they had energy for other enterprises too. In 498 they sent a force in twenty triremes to support the Ionian Revolt. For a distant expedition this was a large force in relation to the contemporary resources of the Athenians; some years later, when they wanted to send seventy triremes against the Aeginetans, they only reached this number of borrowing twenty ships from Corinth at a nominal rent. The Athenian force sent to the Ionians in 498 joined in the sack of Sardis and was recalled at the end of the campaigning season. Some historians have treated the dispatch and recall of this force as indicating changes in policy and in party politics, but such a view is not necessary. It may be better to notice the arguments used by Aristagoras, when he persuaded the Athenians to send the force. According to Herodotus (5.97.1-2; cf. 5.49), he reminded the Athenians of their legendary kinship with the Ionians and he dilated on the good things to be had for the taking in the Persian Empire and on the feebleness of the troops guarding them. Possibly the Athenian force was sent to get booty and was recalled at the most profitable moment, when sizeable booty had been won and the Persians had not yet had time to retaliate.

The eponymous archon of 496/5 was Hipparchus, son of Charmus, a relative of the Peisistratidae. Some have interpreted this as a step towards a rapproachement with Persia; but one may doubt whether Artaphernes was interested in Athenian elections. Furthermore it is not known how close was the link of Hipparchus with the Peisistratidae; at least it was not sufficiently close for him to be expelled in 510. Besides, other cases (chapter 6, p. 151) suggest that the archonship marked not the culmination but an early stage of a political career; if so, the archonship of Hipparchus may not have indicated any significant political or personal change.

Evidence on Athenian internal affairs of the 490s is scanty, but several incidents of 493 are recorded. Miletus had been sacked by the Persians in the previous year, and early in 493 the dramatist Phrynichus produced a play, "The Capture of Miletus." The audience burst into tears; the Athenians fined Phrynichus 1,000 drachmas and gave orders that that play should never be performed again. Some have thought that the play advocated an anti-Persian cause, which was popular, and that a pro-Persian party (or a peace party, seeking to avoid embroilment with Persia) brought about the condemnation of Phrynichus in court. But such an explanation is too rationalistic. Herodotus (6.21.2), who records the incident, may be right in the reason he gives for the fining of Phrynichus: "because he reminded (the Athenians) of their own misfortunes." It may be that his condemnation, like the tears of his audience, was due simply to an outburst of popular emotion not directed in support of any consistent policy. Nor need any political clues be sought in the fact that Themistocles was his choregus when he produced other plays in 477/6.

Themistocles was archon in 493/2. He belonged to the deme Phrearrioi, far out in the southeast towards the promontory of Sunium. In view of the advantages held by the city families such a man needed good connections in order to make his way in politics; Themistocles sought them. He married the daughter of Lysander, who belonged to a city deme, Alopece. He bought a house in another city deme, Melite, where several distinguished politicians of the fifth century resided; evidently it was a fashionable quarter. He stressed his membership in the clan called Lycomidae; after their sanctuary at Phlya was burnt by the Persians in 480 or 479, he restored it. Modern historians have sometimes tried to explain his career by assuming that he had a distinctive policy on the constitution, but recent work (by F.J. Frost) has refuted this. The practice of classifying Themistocles as a democrat cannot be traced before Aristotle; earlier authors mention him quite often and regard him as a distinguished statesman, but they do not attribute to him any view on constitutional questions. He was a controversial figure. About 470 he was ostracized and then tried and condemned in absence; he found asylum in Persian territory. As early as the time of Herodotus the tradition about him was conspicuous for colorful and tendentious anecdotes. Such an end and such a tradition were perhaps to be expected, when a man from far outside the city of Athens tried to compete in politics with the city families.

The main question about the archonship of Themistocles concerns the possibility that he already sought to enhance Athenian sea power. In 483/2 he persuaded the Athenians to engage in a new program of shipbuilding, a program which continued for two or three years. In the sixth century the main harbor used by the people of Athens was that at Phalerum, but early in the fifth century they began to develop more the harbor at the Peiraeus further west. In or soon after 479 Themistocles persuaded the Athenians to complete the fortifications of the Peiraeus. Thucydides (1.93.3), recording this, adds that the fortifications had been begun "previously in his (Themistocles's) archonship which he held for a year among the Athenians." At least Thucydides's sentence has often been understood thus; it was so understood by the scholiast and by many modern historians. They believe accordingly that the work of fortifying the Peiraeus, completed in or after 479, was begun in 493/2, when Themistocles was archon; whether Themistocles himself began it is not clear from the wording on this interpretation of Thucydides's remark, although the coincidence of his archonship with the beginning of the fortifications would be suggestive. But Thucydides's sentence admits an alternative interpretation. It may mean that the fortifications were begun "previously in his office which he (Themistocles) held from year to year among the Athenians;" that is, Thucydides may refer to an office, otherwise unattested, which Themistocles held for a series of years in connection with the shipbuilding program of 483/2.

Two considerations tell in favor of the second alternative. First, it would be strange if the fortifications of the Peiraeus were begun in 493/2 and not completed until fourteen or more years later; the delay is difficult to explain, especially as the Aeginetan War should have made the Athenians alive to the need for completing harbor fortifications. Second, Herodotus (7.143.1), reporting action taken by Themistocles in 481 or 480, describes him as "a man recently come to prominence." This would be erroneous, if the work of fortifying the Peiraeus began in 493/2 and Themistocles initiated it. But Herodotus's remark makes good sense, if the archonship of Themistocles was merely the opening stage of his career and he achieved nothing of importance in 493/2. He would then rise to influence in the 480s. Recent finds of ostraca show that some were cast against him as early as 487/6, although it is difficult to estimate what degree of prominence that implies. Finally, by starting the shipbuilding program in 483/2 and probably by beginning the fortification of the Peiraeus at the same time, Themistocles achieved a place among the leading men of Athens.

If Themistocles as archon in 493/2 was still a relatively unimportant figure, this must be borne in mind in assessing his relationship with another Athenian. Miltiades fled from the Chersonese, as the Persian fleet approached, and returned to Athens in 493 (see chapter 6, pp. 140–142). On his arrival he was prosecuted by his enemies but acquitted. Some historians have supposed that a political link was formed between him and Themistocles. This hypothesis rests on the practice of classifying both men as anti-Persian; Miltiades fled from Persian forces in 493, and Themistocles distinguished himself in resisting the Persian invasion in 480. But the assumption that Athenians in 493 took sides on the Persian question is unproven and unlikely. It can still be observed that Themistocles and Miltiades were both in a sense outsiders in 493; Themistocles belonged to a distant deme; Miltiades had been sent to the Chersonese by the Peisistratidae and had been away from Attica, when the city families were ensuring their ascendancy through the work of Cleisthenes. But this was not enough to bring them together. Moreover, theories which suppose an alliance between Miltiades and Themistocles tend to assume that Themistocles was already prominent and influential in 493. It is still conceivable that in that year Themistocles, beginning his career, attached himself as a hanger-on to the already distinguished and controversial Miltiades, but even this is perhaps unlikely. Miltiades eventually died in prison in 489; if Themistocles had associated with a man thus disgraced, surely his rise in the 480s would have been less rapid.

Herodotus (6.104.2) says that on his return to Athens Miltiades was prosecuted "for his tyranny in the Chersonese." It is difficult to believe that this can have been an offense in Attic law, but Herodotus's words may well indicate the real ground for animosity against Miltiades. As a man who had ruled a distant land for more than two decades and had done something to offend the Persians during the Ionian Revolt, he had a romantic appeal which might make other politicians jealous. His acquittal may attest his popularity.

Who were the other politicians? It is not known who prosecuted Miltiades at his trial in 493. Several men, known from their fortunes in the 480s, must have been active in the previous decade; they belonged to city demes. Of the Alcmaeonidae Cleisthenes disappears from record after his reforms, except for a late and unreliable tradition that he was ostracized. Leadership of the clan passed to his nephew Megacles, who was ostracized in 487/6; later in 486 his team won a chariot race at the Pythian festival. Xanthippus, son of Arriphron, of the city deme Cholargeis, was not an Alcmaeonid but he married Agariste, a woman of that clan; he probably rose to significance in the 490s, for he prosecuted Miltiades in 489 and won a conviction, although the court refused the prosecutor's demand for the death penalty and condemned Miltiades to a heavy fine instead. Apart from the Alcmaeonidae and their associates a little can be presumed about other city families. The family in which the names Callias and Hipponicus alternate with the generations was probably active; Callias had founded the impressive fortunes of the family by buying up the property of the Peisistratidae. Callias belonged to the deme Alopece in the city. Aristeides was a cousin of a Callias of this family, but probably his public career scarcely began before the 480s; he was eponymous archon in 489. The family in which the names Alcibiades and Cleinias alternate belonged to the deme of Scambonidae in the city; it may have counted for much. In 480 Cleinias equipped and manned a trireme at his own expense and commanded it at the battle of Artemisium. His father Alcibiades had collaborated with Cleisthenes in the expulsion of the Peisistratidae.

The service of Cleinias at Artemisium throws welcome light on the social structure of Athenian politics. A man who could provide the crew of a trireme at his own expense could command 200 able-bodied men. Surely he could likewise bring them to vote in the public assembly. A few men of the wealth and initiative of Cleinias could easily command several hundred voters, if they brought them from estates near the city; if such a block voted all one way, it might have a large effect on the outcome, especially as the vote was usually taken by a show of hands. If the city families benefited from the reforms of Cleisthenes, by 490 they may have felt so secure that they could admit outsiders to sensitive positions. Two outsiders appear in the campaign of Marathon. One of them was Miltiades, who was one of the ten generals of 490/89 and was largely responsible for the strategy adopted by the Athenians. Apparently after his acquittal in 493 he became acceptable, at least for operations against Persians. The other outsider was Callimachus, the pole-march of 490/89. As one of the nine archons he may have been at the opening of his career, and his share in the strategy of the battle is far from clear. He belonged to the deme of Aphidna, far away in the northern part of Attica. It was the deme of Harmodius and Aristogeiton, who had tried to overthrow the tyranny in 514. In the campaign of Marathon one consideration affecting Athenian strategy was fear lest Hippias with the Persian forces win a local following in eastern Attica. Evidently no such doubts were felt about Callimachus of Aphidna. It may be relevant that the Athenian state set up statues of Harmodius and Aristogeiton soon after the expulsion of Hippias.

The known events of the 490s suggest that Athenian affairs were guided by short-term policies, not long-lasting plans, and that changes in personal fortunes could be correspondingly swift. Hostilities with Aegina were serious but inter-mittent; aid was sent to the Ionian Revolt but recalled at the end of one season; Phrynichus was condemned because of an outburst of popular emotion; Miltiades was prosecuted but acquitted and presently elected general. Accordingly, as the Athenians refused the Persian demand for earth and water in 491, the reasons should be sought in the immediate situation, not in long-term policies. Possibly some leading men of the city families remembered Artaphernes's former demand for the restoration of Hippias and believed, reasonably enough, that that was still the prce for an accommodation with Persia. But a more immediate reason can be conjectured. When a party of Persian heralds reached Aegina, the Aeginetans gave earth and water; the Athenians sent envoys to Sparta to complain against the Aeginetans. In the first two decades of the fifth century the Athenians regarded Aegina as their most bitter enemy. Perhaps the Athenians took a strong stand against the Persians in 491, not merely refusing to give earth and water but ill-treating the heralds, because they saw Persia as the friend of Aegina.

MARATHON[6]

In 490 a Persian expeditionary force assembled in Cilicia. The commanders were Datis and Artaphernes, the son of the honomymous satrap of Sardis. In Cilicia the infantry and the cavalry embarked and the force proceeded by sea to Ionia.

Coastline of Bay of Marathon. [Courtesy W.K. Pritchett.]

From Samos it sailed westwards through the Cyclades, calling at some of the islands. In Naxos most of the inhabitants sought refuge in the mountains; the Persian troops burned the temples and the city. But they showed ostentatious respect for the sacred island of Delos; Datis offered a large amount of incense there. They demanded hostages and troops from some of the islands. Carystus in southern Euboea at first resisted, so the Persian force besieged the city and ravaged its land, until the inhabitants yielded. Then the Persians proceeded to Eretria, the first of their main goals. The city withstood a siege for six days but on the seventh it was betrayed and the citizens were taken into captivity.

The Persian troops may have numbered ca. 20,000 in all. They included a comparatively small but significant body of cavalry; it may have numbered ca. 800; the difficulty of transporting horses by sea precluded using a larger force. Persian cavalry in the early fifth century consisted of mounted archers; they could inflict considerable losses on hoplites at a distance, but they were at a disadvantage in fighting at close quarters. A few days after the capture of Eretria the Persians sailed towards Attica and landed in the Bay of Marathon. Several reasons favored this choice of landing place. It was the nearest site to Eretria with a good land route leading to Athens. It was one of the few places in Attica which provided pasture for horses in the fall. Moreover Hippias, who guided the force to Marathon, may have expected to find sympathizers in eastern Attica; in 546 his father had landed there and met no organized opposition until he was well advanced thence on the route towards Athens. Within the Bay of Marathon the Persian force landed at the beach now called Schinia. To the west on the landward side an extensive marsh protected this position from attack; on the seaward side the Persian anchorage was sheltered by the promontory of Cynosura.

The Athenian commanders decided not to await a Persian attack in or near the city of Athens; instead they marched to Marathon. This decision was crucial for the development of the campaign and the reasons for it can only be guessed. It was a bold decision. Datis and Artaphernes might try to hold the main Athenian force at Marathon and send part of their own forces by sea to approach Athens by the Bay of Phalerum. Besides, if the Athenians confronted the Persian forces at Marathon, they undertook the risks of a pitched battle, whereas under fifth-century conditions of siege warfare the men defending a city had a tactical advantage over the power attacking it. But the fall of Eretria illustrates the major hazard threatening the defender in a fifth-century siege; perhaps fear of treachery determined the Athenian commanders to march to eastern Attica and prevent the enemy from securing a base, whence he might tamper with the loyalty of some citizens.

The Athenian force probably took the main route from Athens to Marathon, so that it approached the coastal plain from the south through the level land between Mt. Agrieliki and the sea. The whole force totalled perhaps ca. 10,000; it included a small force of Plataeans, numbering perhaps ca. 600. The Greek hoplites were better armed than the Persian forces. They took up a position on high ground facing the plain, so the hills afforded them some protection against Persian attack; unless they chose to move, they could hope to hold their position indefinitely. They were about a mile from the site now marked by the artificial mound called the Soros. This mound was built by the Athenians after the battle as a communal grave for their fallen; its original height was at least twelve meters. Presumably it was erected near the place where the largest number of Athenians fell in the center of the battle lines; so it indicates approximately the position taken up by the Persians before battle was joined.

Herodotus says that the Athenians were commanded by their ten generals and by the polemarch Callimachus, and he tells a strange story of the way they reached the decision to attack. He says that the generals were equally divided but Miltiades persuaded Callimachus to vote for attacking and thus gained a majority; further, the generals took turns to command the whole force for a day and each of those who were for attacking renounced his day of command in favor of

Miltiades; even so Miltiades waited until his own day came before making the attack. Clearly much of this story is mere anecdote. It implies, however, that there was a delay of several days between the Athenian arrival and the battle, and this implication should be accepted, since it is confirmed by another development. Before leaving Athens the generals sent a messenger, Philippides, to Sparta for help. He arrived on the next day; the Spartans declared themselves willing to help, but observed that it was only the ninth day of the lunar month and they must await the full moon before marching out. Eventually a Lacedaemonian force of 2,000 left in haste for Attica and arrived on the third day out from Sparta (Hdt. 6.120); by then the battle had just been fought. Thus the Lacedaemonians reached Attica on the eighteenth of the lunar month and the battle was fought on the seventeenth; there had been a delay since the ninth, when the generals dispatched Philippides at speed.

Since the Athenians were drawn up in a strong position, it is not surprising that they waited several days. The real problem for the student of the battle is to explain why they at last chose to abandon their strong position and attack. Facing this question, some historians have relied on evidence preserved in the Byzantine lexicon called the *Suda* under the rubric, "the horsemen away" (*choris hippeis*). The passage says: "After Datis disembarked in Attica, they say that the Ionians, when he withdrew, climbed the trees and signalled to the Athenians that the horsemen were away; Miltiades, learning of their departure, attacked accordingly and won the victory. Hence the phrase is said to be proverbial for those who disband battle lines." Because of this text some historians have supposed that Datis reembarked part of his force, including his cavalry, in order to sail to the Bay of Phalerum and attack Athens, and he left his rear guard at Marathon to hold the Athenian force there; but the Ionians in the Persian camp climbed trees and signaled his movement to the Athenians; so the latter, learning that the force opposing them was depleted, decided to overcome it before hastening back to the defence of Athens.

The passage in the *Suda* appears to be a compressed and obscure version of some fuller account. The lexicographer cited it to explain a proverbial expression; it is difficult to tell whether the explanation was apt. Possibly the account was invented to explain the proverb. Those who accept this evidence have to suppose that it comes from an Ionian tradition, which somehow escaped mention in ancient accounts of the battle; that is possible, but there are graver objections. It is difficult to conceive of a system of agreed signals, whereby the Ionians could transmit specific and unexpected information to the Athenians over a distance of at least a mile. Moreover, although Herodotus fails to mention the Persian cavalry in his account of the fighting, he probably believed that they took part; for he says (6.112.2) that the Persians were amazed at the Athenian attack, as they saw that the Athenians were few and were advancing at a charge, although they had neither cavalry nor arrows.

Accordingly, it is best to reject the tradition given in the *Suda* and seek in the Herodotean account an explanation of the Athenian decision to fight. Herodotus provides a hint in the speech with which he makes Miltiades persuade Callimachus. The speech may be a free invention by the historian, but it must conform to his beliefs about the strategic and political situation. Miltiades is represented as saying: "If we do not attack, I expect that some great conflict will arise among the Athenians and disturb their views, so that they will join the Persian cause" (6.109.5). To put the matter another way, the grounds for the Athenian decision were political, not military; the commanders feared that, if they postponed fighting longer, there might be treachery among the Athenians. Had not Eretria been betrayed to the Persians a few days before? Even after the victory it was possible to allege in the next years that some Athenians were still loyal to the memory of the Peisistratidae.

The tactics of the battle are clear. The Persian commanders put their best contingents, those drawn from the Persians themselves and from the Sacae, in the center. The Athenians and Plataeans were inferior in numbers but superior in equipment and training. By weakening their center they made their line equal in length to that of the enemy, but they strengthened both wings. According to Herodotus (6.112.1) they advanced the whole distance of eight stades (about a mile) "at the double" or "at a run;" but it is difficult to believe that even well trained men could advance a mile at the double in full armor in summer and then fight. Perhaps the Greeks advanced much of the distance at a marching pace and broke into a run when they were within reach of the enemy's arrows. The Persian forces broke through the Greek center, but the Greeks routed the enemy on the wings; then, instead of pursuing, the Greek forces from the wings turned on the Persian center and put it to flight. The survivors of the Persian force withdrew towards the marsh and Schinia and reembarked on their fleet; they lost only seven ships to the Athenian pursuers.

After reembarking, the Persians sailed round the promontory of Sunium and made for the Bay of Phalerum, in the hope of attacking Athens before the Athenian force returned; they had a journey of about seventy miles, which would take them twelve to fourteen hours. Meanwhile the Athenian troops hurried back to Athens from Marathon, a distance of twenty-three miles; although they were tired from the battle, which had been lengthy, they could make the journey in eight hours or less. Evidently the Athenians arrived first. While the Persians were sailing, they may have been encouraged in their hopes of treachery; Herodotus says that at Sunium a shield was flashed in the sunlight as a signal to them, but interpretation of this incident is difficult (see chapter 8, pp.

202–203). However that may be, the Persians came to anchor off Phalerum. But they found that the Athenian forces had already reached Athens and could defend the city; their hopes of treachery could no longer be fulfilled; and so they sailed back to Asia.

If the views expounded in this chapter about Darius's designs on European Greece are correct, the campaign of Marathon had a precise result. For the Persian forces the sea route through the Cyclades was shorter and cheaper than the land route along the north coast of the Aegean, but in order to use the sea route Darius had to command a base at the European end for disembarking his force. The defeat at Marathon disappointed Darius in his hope of winning the desired base. Ten years later Xerxes, the son and successor Darius, invaded European Greece but he used the land route. The campaign is also highly significant in the development of the Athenian state. When Datis and Artaphernes took Hippias on their journey, they chose a man who not only knew the territory but could still hope to attract followers in Attica. The Athenian generals seem to have been even more alive to the possibility of Athenian treachery; this provides the best explanation both for their original march from Athens to Marathon and for their later decision to fight. Yet these fears and hopes were not realized; the Athenian state had achieved a more effective unity than Eretria. The contrast with the events of 546 is palpable.

NOTES

1. On Homeric similes as a clue to place of composition see Arthur Platt, "Homer's Similes," *Journal of Philology* 24 (1896) 28–38; perhaps the most telling indication is at *Iliad* 9.4–7. For Naucratis see Hdt. 2.178. The Chiote inscription is Meiggs/Lewis 8; and see chapter 5, pp. 120–121. On Miletus under and after Thrasybulus see Hdt. 1.17–22; 5.28–29; 5.92z; Ar. *Pol.* 3.1284a26–33; 5.1311a20–22. The thesis that Ionia was not ahead of European Greece was argued by R.M. Cook, "Ionia and Greece in the Eighth and Seventh Centuries B.C.," *JHS* 66 (1946) 67–98; his argument was criticized by Carl Roebuck, "The Economic Development of Ionia," C.P. 48 (1953) 9–16. Greek recollections of the Mermnad dynasty are given by Hdt. 1.6–56; 1.69–94; Bacchylides 3.23–62. For dedications by Croesus at Ephesus see Tod 1.6.

2. Herodotus records the Persian conquest of the Greek cities of the Asiatic mainland at 1.141–169. His account of Samos is at 3.39–60; 3.120–125; 3.139–149. He mentions a Mytilenaean ship serving under Cambyses in Egypt at 3.13.1. He gives the Greek tyrants present in the Scythian expedition at 4.137–138; for Coes of Mytilene see 4.97 and 5.11. Dates proposed for Croesus's war with Cyrus vary between 547 and 541; Wade-Gery, *Essays* 166 notes 3 = JHS 71 (1951) 219 n. 38 suggests 544. For the Scythian expedition he suggests 514 (Essays 160–161 = ibid. 215). Recent studies of the Samian tyranny include Mary White, "The Duration of the Samian Tyranny," *JHS* 74 (1954) 36–43, and John P. Barron, "The Sixth-Century Tyranny at Samos," *CQ,* N.S. 14 (1964) 210–229. Both White and Barron accept a Eusebian date (532 or 533) for the beginning of the rule of Polycrates and suppose that he had predecessors in the tyranny. That is possible. But the value of

Eusebian dates is disputable; a date ca. 540 would make it easier to accommodate the reported activities of Polycrates; and Herodotus gives the impression that Polycrates was the first Samian tyrant by saying that he won Samos by revolution and at first shared control with his two brothers. The view taken here resembles that of K.J. Beloch, *Griechische Geschichte* I², 1 (Strassburg 1912) 375–376. On the invention of the trireme see J.A. Davison, "The First Greek Triremes," *CQ* 41 (1947) 18–24, and R.T. Williams, "Early Greek Ships of Two Levels," *JHS* 78 (1958) 121–130.

   3. Herodotus gives the expedition against Naxos and the Ionian Revolt at 5.28–6.33; he gives the subsequent settlement of Ionian affairs and Mardonius's campaign of 492 at 6.42–45. For Histiaeus at Myrcinus and Susa see Hdt. 5.11; 5.23–24. A useful study of the Ionian Revolt is offered by J.A.S. Evans, "Histiaeus and Aristagoras: Notes on the Ionian Revolt," *AJP* 84 (1963) 113–128. Mabel Lang, "Herodotus and the Ionian Revolt," *Historia* 17 (1968) 24–36, attempts a highly sceptical treatment of Herodotus's story; but her account of the policy of Histiaeus is less consistent than that given by Evans. The inscription preserving the letter of Darius to Gadates is accessible as Meiggs/Lewis 12. On the excavations at Al Mina (Sueidia) see chapter 1, p. 32 with note 6.

   4. On Mandrocles see Hdt. 4.87–88; on Democedes, 3.129–137. For the building of the palace at Susa see A.T. Olmstead, *History of Persia* (Chicago 1948) 168. On justificatory grievances as Herodotus's way of explaining wars see Sealey, "Herodotus, Thucydides and the Causes of War," *CQ*, N.S. 7 (1957) 1–12. That the Persian elite set a value on conquest is implied by Hdt. 3.120 and 9.122, if attestation were needed. On the value of Demetrias to Antiochus III see M. Holleaux, *CAH* 8.207–208.

   5. The Persian heralds of 491 are given by Hdt. 6.48–49; 7.133. K.J. Beloch, *Griechische Geschichte* II², 1 (Strassburg 1914) 40 note 6, held that they were unhistorical; he has been followed by many, e.g. Hignett, *XIG* 87. Beloch argued that before the battle of Marathon the Persian aim was merely the punishment of Athens and Eretria, not the subjugation of European Greece, and so Darius had no need to seek the submission of the Greek cities. This argument collapses if, as argued above, Darius already planned to reduce Greece and the Persian aim in 490 was to secure Athens and Eretria as bases for landing a force in Europe. Herodotus's account (6.49–93) of the events consequent upon the Aeginetan response to the Persian heralds is circumstantial and difficult to reject. Herodotus says that at Sparta the Persian heralds were thrown into a well. Beloch assigned this to 481, when the Spartans might wish to impress their allies with their determination to resist the Persians, and he held that the story of throwing the heralds into the pit at Athens was a fiction modelled on the Spartan story. It is conceivable that the Athenian ill-treatment of the heralds has been exaggerated, but nothing compels this assumption. Earlier studies of Athenian politics of this period include C.A. Robinson, Jr., "The Struggle for Power at Athens in the Early Fifth Century," *AJP* 60 (1939) 232–237; M.F. McGregor, "The Pro-Persian Party at Athens from 510 to 480 B.C.," *HSCP* supplementary volume 1, 1940 (= Athenian Studies presented to W.S. Ferguson) 71–95; A.W. Gomme, "Athenian Notes. 1" ("Athenian Politics, 510–483 B.C.") *AJP* 65 (1944) 321–339; C.A. Robinson, Jr., "Athenian Politics, 510–486 B.C., " *AJP* 66 (1945) 243–254. Studies of a more recent type include F.J. Frost, Themistocles' Place in Athenian Politics, *CSCA* 1 (1968) 105–124; E.S. Gruen, "Stesimbrotus on Miltiades and Themistocles," *CSCA* 3 (1970) 91–98; Frost's article supersedes previous work on Themistocles. The Aeginetan War is given by Hdt. 5.81; 5.89; 6.87–93; a useful discussion of its chronology is offered by A. Andrewes, "Athens and Aegina, 510–480 B.C.," *ABSA* 37 (1936–37) 1–7. The Athenian expedition of twenty ships to support the Ionian Revolt is given by Hdt. 5.97; 5.99–103. The archonship of Hipparchus in 496/5 is known from Dion. Hal., *Rom. Ant.* 5.77.6; 6.1.1. For Themistocles as choregus to Phrynichus in 477/6 see Plut. *Them.* 5.5; for his marriage see ibid. 32.1; for his house in Melite see ibid. 22.2; for his restoration of the Lycomid sanctuary at Phlya see ibid. 1.4. Other fifth-century politicians resident

in Melite are noted by Sealey, *Essays* 65 (= Hermes 84 [1956] 241). The archonship of Themistocles is attested by Dion. Hal., *Rom. Ant.* 6.34.1. That Thuc. 1.93.3 refers, not to the archonship, but to a special office held in connection with the shipbuilding program was suggested by A.W. Gomme, *AJP* 65 (1944) 323 note 13 and *Comm.* 1.261–262; this view has been strongly defended by C.W. Fornara, "Themistocles' Archonship," *Historia* 20 (1971) 534–540; it has been attacked by D.M. Lewis, *Historia* 22 (1973) 757–8, and W.W. Dickie, ibid. 758–9. Ostraca of 487–6 against Themistocles are noted by F.J. Frost, *CSCA* 1 (1968) 124. Perhaps the most persuasive attempt to associate Miltiades and Themistocles is that of H.T. Wade-Gery, *Essays* 171–179 = ("Themistokles' Archonship," *ABSA* 37 [1936–37] 263–270). The fortunes of Megacles in 486 are known from Ar. *AP* 22.5; Pind. *P.* 7. The marriage of Xanthippus is known from Hdt. 6.131.2 and Plut. *Per* 3.2, and his ostracism from Ar. *AP* 22.6. On Callias see chapter 6, p. 158; for the deme of his family see B.D. Meritt, *Hesperia* 5 (1936) 410. That Aristeides was a cousin of Callias is known from Plut. *Arist.* 25.6. For Cleinias at Artemisium see Hdt. 8.17; for Alcibiades joining Cleisthenes in expelling the Peisistratidae see Isoc. 16.26. Callimachus as polemarch at Marathon is known from Meiggs/Lewis 18 and Hdt. 6.109.2. On the statues of Harmodius and Aristogeiton see F. Jacoby, *Atthis* (Oxford 1949) 339 note 52. The assertion that Cleisthenes was ostracized comes from Aelian, *V.H.* 13.24.

6. Herodotus gives his account of the campaign of Marathon at 6.94–120. Pausanias (1.15.3; 1.32.7) adds the information that some Persians in flight fell into the marsh; he learned this from the reliefs on the Stoa Poikile. It is doubtful whether other literary sources later than Herodotus can be trusted on the Persian Wars; a sceptical view of their value is taken by Hignett, *XIG* 7–25. The present account of the strategy depends largely on Hignett, *XIG* 55–74. For topography see W.K. Pritchett, "Marathon" = University of California Publications in Classical Archaeology, vol. 4, no. 2 (1960) 137–190; idem, "Marathon Revisited," *Studies in Ancient Greek Topography,* Part I = University of California Publications in Classical Studies, vol. 1, (1965) 83–93; idem, "Deme of Marathon: von Eschenburg's Evidence," *Studies in Ancient Greek Topography*, Part II = University of California Publications in Classical Studies, vol. 4, (1969) 1–11. There are two possible sites where the Greeks may have encamped on marching from Athens to Marathon. Their lines may have run from the southeastern base of Mt. Kotroni to the foothills of Mt. Agrieliki; they would be drawn up approximately parallel to the shore. Alternatively their lines may have run along the northeastern edge of Mt. Agrieliki, approximately at right angles to the shore.

8

Persia and Greece II: The Hellenic League

After the failure at Marathon, the Persian high command had to fall back on its plans for using the land route into Greece. A revolt of Egypt in 486 diverted Darius's attention; Egypt, a rich satrapy and the place of an ancient civilization, mattered more to the Persians than European Greece. Darius died later in 486 and was succeeded by his son, Xerxes. Egypt was recovered in 485. During the ensuing four years the Persians carried out extensive preparations for the invasion of Greece. They built a bridge across the Hellespont from Abydus to Sestos; it was supported on anchored boats, and when a storm destroyed the first bridge, a second was built. A bridge was also built across the Strymon river. A canal was dug across the neck of land connecting Mt. Athos to Chalcidice; the Persian fleet was to proceed through this canal, for in 492 the fleet of Mardonius had suffered heavy losses in the storm off Mt. Athos. Depots for storing supplies of food and equipment were set up along the coast of Thrace and in Macedon.

News of these preparations must have reached all parts of Greece, and in 481 many Greek cities joined together in a League to resist the expected invasion. It is not clear how far such resistance was motivated by any consciousness of Greek national unity. In this connection a passage of Herodotus (8.144) is sometimes cited; it is the reply which he puts into the mouth of the Athenians, when they rejected a Persian diplomatic offer in the winter of 480/79. The Athenians are made to say that they will not betray the Greek cause, because they recognize that the Greeks have "the same blood and the same language, common sanctuaries of the gods and sacrifices and similar customs." Such things could be said in diplomacy and propaganda; it does not follow that they supplied real motives. Moreover, Herodotus composed the passage several decades after the event, that is to say, after the defeat of the Persian invasion had itself fostered a consciousness of Greek solidarity. The Greek outlook in 481 may have been different. Some Greek states, such as Argos, refused to join the League formed in that year. Previously some Greek cities had been allies of Persia for a time; this is true of Athens (see chapter 7, p. 175). A brief poem of ca. 500 is the song of a Cretan mercenary, Hybrias, who served the great king and boasted of his calling : "For me the sword and the spear and the fair shield, the defense of the body, are great wealth. With these I plow, with these I reap, with these I tread the sweet wine from the grapes; in virtue of these I am called master of serfs. But as for those who dare not have the sword and the spear and the fair shield, the defense of the body, they all fall at my knee and worship me as master of masters, proclaiming the great king."

In short, most Greeks probably did not come to regard medism, or alliance with Persia, as a disgrace until after they had repulsed the invasion of Xerxes. The reasons why many Greek cities allied in 481 to resist the invasion must be sought in the particular circumstances of those cities, not in any general recognition of Persia as a national enemy. The League of 481 was not an emergent nation but an alliance of sovereign states against a large but temporary danger, and while it operated, differences of opinion arose to strain relations between its members. But in spite of stresses and difficulties, the alliance was successful in a high degree; by the end of 479 it had defeated the Persians decisively and repeatedly. Accordingly, to the student of the Greek city-states the invasions of 480–479 are of interest because he finds Greek cities cooperating effectively in resistance.

SPARTAN POLICY[2]

Sparta was the leading power in the Hellenic League of 481 and so the question must be asked, How did the Spartans come to oppose the invasion of Xerxes? In the middle of the sixth century the Spartans had friendly relations with Croesus of Lydia and Amasis of Egypt, although these relations went no further than exchanges of presents (see chapter 3, p. 86). The conquests of Lydia by Cyrus and of Egypt by Cambyses were accordingly unfortunate for the Spartans, but it does not follow that Spartan material interests were affected. Herodotus tells a strange story of an Asiatic Greek appeal to Sparta straight after the overthrow of Croesus; when the Ionians and the Aeolians had asked Cyrus to renew the conditions which Croesus had observed towards them and he had refused to make any undertaking to any other city but Miletus (see chapter 7, p. 172), they allegedly sent messengers to Sparta to seek help. The story continues that the Lacedaemonians decided not to furnish help, but they dispatched a penteconter; when it reached Phocaea, the crew sent one of their number to Sardis to warn Cyrus not to harm any Greek city, for the Lacedaemonians would not allow it. Cyrus made a contemptuous reply, first asking who the Lacedaemonians were and then saying that he did not fear men who set aside in the middle of their city a place where they gathered to deceive one another on oath. Herodotus explains that Persians do not have market places. Much of this story should be rejected; the account of the penteconter and the envoy sent to Sardis is surely a later fiction, designed to gloss over the Spartan refusal to help the Asiatic Greeks. That the latter did appeal unsuccessfully to Sparta remains possible; if so, it indicates the prominence Sparta had achieved by ca. 544. Even so, nothing in the previous history of the Spartans could lead anyone to expect them to attempt armed intervention on the Asiatic mainland; Spartan inaction in response to the Persian conquest of Lydia did not mean any change in Spartan policy.

Spartan interest in the affairs of the eastern Aegean reached a climax ca. 525, when Samian refugees persuaded the Spartans and the Corinthians to send a force against Polycrates. Herodotus (3.54.1) describes this as "a large expedition." It landed in the island of Samos, defeated some of the enemy outside the walls and began besieging the city. But when the siege had continued forty days, the Lacedaemonians found themselves no nearer to achieving their goal, and so they withdrew. Perhaps during their return journey they put in at Naxos and overthrew the tyrant Lygdamis, but that was small consolation. Their one large-scale attempt to intervene in the eastern part of the Aegean had failed; meanwhile, the consolidation of Persian rule meant that in Sardis there were authorities less willing to develop Greek contacts than the Mermnad dynasty had been. Hence it is not surprising that a new Spartan policy may be recognized in the ensuing generation. Two principles of the new policy can be discerned; in the first place Sparta would continue to assert herself as a land power in the Peloponnese and would try to extend her influence northwards from there; secondly she would not try to assert herself by naval expeditions across the Aegean. Indeed, Sparta made hardly any further attempt to gain influence in Asia Minor or the Aegean before 412. The new policy had consequences for possible relations with Persia. On the one hand, Sparta would not impede the Persian advance in Asia Minor or its offshore islands or even on the north coast of the Aegean in Thrace and Macedon; on the other hand, Sparta would resist any attempt to extend Persian influence into the heartlands of European Greece.

The new policy may be stated thus by an observer who has the advantage of distance in time. To state it is not to imply that any contemporary Spartan formulated it. On the contrary, it is perhaps more likely that Spartan actions in the time of Darius and Xerxes were determined by a series of *ad hoc* decisions, taken as each problem or opportunity arose, not by reference to any long-term goals. An observer' statement of the new policy serves as a summary of the factors to be presumed as governing those decisions. The new policy emerges clearly in the activities of the Spartan king Cleomenes (ca. 520–ca. 490), about whom Herodotus preserves a good deal of information.

Several actions of Cleomenes illustrate the principle of not obstructing the Persian advance beyond the Aegean. Early in his reign, when the Persians conquered Samos (see chapter 7, p. 174), Maeandrius escaped and came to Sparta to seek help. He offered Cleomenes vessels of gold and silver as gifts. But the king refused and, fearing lest Maeandrius have more success in bribing other Spartans, he recommended to the ephors that they expel the alien. Again Herodotus relates a Spartan story that, after the Scythian expedition of Darius, the Scythians planned to avenge themselves and sent envoys to Sparta to propose a military alliance for a grandiose attack on the Persian Empire: the Scythians would cross the Phasis river and advance from the region of the Caucasus into Media, while the Spartans would sail to Ephesus and then march upcountry to join forces with the Scythians. Allegedly Cleomenes associated with the Scythians and learned from them the habit of drinking unmixed wine. The story may be apocryphal or exaggerated; it is difficult to believe that anyone entertained so wild a scheme seriously, or that the Scythians as a whole were sufficiently organized to send an embassy to Sparta. Possibly the story is an inflated account of a real approach to Sparta by a small group of Scythians with a feasible proposal for a raid into Persian territory. In any case there is no record that anything came of the proposal. The constant attitude of Cleomenes to Asiatic prospects can be recognized in events of 499, when Aristagoras of Miletus came to him in search of help for the Ionian Revolt. According to Herodotus, Aristagoras tried to tempt Cleomenes with prospects of plentiful booty and easy fighting against poorly equipped barbarians, but Cleomenes lost interest when he learned that the journey to Susa took three months. Then Aristagoras tried to bribe him with silver, until the king's little daughter, Gorgo, exclaimed: "Father, the stranger will corrupt you, unless you go away and leave him." So Cleomenes withdrew to another building and Aristagoras departed from Sparta. In Herodotus's account the part played by Gorgo is the folklore motif of the "warner," but otherwise the outline of the story makes good sense; Cleomenes refused to help the Ionian Revolt because he did not want to engage in distant enterprises across the sea.

Other actions of Cleomenes sprang from a desire to extend Spartan hegemony within the Peloponnese and northwards beyond it. In 519 he was near enough to Plataea to receive an appeal from that city; he may well have been engaged in bringing Megara into the Peloponnesian League (see chapter 6, pp. 144–145). In his dealings with Athens he tried to bring that city under Spartan influence. When he expelled Hippias in 510, he contracted ties of friendship with Isagoras. Some years later, when Cleisthenes began to win ascendancy in Athens, Cleomenes responded to the appeal of Isagoras and made repeated attempts to establish him in control there. As was seen above (chapter 6, pp. 147–148), these attempts, culminating in an elaborate attack on Attica from three sides, were unsuccessful and they precipitated a crisis within the Peloponnesian League. A congress of the League was called at Sparta and there the Spartans proposed to restore Hippias to Athens; but the Corinthians spoke against the proposal and the allies rejected it. Thereupon Cleomenes and the Spartans gave up their attempts to intervene in Athens. On the whole those attempts had issued in a setback for Sparta, but there were some advantages to assess. The Peloponnesian League had survived a crisis without disintegrating; issues of organization as well as immediate policy were raised at the congress and apparently they were solved satisfactorily (see chapter 3, pp. 84–85). Besides, after the congress Hippias withdrew to Sigeum and continued to enjoy the protection of Artaphernes; this had the effect of bringing relations between Athens and Persia to an end. From the Spartan point of view, if Athens could not be brought into the Spartan sphere of influence, it was something that she was kept out of the Persian sphere.

Within the Peloponnese Cleomenes sought to enhance the Spartan position against Argos. No armed conflict is known between the two cities from the battle of the champions (ca. 544; see chapter 3, p. 84) until ca. 494; possibly a treaty making peace for fifty years was concluded after the battle. The old conflict was revived ca. 494, when Cleomenes invaded the Argolid and inflicted a heavy defeat on the Argives at Sepeia near Tiryns. After the battle he took a picked force of 1,000 men to the temple of Hera and insisted on offering sacrifice; when the priest protested against sacrifice by an alien, Cleomenes had him flogged. When Cleomenes returned to Sparta, he was called to account before the ephors; his enemies complained that he could and should have captured the city of Argos and they alleged that he had accepted bribes not to do so. But Cleomenes satisfied the ephors with his explanations. The question at stake may have been a real issue of policy; Cleomenes's aim was not to capture or destroy Argos but perhaps to bring it into the Peloponnesian League. This aim would explain his insistence on offering sacrifice as well as his failure to advance on the city. But although Argos suffered an internal revolution in consequence of the losses of the campaign, she remained hostile to Sparta.

During much of the reign of Cleomenes Persian influence remained at a distance from the European mainland of Greece, and so the question did not arise, how Cleomenes and the Spartans would respond to Persian encroachment there. The Athenian alliance with Artaphernes of Sardis, made after Cleomenes was driven from the acropolis, did not continue long in effect. But the question was raised in 491, when Darius sent heralds to Greece to demand earth and water. The Aeginetans, among others, gave these tokens of submission, and the Athenians, who were still at war with them, complained to Sparta. Cleomenes responded with vigor; he crossed to Aegina and tried to arrest those most responsible for giving earth and water. But he was opposed by a leading Aeginetan, Crius, who acted on instructions from the other Spartan king, Demaratus. Crius invoked the doctrine that the allies of Sparta were only bound to obey orders issued jointly by both kings (see chapter 3, p. 85); as Cleomenes had come to Aegina without Demaratus, he did not have authority to arrest Aeginetans. So Cleomenes went back to Sparta and tried to have Demaratus deposed by questioning the legitimacy of his birth; the question was referred to the Delphic oracle, which declared that he was not the son of the previous king, Ariston. So Demaratus was deposed and some little time later he fled to Persia. Meanwhile Cleomenes had Leotychidas enthroned in his place; then the two kings went to Aegina, arrested the most powerful men in the island and entrusted them to the Athenians, their most bitter enemies, for safekeeping.

The career of Cleomenes has been estimated variously by modern historians. His policy makes sense on the principles outlined above: he would not attempt naval enterprise across the Aegean to impede Persian expansion there, but he sought to enlarge Spartan authority by land and therefore he resisted any extension of Persian influence into the European heartlands of Greece; Aegina, although an island, was close enough to the shores to concern him. For the most part the Spartan state accepted the policy which Cleomenes executed, but there was some opposition. In the early years of his reign he came into conflict with his half-brother, Dorieus; eventually Dorieus left Sparta and in 510 he led an unsuccessful expedition to found a colony in the western part of Sicily, where he was killed. In the last years of Cleomenes's reign opposition became more intense; Demaratus tried to frustrate his expedition to Aegina by sending instructions to Crius. When Demaratus was deposed and later fled, he may have still had sympathizers in Sparta; certainly a crisis ensued. It was reported that Cleomenes had used corrupt means to induce the Pythian priestess to declare against Demaratus; Cleomenes became so alarmed that he withdrew from Sparta to Sellasia in northern Laconia. Soon the Lacedaemonians came to believe that he was organizing the Arcadians against Sparta. They recalled him, but he began to show signs of madness and his relatives imprisoned him; he committed suicide.

The conflict between Cleomenes and Demaratus may have been purely personal at first, but an issue of policy was at least implied when Demaratus sent instructions to Crius on resisting Cleomenes. The latter was intervening in Aegina because the Aeginetans had given the Persian heralds the tokens of submission; if Demaratus and his sympathizers tried to help the leading Aegine-tans, they could not adhere to the same view as Cleomenes on relations with Persia. Perhaps not all Spartans saw the implication, but if some did, this may explain a curious occurrence of 491. When the Persian heralds demanding earth and water reached Sparta, they were thrown into a well. To refuse their demand was one thing; to ill-treat heralds was another. Possibly the sympathizers of Cleomenes did this because they saw the strength of the opposition within Sparta and they wanted to commit their city to opposing the extension of Persian influence.

When Demaratus fled to Persia, the issue of policy arose more clearly. Demaratus found favor with Darius and later accompanied Xerxes to Greece in 480. So any attempt within Sparta to recall Demaratus implied an accommoda-tion of some kind with Persia. Surely the friends of Demaratus were responsible for those reports about the Pythian priestess which induced Cleomenes to withdraw to Sellasia; they may have been partly responsible for his subsequent misfortunes. The events attending his withdrawal, recall and death must have lasted well into 490. So it is likely that the question of relations with Persia was under consideration in Sparta during 490. This would explain Spartan activity in relation to the campaign of Marathon. When the Athenians appealed to them, the Spartans resolved to send help but they insisted that they must wait until the full moon according to custom; so when at last the Spartans sent a force of 2,000 men, it arrived after the battle and contented itself with inspecting the battlefield. Such behavior may reflect acute and complex difference of opinion in Sparta about policy towards Persia.

Some time after the death of Cleomenes the question of Spartan policy towards Persia arose again. So much may be inferred from a story told by Herodotus. He says that, because the Spartans had ill-treated the heralds of Darius, they were unable to gain any favorable response from the gods at sacrifices; so at last two Spartans, Sperthias and Boulis, volunteered to go to Susa and offer themselves to Xerxes in compensation for the heralds. The story continues that on reaching Susa the two Spartans refused to prostrate themselves before the king, as was the custom of the Persian Empire; even so Xerxes declined to harm them and sent them home, for he did not wish to free the Lacedaemonians from guilt. Diplomatic interchanges in the sixth and fifth centuries were often couched in religious terms. Moreover, when this story reached Herodotus, a generation had passed since the defeat of Xerxes in Greece and medism had become a disgrace; so the Spartans might wish to disguise anything in their record that resembled an approach to Persia. If the reader of Herodotus allows for the religious coloring of the story and for the influences under which it was transmitted, he discovers in it a Spartan attempt at a rapprochement with the Persian king. He must then ask the date of the mission of Sperthias and Boulis. Since the king who received them in audience was Xerxes, they did not travel before 486. A date before 480 is much more likely than a later date, since the Spartans had far more reason to seek Persian friendship before Xerxes was defeated in his attempt to conquer European Greece.

Xerxes apparently refused the offer of Sperthias and Boulis; he sent them away unscathed and emptyhanded. If he was to conquer European Greece, it was important that he should defeat the strongest power there, the leader of the Peloponnesian League. For his purpose an understanding with an unvanquished Sparta would not suffice; it might prove precarious; instead he must demonstrate the superiority of his forces in action. Thus Sparta became committed to a policy of resisting the Persian invasion. In part this was the result of free Spartan choices; on the several issues of policy arising in the time of Cleomenes the Spartans might have chosen otherwise. But in large part their resistance to Xerxes was determined by their geopolitical situation. As the strongest power in European Greece the Spartans resented a would-be intruder; and equally the Persian intruder wished to subdue the Spartans.

ATHENIAN POLICY[3]

After the campaign of Marathon Athenian freedom of choice in relation to Persia was limited. When a state has won a difficult and somewhat decisive battle against a powerful and exotic enemy, it is not likely to make a complete change of policy; the victory exerts a fascination over public opinion. But bitter personal conflicts continued in the next decade and, perhaps partly in consequence of the victory of Marathon, the charge of treacherous dealings with the Persians was used frequently. When Aristotle (*AP* 22.6) says that in the three years 487–485 the Athenians ostracized "friends of the tyrants," this may be true of the first of the three victims, Hipparchus, who had been archon in 496/5 and was a relative of the Peisistratidae; but for the men ostracized in 486 and 485 Aristotle's description may rest on contemporary gossip or later confusion.

Some charges of medism exploited an incident occurring on the day of the battle of Marathon. As the Persian forces were sailing past Sunium on their journey towards Phalerum, a shield was flashed from land in the sunlight to give a signal. The tradition reaching Herodotus said that this signal was given by the Alcmaeonidae; the historian denied this indignantly, asserting that the Alcmaeonidae had constantly opposed the Peisistratidae, but he insisted that a signal was flashed. It is indeed unlikely that the Alcmaeonidae conducted treasonable communications with the Persians in 490; if the work of Cleisthenes had ensured the ascendancy of the city families, a restoration of the Peisistratidae would harm them. If the Alcmaeonidae are exculpated, there is a wide field for conjecture about the identity of those who displayed the shield signal. One may also ask what message the signal conveyed. But another possibility should be considered. On the day of the battle of Marathon a force of Lacedaemonians was advancing at speed by the route which led through the gap between Mt. Aegaleos and Mt. Parnes and past Acharnae; a shield flashed from the height of Sunium may have conveyed a message to them, telling them whether to make for the city of Athens or for Marathon. If political animosity soon misrepresented the shield as a signal to the Persians and blamed the Alcmaeonidae, this merely indicates the prestigious and enviable position which the clan had attained.

The fortunes of Miltiades after the battle of Marathon illustrate some of the factors governing Athenian politics. In 489 he led an Athenian expedition of no less than seventy ships against the island of Paros. He ravaged its territory and besieged the city for twenty-six days, but he could not capture it. A pretext was found for the attack: in 490 the Parians had supplied a trireme to the Persian force on its journey to Marathon. But Herodotus indicates the real motive of the expedition; Miltiades persuaded the Athenians to send it by telling them that he would enrich any who followed him. The quest for booty was an acknowledged aim of policy in the early fifth century; in 499 Aristagoras had persuaded the Athenians to support the Ionian Revolt by telling them of the good things to be plundered in the Persian Empire. Miltiades on his return from Paros was prosecuted by Xanthippus, who accused him of deceiving the Athenian people and demanded the death penalty; the court condemned Miltiades to pay a fine of fifty talents. The condemned man was imprisoned and he died of a leg injury, which he had received during the siege of Paros. It is not necessary to seek divergence of policy in this conflict between Xanthippus and Miltiades. The eminence which Miltiades had gained through the victory of Marathon made him an object of envy. Xanthippus had begun his political fortunes well by marrying an Alcmaeonid; he could advance them further by success in a sensational trial. By 485/4 he was prominent enough to be ostracized.

In 488/7 the Athenians instituted sortition for selecting the nine archons. According to Aristotle (*AP* 22.5), the first board chosen by lot was that of 487/6; all previous archons were chosen by election. The new procedure had two stages; first each tribe chose ten candidates by election and then sortition was used to select ten men from among the hundred candidates. Herodotus (6.109.2) describes Callimachus, the polemarch at the battle of Marathon, as chosen by lot; possibly in 490 the members of the board were chosen by election but they cast

lots for the several functions of eponymous archon, king, polemarch, thesmothetae, and secretary of the thesmothetae. Recent historians have spent much
ingenuity in guessing the reason for the change of 487, but an easy explanation is
readily available. Aristotle (*Pol.* 5.1303a15–16) offers a hint; he says that at Heraea
in the Peloponnese the lot was introduced for choosing magistrates because
candidates had competed in corrupt and excessive ways. When a valuable prize is
to be given to a few among many candidates who all feel equally entitled to it,
none can feel aggrieved if the choice is left to chance; this is still the reason for
tossing a coin. Likewise when voters are removed from the process of final
selection, candidates can no longer bribe or otherwise abuse them. The
introduction of lot for the choice of the archons suggests that political competition had become fierce and ruthless; the same inference might be drawn from the
frequency of ostracism in the 480s.

Apart from personal conflicts, possibly the issue most engaging Athenian
attention was the Aeginetan War. Although the chronology of the operations
reported by Herodotus is obscure, they lasted well into the 480s. This must be
borne in mind in order to understand an Athenian decision taken in 483/2. In
that year an unusually rich vein of silver was discovered at Laureum. At first the
Athenians considered dividing the proceeds equally among themselves; then, on
the proposal of Themistocles, they used the money to build ships. The program
of shipbuilding continued into the next year, and by 480 the Athenians had 200
triremes ready for service. Herodotus says that, in persuading the Athenians to
build warships, Themistocles had in mind the war against Aegina. Some modern
historians have preferred to suppose that he foresaw using the ships against the
Persian invasion; but there is no good reason to doubt Herodotus's view or to
deny the irony of history.

Aristotle, after stating the program of shipbuilding, says that Aristeides was
ostracized in 483/2. Already in the time of Herodotus enmity between Themistocles and Aristeides was almost proverbial. Their recorded activities do not
indicate any clear or sharp difference of policy between them. The ostracism of
Aristeides may have been the outcome of personal conflicts arising from the
controversy about the use of the silver from Laureum. The decision to build ships
may well have raised the political standing of Themistocles enormously.
Aristeides appears to have been a competent, though not a brilliant, statesman,
one who could not compare in native talent with Themistocles. The latter, as will
be remembered, belonged to the deme Phrearrioi, far out to the southeast,
whereas Aristeides belonged to the deme Alopece in the city and was a cousin of
the wealthy Callias of the same deme. Possibly, when the decision to build ships
brought political advantage to Themistocles, the city families put forward
Aristeides as his rival, and the ensuing ostracism disappointed them.

Probably in 482/1 the Athenians recalled those who had been ostracized. Aristotle (*AP* 22.8), reporting this, says that it was done because of the impending invasion of Xerxes. Perhaps Athenian sentiments were mixed; some may have hoped that the men ostracized would be reconciled with their fellow citizens and would join wholeheartedly in resisting the barbarian; others may have thought that such men would be less dangerous if they were brought back to Attica, where they could be watched. Apart from the recall of the ostracized, little can be discerned about political preparations taken by the Athenians against the invasion. Herodotus (7.140–143) says that they consulted the Delphic oracle twice; he gives both responses and an anecdote about Themistocles, who allegedly reinterpreted an apparently alarming response of the oracle as a prophecy of victory at Salamis. It is difficult to discover credible dates for the two consultations; the responses or parts of them may be later fictions. It is likely that the Athenians consulted Delphi, that they differed in opinion and that Themistocles took part in the debates; but the course of the deliberations and of the consultations is lost in the mist of subsequent pride.

The Athenians joined the League formed in 481 to resist the invasion. As observed above, the outcome of the battle of Marathon determined to some extent the Athenian response to a subsequent Persian attack. Furthermore, by joining the League the Athenians gained an immediate benefit. Its members freed them from a troublesome and alarming threat; for the League put an end to the Aeginetan War (see below, p. 207).

THE HELLENIC LEAGUE[4]

In 481 many Greek states set up a League to resist the expected Persian attack. Little information has been preserved about this organization. Herodotus mentions two congresses of the League, a foundation congress held in 481 at an unnamed place and a congress in session at the Isthmus of Corinth early in the campaigning season of 480. At both congresses the member states were represented by envoys or deputies; Herodotus calls them *probouloi* at the second congress. At the first congress the members took an oath, which brought the League into existence. Apparently the oath bound the allies to one another permanently; the Athenians formally abrogated their tie with Sparta ca. 462 (see chapter 9, p. 261), that is, they still recognized the oath as binding until abrogated.

No name is recorded for the League; it can be called "The Hellenic League of 481." After the battle of Plataea the victors dedicated an offering to Apollo at Delphi; it was a gold tripod surmounting a bronze column, which had the shape of three intertwined serpents. The column was removed by the Emperor

Constantine to Constantinople, where it survives. On the serpent column the victors inscribed a list of states under the heading: "These fought the war." The list included cities who had taken part in the fighting of 480–479, even if they were not members of the League of 481. Thus Tenos was inscribed, because a Tenian ship deserted the Persians for the other side just before the battle of Salamis. Even so the list provides some clues to the membership of the League. An approximate classification of the entries on the serpent column into three groups can be discerned. The groups are, first, the Lacedaemonians and the Peloponnesian League; second, the Athenians, Plataeans, Thespians, and several islands including some cities of Euboea; and third, Corinth with her dependent colonies. Theories which would interpret these groups as three subordinate hegemonies within the League are insufficiently grounded; the grouping reflects primarily the convenience of those who drew up the list. But study of the list suggests one important inference about the League. A high proportion of the entries on the serpent column is provided by members of the Peloponnesian League. Out of the total of thirty-one states thirteen are Peloponnesian; the others include Aegina and Megara, which were usually allies of Sparta, and four colonies of Corinth, namely Poteidaea, Leucas, Anactorium and Ambracia. Thus Sparta with her allies including Corinth and her dependencies accounted for nineteen of the entries on the serpent column.

When the Hellenic League was founded in 481, Peloponnesian predominance was less heavy, as the new League probably included several states of Central Greece. Herodotus (7.132.1) gives a list of states which, he says, gave earth and water to Persian heralds in 481; it comprises the Thessalians and others north of the Malian Gulf, the Locrians, the Thebans and the other Boeotians except for Thespiae and Plataea. But the Greek army sent to Thermopylae included forces from Thebes, East Locris and Phocis. Thebes, which headed a federation of Boeotian cities, and East Locris probably joined the Hellenic League in 481; they medized after the battle of Thermopylae, when they had little choice. The Peloponnesian element formed a strong block within the Hellenic League of 481, but the latter was not a mere extension of the Peloponnesian League; the oath founding it gave it separate identity. The weight of the Peloponnesian element is illustrated by a discussion and decision reached at the first congress. A suggestion was made that the Athenians should have command of the naval forces of the new League, but the allies resisted this; they insisted that they would obey a Spartan commander but not an Athenian, and so the Athenians gave up their claim to naval command, although they provided more than half of the federal fleet. The Spartan claim to command the land forces was apparently not disputed. The policy of the Hellenic League was determined by its congresses; it is not clear how often these met. During operations Herodotus's account shows a council of war, which deliberated on strategy; it consisted of the commanders of the contingents from the several cities. Herodotus's account gives the impression that the council was advisory and authority to decide strategy rested solely with the Spartan commander-in-chief. The advantages of unitary command are obvious; in the campaign of Lade in 494 Greek fortunes had suffered because the Ionians resisted the discipline imposed by their chosen commander, Dionysius of Phocaea.

The first congress of the Hellenic League took several decisions. It put an end to wars in progress between its members; the most considerable of these was that between Athens and Aegina. Further the congress sent three scouts to Asia Minor, since Xerxes was already in Sardis with his army. The scouts were captured and, when Xerxes learned of their arrival, he let them inspect his infantry and his cavalry and return to Greece; he wished the Greeks to be alarmed at the size of his force. The first congress also sent envoys to Argos, to Gelon, the tyrant of Syracuse in Sicily, to Corcyra, and to Crete. Strategically the most important of these places was Argos. The Argives remembered their long-standing hostility towards Sparta and their severe defeat by Cleomenes at Sepeia; so they were not willing to join a Hellenic League headed by Sparta. Moreover a Greek tradition reaching Herodotus (7.150–152) said that Xerxes had negotiated with the Argives and reached an understanding of some kind with them; this is credible. Argive troops did not take part in the fighting of 480–479, since Persian forces did not reach or cross the Isthmus of Corinth; but the strategists of the Hellenic League had to reckon with the possibility that Argos might offer the Persians a base within the Peloponnese. The other appeals of the Hellenic League for aid were unsuccessful. Gelon was fighting a war against the Carthaginians and could not spare forces for operations against the Persians. The Corcyreans promised to send help but their sixty ships sailed no further than the west coasts of Lacedaemon, whether because unfavorable winds prevented them from rounding Cape Malea or because they expected a Persian victory. When the envoys of the Hellenic League reached Crete, the Cretans refused their appeal.

In 480 the second congress of the Hellenic League received an offer of help from an unexpected quarter. In Thessaly the Aleuadae, the ruling family of Larisa, were ascendant and held the office of federal king or *tagos*. They had made the Thessalian federation ally with Persia, probably in 492 during the operations of Mardonius. But there was opposition to the Aleuadae within Thessaly; it was probably led by the Echecratidae of Pharsalus. In 480 the dissidents sent envoys to the Isthmus and invited the Hellenic League to send a force in order to hold the passes leading from Macedon into Thessaly. Accordingly 10,000 hoplites were sent under the Lacedaemonian commander Euaenetus; the commander of the Athenian contingent was Themistocles. This force sailed to Halus and then proceeded overland to the Tempe valley, where it could guard the pass leading from Lower Macedon along the Peneus river between Mt. Olympus and Mt. Ossa. But the force only stayed in Thessaly a few days and then returned to the Isthmus. Three other passes led from Macedon into Thessaly; probably the Greek force learned that a large part of the Thessalians adhered to the Aleuadae and the Persian alliance; without united Thessalian support there could be no hope of holding all the passes.

THE STRATEGY OF THERMOPYLAE AND ARTEMISIUM[5]

Xerxes made his expeditionary force gather at Sardis in 481. In the next spring they marched to the Hellespont and crossed it by the bridge which had been built. Then the force proceeded to Doriscus on the Hebrus river; the site had a beach and a large plain, where the Persians had built a fort and installed a garrison; here both the land force and the fleet were counted. The figures given by Herodotus (7.60.1; 7.87) for the land contingents are fantastically high; considerations of time, space and supply suffice to refute them, but modern attempts to discover where Herodotus's statistics went wrong and hence to reach a reliable total have had little success. A possible estimate for the land force at Doriscus is 80,000 to 100,000. For the fleet at Doriscus Herodotus (7.89.1) gives a precise figure of 1,207 triremes. Aeschylus in *The Persians* (lines 341–343; produced in 472) gives the same figure for the fleet when it fought at Salamis later in the year. It is not possible to discern the origin of this figure. Elsewhere Herodotus (8.13 fin.) implies that the Persian ships did not much outnumber the Greek fleet at Salamis. Allowance must be made for losses suffered in storms and action between Doriscus and Salamis, but a total of 1,207 triremes is incredibly high; ca. 600 triremes is a more likely estimate.

From Doriscus the Persian fleet and army proceeded side by side along the coast of Thrace as far as Acanthus on the eastern shore of the Chalcidic peninsula. At Acanthus they separated; the fleet sailed through the canal, which had been cut across the neck of the Athos promontory, and continued round the other promontories of Chalcidice and on to Therma. The army meanwhile marched overland to Therma, and there the whole force was reunited. From Therma the army with Xerxes himself went on ahead through Lower Macedon and Thessaly into the territory of Malis at the head of the Malian Gulf. Herodotus (7.183.2–3) says that, after the departure of the army, the fleet waited eleven days at Therma and then sailed in a single day to Magnesia, where it anchored at Cape Sepias and a neighboring beach. Here Herodotus may have telescoped events; the distance to be traversed by sea was between 90 and 100 miles, and so large a fleet could hardly sail together at more than five miles per hour; possible the fleet sailed in several separate contingents. At any rate Xerxes clearly wished to synchronize the movements of his land force and his sea force; in particular, when they met the Greek forces, he wanted them to be within such distance of one another that communications could pass easily between them. This desire is understandable; if the fleet advanced far ahead of the army, it might be unable to find a friendly coast where it could put in for water; and if the army proceeded much beyond where the fleet could support it, it would be exposed to Greek seaborne raids.

The Greeks likewise sought joint positions for their army and fleet, where communications between the two would not be excessively difficult. The land position chosen was Thermopylae, a narrow defile between mountains and the sea on the south shore of the Malian Gulf. Here the route from Thessaly into Central Greece runs eastward along the shore. At Thermopylae proper, which topographers have come to call "the Middle Gate," the defile was only fifty feet wide; at short distances on either side of the Middle Gate were the West Gate and the East Gate, where the route was wide enough only for a single cart (cf. Hdt. 7.176). The Hellenic League sent a force of about 7,000 hoplites under the Spartan king Leonidas to Thermopylae, and Leonidas decided to hold the Middle Gate; there the mountains to the south were particularly high and precipitous. The fleet was sent to Artemisium, a beach on the northern shore of Euboea. It was commanded by a Spartan, Eurybiades, and consisted at first of 271 triremes, but on the second day of the fighting it was joined by a further Athenian squadron of 53 triremes. Scouts were stationed with triaconters at Thermopylae and Artemisium, so that if either force was overcome the news could be brought to the other (Herodotus 8.21.1).

The aim of the Greek strategy has been reconstructed in more than one way. Until recently it was commonly supposed that the Greeks pinned their hopes on the prospect of naval victory, since at sea they were not so heavily outnumbered as on land; according to this view the task of Leonidas was merely to hold up the advance of the Persian land force, while the fleet was to seek a decisive engagement. This theory rested in part on the eventual outcome of the fighting of 480; at Salamis later in the year the forces of Xerxes were defeated at sea. But it is dangerous to argue from results to intentions, and the theory has been challenged of late (by J.A.S. Evans). Against the theory it is pointed out that the Greeks could have little confidence of naval victory, since their fleet was largely new and untried; the Athenian contingent, which totalled 180 ships in the final fighting at Artemisium, had mostly been raised since 483. The Persian forces included the excellent fleets from Phoenicia and Egypt, and in the most recent sea battle between Greeks and Persians, that of Lade, the Greeks had been defeated. Moreover, the Greek fleet at Artemisium did not behave as if its orders were to seek out and destroy the enemy; instead it tried to cover the land force, it avoided exposing itself, and it retired as soon as it learned of the defeat on land. The land force stationed at Thermopylae was large, about 7,000 men. The force sent to the Tempe valley earlier in the year had been even larger (see p. 207–208); presumably a larger army could have been sent to Thermopylae; in other words, the Greek strategists thought that the force actually sent to Thermopylae was adequate. Relieving forces and supplies could be sent to it, when needed. Furthermore, until he reached Thermopylae, Leonidas did not know of the path through the mountains whereby his position could be turned. Accordingly, it has been suggested that the fleet at Artemisium was intended merely to cover the land position and the Greeks attached their hopes to the engagement on land; the defile of Thermopylae was so narrow that Leonidas could expect to hold up the Persian advance indefinitely, until Xerxes ran short of supplies.

The anchorage chosen by the Persian fleet at Cape Sepias and the neighboring beach was scarcely adequate. This part of the coast of Magnesia now has several beaches, but the level of the sea may have changed since antiquity. At least Herodotus (7.188.1) says that the first of the ships to arrive were beached but the rest had to ride at anchor off the shore, so that they were drawn up in rows as many as eight ships deep. In this position they were especially vulnerable to gales. On the day after they reached the Magnesian coast a storm sprang up and allegedly lasted three days (Hdt. 7.191.2). The damage inflicted was large but it is not easy to assess. Herodotus (7.190) says that at the lowest estimate known to him the Persians lost 400 ships in the storm, but this figure should be considered in relation to his exaggerated total of 1,207 triremes at Doriscus. The correct inference may be that the storm destroyed about a third of the fleet.

On the day after the storm subsided, the Persian fleet sailed round the southeast corner of Magnesia and anchored at Aphetae. The location of Aphetae has been disputed, but the clearest indication is Herodotus's statement (8.8.2) that it was ten miles from the beach of Artemisium; it follows that Aphetae was a position on the south coast of Magnesia. The next development in Persian fortunes is highly problematical. Herodotus's account allows the reader to reconstruct a day-by-day narrative of Persian movements from Xerxes's departure from Therma to the three-day battles at Artemisium and Thermopylae. It appears that the naval battle began two days after the fleet reached Aphetae. Now Herodotus (8.7 and 13) says that, after reaching Aphetae, the Persians detached a squadron of 200 ships to make a wide detour to the east of Euboea and approach the channel between Euboea and the mainland from the south; it would thus block the Greek fleet's line of retreat through the Euripus; but on the night following the first day of fighting a rain storm occurred and destroyed this squadron on a rocky shore called the Hollows of Euboea. To evaluate this information one must first discover what part of the Euboean coast was called the Hollows. Several writers of Roman date mention this place. Some of them (most notably Strabo 10.1.2, p. 445) locate it on the southwest coast of Euboea between Aulis and Geraestus. A storm driving ships ashore here would have to blow from the southwest, but the prevailing winds in summer blow from the northeast. However, one of the geographers (the Epitomator of Strabo, correcting Strabo) identifies the Hollows as the strip of coast facing east between Geraestus and Cape Caphereus. If this is correct, the squadron of 200 ships had sailed ca. 120 nautical miles from Aphetae, a distance which it could cover in the available time of two days.

For several reasons some historians have doubted the historicity of the voyage of the 200 ships. The most telling reasons arise from considerations of strategic probability. If Herodotus's figure for the fleet at Doriscus is much exaggerated, and if it had lost heavily in the storm off Magnesia, the Persians would not be likely to weaken their fleet at Aphetae further by detaching a squadron of 200 ships. If, however, the figure of 200 is an exaggeration and the squadron detached was smaller, that squadron would be all the more vulnerable to attack by Greek contingents held in reserve in such places as Aegina and Athens. Further, the squadron would need places where it could put in for water; the Aegean coast of Euboea had few harbors and was not held by any power favorable to the Persians. On the other hand, those who reject Herodotus's account of the squadron have not found a convincing reason to explain why it was invented. They have suggested that it was devised to lessen the discrepancy between the popular estimate of the original Persian fleet and the actual numbers engaged at Salamis; but this is not persuasive, as Herodotus's account of the squadron is circumstantial. Perhaps it is best to accept his account, while admitting that the squadron may have numbered less than 200 triremes.

Herodotus (8.15.1) says that the battles at sea and on land were fought on the same three days. This has been doubted but it cannot be proved wrong and it allows a credible reconstruction of strategy. Leonidas on reaching Thermopylae learned of the path, called Anopaea, which led through the mountains south of his position and could be used to outflank it; he stationed the Phocian contingent of 1,000 men at a point on this path to guard it. Xerxes began his frontal attack on Thermopylae two days after his fleet had reached Aphetae. The narrowness of the defile neutralized the value of the greater numbers of the Persian forces, and during the first two days of fighting they were unable to make any progress. On the evening of the second day Xerxes sent his crack troops, the so-called "Immortals" under Hydarnes, to proceed by the path Anopaea in the hope of attacking Leonidas in the rear. Hydarnes set off soon after sundown and marched all night; at dawn he reached the Phocian force and attacked it with arrows. The

Phocians were taken by surprise and fled into the mountains. Thus Hydarnes could proceed with his force and descend from the heights at a position somewhat east of the East Gate.

Leonidas received a few hours' warning from his scouts of the approach of Hydarnes. The reasons for the next movements of the Greek forces are not clear. The traditions reaching Herodotus said that several of the Greek contingents fled or, alternatively, that Leonidas dismissed them. On either view the question arises, Why did Leonidas himself not withdraw with his Spartan force of 300? The answer followed by Herodotus said that Leonidas sought to fulfill an oracle, which had said that either Lacedaemon would be plundered by the Persians or a Spartan king would be killed. But even if the romantic character of this explanation can be overlooked, it does not explain why Leonidas kept with him 700 men from Thespiae and 400 from Thebes. The question why Leonidas made his stand on the third day of fighting cannot be answered; for any answer has to assume that in the heat of emergency commanding officers choose those courses of action whose prudence is apparent to a historian pondering the events afterwards in his study.

Meanwhile the naval fighting off Artemisium was indecisive. Losses on both sides were heaviest on the third day and, after the forces had separated, the scout stationed at Thermopylae brought news to the Greeks at Artemisium that Leonidas and his men had been overcome. Thereupon the Greek fleet withdrew through the Euripus. The Athenians persuaded it to put in at Salamis; the immediate aim was to afford protection while the Athenians evacuated Attica, removing their wives and children to Troezen, Aegina and Salamis.

The withdrawal of the Greek fleet from Artemisium illustrates vividly the interdependence of land and sea operations in the minds of the Greek strategists. Their plan of defense had been well conceived. The fleet was not defeated and the losses it inflicted may have been as considerable as those it incurred. At Thermopylae the land force withstood frontal attack successfully and could have continued resistance for a considerable time, had it not been taken in the rear. The plan of defense failed only because the Phocian contingent, set to hold the mountain path, proved to be inadequate or unreliable. From the Persian point of view the nocturnal expedition of Hydarnes was a large risk. The path was not easy to traverse, and Hydarnes could expect to meet resistance when he was out of communication with his base.

SALAMIS[6]

The Persian success at Thermopylae took the Greek strategists by surprise. When Leonidas first took his troops to Thermopylae, the Hellenic League sent messages to the East Locrians and the Phocians, asking for their support and saying that the allies were about to send reinforcements. The reinforcements did not arrive; that is, the Persians forced their way through Thermopylae too soon. Accordingly Greek movements leading to the next battle, that fought at Salamis, do not indicate so clear or consistent a plan as had been pursued at Thermopylae and Artemisium. Counsels may have been divided. On learning of the death of Leonidas many Peloponnesian cities set about building fortifications across the Isthmus of Corinth. This was a reasonable position to choose as a second line of defense, for at the Isthmus, as at Thermopylae, the land route was narrow. The Isthmus was not as good a position as had been held previously, since Xerxes might outflank it by sending a force by sea to land in the Peloponnese. Besides by fortifying the Isthmus the Peloponnesians abandoned Attica, and this displeased the Athenians.

From the Persian point of view the Athenians may have assumed new importance in consequence of the fighting at Artemisium. They supplied by far the largest contingent in the Greek fleet at that battle; according to Herodotus (8.1–2; 8.14.1) the Athenians furnished 180 triremes in a total fleet of 324. Because of the losses in the storm before the battle Xerxes had a smaller fleet to use than he expected. He would compensate for these losses, if he could win over the Athenians or at least persuade them to remain neutral. Once he had penetrated Thermopylae, Central Greece lay open to him and most of its cities yielded; he could expect the Athenians to do likewise, if he threatened their territory and population.

The duration of the Persian march by land to Athens can be calculated from the movements of the fleet. On the day after the battles of Artemisium and Thermopylae the Persian fleet sailed at dawn to Artemisium and stayed there until noon; then it sailed to Histiaea, the northernmost city of Euboea, and seized it. On the next day in response to an invitation from Xerxes the crews went to Thermopylae and inspected the corpses, and on the day after that they returned to Histiaea. Then the fleet waited for three days and in the course of three further days it sailed through the Euripus to the Bay of Phalerum. Thus nine days passed between the end of the fighting at Artemisium and the arrival of the fleet at Phalerum. Evidently Xerxes wanted part at least of his army to secure Athens ahead of the fleet, so that the ships would find a friendly shore at Phalerum; this explains why the fleet waited for three days at Histiaea. It follows that after the battle of Thermopylae the army proceeded without delay, though without excessive haste, to Attica.

If Xerxes hoped to threaten the people as well as the territory of Attica, he was disappointed. When the Greek fleet withdrew from Artemisium, the Athenians persuaded it to put in at Salamis and afford protection, while they evacuated their wives and children from Attica. The Athenian state issued a proclamation inviting the citizens to evacuate their dependents as best they could. So the noncombatants were taken away, some to Troezen, some to Aegina and some to Salamis. Meanwhile ships hitherto held in reserve at Troezen joined the fleet at Salamis.

Such at least is Herodotus's account (8.40–42) of the evacuation of Attica. If he is right, Greek movements between the battles of Artemisium and Salamis were not the result of an elaborate plan conceived in advance. On the contrary, the fleet first put in at Salamis in response to an Athenian request; the evacuation was an emergency measure ordered at the last minute and the Athenian state did little to organize it but relied on the initiative of the individual citizens; and thereafter Herodotus gives a series of deliberations among the Greek naval commanders, deliberations which culminated after some changes of view in a decision to stay at Salamis and fight there. Thus his main narrative does not give the impression that the Greek choice of Salamis for a naval battle was the result of a long-standing plan, conceived even before the battle of Artemisium.

A different reconstruction of Greek strategy has been defended because of an inscription found at Troezen and first published in 1960. It was inscribed in the third century B.C. but it purports to be a copy of a decree proposed by Themistocles in 480. The text orders the evacuation of noncombatants from Attica to Troezen and Salamis; the temple treasurers and priestesses are to stay on the acropolis, but the men of military age are to embark on 200 ships. Much of the text consists of provisions for manning the ships; when ready, 100 of them are to go to Artemisium and the remaining 100 are to guard Salamis and the Attic coast. Since the inscription was published, many studies have appeared on the question whether it reproduces an authentic decree of 480. Those doubting its authenticity can observe that in the fourth century the Athenians looked back to the period of the Persian Wars as an age of glory, and from the middle of the century onwards Athenian orators cited several decrees which purported to be measures of the Persian Wars and were of doubtful authenticity. The phrasing of the inscription resembles mostly the style of the fourth century rather than the fifth, although it has a few terms which passed out of usage well before the end of the fifth century.

Those who claim that the text includes authentic material have to admit that the wording has been modified in transmission. Accordingly the question for the historian becomes, Does the text contain genuine information not known from other sources? Apart from details it purports to provide a major item of new information. It would appear from the decree that even before the battle of Artemisium the Athenians were planning some of the movements they carried out after that battle; their plans already envisaged evacuating Attica and stationing ships at Salamis. Thus a reconstruction based on the decree comes into conflict with Herodotus's narrative; in that account the steps taken to evacuate Attica begin with the proclamation made after the battle of Artemisium, and a

The so-called Themistocles Decree. This inscription was set up at Troezen in the third century. The text purports to be a copy of a decree proposed by Themistocles in 480. See pages 214–216. [Courtesy Alison Frantz.]

series of deliberations lead to the decision to fight at Salamis. But those historians who set a high evidential value on the decree sometimes claim to find traces of a divergent tradition in Herodotus's account. They can point in particular to a passage (7.140–144) where Herodotus is dealing with Greek preparations in 481 and says that the Athenians consulted the Delphic oracle twice; the second response in its last sentence hinted at the possibility of fighting at Salamis, and in Herodotus's account, when the response was discussed in the Athenian assembly, Themistocles interpreted it as holding out the prospect of a Greek naval victory at Salamis. Yet other historians have doubted the authenticity of part or all of the second oracular response; it may have been invented after the event and, if so, Themistocles's interpretation of the response must likewise be fictitious.

There remain serious objections to a reconstruction of Greek strategy on the basis of the "Themistocles decree," as it is called, and the second oracular response to the Athenians. If there is any truth in the reconstruction followed above of the Greek aims in the engagements at Thermopylae and Artemisium, the plans embodied in the Thermistocles decree were not shared by the Greek high command but were peculiar to the Athenians; for, as was argued, the Hellenic League expected to check the Persian advance indefinitely at Thermopylae. Those who accept the Thermistocles decree and the second oracular response must suppose that there were two strategic plans current in Greece in 480, one being held by the Hellenic League as a whole and the other by the Athenians, and moreover the events culminating in the battle of Salamis developed fully in accord with the Athenian plan. But such a coincidence between prior plans and subsequent events hardly ever happens. Special difficulties concern the provision in the decree for evacuating the noncombatants from Attica. Since the evacuation was not carried out until after the battles of Artemisium and Thermopylae, those who seek authentic material in the Themistocles decree have to suppose that its provision for evacuation was merely a plan, whose execution would wait on a further order; yet the passage in the text of the decree gives an unqualified order without any suggestion that a further signal would be required before it could be carried out. Furthermore, if the Athenians planned the evacuation before the battle of Artemisium, one may ask why they did not carry it out before the battle, while there was still plentiful time. After the battle, as Persian forces approached Attica, the Athenians had less than nine days to evacuate an enormous mass of noncombatants; where was the prudence which, foreseeing the need to evacuate, had planned the operation well in advance?

Rather than attempt a reconstruction from the Themistocles decree and the oracles, it is better to rely on Herodotus's detailed narrative (8.40–42). The Athenian decision to evacuate Attica was a novel step, taken after the battle of

Thermopylae. It was a remarkable achievement in cooperation within the Hellenic League; normally a Greek state surrendered to an enemy if it could no longer defend its territory, and most cities of Central Greece came to terms with Xerxes after Thermopylae. The Greek fleet was persuaded to put in at Salamis, in the first place, to cover the evacuation of Attica, and reinforcements joined it there. It stayed at Salamis and eventually fought there in consequence of a series of deliberations, and Herodotus's account of these must be scrutinized next.

According to that account (8.49–64), when the Greek commanders reached Salamis, they met to deliberate and most of them were in favor of retiring to the Isthmus in order to fight at sea in defense of the Peloponnese. Their discussion was interrupted by the arrival of news that the Persians had occupied all Attica and even captured the acropolis. This news caused panic, and some of the commanders did not wait for a decision in council but hastened to their ships and raised sail; the remainder decided to withdraw to the Isthmus and fight a naval battle there. But during the following night Themistocles persuaded Eurybiades to summon another meeting of the council; when it met there was heated discussion, but finally Eurybiades yielded to the arguments of Themistocles; he decided to hold the fleet at Salamis and fight there.

Within this account Herodotus gives a digression on the siege of the acropolis (8.50–55), which evidently took some time. Accordingly, his first meeting of the council should probably be regarded as telescoping two meetings, one held when the commanders arrived in Salamis and the second when the news came of the fall of the acropolis. Herodotus says that those defending the acropolis were few in number and consisted of treasurers of the temple of Athena and poor people; yet he says that the siege lasted "a long time" and his account of the Persian siege operations is impressive. The Persians, he records, took up a position on the Areopagus opposite the acropolis and fired flaming arrows into the wooden barricade set up by the defenders. They sent descendants of Peisistratus to offer terms, but the defenders refused and rolled heavy stones down the slope when the attackers began to climb it. Finally some of the Persians ascended the acropolis by a path so steep that the defenders had not troubled to guard it; they opened the gates, sacked the temple and set fire to the acropolis.

The complexity of these operations may suggest that the acropolis was defended by a more considerable group of people than Herodotus says. Some historians have argued that a garrison was stationed to hold the acropolis. They have relied in part on his statement that the siege lasted "a long time;" in the context of complex siege operations the phrase suggests a period of days or weeks, not hours. They have also drawn attention to the panic which, according to Herodotus, arose among the Greek commanders when they learned of the fall of the acropolis; this seems to indicate that they expected the acropolis to hold out

Aerial view of straits of Salamis. [Courtesy of W.K. Pritchett and American Journal of Archaeology.]

longer and had to abandon previous plans when it fell. If a garrison was stationed on the acropolis, further questions arise. Was the attempt to hold the acropolis a purely Athenian venture or was it decided on by Eurybiades and his advisers in the Hellenic League, and what was the strategic purpose? There is no obvious answer to these questions.

Other historians have rejected the hypothesis of a garrison on the acropolis, since Herodotus says that the defenders were merely treasurers of the temple and poor men. Then they have had to reject as fictitious his account of the ensuing panic among the Greek commanders at Salamis. Even on their view the strategic plans of the Greek commanders remain obscure. Fortifications were being built across the Isthmus of Corinth, but the Isthmus and Salamis were not interdependent positions like Thermopylae and Artemisium. Herodotus (8.57–60) gives arguments supposedly used by Themistocles after the second meeting of the council had dispersed. Allegedly he said to Eurybiades that, if the fleet withdrew from Salamis, its different contingents would each retire to their own cities, and thus he persuaded the Spartan commander to summon the nocturnal meeting of the council; at that meeting he argued first that, as the Greek ships were fewer and heavier than the enemy's, the narrower waters of Salamis were more to their advantage than the open sea at the Isthmus; second that by keeping the fleet where it was the Greeks retained possession of Salamis, Megara and Aegina; and third that by retiring to the Isthmus they would draw the Persian forces on against the Peloponnese. It is impossible to tell whether Herodotus had reliable information about the arguments used among the Greek commanders, but at least the one about preferring the relatively narrow waters of Salamis appears to be a valid strategic consideration, and this may have been the main reason for the Greek decision to stay at Salamis and fight there. Doubtless Herodotus is right too in implying that the influence of Themistocles had a good deal to do with the decision; since the Athenian naval contingent was by far the largest, the view taken by their commander must have carried weight.

After giving the nocturnal council of the Greeks and their decision to fight at Salamis, Herodotus (8.66–69) turns his attention to the Persian camp. He says that Xerxes called a council of the commanders of the naval contingents and through Mardonius asked each his opinion in turn; the others urged him to attack the Greek fleet where it was, but Artemisia, the ruler of Halicarnassus and its neighborhood, advised against this. Yet Xerxes decided for the majority, since he thought that this time the crews would fight better than at Artemisium as he would be able to watch them. Such is the reason Herodotus gives; he does not mention strategic considerations. Obviously he could have had access to even less information about Persian councils than about Greek councils. The role assigned to Artemisia is that of a stock figure of folklore, the "warner." But since Herodotus gives the detail that Xerxes used Mardonius as his intermediary in questioning the commanders, he may well have had some factual information about the Persian deliberations. Accordingly, there need be no doubt that a council was held and a decision was taken to attack the Greek fleet. Strategic considerations leading to this decision can be conjectured. Although Xerxes had brought his forces far into Greece, he had achieved little. For the winter he would have to retreat to such places as Thessaly and Macedon, where there would be an adequate supply of grain; thus he would have to abandon his position in Central Greece. At Thermopylae he had overcome only a small part of the Greek troops, and the fighting at Artemisium had been indecisive. The bulk of the Hellenic land and sea forces were still intact. If Xerxes could destroy the Hellenic fleet at Salamis before the onset of winter, the expenditure of the year's campaign would not have been wasted.

Thus Herodotus gives deliberations leading on both sides to a decision to fight at Salamis. The next item in his narrative (8.70; 8.74–76; 8.78–82) should arouse suspicion. He says that on the night following the Persian council of war alarm arose again among the Greeks at Salamis; they feared that they might be defeated at sea and confined to the island. So they gathered in council again and some of them wished to retire to the Peloponnese. Thereupon Themistocles withdrew secretly from the council and sent his slave Sicinnus with a message to Xerxes; the message said that Themistocles was at heart devoted to the Persian cause and that the Greeks were making ready to flee in alarm, but Xerxes could overcome them if he did not allow them time to escape. Xerxes allegedly responded by ordering some of his ships to move by night to positions where they could prevent any Greek retreat. Then Aristeides, the rival of Themistocles, came from Aegina to Salamis, called Themistocles out from the council, and told him that the Greeks could no longer flee from Salamis since they were surrounded by the enemy. Themistocles brought Aristeides before the council, where he repeated his news, but at first many of the commanders hesitated to believe it. However, a ship of Tenos, which had been conscripted by the Persians but now deserted to the Hellenic cause, arrived straight afterwards and confirmed the report of Aristeides. So the Greeks began preparations for a sea battle.

Patently this account has anecdotal features. Both Aristeides and the Tenian ship arrive at the dramatic moment. Xerxes is portrayed as singularly naive, since he responds precisely in the desired way to a treacherous message from the other side. The whole account is otiose, since Herodotus has expounded how both the Greeks and the Persians had reached decisions to fight. About ten years later Themistocles was driven out of Athens and eventually found refuge in the Persian Empire. The story of the mission of Sicinnus to Xerxes before the battle of Salamis may have been invented, either by Themistocles's enemies when they were working to expel him from Athens or later, when he had settled in Persian territory.

One acceptable item emerges from this dubious account: on the night before the battle of Salamis Xerxes moved some of his ships. Unfortunately Herodotus's indications of the direction of the movements are difficult to interpret. An old theory supposed that Xerxes sent a squadron of ships to sail round the south of Salamis and block the channel in the west between the island and the Megarid. More recently it has been discovered that the sea level has risen since antiquity and in the fifth century that channel was too narrow and too shallow to provide a possible escape route for the Greek fleet.

Promptly after dawn on the day following the Persian movements the Greek fleet sailed out from its anchorage and met the Persian attack. The precise location of the fighting in the area between Salamis and the Attic coast is disputed, but it is clear that the battle was fought in comparatively narrow waters; this neutralized the Persian advantages of somewhat greater numbers and better skill in maneuvering with lighter ships. The outcome was a decisive and unexpected defeat for the Persians; in the next year Persian commanders took care to avoid a naval engagement with the Hellenic League. The battle may have had further significance in the large-scale development of Persian plans. The Persian fleet included well trained and experienced contingents, notably those from Phoenicia and Egypt. It has been conjectured that for the campaign of 480 Xerxes relied on his fleet to win a clear victory and intended his land force primarily to support the fleet by securing coastal positions. This plan had to be abandoned in consequence of the Greek victory at Salamis; for 479 Xerxes instructed his commanders to attempt the reduction of European Greece with land forces alone.

THE CAMPAIGN OF PLATAEA[7]

The battle of Salamis was fought late in September. This is known from a remark made by Herodotus in another context. He says (9.10.3) that the Spartan king Cleombrotus commanded the forces which built the fortifications at the Isthmus and he offered sacrifice to discover whether the omens were favorable for an attack on the Persians, but while he was offering sacrifice there was an eclipse of the sun. The eclipse occurred on 2 October 480. The question of advancing from the Isthmus to attack the Persians could only arise for Cleombrotus shortly after the battle of Salamis. Accordingly, after the battle, Xerxes's most immediate need was to move his forces to winter quarters. Central Greece did not provide enough supplies, so the strongest part of the army was taken to Thessaly and Macedon for the winter; it was entrusted to Mardonius. He was to attempt the reduction of Greece in the season of 479.

Xerxes himself retreated with the rest of the army by the same route as he had come. At the Hellespont he found that a storm had destroyed the bridge, so the fleet carried him and his men across to Abydus. Apart from the question of supplies for the winter, Xerxes had other problems to take into account in placing his forces. The outcome of the fighting at Salamis might encourage Greek cities in the rear of Mardonius's force to rebel. Indeed, Poteidaea did rebel in the winter and, although Artabazus, the second-in-command to Mardonius, besieged it for three months, the city held out successfully. Xerxes was particularly anxious lest the Ionian cities of Asia rebel; they might disrupt communications in the northwestern part of the Empire, as had happened in the early stages of their Revolt of 499–494. Accordingly, after the fleet had conducted Xerxes across the Hellespont, it was stationed at Cyme and Samos for the winter, so that it could keep watch on Ionia. Xerxes proceeded to Sardis with the land forces he had brought back from Europe and there he awaited the outcome of the campaign of 479.

Mardonius's strategic prospects for the new season were good. He could reoccupy Central Greece and he need expect no serious obstacle to an advance by land until he reached the Peloponnesian fortifications at the Isthmus. There an inferior Greek force could check a larger force. In order to turn the Greek position at the Isthmus Mardonius needed a fleet, so that he could send contingents ahead into the Peloponnese. Consequently, the policy of the Athenians became crucial; Mardonius conceived the design of detaching the Athenians from the Hellenic League and winning them as allies, so that their fleet would be at his disposal. He could offer the Athenians good terms and, if they were unwilling to join him, he could threaten to ravage their territory, as the Persians had done in 480.

Mardonius's overture to Athens proved to be the most severe test to the cohesion of the Hellenic League. First he sent Alexander, the king of Macedon, to Athens to seek an alliance. Alexander had been recognized by the Athenians as their friend and benefactor and was thus the proper person to conduct negotiations. The offer he brought was generous: in return for an alliance Mardonius, with the king's approval, would confirm the Athenians in their territory, rebuild the temples destroyed in 480, and grant them whatever additional territory they chose. Herodotus's account of the consequent discussion (8.136; 8.140–144) may have been somewhat embellished in the transmission; it includes patriotic declarations by the Athenians of loyalty to a Panhellenic cause. But much of the account is acceptable. Herodotus may well be right in saying that the Spartans sent an embassy at the same time to discourage the Athenians from accepting the Persian proposal. The Athenians did reject that proposal, but according to Herodotus their reply to the Spartans concluded with an exhortation to them to bring reinforcements to Boeotia before the Persian forces could reach Attica. This recommendation reveals the tension in the Greek plans for 479. From the point of view of the Hellenic League it was good strategy to retire to the fortifications at the Isthmus and abandon everything north of that line, but the Athenians understandably wanted the federal troops to protect Attica by advancing into Boeotia and trying to hold a position there. This latter course was more hazardous, since there was no place in Boeotia where the Persian advance could be impeded so securely as at the Isthmus; but the predominance of the Athenians in the Hellenic fleet gave them special leverage in the deliberations.

Tension within the Hellenic League may be reflected in developments at sea early in the season of 479. The Greek fleet gathered in the spring at Aegina and Herodotus (8.131) says that it numbered 110 ships. This is a surprisingly low figure in comparison with those for the previous year; at the beginning of the fighting at Artemisium Herodotus (8.2.1) gives a Greek fleet of 271 ships, and on the second day of the battle these were joined by 53 more Attic ships (8.14.1); for Salamis he gives a Greek fleet totalling 380 triremes (8.82). His figures for 480 are not beyond dispute, since Aeschylus (*Persians* 338–340) says that at Salamis the Greek fleet numbered 310 triremes. But it is at least clear that in 480 the Hellenic League put at sea a fleet of more than 300 triremes, so the figure for the spring of 479 is surprisingly low. One explanation consists in supposing that the main fighting of 479 was expected on land and so the Greek commanders assigned as much manpower as possible to land operations. The alternative is to suppose that in the spring the Athenians withheld their contingent from the fleet of the Hellenic League because they were dissatisfied with the federal land strategy of falling back to the Isthmus. Against this explanation it can be objected that an Athenian naval contingent, commanded by Xanthippus, took part in operations later in the year and Herodotus, tracing those operations, does not say that it had arrived later than the muster at Aegina. But this objection is not conclusive; Herodotus did not concern himself to emphasize the tension between Sparta and Athens in 479.

In the summer of 479 Mardonius brought his army south from Thessaly into Central Greece. When he reached Boeotia, the Athenians realized that no Peloponnesian force was coming so far north to protect them; so they evacuated themselves and their noncombatants again to Salamis. Hence Mardonius was able to occupy Attica without meeting resistance. Now he made a second attempt to win over the Athenians. His chosen envoy this time was Murychides, a native of the Hellespontine region, and he was sent to Salamis to bring the same offer as Alexander had made previously. The offer was meaningful, since on occupying Attica Mardonius had not at first sacked it. But the Athenians at Salamis would not entertain Mardonius's offer; indeed, the tradition reaching Herodotus said that only one member of the council, Lycides, was in favor of bringing Mury-chides before the assembly and the other Athenians stoned Lycides to death. However, the Athenian attitude towards Sparta was more significant than the details of their behavior towards Murychides. They sent envoys to Sparta to complain that the Lacedaemonians had not marched to Boeotia to check the Persian before he reached Attica; the envoys were to remind their audience of Mardonius's offer and to add a threat that the Athenians would seek a new source of safety for themselves, unless the Lacedaemonians came to their aid. The Athenian threat to join the Persians was effective; although the envoys were detained for ten days by the ephors, an army of 5,000 Spartiates with 35,000 helots as servicing troops was sent north to make for central Greece; it was followed within a few days by a force of 5,000 perioeci.

Before the Lacedaemonian force reached the Isthmus, Mardonius sacked Attica and retired northwards to southern Boeotia. There Thebes afforded a friendly base; moreover, the plain of the Asopus river provided territory where Mardonius could use his cavalry to the best advantage. He had not succeeded in his attempt to win the alliance of the Athenians and the use of their fleet. But by exploiting the difference of view between Athens and Sparta he had gained a great deal; he had drawn the Hellenic defenders north from the Isthmus, where they would have had the advantage of defending a narrow and fortified defile, into ground of his own choosing in Boeotia. Strategically the Greek advance northwards from the Isthmus was hazardous and it meant abandoning a good position; the outcome of the subsequent fighting was paradoxical.

The Lacedaemonian force was commanded by Pausanias, the regent for the Spartan king Pleistarchus, who was a minor. It was joined by the forces of the Athenians and of the other allies, who were mostly from the Peloponnese. According to Herodotus's figures (9.28.2–9.29.1) the Greek hoplites totalled 38,700, the largest contingents being those from Lacedaemon, Athens and Corinth. Probably the Persians outnumbered the Greeks but not heavily; after the defeat at Plataea the surviving Persian army which retreated is given by Herodotus (9.66.2) as 40,000 men, and this is by far the most credible of his figures for Persian forces.

When the opponents reached southern Boeotia, a complex series of skirmishes and maneuvers followed. Mardonius appears to have stationed his men north of the Asopus river, where he had ample room to use his cavalry. Pausanias took up a position further south in the northern foothills of the Cithaeron range; for some days both armies remained on the defensive, since each was on ground favorable to its stronger arm. But Mardonius was anxious to bring the enemy to battle; his need for an engagement can best be explained, not by the strategic situation in European Greece, but by the risks anticipated by the Persians in Ionia. Since the defeat at Salamis the Persian high command no longer had confidence in its naval forces. But a Greek fleet was at sea and was sailing eastwards; it might try to provoke a second revolt of Ionia. If Mardonius could inflict a clear defeat on the Greeks of Europe, this could be expected to deter the Greeks of Asia from revolt.

By brilliant use of his cavalry Mardonius tried to force Pausanias into a situation where he would have to give battle. First Mardonius sent cavalry round the Greek position towards the pass where supplies were brought to the Greeks from further south; the cavalry met a Greek supply train as it was debouching from the pass into the plain and captured it. Four days later the cavalry raided the fountain where the Greeks drew water and disturbed the earth, so that the water could no longer be used. So Pausanias decided to retire to a position closer to Plataea and he began the march by night. But the intended movement was complex and some contingents failed to obey their orders. Soon after dawn Mardonius brought his troops south of the Asopus and attacked. The fighting was indecisive for some time; then the Spartans and Tegeans on the Greek right overcame the Persian wing opposed to them and killed Mardonius himself. The death of the commander decided the outcome of the battle.

Mardonius had fought a good campaign. By bringing his army south of the Asopus for the final attack he left the extensive plain north of the river, where he could best use his cavalry. But this was a reasonable risk to take. The Persian cavalry were mounted archers and, although they had javelins as well as arrows, they were most effective at some distance from the enemy; in close fighting they could be overcome by well armed and well disciplined infantry. In the fighting of 480 and 479 the Greek hoplites were better equipped than any of the various infantry contingents which the Persians could put into the field; in particular, their defensive armor was more comprehensive. Moreover, they had the training and discipline to make this superiority tell. The victory at Plataea was won, not by strategic skill, but by the material equipment and training of the Greek infantryman.

When the enemy had been defeated, the Greeks captured the Persian camp, distributed the booty and buried their dead. Eleven days after the battle they advanced on Thebes and besieged the city for twenty days, until the Thebans surrendered those of their citizens whom they held most responsible for their adhesion to the Persian cause. Thereupon Pausanias dismissed the contingents of his allies, took his Theban prisoners to Corinth and killed them there. Thebes had been a useful position for the Persians, ever since it joined them after the defeat at Thermopylae, and the Hellenic League needed to gain ascendancy over Thebes rather than leaving the Persians so good a position in the heart of Greece. Yet the concentration of the League's efforts on Thebes after the battle of Plataea calls for further explanation; this Hellenic policy allowed Artabazus to retire safely with the remainder of the Persian army through Thessaly and Macedon and, although he suffered some harassment in Thrace, he was able to cross with his force from Byzantium by sea to Asia. One may conjecture that the League concentrated its force against Thebes in response to demands of the Athenians, whose long-standing rivalry with Thebes arose ultimately from border disputes.

MYCALE[8]

In the spring of 479 the fleet of the Hellenic League gathered at Aegina under the command of the Spartan king Leotychides. Two successive groups of messengers came to it and eventually induced it to cross the Aegean. The first group came from Chios. In that island seven men had formed a plot against their tyrant Strattis, but one of them betrayed their scheme, and so the remaining six fled to Sparta to seek help and proceeded thence to Aegina. In response to their entreaty the fleet advanced eastwards but it was unwilling to go any further than Delos. Some time later three messengers from Samos came to Delos. Ships from Samos had fought on the Persian side at Salamis, and Theomestor, the captain of one of them, won there the esteem of Xerxes, who rewarded him by making him tyrant of Samos. Less than a year later some Samians conspired against Theomestor and sent the three messengers to the Hellenic fleet. The messengers appealed to

Leotychides and assured him that Ionia would rise in revolt, if his fleet approached; he was persuaded and the fleet sailed for Samos. The incidents leading to the two messages are of some interest as illustrating the highly factional character of Ionian politics.

The fleet which Xerxes had brought back from Europe spent the winter of 480/79 at Cyme and Samos and gathered at Samos early in the spring. When the fleet of Leotychides approached, the response of the Persian commanders shows how the battle of Salamis had altered their strategic thinking; they dismissed the Phoenician contingent, their best ships, to its home, and they retired with the rest to Mt. Mycale, the mainland promontory opposite Samos, where they could enjoy the protection of the land force stationed there to guard Ionia. At Mycale they beached their ships and built a rampart of wood and stones round them.

Leotychides and his force reached Samos and found the Persians gone. Then the Greek commanders considered retiring to their homes or sailing to the Hellespont; instead they decided to follow the enemy to Mycale and attack. As they sailed past the Persian position, Leotychides brought his ship close in to shore and issued a proclamation to the Ionians who were serving with the Persian force; he urged them to change sides. Then he landed his force somewhere east of the Persian position. The Persian commanders had to consider how to deal with the Ionian contingents in their force. They disarmed the Samians, against whom they had particularly strong suspicions; but they stationed the Milesians to guard the paths leading to the heights of Mycale, since they intended to escape by these paths if they were defeated.

After landing his force, Leotychides led it westwards against the Persians. There was lengthy fighting outside the rampart of the Persian encampment. In the end the Greeks broke through the rampart; most of the enemy fled and eventually reached Sardis; the rest were cut down. The battle was a clear defeat for the Persians, but some attempt must be made to estimate its effect on the political and military situation in Ionia. The risk of revolt among Greeks of Asia Minor in 479 seems to have influenced the calculations of Persian commanders, including Mardonius. During the fighting at Mycale Herodotus (9.103–104) says that the Samians, who had been disarmed, attacked the Persians and the other Ionian contingents followed the Samian lead in this; he says that the Milesians, who had been set to guard the paths to the heights of Mycale, led the fugitives by the wrong paths and brought them to the Greek forces; and he reckons this as a second revolt of Ionia. These reports may have been exaggerated by later Ionian patriotism. The Persians may well have distrusted the Samians more than the people of mainland Ionia, since they could no longer hope to control the islands now that they had disarmed the Phoenician fleet and given up major naval action in the Aegean. If the Persians were willing to entrust their line of retreat to the

Milesians, this shows that they had some confidence in them. Even so, it is likely that the Ionian contingents deserted the Persians during the fighting, once it became clear which way the battle was inclining; that was the obvious way for the Ionian troops to save themselves. Whether their action could commit their cities to revolt is not so clear.

After the battle Leotychides and his fellow commanders had to face the Ionian question. They withdrew to Samos and held a council of war; Herodotus's account of it (9.106) must be scrutinized. He says that the issue was where to settle the Ionians in land controlled by the Hellenic League; Ionia itself would have to be abandoned, since the League could not hope to garrison it permanently against Persian reprisals. He continues by saying that the Peloponnesian commanders proposed to seize the seaports of those Greeks who had medized and transplant the Ionians thither, but the Athenians opposed vigorously any scheme for moving the Ionians, and so the Peloponnesians gave way. "Therefore," he concludes, "they admitted to the alliance the Samians, the Chians, the Lesbians and the other islanders, who proved to be fighting on the same side as the Greeks."

In this account one must distinguish between the deliberations and the conclusion. It is most unlikely that any written or official record was kept of those proposals which were not carried out. In general the historian should beware of allegations about unrealized intentions. The story of a Peloponnesian plan to transplant the Ionians and of its defeat by the Athenians may have been invented by later Athenian propaganda; more than once during the next half-century the Athenians had occasion to assert that they, not the Peloponnesians, were the true friends of the Ionians. But the result of the council of war was a matter of public knowledge and allows no room for dispute; the islanders were admitted to membership of the Hellenic League. It follows that the mainlanders were not. The strategic reason is clear from Herodotus's allusion in his account of the council and from the map; to garrison the many cities of mainland Ionia against possible Persian reprisals would be an enormous undertaking, far beyond the estimated capacity of a League which had just completed two seasons of tough fighting.

From Samos the federal fleet under Leotychides sailed to the Hellespont in the hope of destroying the bridge of Xerxes. When it reached Abydus, it found that the bridge had already collapsed in a storm. Thereupon the Peloponnesians together with Leotychides sailed away to their homes, but the Athenians with their commander Xanthippus decided to stay and make an attempt on the Chersonese; during the following winter they besieged and captured Sestos. This operation may be deemed to begin new developments in the story of the Hellenic League. In 480 and 479 most of its enterprises, with the exception of the Mycale campaign, had been defensive, and for the most part its chief members had collaborated effectively. Admittedly, before the campaign of Plataea Mardonius had exploited by diplomacy a divergence of outlook between the Athenians and the Peloponnesians, and by this means he had succeeded in drawing the federal infantry north to Boeotia; but the ultimate test of military collaboration is success, and in 479 the Hellenic League won the defensive war. With the siege of Sestos a more decisive divergency began to appear between Athenian and Peloponnesian aspirations; it became more pronounced as the League proceeded with offensive operations.

NOTES

1. The Persian preparations are given by Herodotus 7.20–25; 7.33–36. The song of Hybrias is accessible in *Anthologia Lyrica Graeca* (ed. Diehl, second edition) vol. 2, 128.

2. The Spartan response to the Asiatic Greek appeal when Croesus was overthrown is given by Hdt. 1.141.4; 1.152–153. He reports the expedition against Polycrates at 3.39–56. The Spartan deposition of Lygdamis is given by Plut., *On the Malignity of Herodotus* 21 = *Mor.* 859d; schol. Aeschin. 2.77; cf. D.M. Leahy, "The Spartan Embassy to Lygdamis," *JHS* 77 (1957) 272–275. Herodotus gives the activities of Cleomenes in the following passages: 4.148 (Maeandrius); 6.84 (Scythians); 5.49–51 (Aristagoras); 6.108 (Plataea); 5.62–96 (Athens); 6.76–82 (Argos); 6.49–51 and 6.61–73 (Aegina); 6.74–75 (flight, recall and death of Cleomenes). The story of a Scythian appeal to Cleomenes (6.84) is rightly doubted by W.W. How and J. Wells, *A Commentary on Herodotus* II (Oxford 1928) 97–98. At 6.74 the manuscripts of Herodotus say that Cleomenes fled to Thessaly; the emendation "Sellasien" for "Thessalien" is defended by D. Hereward, "Herodotus vi. 74," *CR* N.S.1 (1951) 146. The view of Cleomenes taken here contrasts with that offered by W.G. Forrest, *A History of Sparta 950–192 B.C.* (London 1968) 85–93. The essay by J. Wells, "The Chronology of the Reign of Cleomenes I" in *Studies in Herodotus* (Blackwell, Oxford 1923) 74–94 is useful, although it argues a date ca. 520 for the campaign of Sepeia. For Spartan treatment of the Persian heralds and the mission of Sperthias and Boulis see Hdt. 7.133–137. A further fact may provide an argument for a date before 480 for this mission: the two Spartans met Hydarnes, who held a military command on the coast of Asia Minor (7.135.1). Perhaps he already held this command in the lifetime of Miltiades, who was traduced to him (6.133.1); he was transferred to the command of the Immortals in time for the campaign of 481. Spartan behavior in regard to the campaign of Marathon is given by Hdt. 6.106 and 120. Some historians believe that in 490 the Spartans were threatened by a helot revolt and hence arrived late at Marathon. Such a revolt is alleged by Plat. *Laws* 3.692d and 698e; but Plato is not reliable on historical matters. A defense of Plato's assertion, using numismatic evidence, is offered by W.P. Wallace, "Kleomenes, Marathon, the Helots, and Arkadia," *JHS* 74 (1954) 32–35.

3. On the men active in Athenian affairs in this period see chapter 7, pp. 181–187. Herodotus gives the shield-signal at 6.115 and 121–124; the suggestion that the signal was intended for the Lacedaemonians was made by A.D. Fitton Brown, *Hermes* 86 (1958) 379–380. The Parian expedition of Miltiades and his death are given by Hdt. 6.132–136. On the introduction of sortition for the nine archons see R.J. Buck, "The Reform of 487 B.C. in the Selection of Archons," *CP* 60

(1965) 96–101; E. Badian, "Archons and *Strategoi*," Autochthon 5 (1971) 1–34. Badian offers the interpretation here followed of the choice by lot of Callimachus as polemarch. Badian also argues that the known eponymous archons of 487–457 resembled those of 508–488: they were men of good family who had yet to make their name in politics. But it is still a tenable view that the reform of 488/7 eliminated ambitious men from the archonship; in Badian's lists two of the archons of 508–488 were later ostracized, but this did not happen to any of those of 487–457. On election of archons before 487 see Hignett, *HAC* 321–326. On the ostracisms of the 480s see Ar. *AP* 22.4–8; E. Vanderpool, "The Ostracism of the Elder Alcibiades," *Hesperia* 21 (1952) 1–8; Meiggs/Lewis 21. The shipbuilding program is given by Hdt. 7.144; Ar. *AP* 22.7. Herodotus alludes suggestively to enmity between Themistocles and Aristeides at 8.79.2–3. The date 482/1 for the recall of men ostracized is defended by M. Chambers, *Philologus* 111, (1967) 162–165. For discussion of the Delphic responses to the Athenians immediately before the invasion see Hignett, *XIG* 441–444.

4. The formation and organization of the League are discussed by P.A. Brunt, "The Hellenic League against Persia," *Historia* 2 (1953–54) 135–163. Herodotus gives information on the League and its congresses at 7.132; 7.145; 7.172; 8.3. The inscription on the serpent column is accessible as Meiggs/Lewis 27. The expedition to the Tempe valley is given by Hdt. 7.172–174; for discussion see Hignett, *XIG* 102–104; cf. H.D. Westlake, "The Medism of Thessaly," *JHS* 56 (1936) 12–24.

5. Herodotus gives the fighting at Thermopylae and Artemisium in 7.175–8.21; cf. Hignett, *XIG* 105–192, 371–378. On the size of the Persian forces see Hignett, *XIG* 345–355. G.L. Cawkwell drew my attention privately to Thuc. 6.33.5, a passage implying that the Persian expeditionary force in 480–479 was eventually no larger than the Greek force resisting it. The new reconstruction of the Greek strategy was presented by J.A.S. Evans, "Notes on Thermopylae and Artemisium," *Historia* 18 (1969) 389–406. The main topographical problem about the battle of Thermopylae concerns the path followed by Hydarnes; see W.K. Pritchett, "New Light on Thermopylae," *AJA* 62 (1958) 203–213. On the location of Artemisium and Aphetae see W.K. Pritchett, "The Battle of Artemision in 480 B.C.," *Studies in Ancient Greek Topography*, Part II (Battlefields)–University of California Publications in Classical Studies, vol. 4 (1969) 12–18. For contrasting views on the Hollows of Euboea and the 200 ships allegedly destroyed there see W.K. Pritchett, "The Hollows of Euboea," op. cit. 19–23; Hignett, *XIG* 386–392.

6. Herodotus gives the maneuvering and fighting at Salamis in 8.40–96. Some historians have tried to use information provided by Aeschylus in *The Persians*, a tragedy performed in 472, but the indications there are too imprecise. The account offered here owes much to Hignett, *XIG* 193–239 and 403–408. For Leonidas's messages to the East Locrians and the Phocians see Hdt. 7.203.1; for the fortification built at the Isthmus see Hdt. 8.71–72; for the movements of the Persian fleet from Aphetae to Phalerum see Hdt. 8.23–25 and 8.66.1. The text of the "Themistocles decree" is conveniently available as Meiggs/Lewis 23. An important discussion of the physical character of the inscription is offered by S. Dow, "The Purported Decree of Themistokles: Stele and Inscription," *AJA* 66 (1962) 353–368. There have been many discussions of the question of the authenticity of the text; attention may be drawn to C. Habicht, "Falsche Urkunden zur Geschichte Athens im Zeitalter der Perserkriege," *Hermes* 89 (1961) 1–35; to W.K. Pritchett, "Herodotus and the Themistokles Decree," *AJA* 66 (1962) 43–47; to the comments of J. and L. Robert, *REG* 75 (1962) 152–158; C.W. Fornara, "The Value of the Themistocles Decree," *AHR* 73 (1967–68), 425–433. For discussion of the responses allegedly given by the Delphic oracle to Athens see Hignett, *XIG* 441–444. The hypothesis of an Athenian garrison stationed on the acropolis was first offered by J.B. Bury, "Aristides at Salamis," *CR* 10 (1896) 414–418; see also Sealey, "Again the Siege of the Acropolis," *CSCA* 5 (1972) 183–194. When the Greek council at Salamis received news of the fall of the acropolis and planned to withdraw to the Isthmus, Herodotus (8.57) says that

Themistocles acted on the advice of Mnesiphilus in persuading Eurybiades to convene the council again for a nocturnal meeting; but the role attributed to Mnesiphilus is probably a malicious invention designed to deprive Themistocles of credit; see Hignett, *XIG* 204 and F.J. Frost, "Themistocles and Mnesiphilus," *Historia* 20 (1971) 20–25. The alleged message of Sicinnus is treated with scepticism by Hignett *XIG* 208 and 403–408; its historicity has been defended by G. L. Cawkwell, "The Fall of Themistocles," in B.F. Harris (ed.) *Auckland Classical Essays presented to E. M. Blaiklock* 39–58, especially 42. On the depth of the channel between Salamis and the Megarid see W. Marg, "Zur Strategie der Schlacht von Salamis," *Hermes* 90 (1962) 116–119. I thank G. L. Cawkwell for the suggestion that in 480 Xerxes relied on his fleet for victory. Opinions vary as to just where in the channel between Salamis and the mainland the battle was fought; for discussion with references see the two studies by W.K. Pritchett, "Towards a Restudy of the Battle of Salamis," *AJA* 63 (1959) 251–262 and "Salamis Revisited," *Studies in Ancient Greek Topography*, Part I = University of California Publications in Classical Studies, vol. 1 (1965) 94–102.

7. Herodotus gives the movements of the Persian forces after the battle of Salamis at 8.97–107; 8.113–120; 8.130; he gives the revolt of Poteidaea at 8.126–129; he gives Mardonius's negotiations with Athens at 8.136–144; 9.1–11; he gives the campaign of Plataea at 9.12–89. This section owes much to Hignett, *XIG* 264–344. On the topography of Plataea and its neighborhood see the two studies by W. K. Pritchett, "New Light on Plataea," *AJA* 61 (1957) 9–28, and "Plataea Revisited," *Studies in Ancient Greek Topography*, Part I = University of California Publications in Classical Studies, vol. 1 (1965) 103–121.

8. Herodotus gives the naval campaign of 479 at 8.131–132; 9.90–107; 9.114–121. See Hignett, *XIG* 240–263.

II

The Era of
Hegemonic Leagues

Note

ON THE LITERARY AND EPIGRAPHIC SOURCES FOR PART II

Most of the authors mentioned in the note on the literary sources for Part I are useful for the period treated in Part II. The present note deals with additional sources.

POETS

Among the Athenian tragedians after Aeschylus, SOPHOCLES (ca. 496–406) and especially EURIPIDES (ca. 485–ca. 406) provide in their plays some indication of moods prevalent in Athens, but their work has little direct bearing on political and constitutional history. More importance attaches to Old Attic Comedy, a form of drama which developed a little later than tragedy; the *Suda* says that the first competition in performance of comedy at the Dionysia took place in 486. "Old Comedy" is the term given to the comic dramas of the fifth century; its structure was highly formal with a series of standard items and a simple plot, and its content included plentiful jokes at the expense of contemporary politicians. The works of most writers of Old Comedy, such as CRATINUS (ca. 484–ca. 419), are known only from fragments quoted by later writers. Eleven of the many comedies written by ARISTOPHANES (ca. 450–ca. 385) have been preserved; something can be learned from their frequent remarks about politicians, and they are a valuable source on social conditions.

HISTORIANS

By far the most important source for Part II is the history written by THUCY-DIDES (ca. 455–ca. 400). He was an Athenian and probably a relative of Cimon. In 424 he was put in command of some ships stationed in the Thraceward district; he failed in an attempt to prevent the Spartan Brasidas from capturing Amphipolis and he was exiled for this. Twenty years later he returned to Athens under the amnesty issued at the end of the Peloponnesian War.

He set out to write a history of the war. To achieve a chronologically clear narrative he related in succession the events of each summer and then those of the following winter; his "summer" included spring and fall and lasted about eight months. He asserted that he drew his factual material from his own observation and from oral informants, whose statements he tested; he refrained from saying how he tested them. His exile of twenty years gave him the opportunity to consult people on the Peloponnesian side. Probably he gained some information from Alcibiades. As well as factual material Thucydides included in his work speeches which he attributed to leading figures in the conflicts. These were substantially free compositions by the historian; only the general thrust of each speech can be taken as true to fact. When, for example, Thucydides gives a speech by Pericles urging the Athenians not to yield to the Spartans in the winter of 432/1, it should be inferred that Pericles spoke then in that sense, but the particular arguments in the speech may all be those of Thucydides, not of the historical Pericles.

Thucydides says that he began work on his history as soon as the war broke out. He mentions the end of the war. It follows that he was at work for at least twenty-seven years. It should be expected that in so long a period an intelligent man would modify his views on some points, but attempts to trace the development of Thucydides's ideas have led to few indisputable conclusions. Probably he at first regarded the Archidamian War as a single and complete war, ending in 421, and only learned later to regard the whole conflict of twenty-seven years as one war. Some change can perhaps be discerned in his concept of the causes of the war. But he expresses only a few personal judgements and not much can be said about the way he reached his final opinions.

Digressions are much less frequent in the work of Thucydides than in that of Herodotus, but the younger historian permitted himself some. The digression commonly called the Pentecontaetia (1.89–118) is especially valuable; it surveys events from 478 until the outbreak of the Peloponnesian War in order to reveal the growth of Athenian power.

Thucydides left his work unfinished; it breaks off towards the end of the summer of 411. Several people wrote works intended to continue his narrative. One of these was XENOPHON (ca. 430–ca. 350), an Athenian who in 401 joined the Greek force led by Cyrus from Sardis to Mesopotamia against Artaxerxes II; after the battle of Cunaxa Xenophon was one of the officers who led the Greek troops as they retired to Trapezus (see chapter 15, p. 387). The Athenians passed a sentence of exile against him during his absence. He then served under the Spartan commanders operating in Asia Minor from 399 to 394. Later the Spartans gave him an estate of land not far from Olympia, and he lived there probably until 371. The Athenians repealed the sentence of exile, probably in 369, and Xenophon spent his last years partly in Athens and partly in Corinth.

He composed the *Anabasis*, or "March Upcountry," an extensive account of Cyrus's expedition and the subsequent journey of the Greek troops. His most ambitious work was the *Hellenica*, or "History of Greece." This began where Thucydides's narrative broke off and traced Greek events through the battle of Mantinea in 362. It can easily be divided into two or perhaps three different parts, which differ so much in manner of treatment that they appear to have been composed at different times. Xenophon omitted some major events, such as the foundation of the Second Athenian Sea League; he was less able to construct a clear and causal narrative than Thucydides, and the later part of his work tended to concentrate on Peloponnesian and Athenian events while neglecting those of Central and Northern Greece. Even so he succeeded in preserving a great amount of complex information. Among his many other and lesser works mention may be made of the *Memorabilia*, or "Memoirs of Socrates." This consists largely of anecdotes about Socrates and of imaginary dialogues; in places it is useful for social history.

Another work which continued the narrative of Thucydides is called the HELLENICA OXYRHYNCHIA and is known from papyrus fragments discovered at Oxyrhynchus in Egypt. The larger group of fragments was discovered in 1906. It deals with events of 396–395 and treats them in considerable detail. Like Thucydides, the author arranged his material by summers and winters. He may have taken his account as far as 386 or possibly only to 394. A smaller group of fragments, published in 1949, deals with events of 407/6. The identity of the author is uncertain, although several lost historians have been suggested. The question of authorship has no great significance; the surviving fragments show that the author was careful and well informed. Comparison reveals that at significant points the work agrees with the narrative of Diodorus against that of Xenophon. It has been inferred that Ephorus, Diodorus's source, drew on the *Hellenica Oxyrhynchia*; consequently Diodorus's statements need to be taken more seriously for this period than for that for which Thucydides's account is available.

CTESIAS of Cnidus was a Greek doctor at the Persian court. He was present at the battle of Cunaxa. He wrote a *History of Persia*, which has been lost, but it is known from Photius's summary.

Two authors, whose works are known only from fragments, call for brief note. THEOPOMPUS (ca. 378–after 336) of Chios wrote a *Hellenica* as a continuation of Thucydides. It was extensive in coverage, for it was divided into twelve books but stopped at the battle of Cnidus in 394. He was still more ambitious in his *Philippica*, or "History of Greece in the time of Philip II of Macedon." This work comprised fifty-eight books. The later part of Book X became current separately under the title *Concerning the Athenian Demagogues*; it provided a survey of Athenian history, starting probably with Cleisthenes and continuing to the middle of the fourth century (cf. chapter 10, pp. 272–273). CRATERUS of

Macedon compiled in the third century a collection of Athenian public decrees. He should probably be identified with the Craterus who served as a military commander and political officer under his half-brother, Antigonus Gonatas, the king of Macedon. The collection of decrees is known largely from citations by Plutarch.

PAMPHLETEERS

The manuscripts of Xenophon's works include a short treatise called the *Constitution of the Athenians*. Dates suggested for its composition vary between ca. 441 and ca. 418. It is too early to be the work of Xenophon. The author is often called the Old Oligarch, but this designation is unfortunate, since there is no reason to believe that he was old when he composed his treatise; it is better to call him the PSEUDO-XENOPHON. The author declared himself an enemy of Athens and he addressed himself to her enemies, but his aim was to explain to them why Athenian politics worked efficiently in spite of their radical defects. He provides some detailed information on Athenian practices; how well he understood Athenian politics is a hotly disputed question.

WRITERS OF ROMAN DATE

STRABO (64/63 B.C.–A.D. 21 or later) wrote a comprehensive *Geography*, which sought to be scientific. He had traveled in Rome, Egypt and parts of Asia Minor, and he spent the later part of his life in his native city, Amaseia. The part of his work devoted to Greece has a good deal of antiquarian information, probably drawn mostly from standard works such as Ephorus.

Several of PLUTARCH's Lives, notably those of Cimon, Pericles, Nicias, Alcibiades, Lysander and Agesilaus, are useful for Part II.

BYZANTINE SCHOLARS

HESYCHIUS of Alexandria probably lived in the fifth century A.D. He compiled a comprehensive lexicon, based on compendia of late Hellenistic and Roman date.

INSCRIPTIONS

Documents inscribed by contemporaries on stone and discovered in modern times through exploration and excavation are an important and growing source of information. From the fifth century onwards Athenian inscriptions are especially plentiful, a fact which reflects the power and prosperity attained by Athens. Inscriptions can be classified under several headings; two types may be specified here, namely decrees and lists. The earliest known inscribed decree of the Athenians deals with Salamis and was probably passed late in the sixth century (Meiggs/Lewis 14). Inscriptions bearing decrees of the public assembly become plentiful from ca. 460 onwards. A high proportion of these are honorific, that is, they granted honors to specific persons, often non-Athenians who had promoted the interests of Athens. Probably the men honored saw to it that their honors were inscribed, and this accounts for the plentiful preservation of inscriptions of this class. A good many decrees of more general import have been discovered and they are often highly informative for political history.

Lists are of many kinds. Casualty lists record the men who fell in battle in a single year. Financial lists include the tribute quota lists (see chapter 9, p. 244; chapter 10, pp. 273-275) of the Athenian Empire; these began in 454/3, and are the earliest known major series of financial lists from Athens. Other financial accounts inscribed include the costs of building the Parthenon and the Propylaea (Meiggs/Lewis 59 and 60) and expenses of particular campaigns, such as the operations against the Samian Revolt (Meiggs/Lewis 55).

In a very few cases a whole inscription has been recovered and is fully legible, but usually only fragments of each inscription have been found and the inscribed surface has often been damaged. Reconstruction of the original monument and text is a delicate task. Where a stock phrase, such as those usually occurring in the opening of decrees, can be recognized, supplementary words can be added with some confidence to the extant part of the text, but otherwise caution is necessary and inferences should only be drawn from the letters indisputably legible on the stone.

Systematic study of Greek inscriptions has been in progress since early in the nineteenth century and has been accompanied by attempts to compile collections. Some of these call for note here. *Inscriptiones Graecae* (Berlin 1873-) is an attempt to collect all known Greek inscriptions; the Athenian inscriptions are to be found in the first two volumes, which are now in their second edition (1913-1940), the second volume being in several parts bound separately. The *Athenian Tribute Lists*, by B.D. Meritt, H.T. Wade-Gery and M.F. McGregor (4 vols., Cambridge, Mass. 1939-1953), tries in its first two volumes to collect the quota lists and other texts bearing on the Athenian Empire; the third volume discusses epigraphic and historical questions and attempts a history of the Empire. Two useful selections of epigraphic texts with commentaries are R. Meiggs and D. Lewis, *A Selection of Greek Historical Inscriptions to the End of the Fifth Century B.C.* (Oxford 1969) and M.N. Tod, *A Selection of Greek Historical*

Inscriptions, vol. II: from 403 to 323 B.C. (Oxford 1948). Some texts without commentary are given in G.F. Hill, *Sources for Greek History between the Persian and the Peloponnesian Wars* (new edition, revised by R. Meiggs and A. Andrewes, Oxford 1951). A helpful introduction is A.G. Woodhead, *The Study of Greek Inscriptions* (Cambridge, Eng., 1967).

9

Divergence between Athens and Sparta

For the student of Greek history the center of interest shifts with the Persian Wars. In the archaic period his attention is held primarily by the emergence of the different cities; each of them fashioned a framework of institutions and thereby achieved a sense of identity. By the end of the sixth century a citizen of Athens, for example, thought of himself primarily as a citizen of Athens; he might acknowledge membership in smaller groups, such as a clan, or in larger groups, such as the Ionians, but his city had an overriding claim on his loyalty. Strong political organizations linking many cities together on a lasting basis could only develop after the cities themselves had achieved some degree of sophistication. In this respect the Peloponnesian League, growing in the second half of the sixth century, was a pioneer, and it set a pattern for other leagues, a pattern which may be called "the hegemonic league;" within the league one city was clearly the master, to such an extent that it sometimes behaved arbitrarily towards other members. In response to the attacks of Xerxes and Mardonius many Greek states discovered that they could cooperate effectively. Accordingly, after the defeats inflicted on the Persians in 480 and 479 the center of interest for the student shifts to the attempts of Greek states to fashion lasting structures for interstate cooperation.

For a long time after 479 these attempts took the form of hegemonic leagues. In particular in 478/7 the Athenians founded a new league, the Delian League (the name is modern), and in its subsequent development the Athenians achieved a much more authoritarian position than was held by the Spartans within the Peloponnesian League. Rivalry between Athens and Sparta issued in three wars. The first, the so-called First Peloponnesian War (ca. 460–446) was a somewhat desultory struggle with indecisive results. The second war, called the Great Peloponnesian War or, more often, simply the Peloponnesian War (431–404), ended with a severe defeat for Athens and the destruction of the Delian League. But the severe terms imposed on Athens in 404 were the result of a single battle; they did not reflect the lasting balance of resources between Athens and Sparta. Hence after 404 Athens soon made a considerable recovery and her resentment towards Sparta, together with that of other powers, issued in a complex struggle known as the Corinthian War (395–386). Within a decade of its conclusion Athens set about constructing a new league of less hegemonic and more egalitarian type.

ATHENIAN ENTERPRISE IN THE WINTER OF 479/8[2]

For the Greeks the fighting of 480–479 was paradoxical not only in its outcome –the defeat of a great empire–but also in the methods by which that defeat was accomplished. At least according to the view followed above on the strategy of Thermopylae and Artemisium, the Greek high command put its faith in resistance by land; the fleet was mostly inexperienced and was intended merely to support the land forces. But although the most decisive single battle was fought on land at Plataea, the results achieved in the campaigns of the two years were largely due to naval enterprise. At Salamis the Persian forces were defeated at sea so effectively that they would not risk another naval battle in the Aegean; and although the battle of Mycale was fought on land, it only became possible when Leotychides had the courage to lead a fleet to the Asiatic coast. Thus the fighting gave a new importance to sea power and that meant a new importance for the Athenians, since about two-thirds of the federal fleet consisted of Athenian ships. Even for the Athenians this importance was something novel, since most of their fleet had been built since 483. In the Hellenic League Sparta had command and Athens was merely one of the members, but this relationship between the two cities no longer reflected the actual balance of power.

Two developments in the winter of 479/8 had a bearing on relations between Sparta and Athens; one was the rebuilding of the Athenian fortifications and the other was the siege of Sestos. In 479 the Athenians had evacuated Attica for the second time, and when Mardonius gave up hope of winning them over, he burned the city and destroyed its buildings. When the Athenians returned, they set about rebuilding the city and its wall. Their decision to rebuild the fortifications led to an exchange of embassies with Sparta, and Thucydides's account of this runs as follows. The Spartans, mainly because of the insistence of their allies, sent envoys to try to dissuade the Athenians from rebuilding their city wall. But Themistocles persuaded the Athenians to send him on an embassy to Sparta and to hold back his fellow envoys, until the wall should have reached the minimum height for defensibility. On reaching Sparta he made excuses to postpone presenting himself to the authorities. When rumors came that the Athenians were indeed building their wall, he advised the Spartans to send a further embassy to test the reports. This was done, and Themistocles sent a secret message to the Athenians, bidding them detain the Spartan ambassadors as hostages for his own safety and that of his fellow envoys. Meanwhile the latter arrived, and Themistocles presented himself to the Spartan assembly with a defiant speech; he assured his hearers that the Athenians knew their own best interests, and he boasted that his fellow citizens had resolved on the evacuation of Attica without seeking Spartan advice. "The Lacedaemonians, after hearing him, showed no apparent anger towards the Athenians . . . but they were secretly displeased because they had failed of their purpose."

Such is Thucydides's story. It has suspicious features, such as the secret message sent by Themistocles from Sparta and particularly the secret displeasure of the Spartans at the outcome; if the Spartans kept their displeasure secret, how could Thucydides know about it? Again it is surprising to be told that the Spartans tried to dissuade the Athenians from rebuilding their city wall. Almost every Greek city had its wall; the only known exception is Sparta. It is difficult to imagine that the Spartans had any hope of success, if they urged the Athenians to do without a wall. The figure of Themistocles later attracted anecdotes and exaggerations. But the story of his embassy to Sparta is more probably distorted than invented. That the Spartans were incited to send an embassy by the insistence of some allies is credible; the Aeginetans had been at war with Athens until 481, when the Hellenic League suspended hostilities, and by the fall of 479 they may have been alarmed at the display of Athenian sea power. If the Spartans sent an embassy to discuss differences, whether its main business was the Athenian city wall or something else, Themistocles was the obvious man for the Athenians to send in response. In 480, shortly after the battle of Salamis, he had visited Sparta and the Spartans had extended greater honors to him than to any other foreigner; they gave him an olive wreath and a chariot, and when he left, the royal bodyguard of 300 picked men escorted him as far as the border of Tegea.

The subject and occasion of Themistocles's embassy to Sparta in the winter of 479/8 must remain obscure. But Thucydides's statement of its outcome is fully credible: "The Lacedaemonians . . . showed no apparent anger towards the Athenians." Evidently they were satisfied with Themistocles's explanations and paid no further attention to the complaints of their allies.

In the same winter Athenian naval forces besieged Sestos. They had sailed to the Hellespont from Mycale with Leotychides and the Peloponnesians and, when these latter went home, the Athenian contingent under Xanthippus stayed to make an attempt on the Chersonese. Thucydides (1.89.2) devotes a single sentence to the siege of Sestos, which was held by the Persians; he indicates that the siege lasted through the winter, before the attackers captured the place. He may have felt that the operation had been adequately treated by Herodotus. The latter gives a fuller account (9.114–121), remarking that Persian forces from all parts of the Chersonese gathered in Sestos at the approach of the Greek fleet and indicating that the siege began before the fall. The two historians diverge on a point which may be important for reconstructing events of the next year. Herodotus describes the siege of Sestos as a purely Athenian operation, but Thucydides says that the Athenians had with them "those allies from Ionia and the Hellespont who had already rebelled against the king." These allies are not likely to have been numerous, since Herodotus passed over them in silence, but one may well ask who they were. The allies from Ionia may well have been Samians and perhaps Chians; the phrase does not necessarily imply forces from the Ionian mainlanders. These latter are not likely to have been present at Sestos, since they had not been admitted to the Hellenic League by the council held at Samos after the battle of Mycale (see chapter 8, p. 227). The allies from the Hellespont may have been the forces of Abydus, for Leotychides put in there when be brought the Hellenic fleet to the Hellespont.

When the Athenians stayed to besiege Sestos, their action diverged from that of the Peloponnesians. The Chersonese was of far more concern to Athens than to Sparta; the Athenians already drew part of their grain supply from the land north of the Black Sea, and so they were interested in the sea route through the straits. Moreover the proof they had experienced in the last two years of the value of their warships incited them to maritime enterprises. It was therefore significant that, promptly after the rebuilding of the city wall, the Athenians completed the fortifications of the Peiraeus. These had been begun by Themistocles, probably in 483 (see chapter 7, p. 185), and now he persuaded the Athenians to finish them. Previously the Bay of Phalerum had been the main harbor for the city of Athens; the Peiraeus provided a large and more defensible port, both for a war fleet and for merchant ships. In the same connection Thucydides records a remark of Themistocles: "We must seize the sea." The concentration of the Athenians on developing sea power could easily become a cause of divergence from Spartan policy; Lacedaemon sent only ten triremes to the battle of Artemisium and sixteen to the battle of Salamis. But at the end of 479 the Spartans had not yet decided to withdraw from naval enterprise; there was still no divergence of policy between them and the Athenians.

PAUSANIAS IN COMMAND AT SEA[3]

In 478 Pausanias, the Spartan regent, led a fleet of the Hellenic League to sea; it consisted of twenty ships from the Peloponnese, thirty from Athens and an unrecorded number from other allies. It sailed to Cyprus. This choice of destination is surprising; Persian forces still held places nearer to the heartlands of Greece, such as Eion and Doriscus on the coast of Thrace and Byzantium at the Bosporus. Yet Pausanias's fleet sailed first to Cyprus and reduced much of the island, but there is no secure indication of any attempt to hold it. Evidently the successes of the previous two years had suggested that naval power could be used for the purpose of capturing booty from Persian-held territory.

From Cyprus Pausanias led the fleet to Byzantium and captured it by siege from its Persian garrison. Then troubles developed in the fleet. Thucydides alleges that Pausanias had become violent; so discontent arose among the crews and especially among "the Ionians and those who had recently been freed from the king;" these came to the Athenians, reminded them of their legendary tie of common descent, and asked them to take over command of their forces and protect them against Pausanias. The Athenians accepted their appeal and thus took over leadership of the allied forces, except the Peloponnesian contingents. Meanwhile the Spartans heard rumors about Pausanias; so they recalled him and put him on trial. He was convicted of some offences against individual persons but acquitted on the most alarming charge, that of treacherous negotiations with the Persians. The Spartans sent out Dorcis and others with a small force to replace Pausanias but the allies refused to accept them as commanders. Then the Spartans, after some deliberation, gave up their claim to the command. Thucydides, commenting on their decision, remarks that "they were anxious to withdraw from the Persian War; they considered that the Athenians were competent to command and well-disposed at that time towards them."

The outrageous behavior of Pausanias at Byzantium became a legend. Elsewhere Thucydides gives details: allegedly Pausanias freed Persian prisoners of high rank, who had been captured at Byzantium; he exchanged treacherous letters with Xerxes (Thucydides quotes the supposed text of the letters); he adopted Persian habits of dressing and eating, and he traveled about Thrace with a bodyguard of Medes and Egyptians. His acquittal on the charge of medism at his trial may prompt some doubt about these allegations. His subsequent fortunes call for brief attention here. After the trial he gained a trireme privately from the Peloponnesian town of Hermione, sailed to the straits and occupied Byzantium (477?). Later he was driven out by the Athenians and took up a position at Colonae in the Troad, but the Spartans recalled him. On his return the ephors arrested him, but he gained his release and offered to stand trial; yet no Spartiates could supply adequate evidence to convict him. Eventually the ephors suborned an informer who produced a supposed letter of Pausanias to Artabazus, the satrap of Dascylium, but when they tried to arrest him, he took refuge in the temple of Athena of the Brazen House; the ephors blockaded him there until he starved to death. The repeated failure of his enemies to convict him in court shows that there was no good evidence against him; it follows that the letters quoted by Thucydides were forgeries. His misfortunes show something further; he was what would now be called a controversial figure. Accordingly, by the time when Thucydides wrote, no one cared to defend his memory.

When Pausanias captured Byzantium in 478, he was in a difficult position. A military commander in a captured city has to decide how much license to allow to his victorious troops and how much protection to extend to the vanquished. In Pausanias's case the problem of discipline was compounded, because his troops were drawn from a variety of sovereign cities and because the citizens of the captured city were Greeks like the victors. Furthermore, the story of his bad behavior leaves at least one event unexplained. When he put to sea in 478 his fleet included twenty Peloponnesian ships but these did not join in the eventual transfer of leadership to the Athenians; it is not clear when or why the Peloponnesian ships went home. In a different context Herodotus (8.3.2) makes a brief but revealing comment on the occurrences at Byzantium: "[the Athenians] seizing the occasion of Pausanias's arrogance deprived the Lacedaemonians of the leadership." The account that reached Thucydides of Pausanias's arrogance may be substantially an Athenian story; its exaggerations and obscurities suggest that the Athenians had something to hide.

THE FOUNDING OF THE DELIAN LEAGUE[4]

In consequence of the transfer of naval command at Byzantium the Athenians set up a new league, which came to be called the League of Delos. Thucydides (1.96) gives a little information about its original structure. Its acknowledged purpose, he says, was "to exact vengeance for their sufferings by ravaging the king's land." To this end the member states were to supply warships to the federal fleet, but some of them made cash payments instead. An Athenian magistracy, known as the "hellenotamiae" ("treasurers of the Greeks"), was set up to receive the payments, which were called "tribute." For several years the treasury of the League was kept at Delos and congresses of envoys from the member states met there to determine policy.

At the foundation of the League the Athenians assessed the member states for contributions of ships and tribute. This task was carried out by Aristeides. Thucydides says that the original assessment of tribute was 460 talents. This figure has provoked a good deal of discussion because comparisons have been made with figures supposedly attested later in the history of the League. Sometime after 478 but not later than 454 the Athenians moved the treasury of the League from Delos to Athens, and in 454 they resolved that henceforth, as each payment of tribute came in from a member state, a sixtieth of it should be paid as first fruits to the goddess Athena. The payments of quota to Athena were inscribed on marble, and considerable fragments of the inscribed texts have been recovered by excavation; they are called "the Athenian tribute quota lists" or, less properly, "the Athenian tribute lists." Inferences of two kinds have been thought to have a bearing on the first assessment of the Delian League. First, attempts have been made to calculate the fresh assessment carried out in 454, and the estimates reached lie between 490 and 500 talents. Second, the first quota list, that for the Attic year 454/3, was inscribed with an appendix, whose letters are very poorly preserved. In 1932 the appendix was read (by Wade-Gery) as giving the total quota of the year; the figure as read implied a total tribute of rather more than 383 talents. But between 477 and 454 the League acquired additional members, including wealthy cities like Aegina; and some member states which had originally supplied ships commuted their contributions to payments of cash. Accordingly, many historians have thought that assessment and payment at the foundation of the League must have been far lower than in 454/3, and so they have been puzzled by Thucydides's figure of 460 talents.

Different solutions have been proposed. Some have suggested that in speaking of "assessed tribute" Thucydides meant the whole obligation of member states, whether they chose to acquit it in ships or in money. This would be an unparalleled use of the word "tribute," and it is perhaps easier to believe, as others have done, that Thucydides was simply mistaken in his figure. Again Plutarch (*Arist.* 24.1) says that Aristeides in making the assessment examined the land and revenues of the member states; this would take several years, and so the first assessment may have included a larger membership than that of the League's first year. It has also been supposed that the first assessment was high and the figures were lowered at periodic reassessments.

None of the solutions is wholly satisfactory. Here it will suffice to note that the data of the problem have changed of late and may change again. In 1966 the appendix to the first tribute quota list was reexamined (by W.K. Pritchett); it was found that some of the letters claimed previously are uncertain. In particular, it can no longer be asserted with any confidence that the appendix gave a statement of totals; its tenor is not known. Furthermore the arrangement of the fragments of the quota lists needs to be reexamined. It is not altogether clear how the fragments reached the positions they hold in the current reconstruction. A restudy of their arrangement might lead to changes, which could affect any calculation of the assessment of 454. In the meantime Thucydides's figure of 460 talents is the best evidence for the original assessment of the Delian League.

That figure, however, presents a problem of a different kind. According to Thucydides (1.95.1), the allies who transferred naval leadership to the Athenians at Byzantium in 478 were "the Ionians and those who had recently been freed from the king." This phrase recalls his description of the forces present with the Athenians at the siege of Sestos nearly a year before; he called them "those allies from Ionia and the Hellespont who had already rebelled against the king" (1.89.2). As suggested above, this group of allies was probably not large; in particular, since the council held at Samos after the battle of Mycale did not admit the cities of mainland Ionia to the Hellenic League, forces from those cities are not likely to have been present at Byzantium in 478, for the strategic situation on the mainland of Asia Minor had not changed. But if the group of allies who transferred naval command from Pausanias to the Athenians was small, they cannot have sufficed for a tribute assessment of 460 talents. Perhaps one should suppose that, after the transfer of command was reported at Athens, the Athenians issued a general invitation, asking any Greek states who sympathized with the aims of the League to join it; such an invitation was issued in 378/7, when the Athenians founded a new confederacy. If a general invitation was issued in 478, it is likely that Athenian squadrons toured the Aegean asking and perhaps pressuring cities to join the League; a few years later the Athenians compelled Carystus to join by making war on it, and therefore the hypothesis cannot be ruled out that the Athenians applied coercion to other cities as early as 478/7.

The question of the original extent and membership of the Delian League has been discussed a good deal. Some historians have argued that most of the cities recorded later as members of the League joined it at its foundation; others have argued that the original membership was smaller. The question is difficult because there is evidence extant only on a few cities. It will be best to start with specific cases. Eion at the mouth of the Strymon river did not join the League at its foundation, for the first federal operation consisted in besieging and reducing the town. Further east on the Thracian coast Doriscus was held by a Persian officer, and Herodotus (7.106) says that he alone of the Persian officers in Thrace and the Hellespont was never overcome by the Greeks. On the other hand, Poteidaea and the other cities of Pallene had rebelled against Persian control soon after the battle of Salamis, and Poteidaea withstood a Persian siege in the winter of 480/79; so it is not unlikely that these cities joined the League of Delos at its foundation with a view to futher operations against the Persians.

Indications about some cities of the Aegean may perhaps be extracted from news about events following the battle of Salamis. After the battle the Greek fleet pursued the Persian fleet as far as Andros; then Eurybiades decided against sailing to the Hellespont with a view to destroying the bridge there. Next, Herodotus says, the Greeks besieged Andros and Themistocles, speaking in the name of the Athenians, demanded money from the Andrians, but the latter refused to pay and withstood the siege successfully. Herodotus adds that Themistocles sent messengers with demands for money to other islands; payments were made by Carystus in Euboea, Paros and perhaps some others; yet on raising the siege of Andros the Greek fleet plundered the territory of Carystus. If some islanders were willing to pay money in response to Themistocles's demands in the fall of 480, surely they were still more amenable to Athenian pressure in 478, when the Persians had suffered more defeats. Yet Carystus did not join the Delian League at its foundation; Thucydides (1.98.3) reports that it was compelled to join some years later.

Something more can be learned about the activities of Themistocles from a passage of the contemporary poet, Timocreon of Rhodes. He says: "Leto has conceived hatred of Themistocles, the liar, the unjust, the traitor, who accepted a wicked bribe and refused to restore Timocreon, his friend, to his native city of Ialysus, but took three talents of silver and sailed away to destruction; he restored some unjustly, expelled others and killed others. Then, stuffed full of silver, he gave a ridiculous banquet at the Isthmus, serving cold meat." It has been conjectured that the "banquet" is Timocreon's allusion to the meeting at the Isthmus where the commanders voted to determine which had distinguished himself most at the battle of Salamis. This meeting took place a little while after the battle. Thus Timocreon's remark seems to imply that Themistocles's money-raising operations in the fall of 480 took him as far afield as Ialysus, one of the three cities of Rhodes, and there he altered the balance of internal politics. Timocreon was only interested in his own city, Ialysus; but if Themistocles intervened there, he may also have visited Lindus and Camirus, the other two cities of the island. If he succeeded in giving control to his own partisans in these three cities, they would be likely to join the Delian League at its foundation.

Thus it is probable that the original membership of the Delian League extended as far as Poteidaea in the northwest and Rhodes in the southeast, but it certainly did not include some places, such as Carystus, between these limits. For most of the islands of the Aegean there is no way of telling whether they joined the League at its foundation. Some historians have started by drawing up a list of cities attested in the tribute quota lists for the years beginning in 454; then they have excluded cities known or conjectured to have joined after the foundation, and in this way they have tried to reconstruct a list of foundation members. The case of Carystus proves that this method is unsound. Its payments appear in the tribute quota lists with considerable regularity. One would accordingly presume that Carystus joined the League at its foundation, were it not that Thucydides reports how it was compelled to join some years later.

Controversy about foundation-membership in the League has been most acute with respect to the Greek cities on the mainland of Asia Minor. Arguments have been produced purporting to show that Erythrae, Ephesus, Cyme and other places were not original members of the League, but these are not decisive. Two general considerations should be borne in mind. First, the council held at Samos after the battle of Mycale did not admit the mainland cities to the Hellenic League, and Herodotus's account seems to indicate the strategic difficulty; the Hellenic League lacked the resources to garrison mainland Ionia against Persian reprisals (see chapter 8, p. 227). Surely the same strategic consideration was still valid when the League of Delos was founded. Second, the question should be asked whether the Greek cities of the Asiatic mainland wished to be freed from the Persian empire. Usually Persian rule was not severe (see chapter 7, pp. 172 and 176). Only in the case of Phaselis is there evidence to show whether the citizens wished to join the Delian League. On the expedition which culminated in the battle of the Eurymedon river (469? see below pp. 248 and 250) Cimon put in at Phaselis. As Plutarch reports (*Cim.* 12.3–4), "the Phaselites were Greeks, but they did not admit the expedition and they were not willing to rebel against the king. So Cimon ravaged their territory and attacked their walls." But there was long-standing friendship between Chios and Phaselis, so the Chiote contingent in Cimon's fleet negotiated a settlement; by this the Phaselites paid a sum of ten talents and supplied a contingent to the expedition. The case of Phaselis may not be typical; it lay appreciably further east than most Greek cities of Asia Minor. But at least its behavior should serve as a warning against any assumption that those cities joined the League with unanimous enthusiasm.

In 478, when Greek cities received the invitation to join the Delian League, strategic considerations may have been paramount for most of them. The tribute assessment of 460 talents implies that many states accepted the invitation, but probably these were mostly islands. For the present, at least, they had little to fear from Persian reprisals, since the Persians had withdrawn their best ships from the Aegean; likewise the islands were exposed to the might of the Athenian navy. The situation of the Greek cities on the mainland of Asia Minor was different; they may well have reckoned that they had more to fear from Persian than from Athenian pressure.

THE GROWTH OF THE DELIAN LEAGUE[5]

Thucydides (1.98–101) gives an account of the early operations of the Delian League. It is brief; indeed it is little more than a list with occasional comments. But it is the basic source of information for the events mentioned. Here it will be summarized; then an attempt will be made to discover the dates of the events; hence some picture may emerge of the development of Athenian power.

The first operation of the League was a siege of Eion, the harbor city at the mouth of the Strymon river; the federal forces were commanded by Cimon, the son of Miltiades, and they captured the city from the Persians. Next the League attacked the island of Scyros; it enslaved the inhabitants, who were Dolopians, and installed new settlers. A war was fought against Carystus in Euboea and after some time the Carystians made terms. After that Naxos seceded from the League, but the federal forces besieged it and overcame it. After that Cimon led the forces of the Athenians and their allies eastwards along the south coast of Asia Minor to the Eurymedon river, where the Persians had assembled land and sea forces; Cimon defeated both on the same day, capturing and destroying 200 Phoenician triremes. Some time later Thasos seceded from the League because of a dispute with Athens for control of mines and trading posts on the coast of Thrace. The Athenians defeated the Thasians in a sea battle and began besieging their city. Thereupon the Thasians appealed to the Lacedaemonians to help them by invading Attica. The Lacedaemonians "promised this, without letting the Athenians know, and they intended to carry out their promise, but they were prevented by the earthquake, which had occurred; in it the helots and of the perioeci the people of Thurium and Aethaea seceded to Ithome" (*Thuc.* 1.101.2). The Thasians came to terms with the Athenians in the third year of the siege; they destroyed their fortifications and surrendered their fleet; they were assessed to pay tribute, and they gave up their claims to the mines and the trading posts on the mainland.

In the account paraphrased above Thucydides gives only one numerical indication of chronology; namely, he states the duration of the siege of Thasos. Otherwise he uses vague phrases, like "after that," to arrange the events in order. Later authors give dates for some of the events; some of these appear to be drawn from an *Atthis*, probably the *Atthis* of Philochorus, and so they may be reliable. This may be true of a learned note preserved in the scholia to Aeschines (2.31); the scholiast lists the disasters suffered by the Athenians at Nine Ways, the position on the Strymon river inland from Eion, where the Athenians eventually founded Amphipolis. His note on the first disaster says: "When Lysistratus, Lycurgus and Cratinus advanced against Eion on the Strymon, the Athenians after capturing Eion were destroyed by the Thracians in the archonship of

Phaedon at Athens." Thucydides does not give an expedition to Nine Ways at the time of the siege of Eion and he names Cimon as the commander; but his note on the capture of Eion is too brief to allow an argument from his silence. Possibly while Cimon conducted the siege an expedition was sent under three of his colleagues to try to settle at Nine Ways, but it was overcome. Thus the scholiast provides the Attic year 476/5 as the date of the capture of Eion. Now Aristotle (*AP* 23.5) says that Aristeides assessed the League for tribute in 478/7. It has accordingly been suggested that the business of organizing the League was carried out in the winter of 478/7, so that the federal forces would be ready for action at the beginning of the campaigning season of 477. If this is correct, the first federal operation, the siege of Eion, was protracted and expensive, since it began in 477 but was not completed till the Attic year 476/5. That is possible; fortified towns were difficult to capture by siege. Alternatively, the work of organizing the new League may have occupied the year 477, so that the siege of Eion was begun in 476.

Plutarch (*Thes.* 36) provides more information on the capture of Scyros. In the archonship of Phaedon (476/5) the Athenians received an oracle bidding them recover the bones of their legendary king, Theseus. Scyros was difficult of access, since its inhabitants practiced piracy. So Cimon subdued the island; with the help of divine signs he discovered the bones and brought them back in procession to Athens. An annual festival was held in honor of Theseus. Plutarch may well have learned about the capture of Scyros from the *Atthis* of Philochorus; the latter was interested in religious antiquities and may in turn have derived his information from the traditions of the festival. If the capture of Eion and the oracle about the bones of Theseus both belonged to the Attic year 476/5, it is likely that the two captures belonged respectively to the two campaigning seasons of 476 and 475, since both were major operations.

A more complex argument may indicate the dates of the siege of Thasos. Thucydides says (1.100.3) that, after the Athenians had defeated the Thasians at sea and landed in the island, they sent 10,000 settlers to try to seize Nine Ways; the settlers occupied that site but then they proceeded into the interior and were destroyed at Drabescus by a coalition of Thracian tribes. Elsewhere (4.102.2–3) he summarizes the attempts to found a settlement at Nine Ways. The first, he says, was made by Aristagoras of Miletus when the prospects of the Ionian Revolt were declining; the second was made by the Athenians thirty-two years later and ended in the disaster at Drabescus; in the twenty-ninth year after that the Athenians under Hagnon led a successful expedition to Nine Ways and the name given to this settlement was Amphipolis. The scholiast to Aeschines (2.31), listing Athenian disasters at Nine Ways, says that Hagnon's settlement was founded in 437/6. Thucydides's phrase "in the twenty-ninth year" indicates inclusive reckoning, so the disaster at Drabescus would appear to belong to the Attic year 465/4. Admittedly, the scholiast to Aeschines puts the disaster in the year when Lysicrates was archon, that is, in 453/2; but the name Lysicrates can be emended to Lysitheus, which is the name of the archon of 465/4. Thucydides in his narrative of the Thasian revolt seems to put the attempt on Nine Ways early in the period of the siege, and he says that the Thasians surrendered in the third year of the siege. So the revolt and the siege should be dated ca. 465–ca. 463.

A less secure indication can be found for the date of the battle of the Eurymedon river. Plutarch (*Cim.* 8.8) says that at the competition, when Sophocles first presented tragedies, Apsephion as archon did not choose judges by lot but entrusted the decision between the entries to Cimon and his fellow generals. Apsephion was archon in 469/8; his action suggests that the generals had distinguished themselves and that their expedition had been large enough and serious enough to employ all ten of them. The most likely campaign of the period is that of the Eurymedon river. The tragic competition took place each year at the spring festival called the Dionysia; so it is likely that the Eurymedon campaign was fought in 469.

Thus a skeleton chronology can be established for the operations of the Delian League from ca. 477 to ca. 463. Something can be said about the achievements and their significance. Thucydides was selective in his digression on events between the Persian and Peloponnesian Wars; he recorded events which he considered especially important, or sometimes he mentioned one event as an example for a whole category of similar events. Thus his account of the events of ca. 477–ca. 463 should be taken as illustrative, not exhaustive; and at some points it may be possible to add to the illustrations.

The siege of Eion, for example, may be one of several operations designed to overcome Persian forces which lingered on the Thracian coast. The area was important to the Athenians for several reasons; ship timber could be had from Macedon, there were silver mines in southern Thrace, and futher east the grain route through the Hellespont ran past the Chersonese. Plutarch (*Cim.* 14.1) says that some Persians refused to leave the Chersonese, but Cimon sailed against them with only four ships, captured their thirteen ships, overcame them and thus secured the Chersonese for Athens. Plutarch adds that thence Cimon proceeded against the Thasians, who were in revolt; thus he seems to imply that Cimon fought against Persians in the Chersonese as late as ca. 465. This inference derives some slight support from fragments of an inscribed casualty list; it gives Athenians and allies who fell in fighting at various places, including Thasos and Sigeum. The latter place is opposite the Chersonese and might well be a scene of action in connection with operations there; so the list indicates that there was fighting in the Hellespontine district and at Thasos in the same year. If there were Persian forces in the Chersonese as late as ca. 465, it is not likely that they had been there ever since Xerxes's expedition; Persian troops from all parts of the Chersonese had gathered in Sestos in 479/8, when Xanthippus overcame them. More probably the forces present with thirteen triremes ca. 465 had been sent recently from Dascylium or possibly from Doriscus. Herodotus's remark (7.106) about the latter position is puzzling: he says that in and before 480 Persian commanders were established at many places in Thrace and the Hellespontine district, and later the Greeks overcame all of these except Mascames, the commander at Doriscus, but although they made many attacks on Mascames, these were unsuccessful. Probably the Persian government eventually recalled Mascames and the garrison from Doriscus. After ca. 465 nothing more is heard of fighting by the Delian League against Persian forces in the district of Thrace and the straits; indeed in view of the value of this district for mines and sea routes, it is remarkable that the League did not establish itself there securely against the Persians until so late a date.

The attacks on Scyros and Carystus appear to illustrate a policy of securing the Greek islands for the League. It is not possible to say how extensive such operations were in the years ca. 477–ca. 463, since it is not known how many islands failed to join the League at its foundation. But something can be said about the result. By 431 the League held all the islands of the Aegean except Melos and Thera. These last two islands were Dorian and claimed legendary connections with Lacedaemon. In 416, when the Athenians at last attacked Melos, the Melians resisted in the expectation of help from Sparta. No such help was forthcoming, but the expectations of the Melians may explain the inhibition previously restraining Athenian policy: in the early period of the expansion of the Delian League the Athenians perhaps refrained from attacking Melos or Thera because they did not want to offend Sparta. The other islands of the Aegean may all have been brought into the League by ca. 463.

The victory at the Eurymedon river contributed to the growth of Athenian power in a different way. Since as many as 200 Phoenician ships were destroyed, the Persian preparations must have been large, and it is a reasonable conjecture that the Persian aim was to reestablish a presence in the Aegean. The Delian League showed by its victory that it could protect Greece from any resumption of Persian designs. This outcome mattered particularly for the Greek cities on the mainland of Asia Minor. Possibly many of them had been brought into the League, willingly or reluctantly, before the Eurymedon campaign. In any case that campaign, when Persian forces were defeated on land as well as at sea, showed that the Athenians were now the stronger power on the western and southern coasts of Asia Minor. The strategic situation was no longer the same as had been estimated at the time of the council of Samos after the battle of Mycale (see chapter 8, p. 227).

By ca. 463 the League had probably reached approximately the maximum extent revealed in the tribute quota lists of the years following 454. It held almost all the islands of the Aegean, including the cities of Euboea in the west, most of the Cyclades, and in the east the major islands of Lesbos, Chios, Samos and Rhodes. In the north it held many cities on the coast of Thrace and the peninsula of Chalcidice; further east it held the Greek cities on both shores of the straits. It held most of the Greek cities on the west and south coasts of Asia Minor with some exceptions, such as Magnesia on the Maeander, which was given by the Persian king to a Greek fugitive and does not appear in the tribute quota lists. Crete in the south, Cyprus in the southeast, and in the northeast the Greek cities on the coasts of the Black Sea were outside the League.

By ca. 463 the League of Delos was not only larger than at its foundation; it had also proved that it could maintain itself securely. This became evident when revolts in Naxos, Thasos and perhaps other places were overcome. Within the League the position of Athens was emerging as more patently authoritarian. On the occasion of the revolt of Naxos Thucydides adds a brief digression (1.99) about the general causes of attempts to secede from the League. He notes that many cities chose to commute their ship contributions for monetary payments of tribute, so that they escaped the burden of campaigning; but the Athenians used the additional tribute to increase their own fleet. He also makes the telling remark: "the Athenians were strict in their dealings and burdensome when they brought pressure to bear on allies neither accustomed nor willing to undertake protracted toil." Athenian strictness may have been a major factor in the growth of discontent among the allies.

An act making manifest the enhanced position of Athens may well have been carried out early in the 460s. At some time the treasury of the League was transferred from Delos to Athens. The date is not known; many historians have put the transfer in 454 because in that year the Athenians began paying quotas of tribute to Athena. But the transfer of the treasury and the beginning of quota payments may be independent actions separated by several years. Plutarch (*Arist.* 25.2–3) tells a story that the Samians proposed the transfer of the treasury from Delos to Athens and, when this was under consideration, Aristeides remarked that it was expedient though not just; the context implies that the Samian proposal was carried out. The remark of Aristeides reflects the stock picture of him and may be a fictitious element in the anecdote, but the rest of the story may be true; in particular, there is no apparent reason why fiction would invent the Samians as authors of the proposal. The date of Aristeides's death is conjectural;

the latest political activity attested for him is his assessment of the original tribute of the Delian League, and although many anecdotes clustered around his memory, these do not suggest activity nearly as late as 454. If the federal treasury was transferred to Athens appreciably before that date, a likely occasion for the transfer would be immediately before the Eurymedon campaign; news had come of Persian preparations threatening the Aegean, and so it was reasonable to move the treasury to a place less exposed than Delos.

When the Delian League was founded, the Spartans were content to see the Athenians take over command of naval operations against the Persian Empire. But by the time of the Thasian revolt the League had changed both in extent and in character. This may account for a change in the Spartan outlook. Thucydides's statements (1.101.1–2) about the Spartan attitude to the Thasian revolt deserve some scrutiny. He says that the Thasians, when subjected to siege, asked the Spartans to help them by invading Attica; that the Spartans promised to do so, although they did not let the Athenians know of the promise, and they really intended to invade Attica, but they were prevented by an earthquake and a revolt of the helots and some perioeci. One should be skeptical of unrealized intentions, especially when they are said to have been secret; such allegations could not be checked but they could be invented later, when Sparta wished to pose as the friend of discontented members of the Delian League. It would be surprising if the Spartans considered invading Attica as early as ca. 465; even after the First Peloponnesian War broke out, they refrained for a long time from so extreme a measure; they first invaded Attica in 446. But it is not so easy to doubt Thucydides's statement that the Thasians appealed to Sparta for help. If that is correct, it follows that by ca. 465 many Greeks knew that the Spartan attitude towards Athens was no longer so amicable as it had been in 478.

SPARTA IN THE PELOPONNESE[6]

Sometime in the 470s or 460s an anti-Spartan movement developed in the Peloponnese. The clearest and most reliable information about this is provided by Herodotus (9.35.2). In a digression from the battle of Plataea he talks about Teisamenus of Elis, a seer who in accordance with a prophecy served with the Spartans at five battles which they won. The first was the battle of Plataea; the second and third were "the battle at Tegea against the Tegeates and the Argives, later the battle at Dipaea against all the Arcadians except the Mantineans."

The coinage of Arcadia may throw further light on the Arcadian share in the fighting at Tegea and Dipaea. Several of the towns struck coins independently ca. 500, but later a federal coinage was struck; the coins bore the legend *Arkadikon* ("of the Arcadians"). It is not clear whether the new coinage began somewhat before or somewhat after 480; it continued for a long time, perhaps until 418, when Sparta won another battle at Mantinea (see chapter 13, p. 349). The federal coinage indicates the formation and continued existence of an Arcadian League. While it was current, Mantinea continued striking her own coins but the other towns did not; this suggests, but does not compel, the hypothesis that Mantinea was not a member of the Arcadian League, and this hypothesis would explain the absence of the Mantineans from the battle of Dipaea.

Another digression by Herodotus tells a little more about the policy of Argos. Cleomenes of Sparta defeated the Argives at Sepeia ca. 494 (see chapter 8, p. 199) and Herodotus (6.83) outlines the effects of the defeat. Argos lost so many men that the "slaves" seized control of the city and retained it until the sons of those who had fallen at Sepeia grew up. Then these drove out the "slaves," who therefore seized Tiryns. For a time there was peace between Argos and Tiryns, but then war broke out, and after lengthy fighting the Argives won. The identity of the "slaves" mentioned in this story is difficult to discover; Aristotle (*Pol.* 5.1303a6–8), recording the same incident, calls them "some of the perioeci." Possibly they were some of the people from neighboring communities, such as Tiryns and Mycenae; Herodotus's designation of them as "slaves" may come from their political opponents in Argos. Mycenae and Tiryns each sent a contingent to the battle of Plataea, whereas Argos was neutral during the fighting of 480–479. Evidently Mycenae and Tiryns were independent at the time, and the subsequent war with Tiryns, given by Herodotus as following the Argive expulsion of the "slaves," was an attempt by Argos to win control over that city. Diodorus (11.65) describes a war fought by Argos against Mycenae; the Argives captured Mycenae after a siege and destroyed it. Diodorus relates this under the year 468/7; it may have come shortly after the war against Tiryns and have sprung from the same Argive aspirations to assert or reassert control over their neighbors.

Some historians have supposed that, when the sons of the fallen of Sepeia grew up and expelled the "slaves" from Argos, this revolution caused a change of foreign policy. They have suggested that the battle of Tegea was fought while the regime of the "slaves" was still in control; then the revolution removed Argos from the camp of those fighting against the Spartans, and this would account for the absence of the Argives from the battle of Dipaea. But Argive absence from that battle can be explained just as readily by the fact that Argos was defeated in the previous battle of Tegea. Moreover, in the late 460s relations between Argos and Sparta were still hostile; by 460 Argos and Sparta were at war, and this war continued until 451. It is best to suppose that relations between Sparta and Argos were hostile throughout the period ca. 494–451, although warfare may have been intermittent; the change of regime in the city of Argos did not alter its geopolitical position.

The relation of two other developments to the anti-Spartan movement is not clear. A synoecism was carried out at Elis, that is, the inhabitants moved from their several small towns to form a single large city. Diodorus (11.54.1) reports this under the year 471/0. But there is no evidence that this action or the policy of Elis in consequence was opposed to Sparta. A synoecism was also carried out at Mantinea, where a single city replaced the previous five villages, but it is not even clear whether this occured as late as the period following the Persian Wars. In about the middle of the sixth century the people of Cyrene suffered internal tensions and they invited a man from Mantinea to reorganize their city; this suggests that Mantinea already had an admired and somewhat sophisticated constitution.

The actions of Themistocles have a bearing both on the anti-Spartan movement in the Peloponnese and on consequent relations between Sparta and Athens. No public activities of his in Athens are securely attested after he served as choregos to Phrynichus in 477/6, but Thucydides (1.135–138) gives a digression on his later fortunes. He was ostracized and took up residence in Argos; from there he visited other parts of the Peloponnese. The Spartans claimed that, in investigating the activities of Pausanias, they also had found evidence implicating Themistocles in treacherous dealings with the Persians, and they complained to the Athenians. The latter condemned Themistocles in absence and sent men to arrest him. He fled to Corcyra and thence to Admetus king of the Molossi in Epirus; then he traveled overland to Pydna in Macedonia. There he took a passage on a merchant ship across the Aegean. Landing at Ephesus, he went upcountry to the Persian court and appealed to Artaxerxes. The king treated him favorably and let him settle at Magnesia on the Maeander.

The chronology of Themistocles's movements cannot be determined in any detail. The only certainty is that the king whom he approached was not Xerxes but Artaxerxes, who became king in 465/4. So it is likely that his period of residence in Argos fell in the late 470s or early 460s, that is, at about the time when the anti-Spartan movement developed in Argos and Arcadia. While residing in Argos, Themistocles visited other parts of the Peloponnese; surely the Spartans suspected him of fomenting the anti-Spartan movement, and that was why they trumped up a charge of medism and complained to Athens. The effect of the outcome on relations between Sparta and Athens is difficult to estimate. Themistocles was the Athenian whom the Spartans had trusted most; in 480 they gave him greater honors than they had awarded to any other foreigner (see above, p. 240). When they conceived suspicions against him, they may have felt bitterly disappointed in the Athenians. On the other hand, they had reason to be grateful to the Athenian state for its enthusiastic response to their complaint; on other occasions Athenians were condemned in absence, but the city hardly ever sent men to arrest them outside its borders.

In the 460s an earthquake occurred in Lacedaemon; this provided an oppor-

tunity for the helots and the two perioecid towns of Thurium and Aethaea to
rebel. This Messenian Revolt lasted several years and had a permanent effect on
relations between Spartan citizens and helots. At least after this time Spartan
policy was much concerned with the need to take precautions against the helots,
but that preoccupation cannot be traced with any certainty in the preceding
period. The date of outbreak of the Revolt is much disputed; it may have been as
early as 469 or as late as 464. But two things can be said about relative chronology.
The first concerns possible relationship between the Messenian Revolt and the
anti-Spartan movement in Arcadia. Listing the five victories where Teisamenus
attended the Spartans, Herodotus (9.35.2) gives the battles of Tegea and Dipaea
as the second and third; the fourth was "the battle against the Messenians at
Ithome." After launching the Revolt the rebels took up a position on Mt. Ithome
and presently the Spartans besieged them there. It is not clear at what point in the
course of the Revolt the battle mentioned by Herodotus occurred; so Herodotus's list does not prove that the Spartans had already defeated the Arcadian
League decisively before the outbreak of the Revolt. Yet this is likely on other
grounds; Plutarch's account (*Cim.* 16.4–7) of the outbreak of the Revolt shows
that the crisis for Sparta was serious; if she had still had trouble with the
Arcadians and if consequently there had been a prospect of Arcadian help for the
Messenians, the predicament would have been still more extreme and the
Arcadian complication would have been likely to leave some trace in the sources
on the Revolt. The second matter of relative chronology concerns the fortunes of
Argos. Diodorus (11.65) reports the Argive war against Mycenae after the
outbreak of the Messenian Revolt and says that, because of the Revolt, the
Spartans could not come to the aid of the Mycenaeans. This presents the situation
from the Argive point of view. One can also regard it from the viewpoint of the
Spartans: for them it was fortunate that, during the early and critical stages of the
Messenian Revolt, Argive policy was preoccupied with Mycenae.

After the rebels took up a position on Mt. Ithome, the war continued for some
time and presently the Spartans appealed for help to some of their allies. Help was
accordingly sent by Aegina, a loyal member of the Peloponnesian League. Help
was also furnished by Mantinea, an action which is fully understandable if
Mantinea had stood aloof from the anti-Spartan movement in Arcadia. Help also
came from allies further afield and less constantly bound to Sparta, such as
Plataea, whose only diplomatic bond with Sparta was the Hellenic League of 481.
The terms of that League had not been abrogated. Athens too was a member of it,
and the Spartans appealed to Athens for help against the Messenians; they were
especially keen to get Athenian help, since the Athenians were believed to be
good at siege warfare. To understand the Athenian response it will be necessary to
consider the situation in Athens. In passing one thing may be noted; since the

Spartans appealed to Athens for help in 462, it is very difficult to believe that the Spartans had told the Thasians a few years before that they would take the extreme course of invading Attica.

Cimon served frequently as the commander of naval expeditions in the early years of the Delian League. He commanded the operations at Eion, at Scyros, at the Eurymedon river and at Thasos. Clearly he was a singularly efficient strategist. He was also a capable politician. In 489 his father, Miltiades, was condemned to pay a heavy fine and died in prison (see chapter 8, p. 203); Cimon gave his sister Elpinice in marriage to Callias, a wealthy man who paid the fine. Cimon himself married Isodice, a woman of the Alcmaeonid family. He understood the value of display for winning a political following; when he captured Scyros and brought back the bones of Theseus, the Athenians greeted the relics with a procession and sacrifices. His habitual largesse became notorious: he set no fences or guards around his fields, since he wanted his fellow citizens to be able to help themselves to the crops; a large meal was prepared in his house every day, so that needy Athenians could come in and dine; when he went out, he took with him two or three attendants who gave money and clothes to the poor. Such behavior could win some adherents by conferring material benefits and others by creating an impression of magnificence.

Cimon secured marriage ties with the Alcmaeonidae and with the Callias–Hipponicus family, and the scant indications of the political situation of the 470s within Athens suggest that a complex network of alliances was developing among the city families. Aristeides commanded the Athenian contingent at the battle of Plataea; he was a cousin of a Callias of the wealthy family. Xanthippus, who commanded the Athenian forces at Mycale and Sestos, married Agariste, an Alcmaeonid. The misfortunes of Themistocles–ostracized, condemned in absence and pursued in flight–show how far the city families would go to secure control. As suggested above (chapter 7, pp. 184–185), he was resented not because of any distinctive policy but because he came from the deme Phrearrioi, far outside the city. The prosecutor at his trial was Leobotes, an Alcmaeonid.

By the middle of the 460s Cimon was the most prominent man in Athens. But in Greek practice success provokes the bitter jealousy of rivals; Cimon had enemies. When he returned from overcoming the revolt of Thasos, he was put on trial. The charge was that he could have invaded Macedon successfully but had preferred to accept a bribe from its king, Alexander. Prosecutors were elected by the public assembly; it was a capital trial. Unfortunately the name is known of only one of the prosecutors. That was Pericles, a son of Xanthippus and Agariste, and when his turn came to speak at the trial, he did the accused as little harm as possible, merely rising once to acquit himself formally of his obligation as an elected prosecutor. Two explanations are possible. Born ca. 490, Pericles was young by the standards of Athenian public life in 463; perhaps nothing more was expected of him at the trial. Alternatively, there may have been collusion between Pericles and the defense.

Cimon was acquitted. His enemies must be sought elsewhere. When the Spartan appeal for help against the Messenians reached Athens, Ephialtes spoke against granting aid. For the historian Ephialtes is a puzzling and enigmatic figure. The name, but only the name, of his father, Sophonides, is known; his demotic is not recorded. The subsequent activities of Ephialtes show that he was a determined enemy of Cimon. Previously he had led an expedition of thirty ships far to the east beyond the Chelidonian islands on the south coast of Asia Minor. He conducted this expedition some time after the campaign of the Eurymedon river; it may have been an attempt to out-trump the prestige Cimon had won on that campaign.

When the Spartans appealed to Athens, Ephialtes was not successful in his opposition; Cimon persuaded the assembly to send him with a considerable force to Lacedaemon. But when he arrived there, something went wrong. The Spartans told the Athenians, alone of their allies, to go home. Thucydides (1.102.3) says that they did this "because they were afraid of the daring and innovatory spirit of the Athenians and considered them to belong to a different branch of the Greek nation; they were afraid that, if the Athenians stayed, they might be persuaded by those in Ithome to take some novel action." In writing thus Thucydides came close to admitting that he did not know why the Athenian force was dismissed. Evidently there was an undercurrent of suspicion and opinion in Sparta was divided, but speculation about this is fruitless. Some precise quarrel must have occurred while Cimon was in Lacedaemon.

On his return to Athens, there was a revulsion of feeling against the Spartans, but Cimon's personal fortunes were not at first harmed. Soon afterwards he was entrusted with command of a naval expedition, bound perhaps for Cyprus. But Ephialtes seized the opportunity of Cimon's absence to carry some reforms affecting the Areopagite Council. When Cimon returned, he tried to repeal these measures, but he was ostracized in 462/1. Ephialtes was murdered soon afterwards.

It is difficult to discover what was at stake in the reforms of Ephialtes. The clearest account surviving is given by Aristotle, who says (*AP* 25.2):

"First [Ephialtes] removed many of the Areopagites, by bringing charges against them in connection with their discharge of public business. Then in the archonship of Conon [462/1] he deprived the Council of the additional powers, through which it exercised guardianship of the constitution; he restored some of these powers to the Five Hundred and others to the assembly and the popular courts."

The puzzle is to discover what the powers were which the Areopagus thus lost. Two hypotheses call for brief notice.

One of these concerns the development of the Athenian courts. In the time of Solon most lawsuits were brought to one or another of the nine archons and he gave a verdict; each of the nine archons had jurisdiction over a specific type of case. But after the case had come before the archon, it could—at least if it was a serious case—be referred to the public assembly for decision; when the assembly sat thus as a court of law, it was called the "heliaea." Reference of a case to the assembly could be carried out on the initiative of a litigant, in which case it constituted an appeal against the archon's verdict; alternatively such reference could be carried out on the initiative of the archon, if he preferred not to determine the case on his own responsibility.

In the developed constitution of the late fifth and fourth centuries procedure was different. Instead of the single heliaea there were several popular courts, ten in the fourth century and perhaps as many as twelve before. Jurors were drawn from a panel of 6,000 citizens aged at least thirty years. The standard size for a popular jury was 500, though smaller juries were used for less important cases in the fourth century and larger juries were required occasionally. Moreover the incidence of popular jurisdiction had changed. Each case was brought before one of the nine archons, as before, but he no longer gave a verdict; instead he merely conducted a preliminary hearing, to make sure that the parties had collected their evidence, and then he brought the case before a popular court, which heard the pleas and decided its verdict by majority vote.

The change in the incidence of popular jurisdiction was a change of constitutional principle; when the archon ceased to give a verdict, the popular court became a court of first instance. The numerical change, from the single heliaea of the sixth century to the many popular courts of the developed constitution, was a matter of administrative convenience; the principle of decision by majority vote of a large number of jurors was kept, but more courts were required when the growth of empire and prosperity and the change in the incidence of popular jurisdiction brought far more judicial business.

One of the current hypotheses about the work of Ephialtes says that he effected the change in the incidence of popular jurisdiction, depriving the archon of authority to give a verdict. This hypothesis is difficult to refute, since there is very little evidence on the change. It had come about by the later part of the fifth century, for the extant speeches of the Attic orators assume the fully developed system of courts; but attempts to show that sometime earlier in the fifth century the archon still gave a verdict have not been successful. Against the hypothesis it

Attic red-figured kalpis, ca. 475. Three girls picking fruit. Now in Hearst State Monument, California. [Courtesy California Department of Parks and Recreation and D.A. Amyx.]

can be pointed out that Athenian tradition represented the work of Ephialtes as an attack on the Areopagite Council, not on the judicial function of the nine archons. The change in the incidence of popular jurisdiction may have come about in quite a different way. In the sixth century a man holding office as archon stood on the threshold of a political career and of membership in the Areopagite Council; by giving a verdict in a lawsuit he was almost sure to offend at least one of the parties; he may have hesitated to give offence, especially in cases where powerful interests were involved, and he may have preferred to pass the responsibility on to the popular court. This factor, the reluctance of the individual archon to give a verdict, would operate still more effectively after 487, when the archons were chosen by lot and so there was no longer any likelihood that those selected would be men of ambition. Thus the change in the incidence of popular jurisdiction may have come about, not through specific enactments such as the reforms of Ephialtes, but because of a personal factor, which sprang from the fears of the archons and hardened into custom. Important constitutional changes are not necessarily the result of specific enactments designed to bring them about.

The other hypothesis associates the work of Ephialtes with *euthynai*, that is, with the procedures for calling magistrates to account when they laid down office. In the fourth century the Athenians had two such procedures. First, when a magistrate laid down office, he was required to hand in his accounts to the ten officials called *logistai* within thirty days. The *logistai* brought the accounts before a popular court for ratification or questions. Second, in the three days after the accounts had been ratified any citizen could approach an official of his tribe, called the *euthynos*, with a complaint against the retiring magistrate. The *euthynos* referred private complaints to the touring judges called "deme dicasts" (see chapter 11, p. 298) and public complaints to the thesmothetae, who in turn brought them before a popular court. Both procedures existed by the middle of the fifth century and the general accounting, the procedure involving the tribal *euthynoi*, may have been very old. But doubtless both procedures underwent changes; for example, the *euthynoi* cannot have referred private complaints to the dicasts in the demes before those judges were created in 453/2.

The second hypothesis about the work of Ephialtes consists in supposing that he gave these two procedures virtually their final form and thereby deprived the Areopagus of the task of judging complaints against magistrates. More fully, the general accountability may have been known before 462, but conceivably the *euthynos* brought complaints against retiring magistrates before the Areopagite Council for decision; Ephialtes transferred this function from that Council to the popular court. The financial accountability, the procedure involving *logistai*, may have been instituted by Ephialtes or a little later. This hypothesis goes well beyond the evidence, but it explains why the work of Ephialtes could be regarded as an attack on the Areopagus. His reforms, on this view, deprived the Areopagus of an important function and a function which could be described loosely as constituting guardianship of the laws. As a court for hearing *euthynai* the Areopagite Council had defects; the identity of the jurors was known to the parties beforehand, and as ex-magistrates the Areopagites might have improper sympathy with the accused. Furthermore, Ephialtes's feud with Cimon should not be forgotten. After Cimon returned from Thasos ca. 463, he was tried on a charge of accepting a bribe from Alexander of Macedon (see above, p. 248); since prosecutors were elected by the public assembly, the trial was of the type called *eisangelia* or impeachment. The people who launched that prosecution must have thought that Cimon ought to have been condemned in the previous procedure of *euthynai*.

THE BREACH BETWEEN ATHENS AND SPARTA[8]

The dismissal of Cimon from Lacedaemon caused a sharp change in Athenian alliances. The Athenians felt that the Spartans had suspected them unjustly. They abrogated the link they had contracted with Sparta through the Hellenic League of 481. Further, they made an alliance with Argos, which was at war with Sparta. This brought them into a state of war with Sparta and the ensuing conflict is often called the First Peloponnesian War (ca. 460–446). The Athenians also gained an alliance with Thessaly and one with Megara. The latter alliance was strategically valuable, both for defensive and for offensive warfare. The route northwards from the Peloponnese across the Isthmus led through the Megarid and then branches led into Attica and Boeotia; as long as the Athenians held the Megarid, they were secure against a Peloponnesian invasion of Attica and they were in a strong position to encroach on the Corinthiad or on Boeotia.

The question can properly be asked, Why did the First Peloponnesian War break out? As noted above, relations between Athens and Sparta had deteriorated since 478; the growth of Athenian power through the Delian League evidently alarmed the Spartans. It was also noted (p. 258) that, because of lack of evidence, it is impossible to reconstruct with any confidence the attitude taken by the Spartans in the late 460s. But the question can still be asked from the Athenian standpoint. The dismissal of Cimon from Lacedaemon, however ignominious, need not have provoked a reversal of Athenian alliances; the Athenians might conceivably have contented themselves with blaming Cimon for the failure of policy and retaining their former diplomatic alignment. What was the general political outlook leading the Athenians to treat the dismissal of Cimon as tantamount to a *casus belli*?

The question cannot be answered adequately by classifying Athenian politicians as pro- and anti-Spartan and claiming that the one side defeated the other. Admittedly, Spartan links are attested for some Athenians active in the 460s. Plutarch (*Cim.* 16) expatiates on the pro-Spartan outlook of Cimon, noting among other things that he named one of his sons Lacedaemonius and referring to Cimon's contemporary, Ion of Chios, for the arguments with which Cimon persuaded the Athenians to send him to Lacedaemon. Callias, the brother-in-law of Cimon, was a *proxenos* of Sparta. Again an Alcibiades, of the family in which that name alternated with Cleinias, was *proxenos* of Sparta, but he renounced the *proxenia* and was ostracized; there are archaeological reasons for dating his ostracism within a few years of that of Cimon. Possibly his renunciation of the *proxenia* and the two ostracisms reflect the reversal of Athenian alliances. Ephialtes, on the other hand, opposed the expedition of Cimon to Lacedaemon. Should one see in Athenian events of 462–ca. 460 the victory of an anti-Spartan party, including Ephialtes, over a pro-Spartan party, including Cimon, Callias and Alcibiades?

Policy towards Sparta was, however, not the only issue dividing Ephialtes from Cimon. They disagreed on the measures of Ephialtes concerning the Areopagite Council and there appears to have been hostility of a personal nature between them. Furthermore, another gentleman who had ties with Sparta calls for note. By 431, when the Spartan king Archidamus led a Peloponnesian invasion of Attica, there was formal friendship between him and Pericles, who was then the leading Athenian, and Pericles offered some explanation of this in a speech to the public assembly. A feature of nomenclature suggests that the Spartan ties of Pericles's family went back at least a generation. The name Pericles was not common in Athens; the fifth-century statesman is the first known bearer of the name. The Spartan envoy who brought the appeal for Athenian help against the Messenian Revolt bore the name Pericleidas and he called his son Athenaeus. The Athenian Pericles is not known to have suffered in his political fortunes during the changes of 462–ca. 460. He seems to have proceeded with a normal career. He had taken part, albeit in a curious way, in the trial of Cimon ca. 463 (see above, p. 257). Later tradition associated him with Ephialtes in the reform of the Areopagus, but the better evidence attributed the measures to Ephialtes without naming Pericles. He is next securely attested serving, presumably as general, at the battle of Tanagra in 457.

Cimon, Callias, Alcibiades and Pericles had personal links with Spartans. It does not follow that they constituted a distinctively pro-Spartan party in Athens. The proper inference may be that many leading Athenian families had friends in Sparta. Personal ties were crucial in an Athenian political career; a rising politician looked primarily to his friends (his *philoi*–"his own people") in the city for support. The personal ties of leading Athenians with families outside Attica might well repay study.

Attempts to explain the change in Athenian foreign policy by hypotheses about a pro- and an anti-Spartan party are unsatisfactory for a further reason. To say that an anti-Spartan party defeated a pro-Spartan party merely postpones the question. One must still ask, What outlook among the Athenians enabled the supposed anti-Spartan party to defeat the supposed pro-Spartan party? In other words, what outlook among the Athenians made them respond to the dismissal of Cimon from Lacedaemon by changing their alliances?

Towards answering this question two things may be said. First, although the Athenians allied with Argos, they did not pursue hostilities with Sparta in any extreme fashion in the First Peloponnesian War. In the opening years of the war Athenian operations were directed more against Corinth and Aegina than against Sparta. The first direct confrontation between Athenian and Spartan forces occurred in 457 in the campaign of Tanagra, and that was not due to any Athenian attack on Lacedaemon. From 454 the Athenians abstained from hostilities in Greece and in 451 they made a truce for five years. In 447/6 the struggle was resumed and brought to a new pitch of intensity, but this was due to Spartan initiative.

A second point is suggested by an anecdote which Plutarch (*Cim.* 17.1–2) tells about Cimon's return from Lacedaemon. On his homeward journey he brought his army through the Corinthiad, and a certain Lachartus said that he was crossing the territory of Corinth without first consulting its citizens; as Lachartus remarked, after knocking on a stranger's door one does not go in until invited by the master. Cimon replied by calling to mind the way the Corinthians approached

Cleonae and Megara; they did not pause to knock but tore the doors down. The story may come from a contemporary source and may be substantially true. The complaint of Lachartus may suggest why some Peloponnesians and indeed some Spartans wanted Cimon dismissed from Lacedaemon; perhaps they feared that by his expedition the Athenians were gaining influence with the Peloponnese. If so, one may venture to speculate that this fear may have been well founded. In other words, the diplomatic realignment of 462–ca. 460 marks a change in the methods but continuity in the goals of Athenian policy: by allying with Argos, as previously by sending Cimon to help the Spartans, the Athenians sought to win influence in the Peloponnese.

NOTES

1. Thucydides sketched the history of the period 478–431 in a digression (1.89–118) which ancient scholars called the *Pentekontaetia*. This is the richest single source for the period, but it is a selective account and its indications of date are often imprecise. Most of the other sources are collected in G.F. Hill, *Sources for Greek History between the Persian and Peloponnesian Wars* (second edition, revised by R. Meiggs and A. Andrewes, Oxford 1951). Inscriptions, though often problematic, provide important information for this period; a useful selection is to be found in Meiggs/Lewis. An evaluatory discussion of the sources is given by Gomme, *Comm.* 1. 29–84.

2. The material of this section is drawn from Thuc. 1.89–93; Hdt. 9.114–121. M. Amit, *Athens and the Sea* = Collection Latomus, vol. 74 (Brussels 1965), collects plentiful information about Athenian maritime enterprise and includes a chapter on the Peiraeus.

3. Thucydides reports the naval operations of 478 at 1.94–95; he gives a digression on the later movements of Pausanias at 1.128–134. After the recall of Pausanias Diodorus (11.50) reports Spartan deliberations in the gerousia and the assembly, deliberations leading to a decision not to contest leadership of naval operations with the Athenians; the constitutional procedure implied by Diodorus is difficult to follow, and this may well indicate that his account rests ultimately on genuine material. Plutarch (*Cim.* 6) has still more lurid details of Pausanias's behavior at Byzantium. The chronology of Pausanias's subsequent fortunes is difficult to reconstruct; Justin (9.1.3) says that his second stay at Byzantium lasted seven years; this has been defended by M.E. White, "Some Agiad Dates: Pausanias and his Sons," *JHS* 84 (1964), 140–152, and Meiggs, *AE* 71–73, 465–468. For a conjecture about what was at stake in the dispute at Byzantium see Sealey, "The Origins of the Delian League," *Ehrenberg Studies* 233–255 (criticized by Meiggs, *AE* 462–464).

4. For speculations on the origin of the hellenotamiae see A.G. Woodhead, "The Institution of the Hellenotamiae," *JHS* 79 (1959) 149–152. Attempts to calculate the assessment of 454 were made by Gomme, *Comm.* 1.274–275 and *ATL* 3.19–28. For discussion of the first assessment of the Delian League see M. Chambers, "Four Hundred Sixty Talents," *CP* 53 (1958) 26–32; Meiggs, *AE* 58–65. H.T. Wade-Gery reported his discovery about the appendix to the first tribute quota list in *ABSA* 33 (1932–33: published in 1935) 104–106 and 112. In *ATL* 3.6 he and his colleagues were more confident about the content of the appendix. W.K. Pritchett published the results of his reexamination of the appendix in *GRBS* 7 (1966) 127–129. Hammond, *Studies* 311–345 = "The Origins and the Nature of the Athenian Alliance of 478/7 B.C.," *JHS* 87 (1967) 41–61, offers a

somewhat different reconstruction. Besides insisting on a distinction between "Leagues" and "Alliances," which is difficult to substantiate, he argues two main theses: (1) That the cities of mainland Ionia rebelled against the Persians in the winter of 479/8 and reconstituted the old Ionian League, with which Athens subsequently allied; he interprets thus Aristotle's statement (*AP* 23.5) that the Athenians exchanged oaths with "the Ionians" in 478/7. But Aristotle's phrase does not compel this interpretation. (2) That the Alliance as eventually established was bicameral, one chamber being the Congress of the Allies, where Athens did not have a vote, and the other being the Athenian assembly; he claims that the word *isopsephos*, used of the Alliance at Thuc. 3.11.4, requires this interpretation. Other scholars have supposed that Athens was a member of the allied congress and they have taken *isopsephos* to imply that Athens, like each other member, had only one vote in the Congress; for this sense of the word see Aeschin. 2.116. That the original membership of the Delian League was relatively small is argued by L.E. Highby, "The Erythrae Decree," *Klio* Beiheft 36 (1936) 39–57, and Sealey, supra n. 3, 242–248; the opposite view is defended by Gomme, *Comm.* 1.289–295 and *ATL* 3.194–224. Meiggs, *AE* 56–58, urges that the Greek cities of Cyprus were among the original members of the League; but their omission from the assessment of 425 tells against this view, and the positive arguments for it are indirect. The capture of Eion is given by Thuc. 1.98.1. The revolt of Poteidaea is given by Hdt. 8.126–129. The attempts of Themistocles and the Hellenic fleet to exact money from Aegean islands after the battle of Salamis are given by Hdt. 8.108–112 and 121; at 8.123 he gives the meeting at the Isthmus with the judgement of the commanders. The fragment of Timocreon is preserved by Plut. *Them.* 21.4; its connection with the events of fall 480 was recognized by *ATL* 3.185 with note 10 and 191 note 26; Meiggs, *AE* 414–415, puts Themistocles's visit to Rhodes in 478, arguing that a Greek fleet would not venture so far afield straight after Salamis, when the distribution of Persian naval resources was unknown; but the movements of Themistocles were and are unpredictable.

5. On the chronology of the *Pentekontaetia* the discussion by Gomme, Comm. 1.389–413 is still of basic value. J.D. Smart, "Kimon's Capture of Eion," *JHS* 87, (1967) 136–138, offers a different chronology for the early operations of the Delian League on the basis of the following argument. The archon of 476/5 was Phaedon, and several sources give the name of the archon of 469/8 as Apsephion; but Diodorus (11.63.1) gives the archon of 469/8 as Phaedon or Phaeon (the manuscripts diverge on the spelling). Apparently two archon lists were current in antiquity, one giving Apsephion and the other Phaedon as the archon of 469/8. So Smart suggests that some events, commonly assigned to 476/5, belong to 469/8. Hence he puts Cimon's capture of Eion in 470/69 but the ensuing disaster at Nine Ways (schol. Aeschin. 2.31) in 469/8; the latter would also be the date of Cimon's capture of Scyros (Plut. *Thes.* 36.1), and the operations at Carystus, Naxos and the Eurymedon would be later. Against Smart's hypothesis it can be objected that he must assume that Plutarch moved from one archon list to another without noticing the divergence; in the *Life of Theseus* he assigned the oracle about Scyros to the archonship of Phaedon, but in the *Life of Cimon* (8.8) he recognized an archonship of Apsephion. The suggestion that the Delian League was organized in time to operate at the beginning of the season 477 was made in *ATL* 3.192–193. The argument for 469 as the date of the Eurymedon campaign was developed by F. Jacoby, "Some Remarks on Ion of Chios," *CQ* 41 (1947) 1–17 especially 3 note 1. For the casualty list giving losses at Thasos and Sigeum see Hill B9; D.W. Bradeen, "The Athenian Casualty List of 464 B.C.," Hesperia 36 (1967) 321–328; Meiggs, *AE* 416. Thucydides gives the extent of Athenian alliances in 431 at 2.9.4; he gives the Athenian attack of 416 on Melos at 5.84–116 and indicates Melian reliance on Spartan help at 5.104. The purpose of the Persian preparations frustrated at the Eurymedon river is argued by R. Meiggs, *AE* 77–79. The gift of Magnesia to a Greek fugitive is known from Thuc.

1.138.5; cf. Hill C10 (a). On the transfer of the federal treasury to Athens see W.K. Pritchett, "The Transfer of the Delian Treasury," *Historia* 18 (1969) 17–21 (criticized by Meiggs, *AE* 420–421).

6. A. Andrewes, "Sparta and Arcadia in the Early Fifth Century," *Phoenix* 6 (1952) 1–5, and W.G. Forrest, "Themistokles and Argos," *CQ*, N.S. 10, (1960) 221–241, offer ingenious studies of the anti-Spartan movement but go somewhat beyond the evidence. On the Arcadian federal coinage see W.P. Wallace, "Kleomenes, Marathon, the Helots, and Arkadia," *JHS* 74, (1954) 32–35. The contingents from Mycenae and Tiryns at the battle of Plataea are known from Hdt. 9.28.4. Thucydides (1.102.4) refers to Argos and Sparta as at war by 460; he mentions their peace treaty of 451 at 5.14.4 and 5.28.2. Synoecism at Elis and Mantinea is mentioned also by Strabo 8.3.2.336–337. The Mantinean who reorganized Cyrene in the sixth century is recorded by Hdt. 4.161. Plutarch (*Them.* 20) gives two stories of alleged actions of Themistocles against Sparta after Xerxes left Greece; but they are anecdotal and contribute to the stock pictures of Themistocles and Cimon; they may be inventions or distortions such as grew around the legend of Themistocles. His service as *choregos* is known from Plut. *Them.* 5.5 On the chronology of his later movements see Gomme, *Comm.* 1.397–401; F.J. Frost, "Thucydides I,137,2," *CR* N.S. 12 (1962) 15–16; White art. cit. (supra note 3); P.J. Rhodes, "Thucydides on Pausanias and Themistocles," *Historia* 19, (1970) 387–400. The earthquake at Sparta and the Messenian Revolt are known primarily from Thuc. 1.101–103. On the chronology see Gomme, *Comm.* 1.401–408; D.M. Lewis, "Ithome Again," *Historia* 2 (1953–54) 412–418; N.G.L. Hammond, "Studies in Greek Chronology of the Sixth and Fifth Centuries B.C.: I The Third Messenian War," *Historia* 4, (1955) 371–381; D.W. Reece, "The Date of the Fall of Ithome," *JHS* 82 (1962) 111–120. Plutarch (Cimon 16.8–17.3) says that the Spartans appealed twice to the Athenians for help against the Messenian Revolt and the Athenians sent two successive expeditions under Cimon. This view has been revived by G.A. Papantoniou, "Once or Twice?," *AJP* 72 (1951) 176–181; the case is good, though not conclusive. Thucydides remarks on Spartan anxiety about the helots at 4.80; cf. 5.23.3. Help received by the Spartans from their allies against the Messenians is attested by Thuc. 2.27.2 (Aegina); 3.54.5 (Plataea); Xen. *Hell.* 5.2.3 (Mantinea).

7. For the marriages of Elpinice and Cimon see Plut. *Cim.* 4.8 and 10. On the bones of Theseus see Plut. *Thes.* 36.1–4; *Cim.* 8.3–7. On Cimon's largesse see Theopompus, *F.Gr.Hist.* IIB 115F89; Ar. *AP*27.3; Plut. *Cim* 10.1–7. For the service of Aristeides at Plataea see Hdt. 9.28.6 and Plut. *Arist.* 20.1; for his relationship to Callias see Plut. *Arist.* 25.4–8; for Callias's family see above Table C, p. 168. For the marriage of Xanthippus see Hdt. 6.131.2 and Plut. *Per.* 3.2. An attempt to explain the fortunes of Themistocles by a distinctive policy is made by G.L. Cawkwell, "The Fall of Themistocles," in B.F. Harris (ed.) *Auckland Classical Essays presented to E.M. Blaiklock*, 39–58. For the prosecutor of Themistocles see Craterus, *F.Gr.Hist.* IIIB 342F11 and Plut. *Them.* 23.1; cf. Plut. *Mor.* 605e. For the trial of Cimon see Ar. *AP*27.1; Plut. *Cim.* 14.3–5; *Per.* 10.6. For the opposition of Ephialtes to Cimon's expedition to Lacedaemon see Plut. *Cim.* 16.9; for his father's name see Ar. *AP*25.1; for his expedition beyond the Chelidonian islands see Plut. *Cim.* 13.4. Plutarch (*Cim.* 15.2) says that Cimon was away on a naval expedition when Ephialtes carried his reforms; (Plutarch's accuracy is doubted by R. Meiggs, *AE* 89 note 3); that it was an expedition to Cyprus was suggested by J. Barns, "Cimon and the First Athenian Expedition to Cyprus," *Historia* 2 (1953–54) 163–176. For Cimon's attempt to repeal the reforms see Plut. *Cim.* 15.3; for his ostracism see Plut. *Cim.* 17.3; *Per.* 9.5. For the murder of Ephialtes see Ar. *AP* 25.4; Plut. *Per.* 10. 7–8. The hypotheses on the reforms of Ephialtes are offered by H.T. Wade-Gery, "The Judicial Treaty with Phaselis and the History of the Athenian Courts," Essays 180–200, and Sealey, "Ephialtes," *Essays* 42–58 (= *CP* 59 [1964], 11–22). On the procedure of *eisangelia* see J. Lipsius, "Das attische Recht und Rechstverfahren" (Leipzig, 1905–1915) 176–211. P.J. Rhodes, *The Athenian Boule* (Oxford 1972) 144–207,

accepts the hypothesis that Ephialtes transferred the hearing of *euthynai* from the Areopagus to the popular court. As he observes, in the developed constitution the Council of Five Hundred heard cases of several kinds and could inflict a fine not exceeding 500 drachmas; if a greater penalty was desired, the case was referred to a popular court. Rhodes suggests that the reforms of Ephialtes assigned jurisdiction in these cases to the Council of Five Hundred. But it is perhaps more likely that the judicial functions of the Council of Five Hundred developed form custom than from specific enactment; since the Council dealt with all spheres of public business, it was bound to receive information on alleged offenses of miscellaneous kinds.

8. The change in Athenian alliances is given by Thuc. 1.102.4; 1.103.4. For Callias as *proxenos* of Sparta see Xen. *Hell.* 6.3.4. For Alcibiades see Thuc. 5.43.2; E. Vanderpool, "The Ostracism of the Elder Alcibiades," *Hesperia* 21 (1952) 1–8. For Pericles's friendship with Archidamus see Thuc. 2.13.1. For Pericleidas and his son see Aristoph. *Lys.* 1137–1144; Plut. *Cim.* 16.8; Thuc. 4.119.2. Aristotle associates Pericles with the reforms of Ephialtes in a brief, casual and tendentious passage (*AP* 27.1) but fails to mention him in a more precise and circumstantial account of the reforms (*AP* 25.1–2); cf. Hignett, *HAC* 197. On the importance of *philoi* to a rising politician see W. R. Connor, *The New Politicians of Fifth-Century Athens* (Princeton 1971) 3–84.

10

The First Peloponnesian War

The alliances with Argos, Thessaly and Megara, secured by the Athenians after Cimon's dismissal from Lacedaemon, put them in a strong position for opposing the Peloponnesian League. The Megarian alliance was especially valuable. Megara in the fifth century was a small state poised between the two strong powers of Athens and Corinth; besides controlling a stretch of the land-route between Central Greece and the Peloponnese, Megara had harbors at Pegae on the Gulf of Corinth and at Nisaea on the eastern or Saronic Gulf. Late in the 460s a dispute about borders arose between Megara and Corinth, and this enabled the Athenians to win the alliance of Megara. The Athenians followed this up by building fortifications of the type appropriately called "long walls" to connect the city of Megara to Nisaea. These fortifications consisted of two walls running from the city to the harbor and making them into a joint fortress; the Athenians installed a garrison of their own men. Control of Pegae gave them easy access to the Corinthian Gulf. Further west at the entrance to the Gulf on its northern shore the Athenians captured the town of Naupactus from West Locris. When the Messenians at Ithome surrendered to the Spartans (probably in 460), they gained terms allowing them to leave the Peloponnese in safety; the Athenians settled the refugees at Naupactus.

Corinth could well be alarmed at an extension of Athenian influence into the western Gulf; she kept up ties with her colonies in the northwest at such places as

Leucas, Ambracia and Anactorium, and they were apparently crucial to her commercial interests. The Corinthians were even more alarmed by Athenian control of the Megarid, since this threatened their security at home. A generation earlier Corinth had behaved as a useful friend to the Athenians. When Cleomenes led a Peloponnesian army into Attica in the hope of overthrowing Cleisthenes, it was the Corinthians who frustrated the expedition by mutinying at Eleusis (see chapter 6, pp. 147–148). Somewhat later the Corinthians lent the Athenians twenty ships for the Aeginetan War at a merely nominal charge (see chapter 7, p. 183). But Corinthian policy changed when the Athenians allied with Megara and built the "long walls" there; Thucydides comments (1.103.4), "not least on this account the Corinthians first began to conceive bitter hatred for the Athenians." In the opening operations of the First Peloponnesian War the most vigorous resistance to the Athenians came from Corinth.

The Athenians had resources to spare for warfare against the Persian Empire. They sent a force of 200 ships, drawn from themselves and their allies, to Cyprus; then they received an appeal from Egypt. The satrapy of Egypt was the least secure in the Persian Empire. Its inhabitants inherited a culture more than 2,000 years old and had a strong sense of national distinctness; the deserts on each side made the territory difficult to conquer. Now the rebel leader, Inaros, overturned Persian authority in most of Egypt and in 460 or 459 he sent an appeal to Athens for help. The Athenians responded by ordering the 200 ships to proceed from Cyprus to Egypt. The ensuing operations went at first in favor of the Greeks and the insurgents; they gained control of virtually the whole country including the greater part of the city of Memphis, which stood near the head of the Delta and was therefore the critical position for controlling Egypt; but within Memphis Persian troops together with Egyptian loyalists held out in the fortifications called the White Fortress.

Meanwhile the Athenians acquitted themselves creditably in engagements near the northeastern coasts of the Peloponnese. Following up their Argive alliance, they sailed to Halieis, the town which had the best harbor between Athens and Argos, but when they landed there, they were defeated by a combined force of Corinthians and Epidaurians. A little later an Athenian fleet engaged and defeated a Peloponnesian fleet off Cecryphaleia, a small island between Aegina and the Peloponnesian shore; this was primarily a defeat for Corinth and Aegina, the cities furnishing the largest naval contingents in the Peloponnesian League. Then the Athenians with allies defeated the Aeginetans with their allies off Aegina, capturing seventy of their ships; they landed on the island and began besieging the city. Thus the Athenians resumed that hostility towards Aegina which had issued in warfare in the first two decades of the century. The Peloponnesians sought ways to make the Athenians raise the siege of Aegina; to this end the Corinthians with others invaded the Megarid. But the Athenian reserves under Myronides advanced to Megara and engaged the enemy in two battles; the first was indecisive, but in the second the Corinthians were defeated. The siege of Aegina continued without interruption.

In 457 the conflict took on a new aspect. Sparta sent a force northwards by sea across the Corinthian Gulf into Central Greece; it was composed of 1,500 Lacedaemonian hoplites and 10,000 from their allies. The professed occasion concerned the small state of Doris in the upper valley of the Cephisus river. It consisted of three or four villages and would have been insignificant, but that other Dorians, including the Lacedaemonians, regarded it as their mother city. Recently the Phocians had attacked Doris and captured one of the villages, but the Lacedaemonians compelled them to withdraw and to make an agreement. The size of their expedition to Central Greece suggests that they had a less sentimental purpose and it may perhaps be conjectured. In the later part of the sixth century the Thebans built up a federation in Boeotia, but it was disbanded in 479, when Pausanias marched on Thebes after the battle of Plataea and compelled it to surrender its leaders (see chapter 8, p. 225). In 457 the Spartans may have hoped to restore Theban authority in Boeotia; a strong power on the northern border of Attica would be a check to the Athenians.

While the Spartans were operating in Central Greece, the Athenians sent a naval squadron into the Corinthian Gulf; consequently the Spartans saw that they could not bring their force back to the Peloponnese by sea. They also hesitated to advance through the mountain range of Geraneia into the Megarid, since possession of Megara and Pegae had enabled the Athenians to station garrisons there. So they stayed in southern Boeotia and awaited developments. The Athenians called out their whole available force and gained contingents from their allies, including 1,000 men from Argos; the army they brought to Boeotia numbered 14,000 and it was joined by some Thessalian cavalry. The two armies met at Tanagra; in the battle both sides lost heavily and the Thessalians deserted the Athenian cause. The Peloponnesians won the battle and so they were able to retire through the Megarid to their homes. The campaign of Tanagra showed that Athenian control of Megara was a serious but not an insuperable obstacle to Peloponnesian operations north of the Isthmus. So it is not surprising that the Athenians built additional fortifications of the type called "long walls" to protect their own city. They built two such walls, beginning them before the campaign of Tanagra and completing them shortly after it; one ran from the city of Athens to the Peiraeus and the other ran from the city to Phalerum. Thus Athens and its harbors were envisaged as a large defensible area.

The battle of Tanagra confirmed the general Greek belief in the superiority of the Lacedaemonian hoplite, but it was not decisive for central Greece. Sixty-two days later the Athenians under Myronides invaded Boeotia and defeated the Boeotians at Oenophyta. Hence they gained control over Boeotia and Phocis; they destroyed the fortifications of Tanagra and they exacted 100 hostages from East Locris. A fragmentary inscription from Athens refers to dealings with the Amphictyonic League, which managed the affairs of the Delphic sanctuary; it may indicate that the Athenians made an alliance with the Amphictyony about this time. For the next ten years Athenian influence was paramount in central Greece; its states did not become members of the Delian League and their precise relationship to Athens is not clear, but they were somehow subject to Athenian hegemony; the Athenians made alliances with the Boeotians and the Phocians, so that they could require contingents from them for land campaigns. Any plans the Spartans may have entertained for building up a counterpoise to the Athenians in Boeotia were checked and reversed.

Athenian successes went further. The Aeginetans after a protracted siege surrendered and made terms; they dismantled their walls, handed over their ships and were assessed to pay tribute. In 456/5 an Athenian fleet under Tolmides sailed round the Peloponnese, burning the Lacedaemonian naval station at Gytheum and making raids at Sicyon and elsewhere. By 455 the Athenians were at the height of their achievements.

EGYPT, PEACE AND DISAFFECTION, 454–451[2]

The Athenian expedition to Egypt was at first so successful that king Artaxerxes tried to encourage the Greek enemies of Athens. He sent an envoy, Megabazus, to Lacedaemon to urge the Peloponnesians to invade Attica, but Megabazus could not persuade them. The Spartans may have been deterred by the difficulty of the enterprise, as the Athenians held Megara; but in 457 they sent an expedition to Central Greece by sea and brought it back by land. More probably the Spartans refused to invade Attica because they were not yet willing to push the war to such an extreme. At any rate, when diplomacy failed Artaxerxes assembled a large army and sent it under a commander called Megabyzus to Egypt. Megabyzus defeated the Egyptians and their allies in battle; then he drove the Greeks from Memphis, confined them to the island of Prosopitis between two mouths of the Nile and besieged them there. After a siege of a year and six months he took the position by assault; most of the Greek force perished but the survivors escaped to Cyrene. Inaros, the instigator of the revolt, was betrayed to the Persians and crucified; Amyrtaeus, another leader of the insurgents, held out in a marshy district, but most of Egypt came under Persian rule again. Meanwhile, the

Athenians and their allies sent fifty ships as reinforcements to Egypt. This new force did not learn of the disaster until it landed and was overcome; most of the fifty ships were destroyed.

The Athenians and their allies had operated in Egypt for six years (ca. 460–454). Thucydides gives the impression that both the original force of 200 ships and the reinforcements of 50 ships were for the most part lost; this has sometimes been doubted but for inadequate reasons. This was the greatest single disaster the Delian League experienced in the whole of its existence. At about the same time as the final news came from Egypt another Athenian enterprise ended in failure. Thessaly had allied with the Athenians shortly before the outbreak of the First Peloponnesian War, but at the battle of Tanagra the Thessalian cavalry deserted to the Spartans. Evidently there were divisions within Thessaly. Normally the chief rivals for control of Thessaly were the Aleuadae, who were the ruling family of Larisa, and the Echecratidae, whose seat was Pharsalus. An Echecratid pretender, Orestes, appeared in Athens and the Athenians resolved to restore him. They sent a force drawn from themselves and their allies in Boeotia and Phocis to Pharsalus; it made a landing but could not capture the city, and it had to withdraw, bringing Orestes back with it. A little later an Athenian force of 1,000, commanded by Pericles, sailed from Pegae to Sicyon, where they landed and defeated the Sicyonians. Then they took a force from Achaea, which Athens had brought into subordinate alliance, and sailed to Oeniadae in Acarnania at the northwestern approach to the Corinthian Gulf; but although they besieged Oeniadae, they could not capture it.

After the disaster in Egypt and the failures at Pharsalus and Oeniadae, it is not surprising that the Athenians changed their policy. The next sentence in Thucydides's brief account says (1.112.1): "Later after an interval of three years a treaty for five years was made between the Peloponnesians and the Athenians." The Five Years' Treaty was probably made early in 451; it appears that in the previous three years Thucydides found no enterprise worthy of record. This implies that from 454 the Athenians did not launch any operation on any considerable scale against their enemies. Thus in 454 they abandoned the forward policy which they had pursued since ca. 460. This is the place to consider whether Cimon was recalled from ostracism. He had been ostracized in 462/1 and the standard term for ostracism was ten years. A fragment of the fourth-century historian Theopompus (*F.Gr.Hist.* IIB 115F88) says: "When less than five years had passed, warfare came about against the Lacedaemonians and the assembly recalled Cimon; it thought that because of his *proxenia* he would most quickly make peace. He returned to the city and brought the war to an end." The fragment is preserved as a quotation by a scholiast to Aristeides, the orator of the second century A.D. The scholiast may have compressed the report. It comes ultimately from the tenth book of Theopompus's *Philippica*, where he gave a résumé of Athenian history in the form of a survey of the chief Athenian politicians. The fragment alludes to the campaign of Tanagra as "warfare against the Lacedaemonians" and indicates that that campaign was fought in 457 (cf. below, p. 294, *n.* 1). Plutarch (*Cim.* 17.4–8) has a more dramatic account of Cimon's behavior in relation to the battle of Tanagra. He says that Cimon came to the battle line and asked permission to take his place, but the Council of Five Hundred told the generals not to admit him. So Cimon, hoping to dispel the allegation of friendship with Sparta, exhorted his personal friends to fight vigorously; they set up his armor at his place and fought so vigorously that 100 of them were killed. After the defeat the Athenians recalled Cimon, the decree being proposed by Pericles. Plutarch may draw on a fuller text of Theopompus than the scholiast to Aristeides, or he may use some other source. The detail that the decree of recall was proposed by Pericles may be correct, but Plutarch's account has incredible features; the Council of Five Hundred could not meet on the battlefield to give instructions to the generals.

From the surviving fragments it is difficult to judge the worth of Theopompus's history. At least he was a learned man, and therefore it is reasonable to follow his belief that Cimon was recalled early from ostracism. The difficulty is that the fragment as quoted by the scholiast appears to associate the battle of Tanagra, the recall of Cimon and the conclusion of peace with Sparta in close chronological succession, but peace was not made with Sparta until the Five Years' Treaty of 451. Moreover, after the battle of Tanagra no further activity of Cimon is attested until he led a naval expedition to Cyprus in 451 or 450. One solution (offered by R. Meiggs) consists in supposing that Cimon was recalled only a few months before his ostracism was due to expire; thereupon he negotiated the Five Years' Peace. But this dissociates the recall from the defeat at Tanagra. Another solution would say that Cimon was recalled within a few months of the battle of Tanagra and his influence, together with that of those promoting his recall, is apparent in the change which Athenian policy underwent in 454; henceforth the Athenians abstained from launching enterprises on any considerable scale against the Peloponnesians. The Five Years' Treaty merely confirmed a policy which the Athenians had adopted three years before.

In the period 454–450 the Athenians had to deal with disaffection in the Delian League. Much of the evidence on this is derived from the tribute quota lists, mentioned above (chapter 9, p. 244); their nature must be considered more fully now. In 454 the Athenians decided that henceforth the goddess Athena should receive first fruits from the tribute in the form of one-sixtieth of each payment from each tributary state. Furthermore, they henceforth inscribed these sixtieths or quotas on marble. Several questions arise and have not been answered satisfactorily. One may ask why the Athenians assigned quotas to Athena from the tribute. Some historians have conjectured that quotas had been paid to Apollo while the federal treasury was kept at Delos; but there is no evidence for this and, when it is offered to explain the payment of quotas to Athena, the explanation rests on the unnecessary assumption that the practice of making payments to Athena indicates by a causal connection the date when the treasury was brought to Athens. Again, in Greek religious practice first fruits could be offered to a god in different ratios, and so one may ask why the ratio chosen for the first fruits to Athena was a sixtieth. Furthermore, one may ask why the Athenians decided to inscribe the tribute quotas on stone. This procedure involved some expense. It is not a satisfactory answer to say that by 454 the Athenians had developed the habit of inscribing financial records on stone; several series of such records were inscribed after 454, but the tribute quota lists are the earliest series known to have been inscribed on stone and they may have begun the habit. While precise answers to these questions are difficult to reach, it may at least be supposed that the commencement of the quota lists reflects a general reassessment of policy carried out by the Athenians in 454.

The lists of which fragments have been recovered are lists of quotas; it is not known whether lists of tribute, as distinct from lists of quotas, were inscribed. From 454 onwards reassessments were usually held every four years, that is, in years of the Greater Panathenaic festival. Accordingly, it is often convenient to divide the lists into assessment periods. Certainly at a later stage and perhaps also as early as 454 the payments of tribute were due to reach Athens at the spring festival of the Dionysia. The quota lists for the first fifteen years (454/3-440/39 inclusively) were inscribed annually on a single large stele. More than 180 fragments of this stele have been found. Through the patient labors of several scholars, beginning in the nineteenth century, the fragments have been arranged in plaster to provide a reconstruction of the original monument; it stands in the Epigraphic Museum in Athens. As reconstructed, the stele is at least 3.663 m. high, 1.109 m. wide and 0.385 m. thick. It was inscribed on all four of its vertical faces and in the current reconstruction the inscribed surfaces preserved on the fragments amount to about half of the surface originally inscribed.

For the following reason caution must be observed in drawing historical inferences from the stele. In some cases two preserved fragments are contiguous, making a perfect join, but often this is not so. Clearly the relative positions assigned to the fragments in the plaster reconstruction of the stele may have a bearing on historical conclusions drawn from them. In some cases the epigraphers reconstructing the stele published their reasons for assigning the fragments to their present positions in the plaster, but in many cases this was not done. Moreover, new geological techniques have been developed since World

War II, and if these were applied to the fragments, they might provide new information about the relative positions of the fragments. Meanwhile, calculations depending on the physical length of a list in the current reconstruction must be treated with caution. For the most part historical conclusions must depend on the entries actually preserved on the fragments.

The lists of the first assessment period (454/3–451/0 inclusively) provide indications of disaffection in Miletus and Erythrae. List 1 (454/3) has near the end payments by "Milesians from Leros" (a quota of 300 drachmas, implying a tribute of 3 talents) and by "Milesians from Teichioussa" (the figure is not preserved). No Milesian entries appear in the extant fragments of List 2, but there is an entry (of unknown amount) for "Milesians" without qualification in List 3 (452/1). In 450/49 Miletus paid a tribute of 10 talents. In addition fragments have been found of an Athenian decree embodying regulations for Miletus; although the text is very fragmentary, it mentions a board of five Athenians, who are to be elected and sent to Miletus; it alludes to a garrison; and it has extensive provisions about lawsuits. The regulations mention the Athenian archon Euthynus, whose year was 450/49. Many scholars have accordingly supposed that the decree was passed in that year, but it is perhaps more likely that it was passed a few years later, when there was more trouble with Miletus (see chapter 11, p. 309), and referred to the year 450/49 as somehow epochal in Athenian relations with that city.

From these data it can be inferred that Miletus was in revolt by 454/3; Milesians loyal to Athens had been expelled from the city, but they held out in the neighboring island of Leros and in Teichioussa, an unknown place presumably somewhere in the territory of Miletus. The loyalists paid tribute or perhaps they were allowed the privilege of paying quota only. But the Athenians recovered Miletus in 453 or 452, so that the Milesians are recorded in List 3. Adjustments to the consequent settlement continued to be made in the next few years but were completed in 450/49, so that later the condition of that year could be regarded as standard. These inferences seemed secure until 1971. Then a new fragment of List 1 was found and it includes a reference to Miletus or Milesians. Consequently the condition of Miletus in 454/3 is puzzling. Possibly the reference in the new fragment does not indicate a payment by the city of Miletus but one made by a community which had been founded from Miletus. At least the entries for "Milesians from Leros" and "Milesians from Teichioussa" show that there was some irregularity, and the decree naming the year 450/49 suggests that Athens interfered in Milesian affairs by that date. Thus in spite of the new fragment of List 1 it is likely that Miletus showed some recalcitrance towards the Athenians in 454/3.

The case of Erythrae is clearer. An inscription, copied by a traveler in the nineteenth century and lost since then, gave an Athenian decree imposing regulations on Erythrae. Although the inscription was evidently difficult to read when it was first copied, some of its provisions can be recovered. It mentioned some Athenian officers and a garrison commander, who had been sent to Erythrae. It provided for establishing in Erythrae an annual council of 120 men, chosen by lot. It gave the terms of the oath, whereby the councilors were to swear loyalty to the Athenians and their allies. This oath alluded to men who had recently ruled Erythrae as "tyrants" and as "exiles fleeing to the Medes." Apparently Erythrae had seceded from the Delian League and, when Athens suppressed the revolt, its leaders fled to the Persians. The tribute quota lists may indicate the time of revolt in the first assessment period. Erythrae had five small dependent towns; in the third and fourth assessment periods (446/5–444/3 and 443/2–439/8) Erythrae and its dependencies made their payments separately, but in the second assessment period (450/49–447/6) Erythrae still paid for the whole group. There is no entry for Erythrae itself preserved from the first assessment period, but one of the dependencies, Boutheia, is recorded in List 1 (454/3); the figure is not extant. In List 2 (453/2) Boutheia appears again and its quota is 300 drachmas. In the fourth assessment period, when the dependencies pay separately, the quota for Boutheia is only 16⅔ drachmas. So it is likely that Erythrae was in revolt in 454/3 and 453/2; Erythraeans loyal to Athens held out in Boutheia, and the revolt was suppressed soon afterwards, perhaps at the same time as the trouble in Miletus. This is a possible context for the Athenian decree about Erythrae, but it must be admitted that the decree cannot be dated on internal grounds; the thesis can be defended that the decree marks the suppression of an earlier revolt. In any case the indications in the quota lists imply that Erythrae was recalcitrant in 454/3 and 453/2.

If the chances of preservation have allowed evidence of disaffection in Miletus and Erythrae in the first assessment period to survive, it is proper to guess that disaffection was more widespread then. The mainland coast of Asia Minor was a sensitive area in the Delian League; its cities were subject to the temptations of medism. Entries for some of its major cities, Phocaea, Teos, Myous and Cyme, do not occur in the preserved parts of the first two quota lists; their absence may be due to the fragmentary state of the lists or to disaffection.

A more complex question concerns some of the island cities in the first assessment period. Inferences about these have sometimes been made but depend in part on the lengths of the reconstructed lists. The first list, as presently reconstructed, has room for ca. 140 entries. The second list (453/2) has room for ca. 162 entries, but it opens with 17 entries in the neighborhood of Caria which only appear rarely in the quota lists; the inference has been properly drawn that an

Athenian squadron operated in the Carian district in 453 and compelled these places to pay. Thus List 2, as reconstructed, has room for ca. 145 regular entries. List 3 has room for ca. 145 entries, and List 4 (451/0) has room for ca. 157. But List 4 ends with 12 entries for small places in the Carian neighborhood which only appear rarely in the lists; probably another Athenian squadron was operating there in 450. Thus List 4 has room for ca. 145 regular entries. Accordingly the reconstructed lists of the first assessment period have room for ca. 140 to ca. 145 regular entries each. Towards discovering how many states were assessed to pay at the assessment of 454 historians have made two assumptions. One is that a city which paid once in an assessment period was assessed in the assessment list which opened that period; the other is that a city which paid regularly in three or four of the first six assessment periods (454/3–431/0) was assessed to pay in the other two or three periods. The consequent calculations yield the result that the number of cities included in the assessment of 454 was much higher than ca. 145; one would expect a figure of at least ca. 170. But it is more important to weigh the absentees than to count them. They include several important cities among the Aegean islands. In Euboea Chalcis, Eretria, Histiaea and Styra are absent from the extant parts of the first four quota lists, as are Cythnos, Siphnos, Tenos, Paros and Naxos. Again Ceos, Seriphos and Andros are absent from the extant parts of the first three quota lists but are recorded in List 4 (451/0).

This argument about island cities depends in part on the reconstruction of the stele from the fragments, and from the information hitherto published it is impossible to say how reliable that reconstruction is. Conceivably a new examination of the fragments might show that the first four lists were somewhat longer than previously supposed. But the fact remains that several island states are absent from the fragments of the first three or four lists. This may be due to imperfect preservation of the lists, or it may reflect disaffection. A further consideration, concerning cleruchies, supports the second explanation.

On overcoming a city which had seceded from the Delian League the Athenians often confiscated part of its territory and founded a cleruchy, or settlement of Athenian citizens, there. Plutarch (*Per.* 11.5) gives a list of cleruchies founded near the middle of the fifth century; the list includes a party of 500 cleruchs sent to Naxos and a party of 250 sent to Andros. Diodorus (11.88.3) and Pausanias (1.27.5) say that Tolmides led parties of cleruchs to Euboea and Naxos. A date for these foundations may be inferred from the tribute records of Andros and of Carystus in Euboea, for when land was confiscated to found a cleruchy, the tribute required from the state was usually decreased accordingly. Andros paid a tribute of 12 talents in 451/0 but 6 talents in 450/49 and thereafter; Carystus paid 7½ talents in 451/0 but 5 talents in 450/49 and thereafter. Thus it is likely that the cleruchies were sent to Andros, Naxos and Euboea in 450. The tribute record of the other cities affected by the cleruchies does not conflict with this conclusion, although it is not preserved well enough to support it.

To sum up this discussion of disaffection. In the period 454–450 recalcitrance can be traced in parts of the Delian League, notably on the coast of Asia Minor and in the islands. Disaffection may sometimes have gone no further than a refusal to pay tribute, but in some cases it took the more extreme form of open secession from the League. Since the tribute quota lists, which provide much of the evidence, begin in 454/3, it is difficult to say whether this wave of disaffection started then or somewhat earlier. In 454 the disaster in Egypt and the failures at Pharsalus and Oeniadae doubtless shook Athenian prestige and hence encouraged disaffection. In concrete terms the Egyptian disaster may have caused some people in the islands to expect a Persian fleet to appear once more in the Aegean. But in cities like Miletus and Erythrae on the mainland of Asia Minor the disaffection apparent towards the middle of the century may well have begun before 454. Such places could be reached by Persian land forces from the satrapies of Sardis and Dascylium. They were constantly exposed, according to their point of view, to the threat of Persian interference or to the temptation to seek Persian protection against Athenian interference.

CYPRUS AND PERSIA[3]

In 451 or 450 Cimon led a fleet of 200 ships, drawn from the Athenians and their allies, to Cyprus. Sixty of the ships were dispatched to Egypt to help Amyrtaeus, while the rest besieged the town of Citium. Cimon died during the siege and the fleet ran short of supplies, so it withdrew from Citium. But near Cypriote Salamis it confronted a force of Phoenicians, Cypriotes and Cilicians and defeated them in a combined battle on land and sea. Then the fleet sailed home, as did the squadron of sixty ships which had been sent to Egypt.

After this expedition there were no further hostilities on any large scale between the Delian League and the Persian Empire. Many modern historians believe that the Athenians concluded a treaty of peace with Persia shortly after the expedition, and this has been named "the peace of Callias" after its supposed negotiator. It should be observed that the mere cessation of major hostilities does not itself indicate that a treaty was made. Both sides had more important things to do than fight one another. The Athenians had to deal with disaffection among their allies and the question of their relations with the Peloponnesians had not been finally settled by the Five Years' Peace; besides, the expedition led by Cimon to Cyprus had brought them hard fighting and little gain. To the Persians such places as Babylon and Egypt mattered far more than western Asia Minor or the Aegean.

The positive evidence for a peace of Callias consists of statements made in the fourth century by Athenian orators and some historians. The earliest assertion that a peace was made occurs in a speech which Isocrates prepared for recitation at the Olympic festival of 380. He mentioned with disapproval the peace of 387/6, which the Spartans had brought through negotiations with Persia. He contrasted with it the glorious peace which, he said, the Athenians had achieved with Persia in the days when they were powerful; he alluded to some terms of the Athenian treaty, the most specific being that the king should not send warships west of Phaselis (speech 4. 117–120). In two later speeches (7.80 and 12.59, composed ca. 357 and in 342–339 respectively) Isocrates reiterated the provision about Phaselis and also said that the treaty forbade the Persians to bring land forces west of the Halys river.

It will be noted that Isocrates's first reference to the Athenian treaty occurs in the tendentious context of a contrast with the Spartan treaty of 387/6. Moreover, the language used by Lysias in a funeral speech composed ten years before 380 was a good deal different. Reviewing the achievements of the Athenians in the period when they controlled the sea, he said (2.56) that they displayed such power "that the great king no longer coveted the possessions of others but was willing to give of his own and feared for the rest." If Lysias had known that the Athenians made the Persian king disclaim his former ambitions, this was surely the place to say so.

Athenian orators speaking later than 380 said that a treaty was made but they diverged from Isocrates on its terms. Speaking in 343/2, Demosthenes said that Callias negotiated the treaty, and by its terms Persian land forces were not to come within one day's journey on horseback from the sea, nor were Persian warships to sail west of the Chelidonian islands or Cyaneae. Plutarch (*Cim.* 13.4) reports the opinion of the fourth-century historian Callisthenes. Plutarch himself says that in consequence of the battle of the Eurymedon river peace was made; by its terms the Persians agreed to stay at least a day's journey on horseback from the sea and not to send warships westwards beyond Cyaneae and the Chelidonian islands. Plutarch adds that Callisthenes denied that any treaty was made but said that the Persians observed its restrictions because of the fear which the defeat at the Eurymedon river caused them. Since Callisthenes denied the historicity of a treaty on the terms specified by Plutarch, it follows that an earlier writer than Callisthenes asserted that peace had been made on those terms; the earlier writer may be called Protocallisthenes. His version of the peace was followed by Demosthenes. The sea and land limits he mentioned can be located in part. The rocky Chelidonian islands lay almost due south of Phaselis and were about twenty-five nautical miles from that city; they were a notorious danger to shipping. It is not so easy to be sure what position Protocallisthenes meant by Cyaneae. This was the name of twelve islands at the mouth of the Bosporus. It was also the name of a small town in southern Asia Minor; this, the southern Cyaneae, was about twenty-five miles west of the Chelidonian islands and about four miles from the coast. It has yielded some inscriptions of Roman date, but there is no proof that it was inhabited in the fifth century. There is nothing to indicate what position or line on land could be described as a day's journey on horseback from the sea. Some modern historians have supposed that the position thus designated was Sardis. Herodotus (5.54.2), describing the royal road of the Persian Empire, says that Sardis was three days' journey on foot from Ephesus. At least any place a day's journey on horseback from the Aegean must have been well to the west of the Halys river.

Thus, although Protocallisthenes accepted the tradition of a peace of Callias, he gave land and sea limits further west than those named by Isocrates. For a time in the fourth century there was lively controversy about the peace of Callias; its authenticity was denied by Callisthenes, and Theopompus said that the current account of a treaty with Persia was wrong in important details. In view of the divergence on the limits it should be conjectured that, between 380 and the time when Protocallisthenes wrote, someone produced arguments showing that the limits named by Isocrates, Phaselis and the Halys river, were impossible.

After the controversy had died down writers active later in the fourth century were less careful in specifying limits. In a speech composed in 330 the Athenian orator Lycurgus (*Against Leocrates* 73) said that the treaty forbade the Persians to send warships beyond Cyaneae and Phaselis. If Ephorus's account may be reconstructed from Diodorus (12.4.5), he gave the same sea limits as Lycurgus and said that on land the Persian satraps were not to march within three days' journey of the sea. It is reasonable to equate the latter limit with Sardis in the light of Herodotus's report on the royal road; but to suppose that Protocallisthenes and Demosthenes had the same position in mind when they spoke of a day's journey on horseback is an unsupported guess.

Those modern historians who accept a peace of Callias as authentic often suppose that all the limits named by fourth-century authors were stated in the treaty, and that the different authors have made different selections from the list. They can then account satisfactorily for the places named as sea limits. Phaselis, it is suggested, was the limit for Persian warships keeping close to the southern shore of Asia Minor, and the Chelidonian islands were the limit for such ships if they kept well out to sea. Cyaneae, on this hypothesis, must be identified with the islands near the Bosporus and it was named in the treaty to prevent such Persian enterprises as the activities overcome by Cimon in the Chersonese ca. 465 (see chapter 9, p. 250). But the land limits are more embarrassing. Even if Sardis could be specified, not only as three days' journey from the Aegean on foot, but also as one day's journey from the sea on horseback, it is difficult to believe that the Persians undertook to send no land forces west of the Halys river. Some historians, accepting the peace, have supposed that Isocrates was simply mistaken in naming the Halys (thus R. Meiggs); but this supposition comes close to rejecting the earliest witness to the peace, the witness, that is, who has the best claim to reproduce a fifth-century tradition. Others (as A. Andrewes) have distinguished between the central army of the Persian Empire and the provincial troops controlled by the satraps; they have suggested that the Halys was the limit for the former and Sardis for the latter. But such hypotheses do not explain the chronological pattern of the limits as attested by the fourth-century authors. It is surely no accident that Isocrates, the earliest witness to the peace, named the most extreme limits, whereas his successors named places further west; this would not be the likely outcome, if a text of the treaty named all the places and the different authors selected at random from the list.

Apart from the divergences on the land and sea limits and the divergent views of Theopompus and Callisthenes, there is a further reason to doubt the authenticity of the peace of Callias. That reason is the silence of Thucydides; he fails to mention the peace. To estimate the significance of this silence one must first recognize the nature of his work. As he explained in his opening sentence, he set out to write the history of the war between the Athenians and the Peloponnesians. Later, in his account of events leading to the war, he included a digression (1.89–118) designed to explain the growth of Athenian power between 478 and the beginning of the war. Some readers have been surprised at his failure to mention some developments in the relations between Athens and Persia, and they have tried to explain these omissions by hypotheses about the stages of composition of his work. For example, he fails to mention a peace, now usually called the peace of Epilycus, which the Athenians probably concluded with Persia in 424/3; and he fails to mention at its chronological place a later Athenian alliance with a rebel satrap, Amorges. But to seek special explanations for these omissions is to mistake his purpose. He did not set out to write a general history of the Greeks and their neighbors; the peace of Epilycus was not an incident in the warfare between the Athenians and the Peloponnesians, and Thucydides (8.5.5; 8.19.2; 8.28; 8.54.3) gives sufficient exposition of Amorges's movements when they have a bearing on his account of that warfare.

Accordingly, Thucydides's silence about the peace of Callias must be viewed in relation to his purpose in writing. His digression (1.89–118) on the growth of Athenian power between the Persian and Peloponnesian Wars omits several events known to have occurred in the period. But the peace of Callias, if genuine, was by far the most important of these; moreover, for the following reason it was a significant stage in the growth of Athenian power. A treaty of peace sometimes has more effect on third parties than on the two powers whom it binds directly. As already observed, it is clear that major hostilities between the Delian League and the Persians ceased after Cimon's last expedition. But a possible treaty between Athens and Persia would be highly significant for a third party, namely the allies of Athens in the Delian League. The League had been founded to conduct warfare "against the barbarian;" Thucydides (1.96.1) says so explicitly. If the Athenians made peace with Persia, the question could arise whether the League should continue to exist; if the Athenians succeeded in keeping the League in existence even after they made peace with Persia, this was a decisive step, perhaps the most decisive single step, in the growth of their power. Accordingly, the failure of Thucydides to mention the peace of Callias is a good reason for doubting whether any such peace was made.

THE SUPPOSED CRISIS OF 450–449[4]

Some historians, accepting a peace of Callias, have claimed to trace major effects which it produced in the League of Delos. They suppose that the treaty precipitated a crisis which may be said to have transformed the alliance from a Delian League into an Athenian Empire. Their arguments start from the layout of the quota lists on the stele bearing those of the fifteen years, 454/3–440/39. So attention must now be given to the arrangement of lists on the first stele.

The stele was inscribed on its four vertical faces. The first six lists were inscribed on the obverse; Lists 9–13 were inscribed on the reverse; Lists 14–15 were inscribed on the left lateral face. Since the left face bore two lists, it was supposed until 1933 that the right face bore two lists and that they were Lists 7 and 8, although on this view the extant fragments showed that List 7 was remarkably short. In 1933 H.T. Wade-Gery identified an additional fragment belonging to the right face near the top; hence he was able to show that the writing in the upper part of the right face was not a separate list but appendices to Lists 1 and 2, which were adjacent to it on the obverse. It followed that, below those appendices, there was only one list on the right face. Hence, although the stele bore the lists for the whole period of fifteen years (454/3–440/39 inclusively), it bore only fourteen lists; for one year no list of quota was inscribed.

Some historians have suggested that in that one year all the tribute was assigned to Athena for some special purpose, and so no quota was paid or inscribed. But it is difficult to imagine that all the tribute of a year could be spared from current expenses; and the practice of inscribing itemized quotas on stone shows that the Athenians felt a strong obligation to pay them. Wade-Gery and his colleagues, who together compiled *The Athenian Tribute Lists*, chose reasonably the bolder hypothesis that in one year no tribute was collected. Some features of the first stele indicated the limits between which that year fell. On the obverse the first five lists each bore a serial number; for example, the fifth had the heading: "Under the fifth board [sc. of hellenotamiae], when [–name–] was secretary." The list at the bottom of the obverse bore no number but opened with the heading: "Under the board when Menetimus of the deme Lamptreis was secretary;" provisionally it may be called List X. The list on the right face may be called List Y. It consists of two parts; the first, or "primary part," is the regular list of the year, but it is followed by a long "appendix," giving arrears and supplementary payments. The entries in the "primary part" of List Y follow precisely the same order as List X; this shows that Lists X and Y belong to adjacent years, since the arrangement of entries in the early lists varies and follows no discernable plan. The list preserved in fragments highest on the reverse is List 9; its opening lines are lost but many of the quotas it records are significantly similar to those in the next list below it, where part of the serial number "tenth" is preserved.

From these data it follows that the year for which no quota list has been found came either between List 5 and List X or between List Y and List 9. In other words, that year was either 449/8 or 447/6. Epigraphic indications as to which of these was the year without a quota list are inconclusive. On the one hand, it is remarkable that the heading to List X did not give a serial number; this might suggest that some irregularity immediately preceded List X. On the other hand, List 9 began about ten lines down from the top of the reverse, no fragments having been found from the space above the list; this might suggest that an irregularity immediately preceded List 9 and that the highest lines on the reverse bore some record of it, for example a statement that tribute was not collected in one year but was exacted again thereafter.

If no tribute was collected in one year, whether 449/8 or 447/6, a historical context can be recognized for the anomaly. A failure to collect tribute in 449/8 could be understood as a consequence of the peace of Callias. Alternatively in 447/6 Athens faced revolts in Boeotia, Euboea and Megara (see below, p. 291); with her authority thus weakened some states may have refused to pay tribute and Athens may have remitted her claims on the others as a measure of conciliation. Wade-Gery and his colleagues preferred the first explanation and they claimed to recognize three documents bearing on the crisis following the peace of Callias.

The first of these has come to be called the Congress Decree and is preserved by Plutarch (*Per.* 17). He says that the Athenians on the proposal of Pericles passed a decree inviting all Greek states to send delegates to a congress, which was to meet at Athens. The agenda of the congress was threefold. (1) It was to discuss the Greek sanctuaries which had been burned by the Persians. (2) It was to consider

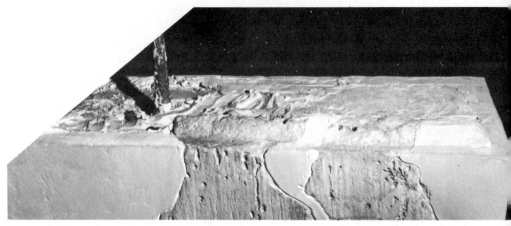

The top of the first stele of the Athenian tribute quota lists. See pages 282–287. [Courtesy W. K. Pritchett.]

the sacrifices which the Greeks had vowed to the gods when fighting the Persians. (3) It was to deliberate about measures for securing the peace of the seas. Plutarch continues his account by saying that the invitations were issued, but the Spartans opposed the plan for a congress; hence some states refused the invitation and the congress did not meet. In this account it is noteworthy that two items of the agenda were predominantly Athenian concerns. The Persians had burned Athens, including its sanctuaries, but had usually respected temples elsewhere, and only the Athenian fleet could maintain the peace of the Aegean. The second item could well arise when a treaty of peace had brought fighting with the Persians to an end. Wade-Gery and his colleagues saw in the Congress Decree an Athenian attempt to gain a new sanction for renewal of tribute, after the peace of Callias had caused non-collection for one year.

A second document was found in a fragment, preserved on papyrus, of an ancient commentary on the speeches of Demosthenes, and it has come to be called the Papyrus Decree. Only the right-hand part of one column and a few letters of the next are preserved in the extant fragment. The column contained explanations of several things mentioned by Demosthenes in speech 22. The speech mentioned the building of the Parthenon and of the Propylaea, and the commentator gave a note on this. In the right-hand part of the column the note mentioned the archonship of Euthydemus, a proposal by Pericles, a reserve of public money, and a sum of 5,000 talents in accordance with the assessment of Aristeides. Euthydemus was archon in 431/0, but the Athenians began building the Parthenon in 447/6 and the Propylaea in 437/6; a decree cited in the papyrus commentary to explain the building of these two works is likely to be not later than 447/6. The name Euthydemus in the papyrus may be an error for the less common name Euthynus, which is that of the archon of 450/49. Wade-Gery and his colleagues restored the papyrus to yield a decree of 450/49, proposed by Pericles, to use for building purposes a reserve of 5,000 talents which supposedly had accumulated from the tribute under the assessment of Aristeides; later they restored further lines of the papyrus to yield another clause in the same decree for transferring 3,000 talents more to Athena in installments. They supposed that this decree was among the measures taken by the Athenians when the congress failed to meet and they resolved even so to continue exacting tribute and to use part of the proceeds for building. It followed that the decision to continue exacting the tribute was taken before the end of the Attic year 450/49.

The third document was a decree, known from an inscription, of which four fragments are preserved. Its general purpose was to tighten up on the collection of tribute. Among its provisions was a requirement that each tributary city should agree with the Athenians on a seal, and it should send to Athens a sealed document stating the amount of tribute it was dispatching; this was to prevent the couriers, who carried the tribute, from allowing it to diminish during the journey. As long as only three fragments of this decree were known, it could be dated no more precisely than "before 426/5;" a decree proposed by Cleonymus in 426/5 sought likewise to tighten up on tribute payment, but as it required each city to choose collectors of tribute, it seemed to mark a more advanced stage than the other decree. A new fragment of the latter was discovered in 1938; it bore the name of the proposer of the decree, Cleinias. This name was not common in Athens; the proposer of the decree could be identified with the Cleinias who was killed in battle at Coronea in 447/6 (see below, p. 291). Mainly for this reason the decree came to be dated not later than 447.

Wade-Gery and his colleagues could present an impressive reconstruction. Cimon, they supposed, died on his last expedition in 450; he had been the chief advocate of continuing hostilities against Persia. Pericles seized the opportunity of his death to alter Athenian policy. Peace with Persia was negotiated in the winter of 450/49; consequently the Athenian claim to tribute lapsed, and no tribute was collected in 449/8. The Athenians tried to call a panhellenic congress in order to get new authorization for levying tribute; when the congress failed to meet, they decided to exact tribute even without such authorization and to use part of the proceeds for building temples in Athens. In the first year when tribute was exacted anew many states were reluctant to pay, and so List X, which was identified as List 7 of 448/7, is exceptionally short. Thereupon the Athenians passed measures, including the decree of Cleinias, to improve the collection of tribute. The supposed effects are reflected in List Y, which is unusually long; it was identified as List 8 of 447/6. In this reconstruction the chronology is a little tight. It was supposed that after the death of Cimon the negotiations with Persia, involving journeys to and from Susa, the attempt to call a panhellenic congress, its failure, and the Athenian decision to resume exacting tribute and use some of the money for buildings all took place before the end of the Attic year 450/49. Again, it is somewhat anomalous that the year without tribute proved to be 449/8, the year after the Athenians had decided to resume exacting tribute.

The problem took on an entirely new aspect in 1964, when W.K. Pritchett published the results he found on examining the top surface of the stele, as preserved in three fragments. At the edge of the top surface he found a smoothly dressed band of stone, ca. 0.032 m. wide and highly polished. Within this band the stone curves upwards to form a ridge, which is ca. 0.03 m. high where best preserved. The band and the ridge were not meant to be seen and they demand an explanation; Pritchett suggested that they served to make a join with a finial stone, designed to rest on top of the stele. The front of the finial might bear a decorative relief; on its reverse and on the uppermost part of the reverse of the main stele there would be room for a quota list. That would be List 8, and Lists X and Y would be Lists 6 and 7 respectively. Critics rejecting this hypothesis have objected that no fragments have been found from the supposed List 8; but it is dangerous to argue from the silence of archaeological evidence. The critics have not offered any satisfactory explanation of the features noted on the top surface of the stele.

An alternative to Pritchett's hypothesis has been proposed by V.F. Allen. Possibly the main stele itself originally rose somewhat higher but above List 1 the obverse was recessed to bear a decorative relief; the smoothly dressed band, which is known only at the front, and the curving ridge would be part of the recessing. Stelae bearing Athenian official documents often had a decorative relief on the obverse above the text, and in the case of the decree giving regulations for Miletus (above, p. 275) the decorative relief was recessed back from the main surface of the stele. On this hypothesis the reverse of the first stele of quota lists rose somewhat higher than previously supposed and offered enough space for List 8.

The features noted by Pritchett on the top surface of the stele demand explanation, and whichever explanation is correct, it can no longer be asserted with any confidence that in one year no tribute was collected. The three documents subsumed by Wade-Gery and his colleagues in their theory of crisis require a little further attention. It has been argued (by R. Seager) that the Congress Decree was a forgery of the fourth century; both the language and the provisions, as summarized by Plutarch, point to the years 346–340 as its time of composition; there is, for example, no trace of diplomatic discussion of the peace of the seas before 346. Athenian orators of the fourth century mention several decrees of doubtful authenticity from the period of the Persian Wars and their aftermath. The decree read into the papyrus commentary on Demosthenes is very uncertain. Since only the right-hand part of the column of writing is preserved, its original width is unknown, and so it can be restored in more than one way. For the decree of Cleinias more than one date is possible. Although the name Cleinias was not common in Athens, it was favored by one family, where it alternated with the name Alcibiades in successive generations; the proposer of the decree may have been an otherwise unrecorded member of that family. The forms of the letters are compatible with a date in the 440s or somewhat later. Against a date in the 420s it has been argued that the letter upsilon in the inscription has a form scarcely attested after 430, but this argument is not strong, since an attempt to date an inscription by the forms of its letters only becomes cogent when it rests on the forms of more than one letter. A date not far removed from 426/5 is likely because of the similarity in spirit between this decree and that of Cleonymus. On the other hand, even if the decree of Cleinias belongs to the early 440s, a credible context can be found for it without the hypothesis of a year without tribute; the quota lists provide evidence of recalcitrance in those years.

DISAFFECTION: 449–447[5]

The lists of the second assessment period (450/49–447/6) offer some indications of disaffection. List 5 belongs to 450/49; and because of the preceding discussion it will be assumed that List X is List 6 of 449/8 and List Y is List 7 of 448/7. As will be remembered, the order of the entries in List 6 and the "primary part" of List 7 is the same; hence it is possible to reconstruct these two lists extensively by using each to supplement the other. Consequently some confidence can be felt in attempts that have been made to calculate the total numbers of regular entries in the three extant lists of the second period.

List 5 consists of five columns. Some entries in the first four columns record "partial payments", that is, cases in which a state paid less than the whole amount required of it. In column V twenty "second entries" are attested or can reasonably be presumed; that is, in twenty cases a state whose "partial payment" appeared in columns I–IV added a "complement" and this appeared in column V. When allowance is made for the "second entries," and for about sixteen states whose names each occupied two lines, it appears that List 5 recorded ca. 163 states as paying tribute. Before a comparison can be made with Lists 6 and 7, attention must be given to eleven cities, whose payments appear in column V of List 5. They are Miletus, Latmus, Myus, Iasus, Priene, Cindye, Caryanda, Madnasa, Pelea, Ephesus and Euromus. They have been called the "southeastern group", since they are in that part of the Delian League. Their payments in List 5 appear to be complete payments, but as they are recorded in column V among the "second entries," it is likely that the payments of the "southeastern group" were made late in the year.

The "southeastern group" appears in the "appendix" to List 7 (List Y) as eleven cities, omitting Priene but including Mylasa; the other ten cities are the same as in List 5. The group does not occur in List 6 (List X) or in the "primary part" of List 7. But much of the "appendix" to List 7 is lost; it may be presumed that the "southeastern group" occurred twice in that "appendix", one set of payments being for year 6 and one for year 7. Why the payments of the group for year 6 were recorded in List 7 is one of several unsolved problems about the relationship between Lists 6 and 7; possibly the explanation should be sought, not in imperial policy, but in unusual behavior by the boards of hellenotamiae. The record of the "southeastern group" seems to be uniform for the three extant lists of the second period; that is, the payments of this group came in late in the year every time but perhaps before the end of the year. Some have tried to explain the lateness of these payments by the distance of the payers from Athens. Yet other payments, such as those for Phaselis and the cities of Rhodes, came from still further afield but arrived at the proper time of the year. So it is better to see in the record of the "southeastern group" some degree of recalcitrance.

The record of the "southeastern group" must be borne in mind in estimating the total numbers of entries in Lists 6 and 7. List 6 has 150 entries. But if the eleven cities of the "southeastern group" are added, on the assumption that their payments arrived so late in year 6 as to be recorded in List 7, then the total of payers for year 6 was 161. The "primary part" of List 7 has likewise 150 cities and, if the "southeastern group" is added, the total of regular payers will be 161. Since List 5 had ca. 163 states as paying tribute, there is little variation in the number of tribute-paying states in the three years. But there is rather more variation in the identity of the payers. About eleven cities recorded in List 5 are absent from Lists 6 and 7, and since List 6 and the "primary part" of List 7 can be reconstructed in full, it is possible to identify these cities. Correspondingly, a similar number of cities was absent from List 5 but appeared in Lists 6 and 7; but since List 5 remains fragmentary, it is not possible to say with confidence which these cities were.

The eleven cities recorded in List 5 but absent from Lists 6 and 7 may be grouped by their districts. Six are in the neighborhood of the Hellespont and the straits; they are Alopeconnesus, Proconnesus, Perinthus, Astacus, Dascylium and Neandria. Two, namely Olynthus and Acanthus, are in the Chalcidic peninsula. Among the islands there is Aegina. Finally there are two small places in the Carian district, namely Erines and Pasanda. Some of these eleven places have irregular records of tribute in other periods. In the case of some, hostility towards Athens is well attested at other times. The arch-example is Aegina; the Athenians had reduced it by siege early in the 450s and it complained to Sparta in 432 (see chapter 11, p. 317). Accordingly, the record of the eleven cities should be understood to indicate some disaffection in 449/8 and 448/7. Not much significance need be attached to Erines or Pasanda, as they were small and the Athenian hold on the Carian district was never secure. But the record suggests serious disaffection in the neighborhood of the straits and in the Chalcidic peninsula. With the behavior of Olynthus and Acanthus that of Poteidaea and Argilus should also be considered, since they lie in the same neighborhood; they are absent from all the fragments of the lists of the second period.

Several other pieces of evidence point to extensive disaffection in the same period. Four fragments of an Athenian decree concerning Colophon have been found. It is so poorly preserved that little can be said about its content, but it contained regulations for Colophon and part of an oath and it used the word *oikistai* (the technical term for founders of a colony). Colophon paid a tribute of three talents in the first assessment period; it is absent from the lists of the second period, and it paid a tribute of only 1½ talents in the third and fourth periods. This record is explained if Colophon rebelled some time in the second period and in the ensuing settlement some of its land was confiscated with a corresponding reduction in tribute. It is known from Thucydides (3.34) that Colophon rebelled in 430, brought in Persian forces and was recovered by the Athenians in 427. Both periods, 449–446 and 430–427, have been suggested as possible contexts for the Athenian decree about Colophon, and the controversy has turned largely on the forms of the letters used in the inscription, but these arguments are not conclusive. Whatever the date of the decree, the tribute record suggests disaffection in Colophon in the second assessment period.

As noted above (p. 277), one method used by the Athenians to increase their control was the foundation of cleruchies. The list given by Plutarch (*Per.* 11.5) of cleruchies founded about the middle of the fifth century includes the dispatch of 1,000 cleruchs to the Chersonese. Several cities had developed there, but in the first assessment period they paid jointly and the sum was 18 talents. By the third and fourth assessment periods (446/5–444/3 and 443/2–439/8) five places in the Chersonese were recorded as paying separately and the total, known from figures preserved for the fourth period, was less than 2 talents. In List 5 the Chersonese was still recorded as paying as a group, but the sum was an irregular figure of between 13 and 14 talents. The Chersonese does not appear in List 6, but in List 7 at least three of the five places attested in the later periods were recorded separately. So it is likely that Athenian intervention, including the founding of the cleruchy, took place in 449 or 448, that is, between the times of List 5 and List 7. Judging from the fourth-century history of the Chersonese, its civilized inhabitants may have welcomed the cleruchy as affording additional protection against Thracian encroachments. Indeed, Plutarch (*Per.* 19.1) says that on his campaign in the Chersonese Pericles not only brought in 1,000 settlers but also built fortifications across the neck of the peninsula against Thracian raids.

Operations related to the campaign in the Chersonese may have left further traces in the documentary sources. List 7 records a payment brought by the people of Abdera to Eion and two payments, of unspecified source, brought to Tenedos. Moreover, an Athenian casualty list names men who fell fighting "in the Chersonese," "in Byzantium," and "in the other wars." The inscribed list bears no date; the suggestion that it belongs to the year when Pericles operated in the Chersonese is attractive. The tribute record of Byzantium in the second assessment period seems to indicate trouble there. In List 5 its sum, 15 talents, may be the regular amount, but it is recorded in the last column, along with "second entries" and the "southeastern group." In List 6 and the "primary part" of List 7 it is recorded with "partial payments" and the "complements" appear in the "appendix" to List 7.

The subject of "partial payments" might merit extensive study. Here it will suffice to note some of the "partial payments" recognizable in the quota lists of the second assessment period. Cos, for example, was recorded with a "partial payment" in the body of List 5 and a "complement" in the last column; the two sums add up to 5 talents. In List 6 and in the "primary part" of List 7 it was recorded with the same "partial payment" as in List 5; two additional payments were recorded in the "appendix" to List 7. Again Tenedos was recorded with a "partial payment" in the body of List 5 and a "complement" in its last column; the two sums add up to 4 ½ talents, the regular figure for Tenedos in the first and third assessment periods. In List 6 it was recorded with a "partial payment" of unknown amount. In the "primary part" of List 7 it appeared with the same "partial payment" as in List 5, and at least one additional payment from Tenedos was given in the "appendix." Tribute records of this type suggest some degree of disaffection, even though the repetition of the same "partial payment" by the same state in different years invites the hypothesis that disaffection may have gone no further than disputing the proper level of tribute due. Accordingly, it is to be noted that "partial payments" in Lists 6 and 7 suggest disaffection in several cities of the straits and of the north Aegean. In the former area, apart from Tenedos, these two lists show "partial payments" in Sigeum, Dardanus, Lampsacus, Cyzicus, Byzantium, Imbros, and Hephaestia in Lemnos. In the north Aegean "partial payments" in the two lists appear for Gale and Sane in the Chalcidic peninsulas, for Thasos, and for Abdera and Aenus on the Thracian coast. It will be remembered that of the eleven cities recorded in List 5 but absent from Lists 6 and 7 several were in the neighborhood of the straits or of the Chalcidic peninsula.

Thus inferences from different sources converge to suggest widespread recalcitrance in the period 449–447. The evidence includes the absence of expected names from the quota lists, the record of the "southeastern group", "partial payments", the payments made at Eion, and a casualty list. Something can be said about Athenian countermeasures in the straits and the north Aegean; a cleruchy was sent to the Chersonese, there was fighting there and at Byzantium, and officers were stationed at Eion and Tenedos. It is not clear whether by 447 the Athenians were gaining the upper hand over the disaffected elements. The narrative of Thucydides shows that events beginning in the winter of 447/6 precipitated a major crisis in the Athenian Empire.

THE THIRTY YEARS' PEACE[6]

For several years after 454 the Athenians abstained from warfare against the Peloponnesians. Some time after the Five Years' Peace of 451 but before the winter of 447/6 the Lacedaemonians made an expedition into central Greece. Thucydides (1.112.5) referred to it as "the so-called sacred war;" evidently that was the Lacedaemonian name for it. They recovered control of the Delphic sanctuary from the Phocians and entrusted it to the people of Delphi. After they had departed, the Athenians made an expedition to Delphi, took control of the sanctuary and entrusted it to the Phocians. Confrontation between Athenians and Lacedaemonians was avoided, and the Athenian ascendancy in central Greece was restored for a time. But the Spartans may have had other things to do in Central Greece.

Probably in the winter of 447/6 trouble came to a head in Boeotia. Exiles hostile to Athens had seized Orchomenus, Chaeronea and some other places. Tolmides led a force, drawn from Athens and her allies, against them; he captured Chaeronea but he was attacked and defeated decisively at Coroneia. By the terms of the capitulation the Athenians withdrew entirely from Boeotia. The force opposing Tolmides at Coroneia included not only Boeotians but also Locrians and exiles from Euboea; the anti-Athenian movement was not restricted to Boeotia.

A little later, perhaps about the spring or early summer of 446, Euboea seceded from the Athenians. Pericles led an army to the island, but while he was away, news came from Megara. The Megarians had rebelled against Athens and killed the Athenian garrison troops, except for those who escaped to Nisaea; they admitted forces from Corinth, Sicyon and Epidaurus, and the Peloponnesians made preparations to invade Attica. Pericles brought his army back from Euboea, but the Peloponnesian force under the Spartan king Pleistoanax reached Eleusis and the plain of western Attica and ravaged the territory. Then Pleistoanax withdrew his force; rumor said, probably correctly, that Pericles had reached a preliminary agreement with him. The agreement offered no safeguards for the Euboeans. Pericles returned to the island and overcame its cities, making terms with most of them; but the Athenians expelled the people of Histiaea, the northernmost city of Euboea, and founded a colony of Athenian citizens on their land; the new settlement was called Oreus. A definitive peace between Athens and the Peloponnesian League was negotiated in 446/5; the parties swore to abide by it for thirty years.

The predicament in which the Athenians found themselves early in 446 was due to a new vigor among the Spartans. About eleven years before they had refused the Persian request, brought by Megabazus, to invade Attica, but in 446 they ravaged its western plain. Some Spartans desired still more severe action against Athens; when Pleistoanax reached his agreement with Athens and brought his men home, he was accused of accepting bribes and he withdrew into exile. Perhaps one aspect of the new Spartan vigor was careful planning. The predicament facing the Athenians in 446 arose because in three sensitive areas, Boeotia, Euboea and the Megarid, revolts occurred in quick succession. The coordination of the revolts suggests that someone coordinated them; that may have been what the Spartans were doing when they went to Central Greece to prosecute "the so-called sacred war." To say this much is not to say that all the revolts of 447/6 followed precisely a grand Spartan design. The hypothesis of coordination between the risings in Boeotia and Euboea is strengthened by the fact that Euboean exiles fought at Coroneia. Possibly during their expedition to central Greece the Spartans negotiated with disaffected elements in Boeotia and Euboea only, and the revolt of Megara was an unexpected windfall.

By the terms of the Thirty Years' Peace the Athenians surrendered Nisaea, Pegae, Troezen and Achaea. The first two of these places were the harbors of Megara; it was logical that the Athenians should surrender them and withdraw their forces, when they had to give up their connection with Megara. It is not clear when in the First Peloponnesian War the Athenians won ascendancy over Troezen; they may have achieved this in connection with the early operations in the Saronic Gulf. Achaea may have been brought into alliance with Athens in connection with the operations of Tolmides or of Pericles in the Gulf of Corinth. Apart from the surrender of these four places by the terms of the peace, the belligerents retained the positions they had reached through warfare by 446. In consequence of the revolts of Boeotia and Megara Athens had to give up her ambitions of land-empire in central Greece. But Athens retained the Delian League and Sparta retained the Peloponnesian League; they were patently the dominant powers on sea and land respectively.

The peace was especially significant for the allies of Athens in the Delian League. The cities of Euboea had by their revolt contributed a great deal to the Spartan success, but in the negotiations Sparta abandoned them. The treatment of Histiaea by the Athenians has already been noted. Some impression of the terms imposed on the other cities of Euboea can be derived from an Athenian

Bust of Pericles. Roman copy. The bronze original was made by Cresilas in the fifth century B.C.

[Courtesy Trustees of the British Museum, London.]

decree about Chalcis. The inscription bearing the decree is well preserved, and the terms are strict but not ruthless. The Athenians undertake neither to impose penalties on any Chalcidian without trial, nor to propose any motion against the Chalcidians collectively or individually without allowing them a hearing; but they add that they will adhere to these provisions "provided that the Chalcidians obey the people of Athens." The oath, to be sworn by all Chalcidians, is highly specific and includes a clause: "I will obey the people of Athens." Additional provisions show that the Chalcidians had made representations about hostages taken by the Athenians; the Athenians reply that they will make no change at present but they hold out some hope of reviewing their decision in future. A significant amendment orders that verdicts imposed by Chalcidian courts on Chalcidians are to be valid, except when the penalty is exile, death or deprivation of civic rights; in cases where any of these penalties is at stake there is to be referral to an Athenian court.

Possibly in the case of one state the Spartans inserted a safeguard into the peace treaty. In 432 the Aeginetans complained to Sparta that in contravention of the treaty their autonomy had been infringed. It has been inferred that the Thirty Years' Peace included a clause guaranteeing the autonomy of Aegina. Even so, autonomy was a flexible concept; the Spartans may have inserted the clause not so much out of concern for the Aeginetans as to provide an occasion for further disputes, if desired. In general, for the allies of Athens in the Delian League the lesson of Euboea was clear; if they rebelled against Athens, they could not count on any help from Sparta.

NOTES

1. The main source for these events is Thuc. 1.103–108. For the chronology two sources have crucial importance. First an inscription (Meiggs/Lewis 33) of the tribe Erechtheis says that the men listed fell in warfare "in Cyprus, in Egypt, in Phoenicia, in Halieis, in Aegina, and at Megara, in the same year." Some scholars have taken "year (*eniautos*)" here to mean a campaigning year, that is, approximately a Julian year; but the view that in this inscription, as generally in Attic practice, the word means the Attic year defined by the archon's term of office is defended by C. W. Fornara, *The Athenian Board of Generals from 501 to 404* = Historia Einzelschriften Heft 16 (1971) 44–46. Second, a fragment of Theopompus (*F.Gr.Hist.* IIB 115F88) says that less than five years had elapsed after the ostracism of Cimon when warfare came about with the Lacedaemonians and the Athenian assembly recalled Cimon in the hope that he would make peace. The recall of Cimon will require consideration later (see pp. 272–273). The warfare mentioned by Theopompus is the battle of Tanagra, and he implies that it was fought in 457, less than five years after Cimon had been ostracized in 462/1. A date in 458 was proposed for the battle of Tanagra in *ATL* 3. 168–173, but the arguments can be answered; cf. R. Meiggs, *CR* N.S. 2 (1952) 99. The inscription indicating Athenian relations with the Amphictyonic League is *I.G.* I², 26 = Hill B21; for discussion see

Meiggs, *AE* 418–420. Pseudo-Xenophon (3.11), Aristotle (*Pol.* 5.1302b29–30) and Diodorus (11.83.1) make brief and obscure allusions to the condition of Boeotia and Thebes after the battle of Oenophyta. The date when Tolmides sailed round the Peloponnese is known from schol. Aeschin. 2.75.

2. The main source for the history of warfare 454–451 is Thuc. 1.109–112. Ctesias (63–65) gives an account of the Egyptian Revolt and says that the force sent by the Athenians was 40 ships. Partly on this basis some historians have tried to scale down the magnitude of the Egyptian disaster, but Thucydides is much clearer and more careful than the later sources; see Meiggs, *AE* 104–108, 473–476, and J.M. Libourel, "The Athenian Disaster in Egypt," *AJP* 92 (1971) 605–615. Three studies by R. Meiggs are valuable towards understanding disaffection in the Delian League in the middle of the fifth century; they are "The Growth of Athenian Imperialism," *JHS* 63 (1943) 21–34; "The Crisis of Athenian Imperialism," *HSCP* 67 (1963) 1–36; and *AE* 109–128. On Miletus see J.C. Barron, "Milesian Politics and Athenian Propaganda, c. 460–440 B.C.," *JHS* 82 (1962) 1–6. The new fragment of the first quota list was published by B.D. Meritt, "The Tribute Quota List of 454/3 B.C.," *Hesperia* 41 (1972) 403–417. For the decree about Miletus see Hill B30; the case for dating it some years after 450/49 is presented by C.W. Fornara, "The Date of the 'Regulations for Miletus'," *AJP* 92 (1971) 473–475. For the decree about Erythrae see Meiggs/Lewis 40. On the Carian entries in the second and fourth quota lists see *ATL* 3.7–9 and 211–212. The totals for the first assessment period were calculated by Gomme, *Comm.* 1.274–275, and by *ATL* 3. 19–28 and 265–268.

3. Thucydides reports Cimon's last expedition at 1.112.2–4. Discussions of the peace of Callias are very numerous. A good starting point is provided by H.T. Wade-Gery, "The Peace of Kallias," *Essays* 201–232 = Athenian Studies presented to W.S. Ferguson = *HSCP* supplementary vol. 1 (1940) 121–156. Wade-Gery presented persuasively the case for believing that a peace of Epilycus was concluded between Athens and Persia in 424/3. For a strong statement of the case against the peace see D. Stockton, "The Peace of Callias," *Historia* 8 (1959) 61–79. Comprehensive accounts of the arguments are provided by C.L. Murison, "The Peace of Callias: its Historical Context," *Phoenix* 25 (1971) 12–31, and by Meiggs, *AE* 129–151; Murison inclines to reject the tradition of a peace of Callias, and Meiggs inclines to accept it. A list of known events which Thucydides omits from his *Pentekontaetia* is provided by Gomme, *Comm.* 1.365–389. A. Andrewes, "Thucydides and the Persians," *Historia* 10 (1961) 1–18, reviews the developments which Thucydides omits in Athenian relations with Persia and makes these the basis for a hypothesis about composition. From two passages in book 8 of Thucydides (56.4 and 58.2) he seeks to defend the authenticity of the peace of Callias, for these passages, stating events of 411, seem to imply that a treaty with Persia was already in force; but a treaty valid in 411 should be that of 424/3. Meiggs (loc. cit.) offers three new arguments for authenticity: (1) Theopompus said that the stele bearing the peace was a forgery, since it was inscribed in Ionic letters and Athens adopted the Ionic alphabet in 403/2. Meiggs comments (p. 131): "It is also a reasonable inference, and the point may be important, that this stele had not been set up recently." But Theopompus's argument only implies that the stele was not widely known to have been set up recently. (2) Meiggs begins his defence of authenticity from the treaty made by the Athenians with Darius II in 424/3 and says (p. 135): "It is difficult to see why, if there had been no previous agreement, Darius should wish to make a treaty with Athens in the middle of the Peloponnesian War. There is considerably less difficulty if the treaty was a renewal." But it is not safe to argue from the silence of our sources about the motives of Persian policy. (3) Meiggs (p. 137) finds tentatively an allusion to the peace in Lysias 2.56 (composed 390), where he translates the crucial words as saying that the king "gave up some of what belonged to him" and infers a deliberate act. But here Meiggs

has not allowed for the imperfect tense of Lysias's verb; Lysias says, not that the king gave, but that he offered or was willing to give of his own. W.R. Connor, *Theopompus and Fifth-Century Athens* (Washington, D.C. 1968) 77–98, makes an important point about the meaning of Theopompus's statement. He also supposes that fourth-century discussion distinguished three supposed treaties of peace, allegedly concluded at different times in the fifth century; but it is not clear that fourth-century publicists were so precise about chronology.

4. H.T. Wade-Gery reported his identification of the fragment from the upper right face of the first stele in *BSA* 33 (1932–33: published in 1935) 104–106 and 112. He offered his thesis of a crisis in 449 in "The Question of Tribute in 449/8," *Hesperia* 14 (1945) 212–229; the theory was restated in *ATL* 3.39–52. The identity of order of entries in Lists x and y was recognized by B.D. Meritt and A.B. West, *AJA* 32 (1928) 281–297. Some epigraphers have claimed to recognize part of the serial number "ninth" in List 9, but this is doubtful; see D.M. Lewis, *BSA* 49 (1955) 25–29, and W.K. Pritchett, *GRBS* 7 (1966) 127. The papyrus preserving part of a commentary on Demosthenes 22 is P. Strassburg 84 verso; for discussion see H.T. Wade-Gery and B.D. Meritt, "Athenian Resources in 449 and 431 B.C.," *Hesperia* 26 (1957) 183–197; Sealey, "P. Strassburg 84 verso," *Hermes* 86 (1958) 440–446. The decree of Cleinias about tribute is accessible as Meiggs/Lewis 46. The death of Cleinias at Coroneia is known from Plut. *Alc.* 1.1. W.K. Pritchett published his findings about the top of the first stele in "The Height of the Lapis Primus," *Historia* 13 (1964) 129–134; "The Top of the Lapis Primus," *GRBS* 7 (1966) 123–129; "The Location of the Lapis Primus," *GRBS* 8 (1967) 113–119. For criticisms see B.D. Meritt, "The Top of the First Tribute Stele," *Hesperia* 35 (1966) 134–140, and "The Second Athenian Tribute Assessment Period," *GRBS* 8 (1967) 121–132. V.F. Allen offered her hypothesis in *The First Tribute Stele and the Athenian Empire 455–445 B.C.* (unpublished dissertation, University of California, Los Angeles 1971). The case for regarding the Congress Decree as a fourth-century forgery was presented by R. Seager, "the Congress Decree: Some Doubts and a Hypothesis," Historia 18 (1969) 129–141; see also A.B. Bosworth, "The Congress Decree: Another Hypothesis," *Historia* 20 (1971) 600–616. Arguments for dating the tribute decree of Cleinias in 425/4 were offered by H.Mattingly, "The Athenian Coinage Decree," *Historia* 10 (1961) 148–188.

5. For analysis of the last column of List 5 see *ATL* 3.30–36. The "southeastern group" was first recognized in *ATL* 3.35–36. Disaffection in the second assessment period is discussed by Meiggs, *AE* 152–174, and by Sealey, "Notes on Tribute-Quota-Lists 5, 6, and 7 of the Athenian Empire," *Phoenix* 24 (1970) 13–28. The Athenian decree about Colophon is accessible as Meiggs/Lewis 47 and the casualty list as Meiggs/Lewis 48. A date in the 420s for the Colophon decree was offered by H.B. Mattingly, *Historia* 10 (1961) 175.

6. The narrative of this section rests mainly on Thuc. 1.112.1–1.115.1. The chronology depends largely on the assumption that the Spartans did not invade Attica until the Five Years' Peace had expired; cf. *ATL* 3.179. Further information on Pleistoanax is provided by Thuc. 5.16; Plut. *Per.* 22. Diodorus (12. 7) gives Callias and Chares as the names of the Athenian enoys who negotiated the Thirty Years' Peace. The Athenian decree about Chalcis is Meiggs/Lewis 52. The Aeginetan complaint of 432 is given by Thuc. 1.67.2; cf. 1.139.1.

11

The Athenian Empire
and the Outbreak of
the Peloponnesian War

ATHENS[1]

Towards the middle of the fifth century the Athenians took several measures altering their constitutional practices. Understanding of the political origins and motivation of these measures has changed a good deal in recent decades. It used to be assumed that the measures were the results of comparatively simple conflicts; on the one side was a party advocating the measures, on the other was a party opposing them, and the outcome was a simple victory of one party over the other. Evidence that could be cited in support of such a reconstruction included a chapter (28) of Aristotle's treatise, *The Constitution of the Athenians*. There he arranges Athenian political leaders of the fifth century in two series; the one consists of the successive leaders of the *demos*, a word meaning here approximately "the common people;" the other consists of the successive leaders of a group which Aristotle calls variously "the notables," "the wealthy," "the others" or "the distinguished." But the list ends with the late fifth century and it has long been recognized that the chapter rests on tendentious political discussions of that period. Recent studies have emphasized the theoretical and unreliable character of fourth-century comments on the politics of fifth-century Athens, and they have discovered political groupings of a less programmatic and more personal kind. Here it will be convenient first to note the constitutional changes and then to say a little about the political scene.

The reforms of Ephialtes were discussed above (chapter 9, pp. 258–261); it was argued that they sought to improve the procedure for hearing complaints against retiring magistrates by transferring that function from the Areopagite Council to the popular courts. In the same context a change in the incidence of popular jurisdiction was noted. In the Athens of Solon a case might be referred to the assembly by a prior authority, which itself had the opportunity of giving a verdict, but in the fully developed constitution popular jurisdiction was exercised at first instance through a large court (*dikasterion*), which often had 500 jurors; now the archon had the merely administrative functions of empaneling a jury, bringing the litigants before it, and having the verdict announced when the jurors had reached it by vote. It was argued that this change came about through the reluctance of archons to accept the responsibility of giving a verdict, especially in difficult cases. It should be added that payment for jury service was introduced on the proposal of Pericles. The original rate was two obols a day; later it was raised to three obols. Fourth-century writers, such as Theopompus and Aristotle, gave this measure a partisan background; they said that Pericles could not compete from his private resources with the largesse of Cimon (on which see above chapter 9, p. 257), and so by introducing jury pay he sought to bribe the populace with public money. This story is patently tendentious. Moreover, judging from the way Athenian orators address juries, pay for jury service was not a bribe for the very poor but compensation paid to people of moderate substance for absence from their gainful activities. The introduction of jury pay may have sought merely to provide sufficient jurors for the growing amount of judicial business. Similar considerations would explain why public pay was extended to the Council of Five Hundred and most magistracies.

Aristotle (*AP* 26.2–4) mentions briefly three further measures taken towards the middle of the century. (1) In 457/6 eligibility for the nine archonships was extended to the third of the Solonian property classes, the zeugitae. From another passage (*AP* 7.4), where Aristotle gives conditions of his own time, it appears that eventually members of the fourth and lowest class, the thetes, were in practice admitted too; when candidates presented themselves for sortition, they were asked their class, but no one gave "thetic" as his and the inquiry into class affiliation was not pursued further. (2) In 453/2 the institution of "deme dicasts" (*dikastai kata demous*) was restored or established. These were judges who toured Attica. Elsewhere (*AP* 53.1–2) Aristotle says that they were chosen by lot, that their number was raised from thirty to forty in 403/2, and that they had authority to decide cases up to a value of ten drachmas. The tradition he followed

(*AP* 16.5) said that they were originally instituted by Peisistratus, but if so, it is difficult to see when or why the practice lapsed; possibly the deme dicasts were first instituted in 453/2. (3) In 451/0 a law was passed, on the proposal of Pericles, to restrict citizenship to those whose both parents were citizens. Previously some people had been recognized as citizens, although their mothers were foreign; Cleisthenes is an example.

The law of 451/0 may mark growing pride in Athenian citizenship, but it is not easy to say how great a change it made, since the immediately preceding conditions are not known. When an Athenian boy came of age in his eighteenth year, his father presented him to his assembly of demesmen; if they were satisfied as to his parentage and age, they added his name to the list of demesmen and this was his proof of citizenship. Conceivably even before 451/0 assemblies of demesmen may have insisted, commonly or increasingly, that both parents of a candidate must be citizens before they would accept him. This is quite uncertain, but because it is uncertain, it is not clear whether the law of 451/0 altered or confirmed previous practice. In general, the three measures noted in the previous paragraph do not show any doctrinaire striving towards a constitutional ideal.

The same may be said of the development of constitutional practice in the middle of the century. Meetings of the public assembly were frequent. In the time of Aristotle (*AP* 43.4–6) it held forty regular meetings each year, and inscriptions show that by the second half of the fifth century it decided all kinds of business. The requirement that matters must be reviewed by the Council of Five Hundred before they came before the assembly did not function as a restriction on the assembly but merely ensured that problems were clarified to some extent beforehand. At an unknown date the Council was divided into ten parts, called prytanies; each consisted of the councilors of one tribe. The year was divided into ten parts, and each prytany was on duty for a tenth of the year. The prytany on duty took its meals in the *Tholos* or office building adjacent to the *Bouleuterion* or council chamber; it summoned daily meetings of the Council and meetings of the assembly.

As business increased with the growth of prosperity and empire, the state undertook more tasks; the method commonly chosen in the fifth century was to create a board of ten men, chosen by lot and drawn one from each tribe. Aristotle (*AP* 24.3) alleges that apart from the Council of Five Hundred no fewer than 700 citizens held offices in Attica each year, but he gives this figure in a passage of patent exaggeration. Even so it is likely that a great many citizens, especially those residing in the city, could expect to hold office at least once in their lifetimes. These officers were chosen by sortition on the assumption that their tasks required no special skill but could be performed by any citizen.

Offices requiring special talent were filled by election. The most important of

Athenian dekadrachm, ca. 479. Obverse: head of Athena. Reverse: owl. [Photo by Hirmer Fotoarchiv, München.]

Athenian tetradrachm, ca. 430/407. Obverse: head of Athena. Reverse: owl. [Photo by Hirmer Fotoarchiv, München.]

Corinthian silver stater. Obverse: Athena. Reverse: Pegasus. [Courtesy Lowie Museum of Anthropology, University of California, Berkeley.]

these was the generalship (*strategia*). Ten generals were elected by the assembly each year and at some stage, probably before 441, the original requirement that one should be drawn from each tribe was abandoned. There was no restriction on reelection; Pericles held office as general for fifteen years in succession (443/2–429/8) and some other men are known to have been elected repeatedly. The generals were primarily military experts, but often they exercised political influence; they had a right of access to the Council of Five Hundred and could propose measures there. Tenure of the generalship brought prestige and there was competition for election. When Athens sent envoys to negotiate with other states, they were elected in the public assembly; so it is likely that service on such embassies brought prestige, but this was not an annual or regular office.

The word *demokratia* was coined about the middle of the century; the earliest author to use it is Herodotus. It was used of the Athenian constitution in its developed form. The original associations of the word are not easy to trace with precision but were quite different from those of such modern words as "democracy" and "government by the people." Indeed, *demokratia* seems to have been coined by critics of the Athenian constitution. Defenders of Athenian practices avoided it or accepted it in an apologetic manner. Somehow it became closely associated with Athens and could not be disclaimed. The force of political terms often resides more in overtones of approval or disapproval than in empirical description. This is true of the word *demokratia*, and its overtones changed towards the end of the fifth century. One should therefore beware of substituting the modern word "democracy" and using this as a clue to the way Athenian institutions worked.

Within the period of the Thirty Years' Peace Pericles achieved an unusual ascendancy. Thucydides (2.65.9) says that the Athenian state was becoming "in name *demokratia* but actually the leadership of the first man;" Plutarch (*Per.* 16.1) says that comic poets called Pericles and his friends "the new Peisistratids." Something must be said here about the way he achieved prominence, and this may throw light on the political scene. Some historians have supposed that Pericles rose to power by advocating a distinctive policy, which contrasted with that of Cimon; in internal affairs, it is suggested, Cimon opposed but Pericles supported the reforms of Ephialtes; abroad Cimon was for continuing operations against Persia and keeping good relations with Sparta, but Pericles preferred to make peace with Persia and oppose Sparta. As noted above (chapter 9, p. 258), Cimon tried to repeal the reforms of Ephialtes, but Pericles's attitude towards them is imperfectly attested; it may not have had much significance, since Pericles was still at an early stage of his career, his earliest known tenure of the generalship being his service at the battle of Tanagra. Towards reconstructing their attitude to Persia a good deal depends on accepting or rejecting the fourth-century tradition of a peace of Callias. If such a peace was made, one might suppose that the death of Cimon gave an opportunity to some Athenians who desired an accommodation with Persia, and one might conjecture that Pericles was among them. But it was argued above (chapter 10, pp. 278–282) that the supposed peace of Callias was not authentic.

The question of their attitudes towards Sparta is complex. During the Messenian Revolt Cimon advocated and led an expedition to help the Spartans (chapter 9, p. 258). In the years 433–431 Pericles encouraged his fellow citizens in an intransigent attitude, which contributed to the outbreak of war (see below, pp. 313–321). But a statesman may change his attitude as time passes. Something may be discerned about the development of Athenian policy during the First Peloponnesian War. The Athenians prosecuted that war with vigor in its early years, but from 454 they refrained from taking the initiative in hostilities against the Peloponnesians. If the fourth-century tradition of Cimon's recall from ostracism is correct, it is reasonable to associate him with this change of policy; Plutarch (*Per.* 17.8) says that the decree recalling him was proposed by Pericles. The latter was rising to prominence in the middle and later years of the First Peloponnesian War; so it is reasonable to associate him with the policy of abstaining from hostilities against the Peloponnesians.

Considerations about the Thirty Years' Peace may strengthen this view of Pericles. He was much involved in the military events leading to the conclusion of peace (chapter 10, pp. 291–292). The question must be asked, whether the Athenians regarded that treaty as a final settlement which would begin a long period of peace, or as securing them an interval to recuperate in order to renew the struggle at a better opportunity. Athenian building policies may provide an answer. The two Long Walls had been built early in the First Peloponnesian War. One, the more northerly, ran from the city to the Peiraeus; the other ran from the city to Phalerum. Perhaps ca. 444–442 a third Long Wall was built; it ran parallel to the northern wall and near to it on its southeastern side. Probably the intention was that this and the northern wall should constitute the chief defenses; the wall running to Phalerum may have been abandoned. The building of the third wall shows at least that people were thinking about the strategy to adopt if Attica suffered invasion. It does not follow that they were planning to renew the war against Sparta, and outlay on nonmilitary buildings suggests otherwise. A good deal of temple building was in progress during the Thirty Years' Peace. In particular, the Parthenon was built on the acropolis in the years 447/6–433/2; a large cult statue of Athena, made of gold and ivory, was completed in 438/7 and put in it; the Propylaea at the entrance to the acropolis was begun in 437/6 but work on it was discontinued in 433/2 because of the approach of war. If on concluding the Thirty Years' Peace the Athenians had looked forward to resuming the war at the earliest good opportunity, surely they would have held back money to form a larger war reserve.

It appears that the Athenians at first expected the Thirty Years' Peace to be a lasting settlement. In 433–432, when they adopted a hostile and provocative attitude towards the Peloponnesians, this attitude marked a change of policy. Pericles should be associated with the later policy and probably with the earlier one too. He may indeed have inherited the policy of cultivating good relations with Sparta from Cimon. Ties of birth and marriage linked the two men. The mother of Pericles, Agariste, was an Alcmaeonid; Cimon married an Alcmaeonid, Isodice. Cimon gave his sister Elpinice in marriage to a Callias of the Callias–Hipponicus family; Pericles divorced his wife and gave her in marriage to a Hipponicus of the same family.

A crucial stage in the rise of Pericles occurred in 444/3, when an ostracism was held to decide between him and his rival, Thucydides, son of Melesias. Thucydides was related by marriage to Cimon and was ostracized. Plutarch (*Per.* 11–14) gives a surprisingly detailed account of the rivalry, summarizing the arguments used on each side. The critics of Pericles, he says, attacked him especially for the building program, complaining that it was an improper use of the money supplied by the allies for warfare. Pericles allegedly replied that, as long as the Athenians protected the allies efficiently from the Persians, they owed them no account of the money and could use it at will, and the building program provided plentiful employment. Plutarch dilates on this last point, specifying the kinds of artisans employed. Until recently historians commonly accepted Plutarch's account, but it is difficult to see how he could have good sources for the arguments used towards 443. Recent studies (especially by F. J. Frost) suggest that Plutarch's account of the arguments has very little value. It was influenced by theorists of the fourth century, men like Aristotle, who insisted on explaining political development by hypotheses of class struggle. In dilating on the theme of employment Plutarch may have had in mind conditions of his own time, when there was widespread unemployment in Greece and people looked to the Roman emperor to finance public works. Archaeological study of the buildings of Periclean Athens suggests that, when the program began, there was a shortage of labor, especially skilled labor.

Recent research offers a new picture of the political scene in the middle of the fifth century. From the time of Cleisthenes until the beginning of the Peloponnesian War nearly all Athenian politicians belonged to demes in or near the city, and this observation can be confirmed against the lists of generals from 441 onwards. Influential families of the city district were the beneficiaries of the Cleisthenic settlement, and politics was largely a matter of alliances and disputes among them. A young man seeking to enter political life relied primarily on his relatives and friends. Issues were usually personal, not programmatic. In this situation Pericles won ascendancy by bringing together a considerable number of influential families. Mention has already been made of his ties with Cimon and with the Callias–Hipponicus family. A Callias of this family was one of the envoys who went to Sparta in 446/5 and negotiated the Thirty Years' Peace. Xanthippus, the son of Pericles, married a daughter of Teisander. The latter was a respected citizen; little is known of his political activity, but an *ostrakon* cast against him has been found; possibly it was cast at the ostracism of 444/3. The marriage between Xanthippus and Teisander's daughter may mark preexisting friendship between the two families. Another daughter of Teisander married Glaucon, who was general in 441/0, 439/8 and 433/2. Yet another daughter of Teisander married Leogoras; the latter's father was general in 447/6 and was one of the envoys sent to Sparta in 446/5. Pericles was also related to Cleinias, who fell at Coroneia in 447 leaving a son, Alcibiades; the latter was brought up under the guardianship of the brothers Pericles and Arriphron. Plutarch (*Per.* 7.5) preserves a revealing piece of information about Pericles's social habits. He devoted himself wholly to work and declined invitations to dinner parties, with one exception; he attended the feast given to celebrate the marriage of his cousin Euryptolemus.

THE EMPIRE[2]

The term "Athenian Empire" is often given to the Delian League in its developed form, when Athenian leadership had become authoritarian. The term is based on fifth-century usage; people spoke of the "rule" (*arkhe*) of the Athenians over their allies. Many steps can be traced in the transition from League to Empire. Those who believe that a treaty with Persia was made in the middle of the century and that it precipitated a crisis in the League have tended to regard that crisis as the crucial step. Others have been impressed by disaffection and the Athenian response to it in the years 454–446, and they have concluded that most of the methods of strengthening Athenian control were developed in that period. But evidence for conditions in the League from 454 onwards is more plentiful because of the survival in part of the tribute quota lists and of some decrees. If there were equally rich evidence for conditions before 454, some of the earlier developments might seem equally decisive. The proper conclusion is that the Empire was constantly in a state of tension and flux; it never settled down to stability under Athenian rule.

In concluding the Thirty Years' Peace Sparta abandoned the members of the Delian League to Athenian discretion. By now only the island cities of Samos, Chios and Lesbos still contributed ships to the federal fleet; hence they were somewhat more secure against Athenian interference than the other allies, who paid tribute. Most of the devices used by the Athenians to control their allies had been developed by 446. They included the dispatch of Athenian political officers to supervise or reform the affairs of an allied city; for example, the decree concerning Miletus orders the dispatch of five such officers, who are to work in conjunction with the local magistrates of Miletus. Sometimes after a revolt had been suppressed an Athenian garrison was sent; the decree concerning Erythrae mentions not only civil officers sent from Athens but also a garrison commander and implies that he was to stay in Erythrae for the future. Cleruchies, as has been seen, were established in the territory of allied cities, especially after unsuccessful revolts.

Sometimes the Athenians intervened in an allied city to modify its constitution. This practice is clearly illustrated by the decree about Erythrae, which sets up an annual Council of One Hundred and Twenty, chosen by lot; it was modeled on the Athenian Council of Five Hundred. To say, as has sometimes been said, that Athens fostered democracies in the allied cities amounts to little, since as noted above (p. 301) the word *demokratia* in the fifth century had emotive force but little empirical content. Athens may often have encouraged allied states to adopt institutions of Athenian type, but the real problem was more personal; within the political class of each city Athens had to ensure the ascendancy of those men who were willing to be her partisans. The Athenians encouraged their individual friends by passing decrees in their honor, especially decrees granting the honorific title of *proxenos*; sometimes this was a prelude to more material benefits, such as speedy procedure in Athenian courts.

Athens interfered in the judicial competence of allied states and the steps taken were designed to protect her partisans. Two policies call for note. First, cases of a particularly serious nature were transferred to Athenian courts. This is first attested in 446 in an amendment to the decree concerning Chalcis (chapter 10, pp. 292–294); this provides that in cases where the penalty is exile, death or loss of civic rights there shall be referral to an Athenian court. It is not clear whether the referral envisaged in the decree was compulsory or voluntary, that is, whether such cases had to be sent to the Athenian court for trial or could be sent there, for example, on appeal. Some later evidence associates the penalties of death, exile, loss of civic rights and confiscation of property, and in a speech of ca. 416–413 the orator Antiphon (5.47) says that no city has authority to put a man to death. Apparently the Athenians developed a doctrine which required referral of cases to Athens, if the major penalties were at stake; the decree about Chalcis may mark an early stage in this development. The second policy consisted in extending special protection to Athenian citizens and to friends of Athens in the allied cities. Several decrees honoring members of allied cities provide that, if the honorand is killed, the city where he dies shall pay a fine of five talents and prosecution shall follow the same procedure as when an Athenian citizen had been killed. Apparently a decree had been passed instituting special procedure, if an Athenian citizen was killed, and this privilege was extended to some citizens of allied states. The adoption of these two policies indicates the intense partisan strife waged between friends of Athens and their enemies in some at least of the cities.

At some time the Athenians passed a decree requiring the allies to use only Athenian coinage, weights and measures. Other coinage in circulation was to be brought to the mint at Athens and exchanged for Athenian coins. Inscribed copies of the decree were to be set up not only at Athens but in the market place of each city; fragments of the inscriptions have been found at several sites within the Empire and a composite text can be reconstructed. The date of the decree is far from clear. Aristophanes in *The Birds* seems to allude to its provisions. In the play a new city of the birds is set up in the sky; presently a seller of decrees arrives and offers, among others, a decree (lines 1040–41) providing that the good people of Cloudcuckooland shall use the same measures, weights and decrees as the citizens of Olophyxus (a small town on the Athos peninsula). *The Birds* was produced in 415/4; it might be inferred that the decree was still recent enough for people to make jokes about it. But in 1938 a fragment of the decree from Cos was published; unlike the fragments found elsewhere this was in Attic, not Ionic, letters. The letter sigma on the Cos fragment was formed of only three strokes, and this form is not certainly attested after 446. Consequently many people supposed that the Coinage Decree was passed not later than 446. Since 1960 criteria for dating fifth-century Athenian inscriptions by letter forms have been under reconsideration, and the Coinage Decree has played an important part in the argument. Agreement has not been reached, but two things may be said about the date of the Coinage Decree. First, except for sigma, the letter forms of the Cos fragment are those of the fully developed Attic alphabet; letters of this kind appear on Athenian inscriptions of the 430's and 420's as well as earlier. Second, an argument which seeks to date an inscription from the forms of its letters has little force if it relies on the form of only one letter.

The Coinage Decree speaks of Athenian supervisory officers as if they were commonly to be found in allied states. It provides that they are to enforce the Decree, and adds that, where there are no Athenian officers, the local magistrates of the cities shall enforce it. Likewise the decree of Cleinias about collecting tribute (chapter 10, pp. 285 and 287) speaks of Athenian officers as widespread, but its date is equally uncertain. It is possible that both decrees belong to the 420s and that Athens first sent out supervisory officers extensively after the Peloponnesian War began in 431. On the other hand, as Athens had to deal with widespread disaffection in the later years of the First Peloponnesian War, it is likely that Athenian officers were to be found in many cities of the Empire in the 440s.

Although no assessments have been recovered from the period when the

Thirty Years' Peace was observed (446/431), something can be learned about assessments from the quota lists. In the assessment of 446 the tribute required from at least thirty cities was reduced, while that of three cities was increased. The corresponding figures in the assessment of 450 were twenty-one reductions and five increases. Evidently in 446 Athens decreased the tribute of many cities in order to meet recalcitrance halfway. The records of quotas show less irregularity in the third assessment period (446/5–444/3) than in the second (450/49–447/6); once Athens had made peace with the Peloponnesian League, she was free to maintain discipline among her allies.

Assessments were usually held every four years in the year of the Greater Panathenaic festival, and so an assessment might be expected in 442. Several features of the ensuing quota lists indicate that the assessment was brought forward a year to 443. In the quota list for 443/2 the cities are grouped for the first time in geographical panels with headings; in the fourth assessment period (443/2–439/8) there are five such headings (Caria, Ionia, Hellespont, Thrace-ward, and Islands) and these headings are given in the same order in all the lists of the period. Again in the quota list for 443/2 the name of one of the hellenotamiae is recorded for the first time; so is the name of the assistant secretary, who remained in office in the next year. Opinions differ as to why the assessment was brought forward a year. Plutarch (*Per.* 13.11) says that Pericles carried a decree adding a competition in music to the Panathenaic festival and was himself chosen to preside at the competition. This probably refers to the Panathenaea of 442. Some have accordingly suggested that the Athenians planned to celebrate the festival of that year with especial splendor and therefore wished to have the business of assessment finished beforehand. The procedure of assessment is best known from the decree ordering that of 425, and in that year the assessment came several months later than the summer festival of the Panathenaea. So it may be that there was in any case no likelihood of a clash between the assessment and the festival, and an alternative suggestion is that the assessment was brought forward a year in order to carry out financial and administrative reorganization.

The assessment of 443 was similar in spirit to that of 446. In the new period (443/2–439/8) it is possible to recognize twelve more cities whose tribute was reduced; these reductions may have been carried out as early as 446. Generally the quota lists show that the years 446–440 were a period of consolidation; the lists have about the same number of cities each year and there is no certain indication of incomplete payments.

The quota lists for the eight years from 439/8 to 432/1 were inscribed on a single stele, which has come to be called "the second stele" as distinct from the one bearing the quota lists of 454/3–440/39. The second stele is very poorly preserved, especially for the lists of the middle 430s. Even so a little can be discerned about the assessments of 438 and 434. In particular, it is possible to recognize eight cities whose tribute was reduced and thirty whose tribute was increased; in at least twelve of the latter cases the increase marked a return to the level obtaining before 446. Apparently by 438 the Athenians felt that they were secure and could cease making concessions. On the other hand, it was not Athenian policy in the 430s to exact the utmost from the Empire; large increases in assessment were to come during the Archidamian War and especially in 425.

ATHENS AND WESTERN GREECE[3]

Until the 440s the Athenians showed an intermittent interest in the Greek cities of Sicily and south Italy. Themistocles named two of his daughters Italia and Sybaris; and when he fled from Argos to Corcyra, he may have considered traveling further west. Action by the Athenian state, not merely individual Athenians, can be inferred from three inscriptions, but dating is difficult. One of them gives an alliance made by the Athenians with Egesta in western Sicily. Only a small part of the inscription is preserved, and so the terms of alliance are not known. The text originally gave the name of the archon, but only its last two letters can be read with confidence; some epigraphers have claimed to discern parts of the two preceding letters and hence have assigned the alliance to the year when Habron was archon (458/7), but the traces are uncertain. The letter forms would allow a date within the First Peloponnesian War or perhaps a little later.

The other two inscriptions give alliances made by the Athenians with Leontini in Sicily and Rhegium in south Italy. In their preserved form these inscriptions belong to the year 433/2; the prescripts, or opening lines stating people who were in office or concerned in passing the decree, name the archon of that year. But in both inscriptions the prescripts are written in a different hand than the substantive provisions, which follow; in the alliance with Leontini the prescript uses somewhat later letter forms than the following lines; and in both inscriptions, where the present prescripts stand, something else was inscribed previously but was erased. These peculiarities have led to the hypothesis that the alliances with Leontini and Rhegium were made at an earlier date, perhaps in the 440s, and renewed in 433/2, but to emphasize the continuity of the old alliances the renewals were not inscribed separately but the prescripts were altered. The inscription concerning Egesta has somewhat older forms of the letters rho and sigma than the substantive provisions in the alliances with Rhegium and Leontini; even so the latter two alliances may be only a few years later than the alliance with Egesta. Possibly all three alliances were made within a few years of

444/3, when the Athenians took a major step in south Italy; it concerned the former city of Sybaris.

In the second half of the sixth century Sybaris and Croton, two Achaean colonies on the southeast coast of Italy, became prosperous rivals. Eventually in 510 the Crotoniates overcame and destroyed Sybaris; the surviving refugees settled in the small towns of Laus and Scidrus. In 452 their descendants formed a new settlement on the site of Sybaris, but a few years later they were again expelled by the Crotoniates. Thereupon they appealed to the Spartans and to the Athenians for additional settlers. The Athenians decided to respond; they gained a favorable oracle from Delphi, and they invited volunteers from the Peloponnese as well as from their own city. The expedition settled near the former site of Sybaris, founding the new colony of Thurii. Plutarch (*Per.* 11.5) includes this in his list of colonies initiated by Pericles. The two leaders of the settlement, Lampon and Xenocritus, were distinguished Athenian interpreters of omens and probably friends of Pericles. After a time strife developed in Thurii between the descendants of the Sybarites and the new settlers; the latter overcame their opponents and invited more settlers from Greece. But in spite of troubles the colony proved permanent. It did not, however, serve as an outpost of Athenian influence in the West but pursued a fully independent policy.

A little can be conjectured about Athenian motives for organizing the expedition to Thurii. Speculations about commercial interests can neither be confirmed nor refuted. Political aims can be discerned with more clarity. The invitation from the former Sybarites, especially when rejected by Lacedaemon, gave the Athenians an opportunity to pose as panhellenic leaders; it is significant that they invited settlers from the Peloponnese, where traditionally Spartan claims were strongest. It is likewise significant that several learned men from outside Athens played some part in developing the colony; among them were Herodotus the historian from Halicarnassus, Protagoras the sophist from Abdera, and Hippodamus the town planner from Miletus. The systematic plan of Thurii suggests that Hippodamus was present at its foundation. It is not clear whether Herodotus and Protagoras joined the colony at its foundation, as commonly assumed, or later.

ATHENS AND THE SAMIAN REVOLT[4]

By 442 the Athenians could believe that the Thirty Years' Peace had enabled them to stabilize control over the Empire. Tribute was coming in more regularly than in the years 454–446. Miletus is not recorded in the quota lists of the third assessment period (446/5–444/3), but it made regular payments in 443/2 and the years immediately following; Erythrae likewise is not recorded in List 9 (446/5) or List 10 (445/4), but appears with regular payments in List 11 (444/3) and the ensuing years. It may well be that disaffection had revived in these two cities towards the end of the First Peloponnesian War but was suppressed within a few years after Athens made peace with Sparta. The foundation of Thurii seems to reflect a mood when the Athenians were confident of attaining panhellenic leadership. The same outlook may be discerned in the celebration of the Panathenaic festival on an enlarged scale in 442.

Confidence or overconfidence appears in Athenian action taken at Samos in 441/0. Warfare had arisen between Samos and Miletus. There had been armed strife between these two cities in the time of Polycrates and even earlier. The issue in dispute towards 441 was control of the small town of Priene, which stood on the mainland between the two cities. This time the Athenians intervened in response to an appeal from Miletus. An Athenian force sailed to Samos; it altered the constitution, exacted 100 hostages and placed them in Lemnos, and installed a garrison in Samos. But some Samians escaped to the mainland and won the alliance of Pissuthnes, the satrap of Sardis. They raised 700 mercenaries, crossed to Samos by night and brought about a revolt of the island. The change in the constitution carried out by the Athenians was reversed; the revolutionaries recovered the hostages from Lemnos, and they handed over the Athenian garrison with the resident Athenian officers to Pissuthnes. They may have sought support from several cities in the Athenian Empire, but the only one to join them in revolt was Byzantium. The quota lists show that Byzantium paid tribute in 441/0, so the revolt must have begun shortly after the Dionysian festival of spring 440.

The Athenians responded by sending a force of sixty ships under Pericles and his fellow generals against Samos. Part of this force defeated the Samian fleet and began blockading the island. The operations continued into the winter of 440/39 and Samos surrendered in the ninth month of the siege. Several features illustrate the strengths and weaknesses of the Athenian position. Additional forces, first of forty and later of sixty ships, were sent out from Athens, so that the total Athenian fleet required to suppress the Samian Revolt was large. Chios and Lesbos also supplied squadrons, first of twenty-five and later of thirty ships, against the Samians. By 446 at the latest Chios, Lesbos and Samos were the only members of the Delian League, apart from Athens herself, who still supplied ships rather than paying tribute. It is noteworthy both that Samos rebelled, although she enjoyed this relatively privileged status, and that Chios and Lesbos did not sympathize with her. During the siege there were rumors that a Phoenician fleet was approaching, and at one stage Pericles sailed southwards with sixty ships to oppose it; this enabled the Samians to break through the blockade and keep their lines of supply open for about fourteen days. The Phoenician fleet did not appear, but the incident shows how uncertain the Greek belligerents were about Persian policy.

When the Samians yielded, Byzantium did likewise and returned to its former status. The Samians made terms, whereby they destroyed their fortifications, surrendered their fleet and gave hostages; they were to pay in installments an indemnity for the cost of the war. It is difficult to estimate the significance of the Samian Revolt in the development of the Athenian Empire, but two points call for note. First, although on intervening for Miletus the Athenians altered the Samian constitution, and although some Samians who escaped into exile prompted the Revolt, there is no trace of any divergence among the Samians during the operations. Apparently once the issue was finally joined, the Samians united in seeking independence of Athenian rule. Second, an allusion made by Thucydides (1.40.5) in another context shows that a congress of the Peloponnesian League met during the Revolt and considered whether to send help to Samos. Opinions among the Peloponnesian allies were divided, but the Corinthians spoke decisively against intervening; they argued that each of the major powers should be free to discipline its own allies. During the First Peloponnesian War Corinth had been bitterly opposed to Athens, but the settlement of 446 had appeased Corinthian fears, especially when Athenian forces were withdrawn from the Megarid.

ATHENS AND THE NORTHEAST[5]

While the Thirty Years' Peace was observed, the affairs of the north coast of the Aegean and of places further to the northeast repeatedly drew Athenian attention. The dates of some actions taken in this theater are uncertain and disputed. It will be best to begin from an event whose date is well attested.

In 437/6 the Athenians founded a colony at the site previously called the Nine Ways in the valley of the Strymon river. It was a little more than three miles from the mouth of the river. The Athenians had tried to found a colony at the same site in 465/4, but that force advanced further and was destroyed by Thracian tribes. The colony of 437/6 was called Amphipolis and established itself successfully as a permanent settlement. As its earlier name indicates, the site was valuable as the meeting point of numerous routes; some led up the valley of the Strymon into Macedon, others led into Chalcidice, and others led eastwards along the coast of Thrace. Amphipolis gave the Athenians access to supplies of ship timber from Macedon and perhaps from elsewhere. Thucydides (4.108.1) also remarks that it supplied Athens with monetary payments. Amphipolis is not recorded in the tribute quota lists, and so the nature of the financial payments is not known.

The foundation of Amphipolis has a bearing on the question of Athenian relations with Perdiccas, who became king of Macedon about the middle of the fifth century. Speaking of conditions in the winter of 433/2, Thucydides (1.57.2) says that by then Perdiccas was at war with the Athenians, although previously he had been their friend and ally. It is not clear when the former alliance came to an end. Possibly Amphipolis was founded at a time when relations were deteriorating; the Athenians may have considered that foundation a better safeguard for their interests than the friendship of Perdiccas.

Some light on Athenian policy in the northeast is thrown by an inscriptio᷉, preserving part of an Athenian decree for sending a colony to Brea. The extant part of the text provides for dispatching the colony and distributing the land to the settlers. It mentions some troops still away on a campaign and provides that they may become members of the colony if they reach Brea within thirty days of their return to Athens. An amendment orders that the settlers are to be drawn from the thetes and the zeugitae; thus the text shows that the Solonian property classes were still recognized in some form. Unfortunately both the location of Brea and the date of the decree are uncertain. The text merely shows that Brea was somewhere in the Thraceward district, one of the districts recognized by the Athenians in recording tribute and quota. A clue to the date has been sought in the reference to soldiers away on a campaign. They have often been identified with the men sent to suppress the Euboean Revolt in 446, and so a date ca. 445 has been suggested for the decree. Advocates of this view have drawn attention to Plutarch's list (*Per.* 11.5) of settlements attributed to Pericles; it includes a group of 1,000 settlers, sent to Thrace to territory near that of the Bisaltae, a Thracian tribe. Nothing is known of the later history of Brea; so on the same view, it is suggested that this colony was abandoned when Amphipolis was founded at a better site. An alternative theory identifies the soldiers away on a campaign with the men sent to suppress the Samian Revolt. Thus a date ca. 438 is suggested and adherents of this view have sought to locate Brea on the eastern shore of the Thermaic Gulf. The letter forms are compatible with either date. Perhaps the most interesting clause in the decree is one providing for defense of the colony, if attacked; aid is to be brought to it, evidently from cities of the neighborhood, "in accordance with the agreements." Thus the decree refers to agreements for defense as known; it indicates that the foundation of Brea was part of a comprehensive plan for defense of some part of the Thraceward district.

Athenian action much further afield in the northeast is known from Plutarch's account (*Per.* 20.1–2) of an expedition of Pericles to the Black Sea. There, as Plutarch puts it, he dealt favorably with the Greek cities but made a display of power to the barbarians. At Sinope he left a force of thirteen ships and some troops under Lamachus to support the opposition to the tyrant Timesileos.

When Timesileos and his associates were expelled, Pericles carried a decree by which 600 Athenian volunteers were to settle at Sinope and take over the land formerly held by the tyrants. Plutarch does not give the date of this expedition. Readers have often sought a date in the early 430s, since in 414 Lamachus was still young enough to die fighting in command of Athenian forces in Sicily. An alternative view would date the Pontic expedition of Pericles before the peace of Callias on the grounds that otherwise the expedition would be a breach of that agreement; but this argument assumes, not only that the peace of Callias is authentic, but also that the Athenians took care to observe its supposed terms. A date in the early 430s seems preferable for the Pontic expedition.

Attention should therefore be given to the kingdom of the Crimean Bosporus, which controlled territory in the Crimea and on both sides of the straits there. Its population was partly Greek and partly barbarian. In the fourth century the Athenians kept good relations with it; their interests demanded this, as much of their grain supply came from the area north of the Black Sea. Very little is known of its history before 438/7, when according to Diodorus (12.31.1) Spartocus founded a new dynasty. So one may conjecture that Pericles on his Pontic expedition sought to establish good relations with Spartocus. Against this hypothesis it must be admitted that Sinope was on the south coast of the Black Sea and Pericles is not known to have approached the northern shores.

THE BREAKDOWN OF THE PEACE[6]

In 431 the Athenians, with their Empire and some other allies, went to war against the Spartans, whose allies included states within and beyond the Peloponnese. The ensuing struggle, the Peloponnesian War (431–404), was interrupted by some years of peace after 421 but it may be said to have lasted twenty-seven years, until Athens was besieged and yielded, giving up her Empire. Thucydides set out to write the history of the war and he prefaced his narrative with an account of the causes. He introduced this account with the statement (1.23.5–6):

As for why they broke the treaty (sc. the Thirty Years' Peace), I have written down first the complaints and the disputes, so that no one may ever inquire whence so great a war arose among the Greeks. Now the most genuine cause, though least spoken of, was this: it was the Athenians, in my opinion, as they were growing great and furnishing an occasion of fear to the Lacedaemonians, who compelled the latter to go to war. But the complaints of each side, spoken of openly, were the following, complaints which led the parties to break the treaty and enter a state of war.

Thucydides's ambition of determining once and for all the causes of the war has not been achieved. The causes continue to be disputed. Opinions vary between two extremes. On the one hand, some historians claim that the war was the result of a long process, namely of the growth of Athenian power ever since 478 and of the Spartan response to that phenomenon; these historians sometimes claim support for their view in Thucydides's statement of "the most genuine cause." At the other extreme, some historians claim that war broke out as a result, perhaps unforeseen, of several incidents occurring and decisions taken in the second half of the 430s; these historians give primary attention to "the complaints and the disputes," as Thucydides calls them. The next step here will be to outline those incidents and the consequent diplomatic interchanges.

Epidamnus had been founded as a colony from Corcyra, probably in the time of Cypselus, and the *oikistes* had been drawn from Corinth (see above, chapter 2, p. 51). Civil strife came to a climax there in the 430s; one party was expelled and it joined the local barbarians in harrassing the city. So the Epidamnians of the city appealed to Corcyra for help and, when they were rebuffed there, they took their appeal to Corinth. In response the Corinthians, calling to mind old grievances against Corcyra, prepared to send additional settlers and troops to Epidamnus. The Corcyreans resented this interference; they sent a fleet to support the Epidamnian exiles and to besiege the city. Thereupon the Corinthians raised a fleet from themselves and their allies and sent it in the direction of Corcyra. The two fleets met off Leucimme, a promontory of Corcyra, in 435; the result of the battle was a severe defeat for Corinth. On the same day the city of Epidamnus surrendered to the force besieging it.

The traditional friction between Corinth and Corcyra had been a small matter; unlike other colonies, Corcyra did not grant perquisites to Corinthians at festivals. Through the battle of Leucimme the conflict was raised to a new scale and it was to be enlarged still further. The Corinthians were unwilling to accept the defeat as final; they spent 434 and much of the next year building ships and gathering rowers from the Peloponnese and other parts of Greece. So the Corcyreans, fearing a new and larger expedition, sent an embassy to Athens to seek an alliance (433). The Corinthians sent a counter-embassy to dissuade the Athenians from helping Corcyra. The Athenians held two meetings of the assembly to consider the question. At the first they were as much persuaded by the Corinthians as by the Corcyreans. At the second they still refused to make an offensive and defensive alliance with Corcyra or, in Greek terms, an agreement to have the same friends and enemies, for this could obligate them to join the Corcyreans in an attack on Corinth and thereby break the Thirty Years' Peace; but they made a defensive alliance, requiring each party to come to the aid of the other, if it was attacked. Shortly afterwards the Athenians sent a force to Corcyra, but it consisted of only ten ships and it had instructions not to fight the Corinthians unless they threatened Corcyrean territory directly.

A large fleet, drawn from Corinth and her allies, proceeded towards Corcyra in 433. The Corcyrean fleet, together with the ten Athenian ships, engaged it in battle among the Sybota islands near the mainland opposite the southern end of Corcyra. As the fighting proceeded, the Athenian ships joined in the action. For a considerable time the Corinthians seemed likely to win; in particular, their left wing put the corresponding part of the Corcyrean line to flight. But late in the day twenty more ships from Athens approached the scene of fighting; the Athenians had decided that the original ten ships were too few for their task. The Corinthians, however, thought that the twenty ships were the vanguard of a larger force, and they retreated; on the next day they prepared to sail home. Thus although Athenian participation in the engagement was slight, it converted a probable Corinthian victory into an indecisive battle.

In the winter of 433/2 another incident developed and this time Athenian provocation was more apparent. The trouble concerned Poteidaea, which held the isthmus of Pallene, the westernmost promontory of the Chalcidice peninsula. Poteidaea was a colony of Corinth and it received supervisory magistrates from the mother city at regular intervals. It was also a member of the Delian League and paid tribute to Athens. Thus it was a place where Athenian and Peloponnesian claims might clash. In the winter of 433/2 the Athenians sent the Poteidaeans an ultimatum; they were required to dismantle the part of their fortifications facing Pallene, to give hostages, and to exclude the Corinthian supervisory magistrates. The Poteidaeans are recorded in the tribute quota list as paying tribute for 433/2 and indeed at a higher figure than usual. But rather than comply with the ultimatum they sent envoys to Corinth; the envoys proceeded with some Corinthians to Sparta and gained some assurance from the Lacedaemonians that these would invade Attica, if the Athenians attacked Poteidaea. Then Poteidaea rebelled against Athens, apparently some little time after the date in the spring of 432 when the tribute was due.

The Poteidaeans were encouraged in their resistance to Athens by Perdiccas, king of Macedon. At an earlier time the Athenians had had an alliance with him but subsequently they alienated him by supporting his rivals in Macedon (see above, p. 312). In the crucial winter of 433/2 an Athenian force of thirty ships and 1,000 hoplites under Archestratus was operating against Perdiccas. The latter accordingly encouraged the Poteidaean revolt; he also urged the cities of Chalcidice and their neighbors, the Bottiaeans, to rebel against Athens. When Poteidaea rebelled, some at least of the cities of Chalcidice joined the revolt and, with the encouragement of Perdiccas, set up a federal state with its capital at Olynthus. The Corinthians responded to the revolt of the Poteidaeans by sending a force, including 1,600 hoplites, under Aristeus to help them. The Athenians, however, sent 2,000 hoplites and forty ships under Callias to operate against Perdiccas and the rebels. Callias joined forces with Archestratus, maneuvered in Macedon and then proceeded against Poteidaea; he defeated the Poteidaeans outside their town and began besieging it from the side where the isthmus lay. Later the Athenians sent reinforcements under Phormion; he completed the blockade of Poteidaea by investing it from the side of Pallene.

These developments throw some light on Athenian plans. During his long reign Perdiccas (ca. 450–413) tried to strengthen his kingdom against pretenders within and against the Athenians, who threatened his approaches to the sea. After the Athenians had broken their original alliance with him, the story of their relations was complex; agreements were made and broken repeatedly. By the winter of 433/2 it was clearly in the interests of the Athenians to reach a definitive settlement with Perdiccas before attempting any new venture in the neighborhood of his kingdom. Their ultimatum to Poteidaea was a new and provocative enterprise, which brought opportunities to Perdiccas. It seems to follow that that ultimatum was not the result of a longstanding and well considered plan for safeguarding Athenian interests in the northeastern part of the Aegean. It is more likely that Athenian counsels were divided; that is, the original dispatch of Archestratus to deal with Macedon may have been brought about by one group, but the ultimatum to Poteidaea was probably brought about by another group pursuing a different policy.

Spartan counsels too were divided. In the winter of 433/2, after the ultimatum had been issued, envoys from Poteidaea and Corinth came to Sparta and received some assurance that the Lacedaemonians would invade Attica if the Athenians attacked Poteidaea. Thucydides (1.58.1) says vaguely that "the authorities" gave this assurance. The ensuing developments show that those authorities did not have power to commit Lacedaemon. After Callias had defeated the Poteidaeans and the siege of Poteidaea had begun, the Corinthians complained to Sparta. Complaints against Athens were received from other allies too. The Spartans accordingly called a meeting of their public assembly; it heard speeches by some of the allies, by an Athenian embassy, and by some Spartans. Then the presiding ephor, Sthenelaidas, formulated the issue in a tendentious way; those, he said, who thought that the Thirty Years' Peace had been broken and that the Athenians were committing injustice were to go to one side, and those who thought otherwise were to go to the other. A large majority of the voters were of the opinion that the Thirty Years' Peace had been broken.

This decision of the Spartan assembly did not lead to immediate military action, and the subsequent delays confirm the inference that Spartan counsels were divided. The meeting of the Spartan assembly took place sometime in the summer of 432, and in consequence of the vote the Spartans invited their allies to send envoys to a congress of the Peloponnesian League. The congress met at

Sparta in about the fall of the year and voted by a majority in favor of going to war. Thereafter military preparations took some time; after giving the vote of the congress Thucydides (1.125.2) comments: "A year did not pass by but less, before the Peloponnesians invaded Attica and openly went to war."

So far some conclusions emerge from this summary of "the complaints and the disputes," as Thucydides calls them. Athenian opinion was divided. When the Athenians allied with Corcyra, they seized the chance to secure a power of naval value for their side, but they showed some caution in making the alliance and following it up. But by the time when they sent their ultimatum to Poteidaea, a decidedly provocative attitude was beginning to prevail among them. Spartan views too were divided, but a significant element, which found a spokesman in Sthenelaidas, was willing to respond to Athenian provocation in a manner at least equally belligerent. There is no indication of any division among the Corinthians. Because of their maritime interests they were the one among the allies of Sparta whom the Athenians could injure most readily. It does not follow, as has sometimes been claimed, that the Athenian quarrel was with Corinth, not Sparta, and that Corinth dragged a reluctant Sparta into war; when Sthenelaidas formulated the issue for the assembled Spartans to vote on, the feeling he expressed was not mere solicitude for an ally.

Other allies of Sparta, besides Corinth, had grievances against Athens, and these deserve some attention. When the Spartans called a meeting of the assembly in the summer of 432, some Aeginetans complained privately that the Athenians had infringed their autonomy in contravention of the Thirty Years' Peace. It has been conjectured that Athens had stationed a garrison in Aegina, but there can be no certainty. More can be said about a complaint which the Megarians presented on the same occasion; the Athenians had passed a decree excluding them from the Athenian market place and from the harbors of the Athenian Empire. Thucydides mentions this decree again (1.139.1), when he relates the diplomatic interchanges which followed between Athens and Sparta in the winter of 432/1 after the congress of the Peloponnesian League; at one stage Lacedaemonian envoys bade the Athenians raise the siege of Poteidaea and respect the autonomy of Aegina, and above all they insisted that there would be no war if the Athenians repealed the decree about Megara.

Thus Thucydides gives repeal of the Megara decree as the chief demand in a Spartan ultimatum. The reader may infer that this was the issue most discussed in Athens in the weeks immediately preceding the outbreak of war. Other sources confirm this impression. Aristophanes in *The Acharnians*, a play produced early in 425, alludes (lines 515–539) to the Megara decree as if it were the sole cause of the war. It is not the business of comedy to weigh historical issues but to make jokes; even so this joke is some indication of popular belief. The fourth-century historian Ephorus treated the Megara decree as the main cause of the Peloponnesian War. Thucydides on the other hand gives far less attention to the Megara decree than to the incidents concerning Corcyra and Poteidaea. Was he overreacting to popular exaggeration of the dispute about Megara, or was his assessment just?

More could be said about the significance of the Megara decree if its antecedents were known. Two possibilities deserve attention. One hypothesis would attribute the passing of the decree to strictly political motives. When relations between Athens and Sparta broke down in the late 460s, the Athenians won the alliance of Megara and were consequently in a position to threaten Corinth and Boeotia. It is suggested that the aim of the Megara decree was to force Megara into alliance with Athens; thus Athens might regain the strategic advantage which she held during most of the First Peloponnesian War. An alternative hypothesis can be offered on the basis of some entries in the tribute quota lists. In the lists of 435/4–429/8 some cities appear under headings indicating that they volunteered to pay tribute. The headings include, for example, "unassessed cities," "cities which assessed themselves of their own accord," and "cities which individuals recorded as paying tribute." The cities appearing under these headings were neither numerous nor intrinsically important. It has accordingly been suggested that in the 430s Athens adopted a policy of inflicting commercial disadvantages on cities which were not members of the Empire. The cities which volunteered to pay tribute would be a small byproduct of this policy, and the Megara decree might be its culmination.

Apart from the disputes about Corcyra, Poteidaea and Megara there may have been others. In another context Thucydides (2.68) mentions troubles arising at the town of Amphilochian Argos on the Gulf of Ambracia. The Amphilochians admitted some people from Ambracia as joint settlers in their town and hence became hellenized. But after a time the Ambraciote settlers expelled the Amphilochians from Argos. So the Amphilochians of the district gained the alliance of their Greek neighbors, the Acarnanians, and these two powers appealed to the Athenians for help. The Athenians sent them thirty ships under the command of Phormion. Directing the combined forces, Phormion captured Argos and "enslaved" its Ambraciote inhabitants, that is, he killed the men and sold the women and children into slavery. This was a severe measure and likely to offend Corinth, since Ambracia was a Corinthian colony. Thucydides does not say when Phormion's intervention took place. Dates suggested vary from ca. 437 to 432, but arguments for each date are inconclusive, since they are drawn from silence, that is, from the failure of Thucydides to mention the incident in passages where one might expect it.

Some historians have thought that particular disputes, such as those concerning Poteidaea and Megara, do not account adequately for the outbreak of the Peloponnesian War and they have looked for a more comprehensive cause. They have been influenced by their understanding of Thucydides's statement about the causes of the war. Thucydides (above, p. 313) distinguishes "the most genuine cause" from "the complaints and the disputes," and many readers have thought that his statement of "the most genuine cause" simply specified the growth of Athenian power and the fear felt by the Spartans in consequence; A.W. Gomme, for example, wrote (*Comm.* 1.152): "the main cause of the war was Athenian imperialism and Spartan fear of her rival." It can indeed be argued that Thucydides in stating "the most genuine cause" meant something more precise, that he constructed his sentence in such a way as to attribute responsibility to the Athenians, and that his judgement must be understood in the light of contemporary views which stressed the Spartan share in responsibility. But at least his statement of "the most genuine cause" mentioned the growth of Athenian power and the Spartan response to this. Somewhat later in his account he returns to this theme. After recounting the disputes about Corcyra and Poteidaea and the meeting of the Spartan assembly, he says (1.88) that the Lacedaemonians voted as they did "not so much because they were persuaded by the arguments of their allies as because they feared lest the power of the Athenians might grow greater, for they saw that the greater part of Greece was already subject to them." To support this view Thucydides inserts a digression (1.89–118), which summarizes the way Athenian power had grown since 479.

Moreover, the present question is not what Thucydides thought about the causes of the war but what the actual causes were. Even if Thucydides had not alluded to the growth of Athenian power in discussing the causes, it could be maintained that the war was caused by Athenian imperialism and the Spartan response to this. Holders of such a view can point to the growth of Athenian power in the first two decades of the Delian League and they can cite plentiful illustrations of Athenian dynamism in the First Peloponnesian War, especially in its opening years. Against this view it has been objected that Athenian power did not grow much in the period 445–435. After the conclusion of the Thirty Years' Peace Athenian policy appears to have aimed at consolidation rather than further expansion, and in this period the Peloponnesians showed little fear of Athens, as their failure to intervene in the Samian War testifies.

Some judgement on the causes of the Peloponnesian War may be reached by approaching the problem from another angle. Thucydides's history of the Peloponnesian War is a model of impartiality, but it is written from an Athenian point of view, and since all subsequent studies draw heavily on it, the war has come to be called "The Peloponnesian War;" had its history been written from a Spartan point of view, it would be called "The Athenian War." Correspondingly, inquiries into its causes tend to become inquiries into Athenian behavior; the attempt is made to trace changes in Athenian policy and to find which actions of the Athenians brought about war. But an inquiry into Spartan policy is equally legitimate, although there is far less evidence; one may ask what actions of the Spartans led to war. The question is especially appropriate because the Spartans were technically the aggressors. When the Spartan assembly met in the summer of 432, Thucydides says that an Athenian embassy was present and in its speech to the Spartans it offered to submit the matters in dispute to arbitration (1.78.4). The first military action of the war was an attack by the Thebans on Plataea (see below, chapter 12, p. 325), and in this the allies of Sparta behaved as the aggressors.

Accordingly, some importance attaches to the stated war aims of the Spartans. As already noted, in the winter of 432/1 the two sides exchanged a series of embassies and recriminations. The last Spartan embassy coming to Athens delivered a brief message, saying: "The Lacedaemonians desire peace, and there would be peace if you would let the Greeks go as autonomous states." The Greek word "autonomous" was ambiguous, but in this context the Spartan ultimatum seems to be a demand that the Athenians should disband their Empire and thereby restore full independence to their allies. Elsewhere Thucydides (2.8.4), explaining the resources of both sides at the beginning of operations, remarks: "There was much more good will towards the Lacedaemonians, especially because they had proclaimed that they were freeing the Greeks." In short, the Spartans voiced an intention of destroying the Athenian Empire, and they achieved this in 404. This amounts to saying that the Spartan war aims were unlimited.

A distinction may be drawn between "wars for limited objectives" and "total wars." In the Samian War, for example, the Athenians pursued the limited objective of bringing Samos back into their Empire; they did not seek to destroy the Samian state. But in a "total war" one side at least seeks to destroy the other as a political entity; in the Peloponnesian War the Spartans sought to destroy the Athenian Empire, although they let Athens survive. In the case of a "war for limited objectives" the historian can hope to specify causes with some precision; he begins his inquiry from the stated war aims. But in a "total war" stated war aims are vague and comprehensive and they are not intended to limit the actions of their author. So the historian can only say that such a war was caused by the whole situation preceding it.

Attention can be drawn to some of the factors in the situation preceding the Peloponnesian War. On the Athenian side it is admittedly correct to observe that for some time after concluding the Thirty Years' Peace the Athenians tried to consolidate the Empire rather than expand it. Even so, they pursued a forward policy on some occasions, for example, in the founding of Amphipolis and in Phormion's intervention at Amphilochian Argos; likewise in 433/2 they renewed their alliances with Rhegium and Leontini. In the late 430s their attitude grew more provocative; although they showed some hesitation in accepting the Corcyrean alliance, they were intransigent in issuing the ultimatum to Poteidaea and in passing the Megara decree. On the Spartan side a miscalculation contributed to the outbreak of war. In 446 the Athenians had yielded and made peace when a Peloponnesian force reached the plain of Eleusis and thus threatened the rest of Attica. Some Spartans must have believed in 432 that the same threat would produce the same effect again, and from 431 until 425 the Peloponnesians invaded Attica almost every year; but although these raids did extensive material damage, they had very little effect on the outcome of the war. Thus one factor contributing to Spartan confidence in 432 was an exaggerated estimate of the effects they could achieve by invading Attica. In other respects little can be said about the views held in Sparta in the 430s; and that is the main reason why the situation precipitating the war remains to a large extent opaque.

NOTES

1. For recent studies of the Athenian political scene in the fifth century see W.R. Connor, *The New Politicians of Fifth-Century Athens* (Princeton 1971); F.J. Frost, "Pericles, Thucydides, son of Melesias, and Athenian Politics before the War," *Historia* 13 (1964) 385-399; idem, "Pericles and Dracontides," *JHS* 84 (1964) 69-72; Sealey, *Essays* 59-74 = "The Entry of Pericles into History," *Hermes* 84, (1956) 234-247. On payment for jury service see Ar. *AP* 27.3; schol. Aristoph. *Wasps* 88 and 300; Theopompus, *F.Gr.Hist.* IIB 115F89, cf. Plut. *Per.* 9.2-3. On the generalship and the abandonment of the tribal rule about candidacy see C.W. Fornara, *The Athenian Board of Generals from 501 to 404* = Historia Einzelschriften Heft 16 (Wiesbaden 1971). The prestige won by tenure of the generalship is known from Aeschin. 1.27; competition for election is attested by Xen. *Mem.* 3.4.1. On the concept of *demokratia* see Sealey, "The Origins of *demokratia*," *CSCA* 6 (1973) 253-295. On the building of the third Long Wall see Gomme, *Comm.* 1.312. On the Parthenon, the cult statue of Athena and the Propylaea see Meiggs/Lewis 54, 59 and 60. On the family ties of Pericles see Table D.

2. On the methods used by the Athenians to maintain control over their allies see Meiggs, *AE* 205-233. On Athenian interference with allied jurisdiction see G.E.M. de Ste. Croix, "Notes on Jurisdiction in the Athenian Empire," *CQ* N.S. 11 (1961) 94-112 and 268-280. On Athenian decrees protecting individual persons in allied cities see R. Meiggs, "A Note on Athenian Imperialism," *CR* 63 (1949) 9-12. Some historians, supposing that Athens fostered democracies in the allied cities and that democracy was the rule of the poor, have tried to explain the conflicts in the Empire as a class struggle; Athens, they hold, promoted the rule of the many poor, called democracy, and her opponents worked for the rule of the wealthy few, called oligarchy. The classic statement of this view is G.E.M. de Ste. Croix, "The Character of the Athenian Empire," *Historia* 3 (1954) 1-41. There have been many subsequent discussions; important criticisms of Ste. Croix's

view were offered by D.W. Bradeen, "The Popularity of the Athenian Empire," *Historia* 9 (1960) 257–269. The Coinage Decree is accessible as Meiggs/Lewis 45. From the extensive bibliography on its date and on the dating value of letter forms the following selection is recommended: H.B. Mattingly, "The Athenian Coinage Decree," *Historia* 10 (1961) 148–188; idem, Periclean Imperialism, *Ehrenberg Studies* 193–224; W.K. Pritchett, "The Koan Fragment of the Monetary Decree," *BCH* 89 (1965) 423–440; R. Meiggs, "The Dating of Fifth-century Attic Inscriptions," *JHS* 86 (1966) 86–98. On increases and decreases in assessment of tribute see Meiggs, *AE* 234–254 and 524–530. The decree ordering a new assessment in 425 is accessible as Meiggs/Lewis 69.

3. For the daughters of Themistocles see Plut. *Them.* 32.2. Suggestions about his goal in fleeing west are offered by Meiggs, *AE* 81. For the alliances with Egesta, Rhegium and Leontini see Meiggs/Lewis 37, 63 and 64. On the destruction of Sybaris see Hdt. 5.44; 6.21. The fullest narrative of the foundation of Thurii is given by Diod. 11.90.3–4 and 12.10–11. The date of foundation is known from Pseudo-Plut. *Mor.* 835d. Strabo (6.1.13.263) says that Athenians took part in the settlement at Sybaris of 452; this may rest on confusion with the later foundation at Thurii, but it is not unlikely that the Athenians took an interest in the district even before 444/3. That Lampon and Xenocritus were friends of Pericles can probably be inferred from Plut. *Per.* 6.2–3 and Anon. *Life of Thucydides* 7. On the connection of Herodotus with Thurii see Suda s.v. Herodotus; cf. F. Jacoby, *RE* Supplement II (1913) 205–209 and 224–229. For the connection of Protagoras with Thurii see Diog. Laert. 9.8.50; for that of Hippodamus see Hesychius and Photius s.v. *Hippodamou nemesis*. A stimulating theory about Athenian political conflicts leading to the foundation of Thurii was propounded by Wade-Gery, *Essays* 239–270 = "Thucydides the son of Melesias JHS 52 (1932) 205–227; it was criticized by V. Ehrenberg, "The Foundation of Thurii," *AJP* 69 (1948) 149–170 and Gomme, *Comm.* 1.386–387.

4. The main source of information on the Samian Revolt is Thuc 1.115.2–1.117.3. Earlier conflicts between Samos and Miletus are known from Hdt. 3.39.4; 5.99.1. For discussion of Samos and the Revolt see Meiggs, *AE* 188–194 and R.P. Legon, "Samos in the Delian League," *Historia* 21 (1972) 145–158; Legon makes the important point that there is no indication of any divergence of policy among the Samians once the Revolt had begun. Athenian documents bearing on the Revolt and settlement are to be found as Meiggs/Lewis 55 and 56.

5. The most informative text on the foundation of Amphipolis is Thuc. 4.102; the date is given by schol. Aeschin. 2.31. A fragmentary inscription, *I.G.*I²,71, gives an Athenian alliance with Perdiccas and other Macedonians, but dates suggested for it vary between ca. 436 and 423/2; see Meiggs, *AE* 428–430. The decree about Brea is accessible as Meiggs/Lewis 49; a date ca. 438 was proposed by A.G. Woodhead, "The Site of Brea: Thucydides I.61.4," *CQ* N.S. 2 (1952) 57–62. The death of Lamachus is given by Thuc. 6.101.6. The date of Pericles's Pontic expedition is discussed by Meiggs, *AE* 197–199. Athenian relations with the kingdom of the Crimean Bosporus in the fourth century are illustrated by Tod 2.167.

6. Thucydides gives the incidents concerning Corcyra and Poteidaea at 1. 24–66, the meeting of the Spartan assembly at 1.67–88, the congress of the Peloponnesian League at 1.119–125, and the diplomatic interchanges of the winter of 432/1 at 1.126–146. He mentions Athenian willingness to submit the disputes to arbitration at 1.78.4; 1.85.2; 1.140.2; 1.145. At 7.18.2 he indicates that the Spartans considered themselves the aggressors. On the chronology of the disputes about Corcyra and Poteidaea see Gomme, *Comm.* 1.196–198 and 222–224. Ephorus's view of the cause of the war is known from Diod. 12.38.1–12.41.1; cf. Plut. *Per.* 29–33. Plutarch gives an account of the events leading to the Megara decree, but its validity has been challenged by W.R. Connor, "Charinus' Megarian Decree," *AJP* 83 (1962) 225–246; it has been defended by G.L. Cawkwell, "Anthemocritus and the Megarians and the Decree of Charinus," *REG* 82 (1969) 327–335. The rubrics

indicating that some states volunteered to pay tribute have been studied by F. A. Lepper, "Some Rubrics in the Athenian Quota-Lists," *JHS* 82 (1962) 25–55; his conclusions are discussed by Meiggs, *AE* 249–252. Renewal of the alliances with Rhegium and Leontini is known from Meiggs/Lewis 63 and 64. An extensive discussion of views on the causes of the war is provided by D. W. Kagan, *The Outbreak of the Peloponnesian War* (Ithaca, N.Y. 1969) 345–374; Kagan rests his own thesis largely on recognition that Athenian power did not grow between 445 and 435. Two financial decrees, proposed by Callias (Meiggs/Lewis 58) have often been dated 434/3 and they can be understood to show that Athens was already preparing for war (cf. Meiggs, *AE* 200–201); but their date is uncertain; a later date has been defended by C. W. Fornara, "The Date of the Callias Decrees," *GRBS* 11 (1970) 185–196. Discussions of Thucydides's views are numerous; mention may be made of A. Andrewes, "Thucydides and the Causes of the War," *CQ* N.S. 9 (1959) 223–239. G. E. M. de Ste. Croix, *The Origins of the Peloponnesian War* (Ithaca, N.Y. 1972), presents a complex thesis with great erudition; his chief claims are (1) that the war was due solely to Peloponnesian aggression, Athenian behavior being constantly correct, and (2) that in passing the Megara decree the Athenians had no ulterior motives but were guided solely by concern for the sacred land of Eleusis, on which the Megarians had allegedly encroached; for criticism and for further discussion of Thucydides's ideas see R. Sealey, "The Causes of the Peloponnesian War," *CP* 70 (1975) 89–109. Divergent dates for Phormion's intervention at Amphilochian Argos are suggested by *ATL* 3.320 note 84 and Meiggs, *AE* 204.

Table D: The family ties of Pericles

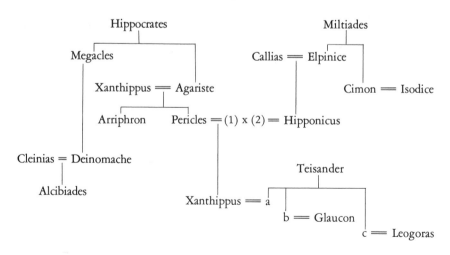

The main sources are: Hdt. 6.131.2; Plut. *Cim.* 4.8; 4.10; 16.1; *Per.* 24.8; 36.2; *Alc.* 1.1–2; Andoc. 1.177–120; Nep. *Cim.* 1.3–4; Athen. 13.589e. For discussion see Davies, *APF* 9–22, 254–270, 455–460.

12

The Archidamian War
and the Peace of Nicias

Thucydides (5.26) argued that the fighting of twenty-seven years from 431 to 404 should be regarded as a single war, and so it has come to be called the Peloponnesian War. Like most of the opinions he expressed, his argument sought to correct contemporary belief. The hostilities which began in the spring of 431 were brought to an end by a treaty made in the spring of 421 and now commonly called the peace of Nicias; *prima facie* these ten years of fighting constituted a distinct war, which is known as the Archidamian War after the Spartan king Archidamus, who was alive in its opening years. Contemporaries of Thucydides indeed regarded those ten years as a distinct war, and since he himself expressed his own view not in the preface but in the middle of his work, it may be presumed that he only reached that view after he had written a good deal of his account. His view rested on his recognition that the peace of Nicias was from the start insecure and bound to collapse. Here accordingly the fighting of the Archidamian War will be sketched in summary fashion; the main question of interest is, Why did the belligerents eventually make peace? Then attention will be given to the question, Why did the peace of Nicias break down?

In the situation of 431 it was difficult for either of the leading protagonists to inflict a decisive defeat on the other. Sparta had an excellent land force and could call out the contingents of her allies; she led Peloponnesian invasions of Attica every year from 431 to 425 except in 429 and 426. In 431, when the Peloponnesian forces approached for the first time, the Athenians withdrew within the fortifications of the city, the Peiraeus and the Long Walls, and they adopted the same measure of defense during the subsequent raids. The Peloponnesians did not try to carry the fortifications by assault and could not entice the Athenians into battle; so although the invasions inflicted large material losses, they had little effect on the outcome of the war. Only a major concentration of naval power could overcome the Athenians; and although some members of the Peloponnesian League, notably Corinth, had considerable fleets, the Athenians were their superiors in numbers of triremes and skill of maneuvering.

For land strategy the Athenian situation in 431 was not nearly as strong as in 460. At the earlier date the Athenians had the alliance of Megara and hence commanded the route leading southwards to the Isthmus and northwards to Boeotia. Possibly the aim of the Megara decree (chapter 11, pp. 317–318) was to force Megara into alliance with Athens, but if so, it was not successful; the Peloponnesians took the precaution of installing a garrison in Nisaea, the harbor of Megara on the Saronic Gulf. In 431 the Athenians made a major raid on the Megarid; later they raided the Megarid twice each year. Finally in 424 two Athenian generals took advantage of civil disputes within Megara and, opening negotiations with a party in the city, they launched a plot to capture it; but their attempt was checked by Peloponnesian reinforcements and they succeeded only in capturing Nisaea. Since the Athenians did not hold Megara, for the opening years of the Archidamian War they adopted a defensive strategy, which Thucydides makes Pericles expound. Its principles were, first, that the Athenians should withdraw within their fortifications and not give battle in Attica, and second, that they should use their naval resources to keep control of their allies. Athenian difficulties were increased by an outbreak of plague in Athens in 430; this caused heavy losses, and the Athenians sent an embassy to Sparta, but it did not achieve peace. The epidemic returned in the winter of 427/6. It is remarkable that Athenian morale was resilient enough to continue the war and keep to a defensive strategy in Attica in spite of the invasions and the sickness. But although the Athenians made maritime raids on the Peloponnese, the defensive strategy adopted in the early years of the war could not inflict a decisive defeat on the enemy; by such a strategy the Athenians could at most hope to hold out until the other side tired of fighting.

The major power which achieved a gain early in the war was Thebes. In Boeotia a confederacy had been restored in consequence of the successful revolt of 447/6 against Athenian control, but Plataea resisted incorporation. Early in the spring of 431, before hostilities had begun elsewhere, a party of Thebans made a surprise attack on Plataea by night; helped by traitors within the town, they entered the gates, but they were overcome. The Athenians responded by sending supplies and troops to Plataea. The Thebans continued operations and had support from their Peloponnesian allies; in particular in 429 the Peloponnesians, instead of invading Attica, marched to Plataea and began a complete blockade. The Plataeans held out for a long time, but Athens sent inadequate support, and in 427 the Plataeans surrendered. The Lacedaemonians yielded to the demands of their Theban allies and executed the captives. About a year later they destroyed the town.

EARLY THEATERS OF WARFARE[2]

The development of the Archidamian War can best be understood by tracing the fighting in the different theaters of warfare. In particular, a distinction should be drawn between theaters where the belligerents had already begun operations when war broke out and those where they first committed forces later. By 431 the Athenians and the Peloponnesians had already come into conflict in Corcyrean waters; the Athenians had helped the Acarnanians and Amphilochians at Argos against the Ambraciotes (chapter 11, p. 318); and the two sides had fought in Chalcidice, particularly at Poteidaea.

Corcyra, which had a valuable fleet, was an ally of Athens at the beginning of the war. But at the battle of Sybota in 433 (chapter 11, p. 315) the Corinthians had captured and kept 250 Corcyreans as prisoners; they trained these men for subversion and later restored them to Corcyra, professedly in return for bail. The returned prisoners sought to bring the alliance with Athens to an end, and the consequent conflict developed into civil war by 427. The troubles continued for several years; both Athenian and Peloponnesian forces intervened. Eventually in 425 the one side with the help of an Athenian fleet destroyed its enemies, and nothing more is heard of internal strife in Corcyra until 410. From the Athenian point of view the troubles in Corcyra meant that Athens was not able to draw on the naval resources of that ally during the Archidamian War.

For operations in the Corinthian Gulf and further towards the northwest the Athenians had a naval base at Naupactus; they had captured it towards the beginning of the First Peloponnesian War and they had installed a settlement of Messenian refugees there. In 430 the Ambraciotes attacked Amphilochian Argos unsuccessfully. In 429 in response to an Ambraciote request a Peloponnesian force together with allies from Epirus and other places in the north invaded Acarnania, but the Acarnanians drove them out. This led to complex fighting in the northwestern theater. In 426 an Athenian force under Demosthenes invaded Aetolia but was driven out and suffered considerable losses. In the fall a Pelo-

Aerial view of the lower Strymon. [Courtesy W.K. Pritchett.]

ponnesian force joined the Aetolians and they advanced against Naupactus, but Demosthenes gained help from the Acarnanians and secured that crucial position. In the ensuing winter the Ambraciotes and the Peloponnesian force made an attack on Amphilochian Argos; but Demosthenes, commanding troops from the Acarnanians and the Amphilochians, defeated the enemy in two battles. The survivors of the Peloponnesian force withdrew, and the Ambraciotes lost so heavily that their city could have been captured easily, but the Acarnanians and Amphilochians did not want it to come under Athenian control. Indeed, shortly after Demosthenes set off on his return to Athens, the Acarnanians and Amphilochians made a treaty of peace and alliance with Ambracia; they did not want Athens to achieve predominance in their neighborhood.

Warfare in Chalcidice proved to be even more unfortunate for the Athenians. The siege of Poteidaea, begun in 432, lasted until the winter of 430/29, when the inhabitants ran short of food and surrendered; by the terms of the capitulation they could leave their city, taking with them a limited amount of clothing and money. Soon afterwards the Athenians sent a colony to Poteidaea. But some cities of Chalcidice remained in revolt; at Spartolus in 429 they defeated an Athenian force sent against them. There was little further change in the situation until 424, when the Chalcidian League (chapter 11, pp. 315–316) and Perdiccas invited Sparta to send them military support. It was difficult for the Spartans to send troops to Chalcidice, since the Athenians controlled the sea, but the problem was solved by Brasidas, the outstandingly brilliant Spartan commander of the Archidamian War. Brasidas raised an army of hoplites, drawing them partly from the helots and partly from Peloponnesian mercenaries, and led them by land to Chalcidice. The bulk of the Thessalians favored the Athenian cause, but Brasidas enjoyed the friendship of some leading men of Thessaly and, to avoid hindrances, he led his men across the territory by forced marches. He was joined by Chalcidian troops and he approached Acanthus; partly by threatening the city's crops and partly by undertaking not to interfere in its internal affairs, he persuaded the Acanthians to join him. Shortly afterwards Stagirus joined him and in the ensuing winter he won over Amphipolis and several Chalcidic cities. The loss of Amphipolis was especially bitter to the Athenians; it had supplied them with valuable revenues and with ship timber, and it controlled routes into Macedon and along the coast of Thrace. Although Brasidas had difficulty in maintaining relations with Perdiccas and although the Athenians sent forces to try to recover parts of Chalcidice, Brasidas continued his operations with considerable success until he was killed in battle outside Amphipolis in 422 (see below, p. 333).

NEW THEATERS OF WARFARE[3]

During the Archidamian War fighting developed in some places where the belligerents were not in conflict as early as 431. In some of the new theaters the fighting, though conducted on a large scale, was ineffectual, that is, it had few or no consequences for the outcome of the war; in others it did have such an effect. Among new theaters of the former type two—Lesbos and Sicily—call for note.

In 428 the city of Mytilene in Lesbos rebelled against Athens. Some Mytilenaeans had been planning revolt even before the outbreak of the war, and in 428 they rose in rebellion before their preparations were complete because they learned that their plans had been betrayed to the Athenians. The latter sent a force of forty ships and these gained control of the harbors, but for some time the Mytilenaeans were able to move freely in much of the island, although Methymna, the second city of Lesbos, supplied troops to help the Athenians. The Mytilenaeans sent an embassy to Sparta to seek help, and the Spartans bade it attend at the Olympic festival in the middle of the summer, so that the allies could hear its plea. The result of the appeal was that the Spartans and their allies voted to send help, but there were delays; the allies were busy with the harvest, and no help arrived in 428. In the fall of the year the Athenians sent 1,000 hoplites as reinforcements under the command of Paches; he was able to build a wall round Mytilene and begin blockading the city. In 427 the prospect of Peloponnesian aid improved; late in the winter of 428/7 Salaethus, a Lacedaemonian, reached Mytilene on a single trireme and brought news that the Peloponnesians were preparing to send a fleet of forty ships.

In 427 the Peloponnesians invaded Attica and devastated the territory more thoroughly than usual. But Mytilene ran short of food. Salaethus armed the populace with a view to making an attack on the Athenians, but instead the people grew restive; they demanded that the men in office should produce supplies of grain or else they themselves would yield to the Athenians. The officers accordingly negotiated a surrender with Paches; by the terms the Mytilenaeans were to send an embassy to Athens, but no restriction was placed on the freedom of the Athenian assembly to decide on a settlement. Meanwhile, the Peloponnesian fleet of forty ships set off across the Aegean; when it reached Icaros and Myconos, it learned that Mytilene had surrendered. The commander, Alcidas, brought his fleet to Erythrae to verify the news; then he sailed back to the Peloponnese as quickly as he could. The Athenian assembly deliberated on treatment of the Mytilenaeans; its first decision was to execute all the adult men and sell the women and children into slavery. But on the next day it met again and reached a milder decision; only those most responsible for the revolt, whom Paches had arrested and sent to Athens, were executed. The fortifications of Mytilene were destroyed and its fleet was confiscated. Later the Athenians founded a cleruchy in its territory; the Mytilenaeans were to work the land and pay a rent to the Athenian cleruchs. It is possible that the cleruchs were recalled a few years later; an Athenian inscribed decree deals with the affairs of Mytilene and, although it is very fragmentary, it appears to be mild in tone and to mention a restoration of land; besides, no Athenian cleruchs in Lesbos are mentioned in Thucydides's detailed account of warfare in the eastern Aegean in 412–411.

Readers of Thucydides have paid a good deal of attention to the revolt of Mytilene, partly because the historian gives an Athenian debate on treatment of the city; he introduces Cleon for the first time, describing him as most influential with the people of Athens, and attributes to him the proposal for executing the men and enslaving the women and children. The revolt is of interest for other reasons too. Mytilene was one of the few cities which still contributed ships to the Delian League instead of paying tribute; it rebelled even though it enjoyed this relatively privileged status. The revolt has been scrutinized for indications of divergent attitudes within Mytilene; when Salaethus armed the populace, they demanded food and threatened to yield to the Athenians, and some historians have inferred that the common people preferred the Athenians, but their action can equally well be explained as due to starvation. The behavior of the Spartans was significant for the further development of the fighting. Previously Sparta had failed to support allies of Athens in revolt, such as the Euboeans in 446 and the Samians in 440. In 428 they and their allies resolved to help the Mytilenaeans, but their fleet did not arrive until too late. Unless Sparta could produce a more efficient commander than Alcidas, there could be little prospect of further revolts against Athens; when Brasidas operated in the Thraceward district from 424 onwards, he proved to be a more efficient commander and was able to win the trust of prospective allies.

A second theater where new enterprise during the Archidamian War produced no substantial result was Sicily. At the beginning of the war the Lacedaemonians instructed their sympathizers in Sicily and south Italy to supply them with ships and money, but there is no indication that this was done. However, the Peloponnesians imported grain from Sicily. Athens had renewed her alliances with Leontini and Rhegium in 433/2 (chapter 11, p. 321). By 427 war had broken out between Syracuse and Leontini, and many other Sicilian cities had joined in as allies of the one side or the other; this gave the Athenians a chance to intervene and they sent a force of twenty ships. Thucydides says that their real motive was to stop the export of Sicilian grain to the Peloponnese, and he adds that the Athenians wished to discover whether it might be possible to bring the affairs of Sicily under their control. It is credible that the Athenians entertained this design; under ancient conditions the only way to stop the export of grain from Sicily to the Peloponnese was to conquer the island. In 425 the Athenians sent a further force of forty ships under Eurymedon and Sophocles; these reinforcements were delayed, since during their outward journey they engaged in operations on the west coast of Lacedaemon and at Corcyra, but they reached Sicily before the end of the campaigning season of 425. However, in 424 envoys from the Greek cities of Sicily gathered in a conference at Gela; Hermocrates, a leading man of Syracuse, argued that it was in their interest to make peace rather than afford the Athenians an opportunity to intervene in their island. Peace was accordingly made and the Athenian force withdrew. The argument of Hermocrates may have been somewhat disingenuous; within a few years civil strife developed in Leontini and the Syracusans intervened to exacerbate it, so that many citizens of Leontini were expelled.

Two new enterprises launched on Athenian initiative had a marked effect on the outcome of the war In 425, when Eurymedon and Sophocles set sail with their forty ships, Demosthenes was allowed to travel with them, and although he held no official position, he was authorized to make use of the ships, if he wished,

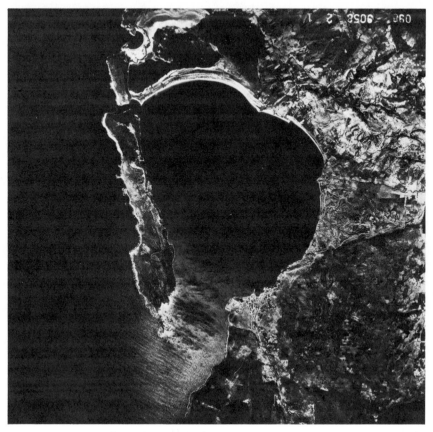

Aerial view of Pylos and Sphacteria. [Courtesy W.K. Pritchett.]

on the journey round the Peloponnese. A storm made the fleet put in at Pylos, a promontory on the coast of Messenia, and encouraged by Demosthenes the men built fortifications. When Eurymedon and Sophocles continued their voyage, they left Demosthenes five ships to hold Pylos. The Peloponnesians came to try to dislodge him and they put a force in the neighboring island of Sphacteria; but Demosthenes beat off their first attack. Meanwhile he sent for help to Eurymedon and Sophocles, who had reached Zacynthus, and they brought their whole fleet to join him. They defeated the Peloponnesian fleet in the bay of Pylos and surrounded Sphacteria.

The Spartans were alarmed for their men in Sphacteria; they made an armistice and sent envoys to Athens to try to negotiate peace. But the Athenians, incited by Cleon, made excessive demands, and negotiations broke down. The Athenian force in Pylos continued besieging the Lacedaemonians in Sphacteria and the siege continued longer than was expected; the Athenians began to run short of food and their water supply was poor. When the matter was discussed in the assembly at Athens, Cleon criticized the generals bitterly and one of them, Nicias, offered to hand over his command to him. Cleon was at first reluctant, but under pressure from the assembly he accepted the commission and boasted that within twenty days he would either kill the Lacedaemonians who were in Sphacteria or bring them back alive. He sailed with reinforcements and joined Demosthenes in the command. Together they launched an attack on Sphacteria and overcame the garrison there. The survivors were captured and brought to Athens; they numbered 292 hoplites and they included about 120 Spartiates. Cleon's boast was accomplished.

This disaster was a serious shock to Sparta. The Athenians maintained a garrison in Pylos for many years. It consisted mostly of Messenians from Naupactus; they harmed Lacedaemon by raids and they were especially able to do so since they spoke the local dialect. Moreover Spartan citizens were a minority in the population of Lacedaemon. Sparta was anxious to recover the captives, and so she refrained from making further raids on Attica and she sought opportunities for concluding peace.

Another enterprise launched by Athenian initiative was decisive through its failure. The essentially defensive strategy advocated by Pericles might enable the Athenians to survive but it could scarcely achieve a clear victory. Traditionally struggles in central Greece were determined by battles fought on the route which led from Boeotia through Megara and the Isthmus into the Corinthiad and the Peloponnese. As already noted, an Athenian attempt on the Megarid in 424 led to nothing more than the occupation of Nisaea. In the same year two Athenian generals, Demosthenes and Hippocrates, launched a more ambitious plan against Boeotia. They were in touch with disaffected elements in the Boeotian cities. The plan was that Siphae, a town in the southwestern part of Boeotia, was to be betrayed to Demosthenes, who was to approach it from Naupactus; on the same day Hippocrates, advancing from Attica, was to seize and fortify Delium, a temple of Apollo which stood in Tanagraean territory near the coast and faced Euboea. Since both operations were to be carried out at the same time, it was expected that the Boeotian forces would be divided and hesitant. But with ancient means of communications it was very difficult to coordinate operations in different places. Moreover the plot was betrayed to the Lacedaemonians and they warned the Boeotian authorities. Demosthenes advanced towards Siphae appreciably before his colleague set off from Attica, but the Boeotians put large forces in Siphae and Demosthenes was unable to take the place. Hippocrates led the Athenians in full force to Delium and fortified the position, but the Boeotians had withdrawn their troops from Siphae and they brought them to Tanagra. The outcome was a battle, which the Boeotians won; the main Athenian force retreated, and sixteen days later the Boeotians overcame the garrison which the Athenians had left in Delium.

This failure had a considerable effect on the Athenian outlook. The defensive strategy, which Pericles had advocated at the beginning of the war, was unsatisfactory, since it could achieve nothing more than mere survival; Pericles, its chief advocate, died in the fall of 429. The obvious alternative for the Athenians was to attempt expansion by land into Central Greece, but the defeat at Delium showed that they could not achieve this. Meanwhile during 424 Brasidas reached Chalcidice and began winning places in its neighborhood; the Athenians were especially sensitive to the loss of Amphipolis.

STEPS TOWARDS PEACE[4]

As appears from the preceding section, by 423 both the Spartans and the Athenians had reasons for wishing to bring hostilities to an end, and in the spring they made an armistice for one year. But Brasidas failed to observe it. Indeed, in the very days when the truce was being negotiated, Scione in Pallene, the western-most promontory of Chalcidice, joined him of its own initiative, and when news of the truce was brought to him, he refused to surrender the city. When the Athenians learned of this, on the proposal of Cleon they passed a decree for executing the whole population of Scione. But Mende, another city of Pallene, also joined Brasidas. A little later the Athenians sent a fleet under Nicias and Nicostratus to Chalcidice; it recovered Mende and invested Scione. It also secured an agreement with Perdiccas, who had quarrelled with Brasidas.

When the truce expired in 422, fighting in the Thraceward district continued on a somewhat larger scale. Cleon led out a further Athenian force and recovered Torone, the chief city of the central promontory of Chalcidice, before Brasidas could come to its aid; Brasidas had captured it with help from inside the city in the winter of 424/3, and feeling was evidently divided there. Advancing by sea from Torone, Cleon captured some smaller towns and proceeded towards his main goal, Amphipolis. Outside that city Brasidas brought him to battle; both commanders were killed in the fighting, but before Brasidas died, he learned that his men had defeated the enemy. The survivors of the Athenian force found refuge in Eion.

A variety of considerations on each side impelled the Athenians and the Spartans to negotiate in the winter of 422/1 in the hope of achieving peace. The defeats at Delium and Amphipolis discouraged the Athenians from continuing the fighting. They were alarmed at the prospect of further revolts among their allies, a prospect which seemed more imminent because of Brasidas's successes in encouraging disaffection in the Thraceward district. The Lacedaemonians were anxious to recover the captives taken at Sphacteria. The garrison maintained by the Athenians in Pylos harassed Lacedaemonian territory and provided a refuge for fugitive helots. Indeed by seizing Pylos Demosthenes had found a new way of harming Sparta, and his example was followed; in 424 Nicias captured the island of Cythera off the southernmost promontory of Laconia and installed a garrison there. Argos also presented a problem. In 451 the Spartans had concluded a treaty of thirty years with the Argives; it was due to expire in 421, and the Spartans did not want to fight the Athenians and the Argives at the same time. They were also alarmed at unrest among their allies.

In addition to these general considerations there were personal factors. The deaths of Cleon and Brasidas removed the two men who were the chief advocates on each side of continuing the war. In Athens Nicias had achieved prominence during the Archidamian War; he had held frequent commands, his most successful enterprise being the capture of Cythera. He was anxious that peace should be concluded while his good fortune held, and he hoped through a treaty to save himself and his fellow citizens from further burdens. Among the Spartans king Pleistoanax was the most vehement advocate of concluding peace. He had been exiled in 446; the charge was that, after leading the Peloponnesian force into Attica and reaching the plain of Eleusis (chapter 10, p. 291), he had accepted a bribe and withdrawn in consequence. In 428 the Spartans recalled him in obedience to the advice of the Delphic oracle. But his enemies were not satisfied; they alleged that his recall had been carried out illegally and they blamed it for every disaster which Lacedaemon suffered. So Pleistoanax wanted to bring the disasters to an end by achieving peace.

The reasons summarized above for concluding peace are given by Thucydides. Possibly something can be added from the study of Athenian finance. At the beginning of the war the reserve of coined silver, kept in the treasuries of Athena and the other gods on the acropolis, amounted to ca. 6,000 talents. In 431 the Athenians set aside 1,000 talents from this as a special reserve to be used only if the enemy brought a fleet against them. Fragments have been found of an inscription recording loans made to the Athenian state from these treasuries in the years from 426/5 to 423/2 inclusively; the same inscription summarizes the loans made in the years 433/2 to 427/6 in order to calculate interest. In spite of difficulties of reading and interpretation, it appears that between 433 and 422 the city borrowed nearly 5,600 talents from the sacred treasuries. This, however, does not necessarily imply that by 422 those treasuries were exhausted. It may be that annual payments were made into them from tribute and perhaps from other revenues; the amount of such payments and consequently the condition of the sacred treasuries in 422 can only be conjectured. It may be more to the point to note that during the Archidamian War the Athenians took new steps to increase revenue. In 428, after Mytilene had rebelled, they exacted an *eisphora* or tax on property in

The Decrees of Callias. See page 323. [Courtesy Louvre Museum. Photograph M. Chuzeville.]

Attica, and it yielded 200 talents. Thucydides says that this was the first time they levied an *eisphora*, and although his statement has been challenged, it cannot be proved wrong. The Athenians took steps to improve the yield of the tribute. Thucydides mentions naval squadrons sent out in 430, 428 and 425 to exact money. A decree proposed by Cleinias sought to improve on collection of tribute by requiring each tribute-paying city to send a sealed statement of the amount it sent; this decree may belong to the period of the Archidamian War, although an earlier date has often been preferred (chapter 10, pp. 285–287). In 426/5 a decree proposed by Cleonymus required each tribute-paying city to appoint collectors of tribute and instituted further steps to improve on the procedure. Moreover in 425/4 a new assessment of tribute was carried out. Reassessments were usually held in the year of the Greater Panathenaea, that is, once every four years, but in 425/4 the reassessment was held without waiting for the Greater Panathenaic year. Parts of the inscribed decree ordering the reassessment and of the list of sums required in consequence have been recovered. The decree is remarkable for the strictness of its outlook; it specifies penalties for any short-comings in procedure. The consequent assessment was ambitious, one might even say unrealistic; it included places which are not known to have paid tribute for many years before and some which are not known to have paid at all. For example, Aspendus in Pamphylia was included; it lay far out to the east on the south coast of Asia Minor and does not occur in the extant fragments of any quota list; Athenian forces may have appeared there in the time of Cimon, particularly during the campaign of the Eurymedon river, but there may have been little prospect of exacting tribute from Aspendus in 425/4. However, the assessment of that year marks a severe increase in the amounts which the Athenians tried to exact from the cities which they in fact controlled. For example, Chalcis and Eretria, which had each paid a constant tribute of 3 talents since the fourth assessment period, were now assessed to pay 10 talents and 15 talents respectively. The total sum demanded was stated at the end of the new assessment list, but unfortunately the first figure of the total is not preserved; so it is not clear whether the sum was rather more than 960 talents or rather more than 1,460 talents. The general scale of assessment in the preserved parts of the inscription suggests that the higher figure is correct. This can be compared with the total of assessment current when the war broke out. Thucydides reports a speech of Pericles summarizing the Athenian resources available for warfare in 431; there Pericles is made to say that Athens receives 600 talents in tribute each year. If the tribute quota lists were the only evidence extant, study of them would suggest a much lower figure, and so some historians have doubted the accuracy of Thucydides's figure of 600 talents or have tried to explain it as including other external revenues as well as tribute. But the quota lists of the 430s are poorly preserved, and so it is better to accept the report of 600 talents as the tribute of 432/1.

It seems likely that by 422 financial factors swayed the Athenians towards peace but their chief effect may have been indirect. There may still have been a considerable sum in reserve on the acropolis, but in order to prosecute the war the Athenians had levied new domestic taxes (the *eisphora*) and above all they had increased sharply the assessment of tribute. This step doubtless made them much more alive to the risk of disaffection among their allies.

Negotiations were conducted during the winter of 422/1. Towards the spring the Spartans required their allies to furnish troops and they announced that they would invade Attica with a view to seizing and fortifying a position there. This stimulated Athenian desires for peace and a treaty was concluded in the spring. It was intended to establish peace for fifty years between the Athenians, the Lacedaemonians and the allies on each side. The general basis of the territorial terms was that each side should restore the positions it had seized by fighting, but exceptions and special provisions were made. The Thebans refused to restore Plataea, since they alleged that they had not seized it by fighting; it had surrendered to them. In compensation the Athenians insisted on keeping Nisaea in the Megarid; they made a similar allegation about it. Panactum, an Athenian fortress on the northern border, had been captured by the Boeotians in 422, and by the terms of the treaty the Lacedaemonians and their allies were to restore it. Correspondingly, the Athenians were required to restore Pylos, Cythera, and the captives taken at Sphacteria. The Lacedaemonians and their allies undertook to restore Amphipolis and other places in the Thraceward district to Athens, but special provisions were made to safeguard some of these. The proper interpretation of these provisions is not wholly clear, but at least in the case of some cities the inhabitants were free to leave, taking their property, and the tribute was not to be raised above the level originally determined by Aristeides. A final clause of the treaty provided that it could be amended by agreement between the Athenians and the Lacedaemonians; this clause did not allow any voice in making amendments to the allies of either side.

THE BREAKDOWN OF THE PEACE OF NICIAS[5]

The treaty concluded in the spring of 421 has come to be called the peace of Nicias because of the part he played in bringing it about. It led to complex diplomacy; after a time new tension developed between Sparta and Athens, and during 420 they stopped negotiating with one another. Thucydides argued that the cessation of hostilities in 421 should not be regarded as peace but merely as an armistice strained by mutual suspicion; the later fighting between Athens and

Sparta, together with the previous war of ten years, constituted in his opinion a single war, lasting until 404. As he recognized, direct hostilities between Sparta and Athens were first resumed in 414, when an Athenian force of thirty ships raided parts of Laconia. Nonetheless, by the end of 420 the Spartans and Athenians had ceased trying to collaborate and were bent on gaining advantages against one another. So the diplomacy of 421–420 must be scrutinized to discover why the peace of Nicias broke down.

Immediately after the conclusion of peace the Spartans faced several embarrassments. The places in the Thraceward district, which they were expected to restore to the Athenians, were not willing to become subject to the Athenians again. Among these places the one to which the Athenians attached most importance was Amphipolis; although Lacedaemonian officers announced the peace terms there, Sparta proved unwilling to coerce the city, and Amphipolis was never restored to Athens. Among their allies Boeotia, Corinth, Elis and Megara had voted against concluding the treaty. The Boeotians made an armistice (described by Thucydides as a "ten-day truce:" his meaning is not clear) with the Athenians, but when a major ally, such as Corinth, holding an important strategic position, refused to accept the peace, the Spartans had cause for concern. The prospect of disaffection within the Peloponnese was especially alarming as the thirty years' peace with Argos was about to expire and the Argives refused a Spartan offer to renew it. Soon after the peace of Nicias had been made, the Spartans met their difficulties by concluding a defensive alliance with the Athenians; if the territory of either party was attacked, the other was to come to its aid, and by a further provision the Athenians should bring aid to Sparta if a helot revolt occurred. This was an astute move on the part of the Spartans, since it meant that neither Argos nor the disaffected members of the Peloponnesian League could look to Athens for support; besides, on concluding the alliance the Athenians restored the captives taken in Sphacteria.

The disaffection within the Peloponnesian League in consequence of the peace of Nicias calls for scrutiny. A congress of the League had accepted the peace terms by a majority vote, but in general the allies of Sparta were displeased at the final clause, which provided that the Athenians and the Lacedaemonians could amend the terms together without reference to their allies. Some of them had particular grievances. The Corinthians were angry because two of their colonies in the northwest, Sollium and Anactorium, had been seized by the Athenians during the war and the peace terms did not require their restoration. The Mantineans had annexed part of Arcadia during the war and were afraid that, now that peace had been made, Sparta might make them give up the territory they had gained. Elis had a dispute with Lepreum, a small town on its border with Arcadia. Traditionally the Lepreates had paid one talent annually to Zeus of Olympia as rent for part of their land, but during the Archidamian War they stopped making the payments, and in the consequent dispute with Elis they enjoyed the support of the Spartans.

These grievances issued in an attempt to form a new league, independent of Athens and Sparta, under the leadership of Argos. The initiative was taken by the Corinthian envoys who had participated in the meeting at Sparta where the terms of peace were sworn. During their return these envoys went to Argos and suggested to the authorities that they should issue a general invitation to the Greek states to join in a defensive alliance. The Argive assembly agreed to the scheme; it set up a board of twelve men with authority to ally with any Greek state except Athens and Sparta, but no agreement was to be made with either of those two powers without reference to the Argive assembly. The first power to join the new league was Mantinea. By doing this Mantinea seceded from its alliance with Sparta, and this action incited many Peloponnesian states to consider following the same course. An embassy from Elis traveled to Corinth and thence to Argos, contracting alliances with both cities. Shortly afterwards Corinth joined the Argive alliance.

For a time it seemed as if the movement launched by Corinth and Argos would produce a third league, headed by Argos and comparable in power to those led by Sparta and Athens. But soon the new movement was checked. The Boeotians and the Megarians declined to join the alliance. Envoys from Corinth and Argos went to Tegea and urged it to secede from its alliance with Sparta and join them in the new league, but the Tegeans refused. The refusal is understandable; Tegea lay immediately north of Laconia and would be the first city to suffer, if the Spartans tried to reassert themselves in the Peloponnese. The Corinthians were discouraged by this setback, but they sent an embassy to urge the Boeotians to ally with them and the Argives. The Boeotians refused to do this, but in response to another Corinthian request a Boeotian embassy accompanied the Corinthians to Athens and asked the Athenians to extend to Corinth the ten-day armistice which they had with Boeotia. The Athenians were unwilling to do this; they replied that the peace of Nicias was open to Corinth if Corinth was an ally of Sparta.

Because of these setbacks the Corinthians gave up their efforts to promote the new Argive league. Indeed, the attempt to develop that league had little effect on subsequent events, but it illustrates some features of the international situation. Corinth proved to be surprisingly weak and ineffectual; it did not have the courage to head the new league but waited on the Argives, and it was easily discouraged when the movement suffered checks. As the chief naval power of the Peloponnesian League Corinth had borne the main burden of fighting at sea during the war; it had lost Sollium and Anactorium, it had not won any ascendancy over Corcyra, indeed it had made no territorial gains. Boeotia was in a much stronger position; it could extort a special armistice from the Athenians, who refused to extend such treatment to Corinth. The Boeotians were not willing to join the Argive league, although they refused to follow Sparta into the peace of Nicias; their policy in the year following the conclusion of peace will deserve attention.

The Athenians and the Spartans exchanged frequent embassies in the summer of 421. In the course of these negotiations the Spartans made a verbal undertaking to join the Athenians in bringing compulsion to bear on those of their allies who refused the peace. But Corinth, Boeotia, and the places which had joined Brasidas in the Thraceward district declined to accept the peace and the Spartans kept postponing any action against them. Sparta recalled her own forces from the north, but her reluctance to proceed against the places won by Brasidas is eminently comprehensible; in the summer of 421 the Athenians recovered Scione by siege and, in accordance with the decree passed previously (above p. 333), they killed the men of military age and enslaved the women and children. The Athenians were especially anxious to recover Amphipolis, but the Spartans protested that they did not in fact control it. The Athenians also wanted the fortress of Panactum restored, but as the Boeotians held it, the Spartans could do little about it. Consequently the Athenians declined to restore Pylos or Cythera. In response to Spartan expostulation they removed from Pylos the Messenian troops and fugitive helots, whose knowledge of the territory and the dialect had enabled them to raid Lacedaemon with great effect; they stationed these men in Cephallenia, from where they could easily be brought back.

In the late summer or fall of 421 a new board of ephors took office in Sparta and two of its members, Cleobulus and Xenares, opposed the policy of peace and alliance with Athens; they wished to strengthen the Spartan position with a view to resuming opposition to Athens. Early in the winter they had an opportunity to launch an intrigue. Envoys had gathered in Sparta from the Peloponnesian League and from Athens, Boeotia and Corinth; their deliberations were inconclusive, but when they made ready to depart, Cleobulus and Xenares approached the Boeotian and Corinthian envoys with a complex scheme. The Boeotians, they suggested, should ally with Argos and then together with the Corinthians they should bring the Argives into alliance with Sparta.

The federal constitution of Boeotia had two organs for determining policy. Ultimate authority belonged to the federal Council of 660 members, elected in equal numbers from the eleven parts into which Boeotia was divided. Further, the eleven boeotarchs served as executive officers and military commanders, and they commonly drafted proposals and brought them before the Council (see chapter 16, pp. 404–405). The Boeotian envoys returning from Sparta disclosed the plan of Cleobulus and Xenares to the boeotarchs. The latter accepted the plan; as a first step they proposed to ally Boeotia with Corinth, Megara and the Chalcidians of Thrace. They did not explain to the Council the ultimate aim of bringing Argos into alliance with Sparta, for the scheme demanded secrecy; they expected the Council to accept whatever they proposed. They were disappointed. The Council did not wish to take action in opposition to Sparta; it was confronted with a proposal to ally with Corinth and it knew that Corinth had in effect seceded from the Peloponnesian League; so it voted against the proposal. Accordingly, the boeotarchs did not try to propose any alliance with Argos to the Council.

Thus the ingenious scheme launched by Cleobulus and Xenares came to nothing. Even so it reveals some features of Boeotian policy. The Boeotians had not followed Sparta into joining the peace of Nicias, but they did not want to take up a position opposed to Sparta; the boeotarchs accepted the scheme of Cleobulus and Xenares, which was designed to strengthen the Spartan diplomatic position, and the Council of 660 rejected the proposal for allying with Corinth because they thought that it was directed against Sparta. Apparently the Boeotians wanted to remain allied to Sparta but they wanted to exercise a decisive voice on the question of relations with Athens. Furthermore, after the scheme was checked, the boeotarchs took no further action; Thucydides (5.38.4) comments: "Among the boeotarchs there was a certain apathy and a willingness to let events take their own course." Perhaps they thought that the passage of time worked in their favor.

Relations between Athens and Sparta came to a crisis over the question of Panactum during 420. When Cleobulus and Xenares had disclosed their scheme to the Boeotian envoys at Sparta, they had added a request that the Boeotians should hand over Panactum to the Spartans, so that the latter could exchange it with the Athenians for Pylos. Late in the winter a Spartan embassy proceeded to Boeotia and made this request formally. The Boeotians in reply demanded that Sparta should make a separate alliance with them. The Spartans were embarrassed. If they made a separate alliance with Boeotia, they would break their verbal agreement with the Athenians to join them in bringing pressure to bear on those of their allies who had not acceded to the peace of Nicias. But the Boeotians insisted, and so the Spartans made a separate alliance with them as the price for receiving custody of Panactum. Then, before handing over Panactum to the Spartan authorities, the Boeotians dismantled its fortifications.

This action had immediate repercussions in Argos. The Argives learned that Sparta had made a separate alliance with Boeotia and that the fortifications of Panactum had been destroyed; they thought that these things had been done with the knowledge of the Athenians and that the Spartans had persuaded the

Boeotians to accede to the peace with Athens. Hence they feared to be isolated. During their diplomatic moves of 421 they had thought that, whatever their relations with Sparta, they could fall back on Athens for support; they had been disappointed when Tegea preferred Spartan friendship to alliance with Argos, and now they feared that they would have to face a coalition embracing not only Sparta and Tegea but also Athens and Boeotia. So in the spring of 420 they sent envoys to Sparta in the hope of renewing their former treaty of peace for another fifty years. The envoys reached agreement on preliminary terms, but these needed to be referred to Argos for ratification; before that could happen, further news came from Athens.

In the spring of 420 three Spartan envoys came to Athens and offered to hand over Panactum. Thereupon the Athenians learned that the fortifications of the place had been dismantled and that Sparta had made a separate alliance with Boeotia; they were indignant and they dismissed the Spartan envoys with an unfavorable response. Some Athenians disagreed with the policy of peace and alliance with Sparta. Among them was Alcibiades, who was beginning a political career; he came of a family prominent and esteemed in Athens since the age of Cleisthenes. When the Spartan envoys were dismissed from Athens, he sent a private message to Argos to suggest that envoys should be sent from Argos, Mantinea and Elis with a view to concluding an alliance with Athens. On receiving this message the Argives learned that the separate alliance between Sparta and Boeotia had not been made with the knowledge and consent of the Athenians; on the contrary, acute tension had arisen between Athens and Sparta. So the Argives desisted from their attempt to negotiate peace with Sparta; instead they sent envoys to Athens, as requested by Alcibiades. The Argive embassy was accompanied by envoys from Elis and Mantinea.

A new embassy of three men from Sparta reached Athens at the same time. Their instructions were to dissuade the Athenians from allying with Argos, to demand the restoration of Pylos since Panactum had been handed over, and to explain that the separate alliance with Boeotia was not directed against Athens. They reported to the Council of Five Hundred and said that they had come with full powers to negotiate. Then, according to Thucydides (5.45), Alcibiades tricked the Spartan envoys. He approached them privately and assured them that he could get Pylos restored to them and the other points of difference settled, provided that they did not admit to the Athenian assembly that they had full powers to negotiate. The Spartan envoys were duly brought before the assembly and said that they did not have full powers to negotiate. Thereupon Alcibiades denounced them for the inconsistency between the statements they had made to the Council and to the assembly, and the Athenians were on the point of making an alliance with Argos, but an earthquake occurred and the meeting dispersed.

On the next day the assembly met again and Nicias persuaded it to postpone dealings with Argos and send him and others on an embassy to Sparta; he and his fellow envoys were instructed to demand that the Spartans should rebuild the fortifications of Panactum, that they should hand over Amphipolis, and that they should break off their alliance with Boeotia unless the Boeotians acceded to the peace of Nicias.

This embassy went to Sparta and expounded its demands. Finally it asserted that the Athenians would ally with Argos, Elis and Mantinea, unless the Spartans abandoned their alliance with Boeotia or the Boeotians joined the peace of Nicias. But Xenares and those who shared his outlook were not willing to give up the Boeotian alliance, and they prevailed in the Spartan assembly. All that Nicias could achieve was that the Spartans renewed their oath to the peace. So he returned to Athens and reported the failure of his mission. Thereupon the Athenians concluded an alliance with Argos, Mantinea and Elis. This agreement can be called "the quadruple alliance." The terms provided that it should be in force for a hundred years. It was a defensive alliance, requiring each party to come to the aid of the others if attacked, and provisions about command and supplies were set out in detail; but it also envisaged the prospect that the four contracting powers might resolve on a common expedition, that is, it did not exclude the possibility of joint offensive action.

With the conclusion of the quadruple alliance the peace of Nicias may be said to have broken down. Athens and Sparta did not yet engage in armed conflict against one another, but they ceased exchanging embassies to try to settle their differences amicably; the policy of cooperation, embodied in the peace and alliance they had concluded in 421, had come to an end. It is accordingly of some interest to ask why the peace broke down.

Attention may be given first to some personal factors, to which Thucydides gives some emphasis. On the Spartan side the new ephors, Cleobulus and Xenares, were not in sympathy with the peace policy. But the intrigue they launched with the Boeotian and Corinthian envoys came to nothing. Xenares is heard of only once later in the negotiations; when Nicias came to Sparta on his final mission, Thucydides says that Xenares and those of his opinion were unwilling to give up the Boeotian alliance. But by then it was scarcely possible to save the policy of cooperation; the demands which Nicias had been instructed to make were large and were not likely to be met, and this time Xenares merely voiced the opinion of a majority of the Spartan assembly.

The influence of Alcibiades is more difficult to assess. Thucydides (5.43) introduces him into the narrative at the point where the Athenians learned with alarm that the fortifications of Panactum had been dismantled and the Spartans had made a separate alliance with Boeotia. The historian gives a full account of the motives of Alcibiades for opposing the peace of Nicias. He thought that a rapprochement with Argos would be more beneficial to Athens, but he also had a personal motive. His grandfather had been *proxenos* of Sparta but had put an end to the tie; Alcibiades himself had sought to renew it by tending the captives taken at Sphacteria, but he had become aggrieved against the Spartans when they preferred to negotiate peace through Nicias and Laches. At the point in the narrative where he is introduced the action taken by Alcibiades consisted in sending a private message to Argos to suggest the dispatch of an embassy. Clearly this action contributed to diplomatic convenience without determining Argive or Athenian policy; it did not alter the considerations which induced the two cities to ally a little later. Alcibiades appears again in the narrative on the occasion when Thucydides says that he tricked the Spartan envoys at Athens and per-suaded them to deny that they had full powers to negotiate. This is a strange story; the reader may wonder what induced the Spartans to listen to Alcibiades rather than to Nicias. But the truth or falsehood of the story matters more for the study of Thucydides's mode of composition than for understanding the nego-tiations of 420. The alleged trick had virtually no effect on the outcome of the negotiations. The Athenians were bitterly aggrieved, not because of the apparent duplicity into which Alcibiades allegedly enticed the Spartan envoys, but because of the condition of Panactum and the separate alliance with Boeotia; when the assembly met again the next day, it sent Nicias to Sparta with instructions to make strict demands on these issues and on Amphipolis, and there is every reason to suppose that his instructions would have been the same, even if the supposed trick had not occurred.

The official attitudes adopted by Sparta and Athens call likewise for attention. In 421 the Spartans committed themselves with some thoroughness to the new policy of entente with Athens. The clause in the treaty providing that Athens and Sparta could amend the terms without consulting their allies made little differ-ence to the allies of Athens, since Athens had long been accustomed to deter-mining alone the policy of the Delian League, but it was an affront to the allies of Sparta, since the Peloponnesian League habitually decided on policy in congresses of all its members; by this clause Sparta attached her hopes for the future to collaboration with Athens instead of relying on her traditional allies. She went further in the same direction by contracting a defensive alliance with Athens shortly after the peace; the clause providing for Athenian help in the event of a helot revolt is especially revealing. The two cities continued exchanging embassies in the summer of 421 and the following winter; this indicates a determined effort to make the peace work. In particular Athens and Sparta relied on direct expostulation with one another in an effort to recover Panactum and Pylos, the places which each desired most. Those of their citizens who wished to break the entente relied, not on persuading the assemblies in their own cities, but on diplomatic approaches to third parties; thus Cleobulus and Xenares launched their scheme with the Boeotians, and Alcibiades sent his message to Argos. On the other hand the outstanding questions were difficult. Amphipolis was to be restored by the terms of peace, but it was virtually impossible for the Spartans to coerce the city; it was difficult for them to restore Panactum, since the Boeotians held it and could demand their own price; and unless the Athenians were satisfied on these two issues, they could retain possession of Pylos. The difficulty of solving these problems provided an opportunity for interested third parties.

Thus the initiative passed to powers of second rank. Three of these, Corinth, Argos and Boeotia, played a large part in the negotiations. Promptly after the peace of Nicias had been made, the Corinthians suggested at Argos their scheme for a new league to be headed by Argos. They did not offer to lead the league themselves; indeed they showed remarkable reluctance to take risks. When the Argives launched the new league, the Corinthians were slow to join it and waited till Mantinea and Elis did so first. A little later, when Boeotia, Megara and Tegea failed to join the new league, the Corinthians gave up promoting it. In the crucial negotiations of 420, which led to the split between Athens and Sparta, the Corinthians are not attested as playing any part. When the quadruple alliance was made, they did not join it but resumed their former collaboration with Sparta. The situation arising once the quadruple alliance was made may well have been what they desired; that is, they may have seen in a renewal of tension between Sparta and Athens the sole prospect of achieving eventually terms more favorable to them than the peace of Nicias. But even if the outcome accorded with Corinthian wishes, it does not follow that Corinthian action contributed effectively to achieving this goal.

Argive policy was likewise ineffectual. The Argives launched the new league in 421 but little came of it; its only lasting significance was that the consequent alliance of Argos, Elis and Mantinea was available in 420 to join with Athens in forming the quadruple alliance. The attitude adopted by the Argives in the spring of 420 discloses the weakness of their policy. When they learned that the fortifications of Panactum had been dismantled and Sparta had allied with Boeotia, they thought that these things had been done with the knowledge of the Athenians and that they would no longer have Athens to fall back on for support against Sparta; so they opened negotiations with Sparta with a view to renewing the thirty years' peace. Argos was not willing to take the risks necessary for exercising decisive influence on international events.

The policy of the Boeotians was more effective. They had some advantages. The Boeotian Confederacy was intrinsically a strong power. It was too far away to be threatened or coerced by the Spartans. It was perhaps the only state which had profited from the Archidamian War; it had secured Plataea and Panactum. The outcome of the intrigue launched by Cleobulus and Xenares shows that the

Boeotians wanted to continue cooperation with Sparta; the boeotarchs agreed to the scheme and saw in it an attempt to strengthen the position of Sparta; the Council of Six Hundred Sixty rejected the proposed alliance with Corinth because they thought that it was directed against Sparta. But Boeotia wanted Spartan policy to oppose Athens. When the Spartans sought custody of Panactum in order to exchange it for Pylos, the Boeotians dismantled the fortifications and insisted that the Spartans make a separate alliance with them. These were unfriendly actions towards the Athenians and the Boeotians could foresee that they would exacerbate relations between Sparta and Athens, even if they could not know in advance that they would finally destroy the entente between those two powers.

The outcome of the peace of Nicias has some general interest for the student of Greek history. By that treaty and the ensuing alliance Sparta and Athens attempted a policy of cooperation; previously they had fought one another bitterly in the Archidamian War and their mutual suspicions went back a good deal further. The change to a policy of cooperation was perhaps greater for Sparta than for Athens, in view of the different relations of each power with its allies. Athens had long been in the habit of taking sole decisions for the Delian League, but in the Peloponnesian League policy had been determined by federal congresses; the clause of the peace of Nicias allowing Sparta and Athens to make amendments and the conclusion of the subsequent alliance between these two powers alone marked a Spartan attempt to seize a more authoritative position. The breakdown of the policy of cooperation was due to many factors. It was difficult to carry out the peace terms, for example, the provisions about Pylos, Amphipolis and Panactum; Sparta was embarrassed by her relations with Argos and by recalcitrance among her allies. The traditional attitude of suspicion and hostility between the two leading powers of Greece persisted; Cleobulus and Xenares voiced it at Sparta, and Alcibiades played upon it at Athens. But the constant negotiations continuing until the quadruple alliance was made show that the Athenians and the Spartans made persistent attempts to solve their differences peacefully. The breakdown of the peace of Nicias was not due to ill will between Sparta and Athens. So far as any one power was responsible for the breakdown, that power was Boeotia.

NOTES

1. A younger contemporary of Thucydides, Andocides (3. 8–9), treated the Archidamian War as a distinct war. The strategy of the Athenians, as expounded by Pericles, is given by Thuc. 1.143.5; 2.13.2; 2.62.2–3; 2.65.7. A classic illustration of Athenian superiority in naval tactics is provided by

Phormion's operations of 429 in the Corinthian Gulf; see Thuc. 2.83–92. On the fortunes of Megara see Thuc. 2.31; 4.66–74. On the plague see Thuc. 2.47–54; 2.59; 3.87. The nature of the disease has often been discussed; in the crowded conditions within the fortifications an epidemic of typhus would be likely, and the case for typhus as the Thucydidean plague has been stated by Sir W. P. MacArthur, "The Athenian Plague: A Medical Note," *CQ* N.S. 4 (1954) 171–174; cf. Gomme, *Comm.* 2. 150–153. That the plague was smallpox is argued by R. J. Littman and M. L. Littman, "The Athenian Plague: Smallpox," *TAPA* 100 (1969) 261–275. For the fortunes of Plataea see Thuc. 2.2–6; 2.71–78; 3.20–24; 3.52–68.

2. The troubles in Corcyra are given by Thuc. 3.70–85; 4.46–48. On operations in and near Acarnania see Thuc. 2.68; 2.80–82; 3.7; 3.94–98; 3.100–102; 3.105–114. The surrender of Poteidaea is reported by Thucydides at 2.70 and the battle of Spartolus at 2.79. For the operations of Brasidas in the north see Thuc. 4.78–88; 4.102–116; 4.120–135; 5.2–3; 5.6–13. G. B. Grundy, *Thucydides and the History of His Age* (Oxford 1948) is a useful introduction to strategic problems of the Peloponnesian War.

3. Thucydides narrates the Mytilenaean revolt at 3.2–6; 3.8–18; 3.25–50. On the Athenian inscribed decree see *ATL* IID 22; B. D. Meritt, "Athenian Covenant with Mytilene," *AJP* 75 (1954) 359–368; Gomme, *Comm.* 2.328–332; P. A. Brunt, "Athenian Settlements Abroad in the Fifth Century B.C.," *Ehrenberg Studies* 71–92. The internal situation in Mytilene is discussed by R. P. Legon," Megara and Mytilene," *Phoenix* 22 (1968) 200–225, and D. Gillis, "The Revolt at Mytilene," *AJP* 92 (1971) 38–47. The affairs of Sicily during the Archidamian War are known from Thuc. 2.7.2; 3.86; 3.88; 3.90; 3.103; 3.115–116; 4.1; 4.24–25; 4.48.6; 4.58–65; 5.4–5. For the operations at Pylos and Sphacteria see Thuc. 4.2–23; 4.26–41. The topography has often been discussed; for the results of a recent inquiry see W. K. Pritchett, *Studies in Ancient Greek Topography*, Part I = University of California Publications in Classical Studies, vol. 1 (1965) 6–29. For the campaign concluding with the battle of Delium see Thuc. 4.76–77; 4.89–101.

4. Thucydides gives the armistice of 423 at 4.117–119, and the ensuing operations at 4.120–5.13; he explains the reasons for making peace at 5.14–17, reproduces the terms at 5.18–19, and dates the peace to ten years after the outbreak of war within a few days at 5.20. At 2.13 he reports a speech of Pericles, made in 431 and including information on the financial reserve and the annual amount of tribute. He records the special reserve of 1,000 talents at 2.24.1. The inscription giving loans of 426/5–423/2 is Meiggs/Lewis 72; among numerous discussions of it attention may be drawn to Gomme, *Comm.* 2.432–436 and 3.687–689. Thucydides gives the *eisphora* of 428 at 3.19.1 and says it was the first to be exacted. The financial decrees of Callias allude to the special vote of permission required for proposing an *eisphora*; many people have dated them 434/3 and inferred that this tax had already been levied by then, the levy of 428 being the first within the Peloponnesian War; but it may be better to assign the decrees to a later date (see chapter 11, note 6, p. 323). Naval squadrons sent to exact money are mentioned by Thucydides at 2.69; 3.19; 4.50. The decree of Cleinias is Meiggs/Lewis 46 (see chapter 10, pp. 285–287). The decree of Cleonymus is Meiggs/Lewis 68. For the assessment of 425 see Meiggs/Lewis 69; for a complete text see *ATL* IIA 9.

5. Thucydides reports the events of this section at 5.21–48. He gives the raid of thirty Athenian ships at 6.105. The Boeotian constitution is known from *Hell. Oxy.* 16 (11); for discussion see J. A. O. Larsen, *Representative Government in Greek and Roman History* (Berkeley and Los Angeles 1955) 31–40. For studies of the politics of 421–420 see D. Kagan, "Corinthian Diplomacy after the Peace of Nicias," *AJP* 81 (1960) 291–310; idem, "Argive Politics and Policy after the Peace of Nicias," *CP* 57 (1962) 208–218; T. Kelly, "Cleobulus, Xenares and Thucydides' Account of the Demolition of Panactum," *Historia* 21 (1972) 159–169.

13

The Middle Stage of the
Peloponnesian War,
419-411

The conclusion of the quadruple alliance in 420 marked the end of the entente between Sparta and Athens, but it did not lead to immediate resumption of hostilities on a large scale. The actions of the Argives soon brought the two major powers into conflict within the Peloponnese, but the Spartans did not press the struggle against Athens with enthusiasm until the Athenians sent a large part of their forces on a distant and hazardous expedition to Sicily. When at last that expedition failed and the whole expeditionary force was lost, the Spartans resumed hostilities on a general scale, trying especially to win the west coast of Asia Minor. Even so, the Athenians continued fighting for eight more years and at times came near to winning the war; only a complex concatenation of circumstances, including cooperation between Sparta and the Persian authorities in Asia Minor, brought about the final defeat of the Athenians and the loss of their Empire.

EPIDAURUS, MANTINEA, MELOS[1]

In 419 the Argives went to war against Epidaurus, a city on the northeast coast of the Argolid peninsula. They alleged as their pretext that the Epidaurians had failed to make a customary offering at the temple of Apollo Pythaeus, which the Argives controlled. In fact the Argives wanted to seize Epidaurus so that they would be secure against any trouble from Corinth and so that the Athenians could bring them troops from Aegina without having to sail round the Argolid peninsula. During 419 the Argives with Athenian support ravaged Epidaurian territory, and in the following winter Sparta sent a garrison by sea to Epidaurus to strengthen the defense. Thereupon the Argives complained to the Athenians because the latter had not prevented the sea journey of the Lacedaemonian force. In response the Athenians, at the suggestion of Alcibiades, added to the inscription bearing the peace of Nicias a sentence saying that the Lacedaemonians did not abide by their oaths; and they brought back a force of fugitive helots to Pylos to ravage the surrounding territory.

In 418 the Lacedaemonians began action on a larger scale to support Epidaurus. They led out their own troops in full force against Argos, and they required their allies, including Boeotia and Corinth, to furnish contingents. This attack led to a complex campaign. When both armies were ready for battle, the Spartan king Agis agreed unexpectedly with a few Argives to make a truce for four months; he withdrew his army and many of the allies of Sparta recalled their contingents. But the Argives, encouraged by the allied troops from Athens, Mantinea and Elis, did not wait for the truce to expire; instead they invaded Arcadia and began capturing places there. So the Lacedaemonians sent out a large force to protect Tegea and this brought the enemy to battle at Mantinea. Those fighting on the one side were the Lacedaemonians and forces from some of the towns of Arcadia. Against them were arrayed the Mantineans and troops from some other towns of Arcadia, the Argives with their local allies from Cleonae and Orneae, and the Athenians. The Lacedaemonians won the battle and the victory made a large difference to their position in Greece. It was the first success they had won in an engagement on any appreciable scale since their defeat at Sphacteria in 425. That defeat had harmed their prestige severely; it had led many Greeks to suppose that the Spartans were cowardly in action and sluggish in policy. The victory at Mantinea restored the traditional image of the Lacedaemonians as the most efficient force of infantry in Greece; little more was heard of recalcitrance among their allies during the Peloponnesian War.

During the campaign of Mantinea forces from the quadruple alliance continued operations at Epidaurus; they built fortifications round the city and began besieging it. The outcome of the battle brought about a change in Argive policy. Pro-Spartan elements began to gain ascendancy in Argos. Early in the winter of 418/7 the Argives accepted a Spartan offer of peace; by its terms the Argives were to withdraw their forces from the territory of Epidaurus and join in compelling the Athenians to withdraw thence. Soon afterwards Argos repudiated its membership in the quadruple alliance and made an alliance with Sparta. In response to an Argive protest the Athenians withdrew their forces from Epidaurus. Once Argos had withdrawn from the quadruple alliance, the Mantineans did not wish to continue their opposition to Sparta; they came to terms with the Spartans and gave up the territory which they had annexed in Arcadia during the Archidamian War. Towards the end of the same winter the pro-Spartans in Argos, helped by Lacedaemonian troops, carried out a revolution and seized control.

In 417 Argos experienced a further revolution. This time the opponents of Sparta seized control. They abandoned their treaties with Sparta, made a new alliance with Athens, and began building long walls from their city to the sea. Warfare continued between Sparta and Argos. Indeed by the end of 417 the Greek states had returned for the most part to their traditional alignments. Sparta had reasserted her leadership over most cities of the Peloponnese. The major realignments, begun in the months following the peace of Nicias, had come to nothing. Argos, as it appeared, could irritate the Spartans but lacked the resources and the initiative to present them with a serious challenge; Corinth, however unhappy with the peace of Nicias, was not willing to abandon her traditional reliance on Sparta.

In 416 the Athenians sent an expedition against Melos. This island and Thera were the only ones among the Cyclades which did not belong to the Athenian Empire. Melos had been settled by Dorians in the age of migrations and it claimed to be a colony of Lacedaemon. Thucydides says that, when the Athenian force reached the island, their spokesmen held a discussion with the magistrates of Melos, and he gives the arguments of the two sides in the form of a conversation. In its wording this "Melian dialogue," like the other speeches given by Thucydides, is largely the historian's free composition, but one of the arguments he attributes to the Melians is likely to have been used by them in fact; they chose to resist the Athenians instead of yielding and making terms because they expected help from Sparta. Because of fifth-century stress on supposed ties of kinship one would suppose that the Melians used this argument, even if Thucydides had not said that they did. Since the Melians refused to submit, the Athenians built fortifications round the city and left a force to besiege it. During the winter of 416/5 the Melians made an unconditional surrender; the Athenians executed the men, enslaved the women and children, and sent 500 colonists to occupy the island.

In introducing the Athenian attack on Melos Thucydides does not give reasons for it. From the dialogue which he gives it would appear that the Athenians wished to complete their control of the Aegean and thus discourage disaffection among the islands. The severities which the Athenians inflicted on

Melos were not unusual; in 421 the Athenians captured Scione in Pallene by siege, killed the men and enslaved the women and children (see chapter 12, p. 340). The attack on Melos, as distinct from the treatment inflicted when it surrendered, may not have been an outrage to Greek sentiment; the force which the Athenians originally sent against the island comprised not only Athenians but also ships from Chios and Lesbos and hoplites from some of the allies, including islanders. Later people called to mind the conquest of Melos as one of several outrages committed by the Athenians in their imperial period. Late in 405, when the Athenians themselves expected to be besieged (chapter 14, pp. 377–378), they remembered the treatment they had inflicted on Melos and other places and feared lest they should suffer the same. In the fourth century the treatment of Melos and Scione was a stock illustration of the enormities of Athenian imperialism. What Thucydides thought about the Melian incident may be inferred from his narrative and his silence; the Melians resisted in the hope of getting help from Sparta but they did not receive any.

THE DISPATCH OF THE EXPEDITION TO SICILY[2]

By 416 war had broken out in the western part of Sicily between the cities of Egesta and Selinus. The latter had the support of Syracuse, which was now by far the strongest power in Sicily. So in 416 the Egestans appealed to Athens for help. The appeal prompted the Athenians to revive their desire of conquering Sicily, but at first they proceeded with caution. They sent an embassy to discover whether the Egestans could provide as much money as they alleged and to find out the condition which the war with Selinus had reached. The decision which the Athenians took in 415 when the embassy returned was to be much influenced by internal rivalries, and so it will not be amiss to consider at this point some changes which the Archidamian War had brought in the Athenian political scene.

Traditionally political life in a Greek city was a matter of rivalries and friendships between those families and influential persons who were wealthy and prestigious enough to command a following. In fifth-century Athens a young man entering a political career sought sympathizers primarily among his relatives and friends. The prizes of public life were the elective offices, that is, generalships and embassies, and successes in lawsuits. A chance remark of Thucydides shows that many Athenian politicians belonged to *hetaireiai* or clubs, each of which sought to promote the interests of its members in lawsuits and elections. The reforms of Cleisthenes (chapter 6, pp. 151–157) brought ascendancy to wealthy families of the city of Athens as distinct from families influential in other parts of Attica. Nearly all the politicians active in the period from Cleisthenes until 431 belonged to demes in the city, so far as their demes are recorded. Pericles achieved his ascendancy by holding together a coalition of city families.

The Archidamian War altered this. In most of the years from 431 until 425 Peloponnesian forces devastated parts of Attica, and the inhabitants withdrew from the countryside to the fortifications of the city, the Peiraeus and the Long Walls connecting them. Living in crowded conditions, they were subject to mass emotions; Aristophanes indicates that at times rumors of plots and of attempts at tyranny were current. Moreover, in consequence of the evacuation of Attica, many people who would otherwise have come only rarely to the city were available to vote. The outcome of votes on policy in the assembly and of elections became more hazardous. This helps to explain why men with no political antecedents achieved prominence in the Archidamian War.

Cleon was a man of this kind. He belonged to a deme within the city, Cydathenae, and his father was wealthy enough to serve in 460/59 as *choregos* or financial producer of an entry at the dramatic competition. But he came from outside of the circle of families who held political initiative before the Peloponnesian War. As far as is known, he was the first of his family to pursue a political career, and the hatred which Thucydides and Aristophanes felt for him may spring from the fact that he was a newcomer to politics. A curious story told by Plutarch tells how Cleon, on deciding to go into politics, called together his friends and renounced his friendship with them. The gesture may have been disingenuous, but it enabled Cleon to pose as the disinterested friend of the people, inaccessible to personal influence. He seems to have introduced a new style in politics; during the Archidamian War new terms, like "lover of the people" (*philodemos*) and "hater of the people" (*misodemos*), became current in political language. Thucydides first introduces Cleon on the occasion of the debate about treatment of the Mytilenaeans after their surrender; he says that Cleon was "the most violent of the citizens and at that time most persuasive to the people." Cleon exercised influence mostly as a speaker in the assembly; he also held a special command for the operation at Sphacteria, and he was general in 422/1, when he was killed at the battle of Amphipolis.

Not only men like Cleon, whose families belonged to city demes but had not previously achieved political prominence, but also men belonging to demes far outside the city began to gain political distinction during the Archidamian War. The change can be traced in the lists of generals, so far as they can be reconstructed, for the period 441/0–412/1. Before the outbreak of the Archidamian War very few men belonging to demes far outside the city were elected as generals, but their number increased steadily in the two decades beginning in 432/1. The political stature which some of these men achieved was more significant than their number. One of them was Demosthenes; his deme, Aphidna, lay far out to the north; the architect of success at Pylos and Sphacteria, he was the most imaginative general Athens produced during the Archidamian War. Another newcomer was Nicias of the deme Cydantidae. He was general in at least five years of the Archidamian War; he won several real, though unspectacular, successes, capturing Minoa, a small island off the Megarid, in 427 and Cythera, off the southeastern promontory of Laconia, in 424.

Considerations of caution swayed Nicias in favor of peace in 421, and the conclusion of the treaty enhanced his prestige. During the next few years Alcibiades emerged as his chief rival. Alcibiades was a man of very different origin. His family had been prominent since the settlement of Cleisthenes. His father, Cleinias, was killed at the battle of Coroneia in 447/6, when Alcibiades was a child; he and his brother were brought up by Pericles as guardian. Alcibiades began public activity during the Archidamian War; he cared for the welfare of the Spartan prisoners captured at Sphacteria and in this way he tried to renew the Spartan proxeny, which his grandfather had held and renounced. But the Spartans chose to negotiate peace not through him but through Nicias; Alcibiades felt rebuffed, and Thucydides gives this as one of his reasons for working in 420 to ally Athens with Argos. The other reason was that he thought that association with Argos would be more beneficial to his city. Later Thucydides introduces Alcibiades again, when he reports the debates held in 415 on sending the expedition to Sicily. He notes Alcibiades's military ability but says that his extravagance in maintaining horses and in other expenditure alarmed many Athenians; they suspected him of aiming at tyranny. In 416 he entered no less than seven chariots in the race at the Olympic festival and he won the first, second and fourth places. Such display brought honor to his city but aroused envy among his political rivals.

By 415 the rivalry between Nicias and Alcibiades was the chief personal issue in Athens, and early in the year an ostracism was held to choose between the two men. But a few days before the vote was to be taken Alcibiades approached Nicias and suggested that they should combine their forces against a third man, Hyperbolus. This was done and Hyperbolus was ostracized. The incident reveals much about the nature of political struggles in Athens. Nicias and Alcibiades each commanded a personal following, whose votes were determined neither by issues nor by political principle but by the wishes of the leaders. Such a following need not have been very large, but it was cohesive and impressive enough to sway the outcome in the assembly decisively, even though the procedure for ostracism was secret voting.

In the spring of 415 the Athenian envoys sent to Egesta returned with some Egestans. They had formed an exaggerated impression of the finances which

Egesta could supply for war. The assembly met and voted an expedition of sixty ships, to be commanded by three generals, Alcibiades, Nicias and Lamachus; they were instructed to help Egesta against Selinus, to restore Leontini (chapter 12, p. 330), and generally to promote Athenian interests in Sicily. Four days later the assembly met again to consider preparations. Nicias spoke and urged the Athenians to reconsider their decision to send the expedition; he felt that it was hazardous to commit a large force to such a distant theater, especially now that Sparta was hostile. But Alcibiades pleaded successfully for sending the expedition; he was supported by the Egestan envoys and by some refugees from Leontini. Thereupon Nicias tried to deter the Athenians from sending the expedition by dilating on its probable high cost. But the assembly was full of enthusiasm; it voted the three generals full powers to decide on the size of the force and the preparations.

At this point a scandal complicated the prospects of Alcibiades. At Athens in the open there were numerous religious objects called herms; these were upright pillars of stone, approximately square in section, with a rough carving of a head at the top; they were associated with the god Hermes. One night all of these were mutilated. Many Athenians were alarmed; the occurrence might be a bad omen for the expedition to Sicily; besides, it might have been committed by conspirators, who sought ultimately to overthrow the constitution and tried meanwhile to bind themselves together more closely by joint perpetration of an outrage. An inquiry was held and rewards were offered for information. Some of the informers alleged another scandal; they said that parodies of the Eleusinian mysteries had been performed in private houses, and their charges implicated Alcibiades. The Eleusinian mysteries were celebrated by the Athenian state twice a year, the greater mysteries in the fall and the lesser mysteries in the spring; they brought participants the promise of a glorious life after death, and it was forbidden to disclose the rites to the uninitiate. Private performance of the rites was accordingly sacrilegious. The two scandals aroused alarm, and the enemies of Alcibiades seized on them to excite suspicion against him. He offered to stand trial before the expedition sailed, but that was not what his enemies wished. The assembly voted that he should sail with the expedition.

The expedition set sail from the Peiraeus about the middle of summer. It comprised 60 fighting triremes and 40 triremes designed to carry hoplites. Forces from the allies and merchant ships carrying supplies had been told to gather at Corcyra. When the force from the Peiraeus joined the muster at Corcyra, the Chians and other allies proved to have furnished 34 triremes, so that the total was 134. The hoplites totalled 5,100, including some from Argos and Mantinea. There were also 480 archers, 700 slingers from Rhodes, 120 light-armed troops drawn from Megarian exiles, and one horse transport carrying 30 cavalry. The

Athenian state sent 30 supply ships and 100 lighter vessels with the expedition, and numerous commercial vessels of these types accompanied it on private initiative.

From Corcyra the Athenian expeditionary force sailed to South Italy and thence to Sicily. Few of the cities of the island showed any desire to join the Athenians, but by a stratagem they seized Catane about forty miles north of Syracuse as a base. Shortly afterwards a special ship, the *Salaminia*, arrived with instructions to arrest Alcibiades; the investigation into the mutilation of the herms and the profanation of the mysteries had continued and charges were to be brought against him. He set sail in his own ship accompanying the *Salaminia*, but at Thurii he escaped and made his way to the Peloponnese. The Athenians tried and condemned him in his absence.

Nicias and Lamachus remained in command of the Athenian forces in Sicily, and early in the winter of 415/4 they began attacking the city of Syracuse. The Syracusans sent envoys to Corinth and Sparta to seek help. It happened that Alcibiades reached Sparta at the same time as the envoys from Syracuse and Corinth, and he joined them in urging the Spartans to send help to Syracuse and to prosecute the war against Athens vigorously at home. In 414 accordingly, Syracuse received a Spartan officer, Gylippus, to direct operations and some triremes from Corinth and her colonies. The Athenian commanders proceeded with the conflict and tried to build siege works. Lamachus was killed in action, and late in the season of 414 Nicias, now alone in the command, wrote to Athens to ask urgently for reinforcements. He asked to be relieved of the command, since he was suffering from a disease of the kidneys. In response the Athenians retained Nicias in command but sent plentiful reinforcements; Eurymedon set off with ten triremes at about the winter solstice, and Demosthenes followed early in the spring of 413 with sixty triremes from Athens, five from Chios and a complement of hoplites. The Syracusans received additional triremes from Corinth and hoplites from Sparta, Boeotia, Corinth and Sicyon. But the fighting of 413 at Syracuse went against the Athenians. After repeated defeats Nicias and Demosthenes tried to retreat by land, but they were overtaken and captured. The two commanders were killed, and the Syracusans set the prisoners to work in quarries under extreme conditions. Thus the whole Athenian expeditionary force together with reinforcements was lost.

Meanwhile, military operations in the Peloponnese and Central Greece increased in scale. In 414 the Spartans and their allies invaded and ravaged the territory of Argos; the Athenians sent thirty triremes to support Argos, and this

Athenian force raided several places on the coast of Laconia. This operation, though of little military significance, had an important consequence for Spartan morale. The Spartans saw that the Athenians had openly broken the peace of Nicias. They felt that in the Archidamian War the injustice had been more on their own side, since they had refused the Athenian offer to submit the disputes to arbitration and the Thebans had attacked Plataea while a state of peace was still supposedly in force. So they considered it only reasonable that they had suffered disasters, such as that at Pylos. But now in 414 they had better expectations, since the guilt for breaking the peace belonged clearly to the Athenians. Further, they saw that the Athenians were at the disadvantage of fighting both in Sicily and at home. So they were enthusiastic for prosecuting the war.

Early in the spring of 413 the Spartan king Agis led a force of Lacedaemonians and their allies into Attica. In addition to ravaging part of the territory, he seized and fortified Deceleia and stayed there with a permanent garrison. This action had been suggested to the Spartans by Alcibiades; furthermore, during the invasions of Attica in 431–425 they had made a point of sparing Deceleia, so possibly they were already thinking of occupying it in those years. Deceleia lay about fifteen miles north of the city of Athens and a little further from the Boeotian border. The garrison under Agis inflicted great damage by continual raids; agriculture in Attica was brought virtually to a standstill and farm animals were killed. Slaves escaping from captivity found a refuge at Deceleia; Thucydides says that as many as 20,000 escaped thus; they may have included many slaves employed in the silver mines at Laureum. Thucydides adds that the import of supplies to Attica became more expensive; previously the route had run from Euboea through Oropus and Deceleia to Athens, but henceforth supplies had to be conveyed by sea round Cape Sunium. Furthermore, because of the danger of attack from Deceleia the Athenians manned their fortifications in relays continually. To meet their financial difficulties the Athenians changed their mode of gaining revenue from the Empire; in 413 they abolished the tribute and introduced instead a duty of a twentieth on goods carried by sea.

Late in the campaigning season of 413 the news arrived of the Athenian disaster in Sicily. The Spartans were encouraged; they expected subject allies of Athens to rebel, and they hoped for naval reinforcements from Syracuse and other Greek cities of Sicily. They planned to prosecute the war at sea in the Aegean. During the winter they gave orders for building a fleet of 100 triremes; they themselves were to build 25 of the ships, and they required the others from their allies in Boeotia, Phocis, Locris, Corinth, Arcadia, Pellene, Sicyon, Megara, Troezen, Epidaurus and Hermione. Appeals were received from some allies of Athens on the east coast of the Aegean, as they were contemplating revolt; approaches were also made to Sparta by the two satraps holding the westernmost provinces in Asia Minor. The satrapy with its center at Sardis governed approximately the territory of the former kingdom of Lydia and was held by Tissaphernes; further north the satrapy of Hellespontine Phrygia was held by Pharnabazus and had its center at Dascylium. The Persian Empire still claimed the Greek cities on the mainland of Asia Minor, although in fact most of them had long been subject to Athens instead of Persia. Recently King Darius II had begun calling both satraps to account for the arrears of tribute theoretically due from the Greek cities.

In the winter of 413/2 messengers came from Lesbos to Agis at Deceleia to seek help for a proposed revolt against Athens; Agis, who had considerable freedom of action, prepared to send them forces. But messengers from Chios and Erythrae went to Sparta with a similar request and they were accompanied by an envoy from Tissaphernes, who invited a Peloponnesian force and offered to provide money for its supplies. Pharnabazus also sent envoys to Sparta to invite the Peloponnesians to the neighborhood of his satrapy. Thus the Spartans had to choose between two possible theaters of operations, a more southerly and a more northerly. On the one hand, they might send the fleet, which was being prepared, to Chios and the Ionian mainland and rely on the financial support of Tissaphernes; on the other hand, they might send the fleet to Lesbos and the Hellespont and rely on the support of Pharnabazus. The Spartans decided for the southerly theater, and this was favored by Alcibiades, who was still influential among them. The reasons for this choice are not clear. The subsequent development of the war was to show that the key to victory over Athens lay in the Hellespont; once her enemies gained control of the narrow waters between the Black Sea and the Aegean, they could stop the supply of grain from the district north of the Black Sea to Athens. But this may not have been evident to the majority of Spartan citizens as early as the winter of 413/2. Early in the spring of 412 a congress of the Peloponnesian League gathered at Corinth and decided on a composite plan, which has the air of a compromise: the fleet was to sail first to Chios and install a Spartan officer there; then it was to proceed to Lesbos and install another Spartan officer there; and finally it was to make for the Hellespont.

Athens, however, made her own preparations and these impeded the execution of Peloponnesian designs. When the news came of the Sicilian disaster, the Athenians decided to economize in administration and build new ships; they set up a standing board of ten *probouloi* to propose measures for meeting the emergency. Hence in 412 to the surprise of their enemies the Athenians were able to send effective naval forces to sea. Soon after the Isthmian festival a Peloponnesian fleet of twenty-one ships set off from Cenchreae on the eastern shore of the Corinthiad, but an Athenian fleet harassed it and drove it to seek refuge in the harbor of Speiraeum in the easternmost part of Corinthian territory. This news at first discouraged the Spartans from naval enerprise, but Alcibiades persuaded the ephors to send him and Chalcideus, the Spartan navarch or annual naval commander, with five triremes across the Aegean. This small force reached Chios and, helped by sympathizers in the city, they persuaded the Chians to rebel against Athens.

The revolt of Chios began a series of risings against the Athenians. Erythrae rebelled promptly, and soon afterwards the Lacedaemonians sailed with three ships from Chios to Clazomenae and persuaded it to join in the revolt. But the Athenians responded vigorously. On learning of the revolt of Chios they voted to draw on the special reserve of 1,000 talents, which had been set aside in 431, and they set about equipping more ships. Their first squadron sent across the Aegean consisted of only eight triremes; it put in at Samos, which was used by the Athenians as their chief base in this and the next year. During 412 both sides sent out larger and larger forces to the eastern Aegean. Proceeding from Chios, the Peloponnesians tried to persuade a series of cities to join the revolt against Athens; during the campaigning season of 412 they won over Teos and Miletus, and forces from Chios persuaded Lebedus and Haerae to join their cause. Chalcideus negotiated a treaty with Tissaphernes for joint prosecution of the war against the Athenians. But the growing Athenian force at Samos achieved some successes. After some Chian ships sailed to Lesbos and persuaded Methymna and then Mytilene to join the revolt, an Athenian squadron of twenty-five ships followed and regained Mytilene and then the rest of the island. Promptly afterwards the same Athenian squadron recovered Clazomenae. A major battle fought on land outside Miletus was indecisive, but in the winter of 412/1 Athenians approaching from Lesbos made a landing in the island of Chios and fortified a position there called Delphinium; thence they were able to harass the Chians and provide a refuge for fugitive slaves. In the same winter the movement of revolt spread southwards; Tissaphernes persuaded Cnidus to rebel, and a little later the Peloponnesian fleet, which had grown to ninety-four ships, sailed to the island of Rhodes and persuaded its three cities to join their side.

THE REVOLUTION OF 411[4]

During 411 fighting on the east coast of the Aegean began to approach stalemate, but drastic changes took place within Athens early in the summer and came near to bringing the war to a sudden and unexpected end. The crucial factor swaying the Athenians in the direction of changes in the constitution was the need for economy since the losses experienced in Sicily. The constitution, as it had developed since the middle of the fifth century, was expensive to run. It provided daily payment for men performing political functions; this included numerous offices, the Council of Five Hundred, and service in the jury courts. Yet in 411 the immediate impulse towards revolution came from Alcibiades and from the officers of the Athenian fleet stationed at Samos.

Alcibiades had made powerful and bitter enemies in Sparta; they included king Agis. In 412 he had sailed to Chios with Chalcideus, who was able to cooperate with him; but Chalcideus was killed in action towards the end of his term of office as navarch. Astyochus, the navarch of 412/1, received orders to execute Alcibiades. The latter fled and found refuge with Tissaphernes; for a time he frequented the satrap's court. Indeed, it is not clear how far the policies pursued by Tissaphernes were his own and how far they were prompted by the advice of Alcibiades. Tissaphernes found collaboration with the Peloponnesians difficult. Some Spartan officers argued that their duty was to liberate Greek cities from Athens, not subjugate them to Persian rule. Moreover, there were financial difficulties. Tissaphernes provided subsidies to maintain the Peloponnesian fleet but he sought to decrease the rate of pay for the crews; Alcibiades encouraged him in this, arguing that the Athenians, who had more experience of naval warfare, paid their crews at a lower rate.

By the beginning of 411 relations between Tissphernes and the Peloponnesians had become difficult. With the concurrence of Alcibiades, he decided that it was not in his interests to bring about a clear victory for either side in the war but rather to ensure that each side weakened the other extensively. Alcibiades had his own goal to pursue; he wanted to have himself recalled to Athens and he thought he could achieve this if he gained a modicum of Persian support for the Athenians. So he exchanged messages with leading men in the Athenian fleet at Samos and offered them a threefold plan: the Athenian constitution was to be changed, so that the men who had brought about the exile of Alcibiades should lose ascendancy; the recall of Alcibiades was to be voted; and Alcibiades was to persuade Tissaphernes to transfer his support from the Peloponnesians to the Athenians. Most of the officers in the Athenian fleet welcomed the scheme. They felt that they had had to bear more than their share of the burdens of warfare, and so they welcomed the prospect of a narrower constitution, which would allow them a greater share in determining policy. The slogan they chose for the type of constitution they preferred was *aristokratia*; in cynical moments they called it *oligarchia*.

Phrynichus, one of the Athenian generals at Samos, opposed the plan. He argued, correctly, that Alcibiades cared no more for the proposed *oligarchia* than for the traditional constitution and that it was of the utmost importance to avoid civil strife. But Phrynichus was in a minority. The leaders of the fleet accepted the threefold plan and they sent Peisander, one of their number, with others to Athens to propose the steps they required. When Peisander reached Athens and addressed the assembly, the language chosen continued to avoid clarity. *Demo-kratia*, a word with imprecise meaning and complex overtones, had been coined in the time of Pericles and adhered to the Athenian constitution. Peisander argued that the Athenians could win the alliance of Persia and overcome the Pelo-ponnesians, if they recalled Alcibiades and "did not conduct their *demokratia* in the same way." There were protests both from the enemies of Alcibiades and from those who objected to a change in the constitution. But when Peisander pointed out that there was no other hope of safety, the assembly acquiesced in the plan and it elected him and ten others as envoys to negotiate with Tissaphernes and Alcibiades. In response to charges made by Peisander, he assembly deposed Phrynichus and one of his colleagues, Scironides, from office, and elected Diomedon and Leon in their stead.

On this visit to Athens Peisander took a further step, which was decisive for the events of the next few months. As noted above (p. 351), there existed in Athens political clubs (*hetaireiai*), each of which tried to help its members in lawsuits and elections. In the case of many clubs, perhaps all, the members were bound together by an oath. An aspiring politician sought support largely through his club. Normally each club competed with the others, but Peisander persuaded the clubs to put an end to their differences and collaborate towards bringing about a change in the constitution. Many members of the clubs saw their opportunity; those who brought about the change in the constitution would retain ascendancy in the new order. During the next few weeks they put forward a specious program, which appealed to the acknowledged need for economy. State pay should no longer be provided for political office but only for those engaged in military or naval service. Accordingly, power was to be restricted to those whose property qualified them for service as hoplites, since they could hold political office without drawing state pay; it was expected that they would number not more than 5,000. The plotters, as they may be called, assassinated some political opponents including Androcles, a popular leader who had done much to bring about the exile of Alcibiades. Since the identity of the plotters was not known, their number was overestimated; no one knew whether his neighbor might not belong to the conspiracy. Soon fear prevailed among the bulk of the population; although the Council and the assembly continued to meet, nothing was proposed which had not been approved by the plotters beforehand.

Peisander and the other ten envoys proceeded to the court of Tissaphernes. But Alcibiades found that he could not persuade the satrap to transfer his support to the Athenians. So, speaking on behalf of Tissaphernes, he made a series of demands for recognition of increasingly exorbitant Persian claims. Hence the negotiations broke down but the responsibility for their failure rested in appearance with the Athenians. Shortly afterwards Tissaphernes visited the fleet of the Peloponnesians and made a new treaty with them. Thus a cardinal item in the threefold plan launched by Alcibiades collapsed, but the effect on the revolutionary movement in Athens and in the Athenian fleet at Samos was paradoxical. When Peisander and his fellow envoys returned to Samos, the Athenian leaders there decided to go ahead with their plans for introducing a more restricted constitution, even though they abandoned the prospect of recalling Alcibiades. Peisander and his colleagues also persuaded some leading men of Samos to set about introducing a restricted constitution in their city. The movement was acquiring an ideological character. One of the generals, Dieitrephes, was sent to the Thracian coast and there he overthrew the democratic constitution of Thasos; a month later Thasos rebelled against the Athenians. Peisander himself was sent with five of the envoys to Athens to take the lead in affairs there.

During the absence of Peisander a development on the northern border of Attica had made the situation more acute. Towards the end of winter the Boeotians with help from some men of Eretria captured Oropus. This position was important because it had easy communications with Eretria; holding it, the enemies of Athens could hope to bring about a revolt of Euboea. When Peisander arrived, a meeting of the assembly was called and on the initiative of the plotters it added twenty new members to the board of ten *probouloi*, which had been in existence since 413; the resulting board of thirty was instructed to report to the assembly on a fixed day with proposals for improving the constitution. When the fixed day came, the assembly was summoned in the temple of Poseidon at Colonus rather more than a mile outside the city wall. The thirty commissioners made only one recommendation, namely that all restrictions on proposing measures should be suspended; this meant that the *graphe paranomon* or indictment for proposing something contrary to the laws ceased to be in force. Then members of the assembly proposed measures, which were carried out and amounted to a revolution. It was resolved that there should be no state pay for political office but only for military and naval service. The list of men qualified by property for service as hoplites was to be drawn up; it was expected that they would number five thousand. They could hold political office without receiving state pay. Above all, a Council of Four Hundred was to be selected in a complex way; five "presidents" were elected in the assembly; they were to choose a hundred men, and each of the hundred was to choose three more. This Council was to rule, in theory as an interim government, in place of the five thousand.

Thus in Athens, as in the fleet at Samos, the plotters chose to proceed to revolution even though they had no longer any expectation of obtaining Persian money through Alcibiades. Indeed, the movement now turned against Alcibiades. The real initiative belonged to a small group, perhaps a dozen men, within the Council of Four Hundred. They included Phrynichus, the enemy of Alcibiades. Another of them was Peisander, who was publicly instrumental in bringing the changes about and proposed the resolution setting up the Four Hundred. Perhaps a more interesting figure in the group was Antiphon, a man who had brought the art of composing speeches to a much higher level of skill than before. He made a point of not speaking in the assembly but outside the public view he was most instrumental in bringing the revolution about.

When the assembly at Colonus was dismissed, the Four Hundred proceeded to the chamber where the traditional Council of the Five Hundred sat. Each of the Four Hundred had a dagger hidden in his clothers and they took with them a standing force of one hundred young men, which the plotters used for intimidation. The Four Hundred made the councilors of the Five Hundred disperse but authorized them to draw their pay for the remaining month of their term of office. Then the Four Hundred occupied the council chamber and organized themselves for the discharge of business. They ruled by terror, killing a few potential opponents and imprisoning and exiling others. They promptly sent out embassies in two directions. One went to Agis at Deceleia, but at first he was unreceptive; he hoped for civil strife in Athens and a little later he made a sally towards the Long Walls. But after his sally had achieved nothing, he welcomed a further embassy from the Four Hundred and advised them to send envoys to Sparta, which they did.

The other embassy, consisting of ten men, was sent by the Four Hundred to Samos to reassure the Athenian fleet, but before it arrived the oligarchic movement there had suffered a series of checks. Those among the Samians who were plotting to change the constitution numbered about three hundred; with the connivance of some leading Athenians they killed Hyperbolus, who had been ostracized from Athens (p. 353), and some others. But their Samian opponents appealed for help to some Athenians, the generals Leon and Diomedon, the trierarch Thrasybulus, and Thrasyllus, who was serving as a hoplite. Leon and Diomedon sent some Athenian ships to support the Samian opposition. When accordingly the three hundred made their attempt at armed revolution, they were defeated; thirty of them were executed and three others were exiled. In a new wave of enthusiasm for democratic constitutions of the traditional type the Samians and the Athenian force in Samos sent a special Athenian ship, the *Paralos,* to Athens to announce the events; they did not yet know that the Four Hundred were in control. When the *Paralos* arrived, the Four Hundred transferred most of its crew to another ship and set them on guard duty near Euboea. But Chaereas, who had sailed with the *Paralos* from Samos, escaped, made his way to Samos, and made exaggerated reports about severities and outrages allegedly practised by the Four Hundred.

When this news was brought to the Athenians in Samos, it produced a strong reaction in favor of *demokratia*. At first the Athenian troops wanted to lynch those who had planned to change the constitution, but they were dissuaded and under the lead of Thrasybulus and Thrasyllus they took an oath to maintain the *demokratia* and civil concord, to continue the war against the Peloponnesians with vigor, and to be enemies of the Four Hundred and not exchange heralds with them. All Samians of military age took the same oath. Further, the Athenian troops formed themselves into a political assembly, deposed their previous generals and elected new ones, including Thrasybulus and Thrasyllus. The ten envoys of the Four Hundred were at Delos, when they received news of these events, and so they paused in their journey there.

In their new enthusiasm many of the Athenian troops relied on the prospect of recalling Alcibiades and gaining through him the help of Tissaphernes. After a time Thrasybulus persuaded the assembled troops to vote the recall; then he sailed to Tissaphernes and brought Alcibiades back with him. So Alcibiades addressed the assembly of the troops; he complained bitterly about the causes which had brought about his exile, but the main content of his speech was a large boast of his influence with Tissaphernes; he insisted that Tissaphernes was willing to go to all lengths to provide financial support for the Athenian cause. The assembly responded by electing Alcibiades general. About the same time the ten envoys of the Four Hundred arrived from Delos and addressed the assembly. They denied Chaereas's allegations of outrages and insisted that rule was to be entrusted to the whole body of five thousand. The assembled troops paid them no heed and wished at first to sail at once to the Peiraeus and overthrow the Four Hundred. Alcibiades restrained them with difficulty and formulated a reply for the ten envoys to take to Athens. He did not object, he said, to the rule of the five thousand, but he insisted that the Four Hundred must be replaced by the traditional Council of Five Hundred; further, he expressed his approval of any economies carried out to ensure supplies to the troops.

Meanwhile in Athens a split had developed among the leaders of the Four Hundred. The cause was frustrated ambition; some of the leaders, such as Theramenes and Aristocrates, had hoped to achieve first place in the new regime but they were disappointed. The message of Alcibiades encouraged them to desert the revolution, since they could hope for support from the fleet. They issued specious demands: they wanted the list of the five thousand published and control transferred to that body. The more resolute of the revolutionaries, who included Phrynichus, Aristarchus, Peisander and Antiphon, found their supremacy threatened and they took two steps. First they sent an embassy, including Antiphon and Phrynichus, to Sparta to try to negotiate acceptable terms of peace. Second, they began fortifying the mole called Eetioneia at the entrance to the harbor of the Peiraeus. They said that they required the fortification to resist the Athenian force in Samos, if it should sail to the Peiraeus; their critics said that they intended to admit Peloponnesian forces at Eetioneia. This charge gained in credibility when a Peloponnesian fleet of forty-two ships gathered at Las on the coast of Laconia; disaffected elements in Euboea had invited it, as they hoped to rebel against Athens; but Theramenes could allege that the fleet was bound for Eetioneia.

The embassy of Phrynichus to Sparta was unsuccessful, and promptly after its return Phrynichus was assassinated. Feeling grew still more tense when the Peloponnesian fleet began its northward journey, raided Aegina and anchored at Epidaurus. Those companies of hoplites who had been set to fortify Eetioneia mutinied and arrested one of the generals. When the Four Hundred in the council chamber learned of this, Theramenes offered to go and quell the mutiny. He went to the Peiraeus and joined the mutineers. They demolished the fortifications which they had been building. Their slogan was that anyone who wished the five thousand to rule instead of the Four Hundred should join them. Their desire was for a return to the traditional constitution, but they clung to the term "the five thousand." For all they knew, the list of the five thousand might already have been compiled and its members might know that they belonged to it; so they might rally to the support of the Four Hundred, if there were an open demand for a return to the traditional constitution. The Four Hundred for their part had fostered general uncertainty by neither publishing the list of the five thousand nor admitting that it had not been drawn up.

On the next day the mutineers marched from the Peiraeus to the city. Picked men from among the Four Hundred approached them with offers of appeasement; they promised that the list of the five thousand should be published and that successive councils of four hundred should be chosen from among them; and it was agreed that an assembly about concord should be held on a fixed day in the theater of Dionysus. When the day came, shortly before the assembly gathered, news arrived that the Peloponnesian fleet of forty-two ships was sailing from Megara past Salamis. The Athenians hastened to the Peiraeus and manned the available ships. The Peloponnesians sailed eastwards past the promontory of Sunium and then north to Oropus. The Athenians sent their ships to Eretria and straight after their arrival the Peloponnesians attacked them. The battle was a defeat for the Athenians. Soon afterwards the cities of Euboea rebelled, except for the Athenian colony at Oreus in the north.

The news of the disaster off Euboea increased the alarm in Athens. The Athenians had only twenty ships left, and in view of their discord with the fleet at Samos they could not expect help from there. The loss of Euboea threatened their supplies. Even so they manned their twenty ships and held an assembly to bring the political conflict to an end. At this meeting they deposed the Four Hundred and entrusted control to the five thousand; the latter were again defined as all those whose property qualified them for service as hoplites; and the rule was reaffirmed that there should be no state payments for service in political offices. At this assembly or one a little later the recall of Alcibiades was voted, although he did not in fact come back to Athens till 407, and friendly relations were reopened with the fleet at Samos. Peisander and some of the other leaders of the revolution escaped to Deceleia. In the next months Antiphon and others were brought to trial and condemned.

The rule of the Four Hundred had lasted about four months. The system replacing it, the rule of the five thousand, has sometimes been called "the intermediate regime;" its nature is problematical and the question has a bearing on the causes of the revolution. The crucial evidence is some remarks of Thucydides. Often his references to the five thousand are distressingly vague; for example, in reporting the assembly which deposed the Four Hundred he says that the Athenians "voted to hand over affairs to the five thousand" (8.97.1). The traditional view has been that in the intermediate regime the right of voting was restricted to "the five thousand," this body being defined by the property qualification for hoplite service. Some passages of Thucydides (8.67.3; 8.72.1; 8.93.2) seem to envisage the five thousand as a deliberative assembly. For example, he says that in the assembly at Colonus, which established the Four Hundred, they were instructed to "convene" the five thousand whenever they thought fit (8.67.3). Again, shortly after taking office the Four Hundred sent ten envoys to report to the fleet at Samos and instructeed them to say that Athenian affairs were in the hands not of a mere four hundred but of five thousand; they were to add that in the past so many citizens had been required to serve abroad that no actual meeting of the assembly had drawn as many as five thousand (8.72.1).

Yet some other passages of Thucydides (8.68.2; 8.92.11) point in a different direction, and a more recent view holds that the intermediate regime allowed the right of voting to all adult male citizens, as was traditional, but restricted eligibility for office to the five thousand defined by the property qualification for hoplite service. Such people could be expected to discharge political offices without receiving state pay. Accordingly, when the assembly which deposed the Four Hundred reiterated the prohibition of state pay for political service, this vote was closely connected to its decision to entrust control to the five thousand. The chief passage of Thucydides that can be cited in support of this more recent view concerns the mutineers at Eetioneia. As Thucydides explains (8.92.11), their desire was for a return to the traditional constitution, and they adopted the rule of the five thousand as their slogan merely for expediency, so as not to alienate any whose names might already be on the list of the five thousand. If this was the mood of the mutineers and their cause was successful, it is not likely that a few days later they would agree to restrict the right of voting to the five thousand; the right of all adult male citizens to vote was an essential principle of the traditional constitution. If this view is correct, the passages of Thucydides which seem to envisage the five thousand as an assembly can still be explained. Since the five thousand were alone eligible for office, they had the responsibility of carrying out any decisions reached in the assembly; so they might make much more effort to attend meetings of the assembly than other citizens.

If indeed the intermediate regime restricted eligibility for office but not the right of voting, this has a bearing on the origins of the revolution. After Peisander made his first visit to Athens, the political leaders drawn from the clubs set about softening public opinion; they issued a specious program, whereby state pay should no longer be provided for political office and power should be restricted to those whose property qualified them for hoplite service, it being expected that they would number not more than five thousand. Clearly the notion of the rule of the five thousand, as expressed in this program, bore the same meaning as that notion of the rule of the five thousand which was achieved upon the overthrow of the Four Hundred. If, accordingly, at the overthrow of the Four Hundred eligibility for office was restricted to the five thousand but the right of voting was not restricted, it follows that the preparatory propaganda issued in Athens between the two visits of Peisander spoke only of a restriction on eligibility for office. This propaganda does not necessarily provide any clue to the motives of those who issued it, but it does show what ideas could sway the mass of the Athenians towards accepting a change in the constitution. If the acknowledged program of the revolutionaries was merely to restrict eligibility for office to those who could afford to serve without pay, then the ideas swaying most Athenians sprang, not from discussions about forms of government, but from considerations of economy.

Among the causes of the revolution motives of three kinds can be distinguished. The ideological element, preference for one form of government over another because of its supposed intrinsic merits, played only a minimal part. Partisans of the revolution among the Athenian commanders at Samos seem to have had some preference for *oligarchia* or *aristokratia*, as they probably called it. In particular, when Peisander failed in his attempt to win the support of Tissaphernes and returned to Samos, the Athenian leaders there not only decided to go ahead with their plans but also encouraged some Samians to try to set up a narrower regime, and at their prompting a constitutional change was carried out in Thasos and perhaps some other allied cities. A second factor was concern for economy. The desire for Persian subsidies swayed the assembly to accept the plans proposed by Peisander on his first visit to Athens. During his ensuing absence the program put about by members of the clubs stressed the need to economize in the administration by suspending state pay for political service. This argument must have had some effect on public opinion, but it is difficult to say how much effect. Thucydides (8.66.1) remarks of this program: "This was a fair-sounding slogan directed to the majority, but those who carried out the change in the constitution intended to keep control of it." The most decisive factors were personal. The rule of the Four Hundred meant in practice the rule of a small group of men, such as Phrynichus, Antiphon and Peisander. A personal consideration of major importance was the question whether to recall Alcibiades. Its magnitude is illustrated by the behavior of Phrynichus. As long as the plan of the revolutionaries included the recall of Alcibiades, he opposed it, but he joined the movement when negotiations with Tissaphernes broke down and the revolutionaries decided to proceed even without Alcibiades. Personal considerations had a crucial effect likewise on the fall of the Four Hundred. Theramenes and a few others among the leaders turned against Phrynichus and his associates because they were disappointed of the first place. They insisted that power should be entrusted to the five thousand and the constitution should be made more equitable, but Thucydides comments (8.89.3): "This was a public slogan for them to proclaim, but most of them took up their cause because of private rivalries. That indeed is the most vulnerable point in an oligarchy which has arisen from a democracy. For at once the members, all of them, claim not merely not to be equal to the general run of citizens but each of them claims to be by far the first."

NOTES

1. The narrative depends on Thuc. 5.53–116. Thucydides reports the capture of Scione at 5.32.1. For later recollection of Athenian outrages see Xen. *Hell.* 2.2.3; Isoc. 12.62–63.

2. The narrative of events leading to the dispatch of the expedition is given by Thuc. 6.1; 6.6–32; 6.42–44. The ostracism of Hyperbolus is known from Plut. *Nic.* 11; *Alc.* 13; *Arist.* 7. Its date is disputed; the date 416/5 has been argued by A.E. Raubitschek, "Theopompos on Hyperbolos," *Phoenix* 9 (1955) 122–126; the date 418/7 was once popular and has been defended by C. Fuqua, "Possible Implications of the Ostracism of Hyperbolus," *TAPA* 96 (1965) 165–179. W.R. Connor, *The New Politicians of Fifth-Century Athens* (Princeton 1971) provides an important inquiry into the nature of the political career in Athens and the change in style brought about by Cleon. For *hetaireiai* see Thuc. 8.54.4; 8.65.2. Rumors of plots for tyranny are mentioned by Aristoph. *Wasps* 463–502. Cleon's father as *choregos* is known from *I.G.* II², 2318 line 34. On generals from demes in different parts of Attica see Sealey, *Essays* 82–94 = *PACA* 1 (1958) 70–78; the lists of generals need to be corrected from C.W. Fornara, *The Athenian Board of Generals from 501 to 404* = Historia Einzelschriften Heft 16 (Wiesbaden 1971). The generalship of Demosthenes is studied by Max Treu, "Der Stratege Demosthenes," *Historia* 5 (1956) 420–447. Nicias's captures of Minoa and

Cythera are given by Thuc. 3.51 and 4.53–57. Thucydides introduces Alcibiades at 5.43 and 6.15; his chariots in the Olympic competition are mentioned at 6.16.2. On the scandal of the herms and the mysteries see Gomme/Andrewes/Dover, *Comm*. 4.264–288.

3. The narrative depends on Thuc. 6.44–8.44. For a recent study of the Sicilian expedition see W. Liebeschuetz, "Thucydides and the Sicilian Expedition," *Historia* 17 (1968) 289–306. At 7.18 Thucydides makes a revealing comment on the outlook which led the Spartans to resume operations against Attica. Herodotus 9.73 reports that the Spartans spared Deceleia during the Archidamian War. Thucydides 7.27–28 gives the effects of Agis's occupation of Deceleia.

4. Nearly all information about the revolution depends on Thuc. 8. 47–98. The account given by Aristotle, *AP* 29–33 adds a few items of value but is mostly problematic. Hignett, *HAC* 268–280 and 356–378 provides a valuable study of the relationship between the two accounts; a different view is offered by M. Lang, "The Revolution of the 400: Chronology and Constitutions," *AJP* 88 (1967) 176–187. A little additional information is provided by [Lysias] 20; in particular this speech says that when the 5,000 defined by hoplite-property were listed, they proved to number 9,000. On *demokratia, aristokratia* and other political terms see J.A.O. Larsen, "Cleisthenes and the Development of the Theory of Democracy at Athens," in M.R. Konvitz and A.E. Murphy (edd.), *Essays in Political Theory presented to George H. Sabine* (Ithaca, N.Y. 1948) 1–16; and Sealey, "The origins of *demokratia*," *CSCA* 6 (1973) 253–295. The crucial evidence on *hetaireiai* is Thuc. 8.54.4 and 8.65.2. The traditional view, that the intermediate regime restricted the right of voting to the 5,000, has been defended by P.J. Rhodes, "The Five Thousand in the Athenian Revolutions of 411 B.C.," *JHS* 92 (1972) 115–127. The other view, that only eligibility for office was restricted, was first presented by G.E.M. de Ste. Croix, "The Constitution of the Five Thousand," *Historia* 5 (1956) 1–23; its implications for the causes of the revolution were developed by Sealey, *Essays* 111–132.

14

The End of the
Peloponnesian War,
411-404

Fighting off the west coast of Asia Minor continued in 411 but was indecisive; there was skirmishing, for example, off Rhodes and in Chios. The Peloponnesians had made a series of treaties with Tissaphernes but they were dissatisfied with the level of the financial subsidies he provided. Meanwhile they received tempting offers from Pharnabazus, and this led them to begin action which was to prove decisive many years later for the outcome of the war; they set about transferring their main forces to the Hellespont. Yet the first steps they took in this direction were small and hesitant. At the beginning of spring 411 a Spartan officer, Dercylidas, was sent by land with a small force from Miletus to the Hellespont. On his arrival Abydus rebelled against the Athenians and joined him and Pharnabazus. Lampsacus joined Dercylidas two days later, but soon Strombichides brought an Athenian squadron of twenty-four ships and recovered Lampsacus; he also put a garrison in Sestus.

Somewhat later in the season the Peloponnesians responded to a further invitation from Pharnabazus, who offered to provide subsidies and win over Byzantium, by sending Clearchus with forty ships north. This squadron tried to avoid the Athenians and it was broken up by a storm. Only ten of the ships reached the Hellespont, but these ten proceeded to Byzantium and persuaded it to join them. Clearchus himself traveled to the Hellespont overland.

Finally in the late summer the new Spartan navarch, Mindarus, took over command and decided to transfer the main Peloponnesian fleet of seventy-three ships from Miletus to the Hellespont. He ran into unfavorable winds and put in at Chios. The Athenians followed from Samos and took up a position in Lesbos to watch for the Peloponnesian fleet. But setting off at night, Mindarus escaped their notice and reached the Hellespont. There he gathered together all available forces at Abydus; his total fleet numbered eighty-six ships. The Athenians, under the command of Thrasyllus and Thrasybulus, pursued from Lesbos as soon as they learned that Mindarus was ahead; their ships numbered seventy-six. Reaching the coast of the Chersonese, they engaged the enemy off the promontory of Cynossema. The result of the battle was a clear victory for the Athenians. Although they captured only twenty-one of the enemy's ships and lost fifteen of their own, the battle restored Athenian morale. It was their first major success since the Sicilian disaster and the ensuing setbacks; they acquired confidence in their own naval capability and ceased to exaggerate that of the Peloponnesians.

A few days after this battle the Athenians recovered Cyzicus, which had seceded from their Empire. The Peloponnesians sailed from Abydus to Elaeus in the Chersonese and sent to Euboea for additional ships. Early in the winter of 411/0 a further battle was fought off Abydus and it proved to be a victory for the Athenians. Even so the Peloponnesians had not been driven from the Hellespontine area. Moreover, the Athenians needed reinforcements and money, and they made their dispositions for the winter accordingly. Alcibiades had reached the Hellespont during the battle of Abydus and he remained there with the main fleet of forty ships based at Sestus. His constitutional position as general was equal to that of his colleagues, but in virtue of his strategic brilliance and his personal hold over the men he probably had the main share in planning operations. Thrasyllus was sent to Athens to ask for men and ships, but he did not return until 409. Squadrons were sent from the Hellespont in various directions to raise money. In particular Thrasybulus sailed to Thasos with this purpose; he had some success and returned to the Hellespont to join Alcibiades towards the end of winter. Theramenes, who had been active in Athens in the fall, sailed to the islands some time later and exacted money at Paros and other places. Then he joined King Archelaus of Macedon, who was besieging Pydna, but he left before the siege was complete and joined Alcibiades in the Hellespont towards the end of winter. Thrasybulus and Theramenes each brought twenty ships, and the combined fleet numbered eighty-six ships.

At about the end of winter Mindarus took his fleet of sixty ships to Cyzicus and captured it by siege. There Pharnabazus joined him with a force of infantry. Alcibiades followed with the Athenian fleet; at Cyzicus he attacked the Peloponnesian forces and defeated them decisively. The whole Peloponnesian fleet was captured, except for the Syracusan contingent which was burned by its own crews. Pharnabazus and the Peloponnesians withdrew from Cyzicus, which promptly joined the Athenians. Alcibiades proceeded to Chrysopolis in the territory of Calchedon and set up a customs station there; he installed a garrison under Theramenes and another general with the task of exacting a tenth from all shipping that came from the Black Sea. Mindarus was killed in the battle and the Athenians intercepted a dispatch sent by his second-in-command to Sparta. It said: "The ships are lost. Mindarus is dead. The men are starving. We do not know what to do."

The battle of Cyzicus improved both the financial and the strategic position of the Athenians. Before the battle the fleet was short of money, whereas the Peloponnesians enjoyed Persian subsidies. After the battle the Athenians had a relatively secure source of revenue in the customs station at Chrysopolis. The news of the battle brought a change of morale in the city as well as in the fleet. At a date probably soon after the battle the Spartans sent an embassy to Athens and offered to make peace, but the Athenians refused.

During 410 some constitutional change was carried out in Athens, but its magnitude is difficult to estimate. The question depends on the view taken of the intermediate regime, which was set up on the overthrow of the Four Hundred in the fall of 411. Two indications show that some further change was carried out during 410. First, early in the Attic year 410/09 a law was passed on the motion of Demophantus for protecting the constitution; its main clause said: "If anyone overthrows the *demokratia* at Athens or holds any office after the *demokratia* has been overthrown, let him be an enemy of the Athenians and let him be killed with impunity, and let his property be confiscated and a tenth of it be assigned to the goddess." The law further provided an oath in corresponding terms to be sworn by all the Athenians. The word *demokratia* had complex implications but in the context of this law it designated the traditional constitution. Secondly, a fund called the *diobelia* or "two-obol fund" was instituted on the motion of Cleophon, a popular leader in the tradition of Cleon. Payments continued to be made into and out of this fund for several years, perhaps as late as 404/3, but its nature is obscure. The name implies that it provided payments to some people at the rate of two obols a day, and an attractive conjecture is that it provided payment for jurors, perhaps also payment for the members of the Council of Five Hundred. At least it is difficult to avoid seeing in the *diobelia* some form of payment for political service.

Those who believe that the intermediate regime restricted the right of voting to the five thousand have to suppose that during 410 the traditional constitution was restored, the suffrage being extended to all adult male citizens; this would be a major change, and the Law of Demophantus would attest its completion. It is then surprising that record of this change in the literary sources is rare or nonexistent. Those, on the other hand, who believe that the intermediate regime restricted eligibility for office to the five thousand but not the right of voting, need not suppose so large a change as occurring in 410. They can point to a statement of Thucydides (8.97.2), made straight after he has recorded the replacement of the Four Hundred by the intermediate regime; he adds that later there were frequent meetings of the assembly, in which the Athenians set up a commission of lawgivers and voted other measures concerning the constitution. Meetings of the assembly dealing with constitutional questions may have continued into 410 and may have carried out a series of modifications, none of them being of such magnitude as the right of all citizens to vote, for on this view that right was not disputed. The introduction of the *diobelia* may have been the most considerable of these modifications. It made possible the admission to office of men who lacked the property qualification for hoplite service. Their admission may have been achieved, not through explicit repeal of the restriction made in the fall of 411, but through its nonenforcement. At least Aristotle (*AP* 7.4 fin.) indicates that in his own time members of the fourth Solonic property class, the thetes, were admitted to the nine archonships through nonenforcement of the law excluding them.

THE ASCENDANCY AND DECLINE OF ALCIBIADES[2]

After the battle of Cyzicus Pharnabazus provided supplies for the survivors of the Peloponnesian crews and set them to build new ships, but a long time was to pass before they would be ready to engage the main Athenian fleet at sea. The operations of the Athenians were impeded by political divisions. Thrasybulus and Theramenes were willing to cooperate with Alcibiades, but the actions of Thrasyllus show that he desired more independence. The fleet in the Hellespont needed reinforcements of ships and men, and Thrasyllus had been sent to Athens to procure these in the winter of 411/0. He stayed in Athens in 410 and repulsed successfully a raid attempted on the city by Agis from Deceleia. At last in 409 he set sail with a force including fifty triremes and 1,000 hoplites; he equipped 5,000 of the rowers to serve as light-armed troops. He did not make for the Hellespont but put in at Samos and from there he waged a campaign of his own in Ionia. He won over Colophon and made a raid into Lydia, but eventually he was defeated by Tissaphernes and some Greek troops near Ephesus. Then at last he sailed north and, after putting in at Methymna, joined Alcibiades at Lampsacus. At first the troops of Alcibiades refused to fraternize with those of Thrasyllus, but during the winter Alcibiades led the entire force towards Abydus and defeated Pharnabazus near there. Then the troops were willing to mix.

Alcibiades planned to devote the season of 408 to capturing Calchedon and Byzantium. First he led the whole Athenian force against Calchedon; it built siege walls around the city and set about besieging it. Pharnabazus came to the aid of the Calchedonians, but the Athenians defeated their enemies in battle outside the walls. Soon afterwards Alcibiades sailed to the Chersonese to raise money, and in his absence Pharnabazus reached an agreement with the Athenian generals. Pharnabazus was to pay the Athenians twenty talents on behalf of the Calchedonians, and henceforth Calchedon was to pay tribute to Athens as before. Furthermore Pharnabazus was to conduct a party of Athenian envoys to king Darius II in the hope of negotiating a settlement, and the Athenians were not to conduct any warlike operations against Calchedon until the envoys expected from the king arrived. In the meantime Alcibiades captured Selymbria on the north coast of the Propontis. He raised extensive reinforcements from the Chersonese and from Thrace, and on his return to the territory of Calchedon he exchanged oaths with Pharnabazus to the agreement. Then he led the Athenian force against Byzantium and besieged it. When the Byzantines ran short of supplies, a small group within the city betrayed it to the Athenians by opening the gates.

By the end of 408 Alcibiades had great achievements to his credit. In the war at sea both the strategic and the financial situation of the Athenians had been restored. Although Peloponnesian forces again operated by land and sea on the west coast of Asia Minor, the Athenians had won a clear predominance in the crucial area of the Hellespont and the Propontis. Alcibiades's achievement was the more impressive because fighting closer to Athens had proved less successful. Agis still held Deceleia and Euboea had not been recovered. Moreover, in 410 the Spartans had launched an attack on Pylos; an Athenian expedition of thirty ships under Anytus could not round Cape Malea because of adverse winds, and the Spartans captured Pylos. In 407 Alcibiades set about visiting Athens to strengthen his political position. He chose a curiously roundabout route. First he sailed to Samos and thence to the Ceramic Gulf, where he exacted 100 talents. He returned to Samos and sailed with twenty ships to Paros. Thence he sailed towards the Lacedaemonian harbor of Gytheum, since he had heard that the Spartans were preparing thirty ships. Learning that the Athenians had elected him general for 407/6 in his absence, he sailed at last to the Peiraeus. Since he was a controversial figure, a large crowd gathered on shore at his approach and discussed his merits and demerits especially concerning the scandal of the mysteries and the revolution of 411. Alcibiades hesitated to land, until he saw his cousin Euryptolemus with other relatives and friends; then he landed and these relatives provided an informal bodyguard for his journey to the city. The movements of his associates illustrate the political divergence apparent a few years earlier. Thrasybulus sailed from the Hellespont to the coast of Thrace, where he recovered Thasos and other places for the Athenian cause; he did not return to Athens in 407. Thrasyllus on the other hand sailed directly from the Hellespont to Athens; he alone had no fear about his reception there.

Alcibiades stayed in Athens rather more than two months. He addressed the Council and the assembly, clearing himself of the charges of impiety. The assembly responded by declaring his command superior in authority to that of the other generals. Alcibiades knew the political value of display and was able to exploit it in connection with the greater Eleusinian mysteries. This annual festival included a procession from Eleusis to Athens, but in recent years the procession had traveled by sea because of the threat from Agis at Deceleia. Alcibiades posted all available troops to provide security and conducted the procession by land. Finally he levied reinforcements, including 1,500 hoplites and 100 ships, and sailed for Samos. On the way he called in Andros, which had rebelled; he defeated the Andrians and confined them to their city.

A change in Persian policy harmed Athenian prospects. Some time earlier the Spartans had sent an embassy to Darius II. In response the king decided to support the Peloponnesians without further hesitation. He sent one of his sons, Cyrus, to western Asia Minor with a special command embracing Lydia, Greater Phrygia and Cappadocia; his authority was to override that of the satraps and he was to have sole command of troops in the three satrapies. The first effect of Cyrus's approach was to stop the journey of the Athenian envoys, who had joined Pharnabazus in accordance with the agreement reached at Calchedon. The Spartan navarch for 407/6, Lysander, was both a competent strategist and a man capable of reaching agreement with Cyrus. Collecting ships from Rhodes, Cos and Miletus, he gathered a fleet of seventy triremes at Ephesus and waited for Cyrus to reach Sardis. When Cyrus arrived there, Lysander visited him to negotiate. The main issue was the rate of pay for the rowers. Lysander persuaded Cyrus to raise it from the standard figure of three obols per day to four obols; this measure was intended to persuade men to desert from the Athenian fleet.

Lysander's opportunity came when Alcibiades sailed away with a few ships from the main Athenian fleet towards Clazomenae, which was under attack by exiles. He left his deputy, Antiochus, in command with instructions not to attack Lysander's fleet. But Antiochus stationed the main force at Notium in the territory of Colophon and advanced with a small squadron towards the harbor at Ephesus. Lysander attacked him and the rest of the Athenian fleet from Notium came to support him. The battle was a defeat for the Athenians, who lost twenty-two ships. Strategically it was not a particularly significant defeat, and a few days later the Athenians withdrew to Samos, where they were safe. But the battle had political repercussions. In Athens the enemies of Alcibiades used it to arouse feeling against him. He was not reelected for 406/5, and the ten generals of that year included Thrasyllus. Alcibiades withdrew to his private fortress in the Chersonese; he was never to be employed in Athenian service again. Thus through political animosities the Athenians lost their most talented strategist.

ARGINUSAE, AEGOSPOTAMI AND THE SIEGE OF ATHENS[3]

Among the Athenian generals of 406/5 the one who at first played the leading role in strategy was Conon. The successor to Lysander as Spartan navarch was Callicratidas and he was much less skillful in dealing with Cyrus. He visited the Persian prince to negotiate about pay for the crews, but Cyrus bade him wait two days. Callicratidas considered it beneath the dignity of a Spartan officer to dance attendance on a barbarian potentate, and he went back to Miletus. Furthermore, Lysander had cultivated good personal relations with leading men in the Greek cities of Asia Minor; many of them were unwilling to transfer their allegiance to Callicratidas, and cooperation became difficult. For these reasons Callicratidas sought to finish the war quickly. He levied additional ships from Chios, Rhodes and other allies, and money from Miletus and Chios. He declared that he would put an end to Conon's rape of the sea. He sailed to Lesbos, attacked Methymna and took it by storm. He had no less than 170 ships with him.

Conon had sailed northwards from Samos in the hope of relieving Methymna, but he arrived too late. Callicratidas cut off his retreat to Samos, drove him to Mytilene and defeated him there. Conon took refuge in the harbor of Mytilene; he had 40 ships, and Callicratidas blockaded him by land and sea. But Conon succeeded in sending the news out to Athens on a swift ship. By an extraordinary effort the Athenians prepared and manned an additional fleet of 110 ships in thirty days. This force sailed to Samos, gained reinforcements from the allies and made for Lesbos. Callicratidas left 50 ships under Eteonicus to continue the blockade of the harbor of Mytilene; with his remaining 120 ships he sailed to meet the enemy, whose force numbered more than 150 ships. The two fleets met at the islands called Arginusae near the mainland opposite Lesbos. The battle was a resounding victory for the Athenians. Callicratidas was killed and the Peloponnesians lost more than 69 ships. Their survivors escaped to Chios and Phocaea.

The battle was fought well before the end of the warm season. When Eteonicus received news of its outcome, he removed his men from Mytilene and brought them together again in Chios. There they were hired out as agricultural laborers to earn their support, until winter began. The battle produced a possibility of ending the war. The Spartans sent an embassy to Athens and offered to make peace on the basis that each side should keep what it held; they also offered to evacuate Deceleia. But Cleophon spoke against these terms. Allegedly he came drunk and wearing a breastplate into the assembly; at least he expressed the feelings of the voters when he demanded that the Spartans should surrender all the cities which the Athenians claimed.

In the aftermath of the battle political tension within Athens was exacerbated. During the fighting twenty-five Athenian ships were destroyed; straight afterwards the eight Athenian generals, who commanded in the engagement, instructed Theramenes and Thrasybulus, who were serving as trierarchs, and some other officers to take forty-seven ships and recover the corpses and any survivors. But a storm sprang up and prevented them from doing this. Six of the eight generals returned to Athens and their political enemies aroused agitation against them on the grounds that they had failed to recover the shipwrecked corpses; Theramenes was active in inciting popular feeling. After debates in the assembly and the Council, the assembly decided to take a single vote on the guilt or innocence of all eight generals without allowing them to plead in their own defense. The vote declared the eight generals guilty, and the six who had returned to Athens were executed.

This verdict diminished the pool of strategic talent, on which the Athenians could draw in electing the ten generals of 405/4. Conon, who had been general both in 407/6 and 406/5, was reelected. On the Spartan side a complication of a different kind arose about the command. Deputies from the allies on the coast of Asia Minor gathered at Ephesus and sent envoys to Sparta to ask that the command be given to Lysander, and messengers came from Cyrus with the same request. Spartan law did not allow the same man to hold the navarchy twice, but the Spartans contrived a subterfuge. They elected Aracus as navarch but selected Lysander as his second-in-command; Lysander was to exercise actual control of operations.

On taking command, Lysander gathered his forces at Ephesus and visited Cyrus, from whom he gained subsidies. Lysander had evidently realized that success in the war depended on control of the straits, since Athens relied largely on grain imported from the district north of the Black Sea. So after brief maneuvers in other directions, Lysander sailed to the Hellespont. Advancing from Abydus, he attacked Lampsacus and captured it by storm. The Athenian fleet followed and anchored at Aegospotami, a beach in the Chersonese opposite Lampsacus. Lysander attacked the Athenians at Aegospotami and defeated them. Conon with eight ships fled and found refuge in Cyprus; another ship escaped and brought the news to Athens; but Lysander captured all the remaining Athenian ships and took them to Lampsacus.

Lysander sailed next to Byzantium and Calchedon. Both cities admitted him and dismissed their Athenian garrisons under truce. Lysander installed a Spartan harmost or supervisory officer to take charge of the two cities and returned to Lampsacus. His aim was to starve the Athenians into surrender, and so as he toured the straits and the Aegean, he sent to Athens any Athenians whom he found. Most cities of the Aegean were willing to join him, and in many he installed Spartan harmosts and oligarchies of local men. These oligarchies came to be called decarchies or "boards of ten," although the members may not have numbered precisely ten in every case. They were narrow regimes and by installing them Lysander entrusted control of the cities to his own friends and partisans. Samos alone refused to join Lysander and remained loyal to Athens; in response the Athenians took the extraordinary step of granting their citizenship to all the Samians.

Lysander appears to have brought the Athenians to battle at Aegospotami early enough in the season for him to intercept the grain fleet, which sailed from the Black Sea each year in the fall. In the winter, while Agis was still at Deceleia, two forces advanced against Athens. Pausanias, the other Spartan king, brought the army of the Peloponnesian League into Attica and advanced to the walls of the city. Lysander brought his fleet of 150 ships to the Peiraeus; on the way he restored Melos and Aegina to the survivors of the original inhabitants, expelling the Athenian settlers. So Athens was blockaded by land and sea, and as food soon began to run short, the Athenians sent envoys to Agis to propose terms; they offered to make peace and alliance with Sparta but they claimed to keep their fortifications including those of the Peiraeus. Agis replied that he had no authority to negotiate and the Athenians should send their embassy to Sparta. They did so, but when the envoys reached Sellasia on the border of Lacedaemon, the ephors told them to go home and added that they must offer more submissive terms, if they desired peace.

This news alarmed the Athenians. The Spartans issued a proclamation demanding destruction of the Long Walls on both sides to a distance of 10 stades (ca. 1¼ miles). Many Athenians thought that partial destruction of the Long Walls was merely a first step, designed to make resistance impossible, and that the Spartans intended to enslave the city in the technical sense, that is, to destroy the town, kill the men of military age and sell the women and children. On the other hand, the Spartan proclamation did not necessarily imply this; possibly the Spartans were willing to see Athens continue in existence as an organized political entity but demanded partial dismantling of the Long Walls to ensure that Athens should not again reach a threatening level of power. Theramenes offered to go to Lysander and stayed away rather more than three months, waiting for famine to make the Athenians willing to accept any terms. When at last he came back, he reported that Lysander bade him proceed to Lacedaemon, as only the ephors had authority to draw up terms. So the Athenian assembly sent Theramenes and nine other envoys with full authority to negotiate terms. The ephors accordingly admitted them at Sellasia and called a meeting of the assembly in Sparta. Embassies from the allies of Sparta were present and many of these, especially the Corinthians and the Thebans, urged that no terms should be made but Athens should be destroyed. But the Spartans refused to do this and preferred to make peace.

The Spartan assembly, with the concurrence of Theramenes and his fellow envoys, drew up two documents, a treaty of peace and one of alliance. By the former the Long Walls and the fortifications of the Peiraeus were to be dismantled. The Athenians were to give up their claims to all their overseas possessions. They were to recall those citizens whom they had exiled. They were to surrender their fleet except for a small number of ships to be determined by the Spartan authorities operating in Attica; the number permitted by those authorities was twelve. But the Athenians were to keep their land, that is, Athens and Attica were preserved intact. The alliance was of the close or "offensive and defensive" type, expressed in the standard Greek formula "to have the same friends and enemies." Moreover, it was explicitly provided that the Athenians should follow the Spartan lead in expeditions on land and sea, that is, Sparta was to determine who the friends and the enemies should be. Theramenes and the other envoys brought these terms back to Athens and the assembly accepted them. Thereupon Lysander sailed into the harbor of the Peiraeus, and the dismantling of the fortifications was begun to the accompaniment of music played by flute-girls; the day was intended to mark the beginning of liberty for the Greeks.

Peace was made in the spring of 404. The Spartan refusal to destroy Athens can be explained by the Theban and Corinthian demand for its destruction. Now that Athens was no longer a rival, Sparta had something to fear from the ambitions of her most powerful allies. So she wanted Athens preserved as a check to Corinth and Thebes. The general effect of the peace was twofold. For the Athenians it meant loss of the Empire but preservation of the city in its traditional territory. For the Spartans the peace brought an ascendancy they had not known before. Not only was Sparta patently the strongest power in Greece, but in many cities its power was cemented through the harmosts and decarchies which Lysander had installed. Yet the outcome of the Peloponnesian War was illusory. The terms of peace and alliance did not reflect the lasting relation of power between the two protagonists. The true balance of resources between them was mirrored more accurately in the situation immediately following the battle of Arginusae, when Sparta offered to make peace on the basis that each side should retain what it held. So it is not surprising that the settlement of 404 was followed less than ten years later by the outbreak of a new struggle, the Corinthian War (395–386). But before coming to that, attention must be paid to a conflict precipitated in Athens by the siege, the peace terms and Lysander.

THE REVOLUTION OF 404[4]

The situation in Athens straight after the conclusion of peace was confused. Theramenes was at the height of his influence. He had negotiated the peace and brought back from Sparta terms which saved Athens from destruction. Moreover, his long sojourn with Lysander in the winter of 405/4 taught the Athenians that he had the Spartan admiral's friendship, and all the Greeks had cause to respect Lysander at the end of the war. Theramenes was an embittered man; he had been elected general for 405/4 but rejected at his *dokimasia*, the scrutiny which every Athenian magistrate had to undergo before taking office and which usually inquired only into such formal qualifications as age and citizenship. Furthermore, by the peace terms the Athenians were to recall their exiles. Indeed, the exiles made a formal entry into Athens on the day when Lysander sailed into the Peiraeus and the demolition of the walls was begun. Doubtless many of the exiles were embittered, although detailed information is available only on one of them, Critias. He was born about 460 but nothing is known about his early career. In 415 he was among those arrested on the charge of profaning the mysteries, but he was released on the basis of information given by his distant kinsman, Andocides. In 411 he proposed the decree recalling Alcibiades from exile. Some time later he was himself exiled through the influence of Cleophon and he went to Thessaly.

Soon after the exiles returned, plotters calling themselves "comrades" (*hetairoi*) set about softening public opinion with a view to making a drastic change in the form of government. They set up a private board of five with the designation of "ephors;" these set up subordinate leaders, one from each tribe, and took charge of propaganda and intimidation with a view to directing votes in the public assembly. But the crucial role was to be played by Lysander. Shortly after his triumphal entry into the Peiraeus, he had sailed away to Samos, the only Aegean city which still held out against him, and begun besieging it. When the plotters in Athens were ready, they sent for him. He came from Samos and attended the decisive meeting of the assembly. There Dracontides proposed electing a board of thirty men, who would have the ultimate task of revising the laws and in the meantime, while they were preparing drafts of legislation, they would have control of the city. Some opposition was voiced. Theramenes spoke in favor of the motion and said that it had the approval of Lysander and the Spartans. Then Lysander spoke. He insisted on election of the Thirty and said that he had the Athenians at his mercy; he explained that they had broken the peace terms by failing to complete the demolition of the fortifications within the prescribed period.

The Thirty were elected. The names had been scrutinized by the plotters beforehand. They included Theramenes, Dracontides and Critias. They brought about selection of a Council of Five Hundred and the other officers required for the year 404/3. The most powerful officers of the new regime were the Thirty themselves, a board of Ten to administer the Peiraeus, and the board of Eleven in charge of the prison and executions. The chronology of the rule of the Thirty is far from clear; perhaps they took office some time after midsummer 404. The question of their ideological composition is difficult. Modern writers have sometimes tried to detect a distinction among the Thirty between "extreme oligarchs" and "moderates" and have tried in particular to explain by this divergence the quarrel which eventually developed between Critias and Theramenes. But the previous actions of Theramenes, his changes of side in 411 and his prosecution of the generals after the battle of Arginusae, point more to ruthless ambition than to constitutional principle as the spring of his actions. Once the Thirty were in power, they are said to have repealed the laws of Ephialtes and of an unknown Archestratus about the Areopagite Council and to have made some reforms in private law; for example, they repealed the restrictive conditions of the traditional law about freedom of bequest. But they are not recorded to have done anything towards designing a permanent form of government; there is not even reason to suppose that they envisaged a large role for the Areopagite Council. Rather their actions show a constant striving to secure and preserve their own control.

The behavior of the Thirty can better be explained by the bitterness of exiles and other frustrated men than by their supposed views on constitutional principle. Moreover, they were not fully independent agents. They owed their appointment to the intervention of Lysander. Some little time after they had taken control they sent envoys to Sparta in the hope of gaining a garrison; the envoys won the support of Lysander, and a garrison of 700 under Callibius was sent to Athens and installed on the acropolis. Nevertheless ideological considerations of a sort played a part in the early stages of the revolution of 404, probably a greater part than in the revolution of 411. A good deal seems to have been said in admiration of Spartan institutions; the choice of the term "ephors" for the private officers set up by the plotters before they seized power illustrates this. Moreover, an incidental remark of Lysias (12.5) shows that on taking power the

Thirty declared that they would purify the city of "unjust men" and turn the rest of the citizens towards "virtue and justice." The word "gentlemen" (*kaloi k'agathoi*) appears frequently in the sources which recount the rule of the Thirty; evidently it featured in their propaganda.

These facts suggest that the terms of the revolutionary ideology were more moral than constitutional. Perhaps for this reason, the fourth-century tradition about the Thirty had a moralistic element. It said that at first they seized, condemned and executed evil men, especially sycophants or those who made a profession of prosecuting on criminal charges, and the city was pleased at this, but later they attacked and killed wealthy men, in order to seize their property, and respected citizens, who might become focuses of opposition. Clearly the distinction between the two types of victim depends largely on the viewpoint of the beholder. The tradition has been further corrupted by the legend of Theramenes. After the revolution had been reversed in 403, men on trial for their association with it alleged that they had been followers, not of Critias, but of Theramenes, who quarrelled with Critias and was executed by him. Thus some people had a material interest in defending the memory of Theramenes and this has colored most of the narrative sources.

It is alleged, for example, that Theramenes criticized his fellow members of the Thirty for the frequent executions and confiscations which they carried out; he urged that they ought to admit more Athenians to share in power and privilege, and for this reason the Thirty drew up a list of three thousand who were to enjoy full civic privileges. The motivation may be doubted, but certainly the Thirty drew up a list of three thousand who were to have full rights. It is not clear what rights were originally reserved to the three thousand. Further, Theramenes allegedly criticized the list of three thousand, saying that "gentlemen" among the Athenians were not necessarily limited to that number, and that those outside the list were more numerous and therefore more powerful than those included. The Thirty responded by disarming all those who were not on the list of the three thousand. The final quarrel is said to have come about between Critias and Theramenes when the Thirty decided to arrest and execute thirty metics or resident aliens in order to seize their property. Theramenes opposed this, and the Thirty called a meeting of the Council of Five Hundred. There Critias denounced Theramenes, calling to mind amongst other things how he had turned against the oligarchy of 411. Theramenes spoke in his own defense and seemed likely to persuade the Council. Thereupon Critias cited one of the new laws, by which members of the three thousand had the right to trial before the Council but the Thirty had authority to execute people who were outside the list of the three thousand; and in the name of the Thirty Critias removed Theramenes from the list. Theramenes took refuge at the altar in the council chamber, but on instructions from the Thirty the Eleven seized him, led him away and executed him. Shortly afterwards the Thirty excluded from the city all those whose names were not included in the list of the three thousand; they drove some of those thus excluded away from their farms in the countryside in order to seize their property. Many of those thus expelled withdrew to the Peiraeus and fled thence to Thebes and Megara.

For a short time after the death of Theramenes the rule of the Thirty seemed secure. His existence had been a threat to the stability of the new regime; the record of his actions in 411 showed that much, even though the legend has obscured his aims of 404 beyond recovery. The Thirty had the garrison of Callibius to defend them and they continued to enjoy Spartan support; Sparta issued an order forbidding Greek states to harbor fugitives from Athens. But some cities, notably Thebes and Megara, refused to comply with the order. Theban opposition was especially significant, since Thebes was strong enough and far enough away to defy Sparta; the Thebans may have been alarmed at the prospect of seeing established permanently in Athens a regime strictly subservient to Spartan wishes. Presently a party of Athenian refugees organized themselves in Thebes, marched southwards across the border and seized the fortress of Phyle in northern Attica. Their leader was Thrasybulus, the politician prominent since 411, and at first they numbered only seventy. Their venture was hazardous, but military fortunes favored them. The Thirty led the three thousand and their cavalry against Phyle; some of their men skirmished with Thrasybulus's men but were driven off. Thereupon the Thirty planned to build a blockading wall around the position at Phyle, but a snowstorm sprang up unexpectedly by night and continued on the following day. This compelled the Thirty with their forces to withdraw to the city; on the way they lost much of their baggage train to the enemy. To protect the countryside from raids the Thirty sent much of the Spartan garrison and some cavalry to a position about two miles from Phyle. But Thrasybulus, whose force had grown to about seven hundred, attacked this force and defeated it, so that it retired to the city.

The Thirty accordingly had to envisage the possibility of being overthrown and they set about securing places where they might withdraw in safety. They visited Eleusis and Salamis, drew up a list of the property owners in both places, and arrested them; then they called a meeting of the three thousand and made them vote for the execution of those arrested. But Thrasybulus, whose force now numbered about a thousand, led his men from Phyle to seize the Peiraeus. Since they were not numerous enough to defend the whole harbor complex, they posted themselves on the hill of Munychia. The Thirty led the Spartan garrison and all their citizen forces towards the Peiraeus, but in the ensuing battle they were defeated. About seventy of the men from the city were killed and these included Critias and some others of the leaders.

This defeat brought consternation and confusion among the men of the city. They gathered as an assembly of the three thousand on the next day; some of them felt committed to the cause of the Thirty and implicated in their deeds; others hoped for reconciliation with Thrasybulus's men, who held the Peiraeus. The assembly deposed from office the surviving members of the Thirty, who withdrew to Eleusis, and set up instead a new board of Ten. It is not clear what instructions were issued to the Ten; although they superseded the Thirty, in their subsequent actions they continued the civil war against the men of the Peiraeus. Skirmishes continued and the men of the Peiraeus manufactured siege engines with a view to attacking the city.

The decision was to be taken in Sparta. Appeals were sent there from the survivors of the Thirty at Eleusis and from the men of the city. Lysander contrived that Sparta made a loan of 100 talents to the men of the city; he himself was sent as harmost to Attica, and his brother Libys, who was navarch, was instructed to blockade the Peiraeus. But Lysander's influence was no longer paramount in Sparta; in particular Pausanias, one of the kings, resented his preeminence. Pausanias won the consent of three of the ephors and led a force of the Peloponnesian League into Attica; of the allies the Boeotians and the Corinthians, still distrusting Spartan policy, refused to join the expedition. Pausanias encamped not far from the Peiraeus; as king he had superiority over Lysander in the field and prevented him from taking any further independent action. He drew Thrasybulus's men into battle and defeated them, but his aim was to bring about a reconciliation. By careful diplomacy he persuaded first the men of the Peiraeus and then the men of the city to send envoys to Sparta in the hope of bringing the civil war to an end. Sparta responded by sending a commission of fifteen men to assist Pausanias in drawing up a settlement.

The settlement made by Pausanias and the commission made Eleusis almost into a separate city from Athens. Any Athenian who had remained in the city was allowed to migrate to Eleusis, provided that he registered his name within ten days. Henceforth residents of Eleusis were not to go to the city nor residents of the city to Eleusis, except during the Eleusinian mysteries. No resident of Eleusis was to hold office in the city, unless he first registered himself anew as a resident of the city. A general amnesty was issued with specific exceptions, namely the Thirty, the Ten who had replaced them in the city, the Ten who had administered the Peiraeus for them, and the Eleven in charge of the prison. On these terms the men of the Peiraeus returned to the city.

It is not clear how many people chose migrate to Eleusis. In 401/0 the separate status of Eleusis was brought to an end. The Athenians alleged, rightly or wrongly, that the people at Eleusis were hiring mercenaries; so they marched on Eleusis, executed the military commanders of the Eleusinians and persuaded the people there to agree to a new reconciliation. A new oath of amnesty was sworn. A good deal was achieved towards preserving the spirit of the amnesties. In particular, although the settlement provided that the two sides, the men of the city and the men of the Peiraeus, should repay separately the loans they had contracted, in fact the Athenians repaid the loan due to Sparta collectively during the ensuing few years. Soon after Pausanias had brought about his settlement, the Athenians appointed a commission of lawgivers to propose revisions in the laws. The commission was at work from 403/2 until 400/399. In consequence a revised code of laws was inscribed on a number of walls set up in the *stoa basileios*. Fragments of these walls have been recovered by excavation. It appears that a large part of the code consisted in a long and systematic calendar of sacrifices; indeed, if the fragments are representative, religious provisions formed a high proportion of the new code.

Thus the work of revising the laws was brought to completion. A commission for this purpose had been set up as early as 410 and had continued until its work was interrupted by the revolution. A little is known of the steps taken to restore the traditional constitution. As soon as the settlement of Pausanias was reached, a provisional government of twenty members was elected. Afterwards, probably at no great interval, a Council of Five Hundred for the year 403/2 was chosen by lot; this was the most characteristic institution of the traditional regime. The steps taken to restore state pay for political service are not recorded. In the 390s a new type of pay was introduced, namely payment for attending the public assembly; the original rate was one obol, but it was soon increased to two and then to three obols. The constitution as reconstructed after the revolution of 404 persisted without change of principle until 322, when Macedonian intervention imposed a new regime.

NOTES

1. The main narrative of military operations depends on Thuc. 8.55–109; Xen. *Hell.* 1.1.1–23. The movements of Theramenes are known from Diod. 13.47 and 49. The Spartan offer of peace is given by Philochorus, *F.Gr.Hist.* IIIB 328F139. The law of Demophantus is known from Andoc. 1.96–98. Payments for the *diobelia* in 410/09, 408/7 and 407/6 are mentioned in financial records for those years, *I.G.* I², 304 A-B (304A is also accessible as Meiggs/Lewis 84); an important study of these documents is W.K. Pritchett, *The Choiseul Marble* = University of California Publications in Classical Studies, vol. 5, (1970). Aristotle (*AP* 28.3) says that Cleophon introduced the *diobelia*. A reference to this fund in a record assigned to 404/3 is restored by A.M. Woodward, "Financial

Documents from the Athenian Agora," *Hesperia* 32 (1963) 144–155, especially 150. K.J. Beloch, "Zur Finanzgeschichte Athens IV," *Rheinisches Museum* 39 (1884) 239–244, argued that the *diobelia* supplied pay for jurors; later (*Griechische Geschichte* II², 1 [Strassburg 1914] 397–398) he suggested that it also supplied pay for the Council of Five Hundred. On the changes of 410 see Sealey, "Constitutional Changes in Athens in 410 B.C.," *CSCA* 8 (1975) pp. 271–295.

2. The narrative depends mainly on Xen. *Hell.* 1.1.24–1.5.17. A fragment of the *Hellenica Oxyrhynchia* 4 provides information on the battle of Notium and supports Diodorus 13.71 against Xenophon. A major problem of chronology arises in Xenophon's account of events of 410–406; see W.S. Ferguson, *CAH* 5.483–485. For a suggestive study of the political relations between Alcibiades, Thrasyllus and their colleagues see A. Andrewes, "The Generals in the Hellespont," *JHS* 73 (1953) 2–9. The recapture of Pylos by the Spartans in 410 is known from Diod. 13.64.5–7; cf. Xen. *Hell.* 1.2.18; Ar. *AP* 27.5. Cyrus's extensive command in western Asia Minor is mentioned by Xenophon at *Hell.* 1.4.3 and specified by him more clearly at *Anab.* 1.9.7.

3. The narrative depends mostly on Xen. *Hell.* 1.5.18–2.2.23. The Spartan offer of peace after Arginusae is given by Ar *AP* 34.1. Plutarch's *Life of Lysander* adds some information, particularly on the harmosts and decarchies set up by Lysander (13.3), on the terms of peace in 404 (14. 4–5), and on the day when the dismantling of the fortifications was begun (15.1). The Athenian grant of citizenship to the Samians is known from Meiggs/Lewis 94; cf. Tod 2.97.

4. The sources for the revolution are Lys. 12 and 13 (especially 12.43–44; 12.71–76); Xen. *Hell.* 2.3–4; Ar. *AP* 34–40; Diod. 14.3–6 and 14.32–33. It is difficult to be precise about the chronology of the revolution; Aristotle (AP 35.1; 39.1) says that the Thirty took office in the archonship of Pythodorus (404/3) and that the reconciliation mediated by Pausanias was achieved in the archonship of Eucleides (403/2). Hignett (*HAC* 285–298, 378–389) reconstructs the order of events, defending Xenophon's account at points where Aristotle's narrative diverges from it. The election of Theramenes as general for 405/4 is known from Lys. 13.10. For the career of Critias and the fragments of his writings see H. Diels and W. Kranz, *Die Fragmente der Vorsokratiker* II⁷ (Berlin 1954) 371–399; on his descent see Davies, *APF* 322–335; the main texts bearing on his career before 404 are Plat. *Tim.* 20d–21a; Andoc. 1.47 and 68; Plut. *Alc.* 33.1. The term *kaloi k'agathoi* occurs frequently in Xenophon's account of the revolution, also in Diod. 14.4.1. Possibly the terms of peace with Sparta included a standard clause providing for the traditional constitution (*kata ta patria*) and this was reinterpreted as a requirement to restore a supposedly ancestral constitution (*patrios politeia*); cf. A. Fuks, *The Ancestral Constitution* (London 1953) 52–62. On the revision of the laws attention should be drawn to three studies by S. Dow: "The Law Codes of Athens," *Proceedings of the Massachusetts Historical Society* 71 (1953–57: published 1959) 3–36; "The Athenian Calendar of Sacrifices: the Chronology of Nikomakhos' Second Term," *Historia* 9 (1960) 270–293; "The Walls inscribed with Nikomakhos' Law Code," *Hesperia* 30 (1961) 58–73. The main literary sources on the revision are Lys. 30 and Andoc. 1.81–87. The provisional government of twenty members is known from Andoc. 1.81. On pay for attending the assembly see Ar. *AP* 41.3.

15

The Corinthian War

It is difficult to estimate how well founded the Spartan supremacy was in 404. There were difficulties for the Spartans to face. Among her allies the two strongest, Boeotia and Corinth, were showing recalcitrance; they disagreed with Sparta about the terms of peace to be made in 404 and they refused to join the expedition of Pausanias to Athens in the next year. Spartans had little experience in administering an Aegean hegemony. The position achieved by Sparta in the last years of the Peloponnesian War brought unexpected opportunities for a few Spartans. Lysander made the most of his chances, but the preeminence he achieved aroused jealousy, notably from Pausanias. Lysander's method of administering subordinate allies was to install narrow regimes, the so-called decarchies, and harmosts with (in some cases) garrisons. Little is known about the fortunes of the decarchies; the case most fully attested is the rule of the Thirty in Athens, which was overthrown by Pausanias in 403, and it seems likely that many or all of the decarchies collapsed in that year, as Pausanias challenged the influence of Lysander successfully.

Apart from political changes, the successes of Lysander in 405/4 had an effect on the Spartan economy. In 404 he brought back a great wealth of booty, including a large amount of gold and silver money. The consequences are not wholly clear, but a strain was placed on the economy of Sparta, which had traditionally excluded coinage in the precious metals. There was also the question of manpower. Spartan citizens were much outnumbered by perioeci and helots. Economic changes could decrease the number of citizens holding full rights, since those who failed to pay their dues to the *phiditia* were reduced to the class of "inferiors." The 292 hoplites captured by the Athenians at Sphacteria in 425 included only 120 Spartiates, but in the next few years Sparta showed herself anxious to recover them; this is some measure of the value she attached to citizen hoplites.

On the other hand the difficulties should not be exaggerated. After Sparta lost control of Messenia in 369, her power declined rapidly, but until then she maintained fully effective leadership over her perioeci and helots. Boeotian and Corinthian recalcitrance was an irritant, but the events following the peace of Nicias (chapter 12, pp. 337–346) showed that Corinthian initiative was limited and Boeotia would rather influence Spartan policy than challenge it. During the Ionian War Spartans had directed naval operations successfully, even though they drew mostly on their allies for ships. The fact that the Spartans won the Peloponnesian War shows that they solved the problems of organization and command.

The question which proved crucial was that of relations with Persia, and complex developments led to an embroilment. Darius II died in 404 and was succeeded by his elder son, Artaxerxes II. Cyrus, the younger son, who had visited his father's sickbed, returned to Sardis and prepared to contest the succession. He spent some years in preparations and gathered a large force of Greek mercenaries. In the spring of 401 he set out on the march upcountry from Sardis. The forces came into conflict at Cunaxa near Babylon in the fall. The royal army, commanded by Artaxerxes and Tissaphernes, killed Cyrus, but the latter's Greek troops remained in possession of the field. Thus a Greek force, tactically superior to anything the Persians commanded, was left at large in the heart of the Persian Empire. Amid privations and skirmishes it made its way north and reached the Black Sea at Trapezus late in the winter of 401/0. The survivors proceeded westwards along the coast and reached Byzantium in the fall. Meanwhile, after the battle of Cunaxa Tissaphernes returned to Sardis but he received the same extensive command as had been given to Cyrus in 407. He promptly sent a demand to the Ionian cities that they should submit to him. Instead they appealed to Sparta for protection, and the Spartans sent a force under a harmost called Thibron in the spring of 399.

Thus Sparta became engaged in operations against the western satraps. Thibron took into his service the survivors of Cyrus's march upcountry. In the fall of 399 he was succeeded in the command by Dercylidas. For the season of 396 Agesilaus, who had recently become king on the death of his brother Agis, came out with large reinforcements and took over the command. Agesilaus sought to portray his campaign as a resumption of the legendary struggle between Europe and Asia; on his outward journey he tried to offer sacrifice at Aulis in Boeotia in imitation of the sacrifice offered by Agamemnon when he sailed against Troy, but the boeotarchs sent a party of cavalry and dispersed Agesilaus's party. Agesilaus continued operations until the spring of 394. The activities of the three commanders were similar. They raided the satrapies of Tissaphernes and Pharnabazus and captured some places; intermittently they opened negotiations with the satraps. Their chief problem was supplies; sometimes they lived off the country, sometimes they exacted contributions from the Greek cities which they protected.

Thus the collaboration between Sparta and the Persian satraps, achieved in the last years of the Peloponnesian War, came to an end. It had been brought about largely by two men, Cyrus and Lysander. By 396 Cyrus was dead. Meanwhile Lysander tried to recover influence through Agesilaus. When Agis died, the succession was disputed, and Lysander was instrumental in ensuring that it passed to Agesilaus instead of to the late king's son, Leotychides. Lysander came out with Agesilaus to Asia Minor in 396 and tried to support his former partisans in the cities. But Agesilaus made a point of refusing the requests of those who had approached Lysander and then sent him away to a subordinate command in the Hellespontine district. In consequence of the Spartan operations Pharnabazus decided in 397 or 396 to send an envoy to European Greece and try to stir up opposition to Sparta there.

THE OPENING OF THE CORINTHIAN WAR[2]

The envoy sent by Pharnabazus was Timocrates, a man from Rhodes. He visited Thebes, Corinth, Argos and Athens and he tried to exploit the rivalries usual among the leading men of Greek cities. The Spartan ascendancy had brought a complicating factor into these rivalries. By supporting one faction in each city and helping them towards control, Sparta had antagonized other factions, which tended to unite against their successful rivals. In Thebes, for example, the leaders of a pro-Spartan group (Leontiadas, Asias, Coeratadas), which had the upper hand, and those of an anti-Spartan group (Ismenias, Antitheus, Androcleidas) can be named. The situation in Athens is most fully attested and shows further nuances. One group, led by Epicrates and Cephalus, sought by all means to oppose Spartan power. By 396 they thought they had found an opportunity in the activities of Conon. The latter was the only Athenian general to escape the rout at Aegospotami; he fled to Cyprus and entered Persian service. By 396 Artaxerxes was preparing a fleet in the eastern Mediterranean to resist the Spartan encroachments in western Asia Minor and he envisaged Conon as one of the chief commanders. The Athenians, at the urging of Epicrates and Cephalus, sent weapons and men to Conon's force. On the other hand, another group of Athenians, whose leaders included Thrasybulus the hero of Phyle, advocated a more cautious policy. As late as the winter of 396/5 Thrasybulus and those who felt as he did were anxious to avoid provoking the Spartans. But the policy of this group was not simply one of keeping good relations with Sparta. The behavior of Thrasybulus later in 395 shows that he was willing to take action against Sparta, once he was convinced of the right opportunity. The issue dividing his group from that of Epicrates and Cephalus was not the abstract desirability of opposing Sparta but the question of the right occasion for opposing Sparta.

The significance of the mission of Timocrates must be understood in the context of the situation within the Greek cities. Fourth-century historians said a great deal about the money he brought with him to distribute as bribes; allegedly he brought fifty talents of silver for the purpose. Presents were a normal courtesy of diplomacy. Timocrates's journey had more decisive implications. In each of the chief cities, Thebes, Athens, Argos and Corinth, it told those politicians who were keen to challenge the Spartan hegemony that they could expect sympathy in the other cities. Furthermore, it told them that Persia was preparing to take action against Sparta and it held out the prospect of Persian subsidies.

A Theban intrigue precipitated an occasion for war in 395. The borders between Phocis and Locris had long been disputed. The Thebans encouraged the Locrians to exact taxes from the territory at issue. So the Phocians raided Locris and carried off booty. The Locrians appealed to Thebes, and in response the Thebans made a raid on Phocis. Thereupon the Phocians appealed to the Spartans. The latter called to mind their longstanding grievances against the Thebans, their refusal to join Pausanias's expedition to Athens in 403 and how they had prevented Agesilaus from sacrificing at Aulis in 396. They welcomed the chance to humble the Thebans and they planned a double attack on Boeotia. Lysander was sent north to collect forces from allies in Central Greece, namely, the Phocians and several small places on the Malian Gulf; he was to bring these forces to Haliartus, a town on the southern shore of Lake Copais in Boeotia. Pausanias was to call out the army of the Peloponnesian League and bring it to Haliartus, where the two forces were to join on a day specified in advance.

Expecting the double attack, the Thebans sent envoys to Athens to seek help. The Athenians voted to send forces to support the Thebans. This Athenian decision is noteworthy for two reasons. First, it was taken although no Spartan force had been attacked or defeated in the field. Second, the man proposing the decree was Thrasybulus, who stood for a more cautious policy than Epicrates and Cephalus; evidently he thought that the right occasion for opposing Sparta had now come. The Thebans were helped, not only by the prospect of Athenian aid, but also by the impossibility under ancient conditions of coordinating the movements of two armies divided by any considerable distance. Lysander in the north won over Orchomenus, but he reached Haliartus before Pausanias and tried to secure the town. The Thebans attacked and defeated him; Lysander himself was killed in the battle. Afterwards Pausanias arrived with the army of the Peloponnesian League, but the Corinthians had withheld their contingent, and some of the other allies only joined the expedition reluctantly. On the day after Pausanias's arrival the force sent by the Athenians reached Haliartus. Pausanias thus found himself opposed by strong forces, including the Theban cavalry. He decided not to fight but to make a truce in order to recover the corpses of Lysander and of those who had fallen with him; by the terms of the truce he withdrew his army from Boeotia.

The operations at Haliartus not only brought about war but encouraged the enemies of Sparta. Shortly afterwards a quadruple alliance was formed between Boeotia, Athens, Corinth and Argos. Little is known about its terms or organization, but at least it set up a *synedrion* or congress in Corinth to direct the affairs of the alliance. This body consisted of envoys from the allies and it seems to have remained continuously in session. The alliance raised a land force from its members and stationed it in the Corinthiad; the strategic aim was to confine the forces of Sparta and her allies to the Peloponnese. The allies sent out envoys to seek support from other cities and they won over several states previously allied to Sparta. Their new adherents included all the cities of Euboea; the cities of Chalcidice on the Thracian coast, where the federation begun in 432 had grown during and after the Peloponnesian War; two colonies of Corinth, Leucas and Ambracia, which chose to follow the lead of their mother city; and the Acarnanians. Furthermore, late in the season of 395 or in the ensuing winter a Theban commander, Ismenias, led a force of Boeotians and Argives to the north. After operating in Thessaly he captured Heraclea Trachinia not far from the head of the Malian Gulf; the Spartans had founded a colony there in 426. He also persuaded the Aenianes and the Athamanes, two small tribes in the same area, to desert the Spartan alliance.

In 394 the Spartans launched two campaigns in the hope of breaking through the allied position in the Corinthiad. First the regular force of Lacedaemon and the Peloponnesian League was sent north. Pausanias had been tried and condemned to death for his failure at Haliartus, and anticipating the verdict, he had withdrawn into exile to Tegea, where he later died; his son, Agesipolis, was under age, so the command passed to Aristodemus, the relative and guardian of Agesipolis. The list of allies who served with the Spartans on this campaign indicates the continuing extent of Spartan control within the Peloponnese; it includes Mantinea, Tegea, Elis, Achaea, Sicyon, Epidaurus, Troezen, Hermione, Halieis, and some small towns in Arcadia and on the borders of Elis. But Phlius

Funeral monument of Dexileos, 394. Found in the Ceramicus at Athens. The inscription says: "Dexileos, son of Lysanias, of the deme Thorikon, born in the archonship of Teisander [414/3], died at Corinth in the archonship of Eubulides [394/3] as one of the five horsemen." [Photo by Hirmer Fotoarchiv, München.]

refused to supply its contingent and claimed to have an armistice with the enemy. The forces on the other side included not only troops from Athens, Boeotia, Argos and Corinth but also men from the cities of Euboea, East and West Locris, Malis and Acarnania. The two armies met near Nemea and the Spartans with their allies won the battle. The Corinthians were so impressed by the outcome that they closed their gates against the fugitives, but an anti-Spartan minority opened the gates, and so the quadruple alliance kept control of Corinth and its territory.

As a second step Sparta sent a message to Agesilaus, recalling him from Asia Minor. He received the instruction in the spring and left 4,000 men to garrison the Greek cities of Asia Minor. He took the rest of his troops, including contingents supplied by the Asiatic Greeks, across the Hellespont and westwards along the north coast of the Aegean. At Amphipolis he received news of the victory of Nemea. He suffered harassment on his march through Thessaly, since the Thessalians mostly favored the Boeotian cause, but he drove off the attackers. He reached the borders of Boeotia at the time of a solar eclipse, which can be astronomically dated to 14 August 394. The quadruple alliance sent a large force to check him, and the two armies met in the plain near Coroneia. Agesilaus defeated the enemy, and in consequence the Thebans made a temporary armistice, allowing him to proceed on his journey. But he crossed the Corinthian Gulf by sea.

The land fighting of 394 had brought the Spartans two victories. But they were unable to dislodge the forces of the quadruple alliance from the position in the territory of Corinth. Indecisive fighting in and near the Corinthiad continued for several years, with the Spartans using Sicyon as their base.

WARFARE AT SEA AND AN ATTEMPT AT PEACE[3]

Developments at sea were more decisive. By 394 the Persian fleet, that had been long in preparation, was ready for operations against the Peloponnesians. The supreme command was held by Pharnabazus, who controlled the Phoenician fleet directly; Conon with a large naval force of Greek mercenaries served under him. Pharnabazus and Conon met and defeated the Peloponnesian fleet off Cnidus; its navarch Peisander, the brother-in-law of Agesilaus, was killed in the fighting. The battle of Cnidus began the overthrow of the Spartan ascendancy in the Aegean. During the remainder of 394 Pharnabazus and Conon sailed among the islands and coastal cities of Asia Minor and expelled the Spartan harmosts; they earned a welcome in the cities by promising not to fortify or garrison their citadels but to allow them autonomy. Only in one place were Spartan forces able to hold out; Dercylidas secured Abydus and from there he seized Sestus, so that the two towns provided a refuge for Spartan harmosts and sympathizers. Pharnabazus attacked Abydus from the landward side and Conon supported him from the sea, but they were unable to dislodge Dercylidas.

In 393 Pharnabazus and Conon set about carrying the naval war into European Greece. They sailed across the Aegean, calling in Melos, and made raids on the coast of Laconia; they installed a garrison in the island of Cythera. From there they sailed to the Isthmus of Corinth and Pharnabazus addressed the envoys of the quadruple alliance. He encouraged them to prosecute the war against the Spartans vigorously and he provided more concrete encouragement in the form of a financial subsidy. Before Pharnabazus returned to his satrapy, he gave Conon permission and money to proceed to Athens and restore the fortifications of the Peiraeus and the Long Walls. So these fortifications were restored in haste, and Athenian tradition credited Conon with the achievement; but an inscription shows that work on the fortifications of the Peiraeus was begun as early as the summer of 394.

Indecisive fighting in the Corinthiad and at sea lasted for several years after 393. Using the money supplied by Pharnabazus, the Corinthians built a fleet and disputed ascendancy in the Corinthian Gulf with the Spartans. Meanwhile in 392 a Spartan diplomatic initiative led to an attempt to make peace. The Spartans sent Antalcidas as envoy to Tiribazus, who had been appointed satrap of Sardis some little time before. Antalcidas was to try to secure at least peace between Sparta and Persia and, if possible, he was to divert Persian support from Athens to Sparta; he was to assert that Conon was using Persian money to win the islands and the coastal cities of Asia Minor for Athens, not for Persia. The other powers learned of the mission of Antalcidas, and so envoys to counterbalance him were sent from Athens, Boeotia, Corinth and Argos. Tiribazus admitted the envoys together to an audience, and there Antalcidas proposed two general principles as the basis for peace: the Persian king should have the Greek cities on the mainland of Asia Minor, and all other Greek cities should be autonomous (on the meaning of "autonomy" see below, pp. 396-397). Tiribazus was favorably impressed by this proposal, but the envoys from the other Greek states were dismayed. The Athenians had recovered their ancient possessions of Lemnos, Imbros and Scyros, and they feared to lose these under the clause providing for autonomy. The same clause alarmed the Thebans, who feared that they might be required to disband the Boeotian federation. Argos and Corinth were likewise perturbed. They had formed a partial union during the war; for Argos the union meant a large increase of power, and although some Corinthians may have opposed it, those in the ascendant benefited from it.

The conference at Sardis brought no immediate end to the war, although it was to find an important echo less than six years later. Tiribazus became convinced that it was in the interests of Persia to support Sparta, but he lacked authority to change his alignment, and so he went to the king. But Artaxerxes was not persuaded; instead he sent Strouthas to take command in western Asia Minor and instructed him to support the Athenians and their allies against Sparta. Meanwhile in Greece the Spartan initiative led to further negotiations. An Athenian embassy of four traveled to Sparta and drew up preliminary terms. These followed mostly the principles enunciated at Sardis, but the Athenian claim to Lemnos, Imbros and Scyros was recognized. When the Athenian embassy returned, it was accompanied by envoys from Sparta. Argos and Corinth sent envoys to Athens to urge rejection of the terms; those two powers realized that Athens was a more significant belligerent than they were. The Athenian assembly was not willing to accept the terms proposed; instead it exiled the four envoys who had drawn up the preliminaries.

The refusal of the Athenians to make peace shows that their ambitions were growing, and a few years later they enlarged their aims further. Probably in 389 Thrasybulus led a fleet of forty ships across the Aegean. One opportunity for action offered itself at Rhodes, where a pro-Athenian party had gained control but the island was under attack from a Peloponnesian squadron of twenty-seven ships. Yet at first Thrasybulus refrained from operating at Rhodes; instead he sailed to the Hellespont and soon won a valuable ally there. The strongest of the Thracian kingdoms was that of the Odrysians, but civil war was in progress between its king, Amedocus, and Seuthes, who ruled the coastal part of the kingdom. Thrasybulus reconciled them and made them allies of the Athenians; their friendship influenced the cities on the European shore of the straits to favor the Athenians. Thrasybulus could likewise be sure of a not unfriendly reception in the cities on the Asiatic shore because of the Athenian understanding with the Persians. He proceeded to Byzantium and made arrangements for levying the tax of a tenth on shipping coming from the Black Sea. He altered the constitution of Byzantium and won the alliance of Calchedon.

From the Hellespont Thrasybulus sailed to Lesbos. There Mytilene had joined the Athenian cause and provided a refuge for pro-Athenian fugitives from the other cities; those cities, of which the strongest was Methymna, were allied to Sparta. Methymna had a Lacedaemonian garrison under the harmost Therimachus and it provided a refuge for pro-Spartan fugitives from Mytilene. Thrasybulus landed his troops at Mytilene and led them and local forces against Methymna. He defeated and killed Therimachus in battle. Hence he was able to win over some of the cities of Lesbos and raise money for his troops by raiding the territory of others. These operations at Lesbos may have been conducted during the winter. In the new campaigning season Thrasybulus planned to advance on Rhodes and as a preliminary he set about raising money. One of the cities he visited for this purpose was Aspendus, but there skirmishes developed between his men and the citizens; in consequence the people of Aspendus attacked Thrasybulus's camp by night and killed him.

The death of Thrasybulus did not bring to an end the operations he had begun, but the political circumstances in Athens are obscure. Shortly before his death attempts were made to recall some of his officers and call them to account on charges of extorting money from the allies; eventually at least one of them, Ergocles, was prosecuted and condemned to death. When Thrasybulus had been killed, Agyrrhius was sent out to succeed him in the command. He was not an obvious choice. He had won popularity in the 390s by introducing pay for attendance at the assembly and later increasing the rate; but there is nothing to indicate that he had had military experience. Succeeding Thrasybulus in command of the fleet on the Asiatic coast, Agyrrhius did not achieve anything noteworthy and after a few months he was replaced by Iphicrates; possibly he had been intended as a mere stopgap until Iphicrates should become available.

Iphicrates had begun his career by serving under Conon, probably in 394 or 393. Later, during the fighting in the Corinthiad, he developed the use of peltasts or light-armed troops; these were more mobile than hoplites and by employing them successfully Iphicrates brought about a great change in the art of war. The achievement which first established his reputation was carried out in 390. The Spartans held Lechaeum, a harbor in the Corinthiad on the Corinthian Gulf, and were using it as a base for attacking the positions held by the quadruple alliance; the garrison included one *mora*, one of the six regiments into which the Lacedaemonian army was divided. Iphicrates succeeded in catching this *mora* on a lengthy march outside Lechaeum and destroying it. In this action he had support from a force of Athenian hoplites under the general Callias, but the victory was essentially the work of the peltasts, and it proved how effective this unconventional mode of warfare could be. Replacing Agyrrhius in 388, Iphicrates brought out reinforcements, including 1,200 peltasts, and took over command of the fleet in the Chersonese. He operated against Anaxibius, who had recently become harmost at Abydus, as this was the sole position remaining loyal to Sparta since 394. Iphicrates brought Anaxibius to battle outside Abydus and killed him, but the Spartans and their allies kept possession of the city.

The operations of Thrasybulus and Iphicrates on the coast of Asia Minor reveal a large development in Athenian war aims. They are the earliest indication that the Athenians were resuming the imperial ambitions of the fifth century. An inscription of 387/6 discloses more about the achievement. It preserves an Athenian decree about relations with Clazomenae; the decree provides that Clazomenae shall pay no other financial obligations to Athens beyond the twentieth. The nature of this twentieth can only be conjectured. It should be called to mind that in 414/3 the Athenians introduced a duty of a twentieth on goods carried by sea; possibly Thrasybulus or his successors revived this. From the same inscription it appears that Clazomenae had been brought into the Athenian sphere of influence by 387/6. This might be of concern to the Persians, for although Clazomenae was technically an island, it lay close to the coast and the king, claiming the mainland of Asia Minor, regarded Clazomenae as his.

THE PEACE OF ANTALCIDAS[4]

A change in Persian policy was decisive for bringing the war to an end. Evagoras, the tyrant of Salamis in Cyprus, had taken part in building up the Persian fleet in the eastern Mediterranean before the battle of Cnidus. By 390 he was in revolt against the Persian Empire, but the Athenians continued to send him ships and reinforcements. Accordingly, the king came slowly to the conclusion that Sparta was the proper power to support in Greece. The Spartans for their part chose Antalcidas as navarch for 388/7 in the expectation that he would negotiate successfully with Tiribazus. Antalcidas and Tiribazus traveled to the heart of the Persian Empire for an audience with the king. They returned to western Asia Minor probably in the middle or later part of the summer of 387 and brought with them a royal rescript giving the proposed peace terms; moreover, they had authority to fight on the Spartan side if the other Greeks rejected the terms. Antalcidas proceeded overland to Abydus and took command of the Peloponnesian fleet there, although his term as navarch had expired. He outwitted and outmaneuvered the Athenian fleet, which had been besieging Abydus, so that it scattered into the Propontis. Then Antalcidas received additional ships from the part of Ionia controlled by Tiribazus and from Syracuse, where the tyrant Dionysius favored the Spartan cause; thus he assembled a fleet of more than eighty triremes in the straits. He stopped the grain ships, which were sailing from the Black Sea for Athens, and diverted them to cities allied to Sparta.

Because of the threat to the grain supply the Athenians were willing to make peace. Although the parties to the quadruple alliance were in form equals and no Athenian leadership was acknowledged, in fact the other allies were not willing to continue the war without the Athenians. So in response to an invitation from Tiribazus the cities sent envoys to Sardis to hear the terms proposed by the king. The royal rescript said:

King Artaxerxes considers it just that the cities in Asia and of the islands Clazomenae and Cyprus should be his, but all other Greek cities, both small and large, should be made autonomous, except for Lemnos, Imbros and Scyros; these latter should belong as of old to the Athenians. Whoever do not accept this peace, I will fight against them, together with any who volunteer, by land and sea and with ships and with money.

The envoys reported the terms to their cities and these accepted the peace after some hesitations, which will require attention shortly.

The treaty thus concluded can be called "the king's peace" or "the peace of Antalcidas." It differed in form from earlier treaties of peace between Greek cities; it was not a bilateral agreement between the belligerents but instead it was designed for all Greek states. Similar agreements were concluded later and came to be called treaties of "common peace." Yet not much significance need be attached to this novelty, which was due to the circumstances of Persian interest in Greek affairs in 392/1 and 387/6. The feature of the peace that most merits consideration is the word *autonomos*, here translated "autonomous;" it can equally well be rendered by "free" or "independent." Study of the usage of this word in the texts of Thucydides and other authors shows that it is systematically ambiguous; at each occurrence it derives its meaning from the context and especially from the condition with which "autonomy" is contrasted. Thus in passages describing the Athenian Empire "autonomous" can designate those cities which supplied ships for federal operations in contrast to those paying tribute; or, when a different contrast is drawn, it can be used of cities which were not members of the Empire as distinct from cities which were. Accordingly, when the word "autonomous" was used without any implied or explicit contrast, it had hardly any factual content. It retained the overtones of enthusiasm which commonly adhere to words expressing freedom, but it became exceedingly vague.

In the peace of Antalcidas the word had this vagueness. Factual application of the terms of peace depended on the distribution of power and above all on the predominant position achieved by Sparta through her new understanding with Persia. This predominance was advertised in the way the peace was formally concluded. After the envoys from the cities had heard the royal rescript at Sardis, they reported back to their cities and these voted to accept the terms. Then the cities sent envoys to Sparta to swear to the peace. Several test cases arose at once. The Theban envoys claimed to swear on behalf of the whole federation of Boeotia, but Agesilaus refused to accept their oath in this formulation and sent them home to seek new instructions. Without waiting for their return he began leading an army northwards, but while he was still in Tegea further envoys arrived from Thebes and agreed in the current phrase to make the cities of Boeotia autonomous. The Boeotian federation was thus disbanded.

Another problem concerned Argos and Corinth. These had formed a close link during the war, a link which was achieved in two stages. At the first stage, probably accomplished in 392, the link took the form later called "isopolity;" that is, citizens of each city could exercise citizenship of the other city provided that they took up residence there. Later, perhaps in 389, the two cities formed a complete union. Their opponents said that at this stage Argos absorbed Corinth, and there was some truth in this judgement, for an Argive garrison was placed in Corinth. When peace was made, Agesilaus threatened war against the Corinthians, unless they expelled the Argive garrison, and against the Argives, unless they withdrew their troops from Corinth. The garrison was withdrawn and the union of the two cities was dissolved. Thus an interesting and perhaps promising experiment in collaboration between two cities was brought to an end through Spartan action. Corinth became a member of the Peloponnesian League again.

In general the peace renewed and confirmed Spartan ascendancy in Greece. The Persians gained control of the mainland cities of Asia Minor and could exact tribute from them. Sparta did not try to dispute this Persian claim again. Consequently the Spartan position in European Greece was stronger after the Corinthian War than after the Peloponnesian War. In the next half-dozen years the Spartans tried to exploit their ascendancy.

NOTES

1. The march of Cyrus's Greek mercenaries is narrated by Xen. *Anab.* The Spartan operations in Asia Minor are given by Xen. *Hell.* 3.1.3–3.2.20; 3.3.1–4; 3.4.1–29. On the booty brought back to Sparta by Lysander in 404 see Plut. *Lys.* 16–17.

2. Xenophon, *Hell.* 3.5, gives an account of the opening of the Corinthian War. An account diverging at some points and giving more detail on the internal situation in the cities is provided in *Hell. Oxy.* 6–7 (1–2) and 16–18 (11–13); for commentary see I.A.F. Bruce, *An Historical Commentary on the Hellenica Oxyrhynchia* (Cambridge 1967). S. Perlman, "The Causes and Outbreak of the Corinthian War," *CQ* N.S. 14 (1964) 64–81, argued that the war began, not because of Spartan interference in the cities, but because of fear of such interference in future. For discussion of the course taken by Athenian politics during the war see Sealey, *Essays* 133–140 = *Historia* 5 (1956) 178–185; and R. Seager, "Thrasybulus, Conon and Athenian Imperialism, 396–386 B.C.," *JHS* 87 (1967) 95–115. Diplomatic and military developments in 395 after the battle of Haliartus are known from Diod. 14.82. The land fighting of 394 is given by Xen. *Hell.* 4.2.1–4.4.1; the Corinthian attempt to exclude the fugitives after the battle of Nemea is mentioned by Dem. 20.52–53.

3. For the naval operations of 394–393 see Xen. *Hell.* 4.3.10–12; 4.8.1–11. The inscriptions about work on the fortifications of the Peiraeus are *I.G.* II², 1656 and 1657 = Tod 2.107. For the negotiations of 392/1 see Xen. *Hell.* 4.8.12–17; Andoc. 3; Philochorus, *F.Gr.Hist.* IIIB 328F149. For the operations of Thrasybulus, Agyrrhius and Iphicrates on the Asiatic coast see Xen. *Hell.* 4.8.25–39. For the political attack on officers of Thrasybulus see Lys. 28 and 29. For the introduction and increase by Agyrrhius of pay for attending the assembly see Ar. *AP* 41.3. For the destruction of the *mora* by Iphicrates see Xen. *Hell.* 4.5.11–17. The inscription about Athenian relations with Clazomenae is Tod 2.114. The chronology of the Corinthian War is uncertain at several points, including the operations of Thrasybulus and Iphicrates; the present account follows the reconstruction by K.J. Beloch, *Die attische Politik seit Perikles* (Leipzig 1884) 346–359; for more recent discussion see T.T.B. Ryder, *Koine Eirene: General Peace and Local Independence in Ancient Greece* (Oxford 1965) 165–169.

4. For the narrative see Xen. *Hell.* 5.1. A good deal has been written about the fourth-century practice of concluding treaties of common peace; previous discussions are superseded by Ryder, *Koine Eirene*. For an important study of relations between Corinth and Argos during the Corinthian War see G.T. Griffith, "The Union of Corinth and Argos (392–386 B.C.), "*Historia* 1 (1950) 236–256.

III

Leagues of
More Equal Type

Note

ON THE LITERARY AND EPIGRAPHIC SOURCES FOR PART III

Many of the sources drawn on in Part I and Part II are useful for Part III. Attention will be drawn here mostly to additional authors.

HISTORIANS

Much of the narrative history of the fourth century depends on Xenophon (see pp. 233-234) and Diodorus (see p. 8), and many of the problems of its first four decades arise because their accounts diverge. Late in life Xenophon composed a short treatise called *Revenues*, in which he proposed steps to improve Athenian finances; it is commonly assigned to a date ca. 355.

For the period of Demosthenes PHILOCHORUS (see p. 90) is a valuable source, as several informative fragments of his *Atthis* have been preserved. ANAXIMENES of Lampsacus (ca. 380–ca. 320) wrote works on history and rhetoric. Fragments of his *Hellenica* and of his *Philippica* have been preserved. Following the tradition of his predecessors, he included in his historical works speeches which were his own free compositions; one of them is extant as speech 11 in the Demosthenic corpus. POLYBIUS (ca. 203–ca. 120), who came from Megalopolis in Arcadia, was deported to Rome in 167 and did not return to Greece until 150. He wrote a history intended to show how Rome gained control of the whole civilized world in the period 220–146. His digressions provide a little information about the fourth century.

ORATORS

The orators Hypereides, Lycurgus, Deinarchus, and especially Demosthenes and Aeschines are a rich source for this period (see pp. 6–7).

WRITERS OF ROMAN DATE

DIDYMUS (ca. 80–ca. 10 B.C.) was a scholar at Alexandria and was nicknamed Chalkenteros ("Bronze-Guts") because of his immense learning and prolific writing. Considerable parts of his *Commentary on Demosthenes* were discovered on papyrus and published in 1904. Probably his Alexandrian predecessors had done relatively little work on Attic prose-writers, and so in expounding Demosthenes he was engaged in research, not compilation. The extant parts of the *Commentary* preserve quotations from Philochorus, Anaximenes and other historians.

DIONYSIUS OF HALICARNASSUS settled in Rome in 30 B.C. and stayed there for many years as a teacher of rhetoric. His most ambitious work was his *Roman Antiquities*, a history of Rome from the foundation to the beginning of the First Punic War; occasionally he gives dates both by Roman consuls and by Athenian archons, and so this work can be useful for reconstructing the archon list. He composed several treatises on Attic prose-writers. One of these treatises, the *First Letter to Ammaeus*, sought to refute the claim that Demosthenes learned his skill in oratory from the rhetorical teaching of Aristotle; it gives dates of the public speeches of Demosthenes. In some of the other treatises Dionysius used chronological arguments on the question of authenticity of speeches attributed to the authors he studied, and these arguments sometimes preserve data of historical value.

POMPEIUS TROGUS lived in the time of Augustus and sprang from a family which came from southern Gaul. He composed a universal history, called *Historiae Philippicae*, in forty-four books; no less than thirty-four of these were devoted to the history of Macedon and of the Hellenistic kingdoms. This work has been lost, except for the "prologi" or brief tables of contents to each book. JUSTIN (in full Marcus Junianus Justinus), who probably lived in the third century A.D., preserved these at the end of an extensive epitome which he made of Trogus's work.

AULUS GELLIUS (ca. A.D. 123–ca. 165) spent most of his life in Rome except for a visit to Athens for additional studies. He wrote his *"Attic Nights"* in twenty books, a collection of discussions on law, history, antiquities, literature and other subjects. POLYAENUS of Macedon, a rhetorician, made a collection of military *Strategems* in eight books and dedicated it to the emperors Marcus and Verus on the occasion of the Parthian War of A.D. 162.

INSCRIPTIONS

As for the late fifth century, so for the fourth century inscriptions provide a great deal of information and additional ones continue to be discovered. Particular attention may be drawn to the decree of Aristoteles (*I.G.* II², 43 = Tod 2.123, see pp. 411–412), which lays down rules for the Second Athenian Sea League, and to the Athenian navy lists (*I.G.* II², 1604–1632), which are inventories of ships and naval supplies drawn up by the annual boards of officers in charge of the dockyards; for an introduction to the study of these lists see J.K. Davies, "The Date of I.G. II², 1609," *Historia* 18 (1969) 309–333.

16

The Decline of the
Spartan Hegemony, 386-371

The history of classical Greece has often been regarded as a study in the behavior of fully independent cities, each intent on preserving its sovereignty unabridged. This approach needs to be corrected, since Greeks of different cities made complex and lasting efforts to develop leagues and federations of very various kinds. Part II of this book was much concerned with leagues of hegemonic type, that is, leagues in which the leading city was very much predominant over the other members. The Athenian Empire was the most ambitious attempt to build up a league of this kind.

However, there were also leagues of a more equal type. In these one city was the recognized leader but its predominance was not unrestricted and the rights of the other members were to some extent guaranteed. An important example is the Boeotian federation as restored in 447/6 and disbanded in 387/6. For federal purposes Boeotia was divided into eleven parts. In some cases one city constituted one part, but in several instances two or three small towns were grouped together to form one of the eleven parts. Thebes together with places it had absorbed counted for four of the eleven parts by 395. Final decision on federal affairs rested with a Council of 660 members, and each of the eleven parts supplied 60 members to the Council. Since Thebes supplied 240 councilors, it had a larger voice in federal decisions than any of the other cities but it did not control a majority. Similarly, executive functions were exercised by an annual board of eleven officers called boeotarchs, one being drawn from each of the eleven parts. Every one of the cities controlled its own local affairs.

The Council of the Boeotian federation was a representative organ, drawing deputies from the different parts of the territory, and a similar pattern of organization may have been adopted in other local leagues of the period, such as the Chalcidian League founded in 432 with its center at Olynthus (chapter 11, p. 315). In the fourth century the evidence, although scanty, suggests that there were several attempts to found local federations; for example, Xenophon (*Hellenica* 4.3.15) says that "the Euboeans" fought on the side of the quadruple alliance against Agesilaus at Coroneia in 394, and the designation suggests that a Euboean federation was in existence.

More interest will attach in Part III to a league of wide extent founded on relatively egalitarian principles. In 378 the Athenians launched their Second Sea League, as it can conveniently be called, and the provisions adopted during the months of its foundation sought to safeguard the allies against Athenian encroachments. The questions will arise, How promising an experiment was this in cooperation between cities, and What causes later brought about the disintegration of the League?

THE SPARTAN OUTRAGES[2]

Between 385 and 379 the Spartans carried out a series of highhanded acts, which became notorious and hence aroused feeling against them in many parts of Greece. They took some of these steps in order to discipline those of their allies who had not responded adequately to their demands during the Corinthian War. The first victim was Mantinea. In 385 the Spartans sent the Mantineans a series of charges. Allegedly the Mantineans had supplied grain to Argos during the war; they had refused to join some federal expeditions and only taken part halfheartedly in others; they had grieved at Spartan successes and rejoiced at Spartan misfortunes. On the basis of this justification Sparta demanded that the Mantineans destroy their city wall. The Mantineans refused, and so Agesipolis led an army against them. At first he undertook conventional siege operations. Then he dammed the river, which flowed through Mantinea, and raised its level so that it undermined the foundations of the city wall and some buildings. Consequently the Mantineans yielded and agreed to dismantle the city wall. But now the Spartans increased their demands; they insisted that the Mantineans abandon their city and dwell henceforth divided into the five villages from which the city had been formed long before. The Mantineans agreed even to this. In response to the intercession of Pausanias, who was still alive in Arcadia, his son Agesipolis allowed sixty leading Mantineans to withdraw into exile.

The next Spartan action concerned Phlius and the opportunity was provided by an appeal of some Phliasian exiles to Sparta; they asserted that, as long as they had been in their city, Phlius had behaved as a loyal member of the Peloponnesian League. The Spartans responded by sending a demand to Phlius for the recall of the exiles. The Phliasians did not wish to face a Spartan expedition, since the exiles had many relatives and friends within the walls and these might betray the city. So Phlius recalled its exiles and provided that their property should be restored to them; anyone who had bought any of the property was to receive compensation from the state, and disputes arising from the settlement were to be decided by a court.

In 382 an opportunity arose for Spartan action far away from the Peloponnese. The Chalcidian federation had been expanding and absorbing many cities of its neighborhood. By 382 it threatened to attack Acanthus and Apollonia, unless these cities joined it. So these two cities appealed to Sparta. The Spartans brought the envoys before their own assembly and before a congress of their allies. The decision was taken to send out the full force of the League, nominally 10,000 men, and each city was permitted to commute its obligation of men for money. Furthermore, since it would take some time to gather this whole army, a force of some 2,000 was to be sent in advance under a commander called Eudamidas. The latter took part of his force ahead and was welcomed in Poteidaea, which he made his base of operations; he instructed his brother Phoebidas to follow with the rest of the 2,000 men.

Phoebidas, traveling northwards by land, encamped outside Thebes, and there a new opportunity offered itself. Thebes was acutely divided between two groups. The one group, led by Ismenias, was hostile to Sparta; it had contrived the issue of a prohibition forbidding any Theban to join the expedition against Olynthus. Indeed, Thebes was in the process of negotiating an alliance with Olynthus. The other group was led by Leontiadas and was favorable to Sparta. Both Ismenias and Leontiadas were in office as polemarchs; this was the chief magistracy and had superseded the boeotarchy when the Boeotian federation was disbanded. Leontiadas, after making a clandestine approach to Phoebidas, led him and his men up the slopes of the Cadmea, the acropolis of Thebes, while the Thebans were preoccupied with a meeting of the Council in the market place, and Leontiadas handed over the keys of the citadel to the Spartan commander. Thus Phoebidas occupied the Cadmea and installed a garrison, and Leontiadas proceeded to arrest Ismenias. About 300 Thebans fled and found asylum in Athens. The Spartan response to these events was mixed. Phoebidas was put on trial and he was condemned to pay a fine. The Spartans kept their garrison on the Cadmea, and they sent there a special court, drawn from themselves and their allies, to try Ismenias; he was condemned to death.

Teleutias, the brother of Agesilaus, led the planned army of 10,000 overland to Chalcidice. He brought the enemy to battle outside Olynthus and defeated them. But in 381 he was killed outside the city in a further action, which resulted in a serious defeat for the Spartans. However, Agesipolis came out with reinforcements and took over the command. He continued operations, ravaging the territory of the Chalcidian cities and capturing Torone, but during the summer of 380 he fell ill and died. Polybiades was sent out as harmost to replace him, and he succeeded in reducing Olynthus by blockade during the next year. When the Olynthians ran short of supplies, they sent envoys to Sparta and made peace; they were required to make a close alliance with Sparta and acknowledge Spartan leadership.*

Meanwhile trouble had developed in Phlius. The returned exiles asserted that the regular courts of the city were not impartial for trying disputes arising from the settlement; they claimed that a special court ought to be set up; apparently they wished it to include jurors drawn from allied cities. When the city refused to meet the demand, the exiles together with their sympathizers went to Sparta; some of them were longstanding friends of Agesilaus. Thereupon the city decreed a penalty against all those who had gone to Sparta without public authorization. But the Spartans responded to the appeal of the exiles by sending an expedition under Agesilaus. He demanded that the Phliasians should hand over their acropolis and, since they were unwilling to do so, he began a blockade of the city. By living on short rations the Phliasians contrived to hold out much longer than was expected, but after a siege of a year and eight months they offered to come to terms. Sparta entrusted the task of drawing up a settlement to Agesilaus. He established a body of a hundred men, fifty being drawn from the exiles and fifty from the other inhabitants. This body was to serve as a court, examining each of the inhabitants and deciding which of them should be executed and which should be spared. It was also to draw up laws for the future government of the city.

Phlius surrendered in 379 and Olynthus later in the same year. The hegemony of the Spartans seemed secure. They had succeeded in carrying out acts offensive to Greek opinion and had overcome all resistance. Such steps as other Greek cities had taken towards independent action since the peace of Antalcidas amounted to little. In 384/3 Athens had made an alliance with Chios, but the terms were carefully drafted to manifest respect for the king's peace. Soon after the surrender of Olynthus the Spartans reorganized their confederacy for military purposes; they divided it into ten parts for levy of troops. Probably an organization of this general type had already been adopted by 382 and is reflected in the decisions taken in response to the appeal of Acanthus and Apollonia. Later the system was reorganized so that Olynthus and the new allies in the Thraceward district constituted one of the ten parts. Probably at the same time the allies adopted a resolution forbidding members of the League to engage in warfare against one another. By 379 the Peloponnesian League, to use its modern name, extended far beyond the Peloponnese and had a much more sophisticated organization than in the fifth century.

THE LIBERATION OF THE CADMEA[3]

A plot launched successfully in 379 freed Thebes from Spartan control and began a series of events which posed a serious challenge to the Spartan hegemony in Greece. The polemarchs in office in Thebes in 379 were subservient to Spartan interests, but their secretary, Phillidas, visited Athens and made a plan with some of the Theban exiles living there. Towards the middle of winter, when the term of office of the polemarchs was due to expire, seven of the plotters came from Athens to Theban territory and they entered Thebes by joining the crowd of people who had worked in the fields and were returning to the city in the evening. On the following evening the seven polemarchs held a feast to mark the end of their term, and when they had drunk heavily, Phillidas offered to bring them women. He brought them the seven plotters in disguise, and these killed the polemarchs. Then Phillidas took three of the plotters to the house of Leontiadas and killed him. Next he took two of them to the prison, released the prisoners and armed them. The conspirators issued a proclamation, saying that the tyrants had been killed and inviting the citizens to parade with their weapons as hoplites or cavalry; the citizens waited until dawn and then gathered in arms. A message was sent to two Athenian generals who were evidently privy to the plot and had stationed their forces at the border between Attica and Boeotia.

The Spartan harmost in the Cadmea sent to Plataea and Thespiae for help. The Plataeans advanced towards Thebes but were driven away by the Theban cavalry. When the cavalry returned to the city and the two Athenian generals arrived with their forces, the Thebans began attacking the Cadmea. The Spartan harmost had only a small force at his disposal, so he made a truce whereby he and his men were to evacuate the Cadmea and withdraw unharmed. As they came down from the citadel, the Thebans arrested and killed some of them because of private grievances.

The Spartans responded to the liberation of the Cadmea by executing the harmost, who had held command there, and by sending an expedition under king Cleombrotus against Thebes. Cleombrotus led his force out while it was still winter and spent sixteen days in the territory of Thebes before returning home, but he inflicted as little damage as he could. The situation was still fluid. The Spartans had lost control of Thebes but they still held positions in Boeotia; moreover, although two Athenian generals had helped the conspirators, Athens had not committed herself irrevocably to the Theban cause. It was in the interests of Sparta to prevent any coalition between Athens and Thebes. Possibly the expedition of Cleombrotus was sent more with a view to making an impression on the Athenians than to any expected effect on Thebes. The expedition was a demonstration of strength, showing that Sparta could send an army into central Greece. At the same time Cleombrotus wanted to avoid hostilities against the Athenians; as he marched north, the Athenians stationed a force under Chabrias to hold the route leading into Boeotia through Eleutherae in Attica, so Cleombrotus chose a different route, through Plataea, which avoided Attic territory. The Athenians were impressed by the show of strength; they tried the two generals who had helped in the liberation of the Cadmea; one of them was executed and the other was sentenced to exile, since he had fled from Attica.

During his return journey Cleombrotus stationed a force of allies in Thespiae under a harmost called Sphodrias and gave him money to recruit mercenaries. Shortly afterwards Sphodrias conceived the design of making a raid on Attica. His aim was to seize the Peiraeus by surprise. He set off from Thespiae early in the night, but when dawn broke he had only reached the plain of Thria in western Attica. Thus the Athenians were warned and they rushed to arms. Sphodrias destroyed buildings and herds of animals in the plain of Thria and then retreated. Three Spartan envoys were in Athens, and when the raid of Sphodrias ended in fiasco, the Athenians questioned them about it; the envoys replied that neither they nor the city of Sparta had any prior knowledge of Sphodrias's plan, and they added that he would certainly be tried and condemned. The situation was still fluid.

Action taken in Sparta precipitated a crisis. A prosecution was undertaken against Sphodrias. Anticipating condemnation, he did not come to Sparta but stayed away from the trial. Yet because of a political intrigue the court acquitted Sphodrias by vote. The influence of Agesilaus was crucial; he admitted that Sphodrias was guilty of the charge, but he argued that he had lived an exemplary life since childhood and that Sparta could not afford to lose such men. The news of the acquittal brought a sharp reaction in Athens. The Athenians put the Peiraeus in a state of defense; they built warships, and when the Spartans sent a further expedition against Thebes, the Athenians sent a force under Chabrias to support the Thebans. The Spartan expedition of summer 378 was commanded by Agesilaus. He found that the Thebans had built a ditch and set stakes to protect the most valuable part of their territory, but after skirmishes and maneuvers he forced his way through the defenses and ravaged the territory right up to the walls. During his return he stationed a force under a harmost Phoebidas in Thespiae. In the ensuing fighting the Thebans defeated and killed Phoebidas, and by a series of expeditions they began recovering their ascendancy over the other cities of Boeotia. But Thespiae was hostile to them and the Spartans sent a further force there by sea.

THE SECOND ATHENIAN SEA LEAGUE[4]

During 378 the Athenians founded a new defensive alliance, which has come to be called the Second Athenian Sea League. Information about its foundation is provided by Diodorus (15.28–30), whose account distinguishes a series of steps, and by a number of Athenian inscriptions. Recent studies have brought the reports of these two sources into harmony and shown that the series of steps sketched by Diodorus is credible.

The first step was the issue by the Athenians of a general invitation, asking Greek states to join them in defending the freedom of them all against Spartan encroachments. The invitation was probably sent fairly early in 378, as soon as the weather was suitable for sailing. Several states responded favorably; these included Chios, which had had an alliance with Athens since 384/3, Byzantium, Rhodes, Mytilene and some other islands. These alliances were merely bilateral agreements between Athens and each of the allies; those allies were not yet bound to one another. An inscription recording the Athenian alliance with Byzantium illustrates this first stage. A second step followed soon afterwards. The Athenians resolved to set up a common *Synedrion* or council of the allies and invite each allied state to send deputies to it. The Synedrion was to sit in Athens and was to remain permanently in session; each ally but Athens had a vote in the Synedrion. Thus final control of policy was divided between two bodies, the Athenian assembly and the Synedrion of the allies. This second step founded the new League; it bound the allies by a multilateral agreement, linking them to one another as well as to Athens. It is illustrated by an inscription preserving part of an Athenian decree about Methymna. The decree notes that Methymna is already an ally of Athens and provides that it shall also become a member of the Synedrion; it is accordingly to be added to the list of allies who belong to that body.

The reason why Athens set about founding the new League should be sought in the uncertain situation following the liberation of the Cadmea. As will be remembered, at the time of Cleombrotus's expedition to Thebes conditions were far from clear. Athens was not at war with Sparta but, since Cleombrotus could reach central Greece unopposed, she felt herself exposed to Spartan pressure. Moreover, straight after the liberation of the Cadmea the Thebans sent an embassy to Sparta to offer submission. Nothing came of these negotiations, since the Spartans demanded that the Thebans should recall their exiles and banish those who had killed Leontiadas and his associates. But the Theban offer of submission to Sparta could well alarm the Athenians; fearing to be isolated, they sought new allies.

The Spartan response to the foundation of the Sea League appears to have been twofold and to reflect division of opinion. On the one hand, a Spartan embassy was sent to Athens; three envoys were there at the time of the raid of Sphodrias. This attempt to reach an understanding with Athens by negotiation may have been the policy of Agesilaus. The alternative course was to try to gain clear military superiority over the Athenians; this policy culminated in the raid of Sphodrias, and he was an associate of Cleombrotus. This raid provoked a sharp reaction among the Athenians. On the one hand, as Xenophon reports and as was mentioned above, they put the Peiraeus in a state of defense by equipping its entrances with gates and they built warships. At the same time, as Diodorus reports, they declared that the Spartans had broken the king's peace and they admitted the Thebans to membership of the Synedrion. The measures reported by Xenophon and Diodorus may be complementary; it has been conjectured that the king's peace limited the armed forces to be maintained by the Greek states and forbade the Athenians to equip the Peiraeus with gates. Furthermore Diodorus, after recording the admission of Thebes to the Synedrion, adds that the Athenians voted to restore land previously held by cleruchies and issued a prohibition forbidding any Athenian to acquire agricultural land outside of Attica. It has been suggested convincingly that these two measures mentioned by Diodorus belonged together. Athens, it is suggested, already feared that Thebes might build up a dangerously strong center of power in Boeotia and she hoped to restrain Thebes by making it a member of the Synedrion. But the other allies, being maritime states, had little interest in admitting Thebes to membership; so in return for their consent to this proposal they extorted a guarantee against the creation of cleruchies, such as had made the Athenians unpopular in the fifth century.

The measures taken by the Athenians after the raid of Sphodrias constitute a third and final stage in the founding of the Sea League. It is illustrated by a well preserved inscription, which gives a decree proposed by Aristoteles in the second half of the Attic year 378/7. It reiterated the general invitation to Greek cities to join the League, and it offered numerous assurances to the allies and prospective allies. They would be free and autonomous, each enjoying the constitution of its choice. No garrisons would be stationed among the allies, no resident officers would be sent to them, and no tribute would be exacted. The guarantee against cleruchies and against Athenian possession of allied land was clearly stated: any land held by Athenians publicly or privately in allied territory was to be restored, and no Athenian was to acquire such land in future. Generally these undertakings sought to prohibit any resumption of the practices which had made the Athenian Empire of the fifth century unpopular.

On the obverse of the inscription bearing the decree, immediately after the text of that document, a list of names of allies was appended. The first six names were inscribed by the same hand as the body of the decree. They were Chios, Mytilene, Methymna, Rhodes, Byzantium and Thebes. These cities had evidently joined the League by the time the decree of Aristoteles was passed. A second hand added the names of four cities in Euboea, namely, Chalcis, Eretria, Arethusa and Carystus, and of Icos, a small island a little further north. These cities joined the League in response to the reiterated invitation and the undertaking about allied land.

At least two more hands can be distinguished among the entries on the obverse of the inscription, and most of the cities inscribed in these two hands appear to have joined the League because of a campaign waged by Chabrias in 377. In that year Chabrias went to Euboea and operated there against Histiaea; then he sailed among the Cyclades. Places whose names were inscribed in consequence of this campaign included Dium in Euboea and several islands, such as Peparethus, Sciathus, Paros and Poeessa. Some more distant places, such as Maroneia on the coast of Thrace and Tenedos near the entrace to the Hellespont, were inscribed among these names and probably joined the League in consequence of the news of Chabrias's expedition, even though he probably did not sail so far away. Perinthus was inscribed in the same group of names; situated not far from Byzantium, it was too far away to be moved by Chabrias's campaign and presumably it joined the League entirely of its own initiative.

After 378 the Spartans continued sending expeditions of the Peloponnesian League against Thebes. In 377 the expedition was led by Agesilaus and he ravaged the territory of Thebes extending eastwards from the city as far as the border of Tanagra. In 376 an expedition with a similar purpose was led by Cleombrotus, but he found that Theban and Athenian troops had occupied the heights of Cithaeron; he could not force his way through or reach Thebes. So a congress of the Peloponnesian League was called and it resolved to equip a fleet with two purposes: the fleet was to intercept the grain ships bound for Athens from the Black Sea, and it was to carry a land army northwards across the Corinthian Gulf against the Thebans. When equipped, the fleet numbered sixty triremes and was commanded by the Spartan navarch Pollis; it took up positions at Aegina, Ceos and Andros in order to intercept the grain ships. But an Athenian fleet under Chabrias brought Pollis to battle off Naxos and defeated him. This victory was decisive for naval ascendancy in the Aegean; Athens remained the strongest power there until 322. But the Peloponnesians, though unable to challenge the Athenians at sea, might still use their fleet for the other purpose of conveying a

The stele of Aristoteles, 378/7, about the Second Athenian Sea League. The lists of members appear in the lower part of the obverse and on the left face. See pages 411–412 and 418–419. [Courtesy R. S. Stroud.]

force northwards across the Corinthian Gulf. Alarmed at this possibility, the Thebans appealed to the Athenians to send a fleet round the Peloponnese; they hoped that this would divert Spartan attention away from central Greece. So in the next year, 375, Timotheus, the son of Conon, led an Athenian fleet round the Peloponnese; he reached Corcyra and persuaded it to join the Sea League. The Spartans sent a Peloponnesian fleet under the navarch Nicolochus against him. The two fleets came to battle off Alyzeia near Leucas; Timotheus defeated Nicolochus and thus gained control of the northwestern theater of warfare.

Meanwhile, the Thebans strengthened their position in central Greece. In 377 Tanagra was still loyal to the Spartans, but already there was internal dissension in Thespiae. In 376 and 375 Boeotia was free from Peloponnesian invasions. So the Thebans were able to march on many of the other cities and recover their ascendancy. They set up a new Boeotian federation, whose constitution differed in some respects from that of the federation dissolved in 386, although few details are known about it. There were only seven boeotarchs instead of the former eleven, and ultimate determination of policy rested, not with a representative council, but with a primary assembly of some kind. But as late as 375 some Boeotian cities, notably Plataea and Thespiae, still guarded their independence against Thebes.

THE PEACE OF 375/4[5]

By 375/4 the major powers were ready to make peace. As between Athens and Sparta the balance of power was clear; Athens had proved herself superior at sea in the battle of Naxos, and the expedition of Timotheus to Corcyra demonstrated the naval superiority of the Athenians anew. But for Athens the expense of maintaining a force in the northwest was a reason for inclining towards peace. Athens indeed had far less reason than Thebes to fight the Spartans. The Thebans had recovered ascendancy over much of Boeotia and they proceeded to attack Phocis. The Phocians appealed to Sparta and the Spartans sent a force under Cleombrotus by sea across the Corinthian Gulf to Phocis. The Thebans saw a serious check to their ambitions in the presence of a Lacedaemonian force based securely north of the Corinthian Gulf; they recalled their own troops from Phocis and guarded the routes leading into Boeotia. The immediate occasion for making peace was provided by the Persian king. He was preparing an expedition against Egypt, which was in revolt; he wanted peace among the Greek cities so that he could draw plentifully on the supply of mercenaries which Greece provided. In response to the invitation brought by his envoys the Greek cities concluded peace on terms very similar to those of 387/6; but this time the Athenian Sea League was recognized as well as the Peloponnesian League.

The way in which this peace came to be broken shortly afterwards is problematic, and it is best to start from Xenophon's account. As he explains, Timotheus was still in the northwest when peace was concluded. The Athenians recalled him, and during his return he restored a party of exiles to the island of Zacynthus. The city itself continued to be controlled by those favoring Sparta and they appealed to Sparta for help. The Spartans responded promptly by dispatching the navarch Mnasippus with a Peloponnesian fleet of sixty ships. He was instructed to pay general attention to affairs in northwestern waters and to attack Corcyra. He sailed to Corcyra and landed in the island; he ravaged the territory and blockaded the city. The Corcyreans appealed to Athens for help. So the Athenians sent Ctesicles with 600 peltasts and asked their ally Alcetas, king of the Molossi in Epirus, to transport the force to Corcyra. Ctesicles completed the journey successfully; he landed in the island of Corcyra by night and brought his men into the city. The Athenians also voted to send a fleet of sixty ships and entrusted the command to Timotheus. In preparation for the expedition Timotheus sailed among the islands of the Aegean to raise additional crewmen. After a time the Athenians decided that he was wasting the season; they deposed him from the command and entrusted it to Iphicrates. The latter equipped his fleet in haste to the number of seventy triremes. Meanwhile the Corcyreans ran short of food and made a sally from the city; in the consequent battle Mnasippus was defeated and killed. A little later his second-in-command, Hypermenes, withdrew the remainder of the besieging fleet to Leucas. Thus the siege of Corcyra had already been raised when Iphicrates arrived; during the journey he had trained his crews and won over the cities of Cephallenia for the Athenian cause. He intercepted and captured ten Sicilian ships sent by Dionysius, the tyrant of Syracuse, which had arrived too late, and he continued operating in the northwest.

Further evidence on some of these events is provided by a speech delivered in court in 362 against Timotheus by Apollodorus, the son of the banker Pasion; Apollodorus brought suit successfully to recover debts. As the speech shows, in Munychion (the tenth Attic month) of the year 374/3 Timotheus was preparing to sail on his voyage into the Aegean and so he borrowed money from Pasion. Later, when Timotheus was deposed from office for delaying his expedition to Corcyra, he was prosecuted by Iphicrates and Callistratus, and the trial was held in Maemacterion (the fourth Attic month) of the year 373/2. It appears that Timotheus's preparatory voyage in the Aegean began in the early summer of 373 and his trial was held early in the following winter. Accordingly, Iphicrates must have set out on his voyage to Corcyra in 372, when the winter was over and sailing became possible.

Something can be said about the personal situation among Athenian politicians. Iphicrates took Callistratus and Chabrias with him to Corcyra; through this and through the prosecution of Timotheus he forged an alliance which was highly influential in Athenian affairs for several years. Iphicrates was the first of his family to attain political prominence. Callistratus was the nephew of Agyrrhius, who had been influential in the 390s; Callistratus himself was general in 378/7 but achieved distinction more as a speaker and politician than as a military commander. Chabrias led a series of successful campaigns in the early years of the Second Sea League. As already noted, in 377 he operated in Euboea and the Cyclades and in 376 he commanded at the battle of Naxos. In 375 he sailed to the coast of Thrace. He found the city of Abdera at war with the Thracian Triballi and expecting a siege; he drove the Triballi away and put a garrison in the city. Several places in the Thraceward district joined the Sea League in consequence of this campaign. Timotheus had cause to feel alarm. His father, Conon, had achieved greater fame than any other Athenian during the Corinthian War and had had opportunities to sail the Aegean winning a local following in many cities. But by 375 Chabrias was winning local adherents on an equal or greater scale. In 373 Timotheus spent several months on his preparatory campaign; evidently he was trying to recover or enlarge the local following of his father.

Diodorus's account of events following the peace of 375/4 differs from that given by Xenophon. He tells how Timotheus restored some exiles to the island of Zacynthus and he names the position they occupied as the fort Arcadia. Thereupon, he continues, the Zacynthians of the city appealed to Sparta for help and the Spartans sent envoys to Athens to protest. Receiving no satisfaction, the Spartans sent a fleet of twenty-five ships under Aristocrates to help Zacynthus. At the same time a pro-Spartan group in Corcyra rebelled and was driven into exile; it appealed to Sparta, and so the Spartans sent out a fleet of twenty-two ships under Alcidas in the hope that together with the exiles he would capture the city of Corcyra. The Corcyreans of the city appealed to Athens, and the Athenians voted to send Ctesicles to Zacynthus and to send a fleet of sixty ships under Timotheus to Corcyra. Then the Spartans sent out a large armament under Mnasippus to Corcyra; his force comprised sixty-five ships and 1,500 troops. He joined the Corcyrean exiles and inflicted a defeat on the Corcyreans of the city. Timotheus sailed towards Thrace, winning new allies and additional ships; because of the delay the Athenians deposed him in his absence from the command, but when he returned with the envoys and ships of the new allies, they restored him to the command. Finally the Athenians sent out two expeditions; Ctesicles with 500 men was sent promptly to Corcyra, where he defeated and killed Mnasippus; and the whole fleet, numbering 130 ships, was sent under Timotheus and Iphicrates, where it intercepted the ships sent by Dionysius.

Diodorus's account is mistaken in at least two points. He duplicates the expedition of Ctesicles, having him sent once to Zacynthus and once to Corcyra;

and he erroneously makes Timotheus share command of the final expedition with Iphicrates. But his account of events preceding the dispatch of Mnasippus deserves some respect, since it is circumstantial: he gives the names of two Spartan commanders, Aristocrates and Alcidas, who led previous naval expeditions. The fleet of Mnasippus was much larger and its departure for Corcyra marked the real resumption of war. Accordingly, the most significant divergence between Diodorus and Xenophon concerns the antecedents to Mnasippus's expedition. In Diodorus's account the Athenians had already voted to send a large fleet under Timotheus to Corcyra when the Spartans dispatched Mnasippus; thus the expedition of Mnasippus was a response to Athenian action, and the main responsibility for the resumption of hostilities rested with the Athenians. In Xenophon's account the expedition of Mnasippus preceded and provoked the Athenian decision to send Timotheus with a large fleet to Corcyra; thus the main responsibility for the resumption of hostilities rested with the Spartans.

A consideration about the navarchy may lend some support to Diodorus's account. It is widely believed that the Spartan navarch took office at the same time as the ephors in the late summer or the fall and, like them, held office for a year. Mnasippus was navarch in 373/2, in the period when Timotheus was prosecuted and Iphicrates set out with the final expedition. It would follow that Mnasippus took office in the late summer or fall of 373. But it appears from the speech of 362 against Timotheus that the latter began his preparatory voyage in the Aegean in the early summer. Hence it can be inferred that the Athenians voted the dispatch of Timotheus before Mnasippus was sent to Corcyra; thus Diodorus's account would appear to be confirmed. It should, however, be added that the hypothesis about the time of year when the navarch took office cannot be proved; and although the reports by Thucydides and Xenophon of the activities of particular navarchs mostly conform to it, they do not do so entirely and other hypotheses may be possible.

A further argument in support of Diodorus's account can be drawn from the speech of Isocrates called *Plataicus* (14). In 373/2 the Thebans seized and destroyed Plataea, and the speech professes to be spoken by Plataean refugees appealing to Athens for help promptly after the destruction of their city. The speech gives the impression that general conditions are peaceful and war has not yet been resumed between Athens and Sparta. This is compatible with the view that peace was observed until some time after the Attic year 373/2 had begun and until Mnasippus sailed on his voyage. But Xenophon's account gives the impression that hostilities were resumed very soon after the peace of 375/4 was concluded. In particular, he says that after the conclusion of peace two Athenian envoys sailed "straightaway" to Timotheus and instructed him to come home; and after he had restored the exiles to the island of Zacynthus and the Zacynthians of the city appealed to Sparta, the Spartans "straightaway" resolved that the Athenians had committed an offense and decided to equip a fleet of sixty ships to sail under Mnasippus. The *Plataicus* of Isocrates seems to show that an interval of genuine peace lasted into the Attic year 373/2, and this may be held to refute Xenophon's implication of a prompt resumption of hostilities. On the other hand, it is not clear how much reliance can be placed on the *Plataicus*. The common assumption that the speech was composed at its dramatic date is not necessarily sound; Isocrates may have composed it some years later, and it is not clear whether he remembered the circumstances of 373/2 correctly or chose to represent them correctly.

Chronological considerations too have a bearing on the choice between Xenophon's and Diodorus's accounts of the resumption of hostilities. At Corcyra in 375 Timotheus ran short of money. Some scholars have stressed this and inferred that he would not be likely to stay in Corcyra through the winter of 375/4. Peace would thus be concluded in the first half of the Attic year 375/4. Aristocrates and Alcidas might be navarchs for 375/4 and 374/3 respectively; there would be an interval of genuine peace, lasting about two years, before the voyage of Mnasippus. Those who take the alternative view suppose that peace was made in the second half of the Attic year 375/4; they draw their main argument from the impression of speed given by Xenophon's account of the resumption of hostilities; they suppose that the interval of peace was negligibly short. The problem depends on the relative reliability of Xenophon and Diodorus.

As observed above (p. 412), a list of names of allies was inscribed on the lower part of the obverse of the stele bearing the decree of Aristoteles. A further list of names was inscribed on the left face of the same stele. This additional list should be divided into two parts. First are the names of twenty-nine allies in the upper part of the left face. The intervals between these entries are short, never amounting to more than a few lines. Second, beneath a blank space equal to sixteen lines, there is a single entry in a different hand: "The demos of the Zacynthians in the Nellos." An old view supposed that this entry was inscribed later than the other twenty-nine, since it is lower down on the stele. A more recent view stresses the difference of hand and the blank space of sixteen lines; it notes that the Zacynthian entry begins on a level with the beginning of the list of allies on the obverse. Presumably the mason inscribing the Zacynthian entry intended to put it level with the list on the obverse and did not see any names inscribed higher up on the left face; that is, the other twenty-nine names were inscribed later than the Zacynthian entry.

The date when the Zacynthian entry was inscribed depends on the identification of the place called "the Nellos." It is not otherwise attested. Some scholars have identified it with the fort Arcadia, where according to Diodorus Timotheus installed the exiles on restoring them to the island of Zacynthus. Alternatively, it may be a place on the mainland where the exiles found refuge before Timotheus restored them to the island; in this case the entry would be easier to understand.

The other twenty-nine entries begin with the following three: "The demos of the Corcyreans. The Acarnanians. Pronnoi in Cephallenia." Pronnoi was one of the four cities on the island of Cephallenia. These three allies, and some others among the twenty-nine such as Alcetas, the king of the Molossi, may have been brought into the League by Timotheus during his northwestern voyage of 375. Indeed, another inscription preserves a decree of the second prytany of 375/4, giving an alliance of Athens with the Corcyreans, the Acarnanians and the Cephallenians; the decree orders that the three names be inscribed on the list of allies. Other entries among the twenty-nine may reflect the expedition of Chabrias to the coast of Thrace in 375 (above p. 416); they include Abdera, Thasos, the Thracian Chalcidians, Aenus and Samothrace. Thus all twenty-nine entries may have been made in 375 in consequence of operations of that year. However, another possibility can also be considered. The decree of 375/4, ordering the addition of Corcyra, Acarnania and Cephallenia to the list of allies, does not distinguish between the four cities of Cephallenia but speaks simply of "the Cephallenians." Yet the entry on the left face of the stele of Aristoteles records only one of the four cities, namely Pronnoi. Possibly the order to inscribe the three new allies was not carried out promptly and circumstances had changed by the time the entries were made on the stele of Aristoteles. In that case the twenty-nine entries may have been made in 373 and the inscribing of them may reflect Timotheus's need to boast of the allies he had secured; some of them were places he had won over on his northwestern voyage of 375, and others were places he may have visited on his preparatory expedition of 373, even if they had been brought into the League by Chabrias two years before.

LEUCTRA[6]

By 371 the Spartans and the Athenians were ready to make peace. The former had failed in their attempt to reassert themselves in northwestern waters. They sent Antalcidas on a further mission to the Persian king; whether he came back with a royal rescript recommending peace in time for the peace conference is not clear and perhaps not crucially important; the Greeks knew that the Spartans were negotiating with Persia with a view to a common peace. The Athenians for their part had reason for alarm at the growing power of the Thebans. The latter attacked and destroyed Plataea in 373/2; those Plataeans who escaped found a refuge in Athens. At about the same time the Thebans attacked and absorbed Thespiae. The Athenians were also concerned about Theban hostility towards

Phocis, a traditional ally of Athens. The position of Thebes, a land power, within the Athenian Sea League was a potential source of friction, since the other members were maritime. The possibility of friction increased when Athens took to levying financial contributions (*syntaxeis*) from the other members of the League. The nature of these contributions is obscure and will require consideration in a later chapter (see chapter 17, pp. 432–433); but it is clear that by the late 370s the Athenians were perturbed because the Thebans did not contribute to the finances of the League. Early in 371 a still more pressing consideration inclined the Athenians towards concluding peace. Iphicrates wintered in the northwest, stationing some of his troops in Corcyra and some in Acarnania; he exacted money from the cities of Cephallenia. He ran short of supplies, and he sent Callistratus to Athens with instructions to procure either money or a treaty of peace.

A peace conference met accordingly in Sparta and agreed to a new treaty of common peace. The Spartans swore on behalf of themselves and their allies, but the Athenians and their allies swore separately. The Thebans at first swore on behalf of themselves alone, but on the next day they came to Agesilaus again and asked that their oath be deemed valid for all the Boeotians. Agesilaus refused to alter the record. The issue at stake was the existence of the Boeotian federation; the Spartans claimed that it infringed the autonomy of the Boeotian cities, and the autonomy of all cities was guaranteed in the peace of 371 as in that of 387/6. Cleombrotus still held his army in Phocis and the Spartan assembly ordered him to march on Thebes. The Thebans called out the army of the Boeotian federation against him and, when he reached Leuctra in Boeotia, they brought him to battle. The result was a severe defeat for the Lacedaemonian army; it lost nearly 1,000 men, including some 400 Spartan citizens, and Cleombrotus himself was killed.

The defeat at Leuctra ended the Spartan reputation for invincibility in hoplite battles, but its immediate effects were not large. The ephors called out the remaining two *morai* and other reserves and sent them north under Archidamus, the son of Agesilaus who was ill. This force was instructed to meet and rescue the survivors of Cleombrotus's army, and as it marched northwards, it was joined by allied contingents from Tegea, Mantinea, Corinth, Sicyon, Phlius and Achaea. The Peloponnesian allies of Sparta were still loyal. The Theban position straight after their victory was by no means secure. They sent envoys with news of their success to Athens, expecting their ally to rejoice; but the Athenian Council, so far from promising military support for the Thebans, did not even offer their herald the usual courtesy of an official invitation to dinner.

The Thebans also sent news to Jason, the tyrant of Pherae, who was their ally. In the previous years he had made himself supreme in all Thessaly and had revived the office of *tagos* or elective federal king. On learning of the battle of Leuctra he called out his mercenaries and his cavalry and marched swiftly southwards to Boeotia. There he offered the Thebans advice about caution in prosperity and negotiated a truce between them and the army of Cleombrotus. He saw that the rising fortunes of the Boeotians made them a potential check to his own ambitions in the north; he wanted Peloponnesian power to continue as a restraint on Boeotia. Thanks to the truce negotiated by Jason, the army of Cleombrotus retired southwards; the relieving force of Archidamus met it in the Megarid and brought the survivors home. Jason was assassinated in 370 and the ensuing internal strife weakened Thessaly severely.

NOTES

1. The organization of the Boeotian federation is known from *Hell. Oxy.* 16 (11). Among many studies of it attention may be drawn to J. A. O. Larsen, *Representative Government in Greek and Roman History* (Berkeley and Los Angeles 1955) 31–40; idem, *GFS* 26–40. On the Chalcidian League see Larsen, *GFS* 58–78.

2. The narrative depends on Xen. *Hell.* 5.2–3. The date of the Spartan action at Mantinea is known from Diod. 15.5.3. Xenophon says that Mantinea was divided into four villages; Ephorus (*F.Gr.Hist.* IIA 70F79) and Diodorus (15.5.4) say that it was divided into five villages; the divergence may somehow reflect contemporary controversies. The trial of Phoebidas is known from Diod. 15.20.2; Plut. *Pelop.* 6.1; Plut. *Mor.* 575f–576a. For the Athenian alliance with Chios see Tod 2.118. The reorganization of the Peloponnesian League is known from Diod. 15.31; the resolution restricting the right of the allies to make war on one another is mentioned by Xen. *Hell.* 5.4.37.

3. The narrative is based on Xen. *Hell.* 5.4.2–46. Plut. *Pelop.* 8–13 gives a somewhat divergent account of the plot, specifying twelve conspirators instead of seven as taking part in the coup. A good discussion of the divergences was offered by Ernst von Stern, *Geschichte der spartanischen und thebanischen Hegemonie vom Königsfrieden bis zur Schlacht bei Mantinea* (Dorpat 1884) 44–57. A more serious crux concerns the Athenian share in the liberation. Diodorus 15.25–27 says that at dawn after the coup the Thebans sent envoys to Athens for help; the Athenian assembly heard them and in consequence of its resolution Demophon, one of the generals, led a force of 5,000 hoplites and 500 cavalry to Thebes. Deinarchus 1.37–40 seems to support Diodorus, since he mentions a decree of the assembly, proposed by Cephalus, for an expedition to help the exiles who had recovered Thebes. But Xenophon's account is more realistic, since it makes the Athenian generals arrive precisely when needed. The decree of Cephalus and the expedition of Demophon probably belong to a later date in 378 after the raid of Sphodrias. This solution of the crux, suggested long ago by George Grote, has been elaborated by A. P. Burnett, "Thebes and the Expansion of the Second Athenian Confederacy: *I.G.* II² 40 and *I.G.* II² 43," Historia 11 (1962) 1–17, especially 15–17. Chabrias's expedition to Boeotia in 378 is known from Diod. 15.32.2–6.

4. The inscriptions mentioned here are Tod 2.118, 121, 122, 123. Earlier studies of the Second Athenian Sea League were superseded by S. Accame, *La lega ateniese del secolo IV a. C.* (Roma 1941). For recent studies see Burnett, art. cit. (supra note 3); G. L. Cawkwell, "The Foundation of the Second Athenian Confederacy," *CQ* N.S. 23 (1973) 47–60. That the Athenians had no vote in the Synedrion appears from the negotiations leading to the conclusion of peace with Philip II of Macedon in 346; see Aeschin. 2.60–61; 2.85; 2.97; 3.69–70; 3.74; Dem. 19.144. The Theban

embassy sent to Sparta straight after the liberation of the Cadmea is known from Isoc. 14.29. Some light is thrown on procedure of the Sea League by an inscribed decree passed by the Synedrion in 373/2; for the text see Accame, op. cit. 230. In the decree of Aristoteles (Tod 2.123) two lines were later erased and these have sometimes been restored to give a reference to the king's peace; but as Cawkwell (loc. cit.) has pointed out, their content is quite uncertain. The narrative of campaigns depends mainly on Xen. *Hell.* 5.4.47–66. Diodorus adds a few items of value, such as Chabrias's expedition to the Cyclades in 377 (15.30.2–5) and the site of the battle of Naxos (15.34.3–15.35.2). Two inscriptions (*I.G.* VII, 2407 and 2408) provide information about the restored Boeotian confederacy; cf. Larsen, *Representative Government* (supra note 1) 71–72.

5. The texts discussed here are Xen. *Hell.* 6.2; Pseudo-Dem. 49.6, 9–10, 22; Diod. 15.45–47. The dispatch of Spartan help under Cleombrotus to Phocis is problematic. After giving Timotheus's northwestern campaign, Xenophon (*Hell.* 6.1.1) says that the Thebans attacked Phocis and the Spartans sent there Cleombrotus with four of the six *morai* or regiments constituting the Lacedaemonian army and a complement of allies. He mentions the force again (*Hell.* 6.2.1) in introducing the circumstances of the peace of 375/4. The same force was still in Phocis in 371, when it advanced into Boeotia and fought at Leuctra (cf. *Hell.* 6.4.17). Yet it is unlikely that two thirds of the Lacedaemonian army stayed in Phocis for three or four years. K.J. Beloch (*Griechische Geschichte* III², 2 [Berlin and Leipzig 1923] 236–237) drew attention to this difficulty and supposed that Xenophon's notice of the dispatch of Cleombrotus has been displaced from 372/1 to 375/4; but this solution treats the text too drastically. It is perhaps better to suppose that Cleombrotus was sent to Phocis with an army of four *morai* or less in 375 or 374; that some of his troops were recalled when peace was made and he stayed for several years with a skeleton force; and that reinforcements were sent to bring his army up to a strength of four *morai* shortly before the campaign of Leuctra. Chabrias's campaign of 375 is known from Diod. 15.36.4. The date of the destruction of Plataea is known from Paus. 9.1.8. The discussion of the problems of the peace of 375/4 owes much to G.L. Cawkwell, "Notes on the Peace of 375/4," *Historia* 12 (1963) 84–95. A different view on some points is taken by Sealey, "*I.G.* II², 1609 and the Transformation of the Second Athenian Sea League," *Phoenix* 11 (1957) 95–111. On the Spartan navarchy see K.J. Beloch "Die Nauarchie in Sparta," *Rheinisches Museum* 34 (1879) 117–130; U. Kahrstedt, *Die Antrittszeit der spartanischen Nauarchen, Forschungen zur Geschichte des ausgehenden fünften und des vierten Jahrhunderts* (Berlin 1910) 155–204. Concerning the entries on the left face of the stele of Aristoteles it should be added that the entry "The demos of the Corcyreans" has been partly restored and the restoration is not certain.

6. The narrative depends on Xen. *Hell.* 6.3–4. Plutarch (*Ages.* 28) gives the date of the peace of 371 as 14 Scirophorion and the date of the battle of Leuctra as 5 Hecatombaeon. An important study of the statesmanship of Epaminondas, the most effective Theban commander at Leuctra, and of related problems is provided by G.L. Cawkwell, "Epaminondas and Thebes," *CQ* N.S. 22 (1972) 254–278. On Thessalian affairs see H.D. Westlake, *Thessaly in the Fourth Century B.C.* (London 1935), and Larsen, *GFS* 281–294.

17

The Theban Hegemony

The battle of Leuctra left the distribution of power between the leading Greek states unclear. The Athenians tried to take advantage of this situation by calling a new peace conference. Envoys from the Greek states gathered at Athens and swore to abide by the terms of common peace already accepted. The agreement made at Athens had a novel feature concerning the question of upholding the peace against infringements. The peace sworn at Sparta in about the middle of the summer of 371 had contained a clause of "voluntary guarantee," as it may be called; if a power contravened the terms, any city which volunteered could come to the aid of the injured party but no city was obliged to do so. The agreement reached at Athens later in the year had instead a clause of "compulsory guarantee;" if a power contravened the terms, all the cities swearing to the peace were required to come to the aid of the injured party. At the conference in Athens the Eleans alone refused to swear to the proposed terms, since they would not acknowledge the independence of three small towns on their borders. It is likely that Sparta took part in the Athenian conference and swore to the terms.

The agreement reached in Athens achieved little in fact towards preserving peace. Its main effect was to stimulate unrest in Mantinea and Tegea. The people of these two cities considered that the Athenian conference afforded them security against Spartan encroachments on their autonomy. Accordingly, the citizens of Mantinea voted to restore and fortify their unitary city in place of the

five villages into which it had been divided since 385. The Spartans sent Agesilaus
to try to dissuade them, but he could not deter them, and because of the
guarantee of autonomy in the recent peace treaty he dared not take military
action. In Tegea in 370 a group led by Callibius and Proxenus launched a plan for
creating a federation of Arcadia. They were opposed by the group hitherto
ascendant, which was led by Stasippus. In the consequent conflict Proxenus was
killed, but Callibius and his associates gained help from Mantinea and overcame
their opponents. About 800 of the followers of Stasippus escaped and appealed
to Sparta for help.

The Spartans responded by sending a force under Agesilaus into Arcadia.
Meanwhile people from many Arcadian cities gathered at Asea and set up the new
federation. Its army was promptly sent to oppose Agesilaus. The result was a
complex campaign of marches and counter marches, and in the course of it
Agesilaus ravaged a good deal of Arcadian territory. The Arcadians received
military support from Argos and Elis and they appealed to Thebes for help.
The Theban force, led by Epaminondas and Pelopidas, arrived in the winter of
370/69, after Agesilaus had withdrawn his army to Laconia. By this time the
Boeotians had confirmed their ascendancy in central Greece, and the list of allies
accompanying their army to the Peloponnese shows how far their influence
extended. It included the Phocians, Euboeans from all the cities of the island,
the Locrians from East and West Locris, the Acarnanians, the Malians and the
people of Heraclea; there were also some cavalry and peltasts from Thessaly. The
army led by the Boeotians joined forces with the Arcadians, the Argives and
the Eleans, and the whole host invaded Lacedaemon. But the Spartans received
reinforcements from some of their traditional allies, including Corinth, Phlius,
Epidaurus and Pellene, and although the Boeotians and their allies came near to
the city of Sparta, they did not attack it but preferred to devastate other parts of
Laconia.

This was the first Theban expedition to the Peloponnese and it achieved some
changes which had lasting effects. First it freed Messenia from Spartan control.
Messenia was made into an independent and fully organized state, and although
the Spartans continued to claim it until 330, they never in fact recovered it. The
loss of Messenia was the crucial blow to Spartan power. The Spartans could no
longer draw on the rich agricultural produce of the Messenian plain; so there was
a drastic decline in the number of Spartan citizens who, through contributions to
the *phiditia*, could enjoy full civic rights and devote themselves to military
exercises and the Spartan way of life.

The Theban expedition of winter 370/69 accelerated a change in the alignment of the leading powers. While the Thebans were still in Lacedaemon, the
Spartans and their allies appealed to Athens for help. The Athenians resolved to

send a force under Iphicrates. No vote of formal alliance between Athens and Sparta is recorded at this point; possibly the Spartans appealed to the Athenians under the terms of the peace conference held in Athens late in 371. Iphicrates led his force as far as Arcadia and tried to harass the Thebans during their return journey, although he achieved little on this expedition. In 369 the Spartans and their allies sent a further embassy to Athens to discuss detailed provisions for military cooperation; decisions were taken in particular about sharing command of the combined forces.

Thus the Athenians departed from their alliance of 378 with Thebes and made common cause with the Spartans instead. There were good reasons for the change. Since Attica and Boeotia were neighbors, their interests could easily clash. There were longstanding border disputes between them, and these were to come to a head again in 366. Both powers might try to strengthen their influence in central Greece. The alliance of 378 had been precipitated by temporary circumstances, the Spartan concern for the Cadmea and the raid of Sphodrias, but once the battle of Leuctra had put an end to Spartan prospects north of the Isthmus, the interests of Sparta and Athens no longer required enmity between them. Among Athenian statesmen Callistratus was most influential in effecting the change in alignment; he had played a leading role at the peace conference of 371 in Sparta, and several decades later he was remembered as the man who brought about the alliance with Sparta. He and his allies, Chabrias and Iphicrates, were to be prominent for several years. Their enemy, Timotheus, had been acquitted at his trial late in 373, but he withdrew for a time into Persian service.

Fighting continued in the Peloponnese in 369 and 368, and although it was far from decisive, it began to reveal strains in the alliances on both sides. In 369 the Thebans sent a second expedition under Epaminondas to the Peloponnese. Its main achievement was to force its way through the Corinthiad in spite of the troops stationed there by the Athenians, the Spartans and their allies to prevent this. It also plundered the territory of some allies of Sparta. Corinth suffered particularly, and in time such losses might diminish the loyalty of Peloponnesian allies to Sparta. The Arcadians began to resent Theban leadership; led by Lycomedes of Mantinea they set about acting independently. They came to the aid of an Argive force, which had found itself in difficulties when attacking Epidaurus, and they made a successful raid on Asine in Laconia. Tension developed between Elis and Arcadia over some small towns on their common border; the Eleans claimed these, but they had rebelled; they professed to be Arcadian and the Arcadian federation supported them. In 368 the Spartan king Archidamus led an army into Arcadia. As he retired, the Arcadians and Argives followed him into Laconia. He brought them to battle and inflicted a heavy defeat; allegedly 10,000 Arcadians were killed. The Lacedaemonians did not lose any men, and so this victory came to be called "the tearless battle." It brought some revival of Spartan morale. No Theban help came to Arcadia for this campaign; indeed, the Thebans and the Eleans showed themselves almost as pleased at the news of the battle as the Lacedaemonians.

The Thebans meanwhile were expanding their interests northwards. In 369 they sent Pelopidas with a force into Thessaly to operate against Alexander, the new tyrant of Pherae. Pelopidas occupied Larisa and held an inconclusive meeting with Alexander; he proceeded into Macedon and achieved a temporary settlement of its dynastic disputes. In 368 Pelopidas and Ismenias were sent to Thessaly on a diplomatic mission without troops. They went on into Macedon and during their return Alexander of Pherae arrested them. The first Theban force sent to rescue them was unsuccessful, but a second force, sent under Epaminondas probably in 367, made Alexander surrender them and agree to a truce of thirty days.

ATTEMPTS TO MAKE PEACE[2]

Early in 368, before the campaign of the tearless battle, Ariobarzanes, the satrap of Dascylium, sent Philiscus of Abydus on a mission to try to negotiate peace. At his invitation envoys from the Thebans and their allies and from the Lacedaemonians gathered in Delphi, but negotiations broke down over the question of Messenia. The Thebans insisted that Messenia should be a party to any common peace, that is, its independence should be recognized, but the Spartans would not agree to this. Philiscus had to content himself with recruiting a force of mercenaries to help Sparta.

Although nothing came of the mission of Philiscus, the idea of achieving peace through Persian mediation was revived. In 367 the Spartans sent an envoy to Susa. On hearing of this, the Thebans likewise sent Pelopidas, who traveled with envoys from Arcadia, Elis and Argos. The Athenians sent two envoys, Leon and Timagoras. The gathering in Susa was the occasion for a change in Persian policy towards the Greek cities. As the Greeks put it, Pelopidas won the king's favor. Evidently the Persian authorities were sufficiently well informed and discerning to recognize that Sparta was no longer the most advantageous power to support; instead they attached some confidence to Theban influence in Greece. The terms recommended by the king, at the suggestion of Pelopidas, included recognition of the independence of Messenia and a requirement that the Athenians should recall their warships from the seas; furthermore, the parties to the peace were to take joint action against any power refusing to accept it. The Athenian envoy Leon protested against the terms; in response the king said that he would be willing to receive and hear any further Athenian embassy proposing amendments to the terms. When the envoys returned to their homes, the Athenians tried and executed Timagoras on a charge of bribery made by Leon. They sent a further embassy to Persia and in consequence the king recognized their claim to Amphipolis.

A peace conference was called in Thebes, where a Persian ambassador was present to read out the royal rescript. The Thebans told the assembled envoys to swear to the terms, but they replied that they had come merely to hear the proposal and they would have to refer back to their cities for authority to swear. The Arcadians were especially displeased because the detailed provisions gave the advantage to the Eleans on the points in dispute between them. Lycomedes went so far as to say that the conference ought not to be held in Thebes but in the theater of hostilities; when the Thebans upbraided him, he and the other Arcadians left the meeting. Since the deputies were not willing to take the oath, the conference dispersed. Thereupon the Thebans set about sending embassies to the different cities and urging them to swear to the peace as proposed in the Persian rescript. But Corinth, which was the first city they reached, declared that it had no need of an agreement with the king and so the Thebans desisted from their efforts.

These negotiations may have lasted into the fall of 367 or the ensuing winter. About a year later some of the belligerents achieved separate treaties of peace, but before that two military developments clarified the situation. One of these began with a third Theban expedition to the Peloponnese. It was led by Epaminondas, probably in 366, and he hoped thereby to recover the obedience of the Arcadians and the other Peloponnesian allies of Thebes. He marched with the Boeotian and allied forces into Achaea, secured a close alliance with the Achaeans and refrained from altering the constitutions of the cities there. When he had retreated, the Arcadians complained to Thebes; they said that since the constitutions had not been altered, the Achaean cities would seize the first opportunity of joining the Spartans. The Thebans were persuaded by this argument and sent harmosts, who altered the constitutions of the Achaean cities and expelled many citizens. Soon afterwards the exiles returned, recovered control of their cities and joined the Spartan cause against the Arcadians.

The other military development took place on the border between Attica and Boeotia. Here the village of Oropus had long been in dispute. It was captured by the Thebans in 411 but recovered by the Athenians between 378 and 373. During the Attic year 367/6 and probably in the second half of the year Themison, the tyrant of Eretria, seized Oropus. The Athenians marched against him with all their available forces, but they were disappointed because none of their allies came to their aid. Even so Themison was outnumbered and, when a Theban force arrived, he and the Athenians agreed to entrust Oropus to the Thebans pending arbitration. Once in possession of Oropus, the Thebans kept it. The incident had the effect of making the Athenians displeased with their Peloponnesian allies and intensely bitter towards the Thebans.

Lycomedes of Mantinea was the first to take advantage of the coolness now developing between Athens and the Peloponnesian League. At his suggestion the Arcadian federation offered to ally with Athens. The Athenians accepted the alliance and thus reached the anomalous position of being allied both to Sparta and to Arcadia, although those two powers were at war. The first decisive steps towards peace were taken by the Corinthians. Athenian troops had been stationed in the Corinthiad to help in resistance to the Thebans. The Corinthians learned of Athenian plans to use these troops to secure control of Corinth, so they made the Athenian garrisons leave. Seeking to pursue an independent foreign policy, the Corinthians raised a force of mercenaries for defense, but they recognized the limitations of their resources and accordingly they opened negotiations with Thebes with a view to peace. With Theban consent they sent envoys to Sparta to ask permission to conclude peace. The Spartans replied that the Corinthians and any other of their allies who wished could make a separate peace, though the Spartans themselves would continue fighting until they recovered Messenia. Thereupon the Corinthians concluded a separate peace with Thebes, but they refused the Theban demand for an alliance, since that would have brought them into hostilities again, though on the opposite side than before. Phlius and Epidaurus made treaties of peace with Thebes at the same time.

These treaties marked the dissolution of the Peloponnesian League. Corinth had traditionally been the second strongest power in that alliance. Phlius had · shown singular loyalty to Sparta during the Theban invasions of the Peloponnese. Epidaurus, being repeatedly threatened by Argos, had looked constantly to Sparta for support. But the loss of Messenia had weakened Spartan resources drastically. Sparta could no longer play a leading role; she could not even overcome the Messenians, and it soon became clear that her conflict with them had only local significance. By the end of 365 she had very few Peloponnesian allies left.

The negotiations leading to the treaties of Corinth and Phlius with Thebes are reported by Xenophon. Diodorus says that in 366/5 the Persian king sent envoys to Greece and persuaded the Greeks to make a common peace; this, he adds, brought to an end after more than five years the war which had begun with the battle of Leuctra. There are several objections to accepting Diodorus's statement. The Athenians were not likely to agree to peace with the Thebans promptly after the loss of Oropus. The Arcadians were not likely to accept a common peace in 366/5, since they had voiced the most vigorous opposition at the peace conference held in Thebes a year before. The Spartans were sure to refuse any agreement recognizing the independence of Messenia. Diodorus's statement of a common peace should not be regarded as an additional item overlooked by Xenophon, since the latter gives a detailed narrative of Peloponnesian events of the years 371–364. More probably Diodorus's statement rests on a misunderstanding of the separate treaties made with Thebes; this misunderstanding could easily come about if the detailed provisions of those treaties were based on those proposed at the preceding conferences in Susa and Thebes. Some historians, however, have accepted Diodorus's statement; their main argument rests on the steps taken to recognize the Athenian claim to the Chersonese, and that will require attention in the next section.

THE CHANGE IN ATHENIAN FOREIGN POLICY[3]

The Second Athenian Sea League had been founded with a view to resisting Sparta. By 369 Athens had become an ally of Sparta, but she kept the League in existence and expanded her maritime aims. She revived her claims to Amphipolis, which she had not in fact held since 424/3, and to the Chersonese, which she had lost in the peace settlement of 404. The occasion when these claims were put forward afresh is problematic. The evidence is some statements made by Demosthenes, Aeschines and Hegesippus in speeches of the 340s. These provide the information that the Athenian claims to the Chersonese and to Amphipolis were each recognized by the Persian king and by all the Greeks; Hegesippus speaks of a vote of the Greeks recognizing that Amphipolis belonged by right to the Athenians. Demosthenes says that the Persian king bribed Timagoras successfully on the embassy of 367, but when he learned that the Athenians had executed the envoy, he recognized Amphipolis as belonging to them; previously he had declared Amphipolis his friend and ally. The statement of Aeschines is especially important. He speaks of a gathering of the Lacedaemonians and other Greeks and calls it an alliance (*symmachia*); he says that king Amyntas of Macedon participated by sending a deputy; and he says that this deputy voted to join the other Greeks in subduing Amphipolis for the Athenians.

The problem is to identify the meeting of the Greeks which recognized the Athenian claims to Amphipolis and the Chersonese. Amyntas of Macedon died in 370/69, and so a date not later than 369 is indicated. An old conjecture was that the recognition was given at the peace conference held in Sparta in 371 before the battle of Leuctra, but since the agreement reached there provided only a voluntary, not a compulsory, guarantee of the peace (see p. 420), the meeting could scarcely be called an alliance. An alternative suggestion was that the recognition was given at the peace conference of 375/4, but a similar objection holds against that; the agreement reached at that meeting was not an alliance but merely a common peace. A better suggestion (that of S. Accame) is that recognition was given early in 369 at the meeting in Athens which drew up detailed provisions for cooperation between Athens and Sparta. This meeting was an alliance and, since it bound the members of the Peloponnesian League and of the Second Athenian Sea League, it could be called a gathering of all the Greeks. Persian recognition of the Athenian claim to Amphipolis need not have been given on the same occasion and was not in fact given until after Timagoras's embassy of 367. In support of this suggestion it should be noted that the Athenians sent squadrons to operate in the northern Aegean from 368 onwards. The command was at first held by Iphicrates, who is recorded to have operated against Amphipolis from 368 to 366 inclusively. Timotheus held the command from 365 to 362 and conducted operations against Amphipolis and the Chersonese.

An alternative suggestion (made by G. L. Cawkwell) admits that the occasion for Greek recognition of the claim to Amphipolis was the alliance of Sparta and Athens in 369, but it notes that Iphicrates is described by Aeschines as "general against Amphipolis," whereas Timotheus is described by Demosthenes as "general against Amphipolis and the Chersonese." It proposes that there was a difference in the commissions of the two generals and that Greek recognition of the Athenian claim to the Chersonese was not given until the supposed common peace of 366/5; indeed, this reasoning has been used as an argument for accepting Diodorus's statement of a common peace in that year. But this argument is not conclusive. Aeschines calls Iphicrates "general against Amphipolis" in a passage where the orator expounds the Athenian concern with Amphipolis; it may well be that Iphicrates, like Timotheus later, was instructed to act "against Amphipolis and the Chersonese" but Aeschines had occasion to mention only part of his task. It is likely that the Athenians sought recognition of their claims to Amphipolis and to the Chersonese at the same time; both claims appear to spring from a revival of Athenian concern for the northern Aegean. The simplest hypothesis is that the claims were recognized at the meeting held in Athens in 369.

It appears that a profound and twofold change in Athenian policy came to fruition in 369. On the one hand, the Athenians changed their alignment among the powers of the Greek mainland; they ceased supporting Thebes against Sparta and began supporting Sparta against Thebes. Steps leading towards this change can be traced back as far as the peace of 375/4. On the other hand, the Athenians put forward afresh their claims to Amphipolis and the Chersonese. Nothing is known about the antecedents of this policy, but something can be said about the steps taken to implement it. The question must be asked, whether it marked a change in Athenian dealings with their allies in the Sea League: did the Athenians abandon the liberal principles of 378 and resume the imperial ambitions of the fifth century? It will be appropriate first to trace the operations in the northern Aegean and then to consider possible new features in Athenian treatment of the allies.

Iphicrates took up the command in the northern Aegean in 368. He operated fruitlessly against Amphipolis and intervened in dynastic disputes in Macedon with some success. While he was still in the north, Timotheus was sent to Samos in 366 with complex instructions. He was to help the satrap Ariobarzanes, whose relations with the Persian king had become strained, but he was not to break the state of peace obtaining between Athens and the king. These instructions appear to reflect the tension lasting between Athens and the king from the embassy of Timagoras until Persia recognized the Athenian claim to Amphipolis. On reaching the eastern Aegean Timotheus found that Ariobarzanes was now in open revolt and that a royal garrison was in Samos. He besieged Samos for ten months until it yielded in 365; the Persian garrison was expelled and Athens sent a cleruchy to Samos.

From Samos Timotheus proceeded to the northern Aegean and took over the command against Amphipolis and the Chersonese in 365. The supersession of Iphicrates reflects known revalries within Athens. Iphicrates, Chabrias and Callistratus had been allied against Timotheus since 373, but for reasons which are obscure the loss of Oropus in 366 harmed the standing of Chabrias and Callistratus; indeed they were prosecuted, although the trials ended in acquittal. There was a corresponding rise in the fortunes of Timotheus. On reaching the northern Aegean Timotheus at first advanced against Amphipolis but, finding that he could achieve little, he entrusted operations there to a fellow general and proceeded to the Chersonese. Here he secured Sestus and Crithote. Meanwhile the Chalcidian League came to the aid of Amphipolis, so Timotheus attacked it. He captured Torone and other cities in Chalcidice, also Pydna and Methone on the coast of Macedon. His final gain was Poteidaea. He returned to Athens in 362 and in the next spring the Athenians sent a cleruchy to Poteidaea at the request of the Poteidaeans.

The gains made by Timotheus were extensive; his admirer, Isocrates, said later that he won no less than twenty-four cities. His influence was correspondingly great on his return. In 362 he threatened in public to prosecute Iphicrates. The latter responded by deserting his former friends and making a marriage alliance with Timotheus; the son of Iphicrates married the daughter of Timotheus. In 362 or more probably 361 Callistratus was driven into exile and condemned in absence to death. The circumstances are obscure and it would be rash to suppose that the eclipse of Callistratus was solely due to the rise in the fortunes of

Timotheus; there were many political groups active in Athens. But for several years after 362 Timotheus may well have outdistanced his rivals in political competition.

So far consideration has been given to the resumption of Athenian claims in the northern Aegean, to the steps taken to implement those claims and to the effects of these actions on Athenian internal politics. The further question must be asked whether this change in policy was accompanied by a change in Athenian methods of dealing with their allies in the Sea League. Traditionally historians have painted a somewhat moralistic picture of the development of that League. When the Athenians founded it in 378, they were guided by the generous principles stated in the decree of Aristoteles; they undertook to abstain from the authoritarian practices which had made them so unpopular in the Delian League of the fifth century. But, it is supposed, as time passed the Athenians forgot their promises of 378/7 and resumed their obnoxious practices of the fifth century. For this reason, it is concluded, some major allies of Athens rebelled in the Social War of 357–355/4, and after that struggle the surviving League was much smaller.

Such an account is suspiciously simple. The Social War will come under consideration in the next chapter. Here attention will be given briefly to authoritarian practices supposedly adopted by the Athenians. Two practices call for note, the foundation of cleruchies and the exaction of financial contributions from the allies. The decree of Aristoteles had forbidden Athenians to acquire land publicly or privately in allied territory. But as noted before, the Athenians sent a cleruchy to Samos in 365 and one to Poteidaea in 361. Yet these expeditions do not necessarily mark a breach of the rules adopted when the Second Sea League was founded. None of the cleruchies known to have been founded in the period of that League was sent to territory inscribed on the stele bearing the decree of Aristoteles; possible the provisions of that decree applied only to states whose names were so inscribed. The dispatch of the cleruchy to Poteidaea was undertaken at the request of the inhabitants of that city; possibly the cleruchs sent to the Chersonese were likewise welcomed by the inhabitants as additional protection against Macedonian encroachments.

The matter of financial contributions is obscure. In the decree of Aristoteles the Athenians undertook not to exact tribute (*phoros*) from the allies. But in fact they exacted payments under the name of "contributions" (*syntaxeis*) from members of the Sea League, and the contemporary historian Theopompus said that the word was merely a euphemism for tribute. The practice of levying contributions was begun by 373, but the common assumption, that contributions were exacted from the very foundation of the League, cannot be proved. It is possible that contributions were first introduced in 373, and that the expedition which Timotheus led in the Aegean in that year had to do with their introduction.

Very little evidence has survived about the "contributions," but this dearth of information may itself be a clue to their nature. In this respect there is a sharp contrast with the tribute exacted in the Delian League in the fifth century. The latter is well attested both by fragments of extensive epigraphic records and by literary references. Inscriptions preserve only a very few allusions to the "contributions" of the Second Sea League and there are no extensive lists of payments. Admittedly, the relative lack of epigraphic records may be due to the accidents of archaeological survival. The paucity of literary references to the "contributions" is more telling. Literary evidence shows that the tribute levied in the Delian League was considered burdensome; literary references do not suffice to show whether the allies found the "contributions" required of them in the Second Sea League a severe burden or not. From this contrast it may properly be inferred that the "contributions" were not a regular annual levy, like the fifth-century tribute, but something much less systematic.

A remark made by Demothenes is accordingly suggestive. Speaking in 342/1, he said that every Athenian commander of a naval expedition exacted payments from the cities where he operated; he made the exaction by bargaining and threat of force; the commander of a large fleet exacted more, the commander of a small fleet exacted less, and the payments were called "good-will offerings" (*eunoiai*). Possibly these offerings were a late and somewhat degenerate form of the "contributions." If so, the "contributions" in their original form may have been, not an annual payment based on a regular assessment, but a matter of *ad hoc* bargaining between the ally who paid them and the Athenian state or its generals. The principle may have been that allied states should supply money as well as ships or troops to campaigns from which they benefited.

The Athenian naval ascendancy in the Aegean suffered some threat in 364. Diodorus reports that Epaminondas addressed an assembly of the Boeotians and urged them to try to gain supremacy at sea. The assembly, Diodorus continues, was persuaded and voted to build a fleet of a hundred triremes; Epaminondas set sail and made for Rhodes, Chios and Byzantium, hoping to detach them from their connection with Athens. An Athenian commander, Laches, retired with his squadron in fear when Epaminondas approached, and the latter reached the cities he desired and won them over. This report of Diodorus is puzzling. Nothing more is heard of naval operations by the Thebans in the 360s or the 350s, and Rhodes and Chios did not rebel against Athens until 357. But the report is too substantial to be rejected entirely. It has been observed that although the Boeotians voted to build a hundred warships, Diodorus does not say that they built a hundred or that Epaminondas's squadron numbered so many. That some tension developed between Athens and Byzantium appears from events of 362; in the fall of that year the Byzantines with help from Calchedon and Cyzicus held up the grain ships destined for the Peiraeus. It is a reasonable conjecture that tension first appeared openly at the opportunity provided by Epaminondas's voyage. Whether the tension amounted to secession of Byzantium from the Sea League has been argued but is perhaps largely a question of definition.

It is difficult to estimate the scale and significance of the Boeotian naval venture of 364, but clearly this challenge to Athenian naval preponderance in the Aegean was not to be dismissed lightly. The Athenians made an adequate response; in each of the years 364–360 they had squadrons under a series of commanders operating in the Hellespont in the fall. Apparently the main task of these commanders was to safeguard the grain fleet at its regular time of sailing each year. By 359 a new understanding may well have been reached with Byzantium, for it is unlikely that any squadron was sent to the Hellespont in that year. Meanwhile, the Athenians continued to assert their claims to Amphipolis and the Chersonese and Athenian commanders operated intermittently against these positions until the outbreak of the Social War, but they achieved little after the return of Timotheus to Athens in 362. Lack of success in those theaters did not mean harm to the Athenians; Amphipolis and the Chersonese were matters of prestige, whereas the grain route from the Black Sea was a vital interest.

THE BATTLE OF MANTINEA[4]

By 365 the Arcadian federation had become one of the strongest powers in the Peloponnese. It had succeeded in preserving its alliances with Boeotia and Elis in spite of tension. The Boeotians had been offended when the Arcadians insisted on pursuing an independent policy. Tension with Elis proved to be more serious; it arose over some townships on the borders. These townships had aspired to independence of Elis and earlier in the fourth century Sparta had supported them. With the decline of Spartan power the Eleans hoped to recover them, but the townships preferred to join the Arcadian federation. In 365 the Eleans seized Lasium, one of the places in dispute, and this action brought about war between Elis and Arcadia. In this and the next year the fighting, though not fully decisive, went on the whole in favor of the Arcadians. They invaded the enemy's territory and they brought about civil war within Elis by supporting a large group who wished to alter the constitution. They occupied Olympia and at the Olympic festival of 364 they entrusted management of the competitions to the Pisatans, the underprivileged part of the population (see chapter 2, p. 41); an armed force of Eleans tried to interrupt the festival but was driven off by the Arcadians.

In 363 and 362 an unexpected development weakened the Arcadians. After occupying Olympia they had drawn on the sacred treasures there in order to pay the federal force. Such use of sacred funds could be considered sacrilege, and now the Mantineans voted to cease drawing on the sacred treasures. The officers of the federation feared to be called to account for the use they had made of the money, and so they called a meeting of the federal assembly in the hope of getting a clear declaration against the new Mantinean policy. But after complex developments the assembly voted to make no further use of the sacred moneys. The immediate result was a change in the composition of the federal force; those who could only serve if they received public pay left the force, and their places were taken by men who could meet the expenses of service out of their own resources. This brought about a change in the balance of power within the federation. The issue seems to have been largely one between Mantinea and Tegea. The changes of 371–370, which had culminated in the founding of the federation, had been carried out without violence at Mantinea but there had been armed clashes in Tegea. It is accordingly likely that opposition had been destroyed in Tegea and so in 363 the Tegeans wished to continue the dynamic policy of the preceding years. But in Mantinea critics had not been eliminated in 370 and by 363 the Mantineans favored more moderate measures.

After the question of the sacred treasures had been raised, those now prevailing in Arcadia opened negotiations with Elis. The two sides agreed to make a treaty of peace. But meanwhile the federal officers who feared to be called to account appealed to the Boeotians for support. Consequently a Theban officer with 300 hoplites was present in Tegea when numerous deputies from the towns of Arcadia gathered there to swear to the peace with Elis. The federal officers and the Theban commander proceeded to arrest many of the deputies. But the next day the city of Mantinea demanded their release and threatened to call out troops from other Arcadian towns. So the Theban commander released the men he had arrested.

The split in the Arcadian League was now complete. The towns adhering to the Theban alliance included Tegea and Megalopolis, which had been founded probably in 368 to secure the southwestern part of Arcadia. The towns on the other side were led by Mantinea. They feared that the Thebans would lead a further expedition into the Peloponnese against them. They believed a report which said, credibly enough, that Epaminondas was arguing that the Arcadians had broken the terms of their treaty with Boeotia by making a separate peace with Elis. So the Mantineans and their sympathizers appealed to Athens and Sparta for help.

The expected Boeotian expedition was led to the Peloponnese by Epaminondas in 362. He brought with him the whole force of the Boeotian League and some troops from Euboea and Thessaly. He was joined in the Peloponnese by forces from Argos, Messenia, Tegea, Megalopolis and some other Arcadian towns. The forces opposing him were drawn from Mantinea and some other parts of Arcadia, also from Elis, Achaea, Sparta and Athens. On reaching the Peloponnese, Epaminondas took up a position at Nemea in the hope of intercepting there any Athenian troops who came to the aid of their allies. But after a time he learned that the Athenians had gone by sea to Lacedaemon. So he advanced to Tegea and made it his base. Meanwhile the forces on the other side gathered in Mantinea. From Tegea Epaminondas made a raid southwards as far as the town of Sparta, but he was driven out by the king Agesilaus. So Epaminondas proceeded northwards from Tegea and drew the enemy into battle at Mantinea. The outcome was indecisive; indeed both sides claimed victory. Epaminondas was killed in the fighting, and the troops of the two coalitions dispersed to their homes.

Although the battle of Mantinea was inconclusive, the campaign had lasting effects. After the battle the Greek cities concluded a treaty of common peace. Messenia was a participant in the treaty and thus its independence was recognized. For this reason Sparta refused to join the peace, but its abstention made virtually no difference. Thus the peace advertised the fact that Spartan power had declined to merely local significance. A change in Boeotian policy was even more significant; henceforth the Boeotians conducted no further expeditions to the Peloponnese. They continued, however, to be effective in the affairs of central Greece and to intervene in Thessaly.

NOTES

1. The narrative depends mainly on Xen. *Hell.* 6.5.1–7.1.32. The question whether Sparta took part in the Athenian peace conference of 371 has been disputed; the case for Spartan participation is presented by Ryder, *Koine Eirene* 131–133; the argument rests mainly on Xenophon's later references (*Hell.* 6.5.10; 6.5.36–37) to oaths binding the Spartans or binding the Athenians to the Spartans. Diodorus (15.66.1; 15.72.3) gives the liberation of Messenia and the name of the tearless battle. That Callistratus was remembered as the man who advised the alliance with Sparta appears from Pseudo-Dem. 59.27. The departure of Timotheus into Persian service is given by Pseudo-Dem. 49.25. A useful study of much of the Peloponnesian material of this chapter is provided by J. Roy, "Arcadia and Boeotia in Peloponnesian Affairs, 370–362 B.C.," *Historia* 20 (1971) 569–599. For the Theban intervention in Thessaly see Diod. 15.67.3–4; 15.71–72; 15.75.2; Plut. *Pelop.* 26–29.

2. The narrative depends mainly on Xen. *Hell.* 7.1.27; 7.1.33–43; 7.4.1–11. For the previous history of Oropus see Thuc. 8.60.1; Isoc. 14.20 and 37. The separate treaty of Epidaurus with Thebes is inferred from Isoc. 6.91. Diodorus gives his statement of a common peace at 15.76.3. Arguments against the hypothesis of a common peace in 366/5 are presented by T.T.B. Ryder, "The Supposed Common Peace of 366/5 B.C.," *CQ* N.S. 7 (1957) 199–205; idem, *Koine*

Eirene 137–139. Arguments for the hypothesis are presented by G.L. Cawkwell, "The Common Peace of 366/5 B.C.," *CQ* N.S. 11 (1961) 80–86. The date of the loss of Oropus is given by schol. Aeschin. 3.85; the circumstances of its loss are given in several passages, most clearly in Xen. *Hell.* 7.4.1 and Diod. 15.76.1.

3. The statements of the orators about recognition of Athenian claims to Amphipolis and the Chersonese are Dem. 9.16; 19.137; 19.253; Pseudo-Dem. 7.29; Aeschin. 2.32. The date of Amyntas's death is known from Diod. 15.59.3. For discussion of the occasion when Athenian claims in the northern Aegean received recognition see S. Accame, *La lega ateniese del secolo IV. a. C.* (Roma 1941) 155–157 and 165–167; G.L. Cawkwell, "The Common Peace of 366/5 B.C.," *CQ* N.S. 11 (1961) 80–86; Ryder, *Koine Eirene* 128–130. The commission of Iphicrates is mentioned by Aeschin. 2.27, that of Timotheus by Dem. 23.149. For the operations of Iphicrates in the northern Aegean see Dem. 23.149; Aeschin. 2.26–29. For the siege of Samos see Isoc. 15.111; Dem. 15.9; Diod. 18.18.9; Nepos, *Tim.* 1; cf. I.G. II², 108. For the operations of Timotheus in the northern Aegean see Isoc. 15.108–113; Dem. 23.150; Dein. 1.14; Diod. 15.81.6; Nepos, *Tim.*1; schol. Aeschin. 2.31; cf. Tod 2.143 and 146. For the marriage alliance of Iphicrates with Timotheus see Pseudo-Dem. 49.66. The trials of Chabrias and Callistratus for the loss of Oropus are mentioned by Dem. 21.64; Ar. *Rhet.* 1.1364a19; 3.1411b6; Aul. Gell. 3.13; Plut. *Dem.* 5.1–3. The exile and final trial of Callistratus are mentioned by Pseudo-Dem. 50.48; Hyp. *Eux.* 1–2; Lyc. *Leocr.* 93. For discussion of Athenian politics in the 360s see Sealey, *Essays* 146–155 = Historia 5 (1956) 192–202. The cleruchs sent to the Chersonese in 353/2 are known from Diod. 16.34.3. The cleruchy sent to Samos in 365 is the earliest known to have been founded in the period of the Second Sea League. Attempts have sometimes been made to infer an earlier cleruchy from *I.G.* II², 1609, but both the date of the document and its reference to a cleruchy are uncertain; see the illuminating discussion by J.K. Davies, "The Date of *I.G.* II², 1609," *Historia* 18 (1969) 309–333; see also G.L. Cawkwell, "The Date of *I.G.* II², 1609 again," *Historia* 22 (1973) 759–761. Theopompus's remark about "contributions" is to be found in *F.Gr.Hist.* IIB115F98. G.L. Cawkwell, *Historia* 12 (1963) 91–93, argues that "contributions" were first introduced in 373. Demosthenes speaks of "good-will offerings" to Athenian naval squadrons at 8.24–25. Epaminondas's naval campaign of 364 is known from Diod. 15.78.4–15.79.1; for discussion are G.L. Cawkwell, "Epaminondas and Thebes," *CQ* N.S. 22 (1972) 254–278, especially 270–273. Pseudo-Dem. 50.4–6 reports how the grain fleet was held up by Byzantium in 362. Athenian commanders in the Hellespont are known from Isoc. 15.108 and 112; Dem. 23.104; 23.153–167; Pseudo-Dem. 50.4–12; 50.14.

4. The narrative depends mainly on Xen. *Hell.* 7.4.12–7.5.27. For discussion see the article by Roy (supra note 1). The common peace concluded after the battle of Mantinea is known from Diod. 15.89.1; cf. Tod 2.145; for discussion see Ryder, *Koine Eirene* 140–144.

18

The Rise of Macedon

Xenophon brought his *Hellenica* to an end with the battle of Mantinea. He did not record the conclusion of the treaty of common peace afterwards; instead he made the comment: "Even greater confusion and disturbance came about in Greece after the battle than before." This remark reflects more the state of mind of its author than the condition of Greece. A relatively stable system of states emerged from the common peace of 362/1 and endured for just over fifteen years. The Peloponnese, now that Boeotian forces were withdrawn, was divided between a number of states varying very much in power; none of them dominated anything beyond its immediate area. Boeotian influence was strong but not unchallenged in central Greece and Thessaly. At sea Athens was clearly the strongest power. The next fifteen years saw three developments: (1) the Athenian Sea League lost many of its members in the Social War; (2) the Thebans became involved in a long and debilitating struggle with Phocis; (3) Macedon under Philip II began to win cities on the northern shore of the Aegean and to encroach on Thessaly. Finally the general balance of power was altered in 346, when unforeseen developments allowed Philip II to secure the route into central Greece.

The extent and effectiveness of the Second Athenian Sea League are difficult to estimate. Diodorus, narrating its foundation, says that seventy cities joined Athens in the League. Aeschines says that in consequence of the Social War the

438

League lost seventy-five members. The names of members were appended to the decree of Aristoteles (see chapter 16, pp. 412 and 418); many, though not all, of the names are legibly preserved, and the space on the stele could accommodate the names of ca. fifty-eight states. New entries were made on the stele during the 370s, but as Athens won new allies in the 360s, they were not added to the inscribed list. Possibly these new allies, though bound to Athens, did not become members of the Sea League or send deputies to the Synedrion. Alternatively, perhaps they should be included in the total of seventy to seventy-five indicated by Diodorus and Aeschines. In that case, the League reached its widest extent ca. 362; it had gained large new accessions through the campaigns of Timotheus.

In the summer of 357 the Athenians had an opportunity to strengthen their position near their own land. Internal strife arose in the cities of Euboea; the contending parties appealed to Thebes and to Athens. The Athenians responded promptly; they were urged to do so by Timotheus, who was now the most influential man in Athens. Within a few days of receiving the appeal they sent a force to Euboea, and within thirty days of its arrival it compelled the Thebans to make a truce and to withdraw their forces. Thus Athens won the upper hand in Euboea and her influence remained paramount there for the next eight years.

Somewhat later in 357 some major allies of Athens, Chios, Rhodes and Cos, seceded from the Sea League. They were joined by Byzantium, which may have been in revolt ever since 364 (see chapter 17, p. 434). The Athenians set about overcoming the rebels and the consequent struggle is called the Social War. A fleet of sixty ships set sail from Athens and, probably in the spring of 356, it brought the enemy to battle at Chios. But there the Athenians were defeated and so the rebels were able to win more allies. Some measure of the rise in the prospects of the rebels is indicated by the special measures which the Athenians took to secure some islands of the Aegean; inscriptions show that they stationed a garrison in Andros and a governor in one of the cities of Amorgos, and doubtless they took similar steps elsewhere. During 356 reinforcements numbering sixty more ships were sent under Timotheus, Iphicrates and his son Menestheus to join Chares, the commander who had survived the battle of Chios, with his remaining ships. The enemy, after raiding several islands, began besieging Samos. The Athenians responded by sailing to the Hellespont in the hope of laying siege to Byzantium. Thereupon the rebels raised the siege of Samos and sailed likewise towards the Hellespont. The two fleets confronted one another near Embata and in spite of a storm Chares against the advice of his fellow generals insisted on giving battle. The Athenian fleet was defeated.

Chares sent complaints against the other generals and they were recalled. He remained in sole command but the defeats at Chios and Embata left him no prospect of making headway against the enemy. Instead, probably in 355, he entered the service of the satrap Artabazus, who was in revolt against the king, and together they defeated the royal army sent against them. Correspondingly Artabazus supplied money with which Chares paid his men. But the Persian king sent an embassy to Athens and demanded the recall of Chares. He threatened to join the enemies of Athens in the Social War and rumor said that he would send a fleet of 300 ships. So the Athenians recalled Chares and made peace with the rebels.

By the terms of peace the Athenians recognized the independence of those allies who had seceded. It is not clear how numerous these were or which states continued to be members of the Sea League after the war. Some major cities, such as Mytilene, remained within the League. The Synedrion of the allies continued to sit in Athens; its activities are attested in the negotiations leading to the peace of Philocrates in 346 (below, p. 455). But in those negotiations it played a merely subordinate part, following the lead of Athens. Athens continued to be the strongest naval power among the Greeks, but henceforth her naval ascendancy rested on her own resources and the support rendered by her allies counted for little.

The question of the causes of the Social War is obscure. Doubtless there was some resentment against Athenian leadership, but that does not explain what precipitated the secession of Rhodes, Cos and Chios. Yet there are some clues and they point to Mausolus, who ruled Caria from 377/6 until 353/2. Though technically Persian satrap, he extended his power and behaved very much as a dynast in his own right. Speaking in 351/0, Demosthenes alleged that Mausolus had contrived the Social War. Demosthenes was not disinterested and he gave no details. But it is attested independently that Mausolus supplied forces to the rebels in time for the battle of Chios. Moreover, within a few years after the end of the war Mausolus and Artemisia, his wife and successor, encroached on the islands of Rhodes and Cos; they installed garrisons in the cities of Rhodes and their opponents there were exiled. Perhaps the immediate causes of the Social War should be sought in the ambitions and intrigues of Mausolus.

The war brought about changes in the internal situation within Athens. Since his successes of 366–362 Timotheus was the most respected man in the city. On his return in 362 his former enemy, Iphicrates, had entered into an alliance with him (see chapter 17, p. 431). But after the battle of Embata Chares sent complaints to Athens against Timotheus, Iphicrates and Menestheus. These three generals were put on trial; Iphicrates and Menestheus were acquitted but retired from public life; Timotheus was condemned to pay a fine but withdrew into exile. Among other statesmen of the older generation Chabrias had been killed fighting as a private soldier at the battle of Chios.

The field was now open for the rise to influence of Eubulus. The beginnings of his career are obscure. He was *thesmothetes* in 370/69, and his nephew Hegesileus commanded the Athenian force at Mantinea in 362, but his major opportunity came after the Social War. He was the first of a series of statesmen who achieved influence by skillful handling of public finance. Little is known about the details of his work. He held office for at least one year as a member of the board of ten in charge of the theoric fund. This fund originally served to provide a dole enabling poor citizens to attend public festivals. The board in charge of it may have been created by legislation which Eubulus proposed. Certainly through his ascendancy the board came to handle large sums; it took charge, for example, of the dockyards and built a new naval arsenal. Moreover, legislation promoted by Eubulus provided that in normal circumstances each year's surplus of revenue over expenditure should be assigned to the theoric fund. There was probably some restriction, perhaps to the effect that in a major emergency the surplus should be used for purposes of defense. In effect this legislation to some degree deterred the Athenians from engaging in armed enterprises. But the pacific tendency of Eubulus's policy should not be exaggerated. As will be seen, his associates resorted to armed action at places, such as Thermopylae and Euboea, where vital Athenian interests were at stake. Nonetheless, after the Social War Athens made less effort in the northern Aegean than in the 360s.

The ascendancy of Eubulus was never fully secure. He had a long feud with another statesman, Aristophon. The latter is credited with political activity as early as 403/2, and his son Demostratus served on the embassy to Sparta which negotiated peace in 371. Thus he was senior to Eubulus in politics, but like Eubulus he first achieved a leading position after the Social War. It was Aristophon who prosecuted Iphicrates after the battle of Embata. He was a close associate of Chares. Evidence on his activities is scanty; it does not suffice to show whether he offered a policy alternative to that of Eubulus. It is not, for example, clear whether he advocated more vigorous measures in the northern Aegean. His rivalry with Eubulus may have been strictly personal.

THE EARLY ACTIVITIES OF PHILIP II[2]

Two regions should be distinguished in the kingdom of Macedon. One, called lower Macedon, consisted of the land watered by the lower reaches of the Axius and Haliacmon rivers. This was the heart of the kingdom. It was ruled by a single dynasty, the Argeadae, since perhaps the seventh century, but in the fourth century until the time of Philip II disputes within the dynasty were frequent and they provided opportunities for intervention and encroachment by Athens and Thebes. The other part of the kingdom was upper Macedon. It consisted of several mountainous cantons in the interior, chiefly Lyncestis, Elimiotis and

Orestis. Each of these had its own dynasty, and the kings of lower Macedon tried with varying degrees of success to assert themselves over the local rulers.

In 360/59 Perdiccas III was killed in a disastrous battle against the Illyrians after a reign of five years. His brother, Philip II, took control and ruled at first as regent for Perdiccas's son; after a few years he killed his nephew and ruled as king. Tradition painted a romantic picture of the first two or three years of his reign; allegedly Macedon was beset by enormous dangers but the heroic ruler overcame them by diplomatic skill and martial force. More precisely, the tradition said that the Illyrians prepared to follow up their victory by invading Macedon; that the Paeonians from the upper valley of the Axius raided the kingdom; that a pretender, Pausanias, had the support of a Thracian king, and another pretender, Argaeus, had the support of Athens, which sent a fleet and 3,000 hoplites to help him. The tradition continued by telling how Philip overcame these dangers by the early part of 357. He withdrew the Macedonian garrison from Amphipolis, which Athens still claimed, and so the Athenian force accompanied Argaeus only as far as Methone; when Argaeus proceeded further, Philip overcame him. A little later Philip sent envoys to Athens and allegedly gave up his claims to Amphipolis. Meanwhile he bought off the Paeonians with gifts and promises; subsequently, when their king died, he invaded their land, defeated them in battle and made them recognize Macedonian overlordship. He bought off the Thracian king with gifts and so Pausanias had to give up his venture. Finally Philip invaded Illyria and inflicted a heavy defeat on the Illyrians; by this he secured the territory running westwards as far as Lake Lychnitis.

This tradition has some suspicious features. It says that the Illyrians were the last of the several enemies Philip dealt with in this period. Yet it also says that the battle where Perdiccas fell was a major victory for the Illyrians and that they promptly prepared to follow it up with an invasion of Macedon. If that is true, it is odd that Philip was free of the Illyrian danger for more than a year and could deal with his other enemies first. It is surely more likely that the battle where Perdiccas fell brought heavy losses to the Illyrians as well as to the Macedonians and that the former were scarcely ready to fight again until Philip attacked them. In other respects the tradition is opaque. All that can be said with confidence is that by the middle of 357 Philip had secured his territory as far as Lake Lychnitis and he could think about expanding beyond the limits recognized by his predecessor.

The first place he attacked was Ampipolis. He brought a large force with siege engines against it and besieged it in the summer of 357. Envoys from Amphipolis came to Athens to seek help just after the Athenians returned from their expedition to Euboea, but no help was sent. Philip succeeded in breaking down part of the city wall and hence captured Amphipolis. He allowed the city to retain its institutions; indeed he used a decree of its public assembly to exile his leading opponents. But he kept Amphipolis under his control and thus he gained a position valuable for communications by land and sea. The siege and capture of Amphipolis had an effect on Philip's relations with Athens. During the siege Philip sent a message to reassure the Athenians; later Athenian orators said that he undertook to hand over Amphipolis to Athens after capturing it, but they may have misrepresented the content of the message. The capture of the city had technically the consequence that henceforth the Athenians considered themselves to be at war with Philip; for they still claimed Amphipolis, although they had not held it since 424/3. But for some time they did little to resist Philip's advance in the northern Aegean.

Promptly after gaining Amphipolis, Philip marched against Pydna and secured it. It was one of the cities which Timotheus had won for the Athenians in the 360s. The next place which he sought to reduce was Poteidaea; apparently he did not so much wish to secure Poteidaea for himself as to deprive the Athenians of the base they held there. The Chalcidian League headed by Olynthus also coveted Poteidaea. Philip regarded Athens as the more formidable rival. So he made an alliance with Olynthus; by its terms he undertook to hand over Poteidaea to the Olynthians after capturing it. Then he besieged Poteidaea and captured it; he brought out the Athenian garrison which he found there, and let it withdraw to Athens, but he sold the citizens of Poteidaea into slavery. He handed over the town together with its land and all its possessions to the Olynthians.

The capture of Poteidaea probably occurred in 356. In that or the next year Philip marched eastwards against the town of Crenides northeast of Mount Pangaeum. This town had been founded a few years before by the Thasians. Philip secured it without difficulty, changed its name to Philippi and enlarged its population with new settlers. The position was valuable because it controlled gold mines; Philip improved the exploitation of the mines and increased their yield. Soon he had ample funds for hiring mercenaries and for diplomacy.

The final step which Philip took to gain access to the coasts was to attack Methone. This city, like Pydna, had been secured for Athens by Timotheus. Philip advanced on it, probably before the end of 355, and besieged it. After a time the citizens surrendered, probably in the summer of 354; by the terms which they negotiated with Philip they were allowed to leave taking one cloak each. Thus by the campaigns of five years Philip had improved the position of his kingdom considerably. In 359 Macedonian access to the sea was blocked by the Chalcidian League, Amphipolis, and the Athenians. By 354 Philip had reduced Amphipolis and he had driven Athenian power from Pydna, Poteidaea and Methone. He had an alliance with Olynthus, and although the growth of his power might lead to tension with the Chalcidian League, there were no overt signs of that yet. Moreover Macedon was a land power, not a sea power; Philip envisaged Thessaly as his next threater for expansion, and his opportunity was provided by a conflict in central Greece.

THE THIRD SACRED WAR[3]

Since the First Sacred War (see chapter 2, p. 47) the affairs of the Delphic sanctuary had been under the ultimate control of the alliance called the Amphictyonic League. As will be remembered, this League consisted mostly of states in the central and northern part of Greece. Its original function had been to watch over the temple of Demeter at Anthela near Thermopylae, but it had also acquired care of the temple of Apollo at Delphi. Each member state sent one, or in most cases two, sacred representatives called *hieromnemones* to the meetings of the Amphictyonic Council. This Council, which transacted the business of the League, held regular meetings twice a year, in the spring and the fall, the word for a meeting being *pylaia*. In an emergency extraordinary meetings of the Council could be called.

Some time after the battle of Leuctra the Thebans made a formal complaint in the Amphictyonic Council because of the seizure of the Cadmea carried out by the Spartans in 382. The Council responded by condemning Lacedaemon to pay a fine. Nothing might have come of this but for a further resolution of the Council. A complaint was made against the Phocians on the grounds that they had cultivated part of the land of Cirrha, which had been dedicated to Apollo and consequently left idle after the First Sacred War. The Council condemned the Phocians to pay a heavy fine within a specified time. When the Phocians failed to pay, the Council ordered that the territory of Phocis should be dedicated to Apollo; at the same time they resolved that other states which had been condemned, for example Lacedaemon, should be required to pay their fines and, if they failed to do so, the Greek states should be invited to take action against them.

The Phocians decided to resist. In this they were led by one of their citizens, Philomelus. He argued that the fine imposed on them was unjust since it was excessive in proportion to the alleged offense. He also reminded the Phocians of their ancient claim to control the Delphic sanctuary. He was elected to supreme command of the Phocian forces. He visited Sparta and had an interview with one of the kings, Archidamus, who gave him fifteen talents. With these and other funds he recruited mercenaries. With citizen troops from Phocis and with his mercenaries he occupied Delphi in about the spring of 355. He executed those citizens of Delphi who opposed him and confiscated their property, but he gave assurances to the rest.

The first of the neighboring states to send troops against him was the Locrians, but Philomelus defeated them at a cliff called Phaedriadae near Delphi. The Locrians appealed to Thebes for help. So the Boeotians voted to go to war against the Phocians and sent envoys to Thessaly and to other members of the Amphictyonic League. Meanwhile Philomelus followed up his victory by making a raid on Locris. Then he set about strengthening his position by diplomacy. He made the Pythian priestess, who customarily uttered oracular responses, mount the sacred tripod, since he desired the sanction of Apollo. When she tried to resist, he threatened her with force, and in desperation she said that he could do as he wished. Philomelus interpreted this ambivalent answer as favorable. He sent envoys with justificatory messages to Athens, Sparta, Thebes and other cities. Athens, Sparta and some other Peloponnesian states made alliances with Phocis. But Theban diplomacy also had been successful; when the fall pylaia of 355 met, it was attended by the Boeotians, the Thessalians and their neighbors in central and northern Greece, and it voted a sacred war against the Phocians.

The Phocians accordingly expected to meet opposition on a larger scale in 354. Philomelus could now draw on large resources and he began the campaign by invading Locris. He was opposed by forces from Boeotia and Thessaly as well as by the Locrians, and towards the end of the campaigning season the Boeotians inflicted a heavy defeat on him at Neon in East Locris. During the rout Philomelus, who had been wounded several times, threw himself from a cliff and was killed, but his fellow general Onomarchus rallied the surviving troops and brought them away safely. After the battle the Boeotians took their forces home. They may have had some expectation that the war was over. Certainly when the Phocians deliberated with their allies, some were in favor of coming to terms, but Onomarchus spoke for the majority when he urged his fellow citizens to continue fighting. The Phocians elected him supreme commander of their forces. He strengthened his position in several ways. Drawing freely on the temple treasures of Delphi and confiscating the property of those Phocians who opposed him, he raised money both for recruiting mercenaries and for diplomacy. He scored a valuable success when he persuaded the Thessalians to withdraw from the war. These preparations probably occupied the winter of 354/3.

In the campaigning season of 353 Onomarchus conducted raids into the territory of several neighboring states, Locris, Doris and Boeotia; he captured Orchomenus before being driven out of Boeotia. But developments further north gave a new turn to the war. In Thessaly Lycophron with his brothers had made himself tyrant of Pherae five years before. But in 353 Thessalians opposing him appealed to Philip of Macedon and he brought an army to support them. Lycophron appealed to Onomarchus, and the latter sent his brother Phayllus with an army of 7,000 men. Philip defeated Phayllus and drove the Phocians out of Thessaly. Thereupon Onomarchus brought his whole force to Thessaly and

Delphi. View of the Temenos or sacred area from the Theater. In the center the Temple of Apollo. In the background the cliff Phaedriadae. [Photo by Hirmer Fotoarchiv, München.]

Delphi. The Sacred Way and the Treasury of the Athenians. [Photo by Hirmer Fotoarchiv, München.]

defeated Philip in two battles. Philip suffered heavy losses and withdrew with the remainder of his forces to Macedon.

At the opening of the campaigning season of 352 Onomarchus was at first free from preoccupations in the north. He invaded Boeotia again, defeated the Boeotians and captured Coroneia. But in the meantime Philip had raised fresh forces. He brought them into Thessaly and advanced against Lycophron. The tyrant of Pherae appealed again to his Phocian ally and Onomarchus brought a large army to his support. But Philip mustered the Thessalian opponents of Lycophron, who proved to be numerous. The ensuing battle has come to be called "the battle of the Crocus Field," and Philip won decisively. Some of the Phocian fugitives reached the coast and were picked up by an Athenian fleet under Chares, but allegedly 6,000 of the Phocians and of the mercenaries in their service were killed. Onomarchus himself fell and was succeeded in the command by Phayllus, who set about raising new funds and recruiting additional mercenaries.

After Philip's victory Lycophron and his associates surrendered Pherae to him; they withdrew with their remaining forces and entered the service of Phayllus. Philip reorganized Thessaly and advanced promptly towards Thermopylae. But there he was checked by an Athenian force under Nausicles, who brought 5,000 infantry and 400 cavalry. Other powers too were alarmed at the prospect of a Macedonian advance into central Greece. Lacedaemon sent 1,000 men and Achaea sent 2,000 to help the Phocians; these two states had been allies of Phocis since early in the Sacred War, but they did little to help their ally until Philip threatened Thermopylae. The political background in Athens to the expedition of Nausicles calls for note. In 343/2 Nausicles and Eubulus appeared together in court to plead for Aeschines; furthermore, a decree of thanksgiving for Nausicles's successful expedition to Thermopylae was proposed by Diophantus, a friend of Eubulus. Thus the Eubulus-group was responsible for the expedition of Nausicles; although it did not pursue Athenian ambitions in the northern Aegean, this group saw that Athenian security would be threatened if Macedonian forces penetrated Thermopylae, and it responded with armed action promptly and effectively. Finding himself opposed at Thermopylae, Philip did not try to force the pass but withdrew to Macedon and then advanced eastwards into Thrace.

THRACE AND THE OLYNTHIAN WAR[4]

To understand Philip's prospects on the northern coast of the Aegean attention must be given to the situation in Thrace. The strongest of the Thracian kingdoms was that of the Odrysae. Their king, Cotys, was assassinated in 360 or

359, and the kingdom was divided into three parts. The easternmost part, situated between the Chersonese and the Hebrus river, was ruled by Cersebleptes, the son of Cotys. The central and western parts were ruled by Amadocus and Berisades respectively; they were probably relatives but not sons of Cotys. The Athenians engaged in complex dealings with Cersebleptes in his early years in an effort to secure the Chersonese; eventually in 357 Chares negotiated a treaty, which embraced the other two kings as well as Cersebleptes, and the Athenians found it satisfactory.

The western kingdom probably stretched from the Strymon river to somewhere near Maroneia. Philip came into conflict with it in 356. At least Diodorus says that three kings, of the Thracians, the Paeonians and the Illyrians, combined against Philip, but he made a surprise attack on them and defeated them. Diodorus gives this information under the year 356/5, and the date is confirmed by an inscription preserving an Athenian decree; it concluded an alliance with the kings of western Thrace, of the Paeonians and of the Illyrians, and it is dated to the first prytany of 356/5. Thereafter western Thrace probably continued to have Odrysian rulers but they were subject to Philip.

The next step in Philip's expansion against the Thracian kingdoms was an expedition which he led as far as Maroneia (see appendix to chapter 18, p. 468). That was probably early in 353. Amadocus, who controlled the neighborhood of Maroneia, prevented Philip from advancing further, but Cersebleptes sent an envoy to Philip at Maroneia to give him assurances; although the content of the envoy's message is not recorded, his mission was evidently a friendly gesture. It seems likely that Philip hoped to exploit rivalry between Amadocus and Cersebleptes. The latter came to realize that Macedonian expansion could ultimately threaten him and so he drew towards the Athenians. In 353/2 he entrusted the cities of the Chersonese, except Cardia, to them; Chares led an expedition to the Hellespont, captured Sestus and installed Athenian cleruchs in the Chersonese.

After Philip was checked at Thermopylae in 352, he returned to Macedon and then promptly led a further expedition into Thrace. He reached a fortress called Heraion Teichos and besieged it late in 352. The events attending the siege are known mainly from a remark of Demosthenes. He says that the Athenians, on learning of the siege, voted to send out a force of forty triremes with a complement of troops. But soon afterwards further reports arrived, some saying that Philip had fallen ill and others that he was dead. So the Athenians desisted from their undertaking; they did not send a fleet to northern waters until the third month of 351/0, and the fleet dispatched then consisted of only ten triremes under Charidemus. Elsewhere Demosthenes says that on this expedition into Thrace Philip expelled some kings and set up others before he fell ill. It is likely that by this campaign Philip gained ascendancy over the central Thracian kingdom of Amadocus. Henceforth the only independent kingdom he had to deal with in Thrace was that of Cersebleptes. The Athenians for their part felt that Philip's eastward expansion had brought him dangerously near to the Chersonese.

Philip's renewed interest in Thrace in 352 was of concern to the Chalcidian League, headed by Olynthus. As will be remembered, in 356 Philip had allied with the Chalcidians and secured for them the site of Poteidaea; indeed, he was so anxious to gain their good will that he gave them the town of Anthemus, which had been constantly in dispute between them and the kings of Macedon. But in 352/1 the Chalcidians made a treaty of peace with Athens. Hitherto the two states had been technically at war because of their rival claims to Amphipolis, but that dispute had ceased to be real when Philip captured Amphipolis in 357. The Chalcidians may well have been prompted to make this approach to Athens by Philip's advance to Heraion Teichos. It is probable that Philip retaliated by a raid against Olynthus. In the speech commonly called "The First Philippic" (4) Demosthenes mentions Philip's "sudden campaigns from his own territory against Thermopylae and the Chersonese and Olynthus and wherever he wishes" (4.17). The date of the speech is given by Dionysius of Halicarnassus as 352/1. If that date is correct, it would appear that Philip made a raid into Chalcidian territory, probably during his return journey from Heraion Teichos. Some scholars, considering this unlikely, have supposed that the speech was made two or three years later and that the allusion was to Philip's major attack on the Chalcidians, the war which he fought against them in 349–348.

In the summer of 349 Philip began a major attack on the Chalcidian League. First he advanced on towns outside the capital city of Olynthus; some of these, such as Mecyberna and Torone, were betrayed to him. Then he approached Olynthus itself. By two victories outside the city he confined its inhabitants within the walls. He besieged Olynthus and it was betrayed to him by two of its leading citizens. Philip plundered Olynthus and sold its inhabitants into slavery. The capture took place in the fall of 348; for straight afterwards Philip celebrated the Olympia, which was an autumn festival for the Macedonians. The war had lasted about a year.

ATHENIAN POLICY TOWARDS OLYNTHUS AND EUBOEA[5]

The Chalcidian League had been founded, with Olynthus as its capital, in 432, when some cities of Chalcidice seceded from the Athenian Empire. Its relations with Athens were usually, though not constantly, hostile. In the years following the king's peace of 387/6 Sparta sought to increase her ascendancy; when envoys from Acanthus and Apollonia appealed to Sparta in 382 for protection against the expansion of the Chalcidian League, they reported that Athens and Boeotia were each negotiating with Olynthus in order to make alliances. But nothing came of the projected alliance of 382 between Athens and the Chalcidian League; indeed, Sparta sent forces against Olynthus and reduced it to the status of a subordinate ally after a long siege (see chapter 16, pp. 406–407). In the 370s the Chalcidian League joined the Second Athenian Sea League and was duly inscribed on the left face of the stele of Aristoteles. But when the Athenians revived their ambitions in the northern Aegean in and after 369, their interests clashed with those of the Chalcidians; the latter might resent Athenian operations at Amphipolis and they might be more aggrieved when Timotheus secured such places as Poteidaea.

As Philip expanded Macedonian power, Olynthus and Athens drew towards one another again and in 352/1 they made a treaty of peace. After Philip went to war against Olynthus, cooperation became close. It is known mainly from three passages of Philochorus, which are quoted by Dionysius of Halicarnassus in his attempt to date the Olynthiac speeches of Demosthenes. Early in the Attic year 349/8 the Olynthians sent envoys to Athens and gained an alliance. Consequently the Athenians sent a force to help them; as described by Philochorus, it consisted of 2,000 peltasts, "the thirty triremes with Chares and another eight which they also manned." The reference to "the" thirty triremes suggests that this squadron was already at sea; it may have been a fleet regularly sent by the Athenians to patrol the northern Aegean. The other eight triremes may have been a volunteer force specially raised for Olynthus; it is known independently that the Athenian state invited rich men to volunteer as trierarchs in order to help Olynthus.

Rather later, probably in the spring of 348, Olynthus made a further appeal to Athens for help. The Athenians responded again; as Philochorus reports, they sent "Charidemus, the general in the Hellespont." He had command of eighteen triremes, 4,000 peltasts and 150 cavalry. Joining forces with the Olynthians, he made raids on the promontory of Pallene and on the district of Bottiaea further inland. It will be remembered that Charidemus had been sent to northern waters with ten triremes in 351. Perhaps he had stayed there ever since, and this would explain why he is described as "the general in the Hellespont." His eighteen ships would be the ten he had held in the Hellespont together with the eight volunteer triremes sent on the previous expedition under Chares to Olynthus.

Finally in the summer of 348 the Olynthians sent a further appeal to Athens. This time they asked for citizen troops instead of mercenaries. The Athenians responded by sending a new force under Chares. As Philochorus reports, it consisted of "another seventeen triremes," 2,000 citizen hoplites, and 300 citizen cavalry in ships specially designed to carry horses. Since the naval squadron is described as "another seventeen triremes," it had probably been raised purposely for the expedition to Olynthus. But this force was delayed by unfavorable winds; it did not arrive until Olynthus had already been betrayed to Philip.

The question to be asked is that of the adequacy of the Athenian efforts to help Olynthus: would a better policy have dictated a larger commitment of Athenian resources? Three speeches which Demosthenes made in 349/8 on the Olynthian question have been preserved. He insists that the Olynthian War is a long desired opportunity to oppose Philip, he urges his fellow citizens to seize it enthusiastically, and he advises them to send out citizen troops instead of mercenaries. But the speeches as preserved fall short of giving precise estimates of the forces to be committed or of their prospects. It can and has been argued that Athenian interests did not require any greater effort to support Olynthus. The positions vital for Athenian security were Thermopylae and the Hellespont. The former was the beginning of the land route which led through central Greece to Attica; by dispatching the expedition of Nausicles in 352 the Athenians had shown that, in alliance with the Phocians, they could hold Thermopylae against Philip. The sea route which brought grain from the area north of the Black Sea led through the Hellespont; by reaching agreement with Cersebleptes and by sending cleruchs to the Chersonese the Athenians secured themselves in that district. Philip's war against Olynthus did not threaten Thermopylae or the Hellespont. In order to help Olynthus more effectively, the Athenians would have had to send larger forces to Chalcidice and maintain them there for a protracted period; the expense would have been enormous. The gain would have been slight; Olynthus had been anything but a constant friend of Athens previously.

These arguments are difficult to refute, but a consequence should be acknowledged. The Olynthians allied with Athens and the Athenians sent them considerable help but not enough to save them from defeat; the city was plundered and its citizens were enslaved. For the future a city which had to choose between resisting Philip and coming to terms with him knew that it could not rely on an Athenian alliance to save it.

In the first half of 348 Athenian attention was drawn to troubles in Euboea. Since 357 the influence of Athens had been paramount there. The troubles which came to a climax in 348 seem to have begun from a change of regime in Eretria. Speaking in 352/1 Demosthenes described Menestratus of Eretria as a friend of Athens and implied that he was tyrant of the city, though without using the word "tyrant." Early in 348 the tyrant of Eretria, who sought Athenian help, was Plutarchus; he had a rival, Cleitarchus. Apparently Menestratus had been overthrown and Plutarchus had gained control, but he was not fully secure. The tyrant of Chalcis was Callias, a man whose ascendancy lasted longer than those of the rulers of Eretria. Callias expressed the aspirations of the Euboeans for independence of foreign influence and for achieving a federal union among the cities of the island. Towards the spring of 348 Plutarchus, finding himself threatened with military overthrow, appealed to Athens for help, and the Athenians sent a force under Phocion. But Callias raised troops from all parts of Euboea and gained some mercenaries from Phocis. Cooperation between Phocion and Plutarchus broke down; Phocion found his force trapped on a hill called Tamynae, but he fought a difficult battle and defeated the enemy. Then he expelled Plutarchus from Eretria. Some time later Phocion left Euboea and was succeeded in command of the Athenian force there by Molossus. Plutarchus was still at large; he captured Molossus alive together with a body of Athenian troops and held them to ransom. Eventually, in about the middle of the summer of 348, envoys came from the cities of Euboea to Athens and made peace. The outcome was that for several years Euboea was free from foreign influence. Plutarchus had been overthrown, and Cleitarchus was able to consolidate his position in Eretria.

Something can be discerned about the political influences which worked in Athens for the expedition to Euboea. Phocion is attested later as an associate of Eubulus. Meidias, another man who enjoyed the good will of Eubulus, had ties of formal friendship with Plutarchus. In 346/5 Demosthenes claimed that he alone opposed the dispatch of aid to Plutarchus. "Alone" may be inaccurate. It seems likely that the Eubulus-group was responsible for the dispatch of Phocion's expedition. Nothing so precise can be said about the Athenian politicians who brought about the sending of limited aid to Olynthus in 349/8, but at least the avoidance of an excessive commitment to Olynthus accords with the general policy of Eubulus. So it can be maintained that in 349/8 the Athenians, under the leadership of Eubulus and his friends, judged their interests correctly. They did not abandon Olynthus, but they did not risk more forces there than they could afford. At the same time they saw that Euboea was much nearer to Attica and could be a serious danger if it fell into hostile hands. Thus they acted correctly in committing a force to Euboea, and although the outcome did not preserve Athenian ascendancy there, at least the island did not fall into the hands of any enemies of Athens, such as the Thebans.

Yet this judgement on the expedition to Euboea would be hasty. The issue confronting the Athenians towards the spring of 348 was not simply whether to send an expedition to Euboea or not. When Plutarchus sought their help, the issue was whether to support him or prefer his rival Cleitarchus. Since the rule of Plutarchus had only recently replaced that of Menestratus, it is not likely that the Athenians had any longstanding commitment to the former. Plutarchus's ties of private friendship with Meidias may help to explain why his appeal received favorable hearing from influential Athenians. The outcome showed that in backing Plutarchus the Athenians made the wrong choice.

THE PEACE OF PHILOCRATES[6]

By the summer of 348 there was little that Philip or the Athenians could expect to achieve by further fighting against one another. Athenian interests in the Hellespont were secure since the dispatch of cleruchs to the Chersonese in 353/2, and although Athens continued to claim Amphipolis, it had long been clear that she had neither any prospect of recovering the city nor any need to do so. The direction of Philip's ultimate ambitions is not easy to discern, but whatever they were, it was to his advantage to achieve peace and, if possible, a good understanding with Athens. When envoys came from Euboea to negotiate peace with the Athenians, they brought a report that Philip too would like to achieve peace with them. Shortly afterwards this news received confirmation. An Athenian called Phrynon was captured by Macedonian pirates and released for ransom. On his return he persuaded the Athenians to send Ctesiphon with him on an embassy to Philip to recover the ransom. When Ctesiphon came back he reported that Philip wished to make peace with Athens.

Thereupon Philocrates, who was to play a large part in the negotiations, carried a decree inviting Philip to send a herald and envoys for the purpose of negotiating peace. A certain Lycinus tried to get the decree invalidated by the procedure called *graphe paranomon*, but when the case came into court, Demosthenes defended Philocrates and the decree was upheld. But a little later news came of the capture of Olynthus; Philip's treatment of the city shocked Greek opinion, and the Athenians did not pursue these steps any further.

The fall of Olynthus led indirectly, however, to serious negotiations. Some Athenians, including Iatrocles and Eueratus, were among the captives; their relatives, supported by Demosthenes and Philocrates, urged the Athenian assembly to intercede, and it sent Aristodemus as envoy to Philip. On his return he at first delayed reporting to the Council. Meanwhile Iatrocles was released by Philip without ransom; he came home and told the Athenians that Philip wanted to make peace with them. So the Council summoned Aristodemus to make his report. This was the Council of 347/6; apparently Aristodemus had delayed his report for about a year. Aristodemus told the Council that Philip wished to make an alliance as well as a treaty of peace. Demosthenes proposed a decree granting Aristodemus a garland as a reward for his services. Philocrates proposed a decree for sending an embassy of ten men to negotiate terms with Philip. When this was passed by the assembly, ten names were proposed and ratified. They included Iatrocles, Ctesiphon, Aristodemus, Philocrates, Aeschines, who was proposed by Nausicles, and Demosthenes, who was proposed by Philocrates.

The first embassy set off in the early or middle part of Anthesterion, the eighth month of the Attic year. When it reached Macedon, Philip admitted it to an audience. Each of the envoys addressed him in turn, and then he gave a feast in their honor. They did not have authority to conclude peace but only to draw up preliminary terms, and the actual situation dictated the principle of the terms; each side was to retain what it held. If the Athenian assembly voted peace on these terms, it would thereby give up its claim to Amphipolis. Philip assured the ten Athenian envoys that he would not encroach on the Chersonese while the Athenians were deliberating about peace; this undertaking amounted to an armistice for the duration of the negotiations. He set off for Thrace when the Athenians began their journey homeward; the message he gave them said that he would soon send envoys to Athens to negotiate.

The embassy returned to Athens early in Elaphebolion, the ninth month. It made its report to the Council and read out a letter, in which Philip offered the Athenians large but vaguely specified benefits if they would make an alliance with him as well as concluding peace. The customary decree inviting the envoys to dine in the Prytaneum was proposed by Demosthenes. Soon afterwards the envoys made their report to the assembly. This meeting voted a decree of Demosthenes for holding a further meeting of the assembly on 8 Elaphebolion, in the hope that Philip's envoys would have arrived by then. They did not arrive so soon, and it was probably at the meeting of 8 Elaphebolion that a resolution of the allied Synedrion was read out; it suggested that the Athenians should await the return of the envoys they had sent to invite other Greek states to the deliberations and then they should hold meetings of the assembly on two successive days to deliberate about peace; but the resolution pledged the allies to accept whatever the Athenians voted. Instead of following this resolution the Athenians voted to hold meetings of the assembly on 18 and 19 Elaphebolion. The period 9–13 Elaphebolion was not available, since it was occupied by the Dionysia. At the meetings of 18 and 19 Elaphebolion the Athenians voted peace. To understand the disappointment they experienced and the decision they took on those days it is necessary to go back and look at other developments, notably an attempt of Eubulus to associate other Greek states with Athenian policy and the situation reached in the Sacred War. These developments may have been causally interconnected.

After the battle of the Crocus Field and the death of Onomarchus, his brother Phayllus received command of the Phocian forces. The most lasting gains of Onomarchus had been the capture of Orchomenus and Coroneia in Boeotia; the Phocians kept these until 346. Phayllus continued operations against the Boeotians and the Locrians but failed to win any permanent advantages. When he died, he was succeeded in the command by Phalaecus, the son of Onomarchus. The war became a series of skirmishes between the Phocians and the Boeotians, and both sides found themselves overstrained. In 347 or the winter of 347/6 internal troubles among the Phocians led to a new development. The Phocians became dissatisfied with the leadership of Phalaecus. He was accused of embezzling funds drawn from the sacred treasures of Delphi. The Phocians deposed him and elected in his stead three generals, Deinocrates, Callias and Sophanes. But meanwhile the Boeotians prepared to appeal to Philip and invite him to intervene in the war.

The dates of the above events cannot be precisely determined. They may have been the reason why Eubulus launched a new Athenian plan, although one cannot be sure about this in view of the chronological uncertainty. In about the middle of Gamelion, the seventh month, or possibly somewhat earlier, Eubulus proposed a decree for sending envoys to the Greek states and inviting them to a conference to deliberate on the question how best to prosecute the war against Philip. The aim of the decree was to build a Greek coalition for resisting Philip; this may have been Eubulus's method of meeting the new situation, which had arisen since the Boeotians were willing to invite Philip and the Phocians were scarcely strong enough to hold the approach to central Greece against him. Aeschines spoke in favor of Eubulus's proposal. He asserted that Philip was gaining influence in Arcadia but that Philip's opponents there would be responsive to an Athenian initiative; he brought an Arcadian friend of his into the assembly to report on the situation. The decree of Eubulus was passed and Athenian envoys were sent to the states of Greece. Aeschines himself served as envoy to Arcadia and returned in time to be elected to the first embassy to Philip. Some of the other envoys had not yet returned in early Elaphebolion. Meanwhile the direction of Athenian policy had changed. When the decree of Eubulus was passed, it envisaged a conference which would deliberate on prosecuting the war against Philip; but when the first embassy was sent to Macedon in the early or middle part of Anthesterion, Athens was seeking to make peace with Philip. A hypothesis suggested (by G.L. Cawkwell) to explain this change depends on an offer made by the Phocians to Athens.

In the early part of 346 there was general expectation that Philip would lead an army southwards from Thessaly into central Greece. The Phocians feared that they were not strong enough to check him. So they sent an embassy to Athens and offered the Athenians custody of the three forts, Alponus, Thronium and Nicaea, which commanded the pass of Thermopylae. The Athenians accordingly voted to send an expedition of fifty triremes with a complement of land forces under the command of Proxenus. But when Proxenus arrived and sought to take over the three forts, he was rebuffed; Phalaecus had recovered control of Phocis and he refused to hand over the forts. Proxenus sent a message to Athens to report this; then he stationed his fleet near Oreus to await developments. The message of Proxenus was read to the Athenians when the assembly was deliberating about the peace negotiations with Philip. The same meeting of the assembly received a report that the Phocians had refused the sacred truce offered by the Athenians for the lesser mysteries of Eleusis.

Any attempt to date this incident must take into account the duration of the truce for the lesser mysteries. This truce began on 15 Gamelion, continued through Anthesterion and lasted until 10 Elaphebolion; the festival itself probably fell in about the middle of the truce. Athens customarily sent out sacred messengers (*spondophoroi*) to offer the Greek states the opportunity of participating in the truce. The purpose of the truce is not recorded. It is sometimes conjectured that the truce was intended to enable participants from all parts of Greece to travel safely to and from the mysteries. Alternatively, acceptance of the truce may have been a way by which the Greek states could associate themselves with the festival. It has been suggested that the spondophoroi visited distant places before they approached places near Athens, so that participants from distant places would have enough time to reach the festival. It is accordingly easy to suppose that the spondophoroi reached Phocis about the end of Gamelion and news reached Athens early in Anthesterion that the Phocians had refused the truce. At the same time the Athenians received the message of Proxenus to the effect that Phalaecus had recovered Phocis and refused to hand over the forts commanding Thermopylae. This message meant the failure of the Athenian plan, launched in cooperation with the previous Phocian regime, to hold Thermopylae against the expected expedition of Philip. The Athenians knew that Phalaecus's resources were not enough to resist Philip; they might guess that Phalaecus would even make an agreement with Philip and open Themopylae to him. On this hypothesis the Phocian rebuff to Proxenus was the reason why in early or middle Anthesterion the Athenians sent an embassy to Philip to negotiate peace terms. By doing so they gave up Eubulus's plan of drawing the Greek states into a conference for the purpose of deliberating on the best way to prosecute the war; but Greek states might still respond to the invitation and join a conference to bring about a general peace to embrace, not only Athens and Macedon, but all the Greek states.

There is, however, a little more evidence about the mission of Proxenus and it suggests an alternative to the hypothesis just outlined. Defending himself in court in 343/2, Aeschines included in his speech a description of the first embassy (2.20–43). In this description he attributed ridiculous behavior to Demosthenes; he failed to cite evidence for his assertions and probably many of them were invented. Even so, this description may provide good evidence for the historian, when it mentions things which were matters of common knowledge at the time when it was spoken. In the course of describing the first embassy, Aeschines told how the envoys were admitted to audience with Philip and alleged that he himself delivered a careful and somewhat defiant address, recounting Athenian services to Philip's ancestors and substantiating the Athenian claim to Amphipolis. Aeschines continued by saying that, after the envoys had withdrawn from the audience and were alone, Demosthenes scolded him for adopting too severe a tone. Allegedly Demosthenes insisted that the Athenians were neither able nor willing to continue the war and asked: "Or do you place your confidence in the fifty ships which have been voted but are never going to be manned?" (2.36–37). This supposed remark of Demosthenes alluded to the fifty ships voted for the expedition of Proxenus; it implied that that expedition had not sailed, much less been rebuffed by Phalaecus, when the first embassy traveled to Macedon and was received in audience by Philip. Aeschines's description of the audience, of his own address to Philip and of his ensuing altercation with Demosthenes may have been fictitious, but the implication about the date of Proxenus's expedition was something which Athenians could easily know when the speech was delivered. Therefore the implication should be accepted; a date should be sought for the journey of Proxenus and for his rebuff by Phalaecus after the first embassy.

A clue is provided by the assembly held on 8 Elaphebolion. It was scheduled in the hope that Philip's envoys would have reached Athens by then. In fact they did not arrive so soon, and therefore further meetings were scheduled for 18 and 19 Elaphebolion. It may be that about 8 Elaphebolion Philip was still completing his plans for Thermopylae and so he held back his embassy a little longer than the Athenians expected. The proceedings of 18 and 19 Elaphebolion are not easy to recover in full from the partisan statements made later by Aeschines and Demosthenes, but something can be discerned. There was a change of mood among the Athenians between the two days. On 18 Elaphebolion a resolution of the allied Synedrion was read out; it was in favor of concluding peace, but it proposed a provision whereby in the ensuing three months any Greek state which wished to do so should be permitted to join the peace on the same terms as the Athenians and their allies. This proposal was designed in the spirit of Eubulus's decree inviting the Greek states to a conference. All those Athenians who spoke on 18 Elaphebolion favored the resolution of the allies. But on 19 Elaphebolion Philip's envoys, Antipater and Parmenion, were present in the assembly, and they insisted on terms of a different kind. Great consternation was expressed in the meeting; Eubulus said that the Athenians must either pass the decree of Philocrates or march to the Peiraeus, levy a property tax for war, and transfer the surplus revenues from the theoric fund to the defense fund. Philocrates proposed a decree embodying terms acceptable to Philip's envoys. It provided for an alliance with Philip as well as a treaty of peace, and it embraced Athens and those of her allies who were members of the Synedrion; it made no provision for other Greek states. This meant in particular that the agreement provided no safeguard for Phocis. This decree was passed. Evidently by 19 Elaphebolion Philip could put enough pressure on the Athenians to make them give up hope of defending Phocis or Thermopylae. This implies that the news of Phalaecus's rebuff to Proxenus reached Athens by 19 Elaphebolion; Proxenus's message reporting the rebuff may have been read out to the Athenian assembly shortly before 19 Elaphebolion or possibly on the morning of that very day.

The decree of Philocrates ordered that an Athenian embassy should travel to Philip and receive his oath to the peace. The same men were elected to this second embassy as to the first. On 3 Munichion the Council passed a decree ordering the second embassy to set off. The envoys proceeded to join Proxenus at Oreus. Then they traveled slowly to Macedon, spending twenty-three days on the journey. They reached Pella, the capital, and waited for Philip to return. Since his dealings with the first embassy Philip had led a campaign eastwards into Thrace; he captured a series of places from Cersebleptes, who survived with his kingdom much diminished. There was no need for the second embassy to make haste. The terms of peace had been agreed by the two sides. Moreover, Philip had promised the first embassy that he would not encroach on the Chersonese during the negotiations; provided that the Chersonese was safe, the Athenians had no interest in helping Cersebleptes nor had they the means to do so. The outstanding question was, What action would Philip take in central Greece after he returned from Thrace? But the Athenians could do nothing about that since their alliance with Phocis had broken down. By the time Philip came back to Pella, embassies had come from a great many Greek states to present their wishes in relation to his expected journey southwards. The Athenian envoys accompanied Philip and his army from Pella into Thessaly and received his oath near Pherae. Then they returned to Athens, arriving on 13 Scirophorion.

The second embassy reported to the Council and, on 16 Scirophorion, to the assembly. The Athenians did not know what measures Philip would take on reaching central Greece, in particular whether he would favor Phocis or Thebes in bringing the Social War to a conclusion. They were in a mood to accept any possible hopes that were offered. They welcomed a long speech made by Aeschines; he said that Philip had been impressed when he (Aeschines) spoke to him against the Thebans; he encouraged his hearers to believe that Philip would restore Thespiae and Plataea and make the Thebans pay the cost of the Sacred War.

When this assembly met, Philip was already at Thermopylae. Phalaecus yielded Nicaea and the other forts to him and withdrew with his 8,000 mercenaries to the Peloponnese. The Phocians surrendered to Philip. But the Macedonian king did not himself impose a settlement concluding the Sacred War; instead he summoned a meeting of the Amphictyonic Council to draw up a settlement. Philip also sent letters to the Athenians, inviting them to send an armed force which would join in bringing the Sacred War to an end. The Athenians decided not to send a force but only an embassy. The composition of this, the third embassy, was largely the same as that of the first and second, but Demosthenes excused himself when he was elected. When the third embassy reached Chalcis, it learned the terms of the settlement made by the Amphictyonic Council. One of the envoys, Dercylus, returned to Athens and reported the news to a meeting of the assembly in the Peiraeus on 27 Scirophorion. The Athenians were alarmed at the severe terms inflicted on the Phocians; they passed a decree, proposed by Callisthenes, for bringing their women and children from the fields into safety, for manning their forts and for putting the Peiraeus in a state of defense. But they instructed their embassy to proceed to Philip and the Amphictyonic Council; its final mission is sometimes called the fourth embassy and it was merely to convey formal congratulations.

The special meeting of the Amphictyonic Council, called to end the Sacred War, assumed that the Phocians had committed sacrilege and treated them accordingly. The debt owed by the Phocians to the Delphic sanctuary was estimated at more than 10,000 talents, and the Phocians were ordered to repay it in annual installments of 60 talents. They were deprived of all weapons and horses and they were forbidden to acquire either of these until they had repaid the debt. Their cities were destroyed, and they were required to live in villages each comprising not more than fifty households. They were excluded from participation in the Amphictyony or the Delphic sanctuary, and the two votes they had previously held in the Amphictyonic Council were transferred to Philip.

Philip stayed in central Greece to conduct the Pythian festival together with the Boeotians and the Thessalians a little later in the summer. Then he returned to Macedon. In prestige the manner of his entry into central Greece had brought him many advantages. He had brought the Sacred War to an end by coming to the aid of the shrine of Apollo against sacrilege. The Thessalians, who were bound to him by alliance since 352, had cause to be pleased with his action; so had the Thebans, since he had joined their cause against the Phocians. Yet Philip had even kept open the possibility that he might achieve a reconciliation with Phocis; for the payments of the Phocian indemnity to the Delphic shrine by installment did not begin until the fall of 343, and the postponement probably reflected Philip's wish. Above all Philip had gained control of Thermopylae; he installed a Thessalian garrison in Nicaea, the chief of the forts commanding the pass.

For Athens the peace treaties of 346, both the peace of Philocrates and the settlement concluding the Sacred War, were disappointing. Admittedly she had done little in the past ten years to help Phocis, beyond the expedition of Nausicles in 352; even so she had been an ally of Phocis, and the outcome of the Sacred War showed that the Phocian cause was sacrilegious. The terms of the peace of Philocrates were realistic; Athens and Philip each kept what they held, and thus Athens gave up her claim to Amphipolis, which she had not held since 424 and did not need. The occurrence of 346 which most alarmed the Athenians was Philip's penetration of Thermopylae, but the peculiar embarrassment of the Athenian position was that Thermopylae was not an issue between Athens and Philip; neither the negotiations leading to the peace of Philocrates nor any conceivable amendments to be made to that treaty in the future could block Philip's route into central Greece. Furthermore, there was no way apparent for the Athenians to remedy their situation. Eubulus's scheme for a general Greek conference to deliberate on prosecution of the war had not been promising; the lesson of the Olynthian War was that an ally who relied on Athenian help against Macedonian attack would perish. Indeed, in 346 the foreign policy of Eubulus and his associates failed. They had made it their aim to protect Athenian vital interests, at Thermopylae and in the Hellespont, but refrain from expensive ventures elsewhere. It was an essentially defensive policy and it was well calculated. But the weakness of a defensive policy is that something quite unexpected, something unforeseen by the policy makers, may happen to the advantage of the other side. In 346 something unforeseen by the Athenians happened when Phalaecus recovered control of Phocis, rebuffed Proxenus, and surrendered Thermopylae to Philip.

NOTES

1. The statements on the number of members in the Sea League are Diod. 15.30.2; Aeschin. 2.70. For the Athenian expedition to Euboea see Diod. 16.7.2; Dem. 8.74–75; 21.174; 22.14; Aeschin. 3.85; Tod 2.153. For the Social War see Diod. 16.7.3–4; 16.21.1–16.22.2; Nepos, *Chabrias* 4; Nepos, *Tim.* 3; Tod 2.152 and 156. On Mytilene see Tod 2.168. For discussion of the chronology see G.L. Cawkwell, "Notes on the Social War," *Classica et Mediaevalia* 23 (1962) 34–49. For the share of Mausolus see Dem. 15.3; Diod. 16.7.3. For encroachment by him and Artemisia on Rhodes see Dem. 15; Vitruvius, *de architectura* 2.8.14–15. For the trial of Timotheus, Iphicrates and Menestheus see Dein. 1.14; Nepos, *Tim.* 3.5; Isoc. 15.129. For the death of Chabrias see Nepos, *Chabrias* 4. On Eubulus and the internal situation in Athens see Sealey, *Essays* 164–182 = "Athens after the Social War," *JHS* 75 (1955) 74–81; G.L. Cawkwell, *Eubulus, JHS* 83 (1963) 47–67. Eubulus's service as thesmothetes is known from an inscription published by B.D. Meritt, Hesperia 29 (1960) 25–28. For Hegesileus see Xen. *Revenues* 3.7; Dem. 19.290. The main text illustrating the growth in the functions of the theoric board under Eubulus is Aeschin. 3.25. The law assigning the surplus of revenues over expenditure to the theoric fund has to be inferred from Dem. 1.19–20; 3.10–13; Pseudo-Dem. 59.3–8; Philoch. *F.Gr.Hist.* IIIB 328F56A. Since this evidence seems contradictory, Cawkwell supposes that the law was changed repeatedly. An alternative hypothesis would be that the law assigned the surplus to the theoric fund except in a major emergency, when

it was to go to the defense fund. For the early activities of Aristophon and his son see Athen. 13.577b; Xen. *Hell.* 6.3.2. For his prosecution of Iphicrates see Polyaen. 3.9.29. For his friendship with Chares see Hyp. fr. 40 = schol. Aeschin. 1.64. For his feud with Eubulus see Dem. 18.162; 19.291; 21.218 with schol.

2. For the distinction between lower and upper Macedon see Thuc. 2.99.1-3. The tradition on Philip's early operations is preserved most fully by Diod. 16.2.4-16.4.7; cf. 16.8.1. For the capture of Amphipolis see Diod. 16.8.1-2; Dem. 1.8; Tod 2.150. For Philip's message to Athens during the siege see Dem. 23.116; Pseudo-Dem. 7.27-28. The enigmatic allegations about his negotiations with Athens at this stage have been discussed by G. E. M. de Ste. Croix, "The Alleged Secret Pact between Athens and Philip II concerning Amphipolis and Pydna," *CQ* N.S. 13 (1963) 110-119. For Philip's capture of Pydna, Poteidaea, Crenides and Methone see Diod. 16.8.3-7; 16.31.6; 16.34.4-5; Dem. 1.12-13; *I.G.* II², 130. A fragmentary inscription giving Philip's alliance with the Chalcidian League is accessible as Tod 2.158. A useful biography of Philip is A. Momigliano, *Filippo il Macedone* (Firenze 1934).

3. The main source for the operations of the Third Sacred War till 352 is Diod. 16.14.3-5; 16.23-33; 16.35-38. A little additional information can be found in Paus. 9.6.4; 10.2.1-10.8.2. There is a brief account in Just. 8.1.1-8.5.6. For the links between Eubulus, Nausicles and Diophantus see Aeschin. 2.184; Dem. 19.86 with schol.; schol. Aeschin. 3.24. For the chronology see Appendix to this chapter.

4. The extensive resources of the Odrysian kingdom were noticed by Thuc. 2.97. A useful study of the kingdom is A. Hoeck, "Das Odrysenreich in Thrakien im fünften und vierten Jahrhundert v. Chr.," *Hermes* 26 (1891) 76-117. Athenian dealings with Cersebleptes 360-357 are known from Dem. 23.8 and 163-173; part of the treaty of 357 is preserved as Tod 2.151. Philip's advance into western Thrace in 356 is known from Diod. 16.22.3 and Tod 2.157. For the continued existence of Odrysian rulers in western Thrace see Dem. 23.173-175, 179-180, 189. Philip's expedition to Maroneia is known solely from Dem. 23.183. For the action of Cersebleptes and Chares in the Chersonese in 353/2 see Diod. 16.34.3-4. Philip's advance to Heraion Teichos is known from Dem. 1.13; 3.4-5; cf. Appendix to this chapter. For Philip's surrender of Anthemus see Dem. 6.20. The Chalcidian treaty of peace with Athens is known from Dem. 23.108-109. On the date of Demosthenes's First Philippic see Sealey, "Dionysius of Halicarnassus and Some Demosthenic Dates," *REG* 68 (1955) 77-120, especially 81-89; J. R. Ellis, "The Date of Demosthenes' First Philippic," *REG* 79 (1966) 636-639. The Olynthian War is recounted by Diod. 16.52.9; 16.53-55. Its duration can be inferred from Dem. 19.192 and 266; that Olynthus fell in the Attic year 348/7 is stated by Philochorus, *F.Gr.Hist.* IIIB 328F156.

5. On the Athenian expeditions to Olynthus see Philoch. *F.Gr.Hist.* IIIB 328F49, 50, 51; Dem. 21.161; Suda, s.v. Karanos. Menestratus of Eretria is known from Dem. 23.124 and Cleitarchus from Philoch. *F.Gr.Hist.* IIIB 328F160. The main sources on the Athenian expedition to Eretria are Plut. *Phoc.* 12-14; Aeschin. 3.86-88; Dem. 21.132-133, 161-164, 197; 39.16; Pseudo-Dem. 59.3-8; schol. Dem. 5.5; schol. Dem. 19.290. On the peace and consequent situation see Aeschin. 2.12; Dem. 9.57; Philochorus loc. cit. On Athenian politicians in relation to the Euboean expedition see Dem. 5.5; 21.110 and 200. The association of Medias and Phocion with Eubulus is inferred from Dem. 21.205-207; Aeschin. 2.184; Hegesileos, the nephew of Eubulus, held a command in Euboea during the expedition, whether under Phocion or after him (Dem. 19.290 with schol.). This section owes a great deal to G. L. Cawkwell, "The Defence of Olynthus," *CQ* N.S. 12 (1962) 122-140. Other discussions are provided by H. W. Parke, "Athens and Euboea, 349-8 B.C.," *JHS* 49 (1929) 246-252; J. M. Carter, "Athens, Euboea, and Olynthus," *Historia* 20 (1971) 418-429. The question whether intervention by Philip contributed to the Euboean troubles of 348 depends

mainly on the reading in Aeschin. 3.87; the view here followed, that Philip was not involved, has been defended by Cawkwell; the alternative view has been restated by P.A. Brunt, "Euboea in the time of Philip II," *CQ* N.S. 19 (1969) 245–265, especially 247–251.

6. The course of negotiations up to the selection of the first embassy is narrated by Aeschin. 2.12–19. Several points in his account can be confirmed from Dem. 18.21; 19.12, 94, 315; Aeschin. 3.62–63. The composition of the first embassy is given by Second Hypothesis to Dem. 19, 4; eight of the names can be confirmed from Aeschin. 2.18, 20–21, 42, 47. The course of the first embassy is narrated by Aeschin. 2.20–43, but on making these assertions in court he failed to support them with evidence, and probably he invented many of them in order to make his opponent, Demosthenes, look ridiculous. Demosthenes 19.163 described the route taken by the first embassy. Philip's undertaking not to encroach on the Cheronese during the negotiations is known from Aeschin. 2.82. The reception given to the first embassy on its return is reported by Aeschin. 2.44–62; he mentions the resolution of the allies at 2.60, and the decision to hold meetings on Elaphebolion 18 and 19 at 2.61. Further evidence bearing on events from the return of the first embassy to the decision to hold the two meetings is Aeschin. 2.65, 109–110; Dem. 18.28; 19.40, 234–235, 253–254; Pseudo-Dem. 7.33. The meeting of 8 Elaphebolion is known from Aeschin. 3.63–68. The development of the Sacred War after the death of Onomarchus is known from Diod. 16.36.1; 16.37–38; 16.39.8; 16.40.1–2; 16.56–60. For the decree of Eubulus see Dem. 19.10–11, 303–306. The consequent negotiations are mentioned by Aeschin. 2.57–60, 79, 164; 3.64–74; Dem. 18.22–24; Diod. 16.54.1. G.L. Cawkwell developed his hypothesis in "Aeschines and the Peace of Philocrates," *REG* 73 (1960) 416–438. The Phocian appeal to Athens and the mission of Proxenus are recorded by Aeschin. 2.132–135; the position taken up by Proxenus at Oreus is known from Dem. 19.155. The duration of the truce for the mysteries is given in *I.G.* I², 6. For the alternative hypothesis see Sealey, "Proxenos and the Peace of Philocrates," *Wiener Studien* 68 (1955) 145–152. For the deliberations of 18–19 Elaphebolion see Aeschin. 2.63–79, 103–104; 3.69–72; Dem. 19.13–16, 144, 278, 291, 307. Antipater and Paemenion are named as Philip's envoys by Dem. 19.69, cf. Aeschin. 3.72. The Second Hypothesis to Dem. 19,5 names Eurylochus as a third envoy, and Aeschines 3.76 may imply that there were three. Aeschines 2.103–104 says that the decree of Philocrates ordered an Athenian embassy to go to Philip and exact the oath from him. The composition of the second embassy is known from Aeschin. 2.97, 108, 126; Dem. 19.175 and 229. Its course is known from Aeschin. 2.91–92 and 97–118; Dem. 19.150–176; Dem. 18.25–32. The date of its return is known from Dem. 19.58. For the report of the second embassy to the Council and the assembly see Dem. 19.17–24, 31–41, 45–50, 58; Aeschin. 2.121–122 and 129. For the third and fourth embassies see Dem. 19.51, 60, 121–130, 172; Aeschin. 2.94–96 and 136–143. For the Amphictyonic settlement of the Sacred War see Diod. 16.59–60, cf. 16.56.6. For the Thessalian garrison in Nicaea see Aeschin. 3.140; Dem. 6.22 with schol.

APPENDIX

THE CHRONOLOGY OF THE THIRD SACRED WAR

Modern studies of this problem begin with A. Schaefer, *Demosthenes und seine Zeit* I¹ (1856) 441–462. Schaefer claimed that Diodorus's account contained a doublet; that is, Diodorus began his account by drawing on one source but, when he had proceeded some way, he turned to another source instead, and in this process he related from the second source events which he had already given from the first, without realizing that he was repeating the same events. Several later scholars took up Schaefer's hypothesis and refined it. Particular value attaches to the treatments by E. Pokorny, *Studien zur griechischen Geschichte im sechsten und fünften Jahrzehnt des vierten Jahrhunderts v. Chr.* (Diss. Greifswald 1913) 1–44, and by P. Cloché *Étude chronologique sur la troisième guerre sacrée* (Paris 1915); in the course of their discussions they tried to locate the *coupure* or place in Diodorus's narrative where he begins to follow his second source. The most recent study of the problem is by N.G.L. Hammond, *Studies* 486–533 = *Diodorus' Narrative of the Third Sacred War, JHS* 57 (1937) 44–78. Hammond argued that Diodorus's account does not contain a doublet.

The Sacred War came to an end when the Phocians capitulated to Philip on 23 Scirophorion in 347/6 (Dem. 19.59). So its beginning can be determined if its duration is known. Most statements about its duration are of three kinds: (1) statements saying that the war lasted ten years (Aeschin. 2.131; 3.148; Diod. 16.59.1; Paus. 9.6.4; 10.2.4); (2) that the war ended in its tenth year (Duris, *F.Gr.Hist.* IIA 76F2, from Athen. 13.560b; Paus. 10.3.1; 10.8.2); (3) that the war lasted nine years (Diod. 16.23.1). It is best to suppose that the war lasted nine years and some months; this hypothesis does full justice to statements of the second and third types. Statements of the first type should be regarded as a loose approximation. Reckoning, then, in Attic years the war began in 356/5. Historians writing accounts of the Sacred War began from Philomelus's seizure of the Delphic sanctuary (Diod. 16.14.3–5); so this was the event taken to mark the beginning of the war. Philomelus probably occupied the sanctuary in the spring or early summer; for previously he had visited Sparta to seek help (Diod. 16.24.1–2), an activity he could well have carried out in winter; and after seizing the sanctuary he drove off a Locrian attack, fortified the sanctuary, and led a campaign into Locris, where he fought two battles (Diod. 16.24.4–16.25.3); these operations should fall within a campaigning season and occupy a considerable part of it. Thus it appears that he carried out the seizure of the sanctuary in the spring or early summer of 355.

A remaining difficulty must be recognized. Diodorus (16.14.3) says that Demophilus, the son of Ephorus, wrote a history of the Sacred War, starting from the seizure of the Delphic sanctuary; Diodorus adds that the war lasted eleven years. He gives this note in his account of the events of 357/6. Likewise Pausanias (10.2.3; cf. 10.3.1) assigns the seizure of the sanctuary to the year 357/6. But the seizure of the sanctuary was a consequence of events occurring at two meetings of the Amphictyonic Council. At the earlier meeting the Council received complaints against the Phocians and condemned them to pay a fine within a specified period; since they failed to pay the fine, the Council at the later meeting ordered that the land of Phocis be dedicated to Apollo. These two meetings may have been the spring pylaia and fall pylaia of 356. Thus an eleven-year duration for the war would be given by an account which began at the point where the Amphictyones first condemned Phocis to pay a fine.

To come to the question of a doublet. Diodorus gives his account of warfare in the time of Philomelus at 16.23-31. Within these chapters three features indicate the presence of a doublet. (1) At 16.23.2 Diodorus explains that after the battle of Leuctra the Thebans brought suit against the Lacedaemonians in the Amphictyonic Council for the seizure of the Cadmea and gained a verdict condemning Lacedaemon to pay a fine. At 16.29.1-3 he says which Greek states allied with the Phocians and which supported their enemies. He adds that the Lacedaemonians collaborated with the Phocians most enthusiastically, because after the battle of Leuctra the Thebans brought suit against the Lacedaemonians in the Amphictyonic Council for the seizure of the Cadmea and gained a verdict condemning Lacedaemon to pay a fine. Thus Diodorus gives his explanation of Lacedaemonian behavior twice. The second account has a detail absent from the first; it gives the amount of the fine, 500 talents, and adds that it was doubled when Lacedaemon failed to pay on time. But when he gives the explanation the second time, he appears quite unaware that he has already given it. This suggests that he moved from drawing on one source to drawing on another without realizing that in the process he repeated information which he had already supplied. (2) At 16.24.3-4 Diodorus says that Philomelus seized the sanctuary, destroyed a Delphic family who opposed him and confiscated their property; "the Locrians who lived nearby" marched against him but were defeated near Delphi and had to retire to their home. By "the Locrians who lived nearby" Diodorus should mean the Locrians of Amphissa in West Locris; they would approach Delphi from the south. At 16.28.2-3 he says that Philomelus exacted money from the Delphians, so that he could pay his mercenaries; the Locrians marched against him but were defeated at the cliffs called Phaedriadae. Although there is no further evidence for the location of Phaedriadae, it is the modern name for a range of cliffs on Mount Parnassus facing southwards towards Amphissa and Cirrha. Thus it would appear that Diodorus has given twice the Locrian attack which was defeated at Phaedriadae. (3) At 16.25.1 Diodorus says that after the defeat of the Locrian attack the Boeotians voted to send a force against the Phocians; Philomelus fortified the sanctuary and gathered plentiful mercenaries, increasing their pay to one and a half times its previous rate. At 16.30.1 Diodorus, who has just explained how several Greek states took sides for or against the Phocians, says that Philomelus expected a Boeotian attack; so he decided to recruit plentiful mercenaries and he increased their pay to one and a half times its previous rate. It seems likely that Diodorus has given the increase in pay twice. This indication of a doublet is less clear than the other two. It is conceivable that Philomelus increased the rate of pay twice, and it must be admitted that in the two accounts (16.25.1–3; 16.30.1–16.31.5) the oucome of the events following upon the increase is different.

These indications, especially the first two, suffice to show the existence of a doublet in Diodorus's account. It is not so easy to be sure about the place of the *coupure*, that is, to discover where Diodorus begins to follow his second source. There are two possibilities. First, at 16.26 Diodorus digresses to give an account of the origin of the Delphic oracle, and at 16.27.1 he returns to his narrative; so some readers, such as Cloché, have put the *coupure* at 16.27.1. On the other hand, at 16.28.1 Diodorus begins events which he assigns to a new year (354/3), and other readers, such as Pokorny, have taken this as marking the *coupure*. Again, it should be admitted that no difference of bias can be traced with certainty between the two accounts.

The military operations under Philomelus were extensive enough to occupy two campaigning seasons and could scarcely be accomplished in less. The battle of Neon was probably fought towards the end of a campaigning season. For after the battle the Boeotians took their forces home; they would not be likely to have done so if there were appreciable time still available before the onset of winter, but could be expected to follow up their success further. The operations under Onomarchus (Diod. 16.32–33; 16.35) likewise suffice for two campaigning seasons. In particular, although Diodorus fails to mark the interval between Philip's two Thessalian campaigns, they should be assigned to different seasons, since the first led to his defeat and expulsion from Thessaly, but the second culminated in his victory at the Crocus Field and his advance to Thermopylae; enough time must be allowed between the two campaigns for Philip to muster fresh forces.

Evidence external to Diodorus helps to provide a date for Philip's second campaign in Thessaly. After his victory Philip advanced to Thermopylae but was checked there by an Athenian force under Nausicles. Dionysius of Halicarnassus (*Concerning Deinarchus* 13, p. 655) says that the Athenian expedition to Thermopylae was sent in the Attic year 353/2. After being checked at Thermopylae Philip withdrew to Macedon and then advanced eastwards into Thrace, where he besieged the fortress of Heraion Teichos. Demosthenes (1.13; cf. 4.40–41) says that his journey from Thermopylae to Thrace was remarkably quick. Further, speaking in 349/8 Demosthenes recalls (3.4–5) that three or four years before news came in the Attic month Maemacterion that Philip was in Thrace besieging Heraion Teichos. Maemacterion was the fifth month of the Attic year. If Philip was at Heraion Teichos in Maemacterion three or four years before 349/8 and if Demosthenes uses inclusive reckoning, as is likely, then Philip was at Heraion Teichos late in 351 or late in 352. But if he had been there late in 351, Demosthenes would have no grounds to call his journey from Thessaly to

Thrace quick. It follows that Philip was at Heraion Teichos late in 352, and hence that his second campaign in Thessaly, concluding with his approach to Thermopylae, was fought in 352.

The events of the opening years of the Sacred War can now be listed; references are to book 16 of Diodorus unless otherwise stated.

Spring or early summer 355: Phocian seizure of Delphi

Summer 355: Locrian attack on Phocians repulsed at Phaedriadae (24.4; 28.3)
> Boetian vote for war (25.1)
> first Phocian invasion of Locris (25.2–3)

Fall pylaea 355: Amphictyonic declaration of war (28.4)

Winter 355/4: Philomelus enlarges his forces (30.1–3)

Campaigning season of 354: second Phocion invasion of Locris, battle of Neon (30.3–31.5)

Winter 354/3: Boeotians retire (32.1)
> Phocians deliberate and elect Onomarchus to supreme command (32.2–4)
> Onomarchus makes financial, military and diplomatic preparations (32.4–33.3)

Campaigning season of 353: first campaign of Onomarchus, he captures Orchomenus (33.3–4)
> Philip's first campaign in Thessaly: he defeats Phayllus but is defeated by Onomarchus (35.1–3)

Campaigning season of 352: second campaign of Onomarchus, he captures Coroneia (35.3)
> Philip's second campaign in Thessaly: he defeats Onomarchus and advances to Thermopylae but is checked by an Athenian expedition (35.3–6; 37.3; 38.1–2; Dion. Hal., Dein. 13. p. 655)
> Philip advances into Thrace and reaches Heraion Teichos (Dem. 1.13; 3.4–5; 4.40–41)

Two other events and their place within this scheme require attention; one is Philip's capture of Methone and the other is the dispatch of Pammenes by the Thebans. Diodorus reports Philip's siege and capture of Methone, once briefly (16.31.6) and once with a little more detail (16.34.4–5). An Athenian decree (*I.G. II²*, 130) of the fifth prytany of 355/4 grants honors to Lachares for bringing something into Methone. This implies that Methone was at least threatened with blockade, perhaps actually besieged, by a date towards the end of 355. Now Diodorus's first report of the siege of Methone synchronizes it with the campaign culminating with the battle of Neon. Such synchronisms in Diodorus's work may be drawn from a date list or similar and strictly chronological source, and so they may be reliable. Thus the indications suggest that Methone fell in 354. After giving his first statement of the capture of Methone Diodorus adds that Philip proceeded to overcome Pagae. No place of that name is known in the areas where Philip was operating, and so the word Pagae in the manuscripts has often been emended to Pagasae. But Demosthenes says (1.13) that, encroaching on Thessaly, Philip took Pherae, Pagasae and Magnesia, arranged the affairs of Thessaly and then departed for Thrace; and it is intrinsically likely that Philip only won

Pagasae when he secured Thessaly in 352. So it is better not to emend the manuscripts of Diodorus; on capturing Methone Philip may have overcome a place nearby but otherwise unknown and called Pagae; or this name may be a corruption of some other place-name.

After giving Onomarchus's first campaign, in which he captured Orchomenus, Diodorus turns to events in Asia Minor; he says (16.34.1–2) that the satrap Artabazus was in revolt against the king and appealed to the Thebans for help; so the Thebans sent him 5,000 men under the command of Pammenes. Diodorus synchronizes this development with the first campaign of Onomarchus. Demosthenes in the speech *On the Symmories* (14.33–34) argues from probability that the Thebans are not likely to join the Persian king in an attack on Greece; he would not need to argue from probability if the Thebans had already sent a force to support a rebel satrap. Dionysius of Halicarnassus (*First Letter to Ammaeus* 4) assigns this speech to 354/3. If that date is correct, the dispatch of Pammenes took place later than the beginning of the Attic year 354/3.

In another speech, which Dionysius assigns to 352/1, Demosthenes (23.183) mentions a meeting which occurred at the Greek city of Maroneia on the coast of Thrace, when Pammenes was there. He says that Philip came to Maroneia; Cersebleptes, the king of eastern Thrace, sent an envoy there to give pledges to Philip and to Pammenes; Amadocus, the king of central Thrace, prevented Philip from advancing further east; and the Athenians learned of the meeting from a letter sent by their general Chares. Philip's eastward march which took him to Maroneia was probably a considerable venture, designed to subdue territory in the western and perhaps in the central part of Thrace; so he would not be likely to interrupt his campaigns of 353–352 in Thessaly in order to undertake it. That is, the meeting at Maroneia probably took place either before Philip's first expedition of 353 into Thessaly or after his advance towards Thermopylae. It is not clear whether Pammenes visited Maroneia on his outward journey to help Artabazus or on his return journey; or he may have interrupted his operations in Asia Minor in order to go to the conference at Maroneia. Demosthenes's reference to the meeting there would allow a date as late as the first half of 351. But since Diodorus synchronizes the dispatch of Pammenes with Onomarchus's first campaign, it is easiest to suppose that Pammenes set off from Thebes for Asia Minor in the winter of 354/3 or spring of 353 and attended the gathering at Maroneia on his outward journey. At that time the Thebans had recently been victorious at the battle of Neon and might suppose that the Phocians would make little more resistance; so they could spare troops for Asia Minor.

19

The Final Struggle
with Philip II

After celebrating the Pythian festival of 346 Philip withdrew to Macedon. He now undertook an extensive scheme of internal colonization, transplanting large bodies of people between the different parts of the kingdom. This policy had several aims. The defensibility of the kingdom could be improved, if the population at vulnerable points was reinforced. The natural resources of Macedon could be better exploited, if reserves of labor were built up at appropriate places. Philip may also have sought to strengthen the unity of his kingdom by detaching disparate populations from their local ties and mixing them together. No details are preserved about the policy of internal colonization, but the measures taken were extensive and probably occupied Philip until the year 345 was well advanced. In 344 he led a large force into Illyria. The fighting was difficult and many Macedonians of high rank were killed, but Philip was successful and captured numerous Illyrian townships. This campaign apparently followed up the policy of internal colonization by securing the northwestern frontier. During his return from Illyria Philip intervened in Thessaly, carrying out a reorganization.

The first months following the peace of Philocrates were highly significant for the development of the outlook of the Athenians and especially for the political position adopted by Demosthenes. Many modern historians have assumed that, confronted with the growth of Macedonian power, Athenian opinion divided into two major parties, anti-Macedonian and pro-Macedonian, with Demosthenes and Aeschines as their respective spokesmen. Admittedly in his speeches Demosthenes exhorted the Athenians repeatedly to take vigorous action against Philip, but the preserved speeches of Aeschines do not accord with the view that he advocated a pro-Macedonian policy. In 343/2 he was tried on a charge of accepting bribes on the second embassy, the prosecutor being Demosthenes, and the speech with which he defended himself successfully has been preserved; again in 330 he prosecuted Ctesiphon for proposing honors for Demosthenes and his speech is extant. In neither speech did he elaborate or defend a policy of friendship with Macedon. In neither did he even claim credit for the peace of Philocrates; on the contrary, in both he assumed that that treaty was a misfortune for the Athenians and stressed the part played by Demosthenes in bringing it about.

The assumption that the Athenians divided into simple categories, for and against Macedon, does less than justice to the complexity of their predicament. A clear clue to their feelings is provided by the decree of Callisthenes, passed on 27 Scirophorion when they learned of the terms imposed on the Phocians; they brought their women and children from the fields into safety, they manned their forts and they put the Peiraeus in a state of defense (see chapter 18, p. 460). Since Philip had brought an army through Thermopylae, there was no place to check him if he advanced into Attica. The position for the Athenians and especially for the ten envoys was peculiarly embarrassing because Philip's penetration into central Greece was not a consequence of the negotiations which had brought about the peace of Philocrates.

For Demosthenes the predicament brought political maturity. For some years he had been trying to achieve a prominent position in public life; the series of his extant speeches, spoken in the assembly, begins in the year 354/3. But there is nothing to indicate that his early speeches had any effect on Athenian opinion; this is true even of the three speeches he spoke on the question of aid to Olynthus in 349/8. In the summer of 348 he appears to have come to the conclusion that he could achieve a leading position in Athens by promoting negotiations with Philip. At least his actions point to this. Shortly before the fall of Olynthus Philocrates carried a decree inviting Philip to send a herald and envoys for peace; when this decree was prosecuted in court, Demosthenes spoke in defense of Philocrates. In 347/6 he was a member of the Council of Five Hundred. When Aristodemus made his report to the Council and said that Philip wished to make an alliance and a treaty of peace, Demosthenes proposed the decree granting Aristodemus a garland. When the first embassy was elected, Demosthenes was nominated to it by Philocrates.

But when the second embassy returned, Philip was already approaching Thermopylae. Demosthenes saw that Athenian policy towards Macedon had failed. During the previous two years, he had associated himself with a memorable aspect of that policy, the steps towards making peace, and although the Athenian negotiations with Philip were not the cause of the advantage Philip had gained in central Greece, Demosthenes could reasonably fear that the Athenians would vent their rage and frustration on their ten envoys. His political insight and skill enabled him to meet his danger. When the second embassy made its report to the Council and it was Demosthenes's turn to speak, he voiced criticisms of the other envoys. A little later he and an associate, Timarchus, gave formal notice of prosecution againt Aeschines; they alleged that during the second embassy he had accepted bribes from Philip and betrayed the interests of Athens. Aeschines countered by bringing a charge of immoral living against Timarchus; if upheld, the charge would disqualify Timarchus from prosecuting. The trial of Timarchus was held in the winter of 346/5 and he was condemned. Demosthenes continued with his prosecution of Aeschines and the case was eventually heard in 343/2.

By lodging the charge against Aeschines Demosthenes dissociated himself from Athenian misfortunes. Likewise in speeches in the assembly he was able to exploit an allegation against Aeschines. During the second embassy Aeschines made an address to Philip, telling what type of settlement the Athenians would wish to see in central Greece; Philip listened with courtesy and perhaps led Aeschines to believe that he was persuaded. When the second embassy made its report to the assembly, Aeschines boasted of his speech; Demosthenes tried to express doubts, but the assembly was in a mood to grasp at any hope offered, and Aeschines and Philocrates shouted Demosthenes down. In speeches of 346 and the next few years Demosthenes magnified the boasts of Aeschines into "promises;" his rival, he said, had promised that Philip would save Phocis and humble Thebes, that he would restore Thespiae and Plataea, and that he would ensure possession of Oropus and ascendancy in Euboea to the Athenians. Demosthenes had been the youngest of the ten envoys sent to Philip and Aeschines had been the next youngest; some Athenians may have found the dispute between them merely amusing, but it enabled Demosthenes to win notoriety.

In the years following the peace of Philocrates Demosthenes achieved political leadership in Athens by advocating resolute opposition to Macedon. Yet he was a realist and knew how to wait for the right occasion for action against Philip. A minor crisis arose in the summer of 346, not long after the Sacred War had been brought to an end. When the Pythian festival was celebrated, the Athenians failed to send their customary deputation to it; in this way they refrained from recognizing Philip's newly-won membership in the Amphictyonic League. So envoys came from Philip and his Thessalian allies to demand recognition of his membership in the Amphictyony; they indicated that a refusal would lead to a sacred war against Athens. The Athenians complied with Philip's request; one of those who spoke in the assembly for compliance was Demosthenes.

In the later part of 346 the international situation was not yet clear to the Athenians. The event which had most alarmed them was Philip's acquisition of the forts controlling Thermopylae. Obviously he would not abandon voluntarily a gain of such strategic value, but he went some distance towards appeasing the alarm felt in Athens and doubtless in other Greek cities when he withdrew his army from central Greece and entrusted Nicaea to the Thessalians to garrison. An incident occurring a few months later showed that Philip's willingness to make concessions was limited. In the early summer of 346 Philip had marched into the kingdom of Cersebleptes and conquered much of it (see chapter 18, p. 459). It was probably in the following winter that the Athenians sent Eucleides as envoy to Philip to request that the peace of Philocrates be enlarged to include Cersebleptes. If these negotiations were in progress in the winter of 346/5 and the Athenians attached some hope to them, that would explain the tone adopted by Aeschines in his speech at the trial of Timarchus. He complained that Demosthenes, who was to plead for Timarchus, was likely "to find fault with the peace which Philocrates and I brought about" (1.174). As long as the Athenians had something to hope for from negotiations with Philip, a public figure could speak with some satisfaction of his share in negotiating the peace; three years later, on the other hand, Aeschines (2.56) insisted that the peace had been brought about, not by himself, but by Demosthenes and Philocrates. Nothing came of the embassy of Eucleides; Philip did not wish to limit his freedom of action in dealing with Cersebleptes.

The failure of Eucleides's mission may have done something to harden the attitude of the Athenians towards Macedon. Certainly by 344 their outlook was becoming clearer. In that year news came to Athens that Philip was intervening in the longstanding disputes in the Peloponnese and in particular that he was preparing to support Argos and Messene against Sparta. Demosthenes was sent on an embassy to Messene and Argos, and he tried to discourage them from accepting Macedonian help; he argued that Philip's friendship had proved treacherous and dangerous to Olynthus and to Thessaly, and so he advised his hearers to beware. But he had little confidence that they would heed him. Soon after he returned, an embassy arrived in Athens with a request concerning the Peloponnesian situation. In the consequent debate in the assembly Demosthenes spoke a speech (6) which is commonly called "The Second Philippic." This speech, delivered in the Attic year 344/3, raises several problems. First, the identity of the embassy addressing the Athenian assembly is not clear. Some historians have thought that it was an embassy from Philip, accompanied perhaps by envoys from Messene and Argos; others have supposed an embassy from Sparta. The question is not of crucial importance for understanding the speech, for the Athenian response to the embassy would become known to all interested parties. Second, it is not clear how serious was the threat of Macedonian intervention in the Peloponnese. In his speech at Athens Demosthenes said that Philip already was sending mercenaries and money to Messene and Argos and was expected to come in person with a large army to the Peloponnese. There is no further evidence for these Macedonian acts of intervention, and so some historians have supposed that the "news" repeated by Demosthenes was a groundless rumor. Yet it is difficult to believe that the Athenians went to the expense of sending Demosthenes on an embassy to Messene and Argos because of a groundless rumor. An alternative possibility is that the Athenian response, whatever its nature, made Philip desist from his intervention in the Peloponnese.

Two passages of the speech are particularly suggestive; they strike a note which was to be echoed in Athenian dealings with Philip for more than a year. At the opening of the speech Demosthenes distinguishes between talking about Philip's actions and doing something to resist them. He complains that hitherto the Athenians have been content to show with mere words that Philip is in the wrong, and he continues (6.4–5):

If even now you are content to have the more just cause to state in words, the matter is easy and does not demand any exertion. But if it is time to see how the present situation can be put right and shall not proceed further without your noticing it until a power complex develops which we cannot even oppose, then our former way of deliberating is no longer the proper way but both those who speak and those who listen must prefer those counsels which are best and promise safety to easy and agreeable courses.

The notion of "putting the situation right," expressed in this passage, is resumed by Demosthenes later in the speech. He complains of those who came back from the second embassy with deceitful promises and expresses alarm lest, when the consequences become large and obvious, the Athenians may grow angry (6.29–33). He continues (6.34):

I am afraid that, while the envoys keep silence about the terms on which they know that they took bribes, your anger may fall upon those who try to put right some of the things which have been lost through the action of the envoys.

In the extant sources these two passages are the first attesting the idea of "putting right" (*epanorthosis*) the situation which had arisen since the peace of Philocrates. That does not necessarily imply that these passages were the first occasion when the idea was expressed. On the contrary, *epanorthosis* may have been a catchword among Athenian speakers in 345–344. It was a highly convenient catchword; no Athenian could deny that the situation needed to be put right, but those who voiced the slogan need have little fear of being required to make precise recommendations for putting the situation right. Some months after Demosthenes delivered speech 6, Philip made a skillful diplomatic retort; he offered to entertain precise proposals for "putting right" (*epanorthosis*) the peace of Philocrates.

THE EMBASSY OF PYTHON[2]

Sometime in the Attic year 344/3 Philip sent to Athens an embassy consisting of Python of Byzantium and envoys from his allies. Through this embassy he declared that he wished to befriend Athens and he complained of those Athenians who spoke against him. Above all he offered to negotiate with a view to "putting right" (*epanorthosis*) the peace of Philocrates. The speech which Python made was well received in the Athenian assembly, but on the proposal of Hegesippus a decree was passed proposing two amendments to the peace as matter for negotiation. First, whereas peace had been made on the basis that each side should keep what it held, the Athenians proposed that each side should keep what rightfully belonged to it. This proposal revived by implication the Athenian claim to Amphipolis. Second, the decree proposed that the other Greek states, who were not parties to the peace of Philocrates, should be recognized as free and, if they were attacked, all parties to the peace should come to their defense. This amounted to enlarging the peace of Philocrates and making it into a treaty of common peace with a guarantee. Thus the response of the Athenians to Python's embassy showed that they intended to engage in singularly hard bargaining. They elected an embassy including Hegesippus to go to Macedon and convey their reply to Philip. Before tracing the consequent negotiations a question of chronology must be raised.

Philip was not the only monarch to take an interest in Athens in 344/3. Artaxerxes of Persia was preparing to recover Egypt, which had been in revolt since 404; eventually he mustered a large army and reconquered Egypt in the winter of 343/2. While making his preparations in 344 he sent envoys to several Greek states to seek mercenaries; he received troops from Thebes, Argos and the Greeks of Asia Minor, but Athens and Sparta refused to send any. Additional light was thrown on these events by the discovery and publication in 1904 of papyrus fragments of Didymus's *Commentary on Demosthenes*. Didymus says (8.7–31) that in 344/3 Philip sent envoys to Athens and the Athenians received an embassy from the Persian king at the same time, but they gave the Persian embassy a needlessly arrogant reply; they said that they would keep the peace with Persia, provided that the king did not attack any Greek cities. Didymus adds that this event was mentioned by Androtion, who spoke in the assembly on this occasion, and by Anaximenes. Then Didymus quotes the passage of Philochorus reporting the Persian embassy. The statement of Philochorus as quoted says that in 344/3 the Persian king sent envoys to the Athenians and asked them to keep their ancestral friendship with him, but the Athenians replied that they would keep their friendship with him, provided that he did not attack any Greek cities.

A large advance towards understanding this information was made by F. Jacoby; Philochorus's arrangement of material was annalistic, and Jacoby recognized that the way in which this quotation from his *Atthis* begins shows that the Persian embassy was the first event which Philochorus recorded under the year 344/3. So that embassy arrived early in the Attic year. It will be remembered that speech 6 of Demosthenes was delivered in 344/3 when a foreign embassy, possibly a Macedonian embassy, was present in Athens. So the relationship of several embassies reaching Athens in 344/3 needs to be determined; they are the Persian embassy, the possible Macedonian embassy of Demosthenes 6, the embassy of Python, and the Macedonian embassy synchronized by Didymus with the Persian embassy.

A solution proposed recently (by G. L. Cawkwell) identifies the three certain or possible Macedonian embassies. That is, it holds that Python's embassy reached Athens at about the same time as the Persian embassy and that Demosthenes delivered speech 6 at the meeting of the assembly which heard Python. But the way in which Demosthenes in speech 6 presents the notion of "putting the situation right" (*epanorthosis*) tells against this hypothesis. He presents this idea as something promulgated by Athenian spokesmen (above, pp. 472–473); this would scarcely be possible, if Python was present and had just stated Philip's offer to entertain proposals for "putting right" (*epanorthosis*) the peace of Philocrates. It is likely that Python's embassy reached Athens sometime later than the occasion when Demosthenes delivered speech 6. For although that speech says a good deal about Philip, it concentrates on the reports of his intervention in the Peloponnese; it says nothing about the offers of Python or the apparent good will expressed through his embassy. Had Philip already adopted so conciliatory a tone, the speech would be singularly inopportune since it failed to take issue with Philip's offer.

The Macedonian embassy synchronized by Didymus with the Persian embassy was probably that of Python. The only information which Didymus gives about this embassy is that it came to Athens at the same time as the Persian embassy. If there were other Macedonian embassies to Athens in 344/3, that of Python was the one which Didymus or his source was most likely to single out as worthy of mention, since it led to serious negotiations. But if a Macedonian embassy was present in Athens in 344/3 when Demosthenes delivered speech 6, and if the Persian embassy reached Athens early in the year 344/3, and if Python's embassy arrived at the same time as the Persian embassy, then a difficulty arises, for it appears that two Macedonian embassies came to Athens in quick succession, that Philochorus did not find the first one worthy of note, and that the second one made the Athenians highly significant offers. Surely those offers mark a new departure in Philip's policy, a new departure which he must have taken some time to think out, and so he must have had the new policy in mind when he sent the first embassy; in that case it is strange that the first embassy did not already make the offers of Python. The difficulty is only somewhat diminished if it is supposed that the foreign embassy present when Demosthenes delivered speech 6 came not from Macedon but from some other Greek state or states. In that case there is only one Macedonian embassy, that of Python, to reckon with, but that embassy came early in the Attic year, if it came at the same time as the Persian embassy, and it came very soon after the news of Philip's aid to Messene and Argos; thus it marked a sudden change of Macedonian policy. Likewise on this hypothesis it is to be noted that Philochorus did not find the circumstances prompting Demosthenes 6 worthy of mention.

A further observation by F. Jacoby may solve the difficulty. Philochorus as quoted by Didymus gave the Persian embassy but did not suggest that a Macedonian embassy was present at the same time; the synchronization of the two embassies may have been constructed artificially by the fourth-century historian Anaximenes. If he predated the embassy of Python by a few months and made it come to Athens at the same time as the Persian embassy, Anaximenes could give a rhetorical conflict of speeches; he could present the Athenians as confronted with a choice between two major monarchies. If the synchronism of the two embassies was invented by Anaximenes for a rhetorical purpose, the actual sequence of events may have been as follows. At about the beginning of the Attic year 344/3 Artaxerxes sent an embassy to Athens and received an arrogant reply. In the summer of 344, whether before or after this incident, the Athenians received reports of Philip's steps to intervene in the Peloponnese and they sent Demosthenes on an embassy to Messene and Argos. Soon after his return an embassy or embassies arrived in Athens, probably from the Peloponnese, and at the consequent meeting of the assembly Demosthenes delivered speech 6. In this speech he used the slogan about "putting the situation right," a slogan which may already have become current in Athens a little earlier. Philip heard of the slogan and some months later, perhaps early in 343, he sent Python to Athens with the offer to entertain proposals for "putting right" the peace of Philocrates.

Something more needs to be said about the supposed choice which the Athenians had to make between the Persian and the Macedonian monarchy. Anaximenes knew and modern historians know that Philip in his last years planned to invade the Persian Empire and his son, Alexander, carried the invasion with spectacular success. The two powers came into conflict as in 340, when Philip besieged Perinthus and Persia sent help to the city. historians who know these later events it is easy to imagine that the poten conflict was already apparent in 344/3. In particular those who assume Athenian leaders were divided between pro- and anti-Macedonians have trie explain the successive rebuffs to the Persian and the Macedonian embassy shift of opinion from a pro-Macedonian to an anti-Macedonian course; they h argued that anti-Macedonian leaders, by raising the question of Amphipol reply to Python, skillfully seduced the majority of Athenians away fro anti-Persian course which they had taken so recently. But it is not easy to c that the bulk of Athenians could be led astray so quickly or so easily. Moreov is not certain that the future hostility between Macedon and Persia could foreseen as early as 344/3. On the contrary, at some time there were go relations between the two powers. Late in 333 Darius III, who had been defeate by Alexander at the battle of Issus, wrote to the victor and reminded him that there had been "friendship and alliance" between their fathers, Artaxerxes and Philip. Some historians have supposed that this alliance was made shortly before 351, when Artaxerxes launched an unsuccessful attempt to recover Egypt. But a date ca. 344 is rather more likely, since by then Macedon was stronger and so its policy was of more concern to Persia. If indeed the alliance was in force in 344/3, the Athenian responses to the Persian embassy and to that of Python showed not a change of policy but consistency.

PHILIP'S NEGOTIATIONS WITH ATHENS, 343–342[3]

In response to the overtures of Python the Athenians sent Hegesippus on an embassy to convey their answer to Philip. The immediate outcome of the negotiations was untoward. Philip was particularly displeased at the resumption of the Athenian claim to Amphipolis. He gave the envoys an unfavorable reply and went so far as to exile from his kingdom the Athenian poet Xenocleides, who had given them lodging. Negotiations were not finally broken off, but the greater part of a year was to pass before Philip sent a new embassy with a letter to Athens to continue the discussion.

Through the embassies of Python and Hegesippus the Athenians became clearer and harder in their attitude to Philip and to those whom they associated with the negotiations of 346. Philocrates was prosecuted by Hypereides, and Demosthenes spoke in support of the prosecution; Philocrates did not await the verdict but withdrew into exile and was condemned in absence to death.

enis was brought to trial and condemned. In 343/2 the case brought by
nosthenes against Aeschines came at last before a court, but Aeschines was
quitted.

The alarm felt in Athens about Philip's plans was increased by news from
Euboea. At the time when Demosthenes prosecuted Aeschines reports current in
Athens said that Philip had sent mercenaries to Euboea and in particular that they
were at Porthmus, the harbor of Eretria. The rumors may not have been well
founded but they caused concern; since Philip could bring an army through
Thermopylae, there was nothing to prevent him from intervening in Euboea.
Accordingly, in the winter of 343/2 the Athenians welcomed overtures from
Callias of Chalcis, the man who had opposed them in 348 (see chapter 18, pp.
452–453). Callias's aim was to create a Euboean federation; he envisaged a
congress of deputies from the cities of the island to sit in Chalcis. For this purpose
he sought foreign support. He went to Macedon in the hope of gaining Philip's
favor, but after a time he found himself unsuccessful. Then he turned to the
Thebans but soon lost their good will too. So far the result of his efforts was that
he had alienated Philip and the Thebans; he had some fear of being attacked by
them. So he sent an embassy to Athens to propose a defensive alliance; Demosthenes supported the proposal and the Athenians concluded the alliance.

In the same winter of 343/2 Philip marched westwards and intervened in the
dynastic affairs of the kingdom of the Molossi in Epirus. He had married
Olympias, who came of that dynasty; her uncle Arybbas was the ruling king.
Now Philip overthrew Arybbas and enthroned Alexander, the brother of Olympias. Arybbas fled to Athens, where the assembly voted him honors; it instructed
the generals of this and the following years to work for his restoration. On the
same expedition Philip marched southwards from Epirus into the district of
Cassopia, which held three small Greek cities. Philip attacked them, overcame
them and added them to the kingdom of Alexander. His march brought him into
the neighborhood of Ambracia, which felt threatened.

The Athenians took military and diplomatic action to check this expedition of
Philip. They sent some troops to Acarnania. Demosthenes, Hegesippus and
others were sent on an embassy to many parts of the Peloponnese; Demosthenes's
journey took him on to Ambracia. At the same time Callias of Chalcis traveled in
the Peloponnese and tried to encourage opposition to Philip. In response to these
embassies several states made alliances with Athens; they included the Achaean
League, Mantinea and some other Arcadian towns, Argos, Megalopolis and
Messene. It is difficult to estimate how effective the new alliances were. A year
later Demosthenes boasted that the Athenian embassy to the Peloponnese
prevented Philip from attacking Ambracia or advancing against the Peloponnese.
Demosthenes may have exaggerated, but his boast may not have been entirely

groundless; on previous occasions, for example at Thermopylae in 352, Philip had yielded at the first show of resistance. When Callias and Demosthenes returned from the Peloponnese, they each addressed the Athenian assembly and presented a plan for a large defensive coalition. In addition to Athens it was to comprise the Euboean cities, Megara and several states of the Peloponnese. Demosthenes envisaged that the prospective members would send envoys to a congress, which was to meet in Athens on 16 Anthesterion. In fact the congress did not meet and little came of the proposed coalition. But at least a Euboean League was founded; it had its seat in Chalcis, and Eretria and Oreus paid it financial contributions comparable to those they had formerly paid to the Athenian Sea League. The alliances with Peloponnesian states which Athens achieved in 343/2 did not in practice last long. Argos, Messene, Megalopolis and the Arcadian towns were neutral during the final war which Athens with her allies fought against Philip from 340 to 338. Nonetheless, the diplomatic and military measures undertaken by the Athenians against Philip in 343/2 had moral significance; at last the Athenians bestirred themselves to offer leadership against Macedonian expansion.

While Philip was away in the west, Demosthenes was sent on an embassy to Thessaly. Nothing is known about what he achieved on this embassy, but Philip had cause to be concerned about the Thessalian situation. So the Macedonian king intervened again in the affairs of Thessaly, probably during his return journey from Epirus. This time he made several changes. He divided Thessaly into four parts, called tetrarchies, for administration; a subordinate ruler was set up for each part. He installed a garrison in the acropolis of Pherae. His intervention in Thessaly in 342 may be the occasion when he replaced the Thessalian garrison, installed at Nicaea in 346, with a Macedonian garrison; certainly he carried out this change by the fall of 340.

At about the time of his return to Macedon from Epirus, Philip made a final attempt at negotiations with the Athenians. He sent them an embassy with a letter. When this was read out in the Athenian assembly, Hegesippus made a speech to rebut Philip's complaints and offers; the speech has been preserved as the seventh in the Demosthenic corpus and it is the source of information about the incident. The letter, it appears, dealt with a series of topics, and on some of them the attitude taken by the Athenians was petty. For example, Philip had captured the small island of Halonnesus from pirates. The Athenians claimed it as rightfully theirs, and Philip offered to give it to them. But the Athenians retorted that they would only accept it if he "restored" it to them, not if the "gave" it to them. But some of Philip's offers were disingenuous. For example, he proposed drawing up agreements for trial of lawsuits concerning Athenians who visited Macedon and Macedonians who visited Athens. But as Hegesippus pointed out, no such agreements had been made with Athens by Philip's predecessors, although private intercourse between Athens and Macedon had been more frequent in their time; moreover, Athens had recently introduced a speedy procedure for trying merchants' cases, and so special agreements were even less needed than before.

The most important topics discussed in Philip's letter were the two proposals which the Athenians had made through Hegesippus's embassy for "putting right" the peace of Philocrates. The first of these proposed that each side should keep what rightfully belonged to it, and it implied resumption of the Athenian claim to Amphipolis. Philip in reply made the implication explicit and insisted that Amphipolis was his. This response was to be expected; it was unrealistic of the Athenians to raise the question of Amphipolis. The other proposal sought to recognize and guarantee the independence of the other Greek states, which were not parties to the peace of Philocrates. Philip in his letter admitted that this proposal was just and declared himself willing to accept it. But as Hegesippus observed, his recent actions did not accord with his words; he had installed a garrison in Pherae, overcome the three cities of Cassopia and advanced towards Ambracia. On this point Hegesippus seems to have the better of the argument. There has been much speculation among modern historians about Philip's intentions towards Greece after the peace of Philocrates. If there was any prospect of achieving understanding and harmony between Philip and the leading Greek powers, the Athenian proposal for recognizing and guaranteeing the independence of the Greek states was the most positive step taken in that direction. But it was not compatible with Macedonian dynamism.

PHILIP'S EASTWARD MARCH, 342–339[4]

In the summer of 342 Philip marched into Thrace. He was to stay away from Macedon until late in the summer of 339. His first step was to reduce the Aegean coast of Thrace, as far as the border of the Chersonese, and parts of the interior. These operations continued into the summer of 341 and during them Philip finally overthrew Cersebleptes.

In 343/2 the Athenians had sent an additional party of cleruchs under a commander called Diopeithes by sea to the Chersonese. Apparently they wished to strengthen their outpost on the Hellespont. But opinion was divided on the amount of support Diopeithes needed; he was not given sufficient funds to raise or maintain troops. So he raised funds on his own initiative by exacting tolls from merchant vessels and by requiring contributions from Greek cities along the Asiatic coast. With these funds he recruited and maintained a force of his own. The issue on which he came into conflict with Philip concerned Cardia, the city near the isthmus connecting the Chersonese to Thrace. It had been an ally of Philip since before the peace of Philocrates. When Diopeithes came to the Chersonese, Cardia refused to admit any of the cleruchs he brought with him; it asserted its independence, whereas Athens claimed the same ascendancy over Cardia as over the rest of the Chersonese. When Philip returned from Epirus to Macedon in 342 and sent his letter to the Athenians, he urged them to submit the dispute to arbitration. They refused and Diopeithes began an attack on Cardia. The people of that city appealed to Philip for help and he sent them an armed force. Diopeithes looked for an opportunity to retaliate; he raided the coast of Thrace, while Philip was away in the interior, and he made good his escape to the Chersonese before the Macedonian king returned.

Accordingly, in the summer of 341 Philip sent a letter of complaint to Athens. The speech which Demosthenes made in the consequent debate has been preserved, but the outcome of the debate is not wholly clear. Demosthenes said that his opponents wished to replace Diopeithes with another commander in the Hellespont and he alleged that their policy would have the effect of disbanding the force which Diopeithes had raised. He may have misrepresented their aims. In 341/0 the Athenian general holding command on the Thracian coast was Chares. Possibly the outcome of the debate was to replace Diopeithes with a commander who had not made himself objectionable to Philip.

Developments in Euboea in 341 gave a new turn to events. Since 348 the situation in Eretria and Oreus had been precariously balanced, with different groups competing for control and some of them sometimes asked for Macedonian support. Thus in Eretria Cleitarchus had gained an advantage with the overthrow of Plutarchus (see chapter 18, p. 453), but he was not secure. Eretria and Oreus were brought into the Euboean League launched by Callias of Chalcis in the winter of 343/2, but internal rivalries continued. Eventually, probably in 342, Cleitarchus appealed to Philip for help. The Macedonian king sent a force of 1,000 mercenaries under Hipponicus, who destroyed the fortifications of Porthmus, the harbor of Eretria, and strengthened the position of Cleitarchus and his associates. Later, but probably still in the year 342, movements against Cleitarchus arose in Eretria twice, but each time he gained forces from Macedon, the first being commanded by Eurylochus and the second by Parmenion. In Oreus the development was similar but simpler. The leader who appealed to Philip for help was called Philistides. At first he gained money from Macedon and contrived to have his chief opponent, Euphraeus, imprisoned. Later Parmenion, after intervening at Eretria, proceeded to Oreus and secured Philistides in control; Euphraeus committed suicide.

Thus the expedition of Parmenion finally installed pro-Macedonian tyrants in Eretria and Oreus. It is unfortunate that the date of this expedition cannot be determined precisely; in particular it is not clear whether Parmenion intervened in Euboea before or after Philip left Macedon for his Thracian campaign. Consequently it is not possible to say whether the absence of Philip in Thrace weakened the maintenance of Macedonian influence in Euboea in 341. In about the middle of the summer of 341 the Athenians made a new alliance with Chalcis and sent an army under Cephisophon to the island. This Athenian force and a Chalcidian force together liberated Oreus from Philistides and from Macedonian influence; Philistides was killed. Early in the new Attic year 341/0 Athenian troops under Phocion operated at Eretria; they overthrew Cleitarchus and freed the city. The Euboean League, which Callias had founded in 343/2, probably resumed its activity; at least the Euboeans are listed collectively among the allies of Athens who fought at Chaeronea in 338. The liberation of Euboea had moral significance beyond its strategic achievement; for the first time the Athenians succeeded, not merely in checking the Macedonian advance as at Ambracia in 343/2, but in pushing it back.

After achieving his aims in Thrace Philip proceeded to the west coast of the Black Sea in about the fall of 341 and won some of the Greek cities there into alliance. He planned to devote the campaigning season of 340 to reducing Perinthus and Byzantium, crucial positions on the north coast of the Propontis. In about the spring he began besieging Perinthus with land forces. He had built a fleet by this time but it was operating against Peparethus. The Perinthians lost heavily in the early stages of the siege, but they received reinforcements, munitions and supplies from Byzantium. After a time another power sent help to Perinthus. Persia was perturbed at Philip's advance eastward. Athens had opened negotiations with the Persian authorities in 341, though without achieving an alliance. The satraps of western Asia Minor, under orders from the king, sent mercenaries, money, food, missiles and other supplies to Perinthus. Sometime in the summer Philip divided his forces and took part of them against Byzantium to besiege it. The rest of his forces were left to continue the siege of Perinthus, but there was little prospect of capturing it.

Relations between Philip and Athens were exacerbated further by an incident occurring during the siege of Perinthus. When the Macedonian fleet had overcome Peparethus, Philip ordered it to sail against Perinthus. But its route through the Hellespont was threatened both by Chares, who held a fleet in the neighborhood, and by the Athenian cleruchs in the Chersonese. So Philip sent a land force into the Chersonese to escort his fleet. Possibly he now sent a letter to the Athenians with a long list of recriminations to justify his action. The risk of Macedonian encroachment on the Chersonese had haunted the Athenian imagination intermittently ever since Maemacterion 352, when Philip was at Heraion Teichos; at last in 340 the risk became a reality.

It is not known at what time in the summer Philip began the siege of Byzantium, but late in the summer a new opportunity offered itself. The merchant ships bringing grain from north of the Black Sea habitually gathered at Hieron near Byzantium before sailing through the Bosporus. This time Chares was in the neighborhood, but he sailed away to confer with the commanders of the forces raised by the satraps. In his absence Philip took a land force to Hieron and seized the grain fleet. The number of ships captured is given variously as 230, 180 and 170; possibly the fleet totalled 230, and 180 or 170 of these ships were bound for Athens. He sent a letter to the Athenians, blaming them for the collapse of relations and saying that he would have recourse to arms against them. Modern historians have often supposed that on seizing the grain fleet Philip expected Athens to respond with a declaration of war, that he wished to provoke such a declaration, and that he sought to show what great harm he could inflict on Athens even before hostilities formally began. That the seizure of the grain fleet was designed to inflict harm on Athens is obvious enough, but to suppose that Philip expected an Athenian declaration of war is wisdom after the event. In the past, notably in 405 and 387, a threat to the grain route through the straits had forced the Athenians to desist from warfare and make peace. When Philip seized the grain fleet, in all probability he expected the Athenians to stop opposing him.

Philip was disappointed. When the Athenian assembly heard Philip's letter, it voted a decree proposed by Demosthenes; by this the Athenians demolished the stele bearing the peace of Philocrates, they manned their ships and set about prosecuting the war. They sent help to Byzantium; help was also sent from Chios, Cos, Rhodes and other places. After a time, perhaps in the winter of 340/39 or the following spring, Philip raised the siege of Byzantium. He made a raid on the Chersonese, but that was poor compensation for his losses. All his undertakings of 340 had failed. Perinthus and Byzantium had withstood him successfully. He had been unable to find a policy for dealing with the Athenians. In 343–342 he had tried to draw them into negotiations, but the effect had been an increase in their distrust of him. When he tried to intimidate them by seizing the grain fleet in 340, his action backfired with a declaration of war against him. Moreover, the array of states sending help to Perinthus and Byzantium—Persia, Chios, Cos, Rhodes and others—showed that in critical circumstances Athenian leadership could still muster allies against Macedon.

In the summer of 339 Philip led an expedition against the Scythians, who dwelled immediately to the north of Thrace. The origin and extent of this campaign are clear only in part. Previously Philip had had friendly relations with Atheas, the king of this tribe of Scythians. Indeed, probably in 340, Atheas found himself at war with his northern neighbors and appealed to Philip for help; Philip sent him a force of troops. But Atheas drove his enemies away before the Macedonians arrived; so he dismissed them and refused Philip's subsequent demand for payment. This incident gave Philip a pretext to intervene. His real object was probably to secure his Thracian acquisitions by a preventive raid. If so, his expedition was successful. He defeated and killed Atheas and captured plentiful booty. But during his return to Macedon he was harassed by the Triballi, a Thracian tribe. The Macedonians had to retire in haste, they lost their booty, and Philip himself was wounded in the right thigh. He reached Pella at last late in the summer.

THE FOURTH SACRED WAR[5]

An opportunity for Philip to intervene in central Greece in the fall of 339 arose from developments in the Amphictyonic Council, and so the composition of that body requires closer attention. The Amphictyony had in principle twelve members, each member being an *ethnos* such as the Thessalians, the Boeotians and the Locrians. Each of these members supplied two voting deputies, called *hieromnemones*, to the Council. Thus from 346 until the fall pylaia of 339 the Thessalian hieromnemones were Cottyphus and Colosimmus, and Cottyphus presided at meetings of the Council. The two votes previously cast by the Phocians were transferred to Philip in 346. In a few cases one of the two votes belonging to an *ethnos* had been permanently assigned to one city, which itself belonged to that *ethnos*. Thus of the two hieromnemones supplied by the Ionians one was chosen by the Athenians and the other by other Ionians; of the two votes cast by the Dorians one belonged to the Dorians of the Peloponnese and the other to their supposed mother city, the small state of Doris near the head of the Malian Gulf. In addition to hieromnemones each member sent advisory officers called *pylagorai*; they could take part in the deliberations of the Council but they could not vote. Thus in 340/39 Athens was represented by the hieromnemon Diognetus and three pylagorai, Meidias, Thrasycles and Aeschines.

Strange things began to happen at the spring pylaia of 339. The extant information is drawn from the accounts given by Aeschines and Demosthenes, when they pleaded against one another in court in 330. Neither of them was bent on telling the whole truth; their attributions of motive and their allegations of unfulfilled intentions should be treated with scepticism. But on the public occurrences they agree for the most part or supplement one another. Aeschines says that the deputation from Amphissa in West Locris was preparing, at the instigation of the Thebans, to propose a motion against Athens; they would demand that the Athenians be fined fifty talents for dedicating gilded shields at the newly rebuilt temple with the inscription: "Spoils taken by the Athenians from the Medes and the Thebans, when they fought against the Greeks" (sc. in the Persian Wars). Meanwhile Diognetus and Meidias had fallen ill of a fever on reaching Delphi. So Aeschines went in front of the Council and brought an accusation against the Amphissans so as to prevent them from making their charge against Athens. He said that they had encroached on the sacred land and harbor of Cirrha, which had been dedicated to Apollo at the end of the First Sacred War; as he alleged, they had cultivated the plain, set up farm buildings, built walls to the harbor and levied tolls on travelers. In fact there was some room for dispute about the boundaries of the sacred land. The hieromnemones listened willingly to Aeschines's charges and, after he had left the meeting, they voted a resolution inviting all Delphians of military age to gather the next morning with shovels and mattocks and join the hieromnemones and pylagorai in an attack on the cultivated land.

The expedition took place the next day; it destroyed some of the buildings and installations of the harbor, but the Amphissans came out with their weapons and drove it away. On the following day Cottyphus called an assembly of the Amphictyones; it was attended not only by the hieromnemones and pylagorai but by all who had come to offer sacrifice or consult the oracle. This assembly voted that the states which were members of the Amphictyony should be invited to send their representatives to a special meeting of the Amphictyonic Council, to be held at a stated time in the summer; the representatives should bring instructions on the proper way to inflict punishment on Amphissa.

When the Athenian deputation came home and reported to the Council and the assembly, Demosthenes spoke against the policy which Aeschines had initiated. He asserted that Aeschines was bringing about an Amphictyonic war against Attica. A decree, advocated by Demosthenes, was passed to the effect that Athens would continue to send its deputation to the regular meetings in the spring and the fall but it would take no part in the special meeting of the Amphictyonic Council called for the summer. Thebes likewise declined to send its representatives to the special meeting. But the other members of the Amphictyony attended the special meeting; it voted an armed expedition against Amphissa and entrusted the command to Cottyphus. He led his force against Amphissa and ordered that city to pay a fine by a stated day. The fine had not been paid when the day came and the Amphictyonic Council gathered for its regular meeting in the fall of 339. By then Philip had returned from his Scythian expedition. The fall meeting of the Council entrusted command of the war against Amphissa to Philip.

The factual outline of events, summarized above, is reasonably clear, but puzzles arise when one asks why they happened. Demosthenes asserts that Philip desired command in a sacred war as a pretext to intervene in central Greece and he

Delphic stater, ca. 346/339. Obverse: head of Demeter. Reverse: Apollo on the Omphalos. The lettering names the Amphictyones. [Photo by Hirmer Fotoarchiv, München.]

Gold stater of Philip II of Macedon, struck towards the end of his reign. Obverse: Apollo with the features of the young Alexander the Great. Reverse: two-horse chariot and the name "Philip". [Photo by Hirmer Fotoarchiv, München.]

bribed Aeschines to bring it about. Modern historians have often supposed that Aeschines was not bribed but that Demosthenes is right in the other part of his allegation; they suppose that the events happened because Philip wanted them to happen and he stage-managed them skillfully from a distance; Aeschines was not bribed but duped. That Aeschines was duped is likely enough. He says that news of the intended Amphissan denunciation of Athens was brought to him "by those who wished to show good will towards our city." This refusal to reveal his sources is suspicious. But whether a sacred war began because Philip desired it is quite another question. Philip was far away in the northeast when troubles began at the spring pylaia; he was still engaged in his Scythian expedition when the Amphictyonic Council gathered for its special meeting. Without modern communications it was scarcely possible to direct complex diplomacy from a distance. Consequently Philip was likely to desire that conditions in Greece should remain undisturbed during his absence; it was not in his interests that a conflict should break out with unforeseeable consequences, which might even lead to impairing the points of advantage he had won, such as his control of Thermopylae.

If Philip was not the prime mover, those who brought about the troubles can perhaps be discerned. Traditionally the leading powers in the Amphictyonic League had been the Thessalians and the Boeotians; rivalry could develop between them. At the spring pylaia of 339 Aeschines became convinced that the Amphissans intended to make charges against Athens. Demosthenes, pleading in court in 330, denied that the Amphissans had had any such intention. The truth about the unrealized intentions of the Amphissans cannot be discerned. The Thebans behaved as allies of the Locrians; they refused to send any deputation to the special meeting, since they did not wish to join in action against Amphissa. Demosthenes dissuaded the Athenians from sending deputies to the special meeting; he may already have envisaged the alliance with Thebes which he achieved some months later. Aeschines says that he was told of the Amphissan intention "by those who wished to show good will towards our city." It is not unlikely that these unnamed persons were the Thessalian hieromnemones, Cottyphus and Colosimmus, or their agents. For the remarkable fact is not Aeschines's predictable reaction, his denunciation of the Amphissans before the Amphictyonic Council, but the prompt response of the Council itself, its decision that an expedition should proceed with shovels and mattocks into the plain of Cirrha the very next day. That decision was taken while Cottyphus presided. He presided likewise at the special meeting in the summer and he took command of the expedition which that meeting voted against Amphissa.

The actions taken at the spring pylaia of 339 and in consequence of it invite the following hypothesis. At the time of that meeting Philip had been away from Greece proper and even from Macedon for nearly three years. Moreover, in 340 he had failed in his attempts on Perinthus and Byzantium. Many Greeks could begin to suppose that they need no longer reckon with him; his influence had been driven from Euboea in 341, and his setbacks showed that he was not as formidable as they had supposed. He might never come back; indeed he was seriously wounded during his return later in the year. When the Amphictyonic Council met in the spring of 339, the members could feel free to pursue their own policies with little or no regard for the possibility of Macedonian intervention. This meant that the traditional rivalry between Boeotia and Thessaly for leadership in the Amphictyony could revive. Perhaps the Thebans took the first step; they may indeed have encouraged their friends, the Locrians of Amphissa, to prepare an accusation against Athens. But the Thessalians learned of this plan in advance and frustrated it with a countermove. They persuaded Aeschines to bring a charge against the Amphissans and, as soon as Aeschines had uttered his denunciation, Cottyphus excited and exploited the feelings of the Council and of the people of Delphi. For the Athenians the issue was whether to join the Theban side or the Thessalian side. Aeschines preferred the Thessalians, and this was understandable; the Athenians had long hated the Thebans, especially since the loss of Oropus. Demosthenes was more reflective; he wanted to keep open the possibility of collaborating eventually with the Thebans, so he dissuaded the Athenians from sending any deputation to the special meeting of the Amphictyonic Council.

What Philip thought about the activities of Cottyphus and Colosimmus may perhaps be conjectured from their subsequent fortunes. They were still the Thessalian hieromnemones at the fall pylaia of 339, but they were not alone. Two other Thessalians, Daochus and Thrasydaeus, were also present. By that time Philip had returned to Macedon and the burning question was whether he would bring an army into central Greece. At the fall pylaia the Amphictyonic Council chose Philip to command the operations against Amphissa. Cottyphus and Colosimmus have never been heard of since. At the spring pylaia of 338 the Thessalian hieromnemones were Daochus and Thrasydaeus. By then Philip had brought his army into central Greece. It seems probable that Philip was displeased at the activities undertaken by Cottyphus and Colosimmus in the spring of 339, and so he had them replaced by two Thessalians whom he found more acceptable.

The papyrus fragments of Didymus's *Commentary on Demosthenes* preserve a quotation from Philochorus, which throws important new light on the developments of 339. Philochorus says that, while Philip was away among the Scythians, the Thebans expelled his garrison from Nicaea and occupied it themselves. Unfortunately it is not possible to determine whether the Thebans seized Nicaea, the fort commanding Thermopylae, before or after the spring pylaia, but this question is not of crucial importance. The Theban occupation of Nicaea decreased very much the likelihood of eventual Macedonian intervention in Greece; accordingly it encouraged the states of central Greece to pursue their own policies without regard to Philip. The information also provides a context for the policy adopted by Demosthenes, when he dissuaded the Athenians from sending any deputies to the special meeting of the Amphictyonic Council. Since the Thebans held Nicaea by then, it was important to Athenian interests that the Thebans should not be left isolated in their rivalry with Thessaly; for then they might come to terms with Philip again and throw open for him the route into central Greece.

Thessaly lay north of Thermopylae, and so Philip could bring pressure to bear on Thessaly even when he did not hold Nicaea. In 339 the Thessalians could muster a majority in the Amphictyonic Council. These facts explain how it came about that the fall pylaia of 339 voted the command against Amphissa to Philip. Information on his next step comes from the same fragment of Philochorus. The latter says that Philip seized Cytinium and Elatea. Cytinium was one of the towns of Doris; it lay south of the highlands which formed the southwestern side of Thermopylae. Elatea in Phocis was east of Cytinium and further ahead on the route leading through the heart of central Greece. Philochorus's statement implies that Philip did not attempt a frontal attack on Thermopylae but outflanked the pass by bringing a force through the mountains. Some details of his route cannot be determined precisely, but it was the same maneuver as Xerxes had adopted in 480. Once Philip had reached Elatea, he held a position ahead of Thermopylae; the Theban garrison in Nicaea could no longer check him and served no further purpose.

The news of Philip's occupation of Elatea reached Athens in the evening and caused acute alarm. The Council and assembly met the next day. The crucial question was, What policy would Thebes adopt? In the assembly Demosthenes delivered the main speech. He argued that Philip had not yet won over the Thebans and there was a chance that they could be persuaded to ally with Athens; for, as he pointed out, if the Thebans had already committed themselves to Macedon, Philip would not be at Elatea but would be approaching the borders of Attica. The Athenians elected Demosthenes as one of ten envoys to go to Thebes and propose an alliance. Meanwhile envoys came from Philip and his allies to Thebes. Philip wanted to secure the Theban alliance for the war against Amphissa and for that against Athens, which had been technically in progress since his seizure of the grain fleet in 340. He proposed that Nicaea should be entrusted to the East Locrians; it stood in fact in their territory. Demosthenes spoke against Philip's envoys and won the alliance of Thebes for Athens. Thus he overcame the longstanding enmity between the two cities. It was the greatest success of his career.

The Athenians promptly sent a force to Thebes; the combined armies advanced into southwest Phocis and took up a defensive position there. Skirmishes were fought in the winter of 339/8 but they were indecisive. When the campaigning season of 338 opened, Philip had scarcely advanced beyond Cytinium and Elatea. He had been engaged in diplomacy. He had tried to win over the East Locrians by offering them Nicaea. He had also taken steps to conciliate the Phocians. At least when the spring pylaia of 338 met, their position had improved, and the changes probably had taken place in the preceding few months. In 346 their cities had been dismantled and they had been required to live in villages; by the spring of 338 some at least of their cities, Elatea, Erochus and Lilaea, were restored. The organized federation of the Phocians was likewise reconstituted. The payments of the indemnity required after the Third Sacred War were diminished. The first installment had been paid in the fall of 343 and had amounted to thirty talents. Thereafter the Phocians paid thirty talents every spring and every fall until the spring of 338 inclusively. No payment was made in the fall of 338. The next payment, made in the spring of 337, amounted to only ten talents. Thenceforth Phocis paid annual sums of ten talents in the spring.

After contracting their alliance, the Athenians and the Thebans sent out embassies to seek additional allies. The effect of the diplomatic activities of both sides appears in the campaign of 338. In the summer Philip brought his enemies to battle at Chaeronea and defeated them there decisively. The forces opposing him were drawn, not only from Athens and Boeotia, but also from Euboea, Achaea, Corinth, Megara, Leucas and Corcyra. The presence of the Euboeans may reflect the Euboean League set up in 343/2 and the alliance which Callias had then negotiated with Athens. But the other states sending troops were acting in response to the embassies of the winter of 339/8; it is noticeable that many of them were traditional associates of Corinth. Phocis was neutral during the campaign.

After the victory Philip negotiated peace settlements with many of the states opposing him. He treated Thebes with severity; the Boeotian confederacy was disbanded and the Thebans lost Oropus. A Macedonian garrison was installed in the Cadmea. Athens still had a fleet far superior to that of Macedon, and this may explain why Philip treated Athens more favorably. The Athenians sent an embassy of three men, Phocion, Aeschines and Demades, to negotiate peace. By the terms the Sea League was disbanded, but Athens kept her overseas possessions of Lemnos, Imbros, Scyros and Samos. Oropus was restored to Athens. In the fall Philip marched into the Peloponnese. He took some territory from Sparta and distributed it between Argos, Messene, Megalopolis and Tegea.

For the winter of 338/7 Philip summoned a meeting of deputies of the Greek states to Corinth. This meeting set up a permanent organization, which has come to be called the League of Corinth. In form it was probably a treaty of common peace with safeguards and additional provisions. The agreement embraced the Greek states south of Macedon; Sparta refused to join because the independence of Messene was recognized. The treaty provided for a Synedrion or congress of representatives, which was to meet in Corinth. The constitutions in force in the member states when they joined the League were guaranteed; federal action was to check any acts of subversion or aggression against member states. There was to be a federal army levied by drawing from the members contingents approximately proportionate to their size. Philip was declared commander of the federal forces and, in accordance with his plans, the Synedrion declared war on Persia.

The explicit terms of the League of Corinth were neither the only nor the most significant feature of the settlement which Philip imposed on Greece in 338. In addition he installed garrisons at crucial positions, including the citadel at Corinth, the Cadmea at Thebes, and Ambracia. The League of Corinth borrowed some features, such as the Synedrion, from previous Greek alliances. Yet the settlement of 338 was designed, not as a constructive experiment towards promoting federal union among the Greeks, but as a means enabling Philip to control Greece and to draw on Greek manpower for military purposes.

Philip was assassinated in 338. His son, Alexander the Great, conquered the Persian Empire, including Egypt and lands stretching as far east as the valley of the Indus river. When Alexander died in 323, disputes arose among his generals, who tried to carve out kingdoms of their own from his empire. Their ambitions brought about a complex series of wars, which lasted more than forty years. By 278 a stable system of states emerged; in particular much of the known world was divided between three dynasties of Macedonian origin, the Ptolemies in Egypt, the Antigonids, who held Macedon and exercised some ascendancy in Greece, and the Seleucids, whose kingdom varied in extent but included Mesopotamia, Syria and parts of Asia Minor. Because of these large changes historians concerning themselves with the early Hellenistic period have often concentrated their attention on the spread of hellenism in the Graeco-Macedonian kingdoms of the Near and Middle East.

The battle of Chaeronea has often been held to mark the end of Greek freedom; from then until the Roman conquest the Greek cities had to reckon constantly with the behavior and wishes of Macedonian princes. Yet the degree of Macedonian ascendancy varied and was often relatively mild; in the third and second centuries there was a good deal of free activity by Greek states. It would be nearer the mark to say that the battle of Chaeronea caused a severe, though temporary, check to the federal movement among the Greeks. In the preceding part of the fourth century this movement had produced local leagues, like those of the Boeotians and of the Euboeans, and one with more than local aspirations, the Second Athenian Sea League. In disbanding the latter Philip may have taken a step of more symbolic than factual significance; by 338 the Sea League probably had few powerful members left. The disbanding of the Boeotian League harmed a real power in central Greece.

The fortunes of the Achaeans on the north coast of the Peloponnese are instructive. Very little is known about their early history, but links of some kind between their settlements may have persised right from the age of migrations. Certainly the Achaean cities constituted an effective federation in the fifth and fourth centuries. But eventually, probably soon after 302, the Macedonians dissolved the Achaean League. Its revival began in 280, when four of the Achaean cities bound themselves together afresh; later the others joined the League. Moreover, by absorbing Sicyon in 251 and Corinth in 243, this League learned to admit non-Achaean cities on an equal basis; thereafter it expanded to gain much of the Peloponnese. Further north the Aetolian League likewise began as a local federation but expanded, absorbing some places outright and drawing more distant communities into association; for a time its links reached some cities of the Peloponnese, some islands of the Aegean, and even Calchedon on the Bosporus. In short, the Greek federal movement, checked in 338, revived in the third century and flourished until it was frustrated by a new conqueror, Rome.

NOTES

1. Philip's policy of internal colonization is known from Just. 8.5.7–8.6.2. For his campaign in Illyria see Trogus, prologue to book 8; Diod. 16.69.7–8; Didymus 12.37–13.12. For his intervention in Thessaly see Diod. loc. cit.; Dem. 6.22; and Appendix to this chapter. On the steps taken by Demosthenes to prosecute Aeschines see Dem. 19.17–18, 103–104, 211–212. Aeschines spoke speech 1 at the trial of Timarchus; its date appears from 1.80 and 157. On the "promises" of Aeschines see Dem. 5.10; 6.28–37; 19.20–23, 74, 102, 112, 220, 325; Aeschin. 2.119–120; cf. Aeschin. 2.136–137; Dem. 18.35–36. On the question of Athenian recognition of Philip's membership in the Amphictyony see Dem. 5; 19.111–113 and 132. The embassy of Eucleides is known from Dem. 19.162 with schol. Two valuable studies of developments after 346 are F.R. Wüst, *Philipp II. von Makedonien und Griechenland in den Jahren 346 bis 338* (München 1938), and G.L. Cawkwell, "Demosthenes' Policy after the Peace of Philocrates," *CQ* N.S. 13 (1963) 120–138 and 200–213. On Dem. 6 see also G.M. Calhoun, "Demosthenes' Second Philippic," *TAPA* 64 (1933) 1–17.

2. The main evidence on Python's embassy is Pseudo-Dem. 7.18–23; see also Pseudo-Dem. 12.18; Dem. 18.136. The Persian reconquest of Egypt is narrated by Diod. 16.40.3–16.51. For the Persian alliance with Macedon see Arrian, *Anabasis of Alexander* 2.14.2. For views which regard the Athenian reply to Python as a skillful maneuver by anti-Macedonians to seduce the assembly see Wüst (supra note 1) 64–77 and, with reservations, Cawkwell (supra note 1) 127–134. On the chronology see also F. Jacoby, *F.Gr.Hist.* IIIb (Supplement) I, 531–533.

3. For the embassy of Hegesippus see Dem. 19.331; Pseudo-Dem. 12.20. For the trial of Philocrates see Dem. 19.116; Aeschin. 2.6; 3.79; Hyp. *Eux.* 19. For that of Proxenus see Dem. 19.280–281 with schol.; Dein. 1.63. For that of Aeschines see Dem. 19; Aeschin. 2. For the reports about the Euboean situation at the time of Aeschines's trial see Dem. 19.83, 87, 204, 326. The

reports may later have proved to be groundless, since nothing is said in Pseudo-Dem. 7 about Macedonian intervention in Euboea. The diplomatic ventures launched by Callias of Chalcis in 343/2 are known from Aeschin. 3.89–105. Until recently they were usually dated to 341/0. The date 343/2 has been proposed by Cawkwell (supra note 1) 210–213. The other date has been defended by P.A. Brunt, "Euboea in the time of Philip II," *CQ* N.S. 19 (1969) 245–265, especially 255–259. On Philip's march to Epirus and Ambracia see Diod. 16.72.1; Just. 8.6.4–8; Tod 2.173; Pseudo-Dem. 7.32; Dem. 9.27; 10.10. For the Athenian response see Pseudo-Dem. 48.24–26; Dem. 9.72; 18.144; schol. Aeschin. 3.83; *I.G.* II², 225. For Demosthenes's embassy to Thessaly see Dem. 18.244; schol. Aeschin. 3.83. For Philip's intervention in Thessaly see Appendix to this chapter; on Pherae see Pseudo-Dem. 7.32; Dem. 9.12; On Nicaea see Pseudo-Dem. 11.4; Philoch. *F.Gr.Hist.* IIIB 328F56b. On Halonnesus see also Aeschin. 3.83. Cawkwell (supra note 1) 132 holds that the proposal to recognize the independence of the other Greek states emanated from Philip; but Hegesippus (Pseudo-Dem. 7.30) says that this proposal was made by the Athenians.

4. For Philip's Thracian conquests of 342/1 see Diod. 16.71.1–2; Dem. 8.2 and 35; Pseudo-Dem. 12.8. On the Cheronese, Diopeithes and Cardia see Philoch. *F.Gr.Hist.* IIIB 328F158; Pseudo-Dem. 7.41–44; 12.3 and 11; Dem.8 with hypothesis. For Chares in 341/0 see *I.G.* II², 228 = Tod 2.174; *I.G.* II², 1628 lines 419–420; 1629 lines 940–941. On Macedonian intervention in Eretria and Oreus the fullest information is given by Dem. 9.57–62; Carystius *apud* Athen. 11.508e; the intervention is mentioned also by Dem. 8.18, 36, 59, 66; 9.17, 33, 63; 10.61, 68; 18.71, 295. The liberation of Oreus and Eretria is known from Philoch. *F.Gr.Hist.* IIIB 328F159–160; it is not clear whether the operations of Cephisophon at Oreus and of Phocion at Eretria constituted two expeditions, crossing from Attica to Euboea, or a single expedition whose commander changed at the beginning of the new Attic year. For the Euboeans at Chaeronea see Dem. 18.237. On the siege of Perinthus see Diod. 16.74–76. On Athenian negotiations with Persia see Dem. 9.71; 10.31–34; Pseudo-Dem. 12.6. For the movements of Philip's fleet and his dispatch of a force to the Cheronese see Dem. 18.70 with schol.; Pseudo-Dem. 12.12–13 and 16; Plut. *Phoc.* 14; *I.G.* II², 228 = Tod 2.174. The letter of Philip preserved as Pseudo-Dem. 12 may have been sent when he dispatched a force to the Chersonese; see Wüst (supra note 1) 133–136; alternatively it may be a literary composition by Anaximenes for his *Philippica*. On the siege of Byzantium see Dem. 18.87–94; Diod. 16.74.2–16.77.3. On the seizure of the grain fleet see Didymus 10.54–11.5, quoting Philochorus (*F.Gr.Hist.* IIIB 328F162) and Theopompus (*F.Gr.Hist.* IIB 115F292); Just. 9.1.5–6. On Philip's letter see Dem. 18.73–78; Didymus 10.15–30. For the consequent Athenian decree see Philoch. *F.Gr.Hist.* IIIB 328F55 *apud* Didymus 1.70–2.2. For the help sent to Byzantium see Plut. *Phoc.* 14; *I.G.* II², 1628 lines 436–438; 1629 lines 957–959; Pseudo-Plut. *Ten Orators* 851A; Diod. loc. cit.; *I.G.* II², 233. For Philip's raid on the Chersonese see Dem. 18.139; Just. 9.1.7; Syncellus 263c. For Philip's Scythian expedition see Just. 9.1.9–9.3.3; Didymus 13.3–7.

5. On the membership of the Amphictyonic Council see Aeschin. 2.116. On Cottyphus and Colosimmus and their successors see W. Dittenberger, *Sylloge Inscriptionum Graecarum* I³ (Leipzig 1915) No. 249A–C and pp. 314–315. The origin of the Fourth Sacred War has to be reconstructed from Aeschin. 3.107–130; Dem. 18.139–159. On Nicaea and Elatea see Philoch. *F.Gr.Hist.* IIIB 328F56b *apud* Didymus 11.40–51. The significance of Philip's seizure of Elatea was clarified by G. Glotz, "Philippe et la surprise d' Elatée," *BCH* 33 (1909) 526–546. For the Athenian response and the alliance with Thebes see Dem. 18.169–179 and 211–217; Aeschin. 3.137–143; Diod. 16.84.1–16.85.1. For the embassies sent out by Athens and Thebes see Just. 9.3.6–8. For the forces opposing Philip at Chaeronea see Dem. 18.237. For Philip's settlement with Athens see Dem. 18.282; Aeschin. 3.227; Plut. *Phoc.* 16; Nep. *Phoc.* 1.3–4; Paus. 1.25.3; Diod. 18.56.6–7; Plut. *Alex.*

28.1; Ar. *AP* 61.6; 62.2. For his treatment of Sparta see Polyb. 9.28.6–7. The structure of the League of Corinth is known mainly from Pseudo-Dem. 17 and Tod 2.177; for recent discussion see Ryder, *Koine Eirene* 150–162.

6. Philip's garrisons are known from Dein. 1.18 (Corinth); Arrian, *Anabasis of Alexander* 1.7.1, Diod. 17.8.7, Plut. *Alex.* 11 (Thebes); Diod. 17.3.3 (Ambracia). It is often and reasonably conjectured that Philip also stationed a garrison in Chalcis. The suppression and revival of the Achaean League is known from Polyb. 2.40–44. On the Achaean and Aetolian Leagues see Larsen, *GFS* 78–89 and 195–240.

APPENDIX

PHILIP'S INTERVENTION IN THESSALY, 344 and 342

In 344, on his return from his Illyrian campaign, Philip intervened in the affairs of Thessaly. The clearest text on this action is a passage in Demosthenes's Second Philippic; speaking in 344/3, the orator reports an address he had delivered recently to the Messenians and quotes himself thus (6.22): " 'What about the Thessalians?' I said. 'When Philip expelled their tyrants and again when he gave them Nicaea and Magnesia, do you suppose that they anticipated that the decadarchy now established would be set up among them?' " Diodorus (16.69.7–8) says that after the Illyrian campaign Philip brought large booty back to Macedon and then went to Thessaly, where he expelled the tyrants from the cities and won the good will of the Thessalians. This report may rest in part on confusion with the actions carried out by Philip in 352. Trogus (prologue to book 8) recorded "how the Illyrian kings were defeated by him (Philip) and Thrace and Thessaly subdued;" this reference to Thrace is puzzling, but the text confirms the fact of intervention in Thessaly after the Illyrian campaign.

In the Third Philippic, spoken in 342/1, Demosthenes seems to mention a further act of intervention by Philip in Thessaly. Listing the injustices committed by Philip against Greek states, the speaker says (9.26): "What is the condition of Thessaly? Has he not deprived them of their constitutions and their cities and set up tetrarchies, in order that they may be in servitude not only city by city but even tribe by tribe?" It should be noted that the passage of the Second Philippic speaks of "the decadarchy" in the singular, whereas the Third Philippic mentions "tetrarchies" in the plural. If the two texts are correctly preserved, Philip intervened in Thessaly a second time, probably on his return in 342 from the campaign which took him into Epirus and towards Ambracia. There is little further evidence on the second intervention; at least Theopompus in book 44 of the *Philippica* mentioned the four divisions of Thessaly and said that Philip set up a ruler over each (*F.Gr.Hist.* IIB 115F208).

The term "decadarchy" in connection with Thessaly occurs only in the Second Philippic. Some readers have regarded it as a textual corruption and have emended the word to "tetrarchy." This emendation is easy to make; if correct, it would follow that Philip intervened in Thessaly to establish tetrarchies in 344 but did not carry out a second act of intervention in 342. But several arguments suggest that the emendation is wrong and that two acts of intervention are likely. The first is drawn from the arrangement of material in Theopompus's work. He mentioned in book 44 the rulers set up by Philip over the four divisions of Thessaly; in book 43 (F206) he mentioned the cities of Cassopia, which Philip subdued on his Epirote campaign. Unless Theopompus departed from chronological order, it appears that Philip set up the Thessalian tetrarchies after he had intervened in Epirus. Second, the Third Philippic (9.12) says that "recently" Philip seized Pherae; the speech of Hegesippus (Pseudo-Dem. 7.32), delivered in 343/2, says that Philip "has deprived the Pheraeans of their city and put a garrison in their acropolis." Unless "recently" in the Third Philippic covers a surprisingly long interval, Philip established his garrison in Pherae in 342, not 344. Third, the Athenians had taken action which was likely to provoke renewed Macedonian intervention. The scholiast to Aeschines (3.83) says that they sent an embassy to Thessaly in 343/2; and Demosthenes (18.244), listing his own diplomatic journeys in apparently chronological order, gives his embassy to Thessaly before that to Illyria.

The nature of the decadarchy of 344 remains conjectural. Unlike the tetrarchies of 342, which were the four distinct parts of the territory, the decadarchy was to judge from the name a single authority for all Thessaly.

(For an argument similar to the above and for references to other discussions see Wüst [supra n. 1] 99–101.)

Note

ON THE ATHENIAN CALENDAR

The Athenians divided the year into twelve months, which bore the following names:

1. Hecatombaeon	5. Maemacterion	9. Elaphebolion
2. Metageitnion	6. Posideion	10. Munychion
3. Boedromion	7. Gamelion	11. Thargelion
4. Pyanopsion	8. Anthesterion	12. Scirophorion.

The Athenians began their year at about the middle of summer. There is no ancient evidence for the view, often asserted, that the Athenians intended the first month of their year to coincide with the first lunar month after the summer solstice. Aristotle says (*Historia Animalium* 5.11.543b): "Other [fishes] breed both in winter and in summer, as was observed previously; as, for example, in winter the bass, the grey mullet and the pipefish; and in summer, about Hecatombaeon, the female tunny, about the time of the summer solstice." Here Aristotle does not say that Hecatombaeon was intended to begin with the first new moon after the summer solstice; his language allows the possibility that Hecatombaeon could begin with the first new moon before the summer solstice.

Festivals werre tied to specific days in specific months; the Dionysia, for example, was celebrated on the five days of 9 to 14 Elaphebolion. The archon controlled the calendar of months. The Athenian months had sometimes 29 and sometimes 30 days; modern attempts to discover a regular pattern in the sequence of months of the two legnths have not been successful. If an average year had equal numbers of months of the two lengths it would have 354 days and would thus fall short of a solar year. To compensate for this the archon had authority to insert or intercalate an additional month into the year. Sometimes the month intercalated was a second Posideion, following the regular Posideion; a second Hecatombaeon, Metageitnion and Anthesterion are also attested in inscriptions.

The archon could also intercalate and suppress specific days within the month. Sometimes he used his power of controlling the calendar for political purposes. Inscriptions of the second century B.C. illustrate the two consequent ways of specifying dates: sometimes they give a single date both *kat' archonta*, that is, according to the archon's reckoning, and *kata theon*, that is, "according to the god (sc. the moon)," in other words, according to the true lunar calendar. Sometimes the two ways of designating the date diverge by as much as thirty days.

Apart from these two calendars, the archon's calendar or calendar of festivals and the lunar calendar, there was a third way of reckoning dates. The Council of Five Hundred drew fifty members from each of the ten tribes. The year was divided into ten parts, and each group of fifty councilors from one tribe was on duty for one of those ten periods. While on duty, the fifty councilors had to sleep and take their meals in the Tholos or office building. The fifty councilors on duty were called *prytaneis* or "presdients" and their period of duty, forming a tenth of the year, was called a *prytaneia* or prytany. Each of the ten prytanies forming the year could be specified by its serial number within the year or by the name of the tribe supplying the fifty councilors on duty.

Speaking of his own time, Aristotle (*AP* 43.2) says that each of the first four prytanies of the year has 36 days and each of the remaining six prytanies has 35 days. His statement implies a year of 354 days. It is conjectured that, in years when an additional month was intercalated, the prytanies had 39 and 38 days and the year had (384 ± 1) days. Although a single sentence of Aristotle is not much evidence, a good working hypothesis consists in supposing that the prytany-calendar was regular, whereas the archon's calendar was not. This hypothesis gains some support from inscriptions of the second century B.C., which specify dates by the three methods: *kat' archonta, kata theon*, and by the calendar of prytanies. In each case the date given according to the prytany-calendar agrees with the date *kata theon*.

Narrating the revolution of 411, Aristotle (*AP* 32.1) says that, but for the revolution, a new Council of Five Hundred was due to take office on 14 Scirophorion. From this statement it appears that in the fifth century the Council of Five Hundred did not necessarily take office on 1 Hecatombaeon; in other words, the archon's calendar and the prytany-calendar did not always agree even as to the day where they put the beginning (or end) of the year. But study of financial records (especially *I.G. I²*, 304B: accounts of 408/7 and 407/6) shows that this modest degree of agreement was reached a few years after the revolution; the Council of Five Hundred for 407/6 took office on 1 Hectombaeon, and thenceforth the archon's year and the conciliar year began on the same day. However, modern attempts to equate specific days of any Athenian calendar with dates given according to the Julio-Gregorian calendar have not been successful.

(Amid the extensive literature on the calendar the following are recommended: W.K. Pritchett and O. Neugebauer, *The Calendars of Athens* [Cambridge, Mass. 1947]; W.K. Pritchett, *Ancient Athenian Calendars on Stone* =

University of California Publications in Classical Archaeology vol. 4, no. 4 [1963] 267–401; *idem*, "The Intercalary Month at Athens," *CP* 63 [1968] 53–54; *idem, The Choiseul Marble* = University of California Publications in Classical Studies, vol. 5 [1970]; for a different view see B.D. Meritt, *The Athenian Year* [Berkeley and Los Angeles 1961]).

Technical Terms

choregia: for each entry in the dramatic competitions at Athenian festivals a rich man was selected to pay the expenses of training the actors and chorus and of producing the plays. He was called the *choregos* and his task was called *choregia*. He selected the members of the chorus. An ambitious *choregos* could win popularity by giving a lavish production.

drachma: a unit of weight and value. Most Greek cities used silver for coinage. The units used most often in calculations were these:

6 obols = 1 drachma
100 drachmas = 1 mina
60 minas = 1 talent.

Originally these were units of weight. When the practice of minting coins began, the design on the coin (which might be a didrachm, tridrachm, tetradrachm, or a smaller denomination) guaranteed that the coin was silver of the specified weight. Late in the Peloponnesian War the standard wage for rowers in the Athenian fleet was 3 obols a day.

graphe paranomon: "accusation of contravening the law," one of the criminal charges recognized by Athenian law. When a decree had been passed by the public assembly, any citizen could bring the proposer to trial by alleging that the decree was contrary to the established laws. When such a prosecution had begun, the new decree was suspended until the case was tried. This charge could only be brought within one year of the passing of the decree. The case was heard by one of the popular courts (see chapter 9, pp. 259–260). This procedure may have been instituted in the middle of the fifth century; it certainly existed by 411, when it was suspended at an early stage in the revolution. It was used frequently in the fourth century.

mora (plural: *morai*): name for the regiments, numbering six, into which the Lacedaemonian army was divided after a reform of the fifth century. Previously the hoplites drawn from Spartan citizens were brigaded in five units called *lochoi* and those drawn from the perioeci were brigaded separately. Sometime between 479 and 418 the system was changed; henceforth the hoplites drawn both from Spartan citizens and from the perioeci were brigaded together in six units called *morai*.

navarch: Spartan commander of the naval force raised from Lacedaemon and its allies. The activities of navarchs are attested in the Peloponnesian War and thereafter until 372. Little is known about the institution; it is commonly believed that the navarch took office in the late summer or fall and held office for a year. The navarch was accompanied by an *epistoleus* ("secretary") or second-in-command, who took control if the navarch was killed.

proxenos: in archaic Greece a man had no rights outside his own city; if he found himself in another city, its laws did not protect him (unless special provisions had been made to encourage aliens, like the provisions with which Solon is credited at Athens). Consequently great importance attached to the relationship of formal friendship (*xenia*) between citizens of different cities; on visiting the other city a man looked to his "friend" (*xenos*) there not only for hospitality but also for protection and general assistance. Starting in the fifth century a similar relationship, called *proxenia*, is attested between a whole city and an individual citizen of another city. The *proxenos* of the Athenians, for example, was expected to help Athenian visitors to his own city and care for Athenian political interests. The Athenian assembly often awarded the title of *proxenos* to individual citizens of other cities as an honor and a reward for past services.

prytany: the Athenian Council of Five Hundred was divided into ten parts, each consisting of the fifty councilors drawn from one of the ten tribes. Each such group of fifty councilors on duty were called *prytaneis* or "presidents" and their period of duty was called a *prytaneia* or prytany. While on duty, the fifty councilors of one tribe had to be available for business at all times, and so they ate and slept in the Tholos or office building. Towards the end of each prytany lots were cast to decide which tribe should have the next tour of duty. Some historians have supposed that the division of the Council into prytanies goes back to its creation by Cleisthenes; others have held, with more probability, that the division was introduced in about the middle of the fifth century, when conciliar business increased, but attempts to associate the system with the reforms of Ephialtes are conjectural.

trierarch: a wealthy Athenian citizen, chosen to bear the financial burden of maintaining a trireme at sea. From early in the fifth century one trierarch was chosen for each trireme which the state sent out, and at first he served also as its captain. Later the trierarch restricted himself to his financial task. From 411 each trierarchy was usually shared by two citizens; reforms in 357 and 340 spread the burden more widely among the wealthiest men. The state supplied the hull and tackle and paid the crew, but the trierarch was responsible for maintenance and repair of the ship.

Map 1. The Peloponnese

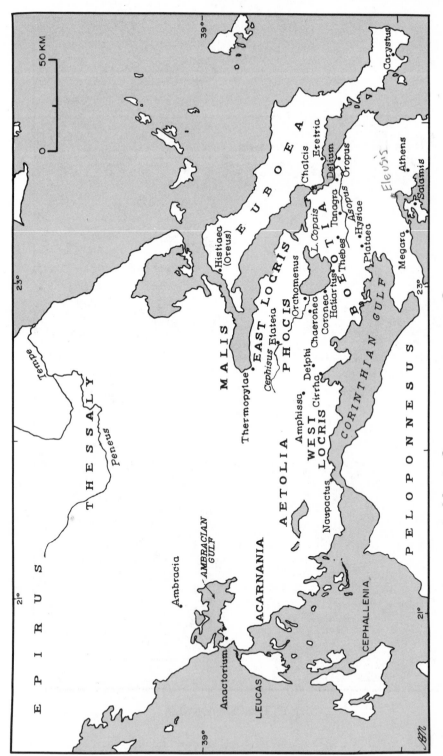

Map 2. CENTRAL AND NORTHERN GREECE

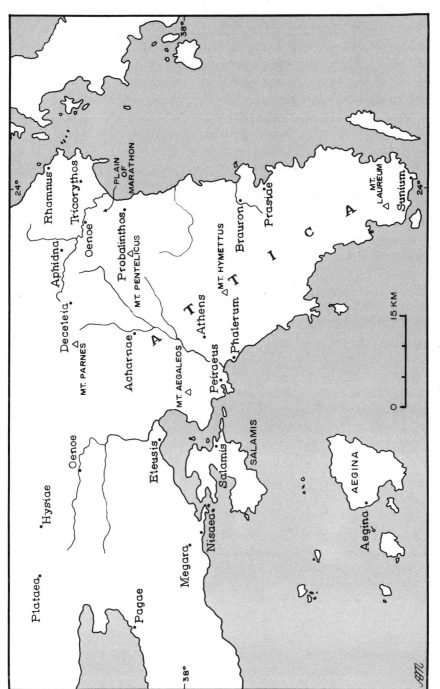

Map 3. ATTICA

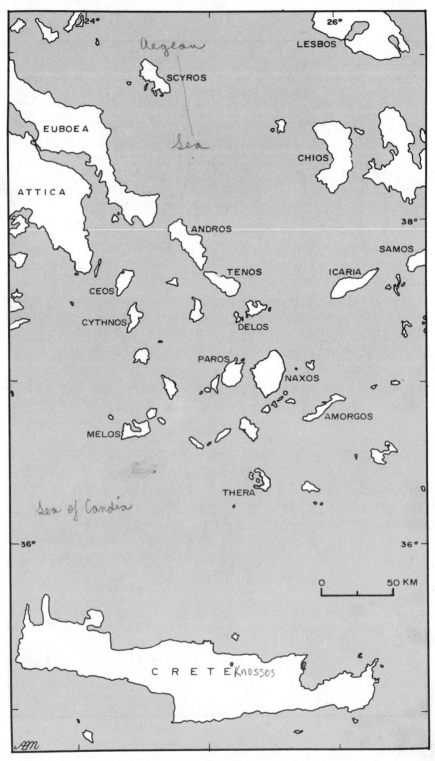

Map 4. THE CYCLADES

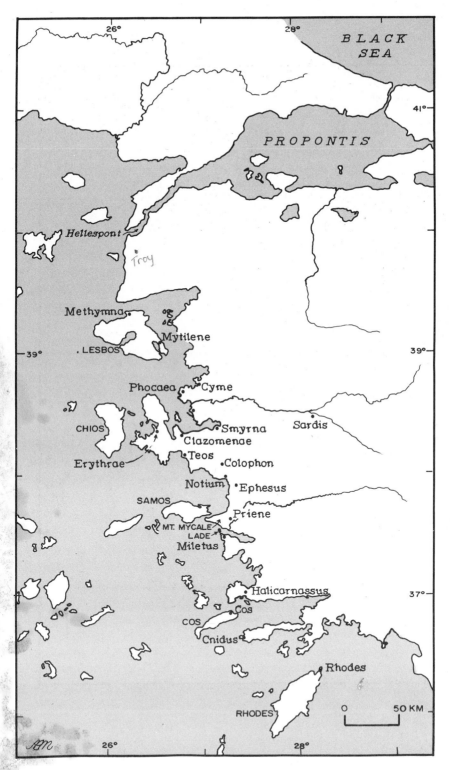

Map 5. WESTERN ASIA MINOR

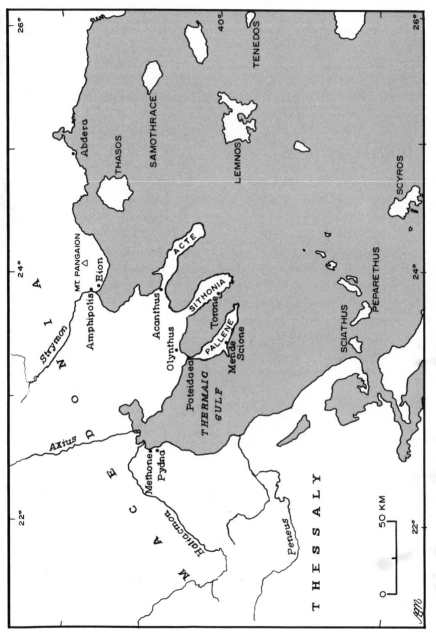

Map 6. THE NORTHWEST AEGEAN AREA

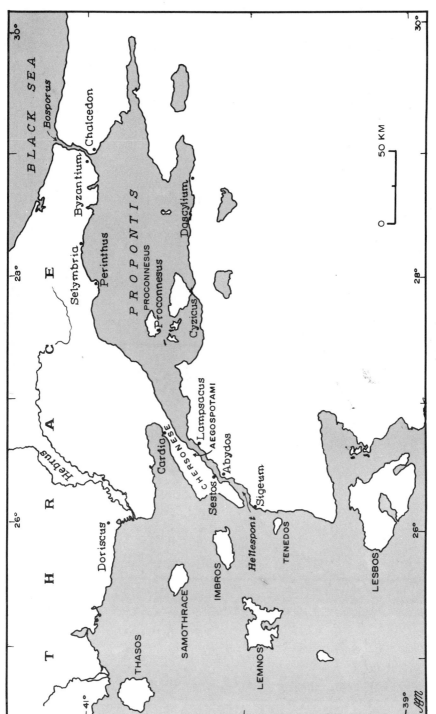

Map 7. The Straits

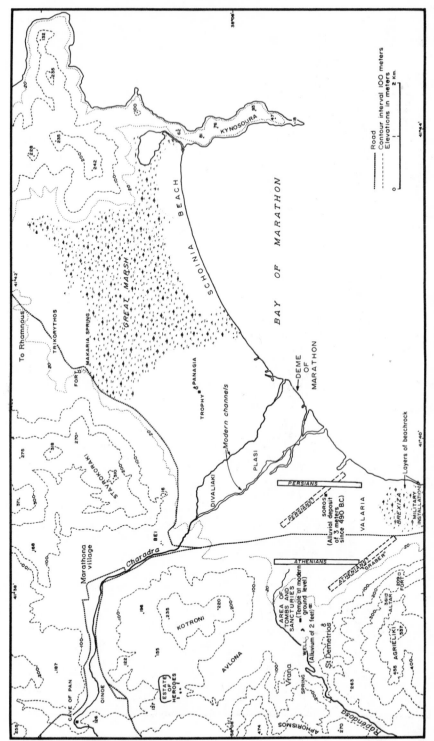

Map 8. The Battle of Marathon.

Index